P9-BAU-863

New York State

China Williams
Becca Blond

Contents

Thousand Islands & St Lawrence Seaway p227

The Adirondacks p203

Capital District & Mohawk Valley p184

Western New York p263

Finger Lakes Region p240

Catskills Region p168

Hudson Valley p146

New York City p55

Long Island p136

Lonely Planet books provide independent advice. Lonely Planet does not accept advertising in guidebooks, nor do we accept payment in exchange for listing or endorsing any place or business. Lonely Planet writers do not accept discounts or payments in exchange for positive coverage of any sort.

Lonely Planet réalise ses guides en toute indépendance et les ouvrages ne contien-nent aucune publicité. Les établissements et prestataires mentionnés dans ce guide ne le sont que sur la foi du jugement et des recherches des auteurs, qui n'acceptent aucune rétribution ou réduction de prix en échange de leurs com-mentaires.

Destination: New York State

The best view is always from the top, and if surveying American culture, history and landscape, New York State is the undeniable summit. This is a state that presided over America's greatest revolution: the Industrial Age. It gave shelter to impoverished immigrants from Europe, Asia and later Latin America, who flooded the gatekeeper, New York City. It drew rebellious artists and rabble-rousers who kicked over the status quo, unleashing reform and the greatest repository of the country's cultural accomplishments.

While New York can't claim the national capital, it is leashed to something much more powerful: New York City, which tells the rest of America what is cool, cultured and artistic. In this electric city, the heroes of arts and media, sports and business are worshiped, while the next generation plots their overthrow from the margins. Joining the pedestrian sea of knowns and unknowns rushing madly towards the prize of 'making it' in the Big Apple is a fierce tide to resist.

Beyond the borders of the world's greatest city is a living canvas of lush forests, sapphire-blue lakes and brooding hills. This harmony of form and color has inspired generations of artists – from the Hudson River school of painters to Jackson Pollock, whose creations can be found in the state's top-notch museums and historic homes. But their inspiration is best enjoyed in natural settings: along the country roads through apple orchards in the Hudson Valley, past vineyards in the Finger Lakes, atop Mt Marcy in the Adirondacks or beside the roar of Niagara Falls. When George Washington viewed these scenes in the 18th century, he accurately predicted that New York State would be the seat of the empire.

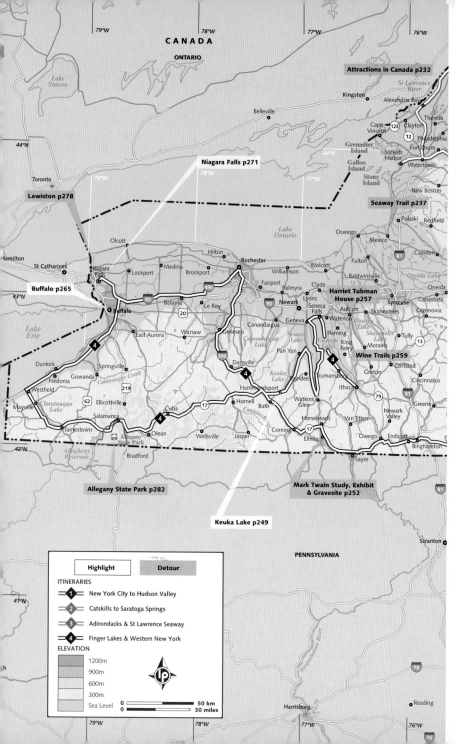

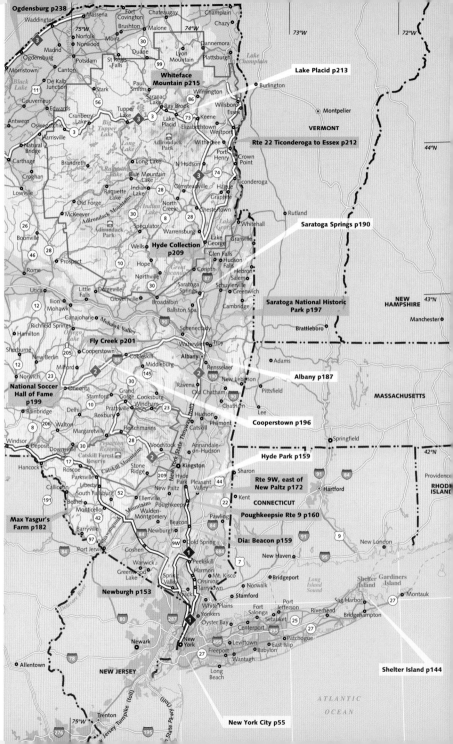

The cultural, artistic and historical legacy of New York State is astounding, as demonstrated in the **Franklin D Roosevelt National Historic Site** (p160) in Hyde Park, the **Women's Rights National Historical Park** (p256) in Seneca Falls and the **Frank Lloyd Wright–designed buildings** in Buffalo (p86).

Food is also key. Pizza receives celebrity status here, while wines from **Long Island** (p144) and the **Finger Lakes** (p259) are drawing raves. Spicy **Buffalo wings** (p270) were born in their namesake city and the restaurants (p176) of quirky **Woodstock** will charm any educated eater.

RICHARD I'ANSON

The bustle and energy never cease on Fifth Avenue (p88)

Mastering the subway system (p135)

COREY WISE

New York City's Empire State Building (p86)

ANGUS OBORN

ANGUS OBORN

The cityscape at night

Drinking a cappuccino in a Greenwich Village (p80) coffee shop and dreaming of a bohemian life

ANGUS OBORN

RICHARD I'ANSON

Browsing or splurging in the shops and galleries of SoHo (p79)

Then there is the state's natural beauty in the waters of the **Thousand Islands** (p229), the brilliant fall colors exploding along the country roads of the **Hudson Valley** (p146) and **western New York** (p263), and the **High Peaks** region (p203) in the Adirondacks.

Want more? There's bobsledding at **Lake Placid's Olympic venues** (p213), horseracing in **Saratoga Springs** (p193) and the National Baseball Hall of Fame in historic **Cooperstown** (p197). Be sure to spend due time in **New York City** (p55), though, before journeying upstate. Ready yet?

A long bike ride through Shelter Island's Mashomack Nature Preserve (p144)

ANGUS OBORN

ROB BLAKERS

The splendid hues
of fall

Water surges over awesome Niagara Falls (p271)

JIM WARK

Getting Started

Better repack that suitcase and throw in more cash, 'cause this state knows how to spend your money. But you won't be disappointed by your spending power: fine meals, fantastic vistas and access to great works of art. You'll definitely need a good map and a lot of patience to tour this big state, best appreciated in digestible portions. And forget about defensive driving – New Yorkers are on the offensive. After a few missed exits on the highway, you'll discover the why New Yorkers are famous for their use of the car horn.

See Climate Charts (p285) for more information.

WHEN TO GO

The best time to visit New York State minus the crowds is late spring (late April to May) before schools close, and early September, after the summer rush. Fall foliage, while spectacular, draws loads of leaf-peeping tourists, particularly on weekends, so be prepared. During the week, accommodations are more readily available and there's less traffic. The Hudson Valley, especially, is glorious in the spring – the tender apple blossoms erupt on the naked branches, spring wildflowers claim the roadside medians, and the formal gardens of the historic homes are awash first in spring bulbs, and then lilacs, followed by roses.

Summer can get hot, and warm air from the Gulf of Mexico can make the humidity stifling. Tourist season is Memorial Day (last Monday in May) to Labor Day (first Monday in September). In the Adirondacks, summer comes a little later, usually July and August. 'Mud season' arrives after the first thaw of spring, and anywhere from late May to early July the 'fifth season' arrives with its prominent, hungry guest, the black fly. It bites.

A brief siesta is taken after Labor Day. Mid-September through October sees one last surge of tourism, when people come to see the magnificent fall colors of the forests. Visitors often combine this with some early Christmas shopping in New York City.

DON'T LEAVE HOME WITHOUT

It's best to start light and pick up items along the way.

- Clothes – If New York City is your first stop, you'll need an urban look (smart black shirt, hip dress shoes, and if you must wear jeans, they should be designer). For upstate, you can go casual with fleece and flannel. Swanky restaurants in the Hudson Valley will want business casual.

- Cash – Small hotels and restaurants don't take credit cards, so be sure to have cash on you.

- CDs – If you're driving through the region, you'll want to escape radio-torture with your own music.

- Specialty equipment – If you plan to go camping or hiking, bring the appropriate gear from home as these items are expensive to buy in outdoor destinations.

- Maps – If you want to explore the backroads, you'll need a good county map.

- Odds & ends – Photocopies of important documents, such as passport, credit cards and traveler checks, Swiss Army knife (pack in your check-in bag for airline travel), sewing kit and earplugs.

The least hospitable months are November to February, when it's cold and rainy and daylight hours are short. A brief ski season generally runs from December to January.

COSTS

New York City is ridiculously expensive, but costs in the rest of the state are more sane. Thrifty travelers to NYC will feel moral outrage over paying $1 for a pack of gum or $20 for a plate of macaroni and cheese. Just remember that space is at a premium in New York City and the cost of density trickles down to everyone. But don't let penny-pinching disturb New York's signature hedonism; a realistic daily budget, including accommodations, is $200 to $250.

Upstate, costs vary by location. Popular tourist sights like Lake Placid and Niagara Falls are priced accordingly, and the Finger Lakes wine country has food and lodging options for all budgets. In the high season (summer and fall), accommodations are inflated, but state-run campgrounds are an amazing bargain and have top-notch scenery. Expect a daily budget outside NYC to be $100 to $150.

If you plan on traveling outside New York City, it is smarter to rent a car than to take public transportation. Because rental car rates in New York City are high, shop around for cheaper rates offered in outlying cities accessible by train or bus.

TRAVEL LITERATURE

The classic US travel series is the *WPA Guides to America*, published in the 1930s as part of the New Deal project to employ writers. The guides to New York were published in 1939 and are so wonderful that they stand on their own today as good reading. A century earlier, Charles Dickens recounted his travels through America as a literary star in *American Notes* (1842). Although your own journey may not be as colorful or as disappointing, Americans never tire of seeing themselves through critical European eyes.

For literary New York try *The Tavern Lamps Are Burning: Literary Journeys Through Six Regions and Four Centuries of New York State*, an exhaustive anthology of writings about New York State by many great American writers. *Remember the Catskills: Tales by a Recovering Hotelkeeper*, by Esterita 'Cissie' Blumberg, recounts the heyday of the Catskill's Borscht Belt resorts. *Here Is New York* (1949) is a classic, novella-sized essay on New York by the elegant *New Yorker* writer EB White. His observations on the city remain insightful – even today.

INTERNET RESOURCES

Lonely Planet (www.lonelyplanet.com) In the Thorn Tree section, you can post questions to a network of travelers eager to give advice on where to stay and what to see. The subwwway section links you to the most useful travel resources elsewhere on the Web.

NYC & Company (www.nycvisit.com) New York City's visitors bureau has general travel information as well as hotel listings.

National Scenic Byways (www.byways.org) Operated by the US Department of Transportation, this site provides maps and descriptions of New York's scenic backroads.

New York State Tourism (www.iloveny.com) The official state tourism site has travel ideas, accommodations listings and activities guides.

New York Times (www.nytimes.com) An online version of one of the country's premier newspapers. One useful section for the traveler is the 'Journeys' column, which profiles destinations throughout the state.

Foliage Network (www.foliagenetwork.com) Provides color-coded maps for building an itinerary for an autumnal outing in New York State.

HOW MUCH

In New York City:

Hotel room high/low season $200/150

Cup of coffee $2

Pint of beer $7

Restaurant dinner per person $30–40

Taxi (Midtown to East Village) $7

Parking per day $25–30

Outside NYC:

Hotel room high/low season $150/75

State campground $14–18

Full tank of gas $25–30

Cup of coffee $1.50

Pint of beer $3.50

Restaurant dinner per person $25

TOP 10S
NEW YORK ON FILM

While New York City has been the setting for countless quality films, movies shot upstate are few and far between. An evening viewing any of these titles will get you ready for your trip.

- *King Kong* (1933)
  Director: Merian C Cooper

- *A Tree Grows in Brooklyn* (1945)
  Director: Woody Allen

- *West Side Story* (1962)
  Director: Robert Wise

- *Woodstock* (1970)
  Director: Michael Wadleigh

- *The French Connection* (1971)
  Director: William Friedkin

- *Manhattan* (1979)
  Director: Elia Kazan

- *Ghostbusters* (1984)
  Director: Ivan Reitman

- *GoodFellas* (1990)
  Director: Martin Scorsese

- *25th Hour* (2002)
  Director: Spike Lee

- *Miracle* (2004)
  Director: Gavin O'Conner

FESTIVALS & EVENTS

Many of New York's festivals – New Year's Eve, Macy's Thanksgiving Day Parade – are destinations in themselves, but they aren't the only offerings. Consider these regional winners:

- Lucy-Desi Days (Jamestown),
  May (p282)

- Tulip Festival (Albany),
  May (p188)

- Ithaca Festival (Ithaca),
  late May (p245)

- Saratoga Springs Racing Season (Saratoga Springs), late July to August (p193)

- Chautauqua Institution Summer Series (Chautauqua), May to August (p278)

- Professional Baseball Season (New York City), March to October (p130)

- Woodstock Film Festival (Woodstock), September (p174)

- Adirondack Canoe Classic (Fulton Chain of Lakes, Adirondacks), September (p225)

- Haunted Halloween (Tarrytown and Sleepy Hollow), October (p153)

- Decorated historic homes for the Christmas season (along Hudson River), December (p155)

TOP READS

To list the great New York stories is to name some of America's best works of fiction.

- *Catcher in the Rye*
  JD Salinger

- *The New York Trilogy*
  Paul Auster

- *Invisible Man*
  Ralph Ellison

- *Last of the Mohicans*
  James Fenimore Cooper

- *World's End*
  TC Boyle

- *Stories of John Cheevers*
  John Cheevers

- *Nanny Diaries*
  Emma McLaughlin & Nicola Kraus

- *Amazing Adventures of Kavalier & Clay*
  Michael Chabon

- *Another Country*
  James Baldwin

- *Great Gatsby*
  F Scott Fitzgerald

Itineraries

There's no 'right' way to see this region, but it may help to have some sample itineraries. In summer and fall try to visit cities on weekends and country towns and resorts on weekdays. This will help you find lower prices and avoid the crowds.

CLASSIC ROUTES

NEW YORK CITY TO HUDSON VALLEY   One Week

When you tire of New York City, follow the fashionable route used by many city-weary socialites of the Gilded Age to the bucolic Hudson Valley.

If you only have a week, base yourself in New York City. In the first two days, visit the top attractions – the Statue of Liberty (p70), Ellis Island (p71) and the Empire State Building (p86). Get an outside perspective of New York City's skyline by crossing the Brooklyn Bridge or riding the Staten Island Ferry (p103).

Then take another day or two to visit Museum Mile, including the Frick Collection (p90), the Guggenheim (p91) and the Metropolitan Museum of Art (p91). Loop home after a day of art-gazing with a stroll through Central Park (p89).

Don't miss the Museum of Modern Art (p88) and be sure to work in a wandering tour through New York's famous neighborhoods – SoHo

(p117), Chinatown (p115) and Greenwich Village (p118). On any night, take in a famous bar, Broadway show or a club show.

For excursions, do a day trip to the lower Hudson Valley. Tarrytown (p153) was the home of Washington Irving and the inspiration for his Sleepy Hollow stories. Further north, the Museum of the Franklin D Roosevelt Library (p160) and Eleanor Roosevelt's cottage, Val-Kill (p160), are historic landmarks. To return home, cross over to the western bank of the Hudson River, traveling south through to West Point (p151), the US military academy, and the pretty state parks of Harriman and Bear Mountain (p150).

CATSKILLS TO SARATOGA SPRINGS   One to Two Weeks

Use Woodstock (p174) as a base to explore the surrounding region. You can easily drive Rte 212 west to Rte 30 north to Rte 23 east and spend the night in Windham (p179), a charming little ski town. From the Catskills head north to Albany (p187). Spend an afternoon wandering the capital city's graceful streets and eating at Miss Albany Diner (p189) or Jack's Oyster House (p189). From Albany continue north to Saratoga Springs (p190). During the summer season you'll want at least three days here to check out the horseracing, ambience and museums. The town was famous in the 19th century for its European-like spas, such as the Lincoln Baths (p192).

A bit of a detour, Cooperstown (p196) offers the National Baseball Hall of Fame (p197), the Fenimore Art Museum (p199) and the Farmers' Museum (p198). Otsego Lake (p199) on the edge of town is a must, if only to recover from a busy trip to Cooperstown.

Woodstock is just a few hours' drive (80 miles) north of New York City, but light-years away. Once you get here, don't be in a hurry to leave. Albany is 40 miles up the road and Saratoga Springs is another 25 miles north. This trip could eat a week, or a little more if you're feeling slow.

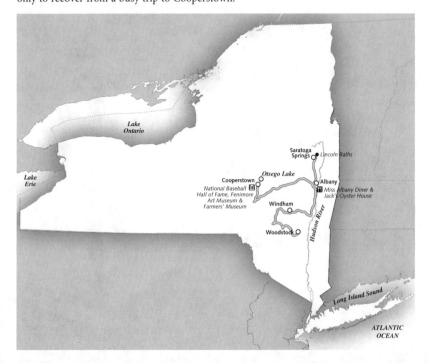

ADIRONDACKS & ST LAWRENCE SEAWAY   One to Two Weeks

One of the largest wilderness areas in the northeast, Adirondack Park (p203) has scenic drives, breathtaking hikes and languid paddling trips. A good southern base is Lake George (p207), which can entertain a family with disparate tastes. From Lake George, travel Rte 9N/22 through the picturesque villages of Westport (p212) and Essex (p212) that look out over Lake Champlain (p212).

Alternatively you can travel Rte 73 through the Keene Valley into the bosom of the High Peaks region (p216). Two-time host of the winter Olympics, Lake Placid (p213) is a good base for hiking trips to New York's tallest mountain, Mt Marcy (p216). If canoeing is your calling, use Saranac Lake (p221) or Blue Mountain Lake (p224) as a base to explore the St Regis Wilderness Canoe Area (p205) or the Fulton Chain of Lakes (p225), respectively. Blue Mountain is also home to the excellent Adirondack Museum (p223). Exit the park west via Rte 28.

For an out-of-the-way adventure, you could exit the park via Rte 3 west toward Watertown and head north on I-81. Stop off at Alexandria Bay (p229) to explore the islands in the St Lawrence Seaway. Do day trips to the small towns of Massena (p238) and Ogdensburg (p238), and before cruising home, spend at least one night in picturesque Sackets Harbor (p237).

This escape to the wilderness can be done as a week's stay in a cabin in one location or as a two-week road trip. It takes in lakes, mountains and pretty little towns.

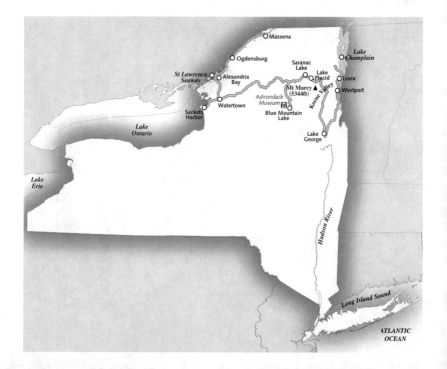

FINGER LAKES & WESTERN NEW YORK   One to Two Weeks

Start in Ithaca (p242), a cultural gem on the southern tip of Cayuga Lake. Then drive west in a zigzag fashion between the lakes. Seneca Falls (p256) on Rte 96 is home to the women's suffrage movement, and Keuka Lake (see boxed text, p249) is famous for several wineries. Further west is the beautiful but less-frequented Canandaigua Lake (p258).

Heading north on I-390 toward Rochester (p260), you can visit George Eastman House (p260), the home of the Kodak founder and one of the best photography exhibits in the state. Continue west to Buffalo (p265) with its Frank Lloyd Wright homes (see boxed text, p269) and Albright-Knox Art Gallery (p267). A trip to nearby Niagara Falls (pp271 and 277) should be based in Buffalo, as sleeping and eating options are more interesting.

To loop back around, swing south to Chautauqua (p278), home of the Chautauqua Institution, an American classic since 1874. Follow Rte 17 – one of the state's most scenic roads – east through Corning (p250), home of the Corning Museum of Glass (p251), and Elmira (see boxed text, p252), where Mark Twain used to summer.

This quintessential summer-vacation road trip deserves at least a week and a half, taking in lush Ithaca, historic Seneca Falls, wineries at Keuka Lake and Niagara Falls.

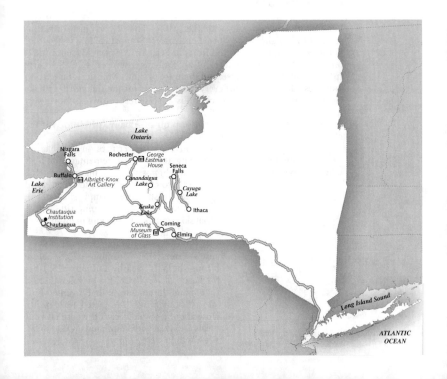

TAILORED TRIPS

FALL FOLIAGE

If you're coming from New York City, shoot straight up the spine of the state along the scenic Taconic State Parkway to a cozy B&B in the Hudson

Valley (p146) or to the hiking trails in the Adirondacks (p203). The Taconic Parkway is a highway masterpiece that dips and crests through vistas of autumnal colors unraveling in the distant landscape. If you're pressed for time, Hudson (p165) in the Hudson Valley is a good base for exploring the surrounding countryside.

But for the outdoorsy types, any spot in the Adirondacks will fit the bill for a walk in the crisp autumn air scented by wood stoves and freshly fallen leaves. Consider making Lake George (p207) or Lake Placid (p213) a base for day-time hikes or scenic drives.

CHILDREN ABOARD

Landing in New York City with kids (p105)? The city isn't just stuffy museums or all-night dance clubs. South Street Seaport (p75) has beautiful tall-masted ships to tour; the Intrepid Sea, Air & Space Museum (p89) might ignite the imagination of an evolving engineer; FAO Schwartz (p132) is just plain paradise; and there are Broadway musicals targeted to kids these days. Then stuff everyone in the car for the trek north to Lake George (p207), the Adirondacks' most diverse resort town, or northwest to Niagara Falls (pp271 and 277).

En route to either destination, stop off in Albany (p187) to visit the New York State Museum (p188).

Lake George has fun parks, a souvenir strip, cruises on the river, as well as strenuous hiking and canoeing. If you've got elementary and high schoolers to entertain, Lake George might possibly turn ingrates grateful.

You can also continue north to Lake Placid (p213) for a visit to the Olympic sites (p213); kids can take a bobsled training ride, watch aerial ski jumpers, or even join in on summer camp activities.

If you're Niagara-bound, stop off at Syracuse's Erie Canal Museum (p253) before hitting the falls. Nearby Buffalo (p265) has the kazoo factory (p267), a bicycle museum (p267) and the restaurant that invented Buffalo chicken wings (see boxed text, p270). How about a whole vacation where all your meals are eaten with your hands? OK, too far. Are we there yet?

FOR CULTURE BUFFS

Ithaca (p242) and Saratoga Springs (p190) are two of the most culturally blessed towns in the state, and much more navigable than New York City. Saratoga Springs, in fact, has the best of both worlds in the summer – in addition to horseracing, the city is the summer home to the New York City Ballet and the Philadelphia Philharmonic Orchestra. After a day at the races, travel further north to the state capital of Albany (p187) for a stroll through the Albany Institute of History & Art (p187) – which has a large collection of Hudson River school landscapes – and the New York State Museum (p188).

On the other hand, Ithaca – home to Cornell University (p244) – has natural and man-made beauty, while also being within striking distance of the Finger Lakes' wineries (see boxed text, p249), a culture buffs favorite beverage. In nearby Elmira (see boxed text, p252) is a historic site dedicated to every cynic's patron saint, Mark Twain.

WEEKEND ESCAPES

Need to leave the city for a few days? A delicious tonic is the bucolic Hudson Valley (p146). This region is an easy day trip that skirts along the mighty river past historic homes of grand proportions (like Kykuit, p154, in Tarrytown), tidy romantic villages (Rhinebeck, p162) and historical heavy hitters (Home of Franklin D Roosevelt National Historic Site, p160, in Hyde Park). In summer and fall visit pick-your-own orchards and farms celebrating the abundant harvest. On your way back home cross over to the other side of the Hudson to visit funky New Paltz (p171) or the state parks of Harriman and Bear Mountain (p150).

Also within striking distance are the summer resorts of Long Island (p136). Some of the country's prettiest beaches are accessible by public transportation from New York City. You can reach the family-oriented Robert Moses State Park (p138) in about an hour by train from New York City's Penn Station. The more exclusive Hamptons (p139), at the southern fork of Long Island, and the wineries of the North Fork (p144), are both about three hours away by car or train.

The Authors

CHINA WILLIAMS
Coordinating Author, New York City, Long Island, Hudson Valley & Adirondacks

Way back when the nation was young, Philip and Louisa Lewis left their home in western New York in a covered wagon, crossing the frozen lakes to the Ohio frontier. Seven generations later, their descendant returned to the ancestral lands to hike the Adirondacks, cruise Hudson Valley and Long Island back roads and prowl New York City's sights, attractions and nightlife. A gypsy in her personal life too, China has lived in more places than it is interesting to recount, but presently she lives in Portland, Maine, with her husband, Matt.

My New York State

My favorite place is the Belvedere (p222), an Italian restaurant and bar, in Saranac Lake. It isn't someplace I would go out of my way for, but I was glad I found it. The night I visited, the 'Bell' was in full swing; it was a Friday night and people were getting their swerves on. I befriended the entire bar that night. Bleary eyed from whiskey sours, one woman hugged me on my way out. A more sober woman invited me on her pontoon boat, an invitation I accepted and enjoyed. Throughout my research trip, I would remember the Bell's tangy pasta dish washed down with a Bud in a bottle and would smile.

BECCA BLOND
New York State Outdoors, Catskills, Capital District & Mohawk Valley, Thousand Islands & St Lawrence Seaway, Finger Lakes & Western New York

In her free time Becca likes to set cross-country road trip records in her old blue Tercel, so she jumped at the opportunity to explore vast amounts of New York. A native of Washington DC, Becca now calls Boulder, Colorado, home. In between traversing the globe for Lonely Planet, she chases wildfires for the *Denver Post* and spends as much time outside under the blue skies as possible.

My New York State

My favorite trip was driving through the Finger Lakes in the fall. The air was crisp, and the trees were stunning reds, yellows and oranges. The ground was golden. The sky was a deep, deep blue and the lakes sparkled in the sunlight. There are so many magnificent drives in that part of the state, where the towns are mostly pristine. The wineries, sumptuous food in Ithaca (p245), the story of Mark Twain's life in Elmira (p252), or the history of the American women's suffrage in Seneca Falls (p256) – there was just so much to pass the time.

Snapshot

Job losses, record winter temperatures, another win for the Yankees – the early years of the 21st century looked like a photocopy of every other year for New York State. One defining characteristic was the extraordinary number of financial scandals surrounding the New York Stock Exchange (NYSE). At the top of the scoundrel list was Richard Grasso, NYSE Chairman, who was hailed as a savior for returning the NYSE back to working order after the terrorist attacks of September 11. His fanfare soon died when he left the exchange in the summer of 2003 with a $140 million package, an unthinkable sum for the chief of a regulatory agency. (Does Tom Cruise even make that much?) News of Grasso's paycheck came at the end of a long series of scandals involving insider trading at the exchange. The new chair of the NYSE is now considering eliminating the 'open outcry' method of trading (a 200-year-old tradition) in favor of an electronic system that would reduce human abuses.

While the NYSE imploded, the town of Rochester was dumped by its corporate creator, Eastman Kodak, when the company announced 4500 layoffs over a three-year period in an effort to reposition itself in the digital market. Kodak is one in a long line of manufacturing giants that have severed ties with their upstate New York centers. Since 2001, the state has lost more jobs than the national average, many of those in manufacturing. But politicians remain upbeat and point to New York's emergence as a leader in the nanotechnology field (the study of nano-sized matter) as a promising indicator; one-third of the science's discoveries occurred at New York–based research facilities. Many laid-off factory workers who are now working odd jobs are unimpressed and criticize the state government for rampant spending that is expected to result in a $6 billion deficit in 2004.

Although financial matters look bleak, New York continues good New England social ideals. Governor George Pataki handed the First Amendment an early Christmas present in 2003 when he granted a posthumous pardon to comedian Lenny Bruce. During a 1964 show in New York City, Bruce was arrested and later convicted on obscenity charges; police reported hearing 100 obscene words during Bruce's show. The fear of going to prison is believed to have precipitated Bruce's lethal drug overdose.

Lenny Bruce might have emitted a few obscenities regarding New York's most talked-about legislation – the statewide smoking ban. Enacted in mid-2003, smokers cursed the legislature that dared interfere with their primary hobby. As winter neared, bar owners were sure that patrons would stay at home rather than shuffle into the cold for a smoke. And as the freeze set in, the glow of the Budweiser sign beckoned people to share some suds and companionship. In a recent *New York Times* article, the owner of McSorley's Old Ale House said that the ban 'may be helping us because it's driving people to drink.'

FAST FACTS

New York State population: 18.9 million

Percentage of foreign-born persons: 20%

Total land area: 47,939 sq miles

Total inland water area: 1637 sq miles

Primary industries: printing and publishing, manufactured goods (cameras, film, copy machines, medical and surgical equipment), farming (dairy, animal feed crops)

State flower: rose

Number of High Peaks in the Adirondacks: 46

Start to finish time, Lake Placid bobsled: 43 seconds

Number of World Series baseball titles won by the New York Yankees: 26

History

New York's success, wars and ancestral heritage can be attributed to its waterways, which were the primary highways into the northern interior of North America. The Hudson River to Lake Champlain into Canada, Finger Lakes to Susquehanna River to the Chesapeake Bay – rivers and lakes with portages between were traversed by early Native Americans, Dutch, French and English and eventually led to New York's industrial dominance in the emerging nation.

The Epic of New York City (1966), by Edward Robb Ellis, is a massive personality-based history of the city from the days when Native Americans were the region's only residents to the mid-1960s.

NATIVE AMERICANS

There were two major groups of Native Americans in this region when Europeans began to arrive – the Algonquians and the Iroquois. Algonquian is a linguistic term commonly applied to tribes that spoke variations of the same family of languages. Algonquian-speaking tribes occupied the Hudson Valley and Long Island. They were made up of the Lenni-Lanape (meaning 'Original People', but called the Delaware by the British), Shawnee, Mohegan (or Mohican) and Munsee.

The Iroquois were a military and political confederacy of different Native American tribes that occupied central and western New York. They included the Cayuga, Mohawk, Oneida, Onondaga and Seneca peoples who together formed the powerful Iroquois Confederacy in 1570.

DID YOU KNOW?
The Dutch introduced the game of bowling and the myth of Santa Claus to its American colony of New Netherlands.

EUROPEAN ARRIVAL & COLONIALISM

The first European credited with visiting the region is the Italian navigator Giovanni da Verrazano, who sailed into New York Bay in 1524. In 1609, the English explorer Henry Hudson anchored the *Halve Maen* (Half Moon) in New York Harbor for 10 days before continuing up the river. 'It is as beautiful a land as one can hope to tread upon,' reported Hudson. Hudson's ship got as far as present-day Albany and he claimed all that he saw for the Dutch East India Company, for whom he was working.

Charged with finding the fabled Northwest Passage to India, Hudson instead found a wilderness that offered another profitable commodity: fur pelts. (Two years later another attempt to find the Northwest Passage, in the Canadian bay that bears his name, he was set adrift with eight others by his own crew and never seen again.) Trading posts were established and the company created an offspring with a more accurate geographic name – the Dutch West India Company – in 1621 with the aim of gaining dominance over the Atlantic trade.

DID YOU KNOW?
In the 1640s New Amsterdam was such a hard-drinking town that it faced a bread shortage because too much wheat had been diverted to the beer breweries.

Hudson was followed by Dutch explorers, and in 1624 settlements were established, in what was subsequently named New Netherlands. The first permanent settlement was established by a handful of Walloon families, French Protestants who fled the Spanish-ruled Netherlands looking for religious freedom. They called their settlement Fort Orange (present-day Albany). Two years later a settlement was established at New Amsterdam, the southern end of Manhattan Island.

In 1647 a new governor named Peter Stuyvesant arrived to impose order on what the Dutch government considered an unruly colony.

1524   **1609**

Giovanni da Verrazano sails into New York Harbor	Henry Hudson reaches the mouth of the Hudson and claims the wilderness for the Dutch

His ban on alcohol and curtailment of religious freedoms caused unrest among the settlers. In order to consolidate its control over the Atlantic colonies, the English sailed four warships into the New Amsterdam harbor in 1664, and in a bloodless takeover the young colony became New York. The Dutch settlers were allowed to keep their own language, religions and customs. Today there are still remnants of New York's Dutch heritage, especially in Albany as well as in the state's influential family names (like the Roosevelts), architecture and geographic and town names.

FRENCH & INDIAN WAR

In the early 1750s, fur traders and land speculators in the American colonies began to eye lands claimed by France east of the Appalachian Mountains. The French had built a line of forts from Lake Erie to western Pennsylvania from which they controlled their territory. The French even held the only portage around the strategically important Niagara Falls. Aggravated by rivalries in Europe, North America became an extended theater for war between the English and the French.

In 1754, the British colonial government sent young George Washington and 150 troops to dislodge the French. Washington failed, as did a force of 1500 men under British General Braddock (known as the Battle of Fort Necessity). The British and American troops fared poorly against the French and their Indian allies until 1757, when William Pitt became prime minister of England. Pitt borrowed heavily to pay for a vast infusion of troops and ships that helped change the course of the war. In 1759, the Anglo-American forces captured Fort Niagara on eastern Lake Erie, Fort Crown Point on southern Lake Champlain, and Quebec. When British and American troops captured Montreal in July 1760, French resistance in the New World collapsed. In 1763 the Peace of Paris agreement gave Britain all of North America east of the M ississippi, as well as Florida and Canada.

Despite their alliance with the Iroquois, the British were less conciliatory than the French in their relations with Native Americans. In 1763 an Ottawa Indian, Pontiac, emerged as a prophet and led attacks on British forts throughout western New York in an attempt to drive the British out. Pontiac's fighters at first overwhelmed a number of forts, but by 1764 found that they couldn't succeed. With the defeat of Pontiac, the last impediments to further westward colonial expansion in New York were swept away.

BREAK WITH BRITAIN & INDEPENDENCE

To finance the French and Indian War, Britain raised taxes in the colonies and introduced stricter controls on trade. By that time, opposition to the excesses of British colonial rule had developed and was given voice by John Peter Zenger's influential New York City newspaper, the *Weekly Journal*. On July 9, 1776, New York representatives signed the Declaration of Independence and joined the struggle against Britain.

Strategically, the British focused their military campaign on New York State, which they viewed as a keystone between the New England and southern colonies.

New York State hosted the first skirmish between British and rebel forces in 1775 when the independence movement was in its infantile insurgency state. Ethan Allen (with help from Benedict Arnold) and his

American Notes (1842), by Charles Dickens, includes reflections on New York City. He describes the life of one of the city's many roving pigs as 'a gentlemanly, vagabond kind of life, somewhat answering to that of our club-men at home.'

www.adirondack museum.org – The Online Exhibits page of the Adirondack Museum website has interesting essays on features of Adirondack history.

www.nyhistory.org – The New York Q&A section on the Library Collections page of the New-York Historical Society website arms visitors with a plethora of trivia.

1626	1788
Dutch settlers begin building New Amsterdam, later known as New York City	New York becomes the 11th US state

Green Mountain Boys ensured American control of Lake Champlain by successfully ousting the British from Fort Ticonderoga. This and other skirmishes total nearly one-third of the revolutionary battles occurring in New York. In August 1776, New York City was seized and burned by British troops; the occupation lasted until 1783. Toward the end of the war, General George Washington made his headquarters at Newburgh on the west bank of the Hudson River while waiting for the peace treaty to be signed. It was here that his troops offered to crown him king of the new nation. Washington indignantly declined.

NAME DROPPING: A WHO'S WHO OF NEW YORK HISTORY

- Susan B Anthony (1820–1906) – The foremost leader of the women's suffrage movement, Anthony campaigned from her home in Rochester. Claiming she had the right to vote under the 14th Amendment, Anthony tried unsuccessfully to cast her vote in the 1870s.

- Cass Gilbert (1859–1934) – One of the country's main proponents of the Beaux Arts style, Gilbert used a mixture of classical architecture and elaborate ornamentation. He built New York City's Custom House (1907), now the National Museum of the American Indian, and the Woolworth Building.

- Horace Greeley (1811–72) – One in a long line of reformers, Greeley founded the *New York Tribune* in 1841 and used its pages to rally for abolition of slavery, women's suffrage and universal public education.

- Jacob Riis (1849–1914) – A Danish reporter and photographer exposed the bleak squalor of urban tenements in his book *How the Other Half Lives: Studies Among the Tenements of New York*. His work helped dispel the myth that immigrants were genetically predisposed to a life of poverty and crime, but were instead unnecessarily blocked from success by inadequate and unsanitary housing conditions.

- John D Rockefeller (1839–1937) – Cofounder of Standard Oil Company, Rockefeller amassed an empire by ruthless and inventive practices. By buying up or outpricing his competitors, Rockefeller controlled close to 90% of the American oil refining industry and breaking up his monopoly was the primary aim of the government's 1890 antitrust act.

- Elizabeth Cady Stanton (1815–1902) – Co-organized the first convention for women's right, which was held in Seneca Falls in 1848; the convention called for the right to control property, legal control over earnings and the right to vote. The legislature honored the first two requests within 15 years, but the last demand came 60 years later.

- William 'Boss' Tweed (1823–78) – At the peak of his career as boss of the Tammany Hall political machine, Tweed was president of the New York City county board of supervisors, street commissioner and state senator. His handpicked cronies held all the other offices he didn't have time for. He bought votes from new immigrants and lined his pockets with bogus city contracts. In 1871, Tweed was finally tried and convicted of graft and corruption.

- Cornelius Vanderbilt (1794–1877) – Born to a modest Staten Island farming family, Vanderbilt started up a ferry company when he was 16 to transport commuters between New York City and Staten Island. He then graduated to a steamboat shipping company. After the Civil War, he gained control of the New York Central Railroad and connected New York City to Chicago.

- Stanford White (1853–1906) – Architect and socialite, White's firm McKim, Mead & White designed the former Penn Station, the Washington Square Park Arch and other Gilded Age masterpieces.

1825	1827
The Erie Canal opens	Slavery is abolished in New York State

New York City was awarded the honor of the nation's first capital, even though there was no constitution, no president and only a handful of representatives who spent their days in debate. At the corner of Wall and Broad Sts in the Federal Hall, the meeting house of the new government was the site where George Washington was sworn in as president. Five years later, the seat of the government relocated to the District of Columbia, a move that was probably driven by a dislike of the city by the founding fathers. Thomas Jefferson later said that he regarded New York to be a 'cloacina [sewer] of all the depravities of human nature.'

Though not the first group in history to pick the wrong side, the Iroquois, who had sided with the British, paid a far worse price than the average lottery loser. Beset by military defeats, disease and continuing encroachment by European settlers, the Iroquois communities around the Finger Lakes were devastated for good in 1779, when General George Washington sent a heavily armed expedition to punish the Native Americans for their isolated and brutal attack on a Scottish and Irish community near Otsego Lake. Entire communities were wiped out, and much of the land was deeded to Revolutionary War veterans as payment for service.

ERIE CANAL & CIVIL WAR

New York's natural arteries were augmented with a 363-mile 'ditch' (the Erie Canal) that connected Buffalo (on Lake Erie) and Albany (on the Hudson River) in 1825. A keg of Lake Erie water was poured into New York Bay, as part of a ceremonious 'marriage of waters.' The canal provided a shortcut into the heartland of the interior, opening up the farms of the Midwest to the distribution point of New York City's harbor. Canal boats transported people, wheat, salt, glass and other items to new markets in less time and with less expense. What would have taken three weeks to send to market, now took eight days. From Albany to Buffalo, towns and cities prospered along with the canal's economic success. Rochester, for example, emerged as a wheat and flour producer.

By the 1850s, George Washington's prophecy, a generation earlier, of New York State becoming the 'seat of the empire' was realized. It was the country's leading industrial center, producing iron casting, cotton textiles and agricultural goods. A more subtle revolution occurred in New York State at this time. Thanks to the increase in commerce, merchants began replacing the landed gentry as the ruling class, contributing to much of the power structure that exists today.

In 1827 New York State had abolished slavery within its borders just as other northern states had done. As the US expanded westward, the Congress fought bitterly over the extension of slavery into these new territories. Compromises were soon exhausted, and with the election of the antislavery candidate Abraham Lincoln in 1860, South Carolina became the first of 11 southern states to secede from the Union, marking the beginning of the Civil War. Raising an army to force the southern states back into the Union fell upon the northern states. In New York, draftees could pay a $300 fee to opt out of military service, ensuring that the burden of fighting fell to the poorer citizens (in this case recent Irish immigrants). In response, the three-day Draft Riots of 1863 destroyed the draft lottery building, burned whole sections of New York City and killed 1200 people.

The Hudson (1989), by Carl Carmer, recounts history in novelistic fashion with vivid details and compelling characters.

New York: An Illustrated History (2003), by Ric Burns, James Sanders and Lisa Ades, is an essay-driven, 500-photograph tome on New York City's career from frontier to megalopolis. Transcripts from the companion PBS documentary and interviews accompany this book.

1848	1861–65
First women's rights convention is held in Seneca Falls	Civil War

Ethnic New York (1995), by Mark Leeds, is a good neighborhood-by-neighborhood guide to New York City.

Over 500,000 troops from New York fought for the preservation of the Union. Of these, nearly 60,000 died on the battlefield – ironically, about the same number of Americans who died 100 years later in Vietnam. The Civil War ended in 1865, partly due to the superior industrial resources of the North (New York in particular).

IMMIGRATION & THE GILDED AGE

The country's primary port, New York City, also became the gateway for another import – immigrants. Europeans abandoned their decrepit farms or political turmoil at home to find jobs in New York's manufacturing cities. In the 1840s close to three million immigrants arrived in New York, many of whom were unskilled, poor and Catholic, an unwelcome religious affiliation in the largely Protestant state. In the 1860 census, one-quarter of the state and 45% of New York City's population was foreign-born. They originally hailed from Ireland, Germany, Italy, Poland and China. Joining the emerging industrial machine, immigrants became like interchangeable parts, swapped out with new arrivals and stored in damp, cramped ghettos.

Meanwhile the industry titans made unimaginable sums of money in the new technologies: railroads, steamboats and oil refinery. Their headquarters and showpiece homes were in New York City. The fortunes made during this period, referred to as the Gilded Age, made every other wealthy family in the history of the US seem like paupers, and the purchasing power of this era rivaled the excesses of European aristocracy.

To mediate the widening economic gap, New York became a staging ground for social and political reform movements, including women's suffrage, labor unions and tenement-housing codes. Theodore Roosevelt, a New York native son, used his presidency (1901–09) to curb the ruthlessness of the Gilded Age through federal oversight of interstate commerce and antitrust laws. He also set aside forest reserves and conservation areas at a time of rapid development. Even the industries' barons bought their way into progressivism by founding educational and cultural institutions, such as New York City's Frick Collection and the Museum of Modern Art.

MODERN TIMES

After WWII, there began a trend in New York State that continues to the present time: the exodus of large manufacturing companies, such as

---

PRESIDENT OF THE PEOPLE: FDR

One of the most popular presidents of modern America, Franklin D Roosevelt (FDR) was born to an influential New York family whose lineage could be traced back to Dutch fur traders and included founders of the Bank of New York, another US president (Theodore 'Teddy' Roosevelt) and railroad tycoons. Despite privilege and pedigree, FDR developed a keen sense of social responsibility that manifested itself, during his presidency, in work and relief programs that helped offset the economic disaster of the 1930s. At the age of 39, just as he was poised to make a bid for the White House, he contracted polio and never regained the use of his legs. Only a temporary setback, FDR resumed the political stump three years later and was elected president four times. Not bad for a man confined to a wheelchair and who never finished his law degree at Columbia University.

1883	1929
The Brooklyn Bridge is completed	The stock market crashes and an economic depression follows

GOTHAM BEGINNINGS

Now synonymous with a hulking city haunted by evil geniuses in the comic books *Superman* and *Spider Man*, New York City's alter ego was first applied by Washington Irving and his friends in a collection of humorous essays on the city, titled *Salmagundi*. The term Gotham refers to an old story about a 13th-century village in England of the same name. One day King John arrived in town looking for an idyllic spot to build a castle, someplace where hard-working villagers would lend a dutiful hand in order to maintain the royal possession. Once the villagers were wise to the king's plan, they conspired to scare him away. In plain view King John spotted one villager trying to rake the reflection of the moon out of a small pond. Other villagers joined in the fun and King John left disgusted with their imbecility. The villagers boasted 'more fools pass through Gotham than remain in it.'

Nestlé, Nabisco, GE and Kodak, from the dependent population centers of Syracuse, Rochester and Beacon, to name a few. New York ceded its role as national engine to new markets in California and Texas, along with other hulking factory states, like Pennsylvania and Ohio, became better known as 'the rust belt.' Job losses, the advent of suburbs and the emergence of a social safety net hacked away at the viability of New York's once-thriving cities, most notably New York City. Between 1950 and 1970, more than one million families left New York City for the outlying suburbs. A city without a strong economy is a broken-down place that feeds upon its own destruction. Those who could afford to get out did, leaving behind the struggling or unemployed families too poor to move to new opportunities – often these lines were racial, fueling a statewide struggle between white and black. Simple questions of economics were tainted by irrational sentiments of racial discrimination. New York State wasn't alone in this argument, the 1960 and '70s ushered in social upheaval and divisive political cleaving across the country.

Amidst the tumult, New York State served as the stage for one of the hippie generation's greatest accomplishments: Woodstock. In the rural heartland of New York State, a three-day music concert briefly created an idyllic commune of counter-culture aspirations. The state responded with such severe legislation that the event could never be truly duplicated.

Interestingly, during such unpredictable times, New York elected Nelson Rockefeller, descendant of the industrial revolution's most despised leader, to the office of governor four times starting in 1958. A moderate Republican, Rockefeller established the SUNY (state university) system, built low-income housing and the Albany Mall, the ultramodern home of the state government, and funded arts and environmental protection.

Moving into the last decades of the 20th century, tourism became an economic salve for the state's struggling cities. The transformation of New York City from crime-ridden ghetto to family-friendly outing served as the model for other cities. Beacon attracted a cutting-edge museum, Hudson became the antiquers' weekend therapist and Buffalo was heralded as a phoenix rising.

But the end of the 1990s stock market boom and the 2001 terrorist attacks on New York City have brought a dose of uncertainty to the state. Fear of recession and another terrorist attack make many New Yorker skeptical of the government's political promises.

DID YOU KNOW?

Six New Yorkers have been elected president, including two of the country's most popular chief executives, Theodore Roosevelt and his cousin Franklin D Roosevelt.

1946	2001
New York is chosen as the site for the United Nations	Attacks on the World Trade Center

The Culture

New York State enjoys one of the most culturally rich environments of any state in the Union. The wealth of the Gilded Age bestowed to the public fine collections of art and architecture, and New York City is both a receptacle of and muse for artistic endeavors.

REGIONAL IDENTITY

There are two distinct New Yorks: the swathe that falls within the influence of New York City (specifically Long Island and Hudson Valley) and that amorphous area called 'upstate' (which refers to everywhere else). The landscape of the Hudson Valley might be pastoral but the people are not. Many of the residents are city refugees who followed the river north to buy a Victorian fixer-upper or to claim a tidy yard for their yellow Labrador. The tastes and aesthetics are sophisticated and catered to by upscale bistros and antiquarian bookstores. Meanwhile, the local people who grew up on small family farms just shrug and hope that the property taxes don't increase too much and force them to sell to a developer.

Upstate New York was once the industrial muscle of the country. Rochester, Syracuse, Buffalo – these were boom towns where new immigrants and Southern blacks moved to get good paying factory jobs. Once the factories folded, these towns became places that people move away from rather than move to. Rusting alongside these factory cities is the beleaguered economy of the Adirondacks. Life in this remote place has always been hard, jobs scarce, winters brutal. But as a reward, the residents of the Adirondacks had the undiluted work of the Creator to admire and play in.

While its rural landscape of small family farms and stone fences mimics New England, New York's character is quite different. A steely spirit, one of self-reliance with a streak of bravado, was forged in the company towns and small hamlets. While New Englanders rally around the town hall to decide local matters, New Yorkers prefer to focus their civic energies on the local fire house, where fearlessness and action are required rather than the seemingly ineffectual process of debate.

This is also an immigrant state, holding dear to the memories of a homeland, whether the exodus occurred in colonial or modern times. Enclaves of ethnicities maintain distinct identities within the larger framework of being New Yorkers. Near the Canadian border many of the inhabitants have surnames and traditions tied to French Canada, while other regions in the interior claim Irish, Scottish, Polish and Italian heri-.tage. A visitor bearing the ancestral coloring of these motherlands will be greeted with friendly toasts from old-timers smoking pipes in front of the downtown fire houses.

New York shares a united devotion to the arts and education. It has the nation's largest public school system and a supervisory board that dates back to 1784. The state proudly boasts some of the country's most prestigious universities – Columbia, New York University, Cornell – and a remarkable public university system. If a town is too small to support a museum or historic homes, then it will surely have a dusty used bookstore, a well-stocked library or an amateur theater company. It also has all of New York City's many cultural events just a short trip away.

Radio first appeared in the US when its inventor, Guglielmo Marconi, broadcast a commentary from New York Harbor on the America's Cup yachting race in 1899.

LIFESTYLE

An ongoing debate, of course, is what constitutes 'upstate' New York. This is more an argument of lifestyle and values than of geography. Folks in the Adirondacks' North Country refer casually to 'downstaters' as occupants of a different reality. On the other hand, it's not unusual to hear New York City dwellers discuss a trip 'upstate,' only to find out they went to Poughkeepsie, where commuter trains carry people in and out of the Big Apple every day of the week. A resident of Westchester County had the best definition of upstate: 'Any place north of where you are.' An even better divining rod is the local coffee shop. If a town has a spot where the local men gather to drink coffee and swap jokes, you're in upstate. If the residents get their coffee to go, you're in downstate.

To the residents of New York City and its satellites, time is precious and is best used making or spending money. One of the most frequently quoted reasons for living in New York City is that you can get anything you want anytime. (Except you can't buy a bottle of wine at a liquor store on Sunday, but why burst their bubble?) No appetite goes unsated, and no expense goes unnoticed.

Upstaters, on the other hand, are austere in their tastes and indulgences. They are even reserved in political matters. New York cleaves between a heavily Democratic New York City and Republican-leaning voters in the rest of the state. In lean times, upstate often accuses the state legislature of spending too much money and attention on the problems of New York City. Without noticing the poverty and crime in their own backyard, upstaters sometimes heap criticism on an easy target – the urban poor.

Well hidden in the endless debates about the points on the compass, both 'states' love self-reflection. Like catching a glimpse of oneself in a mirrored window, New York State has been written, photographed, filmed and debated about so much that it is secretly admiring itself when it points to the metropolis or the country and sees 'otherness.'

> 'If a town has a spot where the local men gather to drink coffee and swap jokes, you're in upstate'

POPULATION

With 18.9 million residents, New York is the third most populous state in the nation, behind California and Texas. Sixty-seven percent of that total are white, 15.9% are African-American, 12.5% are Hispanic, 3.6% are Asians and 0.9% are American Indian.

Approximately half of all state residents live in New York City. About 35.9% (2.8 million) of the city's residents claim foreign birth. Percentage-wise Los Angeles outpaces New York City at 40%, but NYC still holds on to its historic role as the gateway to America with 1.3 million more recent immigrants than LA. The city is home to the largest Chinese population in the US, along with the country's largest bloc of Asian Indians. New York City claims to have the largest Jewish population outside of Israel and the largest population of Russian-speaking and Orthodox Jews in the US. More native Greeks live in Astoria, Queens, than anywhere outside Athens; more native Russians, more native Irish, and so on. These claims are difficult to prove using statistics, but a walk through several of the city's neighborhoods leaves the impression that these assertions are probably not far off the mark.

There are three million African-Americans living in New York, typically centered in urban areas, such as New York City, Buffalo and Rochester. Although New York State's percentage of African-American residents is quite low at almost 16% (compared to 60% in the District of Columbia), in actual numbers more African-Americans live here than in any other state.

Hispanics make up 12.5% (about 2.4 million people) of the state's population. About half of New York City's two million Hispanic residents are of Puerto Rican descent and began migrating from the island in significant numbers during the Depression. Over the past 20 years there has been an influx of Latinos from many other countries, such as Ecuador, Colombia, Dominican Republic and El Salvador.

SPORTS

The major football teams in this region are the New York Jets and New York Giants (who actually play at the Meadowlands Sports Complex in New Jersey). The other main team in New York is the Buffalo Bills, with wildly loyal fans who brave subzero temperatures to watch their team play in upstate New York.

'Football makes the winters go by, but baseball keeps the state's blood pumping'

Football makes the winters go by, but baseball keeps the state's blood pumping. Two of the most famous baseball clubs in the US are the New York Yankees (the most successful team in baseball history), who play at Yankee Stadium in the Bronx, and the New York Mets, who play at Shea Stadium in Queens. Minor league teams pop up all over the state.

In basketball the region's major clubs are the New York Knickerbockers (Knicks), whose games are filled with almost as many celebrities as the big Hollywood awards shows.

Ice hockey is also popular, and teams compete in the National Hockey League (NHL) for the Stanley Cup. The main clubs are the New York Rangers, New York Islanders and Buffalo Sabers.

In New York City, Madison Square Garden is a world-famous sports venue. Flushing Meadows, in Queens, is the site for pro-tennis' US Open tournament, held in September.

Thoroughbred horseracing is popular, and national events are held in summer at the Saratoga Race Course in Saratoga Springs, also home to the National Museum of Racing.

MULTICULTURALISM

Immigration has never been regarded favorably by those who had come before. When the Native American tribes looked up from their sylvan hunting grounds and saw the Europeans' strange sailing ships, they knew that the old days were numbered. Since then, the immigrants' descendants, self-crowned as natives, looked to the newcomers with primal disgust. The English and Dutch, who had arrived to find a frontier, abhorred the Italians and Irish who followed some one hundred years later. The 'original' colonists termed themselves nativists (a laughable appellation by today's definitions) and, in the 1800s, formed a powerful political party (Native American Democratic Association) to counter the immigrant threat. Within several generations, the Americans (now a polyglot of Italian, Irish, English and Dutch) looked suspiciously at their replacements, African-Americans who were migrating from the rural South to manufacturing jobs. Blacks were branded as outsiders, although many could claim longer American lineage than their accusers. Then came the Chinese, and Colombians, and in 1990 Hispanics displaced Italians as the state's second-largest ethnic group. It wasn't until the civil rights struggle of the 1960s that the state, and the nation, began to recognize the errors of relegating US inhabitants to second-class status. Although personal opinions may still reflect xenophobia, the state's institutions are held to a higher standard. In fact, some communities, like Schenectady, see immigrants as a way to resuscitate declining populations and tax bases. The Schenectady mayor has even identified a preferred immigrant group, the Guyanese, and maintains a website (www.guyaneseopportunities.com) to advertise his town's advantages to Guyanese families and entrepreneurs.

MEDIA

New York didn't invent journalism, but it did perfect the profession into an industry. A New York City court case in 1733 set the legal precedent for a free press, which would later be ensured by the Constitution and regarded as integral to the new republic's checks-and-balances system. Penny papers, political leaflets and foreign-language rags proliferated throughout the state, printed by small-time presses or enterprising idealists, like Frederick Douglass, whose influential African-American paper *North Star* was published in Rochester in 1847. The undeniable center of the newspaper age was New York City, which attracted generations of emerging writers and activists who first tested their pens in the paper trade. The evolution of news gathering took a major leap forward thanks to Samuel Morse's (a native New Yorker) invention of the telegraph and the formation of wire services, including the Associated Press (AP). Wire services also gave rise to feature-length magazines, many of which survive today. But New York's most notorious invention was 'yellow journalism' (irresponsible, even fabricated reporting), which eventually evolved into the less insidious tabloid. In the early 20th century, the media business was modernizing into an industry. The do-it-yourself dailies were being swallowed up by a few profit-driven companies dictated by the concerns of the advertisers. By 1940, New York's 20 dailies had shrunk to eight. Even the new technologies of radio and TV, whose newsrooms were headquartered in New York City, followed a similar model. Today New York holds the ceremonious crown of media capital but many news outlets (TV, radio and print) have been absorbed into mega-conglomerates, many of which are no longer based in New York.

American Visions: The Epic History of Art in America (1997), by Robert Hughes, is a 350-year art history that is well written, some say witty.

ARTS

New York City remains the most important center for the arts in the US and, historically, has helped shape much of the country's artistic and cultural life.

Painting

Documenting New York's role in American painting are the prestigious museums – Metropolitan Museum of Art (p91), the Museum of Modern Art (MoMA; p88), the Frick Collection (p90), the Whitney Museum of American Art (p91) and the Guggenheim Museum (p91). The Albany Institute of History and Art (p187) has an excellent collection from the Hudson River school of painting.

AMERICAN LANDSCAPE

From about 1825, landscape painting became the strongest current in American art. It reflected the trend of territorial expansion and took a romantic, sometimes allegorical view of a wilderness that was rapidly disappearing in the eastern states. Asher Durand (1796–1886) and Thomas Cole (1801–48) were the leading figures of the Hudson River school, which initially concentrated on the Catskill Mountains in New York State. Their 'luminist' emphasis on atmosphere and light was developed in the landscapes of Cole's student Frederic Edwin Church (1820–1900), who extended his subject matter to monumental paintings of New York's Niagara Falls, the Andes and the tropics.

AMERICAN REALISM & MODERNISM

In the early 20th century, a group of artists began to paint with the eye of the muckraking journalist – in New York, of course. Rejecting impressionism, which they saw as too refined, they insisted on a realism that represented urban, working-class life. They were later known as the Ashcan school. The best example is George Bellows (1882–1925), who portrayed the poor of lower Manhattan and the brutality of boxers.

Evolving at this time were imitations of European moves toward abstract art. A young French painter, Marcel Duchamp (1887–1968), caused a sensation at the 1913 'Armory' show (officially called the International Exhibition of Modern Art) with his cubist *Nude Descending a Staircase*, which most critics noted didn't seem to portray a recognizable nude *or* a staircase. Duchamp told the newsman that was exactly the point, and thus the New York school of Dada was begun.

Taking its name from the French slang for hobbyhorse, the Dada movement was led by Duchamp, fellow countryman Francis Picabia and American artist Man Ray (1890–1976), who became known for their antiwar attitudes and deconstructive art that sought to shock and offend. By the 1920s, most of the Dadaists had moved on – Ray to photography and Duchamp to full-time celebrity – but the Dada movement remained influential.

Others practiced a hybrid form of expression, as in the paintings of Charles Demuth (1883–1935) and Charles Sheeler (1883–1965). Usually using urban and industrial America as their subject matter and identified by straight lines and geometric planes, their work was known as cubist realism. The popular Georgia O'Keeffe (1887–1986) did the same with desert flowers and landscapes. In the mid-20th century she spent much of her time at New York's Lake George with her husband Alfred Stieglitz (who had introduced cubism to the US).

Painting thrived in Harlem during the Harlem Renaissance of the 1920s and '30s. One of the most prominent artists was Aaron Douglas (1899–1979), who did illustrations for such publications as Eugene O'Neill's *The Emperor Jones* (1926) as well as murals of black Americans and Africans.

POST WWII

American art flourished after WWII with the emergence of a new school of painting defined by Jackson Pollock (1912–56) and Willem de Kooning (1904–97). Known as abstract expressionism, it combined spontaneity of expression with abstract forms composed haphazardly and dominated art until the mid-1980s.

From the 1950s other artists began to borrow images, items and themes from popular culture, enlarging, coloring and combining them in the pop-art style made famous by Roy Lichtenstein (1923–97), Jasper Johns (born 1930) and Andy Warhol (1928–87). Warhol worked in many different media – drawing, painting, sculpture, silk-screening, photography, film, video and music. Accessible, enjoyable and popular, pop art was also identifiably American in its imagery.

In the 1980s Warhol's legacy of artist-as-celebrity spawned a host of well-known painters and illustrators, many of whom broke out from New York's SoHo gallery scene, among them Julian Schnabel, Kenny Scharf and the late Keith Haring, who began his career as an underground graffiti artist.

The avant-garde art scene is now more international than American. Even New York's avant-garde art scene has migrated out of its birthplace, SoHo, to warehouses in Chelsea and Brooklyn.

SMILE FOR THE CAMERA

New York City's photogeneity pushed the new technology into an art form, especially under the guidance of Alfred Stieglitz (1864–1946). The city's role as a publishing center also provided work opportunities for photographers. *Life* magazine was influential in the development of photojournalism and kept a large staff of photographers corralled for grazing the city's streets as well as the world's. Margaret Bourke-White (1904–71) covered WWII and the Korean War and was one of the first female photographers assigned to cover the US armed forces. Another photographer was Alfred Eisenstaedt (1898–1995), a portraitist and news photographer who took the famous image of a sailor kissing a nurse in Times Square at the end of WWII.

Weegee (1899–1968), whose real name was Arthur H Fellig, was a press photographer noted for his on-the-spot street photography. William Klein and Richard Avedon were fashion photographers who worked for magazines like *Vogue* and *Harper's Bazaar* in the 1950s and '60s. Avedon's work also included portraits and shots of Vietnam War protesters and the civil rights movement.

In more recent years, Stephen Meisel, Herb Ritts and Annie Leibowitz have become as famous for their commercial work as their more artistic endeavors. Nan Goldin charted the lives (and many deaths) of her transvestite and drug-addicted friends from the 1970s to the present day. Cindy Sherman specializes in conceptual series (such as those inspired by movie stills and crime-scene photos).

Literature

As New York City developed into the publishing capital of the US – a position it retains today – it attracted writers from all over the country.

18TH & 19TH CENTURIES

An essayist and short-story writer, Washington Irving (1783–1859) was the first American literary figure to receive international recognition. His country estate was called Sunnyside, on the Hudson River near Tarrytown, and the area around it is described by him in the stories 'Sleepy Hollow' and 'The Legend of Sleepy Hollow.' He also wrote a widely praised satire, *History of New York* (1809), under the pen name of Dietrich Knickerbocker.

In tribute to the book, a group of writers adopted the term 'Knickerbocker' for their movement to develop a recognizably American literature. Foremost among them was James Fenimore Cooper (1789–1851), who drew images of the landscape and pioneer life on the American frontier in his *Leatherstocking* stories and of Native Americans in such works as *The Last of the Mohicans* (1826).

The Knickerbockers were satirized by literary critic, poet and gothic horror-story writer Edgar Allan Poe (1809–49), who lived for a time in Philadelphia before settling in New York City. Among his most famous works are 'The Pit and the Pendulum,' 'The Black Cat' and 'The Raven.' Margaret Fuller (1810–50), a contemporary of Poe and a fellow reviewer, wrote *Woman in the Nineteenth Century* (1845) disclosing conditions in prisons and hospitals. It helped inspire the later feminist movement in the US.

Prior to the Civil War, a group of writers became known as Pfaff's Cellar because they used to meet at a place by that name on Broadway. Its leading member was Long Island's Walt Whitman (1819–92), whose exuberant poetry celebrated the plurality of American democratic society. His life work is contained in *Leaves of Grass* (originally published in 1855 and enlarged in later editions), which is considered one of the masterpieces of world literature. True to New York fashion, it earned him the distinction of having a mall named after him on Long Island.

New York City is the main magazine- and book-publishing center in the country and its multibillion-dollar industry produces more magazines per month than any other city in the nation.

THE NEW YORKER

Founded in 1925, the *New Yorker* began life as a humor magazine in a small office with one typewriter. Directed at a cultured, literate audience, the magazine's typical reader was depicted on its first cover by a cartoon of a monocled dandy watching a butterfly. This cover illustration is reused every year on the anniversary of the first edition.

Early contributors to the magazine were the members of the Algonquin Round Table, an influential and witty group of 1920s literary figures, including Dorothy Parker, who regularly lunched at the Algonquin Hotel. A surviving anecdote from those early days was when founding editor Harold Ross chased down Dorothy Parker, asking her, 'I thought you were coming into the office to write a piece last week. What happened?' Parker replied, 'Somebody was using the pencil.'

Other contributors over the years have included JD Salinger, Rebecca West, Ogden Nash, John Cheever, EB White, Marianne Moore, Raymond Carver, Ann Beattie, Rita Dove and John Updike.

Illustrations have always been a signature of the magazine, which has used the work of Rea Irvin (who designed the illustration for the very first cover), Charles Addams, Peter Arno and James Thurber.

Writing New York: A Literary Anthology (2000), edited by Phillip Lopate, is the single best overview on New York City as the star in American literature.

Henry James (1843–1916), though he lived mostly in England, grew up in New York City and returned from time to time in later life. In *Washington Square* (1881) he described upper-class life in that area before the Civil War. The row houses that were occupied by New York society still line the northern edge of Washington Square Park.

A close friend of James' was Edith Wharton (1862–1937), who chronicled the Gilded Age of New York City in the Pulitzer prize–winning *Age of Innocence* (1920) and other works.

JAZZ AGE TO MODERN AGE

From the early 20th century onwards, Greenwich Village rose to prominence as an artistic and literary colony. Among these artists were the playwright Eugene O'Neill (p35) and the poet ee cummings (1894–1962). Some of the early short stories of F Scott Fitzgerald (1896–1940) were published here, too, and with the success of his first novel, *This Side of Paradise* (1920), he became the chronicler and self-styled representative of the Jazz Age. A later collection of his short stories was published under the title *Tales of the Jazz Age* (1922). Many of his works feature upper-crust New York, and Long Island was the site for *The Great Gatsby* (1925), which has been acknowledged as one of the finest American novels.

By the end of WWI, Harlem had become a vibrant, predominantly black neighborhood with a growing self-assertiveness and authors writing on the African-American experience. The publication in 1917 by the short-lived Greenwich Village magazine *Seven Arts* of Claude McKay's story 'Harlem Dancer' is said to mark the start of the Harlem Renaissance, which reached its peak in the 1920s and '30s. As well as McKay, its leading authors included Wallace Thurman, Jean Toomer, Langston Hughes, Countée Cullen and Zora Neale Hurston. McKay's novel, *Home to Harlem* (1928), about a black army deserter, was a best-seller. Hurston's *Their Eyes were Watching God* (1937) became an important piece of feminist work.

One of the early important Beat novels was William S Burroughs' *Junkie* (1953), a stark account of his early life as a drug addict. In 1956, Allen Ginsberg gave poetic voice to his generation in *Howl and Other Poems*. When Jack Kerouac's *On the Road* (written in one sitting, it's said, on a large ream of typewriter paper in the Chelsea Hotel) hit the bookstores in 1957, it became the compulsory reading of a generation.

In the same period JD Salinger's *Catcher in the Rye* (1951) spoke to a generation of disaffected young Americans.

Thomas Pynchon portrayed the restlessness of younger New Yorkers in *V* (1963). Alternatively, a group of writers including John Cheever and John Updike set out to document northeastern life of the upper-middle class during this time.

A newer, more energetic style of writing dominated the 1970s and '80s. Don DeLillo's *Great Jones Street* (1973) and Mark Helprin's *Winter's Tale* (1983) are prime examples of their disturbing view of society. Paul Auster, who lives in Brooklyn, won many followers abroad for his *New York Trilogy* (1990) and wrote the screenplay for the Brooklyn-based movie *Smoke*.

The works of EL Doctorow (born 1931), including *Ragtime* (1975), *The Book of Daniel* (1971) and *World's Fair* (1985), are loftier ruminations on New York in its various eras, from Gilded Age boomtown to cold war ideological battleground.

Jay McInerney was first blessed, then cursed with association to the yuppified early 1980s with his blockbuster first novel *Bright Lights, Big City* (1984). *Bonfire of the Vanities* (1987) by Tom Wolfe (born 1931) followed up with its comic canvass of a city out of control and split along racial lines. Tama Janowitz, author of *Slaves of New York* (1986), covers much of the same ground, as does essayist Fran Lebowitz.

In the 1990s, new writers and spoken-word performers emerged in the East Village of New York City, debuting their work at various cafés, but for the most part the generation-X novelists have been based on the West Coast. One literary lion, Jonathan Lethem, crowned the poet of Brooklyn, has written several novels about race and broken families. His books *Fortress of Solitude* (1999) and *Motherless Brooklyn* (1999) continue to cultivate fans. Another much-heralded writer is Michael Chabon, whose book *The Amazing Adventures of Kavalier & Clay* (2001) divides its time between New York and Prague.

New York Days (1993), by Willie Morris, describes the 1960s literary era and new journalism, as well as the backstabbing in the profession.

www.albany.edu /writers-inst – The New York State Writers Institute is a nonprofit organization that hosts writing workshops, film series and lectures on the craft of writing. They also recognize modern poets and writers with literary awards, and the website provides biographies on past winners.

Music

New York's most heralded period was the Jazz Age, when Harlem musicians ushered the brass bands from New Orleans into the abstract art form of bebop. After prohibition forced the closure of many clubs in Chicago, jazz musicians converged on New York City in the 1920s and '30s. At venues like Harlem's Cotton Club, big-band orchestras led by such notables as Count Basie and Duke Ellington played to mixed crowds. Even Satchmo, Louis Armstrong, found his greatest fame in the Big Apple. After winning a talent contest at Harlem's famed Apollo Theater in 1934, Ella Fitzgerald went on to become one of the great jazz singers. Billie Holiday learned her trade in New York's nightclubs before headlining at the Apollo.

In the 1940s Dizzy Gillespie, a celebrated jazz trumpeter, invented the bebop school of jazz improvisation with Charlie Parker and Thelonious Monk.

Folk music had been around since colonial times, but Greenwich Village gave the music a modern and political edge that started in the 1930s with Woody Guthrie and Pete Seeger and peaked in the 1960s with Bob Dylan, Joan Baez and Peter, Paul & Mary. Simon & Garfunkel, from Queens, also had their roots in this music.

In response to the idealism of the folk scene, a new generation of musicians tossed aside harmonies for raw rock and roll. An Andy Warhol darling, the Velvet Underground, led by Lou Reed and John Cale, presaged the music of punk rock with their tribute songs to heroin addiction.

Tin Pan Alley, which dominated American popular music from the 1890s to the 1960s, originally referred to an area of New York City where music publishers and composers were centered. Among its most influential composers were Irving Berlin, George and Ira Gershwin, Oscar Hammerstein and Cole Porter.

CBGB, a club on the East Side, became the epicenter of the punk scene. Most often cited by modern musicians as an inspiration, the Ramones played their instruments loud and fast; most of their songs were under two minutes long. CBGB was the proving ground for other bands like Television, Talking Heads and Blondie.

In the discos and streets of the South Bronx a music revolution occurred: the African-American tradition of oral posturing, known as rap, was paired with music. It started out as party music through the work of Afrika Bambaataa, Grandmaster Flash and Harlem's Sugar Hill Gang, but became heavy-hitting commentaries on ghetto life. In the 1980s, Public Enemy's hard-edged political and racial rhymes earned them critical recognition as the genre's greatest act. Even the Beastie Boys, who started out as a hardcore band, carved out a respectable rap niche long before Eminem breathed into a microphone. When rap found a melody as well as the beat, it became hip hop, of which De La Soul and A Tribe Called Quest are its best representatives. Recent promoters of the New York sound include Busta Rhymes and Lil' Kim.

AIA Guide to New York City (2000), by Norval White and Elliot Willensky, is the most comprehensive guide to architecture in New York City detailing the buildings' history, anecdotes and architectural styles.

Although rap and cutting-edge music have drifted to other cities, New York City has experienced a very minor but highly publicized emergence of guitar-revival bands. Among the grittiest, the Yeah, Yeah, Yeahs, led by singer Karen O, have revived the aging face of punk rock with a sprinkle of new-millennium attitude. Their reign may be brief, but at least rock is back.

Architecture

America's early architectural styles reflect the different origins of the European settlers, predominantly Dutch and British.

The stoop – a wide set of stairs leading to the front door of many buildings in New York City – was a Dutch feature serving, as it does today, as a patio for visiting with neighbors or enjoying a sunny day. Kingston and Albany retain the best surviving examples of the distinctive Dutch stone cottages.

The historic homes along the Hudson River valley serve as a textbook for American architecture. Clermont, the home of the influential Livingston family, is an example of Georgian architecture, one of the earliest British styles to be introduced to America. Named after the British monarch, the Georgian period lasted roughly from the start of the 18th century until the American Revolution. The red-brick buildings are simple and symmetrical, with delicate glass fanlights over large, elegant doorways. After the revolution the style was modified slightly and became known as Federal.

From the late 18th century, neoclassical architecture based on Roman and Greek designs became popular. Many institutional buildings on Wall St in New York City were modeled on these design elements. The architects of this style also designed Gothic Revival buildings, another popular style of the 19th century. It was given expression in Trinity Church (1846; p72) and the Woolworth Building (1913; p76) in New York City.

But the skyscraper is New York's must stunning addition to the manmade landscape. The 19th-century attempts to build a vertical city were limited structurally by the thickness of the buildings' walls (which supported successive stories). The creation of a metal skeleton (which was first applied in Chicago in 1883) allowed adequate weight distribution and the invention of the 'vertical train' (or elevator) in 1853 made it possible for New York to grow vertically.

Theater

The theater is one of New York City's most noteworthy artistic institutions. At the end of the 19th century and for more than two decades into the 20th, vaudeville (song-and-dance variety acts) was the most popular form of theater in the country. The main venue in New York City was the Palace Theater in Times Square and the most famous vaudeville impresario was Florenz Ziegfeld (1867–1932), best known for his lavish revues, the Ziegfeld Follies.

One of the great playwrights of the early 20th century was New York-born Eugene O'Neill (1888–1953), who won three Pulitzer prizes for his plays in the 1920s. In 1936 he also won the Nobel prize for literature. *The Iceman Cometh* (1946) was his last Broadway play before he died, and *Long Day's Journey into Night* (1956) was produced posthumously.

Neil Simon (born 1927), possibly the modern playwright most closely associated with New York, has written many comedies set in the city. He received a Tony award for *Biloxi Blues* (1985), then again for *Lost in Yonkers* (1990), for which he was also given the Pulitzer prize. He now has a Broadway theater named after him, though his New York production, *London Suite* (1994), actually opened Off Broadway, downtown.

Musicals have always been a mainstay of New York theater, and the Tin Pan Alley composers wrote many of the most memorable. George and Ira Gershwin straddled classical and contemporary music in such works as the opera *Porgy & Bess* (1935). Cole Porter wrote the music and lyrics for *Kiss Me Kate* (1948) and *Can Can* (1953). Stephen Sondheim (born 1930) wrote varied and experimental popular Broadway fare including the lyrics for *West Side Story*, and music for *A Funny Thing Happened on the Way to the Forum* (1962) and the Pulitzer prize–winning *Sunday in the Park with George* (1984).

www.laguardiahs.org – Remember the movie *Fame*? Well, the Fiorello H LaGuardia High School of Music, Art & Performing Arts, a publicly funded arts high school, served as the basis for the movie. Check the website's performance calendar for student plays and events.

Dance

The School of American Ballet was founded in 1934 by Russian-born choreographer George Balanchine (1904–83). He then became artistic director of the New York City Ballet when it was founded in 1948 and turned it into one of the best ballet companies in the world.

Modern dance, which challenged the strictures of classical ballet, was pioneered by Isadora Duncan (1877–1927), who spent four years in New York City before heading for Europe. Basing her ideas on ancient Greek concepts of beauty, she sought to make dance an intense form of self-expression.

In Los Angeles in 1915, Ted Shawn (1891–1972) and Ruth St Denis (1879–1968) formed Denishawn, a modern-dance company and school, which moved to New York in 1920 and remained the nation's leading company into the '30s. Its most influential student was Martha Graham (1894–1991), who founded her Dance Repertory Theater in New York. In her long career she choreographed over 140 dances and developed a new dance technique, now taught worldwide, aimed at expressing inner emotion and dramatic narrative. Her two most famous works were *Appalachian* (1944), dealing with frontier life, and *Clytemnestra* (1957), based on Greek myths.

Paul Taylor (born 1930) and Twyla Tharp (born 1942), two students of Martha Graham, succeeded her as the leading exponents of modern dance. Another student of Martha Graham, Alvin Ailey (1931–89) set up the Alvin Ailey American Dance Theater in 1958. His most famous work is *Revelations* (1960), a dance suite set to gospel music. Mark Morris (born 1956) is a celebrated dancer and choreographer who formed his own dance group in 1988, which performs at the Brooklyn Academy of Music.

Cinema

Canadian Bacon
(1994) – A political spoof
by Michael Moore about
a cold war with Canada.
In one of his last movies,
John Candy plays the
bumbling police chief
of Niagara County, NY,
who organizes a skirmish
into enemy territory by
spreading garbage in
a Canadian park, loses
one of his deputies and
leads another sortie to
the capital (Toronto)
to rescue the war's first
hostage.

Oh New York, everyone's favorite costar. Celluloid captures her every feature from elegant and uplifting to dehumanizing and depraved. The stories that unfold in this concrete jungle have shaped America's psyche for generations.

Even the early talkies cast New York in a leading role. In *King Kong* (1933) a giant ape escapes his cage and terrorizes the city, climbing up the Empire State Building with a screaming hostage and swatting at fighter planes as if they were gnats.

Adorable and free-spirited Holly Golightly, played by Audrey Hepburn, takes her breakfast before she retires for the night in front of Tiffany's bejeweled window displays in the classic *Breakfast at Tiffany's* (1961).

Capturing the dark reality of wanting to 'make it' in New York, *Midnight Cowboy* (1969) is the story of a small-town hustler, played by Jon Voight, who teams up with the seedy, streetwise Ratso Rizzo, played by Dustin Hoffman. More from New York's underbelly, *Taxi Driver* (1975), directed by Martin Scorsese, stars Robert de Niro as a psychotic ex-Marine who drives a taxi at night.

Do people like this really exist or are they all just babbling characters that live inside Woody Allen's head? In *Annie Hall* (1975) viewers get the pleasure of meeting Allen's most charming and entertaining version of a neurotic, sex-obsessed New York.

Ridiculously dated but remarkably cool, *Saturday Night Fever* (1977) put disco-crazed John Travolta in all the teen-fan magazines.

In *Do the Right Thing* (1989), wiry Spike Lee recreates a racially motivated clash in Brooklyn, a stark reminder that America will never 'get over' its racial issues.

More lighthearted, the character-driven movies of *Smoke* (1995) and *Blue in the Face* (1996), written by Paul Auster and directed by Wayne Wang, star Harvey Keitel as a cigar-store clerk in Brooklyn.

Capturing three days of peace and music, the documentary *Woodstock* (1970) will make you glad you didn't eat the brown acid, and eternally grateful that the farmer who owned the land allowed all those kids and musicians to roll around in his mud.

Environment

Blessed with a stunning and exploitable natural landscape, New York has suffered the consequences of unregulated development and industrialization. With aggressive environmental controls, the state cleaned up many of the polluted rivers and lakes, halted the devastating effects of acid rain and set aside wilderness areas to preserve remaining or repopulated forests. It also served as a leader for the nationwide efforts of environmental protection during the historic passage of the Clean Water and Clean Air Acts.

THE LAND

As the continental glacier receded roughly 10,000 years ago, it left its dramatic legacy across the region. Valleys were carved and broadened, hills were rounded and gorges and waterfalls were created. Glaciers sculpted the Finger Lakes. This upheaval in topography bestowed an abundance of lakes and rivers: the Atlantic seacoast, two of the Great Lakes (Erie and Ontario), the Finger Lakes of central New York, Lake George, Lake Champlain and thousands of smaller lakes and ponds across the state, the St Lawrence Seaway and its 'Thousand Islands' and an engineered canal system that connected many of the natural waterways and sustained much of New York's westward expansion.

From shifting sand dunes in eastern Long Island to blue mountains in the Adirondacks, the land encapsulates all the variety of the East Coast. Though not particularly high in elevation, the Adirondacks are striking for their range, beauty and age. The ancient range was once covered by a continental glacier, resulting in a gently worn landscape of low relief highlighted by a number of dramatic peaks, known collectively as the

---

POETRY OF THE WOODS

The pastoral poetry of many famous American poets, including Walt Whitman and Henry Wadsworth Longfellow, was inspired by the rugged and wild country of the northeast. It often evokes the mystery Americans found in the thick woods and Native American ways; below is a portion of *The Adirondacs*, a poem written in 1858 by Ralph Waldo Emerson (1803–82).

...we swept with oars the Saranac,
With skies of benediction, to Round Lake,
Where all the sacred mountains drew around us,
Taháwus, Seaward, MacIntyre, Baldhead,
And other Titans without muse or name.
Pleased with these grand companions, we glide on...
Through gold-moth-haunted beds of pickerel flower,
Through scented banks of lilies white and gold,
Where the deer feeds at night, the teal by day...
The wood was sovran with centennial trees –
Oak, cedar, maple, poplar, beech and fir,
Linden and spruce. In strict society
Three conifers, white, pitch and Norway pine,
Five-leaved, three-leaved and two-leaved, grew thereby...
'Welcome!' the wood-god murmured through the leaves,
'Welcome, though late, unknowing, yet known to me.'

Ralph Waldo Emerson

High Peaks. The highest of these is Mt Marcy (5344ft), and the rest range from 4000ft to 5000ft. Much of the Adirondack range is covered by forests, and most areas are protected from extensive development.

Just south of the Adirondacks, the Appalachian Plateau stretches between the Allegheny Mountains and the Catskills. This plateau extends to the shores of Lake Erie and Lake Ontario, where it forms a fertile plain that has been the basis of extensive agriculture.

The drainage of New York makes its way in several directions. Most of the Adirondack waterways drain into the St Lawrence system. Parts of the Catskills drain into the Delaware River and into Delaware Bay. The source of the Hudson River is Lake Tear of the Clouds in the Adirondacks, the highest lake in the state. From there, the Hudson ranges over 306 miles until it reaches New York Bay.

Birding in Central & Western New York: Best Trails & Water Routes for Finding Birds (2001), by Norman E Wolfe, provides you with the where, when and what of birding in the Finger Lakes region and surrounds.

WILDLIFE

The region was drastically altered by the influx of European settlers. Forests were cleared for lumber and farms and animals were trapped for their pelts. The bounty of the forests fueled further exploration and settlement of the state.

Animals

Before the arrival of Europeans, the region boasted many species, including black bear, Canada lynx, elk, bison, wolf and panther. Some, like the panther, have disappeared and others exist only in small numbers. Commonly seen among the region's smaller mammals are beaver, chipmunk, fox, opossum, rabbit, raccoon, squirrel, skunk and woodchuck. Of the larger mammals the white-tailed deer is widespread, but the black bear is largely restricted to the remote regions of the Appalachian Plateau and the Adirondack Mountains.

Two poisonous snakes are the timber rattlesnake, found mostly on mountains, and the copperhead, common on rocky streambeds; nonpoisonous snakes are far more common.

Birds that can be seen all year are the bluebird, blue jay, bobolink, eastern meadowlark, goldfinch, red-tailed hawk, owl and woodpecker. Migratory birds include the hummingbird, hawk, falcon and bald eagle. Along lake shores and the Atlantic coast are the gull, heron and osprey. Game birds include the wild duck and turkey, grouse, partridge, pheasant and quail.

Among the numerous varieties of fish found in the region's fresh waters are black bass, catfish, crappie, walleyed pike, pickerel, salmon,

---

TOP FIVE NEW YORK PARKS

- Adirondack Park (p203) – The High Peaks region around Lake Placid gets all the glory, but the lakes around Blue Mountain are heaven on earth.

- Catskill Forest Preserve (p170) – Waterfalls, winding mountain roads and wacky Woodstock will bring out the inner tree-hugger in everyone.

- Fire Island (p138) – This car-less preserve has a wide blonde beach and a castaway feel within reach of New York City.

- Niagara Reservation State Park (p274) – If you're convinced the topography of the East Coast is too subdued, make a trip to this impressive gorge.

- Harriman & Bear Mountain State Parks (p150) – Just outside of New York City, these adjacent parks in the scenic Hudson Highlands give cooped-up city folk a chance to ramble in the woods.

FOREVER WILD

In the 1890s, the citizens of New York acted to make the Adirondacks and the Catskills part of a publicly owned forest preserve. The spirit of this effort is found in the 'Forever Wild' clause of the New York state constitution. It proclaims: 'The land of the state, now owned or hereafter acquired, constituting the Forest Preserve as now fixed by law, shall be forever kept as wild forest lands. They shall not be leased, sold or exchanged, or be taken by any corporation, public or private, nor shall the timber thereon be sold, removed or destroyed.'

trout, muskellunge and whitefish. Salt waters contain bluefish, marlin, tuna and flounder as well as crabs, clams and oysters.

Plants

Much of the region was covered by virgin forest when Europeans first arrived. During the 18th and 19th centuries most of the original forests were cleared for farmland or used for lumber and charcoal. Since the end of the 19th century, however, preservation and reforestation has been successful. Over half of New York is covered by forest, the vast bulk of which is new growth intermixed with a number of smaller areas of pristine, old-growth trees.

The Adirondacks: Wild Island of Hope, Creating the North American Landscape (2002), by Bill McKibben and Gary A Randorf, explores the 'second-chance' wilderness of the Adirondacks through photographs and essays.

There are many different species, but most of the region's forests are dominated by northern broad-leaved hardwoods. Beech and sugar maple are the main ones, but others include ash, basswood, birch, cherry, hickory, red maple, walnut and oak. Some forests, especially along the Atlantic coast, are made up chiefly of softwood conifers such as cedar, fir, hemlock, spruce and white and yellow pine.

Wildflowers common to the region include the azalea, black-eyed Susan, daisy, buttercup, honeysuckle, mountain laurel, orchid and violet; dogwood trees are also common.

Endangered Species

A too common story by now, of course, is the impact rapid industrialization has on the land, water and natural resources of any region on earth. In the late 1800s, when commerce and industry were in full swing in New York and much of America, the land was suffering. Destructive logging practices and the pollution of lakes and rivers by careless manufacturing interests were taking their toll on New York's abundant wildlife. The reduction in wildlife habitats has meant that animals like the black bear and bobcat are restricted to small, remote woodland areas.

DID YOU KNOW?

A native species of New York, the wild turkey was nominated by Ben Franklin to be the national bird. Oddly, the eagle won the title.

At one time predatory birds like the hawk, falcon, osprey and bald eagle were threatened with extinction by hunters and the widespread use of chemicals (which become increasingly concentrated the further up the food chain). But their numbers have recovered since they were protected by the federal Migratory Bird Treaty Act of 1972, the Endangered Species Act of 1973 and the 1972 ban on the chemical DDT. The official status of the bald eagle in the US was upgraded from 'endangered' to 'threatened' in 1993, like that of the peregrine falcon in 1999. The bluebird was close to extinction, but its numbers are gradually returning.

Nevertheless, some chemicals, though banned, persist in the environment, and natural habitats continue to diminish. The alpine areas of the Adirondacks remain the most vulnerable to airborne pollutants and damage from hikers and others who visit the area. The Boots rattlesnake root and the alpine birch are two suffering species that are drawing attention. Much of the forest habitat of New York has improved quite a bit over the

---

LOVE CANAL

Love Canal was an unfinished canal in Niagara Falls that the Hooker Chemical Company used as an illegal dumping site of chemical by-products. In 1977 the company sold the land to the city, which built a school and houses on the site. Residents reported mysterious explosions, skin burns after handling the soil and high incidences of respiratory problems, miscarriages and liver and kidney diseases. Through public pressure, the state finally identified the site as a toxin chemical dump and evacuated Love Canal residents in 1978 and 1979.

Niagara Falls State Park in northwestern New York was the first state park in the nation.

years, due primarily to the great efforts of volunteers and nature-lovers who treat the land with the respect it requires. The habitat is so improved, in fact, that the beaver, once trapped to near-extinction, is now returning in numbers great enough to allow it to be hunted. The same is true for wild turkeys and even Canada geese, whose steadily increasing population is unpopular with farmers who blame them for increasing crop damage.

According to the New York State Department of Environmental Conservation (DEC), other waterfowl, such as the mallard, are dwindling in number due to general environmental factors. As more has been learned about the effects of acid rain, fish restocking efforts have grown. Pike, bass, perch and minnows are among the species being restocked in great number. To help restore the plankton to the ponds and lakes of the Adirondacks, the DEC is liming these bodies of water. Plankton accumulates near the surface, and its absence in an otherwise clear pond is not a good sign; the sighting of a mallard on the pond is a much better sign.

www.nysparks.state .ny.us – Search for a state park by region or activity, or access an alphabetical list of parks and historical sites on the New York State Parks' website.

STATE PARKS

Among New York State's extensive system of public lands, the Adirondack Forest Preserve (established in 1885) is pristine wilderness, protected by the 'Forever Wild' clause in the state's constitution. The preserve constitutes roughly 40% of the much larger Adirondack Park, a mixture of public and private lands. The region is a year-round center not only for wilderness exploring, but also for hiking, canoeing, rock climbing and skiing. Lake Placid is in the heart of the High Peaks region.

Just northwest of the Adirondacks, in the Thousand Islands region, Wellesley Island State Park is a wildlife sanctuary, popular camping area and home to an excellent nature center.

Closer to New York City, Bear Mountain State Park and Harriman State Park are popular hiking and mountain-biking destinations. Also close to New York City is the Rockefeller State Park Preserve, about three miles north of Tarrytown, a peaceful and secluded wooded area, great for walking and bird-watching.

Further north (but less than two hours by car from New York City), one of Washington Irving's favorite haunts, the Catskill Forest Preserve, is home to Kaaterskill Falls and the art- and music-lovers' town of Woodstock. Minnewaska State Park is nearby, near the town of New Paltz, and is a popular hiking and rock-climbing area.

Further west, in the Finger Lakes region, Taughannock Falls State Park is home to the highest waterfall in the state. Letchworth State Park, south of Rochester, is referred to as the 'Grand Canyon of the East' – rather unfair, because it is a stunning site on its own merits – and takes in the 600ft-deep Genesee River Gorge. Continuing west, Niagara Reservation State Park is home to Niagara Falls, the largest (not the highest) waterfall of all.

Nationally Protected Areas
There are no national parks in this region, but there is one national seashore (Fire Island National Seashore, just off the southern shore of Long Island) and a national forest (Finger Lakes National Forest in central New York). The National Park Service (NPS) also administers a number of national monuments, memorials, historic sites, trails and rivers throughout the region.

ENVIRONMENTAL ISSUES
Much of upstate New York's outdoor sparkle – from the High Peaks of the Adirondacks to the shimmering Finger Lakes – dims a bit when the impact of a modern industrial society is taken into full account. The good news is that several organizations are working to check this impact, including efforts to bring environmentalists and commercial enterprises closer together; land use, wildlife preservation and agricultural practices are now topics for debate and compromise.

New York State Conservationist, a bimonthly magazine published by the State Department of Environmental Conservation, covers ecological and environmental issues for a lay audience.

Acid rain is a continuing problem in the industrial northeastern US and the Great Lakes region, as well as much of New York state. Airborne pollutants from as far away as Chicago, Detroit and Cleveland join the airstream, finding their way eventually to waterways. Most of the alpine areas in the Adirondacks are affected not only by acid rain, but by human activity as well. There are vigorous efforts to arrest erosion and to educate hikers and others who enjoy the land.

Newcomers to acid-rain impact need to know a deceptive fact: the acid affects all life forms, from plankton to minnows to dazzling brook trout – so much so that a small lake may look 'clearer' than ever. But clear does not mean clean, despite what the advertisers tell us; a little murky algae on the edges is what we want. (Algae is a living organism quite vulnerable to acid pollutants.) Many of the mountain lakes, in addition to the larger Finger Lakes, have increased acid levels, though acid rain isn't the only villain. In Lake Ontario, a combination of pollutants have led to contaminated fisheries; although locals continue to fish, ongoing studies suggest that nearly half of all the fish in the lake are unsafe to consume on a regular basis.

There are positive signs that environmental efforts are working. In the Adirondacks, moose are returning in greater numbers, mostly from Canada. The same is true for many birds of prey, including the bald eagle, peregrine falcon and osprey.

The ongoing efforts to preserve many of the wilderness areas of the Adirondacks and elsewhere call to mind the definition of wilderness as stated in the national Wilderness Act (1964): 'A wilderness is hereby recognized as an area where the Earth and its community of life are untrammeled by man, where man himself is a visitor who does not remain.'

SAILING FOR THE HUDSON
Activist and folk singer Pete Seeger joined with a group of friends in 1966 to 'build a boat to save a river.' Their idealistic plan hatched a replica of a Dutch sailing sloop, called *Clearwater*, which would educate people about river health, conservation and pollution. At this time the Hudson was a dumping ground for raw sewage and industrial waste. The *Clearwater* helped ignite conservation attempts on the river and even sailed to Washington, DC, to lobby for passage of the Clean Water Act. Today the sloop and the affiliated environmental group monitor activities on the river and introduce visitors to educational exhibits. Visit the Clearwater organization's website (www.clearwater.org) for a schedule of sailings and volunteer opportunities.

New York State Outdoors

Although New York is heavily urbanized, the pursuit of outdoor activities opens up some of the most beautiful and fascinating corners of the state, far away from the hustle of big cities. Many activities are within the reach of the tightest budget, and a walk or cycle in the countryside will almost certainly be a vacation highlight. New York's mountains are popular destinations for rock climbing, mountain biking and hiking, while its lakes and rivers draw anglers, rafters and canoeists. Wildlife enthusiasts can choose from dense woodlands, glacial lakes or coastal wetlands. For those with the money, skiing and golf are readily available.

www.fingerlakestrail .org – If you're interested in finding out more about hiking the 552-mile Finger Lakes Trail, visit this website.

New York's natural treasures include the six-million acre Adirondack Park, which is wild and remote mountain country; the long, narrow lakes, waterfalls and gorges of the Finger Lakes region; the rock climbing and skiing mecca of the Catskills; and the watery wilderness of the Thousand Islands.

Recreational programs for handicapped people are offered by **Disabled Sports USA** (☎ 301-217-0960/3; www.dusa.org; Suite 100, 451 Hungerford Dr, Rockville, MD 20850). New York's Department of Environmental Conservation has an online publication *Opening the Outdoors to People with Disabilities* that can be viewed at www.dec.state.ny.us/website/dfwmr/openout.htm.

HIKING & BACKPACKING

On foot and on the trail are some of the best ways to appreciate the mountains, public forests, wilderness areas and river and coastal regions of New York. Perhaps because the region is so crowded, a high premium is placed on open space and the chance to find fresh air; every weekend thousands of people take to the parks and the countryside.

A vast network of trails traverses the region's most stunning scenery and wilderness. The 2158-mile **Appalachian Trail** – which passes through 14 states, from Maine to Georgia, following mountain ridges ranging in height from about 500ft to 1200ft – enters New York State from Connecticut in the rural area north of Pawling and heads southwest through the small farm communities of the Hudson Valley, the rocky cliffs of the Hudson Highlands and the weather-beaten Ramapo Mountains.

The 4200-mile **North Country National Scenic Trail** – 1600 miles have been completed – is planned to run from Lake Champlain in New York to Lake Sakakawea in North Dakota, and will link the Appalachian Trail with the West Coast's Lewis & Clark and Pacific Crest Trails. The trail runs through the Adirondack Mountains and connects with the 552-mile **Finger Lakes Trail**, which runs east–west from the Catskill Mountains, through the state's southern tier into the Allegheny Mountains and the wooded Allegany State Park.

Through the efforts of organizations like the Rails-to-Trails Conservancy, many abandoned railroad lines are being converted into trails for public recreational use. There are now over 700 trails nationwide and more than 100 in New York. The same process is occurring along 338 miles of the Erie Canal, which is being converted into a trail that will ultimately link the Hudson and Niagara Rivers.

The Adirondack's **High Peaks** (p216) region, including Mt Marcy and other mountains over 4000ft, provides single- and multi-day challenges to hikers; there are 46 peaks in and around Lake Placid of varying levels of difficulty. After summiting these peaks, true outdoor addicts hold the coveted titles of being '46-ers.' These trails are heavily used, especially in summer.

The best times for hiking and backpacking are the spring and fall, when temperatures are not too extreme. Fall is especially beautiful when the trees put on a breathtaking display.

Information

For travelers with little hiking experience there are many short, well-marked, well-maintained trails with restroom facilities at both ends and interpretive displays along the way. These trails are usually marked on maps as nature trails or self-guided interpretive trails.

The following private clubs can provide hiking information:

Adirondack Mountain Club (☎ 518-668-4447, 800-395-8080; www.adk.org; 814 Goggins Rd, Lake George) Maintains trails and leads excursions and workshops in New York's Adirondack and Catskill Parks.

Appalachian Mountain Club (☎ 212-986-1430; www.outdoors.org; 5 Tudor City Place, New York) America's oldest conservation and recreation organization sponsors a wide variety of outdoor activities.

Finger Lakes Trail Conference (☎ 716-288-7191; www.fingerlakestrail.org; 202 Colebourne Rd, Rochester) Maintains trails in New York's Finger Lakes region.

North Country Trail Association (☎ 616-454-5506; www.northcountrytrail.org; 221 E Main St, Lowell, MI) Maintains North Country National Scenic Trail.

Rails-to-Trails Conservancy (☎ 202-797-5400, www.railtrails.org; Suite 300, 1400 16th St NW, Washington, DC) A private nonprofit organization that manages public trails created from former rail lines.

Safety

Weather conditions and terrain vary significantly from one region, or even from one track or trail, to another. These differences influence the way you should dress and the equipment you should carry. Carry a rain jacket and light pair of long underwear at all times, even on shorter hikes. Backpackers should have a pack-liner (heavy-duty garbage bags work well), a full set of rainwear and food that doesn't need cooking.

Obtain reliable information about physical and environmental conditions along the route you intend to take (eg from park authorities or a reputable local guiding operation).

If possible never hike alone, but if you travel solo let someone know where you're going and how long you plan to be gone. Travelers seeking hiking companions can inquire or post notices at ranger stations, outdoors stores, campgrounds and hostels.

Forging rivers and streams is another potentially dangerous, but often necessary, part of hiking. On maintained trails bridges are usually available for crossing bodies of water, but not in wilderness areas where bridges are taboo. If you have to cross a river in a wilderness area, on reaching it unclip all your pack straps – your pack is expendable, you are not. Avoid crossing barefoot – river cobblestones suck body heat out of your feet, numbing them and making it impossible to navigate. Bring a pair of lightweight canvas sneakers to avoid sloshing around in wet boots for the rest of your hike. Although cold water makes you want to cross as quickly as possible, don't rush. Take small steps, watch where you put your feet and keep your balance. Using a staff for balance is helpful, but don't rely on it to support all your weight. Don't enter water higher than mid-thigh; any higher and your body gives the current a large mass to work against.

If you get wet, wring out your clothes immediately, wipe off as much excess water from your body and hair as you can and put on some dry

'If you travel solo let someone know where you're going and how long you plan to be gone'

clothes. Synthetic fabrics and wool retain heat when they get wet, cotton doesn't.

People with little hiking or backpacking experience shouldn't attempt to do too much too soon. Know your limitations, know the route you're going to take and pace yourself accordingly. Remember, it's OK to turn back or not go as far as you originally intended. Plan your water supply and be careful with fires. Be very careful when walking during the hunting season (Thanksgiving to mid-December).

Bears are a problem in the High Peaks region of the Adirondacks. They regard humans as food sources and usually show up just in time for dinner. Keep your distance even if it means abandoning your food.

Laws & Regulations

Most National Park Service (NPS) areas require overnight hikers to carry backcountry permits, available from visitors centers or ranger stations. These must be obtained 24 hours in advance and require you to follow a specific itinerary. Most wilderness areas don't require permits for hiking and backpacking.

www.nysparks
.state.ny.us – For all the information you could ever want or need about state parks in New York.

State game lands don't allow fires, and in other areas during periods of fire hazard (usually summer and early fall) there are constraints on building open fires.

Discourage the presence of wildlife by not leaving food scraps behind you. Place gear out of reach and tie packs to rafters or trees. Do not feed wildlife, as this can lead to animals becoming dependent on handouts, to unbalanced populations and to other problems.

Responsible Hiking

The popularity of hiking places great pressure on the environment. Backcountry areas, especially, are composed of fragile environments that can't support a flood of human activity. A code of ethics has evolved to deal with the growing numbers of people in the wilderness. Most conservation organizations and hikers' manuals have their own backcountry codes, which outline the same important principles: minimizing impact, leaving no trace and taking nothing but photographs and memories. Above all, even if it means walking through mud or crossing a patch of snow, stay on the main trail.

Please, consider the following tips when hiking and backpacking, and help preserve the ecology and beauty of New York.

GARBAGE

Carry out all your garbage. Don't overlook those easily forgotten items such as silver paper, orange peel, cigarette butts and plastic wrappers. Empty packaging weighs little anyway and should be stored in a dedicated garbage bag. Make an effort to carry out garbage left by others.

Never bury your garbage: digging disturbs soil and ground cover and encourages erosion. Buried garbage will more than likely be dug up by animals, who may be injured or poisoned by it. It may also take years to decompose, especially at high altitudes.

Minimize the waste you'll have to carry out by taking minimal packaging and no more food than you will need.

Don't rely on bought water in plastic bottles, because disposal of them creates a major environmental problem; use iodine drops or purification tablets instead.

Sanitary napkins, tampons and condoms should also be carried out despite any inconvenience. They burn and decompose poorly.

HUMAN WASTE

Contamination of water sources by human feces can lead to the transmission of hepatitis, typhoid and intestinal parasites such as Giardia, amoebas and roundworms. It can cause severe health risks not only to members of your party, but also to local residents and wildlife.

Where there is a toilet, please use it. Where there is none, bury your waste. Dig a small hole 6 inches deep and at least 320ft from any watercourse. Consider carrying a lightweight trowel for this purpose. Cover the waste with soil and a rock. Use toilet paper sparingly and bury it with the waste. In snow, dig down to the soil; otherwise, your waste will be exposed when the snow melts.

www.iloveny.com – The recreation section of the state's official tourism website offers information on all sorts of outdoor activities statewide – from skiing to rock climbing.

WASHING

Don't use detergents or toothpaste in or near watercourses, even if they are biodegradable.

For personal washing, use biodegradable soap and a water container (or even a lightweight, portable basin) at least 160ft away from the watercourse. Disperse the wastewater widely to allow the soil to filter it fully before it finally makes it back to the watercourse.

Wash cooking utensils at least 160ft from watercourses, and use a scourer, sand or snow instead of detergent.

EROSION

Hillsides and mountain slopes, especially at high altitudes, are prone to erosion. It is important to stick to existing tracks and avoid shortcuts that bypass a switchback. If you create a new trail straight down a slope, it will turn into a watercourse with the next heavy rainfall and eventually cause soil loss and deep scarring.

If a well-used track passes through a mud patch, walk through the mud; walking around the edge will increase the size of the patch.

Avoid removing plant life that keeps topsoil in place.

FIRES & LOW-IMPACT COOKING

You should not depend upon open fires for cooking. The cutting of wood for fires in popular trekking areas can cause rapid deforestation. It's best to cook on a lightweight kerosene, alcohol or Shellite (white gas) stove and avoid those powered by disposable butane gas canisters.

Fires may be acceptable below the tree line in areas that get very few visitors. If you light a fire, use an existing fireplace rather than creating a new one. Don't surround fires with rocks, as this creates a visual scar. Use only dead, fallen wood. Remember the adage 'the bigger the fool, the bigger the fire.' Use minimal wood, just what you need for cooking. In huts, leave wood for the next person.

Ensure that you fully extinguish a fire after use. Spread the embers and douse them with water. An extinguished fire is only truly safe to leave when you can comfortably place your hand in it.

CROSS-COUNTRY SKIING

Cross-country skiing (also called ski touring or Nordic skiing) allows you to experience quiet, natural beauty at close quarters and escape the crowds and relatively expensive lift tickets at ski resorts. The sport appeals to beginners in particular, because they can be on their way with only a few lessons.

Public lands operated by NPS, US Forest Service (USFS) and the US Army Corps of Engineers, in addition to state parks and forests, Rails-to-Trails Conservancy and private lands support hundreds of cross-country

DOWNHILL SKIING & SNOWBOARDING

The Adirondacks and Catskills provide the region's best skiing and snowboarding. Boards are allowed at most ski areas and many have half-pipes, snowboard lessons and rental equipment.

There are dozens of resorts offering great opportunities for skiing as well as other snow-related sports. Facilities range from day-only ski areas to resorts that are self-contained mini-cities and offer gentle slopes for the learner and challenging verticals for more accomplished skiers.

The skiing season lasts from about mid-December to early April, though it's sometimes possible to ski as early as November and as late as May. State tourist offices have information on resorts, and travel agents can arrange full-package tours including transport and accommodations. Many resorts are close to towns so it's quite feasible to travel on your own to the slopes for the day and return to town at night. If you have travel insurance make sure that it covers you for winter sports.

Ski areas are often well equipped with accommodations, eateries, shops, entertainment venues, child-care facilities (both on and off the mountain) and transport. In fact, it's possible to stay a week at some of the bigger places without leaving the slopes. Ski areas have at least one comfortable base lodge with a rental office, ski shop and lockers. There are also cafeterias and lounges or bars where visitors can relax in warmth. You don't have to buy a lift ticket or pay to enjoy the base lodge.

Equipment rentals are available at or near even the smallest ski areas, though renting equipment in a nearby town can be cheaper if you can transport it to the slopes.

Belleayre Mountain Ski Center

This casual state-owned resort (p178) in the Catskills offers a rustic state park atmosphere and has something for everyone – from the child wobbling on her first pair of skis to the expert snowboarder rushing down the steep terrain. The mountain has a 1404ft vertical drop and is divided into upper and lower mountains. The upper mountain caters almost exclusively to black diamond terrain, while the bottom mountain has an extensive beginner trail system. Offering good value for money, it has been rated one of the top resorts on the East Coast. It offers discounts for those under the age of 22, and for midweek, early season and multi-day skiing. The resort offers 4 miles of free cross-country skiing.

- Nearest town: Highmount
- One-day lift ticket: $42
- Information: ☎ 845-254-5600; www.belleayre.com

Ski Windham

A popular family and singles destination, this ski resort (p179) is in a charming town with good eating and sleeping options. Located in the Catskills, it's just¹ 120 miles from New York City, making it a feasible day-trip option. With a 1600ft vertical drop, the resort offers trails like Wooly Bear, perfect for beginners, and Upper Wheelchair, a wicked advanced run. There is also a snowboard park and a 400ft half-pipe. Don't feel like skiing? Check out snow tubing in the mountain adventure park. You can race down 14 runs lying on your back in a canvas-covered tube. Tubing costs $25 for the day, or $15 for two hours.

- Nearest town: Windham
- One-day lift ticket: $40/50 weekday/weekend
- Information: ☎ 518-734-4300; www.skiwindham.com

Whiteface Mountain

Near Lake Placid, this resort (p215) hosted the 1932 and 1980 Winter Olympic Game alpine competitions. With the greatest vertical drop (3430ft) in the eastern US, it offers 65 miles of trails and has been rated the number one ski resort in the eastern US more than once by *Ski Magazine*. There is a heated gondola, trails for all levels of skiers and a terrain park and half-pipe for snowboarders. Expert riders can test their skills on 'the slides,' 35 acres of out-of-bound skiing in a pristine alpine setting.

- Nearest town: Lake Placid
- One-day lift ticket: $55
- Information ☎ 518-523-1655; www.whiteface.com

trails; some trails are operated under special-use permits by private industries. New York's Finger Lakes region provides some of the best views; trails near Ithaca, Buttermilk Falls State Park, Keuka Lake State Park and Finger Lakes National Forest are popular. Among the best places is Robert Moses State Park in the Thousand Islands region. In the Hudson Valley, good spots are Bear Mountain, Mills-Norrie and James Baird State Park, while in the Capital District & Mohawk Valley you'll find decent trails in Saratoga National Historic Park and Chenango Valley State Park.

Many ski resorts also provide groomed ski trails, but most cross-country skiers prefer to avoid the downhill crowds by visiting dedicated cross-country areas and backcountry trails.

Equipment rentals are available at outfitters like REI, Eastern Mountain Sports and other places near the trails. The **Cross-Country Ski Areas Association** (☎ 603-239-4341; www.xcski.org; 259 Bolton Rd, Winchester, NH 03470) has information on guided tours and publishes *The Best of Cross-Country Skiing*, a guide to the sport in North America. Most cross-country trail distances are given in kilometers (to convert trail distances into miles, see the conversion chart on the inside front cover of this book).

ROCK CLIMBING & MOUNTAINEERING

If you want to really push yourself, to feel your hands sting and your legs burn, to experience the adrenaline rush of making it to the top minutes after you thought your body was going to give out, then rock climbing might be the adventure sport for you. The premier rock-climbing destination is the Shawangunk Mountains of the Catskills region – especially popular are spots in the Minnewaska State Park (p171), near the village of New Paltz, and the Mohonk Preserve (p171). In the Adirondacks, Lake George (p107) and Lake Placid (p213) have many worthwhile climbing areas. Rock climbing is best experienced in the fall and spring, when temperatures are not too hot or too cold.

The **Access Fund** (☎ 303-545-6772; www.accessfund.org; 207 Canyon Ave, Boulder, CO 80302) is a nonprofit organization working to keep climbing areas open to the public by purchasing or negotiating access to key sites. Action alerts on legislation affecting climbing are posted on its website.

'If you want to really push yourself, rock climbing might be the adventure sport for you'

Safety

Rock climbing and mountaineering are demanding activities requiring top physical condition. They also require an understanding of the composition of rock types, their hazards and other hazards of the high country, and familiarity with equipment including ropes, chocks, bolts, carabiners and harnesses.

Rock climbers and mountaineers categorize routes on a scale of one to five. Class I is hiking, while Class II involves climbing on unstable materials like talus and may require use of the hands for keeping balance, especially with a heavy pack. Class III places the climber in dangerous situations involving exposed terrain, with the likely consequences of a fall being a broken limb. Class IV involves steep rock, smaller holds and great exposure, with obligatory use of ropes and knowledge of knots and techniques like belaying and rappelling; the consequences of falling are death rather than injury. Class V divides into a dozen or more subcategories based on degree of difficulty and requires advanced techniques, including proficiency with rope.

Climbing is potentially hazardous, though serious accidents are more rare than frequent. Nevertheless, climbers should be aware of hazards that can contribute to falls and very serious injury or death. Weather is an important factor, as rain makes rock slippery and lightning can strike an exposed climber; hypothermia is an additional concern. In dry weather, lack of water can lead to dehydration.

Minimum Impact

Many climbers follow guidelines similar to those established for hikers to preserve the resource on which their sport relies. These include concentrating impact in high-use areas by using established roads, trails and routes for access; dispersing use in pristine areas and avoiding the creation of new trails; refraining from creating or enhancing handholds; and eschewing the placement of bolts wherever possible. Climbers should also take special caution to respect archaeological and cultural resources, such as rock art, and refrain from climbing in such areas.

Instruction

Travelers wishing to acquire climbing skills can do so at several schools and guide services, including:

Adirondack Mountain Club (☎ 800-395-8080; www.adk.org; 814 Goggins Rd, Lake George, NY 12845)

Alpine Adventures (☎ 518-576-9881; PO Box 179, Rte 73, Keene, NY 12942)

Ascents of Adventure (☎ 518-475-7519; 147 Cherry Ave, Delmar, NY 12054-2522)

Mountain Skills Climbing School (☎ 914-687-9643; 595 Peak Rd, New Paltz, NY 12484)

CANOEING, WHITE-WATER RAFTING & TUBING

The myriad lakes and rivers in the Adirondacks have inspired generations of canoeists. The Fulton Chain of Lakes (p225) and the St Regis Canoe Wilderness Area (p221) are two popular places for day-long paddles or water-running. The Adirondack Canoe Classic starts in Old Forge (p225) and hops from waterway to waterway for 90 miles to the finish line in Saranac Lake (p220).

www.americanwhite water.org – The American Whitewater Affiliation can give you information about rafting and tubing in the region, as well as a general overview of the sports.

The Delaware River (p183), in the southeastern portion of the state, is a popular NPS-designated Wild & Scenic River – particularly scenic stretches pass through the Catskill towns of Narrowsburg and Barryville. The Genesee River in Letchworth State Park, in the Finger Lakes region, runs for 17 miles beneath a 600ft gorge. Other New York options include the Hudson River, where early spring rapids provide some of the most challenging opportunities; Esopus Creek (p177), which is a center for tubing, near Phoenicia in the Catskills; and Lake Placid (p213) in the Adirondacks.

White-water trips take place in either large rafts seating a dozen or more people, or smaller rafts seating half a dozen; the latter are more interesting and exciting because the ride over the rapids can be rougher and because everyone participates in rowing. Rivers are classified on a scale of I to V, I being suitable for beginners with tiny rapids that provide little possibility of capsizing, while Class V rapids should not be tried by anyone other than experienced river runners as the possibility for capsizing, and even drowning, is real. Most commercially run rivers in the state have Class II to IV rapids, with the norm being Class III – which provide a fun, yet safe, ride and are appropriate for inexperienced rafters. Rapids can change with water levels, so if you're looking for the wildest action head out in the spring when rivers are highest due to snow runoff. Some trips may have restrictions regarding experience, age and/or weight.

Tubing is popular on smaller streams and rivers, but is often available only when spring runoff has lessened and the current isn't as rough. Often, you rent a 'tube' – or the inner tube of a tire – which may or may not be fitted with handles or seats. Then, much like white-water rafting, tubers (people, not the root vegetables) are 'put in' at the head of a river and they float downstream. It's lots of fun, especially if you have a group on a warm sunny day.

Outfitters provide white-water experiences ranging from short, inexpensive morning or afternoon trips to overnight stays and three- or four-day expeditions. For information on white-water rafting and tubing, contact the **American White-Water Affiliation** (☎ 301-589-9453; www.americanwhite water.org; 1430 Fenwick Lane, Silver Spring, MD 20910). The organization works to conserve and restore the nation's white-water resources and promote white-water activity. For canoeing, you can either bring your own equipment, rent the equipment you need or sign on for a complete guided tour, including meals and shuttle service.

www.dec.state.ny .us – Fishing is big sport in many parts of the state. To learn more about charters, licenses, regulations and publications head to the website of the Department of Environmental Conservation.

Safety

While it's not unusual for participants to fall out of the raft in rough water, serious white-water injuries are rare and the huge majority of trips are without incident. Outfitters give orientation and safety lectures before heading off; trips have at least one river guide experienced in white-water rafting and trained in safety procedures and lifesaving techniques. You don't have to be able to swim to participate, but you must wear a US Coast Guard–approved life jacket and should be in reasonably good physical condition. Keep your feet and arms inside the raft.

FISHING

The Atlantic coastline, the hundreds of lakes and ponds and the thousands of miles of rivers and streams make New York State a prime fishing region. Freshwater fish include varieties of trout, salmon, bass and pike, as well as muskellunge (muskie), sauger, shad and walleyed pike; in the Atlantic you'll find bluefish, flounder, giant tuna and even shark.

The streams of the Catskill Mountains are said to have some of the country's best trout fishing, and the lakes of the Adirondacks, including the 469 sq miles of Lake Champlain and the Ausable River, are home to bass, pike and salmon. Some of the best bass and muskellunge fishing (along with scenery) are reputedly found along the St Lawrence River in the Thousand Islands region. Lake Chautauqua (p278) in the far southwest corner of the state is noted for its giant muskellunge. Stream and ice fishing is popular in Allegany State Park (p282). In the fall, Montauk (p141) becomes the site of huge 'fish boils,' where the ocean seemingly boils with schools of albacore and bluefin tuna.

Anglers are required to have the appropriate state license and to abide by whatever seasonal or territorial regulations are in place. The same stream may have several sections with quite different restrictions on types of hooks, bait, seasons and what size and type of fish can be kept. It can be complicated so ask for current regulations at bait or sporting-goods stores, fish and wildlife offices or some state campgrounds where you can also buy a license.

Fishing licenses are issued to resident and out-of-state anglers (the latter are more expensive) and can be bought for a year or shorter intervals. There are numerous types of licenses. Generally you'll pay about $20/$35 for a day/ seasonal out-of-state license, with discounts for students and seniors. Up-to-date information on licenses, regulations, charter boats and publications is available from the **Department of Environmental Conservation** (☎ 518-457-3521; www.dec.state.ny.us; Room 111, 50 Wolf Rd, Albany).

Food & Drink

New York State is home to master chefs and sophisticated eaters, primarily centered around the culinary capital of New York City, but extending deep into the Hudson Valley and beyond. The state's diverse ethnic makeup ensures that more pedestrian dishes are hearty, tasty and widely available. And no other region does America's favorite junk food, such as hot dogs, pizza and pretzels, like the small-time operations in New York State.

STAPLES & SPECIALTIES

Fresh seafood and shellfish, such as clams, oysters and lobster, harvested from the Atlantic Ocean appear in New York's markets and restaurants. New York City's famous Fulton Fish Market (p75) is a primary land-distribution site for the day's catch. Brook trout is a freshwater cousin coaxed from the shallow streams of upstate New York to the frying pans of local and commercial cooks.

For over 300 years, New York State has devoted part of its farmland to apple orchards. Along the country roads of the Hudson Valley, rows of squat, gnarled branches pregnant with fruit celebrate the fall harvest. As many as 14 varieties of apples might appear at these farm stands. Some, like the tart Paula Red, are best used for baking pies, while others, like the sweet Cortlands, can be attacked on your way out of the parking lot.

Many farmers sell their crop at small roadside stands on secondary roads or invite visitors to buy what they can pick. Others transport the harvest to farmers' markets in the closest major town. In the spring, you'll find asparagus, spinach and fresh salad greens. By June the strawberries have ripened, leading the way for the harvest deluge of tomatoes, corn, eggplant, melons and blueberries. In the fall apples and pumpkins usher the growing season to a close. Contact the towns' chambers of commerce or visitors centers for the farmers' market schedules and locations. Even New York City boasts a farmers' market in Union Square (p85).

DELI SPEAK

The Jewish delis in New York introduced the rest of the culture to Yiddish, a Germanic hybrid language. Thrown into the fast-paced environment of the deli counter are other abbreviated terms to save time and breath. Here is a quick primer, so you don't have to expose your deli virginity.

- blintz – a small crepe
- challah – braided egg bread
- gefilte fish – a Jewish holiday dish of ground white fish (carp or pike) mixed with egg, matzo meal and seasonings and then chilled with its own stock, typically served with horseradish or dill pickles
- knish – a stuffed pastry shell
- lox – smoked salmon
- nosh – to eat a little something, to snack
- schmear – otherwise known as cream cheese spread on a bagel; at some delis you get to choose between onion, vegetable and strawberry schmears
- stay or go – off-handedly tossed at a customer after placing an order; translation: 'Would you like to eat your order at the restaurant or take it home to eat it?'

The different immigrant groups that make up the USA's cultural mosaic contribute enormously to the diversity of cuisine. Buffalo boasts a number of regional specialties like beef-on-weck, char-grilled hot dogs and Buffalo wings. Beef-on-weck claims German heritage, reputedly invented by a tavern-keeper to sell more beer; it is thin slices of slow-roasted beef stuffed into a hard roll crusted with pretzel salt and caraway seeds with a dollop of horseradish (taster's discretion). Everyone's favorite pub grub, Buffalo wings are fried chicken wings tossed in a spicy Tabasco-like sauce. Anchor Bar (p270), the restaurant that found a purpose for the otherwise unwanted pieces of the chicken, serves Buffalo wings to varying degrees of spiciness. The suicidal rating will have you seeing stars. Other imports from Western Europe, mainly by Jewish refugees, include pastrami, knishes, matzo ball soup, sauerkraut and the deli tradition of a huge plate of sweet and sour pickles to accompany every meal.

Italian food seems commonplace to Americans now. But in the not so distant past, pizza was a foreign term. Today, pizza counters are New York City's most reliable food stops. New Yorkers love to sample and argue over which pizza-maker does the best slice. The winning criteria are usually a crisp crust, gooey but not oily cheese and a tangy red sauce. When you meet that perfect slice, you'll be in love. Specific to Binghamton (p201), spiedies (*speed*-ies) are an Italian invention of marinated meat, skewered and cooked over a charcoal grill. Traditionally lamb was the meat of choice, but chicken and pork have become common standbys as they are more readily available in the New World.

DRINKS

Before the American Revolution, Brooklyn emerged along with Philadelphia as the colony's major brewing centers. German immigrants established small local beer-making factories specializing in lagers in an area of Brooklyn known as Brewer's Row. Prohibition and beer consolidation in the Midwest brought an end to this local industry, but the recent microbrew-revival has seen a rebirth of delicious New York–brewed beverages. A former Associated Press correspondent, Steve Hindy started out as a home-brewer while stationed in Arabic countries where alcohol was forbidden. With the help of recipes from a fourth-generation brewmeister and business support from his downstairs neighbor, he formed Brooklyn Brewery, best known for its Brooklyn Lager and Brown Ale, widely available in and around New York. The brewing facility in Williamsburg is open for tours (p101).

One of the few survivors of the beer wars, the makers of Saranac beer have been around since the late 19th century. The patriarch FX Matt came to Utica in 1885 after an apprenticeship in a Black Forest brewery in Germany. He worked for several Utica companies before taking over the West End brewery. The family survived prohibition by switching to soft drinks, and now Matt's descendants have created a successful craft beer under the label Saranac (try their Pale Ale).

Microbrews are tasty, but they won't win you friends outside of yuppie circles. The working-man's brew of choice is Genesee Cream Ale (which tastes more like water than cream), a Rochester brand name that dates back to the 1870s. If you're invited on a fishing trip, bring along some Gennys and some Buds (for the high rollers).

Long Island and Finger Lakes wines have slowly emerged from under California's domination of the American wine industry. In the North Fork area of Long Island, Lenz and Paumanok (see boxed text on p144) have won international awards for their merlot and chenin blanc, respectively.

New York Cookbook (1992) is a pot-luck helper book by Molly O'Neil, a *New York Times* food writer, who collected the recipes and stories of New York City. Readers rave about her Peking duck recipe.

An Adirondack Guide's Cookbook (2001), by John Gibbons, teaches the hearty outdoors types how to turn a campfire into a culinary wonder. The foil dinners save campers from canned-bean monotony.

Hudson Valley Harvest: A Food Lover's Guide to Farms, Restaurants and Open-air Markets (2003), by Jan Greenberg, is a comprehensive guide to the valley and is perfect for a weekend away or a recent transplant.

CELEBRATIONS

One way to sample New York's bounty is to visit a local harvest or heritage festival. Buffalo hosts festivals celebrating its Italian and Polish heritage, Poughkeepsie honors it Hispanic residents, Nyack celebrates the Greek fishing culture, the Thousand Islands pay homage to the area's French and Irish culture. And in summer, New York City's streets are closed off to traffic for street festivals dedicated to the neighborhoods' predominant ethnicities.

Another great celebration to watch for is New York City's Restaurant Week (www.restaurantweek.com), when three-course lunches and dinners are offered for unbelievable bargains at some of the city's best restaurants.

WHERE TO EAT & DRINK

Vintage diners made to look like chrome-and-steel railcars appear all over New York State. Many of these lunch counters are survivors from the 1920s to '40s, the heyday of the streamline aesthetic. Some diner cars can also claim a birth on the banks of Lake Erie in western New York, where many diner-car manufacturers were headquartered. Bottomless cups of weak coffee, Frisbee-sized pancakes and eggs any style – breakfast is the diner's most famous meal. But in New York, many diners are owned by Greek families who have introduced dishes, like spanakopita and gyros, into the lengthy menus of American standards.

FOOD FESTIVALS

Cayuga Nature Center's Maple Sugar Festival (☎ 607-273-6260) In the bleak mid-winter, Ithaca (p242) taps its maple trees for the sweet sap. Festivities include demonstrations and maple foodstuff.

Dairy Princess Pageant & Dinner (☎ 315-376-5270) In April, Lowville (in the Adirondacks) celebrates Lewis County's dairy industry by crowning the town's (not the herd's) best looking contestant. Food, crafts and demonstrations accompany the event.

Ninth Avenue International Food Festival (☎ 212-333-7222) In mid-May, New York's most famous street fair (p108) converges on the Hell's Kitchen area of Ninth Ave (between 37th and 57th Sts). The street is closed to car traffic and the ethnic restaurants that line this corridor set up informal kitchens for two days of pedestrian-friendly grazing.

Strawberry Festival (☎ 585-589-7727) In early June, Albion (in Western New York) welcomes the beginning of summer with vendors, games and strawberry-inspired foods.

Father's Day Ice Cream Social (☎ 845-473-5957) In late June, dads accompanied by a child get in free to sample various flavors of ice cream, a tradition started by Mrs Vanderbilt at her Hyde Park home (p161).

Finger Lakes Wine Festival (☎ 607-535-2481) In mid-July, Watkins Glen (p248) celebrates the region's favorite fermented drink with over 60 Finger Lakes wineries.

Annual Long Island Wine Classic (☎ 631-537-3177) In late August, *Wine Spectator* organizes a high-flight tribute to Long Island's wines with New York City's top chefs in Bridgehampton.

National Buffalo Wing Festival (☎ 716-565-4141) In the beginning of September, Buffalo (p265) hosts a wing-sparing match between national wing sauce makers.

International Pickle Day (☎ 212-226-9010) In early September, New York City's Lower East Side (p78), once home to pushcart pickle vendors, now hosts this annual pickle celebration with more than a dozen vendors sampling and selling sweet-and-sours, pickled mangoes, garlic, kimchi and sauerkraut.

Tavern Days (☎ 914-631-8200) In mid-September, Croton-on-the-Hudson toasts microbreweries with 17th-century inspired games and festivals at the Van Cortlandt Manor (p155).

Hudson Valley Garlic Festival (☎ 845-246-3090) In late September, Saugerties hosts an odiferous festival to everyone's favorite root vegetable, garlic.

Apple Harvest (☎ 607-277-8679) In October, Ithaca (p242) picks, presses, bakes and noshes on apples.

Central New York Great Pumpkin Festival (☎ 315-343-7681) In October, Oswego selects the community's biggest pumpkin.

The summer sees the annual awakening of the roadside ice-cream stand, a New England tradition. Soft-serve ice cream or heart-stopping hot dogs slathered in chili and other indescribable red sauces are gulped down at picnic tables alongside leather-clad motorcycle drivers and a minivan full of kids. Giving yourself a mild stomachache from too much junk food is a quintessential summertime activity.

Most downtowns have an upscale bistro that the local residents regard as proof of their cosmopolitan tastes. While the food is usually solid, the options lack a region-specific personality and the decor tries hard to replicate New York City. Family-style Italian restaurants dating back at least a generation are as much a fixture in most small towns as the local courthouse. Popping up in more and more towns throughout New York are restaurants catering to the most recent wave of immigrants: Latinos from Central and South America. If your Spanish is up to snuff or you've mastered the art of pointing, you'll be in for a tasty treat.

Nothing compares to New York City for diversity and magnitude of restaurants. Manhattan alone leads the entire country in a dizzying number of exceptional gourmet restaurants and cutting-edge fusions. Then there are the numerous pizza parlors, closet-sized coffee shops serving down-home Cuban food, Chinese restaurants, Vietnamese noodle joints – the possibilities are endless. Hard to believe, but jaded chowhounds consider Manhattan's ethnic choices to be too limited, so they venture to Queens where a slice of almost every world population has established a thriving community and a small deli counter or restaurant.

VEGETARIANS & VEGANS

Vegetarians are in luck. New York, especially New York City, has embraced the non-meat eating culture. New York City has a whole universe of interesting meat-alternative restaurants, including the local chain Zen Palate, which uses soy- and wheat-substitutes in Asian-inspired dishes. NYC also has a juice stand on almost every corner and Chinese and Indian restaurants usually specialize in non-meat dishes. Most upscale restaurants will offer a vegetarian item, but quality is inconsistent, especially if the restaurant's specialty is in other arenas. In this case, vegetarians are better off ordering a fish or seafood dish, which will be more lovingly prepared. Even in the most macho of towns, you'll be able to find a health food store to supply basics for self-catering when the restaurant options run dry. Vegans will have a harder go of it outside New York City.

WHINING & DINING

Most restaurants offer a kids menu with smaller sizes, smaller prices and no funny ingredients like spices or garlic. Kids will probably feel most at home in the diners, but even pub-restaurants accommodate families with highchairs and crayons for meal-time artists.

New York City's restaurants are very cramped and can hardly shoe-horn in their patrons – forget about dragging in a tank-sized baby stroller. Consider carting the rugrats around in a fold-up number or look for outdoor seating where you can park your kid's wheels.

An interesting option to the fast-food restaurants are the local fundraising suppers held in communities across the state. Churches, fire houses and schools host inexpensive Italian and Greek suppers as modest money-makers. Meals are donated by community members, and unlimited plates, eaten family style, cost anywhere from $5 to $8. These are great ways to try some of the region's home cooking (dessert is included) and chat up some locals. Check the local papers for a schedule of public suppers.

www.chowhound.com – People who proclaim eating as their primary hobby flex their culinary knowledge on this bulletin board.

www.nytimes.com /pages/dining – Visit the *New York Times'* Dining & Wine page for reviews of New York restaurants, food trends and helpful hints on how to be a cultivated connoisseur.

www.roadfood.com – Jane and Michael Stern wrote *Roadfood*, a survey of America's hometown specialties and restaurants. This website takes their cause further, allowing visitors to post and search reviews by other 'roadfooders.' It has over 50 New York eateries on their message board.

HABITS & CUSTOMS

Upstate New Yorkers don't greatly differ from the rest of Americans in their eating rituals. Most people eat their meals at home, except for the office lunch crowd and the special occasion dinner crowd. It is recommended to make reservations for upscale restaurants on the weekends, but weekdays tend to be more relaxed.

Food culture in New York City, however, is its own beast. Most home kitchens are so small and most daily routines are so busy that New Yorkers rarely cook their own meals. During a recent power outage in New York City, a reporter asked a bystander if he was worried about the food in his fridge going bad. He responded by holding up a bottle of beer and saying 'This was all that was in there.' Breakfast (usually a bagel and coffee) is grabbed from a small metal cart en route to the subway station. Lunch might come from a sidewalk cart too, where brightly spiced dishes of meat and rice sizzle on an open-air grill. After perusing a small library of takeaway menus and calling in an order, dinner arrives at their door thanks to a sweaty bicycle deliverer. Refrigerators and stoves in New York City are lonely places.

Getting reservations for the *in* restaurants in New York City is near impossible unless you have a heavy-duty celebrity name. You also might have luck hitting restaurants at odd hours: just after the lunch crowd shuffles back to the office (around 2pm) or before or after the dinner rush (5pm or 10pm). If you're traveling alone, many restaurants have small bars where you can eat in a less conspicuous place than at a table by yourself. The bartenders are usually good chatters on local topics and can steer you to interesting wine pairings.

Tipping is a uniquely American convention of wealth-redistribution, a task that government can't be trusted with. You should tip 10% to 15% in a lunch spot and 20% in an upscale restaurant. If you are unhappy with the service, you should tip only 15% and complain to the manager. Coffee shops often have tip jars beside the register; this is an individual call not yet decreed upon by etiquette mavens.

In bars, you should tip the bartender $1 for every drink. In upstate bars, New Yorkers have a curious tradition for paying the bartender. Upon ordering a drink, regulars put however much money they plan on spending on the counter beside their drink. The bartender then subtracts the right amount from the pile as a new round is ordered. It is a funny sight to see a row of Budweiser bottles sitting beside green piles of bills.

There is no smoking in bars or restaurants in New York State.

COOKING COURSES

The country's preeminent cooking school, the **Culinary Institute of America** (p162; ☎ 800-888-7850; www.ciachef.edu) offers continuing education classes to budding and stagnate culinaries. The kids program teaches children aged 10 to 13 years how to make pizza from crust to toppings in an afternoon hands-on class. Taller cooks can learn the techniques for making French bistro classics, find out how to get a cookbook published or figure out how to 'marry' wine and food.

New York City

CONTENTS

This is the gospel according to New York: In the beginning God created New York City. Then he created other places, somewhere else, but New Yorkers aren't sure where or why. Welcome to the Center of the World.

New York is all-consuming and unconquerable. The man-made mountains of skyscrapers blot out the sky and obscure the horizon, so that the citizens only see and dream 'New York.' Below ground the city is just as domineering, having anchored itself deep into the bedrock, feeding intravenously from far-away aqueducts. It is the greatest machine that human hands have ever wrought and it circulates its human components through capillaries of streets, subway tunnels and elevators. Motion and noise are everywhere, and joining the collective push towards something, anything, is contagious and pervasive. Through its magnificent knack for self-expression, reinvented by each generation, New York insinuates itself into the imagination of every young mind, ensuring a ceaseless stream of new talent and creative legends.

When slums still existed in Manhattan, it was a Noah's Ark of human diversity – foreign and native, aristocrat and peasant, rebel and conformer – compacted into a cramped island. Of late, soaring rents have chased the bohemian artists to Brooklyn and immigrants to Queens. But gentrification has also opened up transitional zones, like Hell's Kitchen and Alphabet City, where some of New York's edginess is still tangible.

HIGHLIGHTS

- **Best Night Out**
  Staying out till dawn in the Lower East Side (p125).

- **Best Museums**
  Visiting one (or all) of the following museums: Frick (p90), MoMA (p88) and Guggenheim (p91).

- **Best View of Manhattan**
  Walking over the Brooklyn Bridge (p75), a proud monument to humankind's ingenuity.

- **Best-Looking Woman in New York City**
  The classic beauty of the Statue of Liberty (p70) earns her the title of 'hotty of the harbor.'

- **Best Chance to be a Critic**
  Booing or cheering young talent at the famous Apollo Theater's amateur night (p95).

- **Best Way to Spend a Morning**
  Drinking a cappuccino in a Greenwich Village (p80) coffee shop and dreaming of a bohemian life.

- **Best Neighborhoods for Eating**
  Chowing your way through Hell's Kitchen (p122) and East Village (p119).

- **Best Trick to Look Like a Local**
  Getting a morning coffee to go from the corner carts and jaywalking like a pro.

- **Best Way to Get Around**
  Mastering the subway system (p135).

ORIENTATION

New York City consists of five 'boroughs' – entities that came together in 1898 to form 'Greater New York City.' A series of islands makes up the city's 309-sq-mile land mass. Manhattan and Staten Island stand alone; Queens and Brooklyn comprise the western end of Long Island. Only the Bronx is connected to the US mainland.

The water gap between Brooklyn and Staten Island – the narrows through which the first Europeans entered the area – serves as the entrance to New York Harbor. Manhattan itself is bordered by two bodies of water: on the west by the Hudson River and on the east by the East River, both technically estuaries subject to tidal fluctuations.

Most of Manhattan is easy to navigate, thanks to a street plan that created the current grid system of 14 named or numbered avenues running the north–south length of the island, crossed by east–west numbered streets.

Above Washington Square, Fifth Ave serves as the dividing line between the 'East Side' and the 'West Side.' Most New Yorkers give out addresses in shorthand by listing the cross-street first and the avenue second, eg 'we're at 33rd and Third.' If you are given an address on an avenue – such as '1271 Sixth Ave' – be sure to ask for the nearest cross-street to save time.

In the oldest part of New York City, from 14th St to the southern tip of Manhattan, travel becomes a bit trickier. Streets that perhaps began as cow paths or merchants' byways snake along in a haphazard manner, which is why it is possible today to stand at the corner of W 4th St and W 10th St in Greenwich Village.

Broadway, the only avenue to cut diagonally across the island, was originally a woodland path used by Native Americans; it runs, in some form, from the tip of the island all the way to the state capital of Albany, 150 miles away. Today, Wall St stands at the place where, in 1653, the Dutch residents of New Amsterdam constructed a wooden barrier at the town's northern border to ward off attacks from hostile natives.

New York neighborhood names can be purely geographical (Lower East Side), ethnically descriptive (Chinatown) or occasionally just plain scary (Hell's Kitchen). Tribeca is the name given to the 'Triangle Below Canal St' while SoHo is the area south of Houston St.

The Upper East Side and Upper West Side include the areas above 59th St on either side of Central Park. Midtown generally refers to the largely commercial district from 59th St south to 34th St, an area that includes Rockefeller Center, Times Square, the Broadway theater district, major hotels, Grand Central Terminal and the Port Authority Bus Terminal.

Significant neighborhoods in the Outer Boroughs include Brooklyn Heights, Park Slope, Williamsburg and Brighton Beach in Brooklyn; Arthur Ave, Riverdale and City Island in the Bronx; and Astoria, Jackson Heights, Forest Hills and Flushing Meadows in Queens.

Maps

Lonely Planet publishes a laminated, pocket-sized map of New York City available at bookstores. If you want to explore the city at large, buy a five-borough street atlas by Geographia and Hagstrom.

Subway stations distribute free subway maps and have detailed street maps of the surrounding neighborhood next to the ticket booths.

You can purchase maps at the **Hagstrom Map & Travel Center** (Map pp64-5; ☎ 212-398-1222; 57 W 43rd St btwn Fifth & Sixth Ave).

INFORMATION
Bookstores

Books and Co (Map pp66-7; ☎ 212-737-1450; 939 Madison Ave) Hosts major authors for readings.

Books of Wonder (Map pp64-5; ☎ 212-989-3270; 16 W 18th St) Children's books.

Coliseum Books (Map pp64-5; ☎ 212-803-5890; 11 W 42nd St btwn Fifth & Sixth Ave) Huge selection of paperback fiction and out-of-print titles.

Complete Traveller (Map pp64-5; ☎ 212-685-9007; 199 Madison Ave at 35th St) First editions and old Baedeker guides.

Gotham Book Mart (Map pp64-5; ☎ 212-719-4448; 41 W 47th St) Premier stand-alone shop; its trademark shingle declares that 'wise men fish here.'

Rizzoli (Map pp64-5; ☎ 212-759-2424; 31 W 57th St btwn Fifth & Sixth Ave) Art, architecture and antique prints.

St Marks Book Shop (Map pp60-1; ☎ 212-260-7853; 31 Third Ave) Political literature, poetry and academic journals.

Strand Bookstore (Map pp60-1; ☎ 212-473-1452; 828 Broadway) New York institution boasts having 8 miles of used books and review copies.

0   1 km
0   0.5 mile

Ⓐ   Ⓑ   Ⓒ   Ⓓ

①
②
③
④
⑤
⑥

Jacqueline Kennedy Onassis Reservoir

Guggenheim Museum

Metropolitan Museum of Art

UPPER WEST SIDE

UPPER EAST SIDE

Carl Schurz Park

Hudson River

Central Park W

W 86th St
W 81st St
W 79th St
W 77th St
W 72nd St

W 66th St
W 60th St

Tenth Ave
North Ave

E 86th St
E 79th St
E 72nd St
E 65th St
E 59th St
E 57th St

The Lake

Frick Collection

Central Park

Lincoln Center

West End Ave (Eleventh Ave)

Fifth Ave
Park Ave
Lexington Ave
First Ave
York Ave

Rockefeller University

John Jay Park

Roosevelt University

Roosevelt Island

Rainey Park

Main Ave
Vernon Blvd
21st St

34th Ave
44th Dr

LONG ISLAND CITY

Jackson Ave

Queensboro Bridge

WEST NEW YORK

See Upper West Side, Upper East Side & Central Park Map (pp66–7)

Dewitt Clinton Park

MIDTOWN

Rockefeller Center

TIMES SQUARE

Worldwide Plaza

THEATER DISTRICT

Port Authority Bus Terminal

HELL'S KITCHEN

WEEHAWKEN

Lincoln Tunnel

Twelfth Ave (West Side Hwy)

Jacob Javits Convention Center

GARMENT DISTRICT

Bryant Park

Grand Central Terminal

United Nations

Saint Gabriels Park

Queens-Midtown Tunnel

Newtown Creek

W 42nd St
W 40th St
W 39th St
W 34th St

E 42nd St
E 39th St
E 34th St

Penn Station

Broadway

LITTLE KOREA

CHELSEA

Chelsea Park

FLATIRON DISTRICT

Madison Square Park

Bellevue Medical Center

24th Street Park

W 23rd St

E 23rd St

Eighth Ave
Seventh Ave
Sixth Ave
Fifth Ave

North Ave

Third Ave
Second Ave
First Ave

FDR Dr

East River

Elevanth Ave

GRAMERCY

Gramercy Park

STUYVESANT TOWN

Stuyvesant Square

UNION SQUARE

Irving Pl

E 14th St

See Chelsea & Midtown Manhattan Map (pp64–5)

NEW JERSEY

HOBOKEN

WEST VILLAGE

GREENWICH VILLAGE

Washington Square Park

New York University

EAST VILLAGE

Tompkins Square Park

ALPHABET CITY

East River Park

Sixth Ave (Avenue of the Americas)

Fourth Ave

Second Ave

First Ave

Pitt St

Franklin D Roosevelt Dr

Williamsburg Bridge

Hudson St
Greenwich St
Thompson St

NOHO

SOHO

Broadway

Christie St
The Bowery

E Houston St

LOWER EAST SIDE

Delancey St

Corlears Hook Park

Ferry to Hoboken (NJ)

Holland Tunnel

Canal St

TRIBECA

Lafayette St

LITTLE ITALY

CHINATOWN

W H Seward Park

South St Viaduct

See Downtown Manhattan Map (pp60–2)

Confucius Plaza

Rutgers Park

Rockefeller Park

Federal Plaza

City Hall Park

Police Plaza

TWO BRIDGES

Manhattan Bridge

DUMBO

Cadman Plaza W

Adams St

West St

Church St

LOWER MANHATTAN

Brooklyn Bridge

Fulton Landing

World Trade Center Site

North Cove

Battery Park City Esplanade

Maiden La

Wall St

Beaver St

FINANCIAL DISTRICT

BATTERY PARK CITY

Pier A

Hudson River

JERSEY CITY

Brooklyn Heights Promenade

BROOKLYN HEIGHTS

Columbus Park

See Lower Manhattan Map (p63)

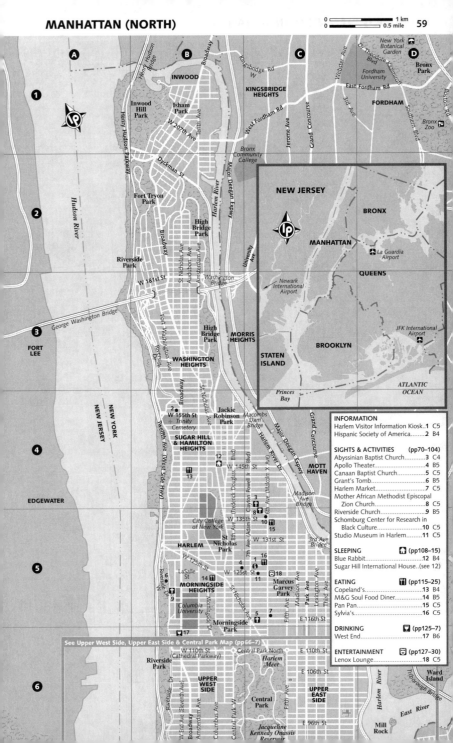

0 —————— 1 km
0 —————— 0.5 mile

INFORMATION
Harlem Visitor Information Kiosk..**1** C5
Hispanic Society of America........**2** B4

SIGHTS & ACTIVITIES (pp70–104)
Abyssinian Baptist Church...........**3** C4
Apollo Theater..........................**4** B5
Canaan Baptist Church................**5** C5
Grant's Tomb............................**6** B5
Harlem Market..........................**7** C5
Mother African Methodist Episcopal
    Zion Church...........................**8** C5
Riverside Church.......................**9** B5
Schomburg Center for Research in
    Black Culture.......................**10** C5
Studio Museum in Harlem........**11** C5

SLEEPING (pp108–15)
Blue Rabbit.............................**12** B4
Sugar Hill International House..(see 12)

EATING (pp115–25)
Copeland's.............................**13** B4
M&G Soul Food Diner..............**14** B5
Pan Pan................................**15** C5
Sylvia's.................................**16** C5

DRINKING (pp125–7)
West End...............................**17** B6

ENTERTAINMENT (pp127–30)
Lenox Lounge.........................**18** C5

A **B** **C** **D** UNION SQUARE

W 16th St
W 15th St
E 15th St

1
8th Ave-
14th St
14th St
33
6th Ave-
14 St
W 14th St
130
WEST
VILLAGE
97
135
W 13th St
W 13th St See Chelsea, Midtown Manhattan & Times Square Map (pp64–5)

Little W 12th St
W 12th St
77
E 12th St
113
57
E 11th St
Gansevoort St
73
109
56
45
14
Horatio St
Jane St
Abington
Square
139
41
28
GREENWICH
VILLAGE
W 9th St

2
MEATPACKING
DISTRICT
98
23
W 8th St
Bank St
W 11th St
Perry St
Charles St
9
61
MacDougal
Al
Washington Sq
Mws
W 12th St
Bethune St
124
50
37
1
62
49
Washington Sq North
70
Waverly Pl
Christopher St-
Sheridan
Square
Washington Pl
Washington
69
107
116
W 4th
St
140
Washington Sq
Park
30
New York
University
W 3rd St

3
West St
87
108
67
68
82
89
21
128
Washington Sq South
W 3rd St
76
112
Bradford St
88
141
16
34
65
54
Minetta La
127
Weehawken St
85
10
31
91
100
Bleecker St
93
Morton St

4
Leroy St
St Luke's Pl
James J
Walker
Park
Houston
St
105
133
W Houston St
137
Clarkson St
King St
94
Prince St
4
26
75
Charlton St
Vandam St

5
Hudson River
SOHO
36
Spring St
Dominick St
131
Collister St
Broome St
142
145
111
See Lower Manhattan Map (p63)

Broome St
Grand St
84
Watts St
Holland Tunnel
Canal St
Canal St
Canal St
Desbrosses St

6
Vestry St
Lispenard St
Laight St
Hudson
Square
Walker St
Hubert St
Beach St
White St
TRIBECA
Moore St
North Moore St
Franklin St
Franklin St

0 — 400 m
0 — 0.2 mi

E 16th St

E Irving Pl

Stuyvesant Square **F**

First Ave Loop

G 14th St Loop

H

14th St-Union Sq

3rd Ave

E 15th St

1st Ave

E 14th St

E 14th St

1

122

146

E 13th St

E 13th St

Broadway

•7

144

52

86 150

E 12th St

E 12th St

Third Ave

5

E 11th St

24

47

E 10th St

E 10th St

44

Stuyvesant St

•11

Second Ave

138

136

EAST VILLAGE

90

148

E 11th St

E 10th St

13

2

E 9th St

6

92

102

E 9th St

149

96

First Ave

Ave A

Tompkins Square Park

Ave B

E 9th St

106

E 8th St

8th St NYU

15

E 8th St

Astor Place

•18

St Marks Pl

55

17

60

118

151

E 7th St

E 7th St

Lafayette St

29

Mercer St

•12

E 6th St

E 6th St

53

E 5th St

E 5th St

Broadway

147

38

114

•12

143

78

ALPHABET CITY

Ave C

132

121

E 4th St

E 4th St

3

Great Jones St

E 3rd St

E 3rd St

Bond St

NOHO

E 2nd St

101

74

Bleeker St

Bleecker St

129

126

East Houston St

Hamilton Fish Park

The Bowery

117

125

Broadway-Lafayette St

2nd Ave

119

Attorney St

Pitt St

E Houston St

103

64 79

134

4

43

120

35

Jersey St

40

115

104

LOWER EAST SIDE

Stanton St

Ridge St

42

Prince St

80

NOLITA

Chrystie St

Eldridge St

99

123

51

Clinton St

Prince St

Crosby St

Lafayette St

Mulberry St

Mott St

Elizabeth St

46•

22

72

Williamsburg Bridge

58

20

Delancey St-Essex St

Spring St

48•

63

95

81

83

Bowery

Kenmare St

Delancey St

Delancey St

Broome St

Essex St

Ludlow St

Norfolk St

Suffolk St

8•

27•

39

66

LITTLE ITALY

59

Orchard St

Allen St

32

5

110

71

Grand St

Grand St

2

25

Broadway

Lafayette St

Centre St

Baxter St

Mulberry St

Mott St

Elizabeth St

The Bowery

Sarah D Roosevelt Parkway

Forsyth St

Howard St

Hester St

W H Seward Park

East Broadway

Mangin St

Canal St

Canal St

Canal St

East Broadway

Jefferson St

Clinton St

Madison St

Henry St

Rutgers St

Cherry St

6

Cortlandt Al

19

East Broadway

CHINATOWN

Bayard St

Columbus Park

Confucius Plaza

Pike St

0   500 m
0   0.3 mile

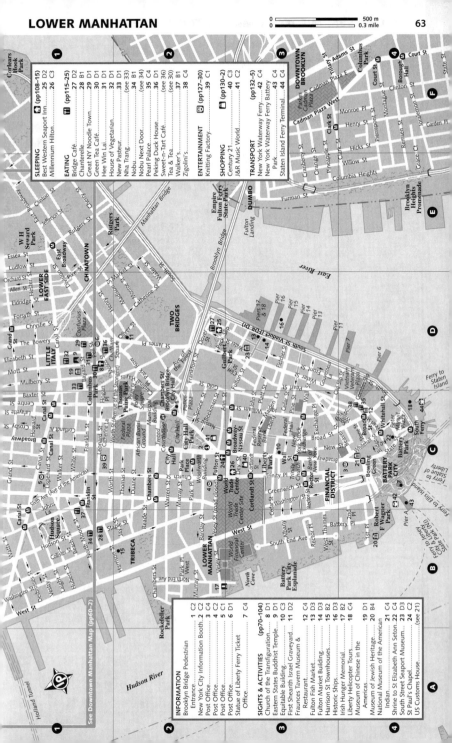

See Downtown Manhattan Map (pp60–2)

INFORMATION
American Express	1 F2
Australian Consulate	2 F3
Books of Wonder	3 E6
Canadian Consulate	4 E2
Coliseum Books	5 E3
Complete Traveller	6 F4
Duane Reade	7 D1
German Consulate	8 G2
Gotham Book Mart	9 E2
Hagstrom Map & Travel Center	10 E3
Italian Consulate	11 F5
Japan Society	12 G2
Kinko's	13 F2
Mid-Manhattan Library	14 E3
NYC & Company - the Convention & Visitors' Bureau	15 D2
Post Office	16 F1
Radio City Post Office	17 D2
Rizzoli	18 E1
Times Square Post Office	19 D3
Times Square Visitor Center	20 D2
TKTS Booth	21 D2
Travelex	22 D2
UK Consulate	23 F2

SIGHTS & ACTIVITIES (pp70–104)
Chelsea Art Museum	24 C5
Chelsea Piers	25 C5
Circle Line	26 B3
Dia: Chelsea	27 C5
Flatiron Building	28 E5
GE Building	29 E2
Gramercy Theatre	30 F5
International Center of Photography	31 E3
Liberty Helicopter Tours	32 B4
Metropolitan Life Tower	33 F5
MTV Studios	34 D3
Museum of Modern Art	35 E1
Museum of Television & Radio	36 E2
NBC Studios	(see 29)
National Arts Club	37 F6
One Times Square	38 D3
Pierpont Morgan Library	39 F4
Players Club	(see 37)
Prescriptive Fitness Gym	40 D1
Transportation Alternatives	41 E4
Whitney Museum of American Art at Altira	42 F3
World Yacht	43 B3

SLEEPING (pp108–15)
Algonquin	44 E3
Ameritania Hotel	45 D1
Big Apple Hostel	46 E2
Broadway Inn	47 D2
Chelsea Center Hostel	48 D4
Chelsea Inn	49 E6
Chelsea International Hostel	50 D6
Chelsea Pines Inn	51 D6
Chelsea Savoy Hotel	52 D5
Colonial House Inn	53 D5
Doubletree Guest Suites	54 D2
Gershwin Hotel	55 E5
Gramercy Park Hotel	56 F5
Herald Square Hotel	57 E4
Hotel 17	58 F6
Hotel Chelsea	59 D5
Hotel Edison	60 D2
Hotel Stanford	61 E4
Inn at Irving Place	62 F6
Majestic Hotel	63 D1
Novotel	64 D2
Paramount	65 D2
Plaza Hotel	66 E1
Portland Square Hotel	67 E2
Ritz Carlton	68 E1
Royalton	69 E3
Salisbury Hotel	70 E1
Sherry Netherland Hotel	71 E1
W Hotel	72 D2
Waldorf-Astoria	73 F2
Wellington Hotel	74 D1
Wolcott Hotel	75 E4

EATING (pp115–25)
Aquavit	76 E1
Basilica	77 D2
Brasserie Les Halles	78 F5
Burger Joint	79 E1
Chelsea Market	80 D6
Dae Dong Restaurant	81 E4
Empire Diner	82 C5
Ess-a-Bagel	83 F2
Gramercy Tavern	84 F6
Grand Sichuan	85 D2
Hangawi	86 E4
Island Burgers & Shakes	87 D2
Joe Allen	88 D2
La Bonne Soupe	89 E1
Le Cirque 2000	90 F2
Madras Mahal	91 F5

0 — 400 m
0 — 0.2 miles

Mee Noodle Shop....................92 G2
Mee Noodle Shop....................93 D1
Michael Jordan's Steakhouse.94 F3
Munson Diner.........................95 C2
Oyster Bar & Restaurant......(see 94)
Rocking Horse Café................96 D6
The Half King.........................97 C5

Uncle Nick's..........................98 D2
Union Square Café..................99 E6
'wichcraft.............................100 F6
Zen Palate...........................101 D2

DRINKING (pp125–7)
Barracuda............................102 D5
Old Town Bar & Grill.............103 F6
Pete's Tavern........................104 F6
Rainbow Room...................(see 29)
Russian Vodka Room............105 D2
Siberia.................................106 D3
Single Room Occupancy.......107 D1
xl..108 D6

ENTERTAINMENT (pp127–30)
Ambassador..........................109 D2
Avalon.................................110 E6
Booth..................................111 D2
Broadway.............................112 D1
Circle in the Square..............113 D2
City Center...........................114 E1
Ed Sullivan...........................115 D1
Eugene O'Neill......................116 D2
Ford Center Theater.............117 D3
Gershwin..............................118 D2
Helen Hayes.........................119 D3
Imperial...............................120 D2
Irving Plaza..........................121 F6
John Golden.........................122 D2
Joyce Theater.......................123 D6
Lunt-Fontanne.....................124 D2
Majestic...............................125 D3
Marquis...............................126 D2
Music Box............................127 D2
Nederlander.........................128 D3
Neil Simon...........................129 D2
New Amsterdam....................130 D3
Palace Theater.....................131 D2
Plymouth.............................132 D2
Shubert...............................133 D3
Town Hall............................134 E3
Walter Kerr..........................135 D2
Winter Garden Theater.........136 D2

SHOPPING (pp130–2)
Academy Records & CDs.........137 E6
B&H Photo-Video..................138 D4
Bergdorf Goodman................139 E1
Brooks Brothers....................140 F3
Brooks Brothers....................141 E2
Cartier.................................142 E2
Chelsea Flea Market..............143 E5
Christie's New York...............144 E2
Dave's New York Army & Navy.145 E6
Disney Store.........................146 E1
FAO Schwartz.......................147 E1
Garage Antiques Building......148 E5
Gianni Versace.....................149 E2
Gucci..................................150 E1
Henri Bendel........................151 E1
Louis Vuitton.......................152 E1
Metropolitan Art & Antiques
    Pavilion...........................153 E6
NBA Store............................154 E2
Niketown.............................155 E1
Paragon Athletic Goods........156 F6
Saks Fifth Avenue................157 E2
Tiffany & Co.........................158 E1

TRANSPORT (pp132–5)
Aer Lingus............................159 F1
Aeromexico...........................160 E1
Air Canada...........................161 E2
Air France............................162 E1
American Airlines..................163 E2
British Airways......................164 E3
Continental..........................165 F3
Delta...............................(see 165)
Finnair.............................(see 165)
Singapore Airlines.................167 F1
Swiss Air..........................(see 165)
United.............................(see 165)
US Airways...........................168 F3
Virgin Atlantic...................(see 165)

A   **B**   **C**   **D**

EDGEWATER

GUTTENBERG

WEST NEW YORK

Hudson River

Riverside Park

Riverside Park

UPPER WEST SIDE

INFORMATION		
Alliance Française	1	F6
Asia Society	2	F5
Books and Co	3	F5
Czech Center	4	F4
French Consulate	5	E5
Goethe Institute	6	E4
Italian Cultural Institute	7	E5

SIGHTS & ACTIVITIES	(pp70–104)	
Children's Museum of Manhattan	8	C4
Cooper-Hewitt National Design Museum	9	E3
Frick Collection	10	E5
National Academy of Design	11	E3
New York Road Runners' Club	12	E3
Temple Emanu-El	13	E6

SLEEPING	(pp108–15)	
Hostelling International - New York	14	C1
Hotel Newton	15	C2
International Student Center	16	D3
On The Ave	17	C4

EATING	(pp115–25)	
Café con Leche	18	C4
Café Greco	19	F5
Café Lalo	20	C4
Fairway Market	21	C5
Favia Lite	22	F6
H&H Bagel	23	C4
Hungarian Pastry Shop	24	C1
Lexington Candy Shop	25	F4
Taqueria y Fonda la Mexicana	26	C1
Tibet Shambala	27	C4
Zabar's	28	C4

DRINKING	(pp125–7)	
Saints	29	C1
Subway Inn	30	F6

ENTERTAINMENT	(pp127–30)	
Frederick P Rose Hall (Jazz at Lincoln Center)	31	D6
Iridium	32	D6
Lincoln Plaza Cinemas	33	D6
Merkin Concert Hall	34	C5
Symphony Space	35	C2

SHOPPING	(pp130–2)	
Barney's	36	F6
Bloomingdale's	37	F6
Calvin Klein	38	E6
Diesel	39	F6
Giorgio Armani	40	E6
Givenchy	41	E6
Missoni	42	F4
Polo/Ralph Lauren	43	F5
Sotheby's	44	G5
Yves St Laurent	45	F5

TRANSPORT	(pp132–5)	
Roosevelt Island Tram Station	46	H6
Roosevelt Island Tram Station	47	F6

Cathedral of St John the Divine

W 112th St
W 111th St
Central Park

Twelfth Ave (West Side Hwy)

Riverside Dr

24
29
26
14

W 110th St (Cathedral Parkway)
110th St
W 109th St
W 108th St
W 107th St
W 106th St (Duke Ellington Boulevard)
W 105th St
W 104th St
W 103rd St
W 102nd St
W 101st St
W 100th St
W 99th St
W 98th St
96th St
W 97th St
W 95th St
W 94th St
W 93rd St
W 92nd St
W 91st St
W 90th St
W 89th St
W 88th St
W 87th St
86th St
W 85th St
W 84th St
W 83rd St
W 82nd St
W 81st St
W 80th St
79th St
W 78th St
W 77th St
W 76th St
W 75th St
W 74th St
W 73rd St
72nd St
W 71st St
W 70th St
W 69th St
W 68th St
W 67th St
W 66th St
W 65th St
W 64th St
W 63rd St
W 62nd St
W 61st St
W 60th St
W 59th St

Cathedral Pkwy (110th St)

Columbus Ave
Amsterdam Ave
Manhattan Ave
Central Park West

103rd St
The Pool

35
15

American Museum of Natural History

81st St-Museum of Natural History
Swedish Cottage Marionette Theater

New-York Historical Society

The Lake

The Dakota
72nd St

Tavern on the Green

66th St-Lincoln Center

Lincoln Center

59th St-Columbus Circle

West End Ave (Eleventh Ave)
Broadway
Amsterdam Ave
Freedom Pl
Twelfth Ave (West Side Hwy)

27
8
20
28
18
23
17
21
34
32
33
31

See Chelsea, Midtown Manhattan & Times Square Map (pp64–5)

NEW YORK CITY IN...

Two Days

First stop, one or all of the museums along Museum Mile with a homeward-bound stroll through Central Park. Grab lunch at the Grand Central Oyster Bar or a romantic dinner at Babbo or Nobu (make reservations way in advance). You should also wander through New York's neighborhoods – Greenwich Village, Chinatown, Little Italy, Lower East Side – window-shopping, noshing and conversing. Grab a midday or evening meal at Grand Sichuan, Sweet-n-Tart Café or Katz's Deli. Don't forget to party till the break of day with the young kids in the Lower East Side or at the jazz joints in the Village.

Four Days

The view of Manhattan's skyline from the Staten Island or Statue of Liberty ferries is a spectacular sight in real life. Visiting Ellis Island is also an educational homage for all immigrant Americans. If you're in Lower Manhattan, don't forget to walk across the Brooklyn Bridge for yet another perspective on Gotham. Then counter irrational patriotism with shopping therapy along Fifth Ave or at the funky boutiques in the East Village. If your visit is timed right, you'll be able to catch amateur night at the Apollo or a Sunday gospel service in Harlem.

Seven Days

Now you have time to visit the boroughs. You can foray out to Queens for an eating expedition in neighborhoods of recent arrivals or shoot for the roller coaster at Coney Island. Or for borough-phobes, you can do a weekend gallery tour of Chelsea, hit the 10th St Baths in the East Village, or join a walking tour for quirky historical information. If you're inundated with concrete, escape to a patch of green on Roosevelt Island.

Three Lives (Map pp60-1; ☎ 212-741-2069; 154 W 10th St) Greenwich Village institution carrying biographies.

Unoppressive Non-Imperialist Bargain Books (Map pp60-1; ☎ 212-229-0079; 34 Carmine St) Publishers' overstocks.

Cultural Centers

Alliance Française (Map pp66-7; ☎ 212-355-6100; 22 E 60th St btwn Park & Madison Ave)

Asia Society (Map pp66-7; ☎ 212-288-6400; 725 Park Ave at E 70th St)

Czech Center (Map pp66-7; ☎ 212-288-0830; 1109 Madison Ave at E 83rd St)

Goethe Institute (Map pp66-7; ☎ 212-439-8700; 1014 Fifth Ave)

Hispanic Society of America (Map p59; ☎ 212-926-2234; 613 W 155th St at Broadway)

Italian Cultural Institute (Map pp66-7; ☎ 212-879-4242; 686 Park Ave)

Japan Society (Map pp64-5; ☎ 212-832-1155; 333 E 47th St btwn First & Second Ave)

Swiss Institute (Map pp60-1; ☎ 212-925-2035; 3rd fl, 495 Broadway)

Emergency

For police, fire and ambulance, dial ☎ 911; it's a free call from any phone. For non-emergencies call ☎ 311.

Internet Access

Free Internet access is available at the following locations:

New York Public Library's main branch (Map pp64-5; ☎ 212-930-0800; Fifth Ave at 42nd St) Free half-hour Internet access.

Times Square Visitor Center (Map pp64-5; ☎ 212-768-1560; www.timessquarebid.org; 1560 Broadway btwn W 46th & W 47th St; ☉ 8am-8pm)

New York City also has public 'hot spots,' open to anyone with wireless Internet capability. These include the following parks: City Hall, Bowling Green, South Street Seaport and Bryant Park. Verizon also has subscriber-accessible hot spots within 300ft of their pay phones; see their website for a map (www.verizon.net/wifi).

Internet Resources

Gawker.com (www.gawker.com) Catty gossip about anyone who dares to pose for the camera.

Manhattan Users Guide (www.manhattanusersguide.com) Dedicated to covering all the latest and greatest openings of stores, restaurants and bars.

New York Times Travel section (www.nytoday.com) Resources for in- and out-of-towners with entertainment listings and an archive of reviews.

NYC & Company (www.nycvisit.com) The Convention & Visitors' Bureau for general information and rush hotel reservations.
NYC Subways (www.nycsubway.org) Unofficial site detailing the transit system, from practical information to historical trivia.

Libraries

All public libraries are closed on Sunday; for a list of other branches, visit www.nypl.org.
Jefferson Market Library (Map pp60-1; ☎ 212-243-4334; 425 Sixth Ave at 10th St)
Mid-Manhattan Library (Map pp64-5; ☎ 212-340-0833; 455 Fifth Ave)
New York Public Library (Map pp64-5; ☎ 212-930-0800; Fifth Ave at 42nd St)

Media

New York Times The nation's premier newspaper, with more foreign bureaus and reporters than any other publication in the world. Its Weekend Section, published on Friday, is an invaluable guide to cultural events.
Wall Street Journal A must-read for financial workers.
Village Voice Distributed free in Manhattan each Wednesday; it is well known for nightlife listings for the mainstream clubs and music venues. It's also the best-known source for fee-free rental apartments and room-mate situations.
New York Magazine Follows the city scene for restaurant-obsessed readers.
New York Observer A weekly newspaper about local media and politics; lists literary readings and parties.
Time Out New York The most comprehensive listings of bars, restaurants and goings-on.

Medical Services

All hospital emergency rooms are obligated to accept sick visitors without regard to an ability to pay. However, showing up without insurance or money will virtually guarantee a long wait unless you are in extremis. For locations of hospitals nearest you, check the yellow pages.
New York University Medical Center (Map pp64-5; %212-263-5550; 462 First Ave at 33rd St)
Planned Parenthood (☎ 800-230-7526, 212-965-7000 for appointments; locations: 26 Bleecker St at Mott St, Manhattan; 44 Court St, Brooklyn) Women's health and reproductive issues.

New York has many 24-hour pharmacies, which is really the term for a convenience store with a drugs counter.
Duane Reade pharmacy Midtown (Map pp64-5; ☎ 212-541-9708; 224 W 57th St & Broadway) Greenwich Village (Map pp60-1; ☎ 212-674-5357; 378 Sixth Ave & Waverly Place)

Money

Banks and ATMs are widespread in Manhattan and the boroughs. Banks are normally open weekdays, usually 9am to 3pm. The Chase Manhattan branch at the corner of Mott and Canal Sts in Chinatown is open daily. Several other banks along Canal St also have weekend hours.
American Express (Map pp64-5; ☎ 212-421-8240; 374 Park Ave at E 53rd St)
Travelex (Map pp64-5; ☎ 212-265-6049; 1590 Broadway at 48th St; ☼ 9am-7pm Mon-Sat, 9am-5pm Sun) Formerly Thomas Cook Foreign Exchange.

Post

General Post Office (Map pp64-5; ☎ 212-330-3002; James A Foley Building, 441 Eighth Ave, New York, NY 10001; cnr W 33rd St; ☼ 24hr) Receives poste restante marked 'general delivery.'
Rockefeller Center post office (Map pp64-5; ☎ 212-265-8024; 610 Fifth Ave; ☼ 9:30am-5:30pm Mon-Fri)
Franklin D Roosevelt Station (Map pp64-5; ☎ 212-330-5508; 909 Third Ave at E 55th St; ☼ 7:30am-8pm Mon-Fri, 9am-4pm Sat)

Telephone & Fax

There are thousands of pay telephones on the streets, but they are dwindling in number because many people rely on their cell phones. Public pay phones can also be found in the lobbies of large hotels.
Kinko's (Map pp64-5; ☎ 212-308-2679; 16 E 52nd St btwn Madison & Fifth Ave; ☼ 24hr) Offices throughout the city offer fax, computer and photocopying services.

Toilets

New York City doesn't have a lot of public toilets, and you should head to department stores such as Macy's, Saks Fifth Avenue and Bloomingdale's or use a hotel lobby. If you're discreet and well dressed, it's also possible to walk into a crowded bar or restaurant to use the bathroom.

Tourist Information

NYC & Company – the Convention & Visitors' Bureau (Map pp64-5; ☎ 800-692-8474, outside US ☎ 212-397-8222; www.nycvisit.com; 810 Seventh Ave at 53rd St; ☼ 8:30am-6pm Mon-Fri, 9am-5pm Sat & Sun) Call the 24-hour phone line to order promotional and tourist publications for New York City. To speak directly with a multilingual counselor, call ☎ 212-484-1222.
Big Apple Greeters Program (☎ 212-669-8159; www.bigapplegreeter.org) Five hundred volunteers welcome visitors to the city by offering free tours of lesser-known

neighborhoods. Some greeters are multilingual and specialize in helping the disabled. Reservations must be made in advance.

Useful Organizations

AIDS Hotline (☎ 800-872-2777)
Alcoholics Anonymous (☎ 212-647-1680)
Crime Victims Services (☎ 212-577-7777)
Gay & Lesbian National Hotline (☎ 212-989-0999)
Legal Aid Society (☎ 212-577-3300)

DANGERS & ANNOYANCES

Although panhandlers and hustlers are not as prevalent in New York as in years past, appeals for money come in dozens of forms, including pitches for a dubious support group ('I'm a member of the United Homeless Organization'), unsubtle appeals to tourist fear ('I don't want to hurt or rob anybody'), and the shoulder-shrugging appeal for help ('I just got locked out of my car and need money for a cab'). Giving money is a personal decision, but remember that a sad story to a stranger is usually a well-rehearsed story.

If you wish to donate to a legitimate organization that helps people in need, contact **Citymeals-on-Wheels** (☎ 212-687-1234), which reaches out to feed hundreds of hungry people each day.

Hustlers often set up three-card-monte games – 'players' try to pick the red card out of three shuffled on the top of a cardboard box. This variation on the shell game is widely known to be a no-win scam. Yet, enough tourists play along (or get their wallets lifted while watching) to make it a common sight on downtown streets during the weekends. Readers have written us with tales of friends who have been taken in by this, and as long as there's a gullible player willing to shell out money, this scam will continue.

Solo travelers, especially women, should avoid riding the subway after midnight. The cars tend to be deserted or haunted by strange types looking for victims. The area around Port Authority is still pretty dodgy, so keep your bags close and your guard up.

SIGHTS
Lower Manhattan   Map p63

The southern tip of the island is the oldest section of the city. It was here that a frontier outpost was hacked out of the forest by the Dutch. Colonial-era fur-traders were soon replaced by 19th-century power players,

and it was here that the country's financial institutions sprouted from within massive Beaux Art temples. Capitalism of the 20th-century worshipped in gravity-defying skyscrapers, epitomized by the World Trade Center (WTC). It is also here that the US suffered its worst foreign attack since Pearl Harbor; an attack that destroyed the twin towers of the WTC. This is a scarred district that few New Yorkers visit for pleasure. The hole in the skyline, the Statue of Liberty and Ellis Island's memorials to human struggle, the daily but irreverent practice of commerce – these sights have renewed poignancy now that history has disrupted a period of complacency.

STATUE OF LIBERTY
Prior to September 11, 2001, visitors could climb the 354 steps to the statue's crown, the equivalent of a 22-story building. Due to heightened security, visitors are only allowed to tour the grounds at the base of the statue (Map p63). These precautions are liable to change without warning so stay tuned to the National Park Service's website (www.nps.gov/stli). Despite the statue's restricted access, the 15-minute ferry ride is spectacular for the views of Manhattan, although this view comes free-of-charge and with less hassle on the Staten Island ferry (see p103).

Circle Line (☎ 212-563-3200; www.circleline.com; Battery Park; tickets adult/senior/child $10/8/4, audio tour $6; ◷ every 30min 9am-4pm) runs the only boat service from Manhattan to the Statue of Liberty and nearby Ellis Island. They accept cash or traveler's checks only. To take in both sites is an all-day affair, so arrive early and count on crowds, especially in summer. Boat schedules change with the season and mid-afternoon trips have time to visit only one site. The main ticket office is housed inside Castle Clinton (see p72).

Ferries also leave from Liberty State Park on the New Jersey side of the harbor.

MANHATTAN

☎ 212 / pop 1.5 million

For most visitors, Manhattan *is* New York City. Even the residents of the outer boroughs refer to it as 'the city,' a tacit acknowledgment of the island's primacy.

STATUE OF LIBERTY

The most enduring symbol of New York City – and indeed, the New World in general – can trace its origins to a Parisian dinner party in 1865. There, a group of intellectuals who were opposed to the government of Napoleon III gathered in the house of political activist Edouard René Lefebvre de Laboulaye to discuss ways to promote French Republicanism. The notion of building a monument honoring the American conception of political freedom intrigued sculptor Frédéric-Auguste Bartholdi, a fellow dinner guest, and he dedicated most of the next 20 years to turning the dream into a reality.

Laboulaye and Bartholdi decided that the structure should end up in the US. Bartholdi traveled to New York in 1871 to choose a site for the work (modeled on the Colossus of Rhodes). Soon afterward, the pair held a lottery to raise $250,000 to cover the cost of construction of the statue, which, incidentally, included a metal skeleton by railway engineer Alexandre Gustave Eiffel, who later became world-famous for his eponymous Parisian tower. Meanwhile, in the US, a campaign by the New York *World* newspaper beat the drum for the project. In 1883, poet Emma Lazarus published a work called *The New Colossus* in support of a fund for a pedestal for the statue. Her words have long since been associated with the monument:

Give me your tired, your poor
Your huddled masses yearning to breathe free
The wretched refuse of your teeming shore
Send these, the homeless, tempest-tost to me
I lift my lamp beside the golden door!

On October 28, 1886, the 151ft *Liberty Enlightening the World* was finally unveiled in New York Harbor before President Grover Cleveland and a harbor full of tooting ships.

By the 1980s a restoration of the statue was in order, and more than $100 million was spent to shore up Liberty for its centennial. Substantial work was required to restore the rotting copper skin, and a new gold-plated torch, the third in the statue's history, was installed. The older stained-glass torch is now on display just inside the entrance to the staircase, near a fine museum that describes the statue's history and its restoration.

ELLIS ISLAND

More than a government institution, Ellis Island symbolizes the American birth of over 15 million people. Escaping persecution, famine or hopeless conditions across Europe, the ship-borne immigrants were unloaded, recorded and examined on this island before being discharged into their new and uncertain future. In service from 1892 to 1954, Ellis Island became the main entry point for US naturalization and on an average day swelled with as many as 5000 newcomers.

A $160 million restoration project turned the impressive redbrick building into an **Immigration Museum** (☎ 212-363-3206; audio tour adult/child $6/4; ⓨ 9:30am-5pm) covering the history of the island. The exhibitions begin at the Baggage Room and continue on the 2nd floor where medical inspections took place and foreign currency was exchanged. At all points, the exhibits emphasize that, contrary to popular myth, most of the aliens were processed within eight hours, and conditions were generally clean and safe. The 338ft-long Registry Room includes a beautiful vaulted tile ceiling made by immigrants from Spain.

There is a 50-minute audio tour of the facility narrated by Tom Brokaw. Much more moving are the recorded memories of real Ellis Island immigrants that were taped in the 1980s and are available through phone banks in each display area. Visitors can also take in **Ellis Island Stories** (adult/child $3/2.50; ⓨ May-Oct), a 30-minute play about the experience of arriving at Ellis Island. *Island of Hope, Island of Tears* (free) is a 30-minute film on the immigrant experience that is worth checking out. Admission to the play and the movie are on a first come, first served basis.

Barely visible up the slip from the boat docks are the rotting remains of *Ellis Island*, a passenger ferry that sank in 1968 after years of neglect.

Ellis Island is usually visited in conjunction with the Statue of Liberty. See p70 for Circle Line ferry prices and details.

BATTERY PARK CITY

This 30-acre waterfront swath stretches from Chambers St to Pier 1 on the southern tip of the island. It's a fantastic getaway from Manhattan's madness, with glorious sunsets and views of the Statue of Liberty.

In the northernmost section of the park, green lawns and playgrounds serve as downtown Manhattan's communal backyard. Every corner of open space is usually claimed by a family or a Frisbee game. Heading south, the park evolves into something of a monument alley. The latest addition is the **Irish Hunger Memorial** (cnr Vesey St & River Terrace), which is more of a landscape artwork than an emotional fish-hook. At an ordinary street corner, a tilted ramp with a rambling path displays a re-creation of the Irish countryside complete with a stone cottage and green fields. Marking the 150th anniversary of the famine in Ireland, the quarter-acre site represents the maximum amount of land an Irish family could have owned in order to receive famine relief from British overseers.

More a personal history than a textbook account, the **Museum of Jewish Heritage** (☎ 212-509-6130; 18 First Place, Robert F Wagner Park; adult/child $7/5; ☽ 10am-5:45pm Sun-Wed, 10am-8pm Thu, 10am-5pm Fri) uses family memorabilia and video interviews to describe Jewish culture, diaspora and assimilation. The 2nd floor is devoted to the Jewish holocaust and traces the struggle of ordinary people sucked into turbulent times.

In Battery Park proper looms the shell of **Castle Clinton**. Built in 1811 and designed by John McComb (the first major New York–born architect), the imposing fortress, with its 8ft-thick walls and rusticated gate, once brimmed with 28 guns set in the embrasures. Back then, the fort stood on an island that was hundreds of feet from the shore; landfill has since joined it with Manhattan. Its guns were never fired in anger, and in the 1820s the government decommissioned the fort and turned it into Castle Garden, a concert hall-cum-resort that is said to have hosted up to 6000 people beneath a domed roof. Castle Clinton has had a colorful history: in 1855 the government turned it into

a processing center for immigrants, and in 1896 the renowned architecture firm of McKim, Mead & White converted the building into an aquarium (a purpose it served until 1941). Today, it is the site of the ticket office for the Statue of Liberty ferry.

Not technically within the boundaries of Battery Park City, **Shrine to St Elizabeth Ann Seton** (7 State St) commemorates the first American Catholic saint. This delicate Georgian home, set in redbrick, dates from 1793 and is the lone survivor of a series of graceful row houses that once hugged the shoreline (due to landfill, it's now set well back from the river). A Federal-style west wing was added in 1806, reputedly by John McComb. This section of the structure is enlivened by a curved porch and a double colonnade of attenuated Doric and Ionic columns that were supposedly made from recycled ship masts.

NATIONAL MUSEUM OF THE AMERICAN INDIAN

Established by oil heir George Gustav Heye in 1916, this **museum** (☎ 212-668-6624; 1 Bowling Green; admission free; ☽ 10am-5pm), an affiliate of the Smithsonian Institution, lives in the former US Custom House. It does little to explain the history of Native Americans, but instead concentrates its collection on Native American identity as reflected in its million-item collection of crafts and everyday objects. Computer touch-screens offer views on Native American life and beliefs, and working artists are often available to explain their techniques.

Ironically the building is more compelling than the exhibits. This Beaux Arts monument to commerce was built to collect federal duties imposed on foreign goods in the days before income tax. Walls, doors, ceilings and floors are festooned with shells, sails, sea creatures and other sea imagery. The glorious elliptical rotunda is a 135ft-long room encircled by Reginald Marsh's murals (added in 1937) portraying everything from the great explorers of America to Greta Garbo. It is simply one of the most sumptuous Beaux Arts buildings ever built.

TRINITY CHURCH

By the mid-19th century, everything new, from courthouses and banks to privies, was designed to look like Greek temples, and people quickly tired of the austerity of the ancients. British-born Richard Upjohn rectified this homogeneity with the richly decorated **Trinity Church** (☎ 212-602-0872; cnr Broadway & Wall St; 🕑 9am-4pm Mon-Fri, 10am-3:45pm Sat, 1-3:45pm Sun). A brownstone with buttresses and finials, Trinity also donned a 280ft octagonal spire that was the premier 'skyscraper' of colonial New York's skyline. Its appearance proved a revelation to a citizenry craving more transcendental and less rationalist forms. Upjohn's church helped launch the picturesque neo-Gothic movement in America.

The long, dark interior of the church includes a beautiful stained-glass window over the altar. Trinity, like other Anglican churches in America, became part of the Episcopal faith following US independence. A pamphlet describing the history of the parish is available for a small donation.

NEW YORK STOCK EXCHANGE
One of the world's largest stock exchanges, the **New York Stock Exchange** (NYSE; ☎ 212-656-3000; www.nyse.com; 8 Broad St) dates back to 1792 when 24 traders signed an exchange agreement, creating a market to sell the stock of three recently incorporated banks; this momentous event took place under a buttonwood tree in a less urbanized Manhattan. The exchange really came of age during and after the Civil War when railroads

and other industries boomed across the country. In 1903 the NYSE graduated to its present home, an imposing rendition of a Romanesque temple.

A complicated and influential auction of stocks for 2800 companies, from blue chips to technologies, takes place weekdays from 9:30am to 4pm; the start and close of the day is ceremoniously marked by the ringing of the bell, an honor given to dignitaries or celebrities. On an average day, more than 1.3 billion shares, exceeding $35 billion, change hands on the trading room floor.

The NYSE building is presently closed to visitors; the cordoned-off streets and armed security outside of the building is a continuous reminder of New York's vulnerability as a terrorist target.

FEDERAL HALL
As Americans sought a way to define their new nation, they looked to the ancient democracy of Greece and the republic of Rome for examples to emulate. Classical architecture, as classical government had, gave expression to the official architects of the young republic. The finest surviving example in Lower Manhattan is **Federal Hall** (☎ 212-767-0637; 26 Wall St; 🕑 9am-5pm Mon-Fri). The present building is the third to occupy the site, and each previous building served a

---

BUILDING BONANZA

For a short but comprehensive tour of the city's man-made landscape, it's best to spend a day downtown near Wall St. Though famous as the world's financial capital, this area of urban canyons is an unrivaled museum of architecture. Along the cramped and circuitous side streets and the grand avenue of Broadway you will find Federal homes, Greek Revival temples, Gothic churches, Renaissance palazzos and one of the finest collections of early-20th-century skyscrapers. Although no Dutch buildings survive from the early 17th century, the paths and lanes mapped out by the engineer Cryn Fredericksz in 1625 have restrained and influenced every architect who ventured to build here.

A few standouts in the collection include:

- Woolworth Building (p76)
- St Paul's Chapel (p74)
- Equitable Building (corner of Broadway and Cedar St)
- Trinity Church (p72)
- Federal Hall (p73)
- US Custom House (now the National Museum of American Indian; p72)
- Clinton Castle (see Battery City Park, p72)
- Shrine to St Elizabeth Ann Seton (see Battery City Park, p72)

WORLD TRADE CENTER SITE

The massive twin towers of the World Trade Center (WTC) once rose 1350ft above the square at the corner of Church and Vesey Sts. That was prior to September 11, 2001, when two commercial planes were commandeered by terrorists and purposely steered into the two towers shortly after rush hour on a sunny work day. In the midst of the evacuation effort, first the south tower, then the north tower collapsed, taking with them the lives of 2000 people from more than 60 countries. On that day, New Yorkers beheld the indiscriminate force of annihilation, leaving survivors with heavy burdens of sorrow. Grieving varies in its duration and expression, but a tangible scar on the city's psyche is still evident today.

The site – once a symbol of US economic domination, then a horrific mass grave – has been transformed once again into a construction zone nearly indistinguishable from other projects except for the crowds of tourists who mill about the sidewalk and snap pictures for morbid scrapbooks. Not long after the attacks, Larry Silverstein, the developer who leases the land from the Port Authority of New York, announced plans to rebuild on the site and solicited proposals from top architectural firms. Decision makers, especially business interests, were eager to rebuild so as to dissuade displaced companies from relocating outside of Manhattan. Average New Yorkers were eager to fill the gaping hole in the skyline. But agreeing on how to erase the void and how to remember the victims has been ardently debated.

Close to a year's worth of debate has yielded the final plan for the replacement towers. Recapturing the title of the world's tallest building, the towers will rise 1776ft, but offices will only occupy space from the ground level to the 70th floor (more than 200ft less than the original twin towers). The remaining space will be an open-air structure filled with cables and windmills that may generate power for the building. Also on the site will be a memorial to the victims of the attack. 'Reflecting Absence,' designed by Michael Arad, an architect with the New York Housing Authority, will transform the footprints of the two towers into sunken reflecting pools with an underground interpretative center.

different function. This was the location of the British City Hall during colonial times, and where John Peter Zenger, a newspaper publisher, was jailed on charges of libel. The ensuing court case won a major victory for freedom of the press, which was later incorporated into the new nation's Bill of Rights. This is also the meeting place for the first US Congress, and where Washington took the oath of office as the first president of the United States; the exact location is marked by a huge statue of Washington.

It later became the US Customs House and is now a small museum dedicated to post-colonial New York. Free guided tours of the building leave every hour on the half-hour from 12:30pm to 3:30pm.

FEDERAL RESERVE BANK OF NEW YORK

Looking like a stone prison, the **Federal Reserve Bank of New York** (☎ 212-720-6130; 31 Liberty St) contains more than 10,000 tons of gold reserves stored in high-security vaults drilled 50ft into Manhattan's bedrock. A tour of the Fed (by appointment only) will give you a glimpse of a small part of the fortune, as well as exhibits of coins, counterfeit currency and more than you've ever wanted to know about banking history.

ST PAUL'S CHAPEL

One of the few remaining constituent chapels of Trinity parish, **St Paul's** (cnr Fulton St & Broadway; ⏰ 10am-6pm Mon-Sat) has survived almost every tragedy that has struck this end of the island. A blaze that raced through the city during the Revolutionary War almost claimed St Paul's, but citizens climbed to the roof and extinguished the flames that threatened this schist and brownstone church. Designed in 1764 by Thomas McBean, the chapel is now the last remaining colonial building in the area and one of the greatest Georgian structures ever built in the country. It was here, within the airy interior of fluted Corinthian columns and Waterford chandeliers, that President George Washington attended services when New York served as the nation's capital. His personal pew is still on display.

St Paul's historic tenacity proved vital more than two hundred years later after the attacks on the WTC. On the perimeter of 'ground zero,' St Paul's fed and cared for weary emergency workers responsible for the clean-up of the destroyed buildings and the recovery of victims' bodies. A tribute to the crews and church volunteers now occupies the side aisles of the church arranged in 12 symbolic stations. This exhibit affords a personal and private way to grieve for the lives destroyed on that day.

FRAUNCES TAVERN MUSEUM & RESTAURANT

Located on a block of historic structures, **Fraunces Tavern** (☎ 212-425-1778; 54 Pearl St; adult/child $3/2; ☺ 10am-5pm Tue, Wed & Fri; 11am-5pm Thu & Sat) is one of the final examples of colonial-era New York that remains largely intact.

Here stood the Queen's Head Tavern, owned by Samuel Fraunces, who changed the name to Fraunces Tavern after the American victory in the War of Independence. It was in the 2nd-floor dining room on December 4, 1783, that George Washington bade farewell to the officers of the Continental Army after the British relinquished control of New York City. In the 19th century, the tavern closed and the building fell into disuse. It was also damaged during several massive fires that

swept through old downtown areas and destroyed most colonial buildings and nearly all structures built by the Dutch. In 1904, the building was bought by the Sons of the Revolution historical society and returned to an approximation of its colonial-era look – an act believed to be the first major attempt at historic preservation in the US.

SOUTH STREET SEAPORT

Rounding the tip of the island towards the East River is the South Street Seaport, the primary port of call from 1815 to 1860. Ships delivered passengers here from the first regularly scheduled trans-Atlantic service and received goods originating from the recently opened Erie Canal. With shifting transportation trends, the South Street Seaport fell into disuse and was all but abandoned until its revival as a tourist destination in the 1980s. This 11-block enclave of shops and historic sights combines the best and worst in historic preservation. Significant buildings from the 18th and 19th century are physically preserved, but the run-of-the-mall stores stuck inside do little to preserve any regional identity. Regardless of commercial ideals, families find that the

BROOKLYN BRIDGE

Celebrated by poets and painters, Brooklyn Bridge became an icon for America's Gilded Age of prosperity and optimism. An engineering marvel, the bridge earned two superlatives when it opened in 1883: the world's first steel suspension bridge and the longest span. It is a magnificent example of urban design, and a glimpse of its spiderweb cables fretted between the arched supports inspires an indescribable desire to cross its outstretched path.

The story of the bridge's birth incorporates elements of high drama. Plans for a suspension bridge spanning the East River were drawn up by the Prussian-born engineer John Roebling, who was knocked off a pier by a ferry in Fulton's Landing in 1869 and died of tetanus poisoning before construction of the bridge began. His son Washington Roebling supervised construction of the bridge, which took 14 years and was plagued by budget overruns and the death of 20 workers. The younger Roebling was stricken by the bends while helping to excavate the riverbed for the bridge's western tower and supervised the project largely from his bed. There was one final tragedy to come in June of 1883, when the bridge opened to pedestrian traffic: someone in the crowd shouted, perhaps as a joke, that the bridge was collapsing into the river, setting off a mad rush in which 12 people were trampled to death.

There's no fear of collapse today. The bridge enters its third century following an extensive renovation in the early 1980s. The pedestrian walkway that begins just east of City Hall affords a wonderful view of Lower Manhattan, and you can stop at observation points under both stone support towers and view brass panorama histories of the waterfront at various points in New York's past. Once you reach the Brooklyn side (about a 20-minute walk) you can bear right to walk down to Cadman Plaza West to a park that will bring you to Middagh St, which runs east to west in the heart of Brooklyn Heights. Bearing left brings you to Brooklyn's downtown area, which includes the ornate Borough Hall and the Fulton St pedestrian mall.

Seaport entertains kids of varying ages and the area is picturesque and user-friendly.

Schermerhorn Row (Fulton St btwn Front & South St) is a block of old Federal-style warehouses that originally housed merchants and traders connected to the port business. On a cobblestoned street, the row supports 1st-floor retail space and 2nd-floor exhibit space for the expanding **South Street Seaport Museum** (☎ 212-748-8600; 12 Fulton St; admission $5; ☑ 10am-5pm). Permanent exhibitions offer a glimpse of the seaport's history and a survey of the world's great ocean liners. At Pier 16 stands the museum's collection of tall-masted sailing vessels, including the *Peking* and *Wavertree* and the lightship *Ambrose*; call the museum for a tour schedule of the ships. Walking tours of the waterfront are held in the afternoon.

Fulton Market Building (Fulton St), built across the street from Piers 16 and 17 in 1983 to reflect the redbrick style of its older neighbors, and **Pier 17**, beyond the elevated FDR Dr, are both shopping and restaurant arcades.

Tickets for harbor tours are offered by **Circle Line Cruises** (☎ 212-563-3200; www.circleline.com) and can be bought from a booth on Pier 16. **New York Waterway** (☎ 800-533-3779; www.nywaterway.com) tours have varying prices and durations; tours depart from Pier 17.

Fulton Fish Market (Front & South St btwn Fulton & Beekman St) has lived at Pier 17 for more than 130 years; this is where most of the city's restaurants get their fresh seafood. Fishmongers sling fish from one storage container to another in the wee hours of the night (midnight until 8am). By midday the only evidence of the market's activity is lingering smell of rotting fish guts. The facility has long been thought to be controlled by an organized crime family, and a federal and city government crackdown on corruption led to months of labor unrest and a suspicious 1995 fire that destroyed part of the market. In 2001, Mayor Giuliani announced a deal that would move the fish market to Hunt's Point in the South Bronx; the move should be completed by the end of 2004.

CITY HALL

Along Park Row near the entrance to Brooklyn Bridge, **City Hall** (☎ 212-788-6865; cnr Park Row & Franfort St) has been home to New York's government since 1812. In an example of the half-baked civic planning that has often plagued big New York

projects, officials neglected to finish the building's northern side in marble, betting that the city would not expand uptown. The mistake was finally rectified in 1954, completing a structure that architecture critic Ada Louise Huxtable has called a 'symbol of taste, excellence and quality not always matched by the policies inside.'

Free public tours are offered every Friday at 2pm and visit the historic aspects of the building. In 1865, Abraham Lincoln's coffin was placed on the 2nd floor on its way from Washington, DC, to Springfield, Illinois, so that New Yorkers could pay their respects to the defender of the Union. The Governor's Room, a reception area used by the mayor for important guests, contains 12 portraits by John Trumbull of the founding fathers, several examples of Federal furniture, including George Washington's writing table, and the remnants of a flag flown at his 1789 presidential inaugural ceremony. Peeking into the City Council chambers may reveal the lawmakers deliberating the renaming of a city street in someone's honor, an activity which accounts for about 40% of all the bills passed by the 51-member body.

The steps of City Hall are a popular site for demonstrations and press conferences by politicians, including the mayor. Don't be discouraged by the less than welcoming security presence.

WOOLWORTH BUILDING

Across Broadway from City Hall Park, the **Woolworth Building** (233 Broadway btwn Park Pl & Barclay St) held the transitory title of 'tallest building' for a brief stint from 1913 until 1929 when the Chrysler Building deposed it. Frank Woolworth, head of the famous department store chain, reputedly paid the $15 million price tag with nickels and dimes. Radiating with Gothic details and culminating in an elegant crown, this cathedral of commerce also boasts a most distinguished interior, with stained-glass ceilings and gold marble walls. Caricatures in bas relief depict the creation of the building – Woolworth counting his change and Cass Gilbert with a model of the site, among others.

Chinatown & Little Italy   Map p63

Virtually a self-sufficient enclave, **Chinatown** more successfully replicates the rhythms of its residents' ancestral home than any other immigrant district in New York. Commerce fills every nook and cranny of the cramped area. Small-time shoe repairers or fortune tellers claim a coveted piece of sidewalk for their daily business. Vegetable-sellers unload boxes of bulbous melons, prehistoric-sized greens and spiny fruits into decor-less stores that spill out into the street. Plastic goods, herbal medicines and dried fish are sold at variety shops so stuffed with goods that it's hard to find the shopkeeper.

With about 130,000 Chinese-speakers, Chinatown represents the largest concentration of Chinese in the western hemisphere. Chinese immigration to Mott and Pell Sts dates as far back as 1875, and the neighborhood continues to grow out of its common definition (south of Canal St and east of Centre St) into historic Little Italy and the Lower East Side.

While Chinatown represents a dynamic neighborhood, **Little Italy** today is merely a monument to New York's Italian heritage, confined largely to Mulberry St, north of Canal St. This was once a vital Italian neighborhood of shopping housewives, crowded wash lines and thriving markets. Film director Martin Scorsese grew up on Elizabeth St, and drew on his Little Italy experiences when filming works like *Mean Streets* and *GoodFellas*. Although many of the apartment buildings in this 10-block radius are still owned by Italian Americans, there was an exodus from Little Italy in the mid-20th century. For that reason, there are few cultural sites, but there is an abundance of street life, especially when, on weekends, Mulberry St becomes a pedestrian zone between Broome and Canal Sts and the restaurants set up outdoor tables.

Between Lafayette and Chrystie Sts, Little Italy begins to take on a more cosmopolitan character, as the overflow of SoHo-style shops, cafés and restaurants make their way into the area known as Nolita ('North of Little Italy').

The subway station at Grand St makes a good starting point for touring Little Italy.

MUSEUM OF CHINESE IN THE AMERICAS

This small heritage **museum** (☎ 212-619-4785; 2nd fl, 70 Mulberry St; adult/child $3/1; ☻ noon-5pm Tue-Sun), in a former public school building, briefly sketches the Chinese immigrant experience with historic photographs and artifacts.

Some displays are intensely personal, like the translated letter from a wife in China to her husband in the US. In cloaked formality, she informs him of her struggles during his absence. Special exhibits focus on aspects of Chinese culture in the western hemisphere or on intergenerational memories of world events. The museum also sponsors walking tours (call for times and reservations; $10) and public workshops (paper lantern making, Chinese opera demos).

OTHER CHINATOWN SIGHTS

In the southwest corner of Columbus Park, the five-way intersection of Baxter, Worth and Mosco formed the nexus of Five Points, New York's most infamous slum. The book *Gangs of New York*, by Herbert Asbury (and Scorsese's film adaptation), portrays the mid-19th-century gangs, like the Plug Uglies, Forty Thieves and Dead Rabbits, who fought over this turf. Many of the shabbily constructed buildings from this time were razed in hopes of urban renewal.

Eastern States Buddhist Temple (☎ 212-966-4753; 64B Mott St) is a busy storefront shrine with dozens of golden and porcelain Buddhas on display. You can buy a fortune for a donation and watch the devout make their offerings.

Church of the Transfiguration (29 Mott St) began as an Episcopal church in 1801 and was purchased by the Roman Catholic Church 50 years later to meet the needs of what was then an Irish and Italian neighborhood. In the 1890s the ascendant and spiteful Irish church leaders forced Italian patrons to worship in the basement. The church got its first Chinese pastor in the 1970s and today holds services in Cantonese and Mandarin.

Chinatown began in the winding of Doyers St (near the south corner of Confucius Plaza) in the 1870s when Chinese railway workers, fed up with racial discrimination in the American West, moved to New York City in large numbers. During Chinese New Year celebrations in late January and early February, papier-mâché dragons snake their way around this corner to the sounds of firecrackers shooing away evil spirits.

When the neighborhood was still an Irish neighborhood, Chatham Square was where public auctions took place to sell the goods of Irish debtors in the early 19th century. St James Place brings you to **First Shearith Israel Graveyard**. This cemetery, which dates back to the 1680s, served early Portuguese and Spanish immigrants who fled to New Amsterdam to escape from the Inquisition; it is the oldest Jewish cemetery in the US.

LITTLE ITALY SIGHTS   Map pp60-1

On an odd wedge of street, the **Old Police Headquarters** (240 Centre St) looks more like an institutional refugee from the nation's capital than an arm of city government. It is easy to walk past the old edifice and not notice its grandiose French Baroque details, an effect that urban critics attribute to a lack of public space needed to frame the building. It was converted into apartment units in 1988. Lifestyle maven Martha Stewart once owned an apartment here.

Old St Patrick's Cathedral (☎ 212-226-8075; 263 Mulberry St; ☉ 8:30am-8pm Mon-Fri, 9am-1pm Sat) appears bland and unimpressive due to a fire that destroyed much of its exterior. But the structure served as the city's first Roman Catholic cathedral from 1809 to 1878, until its more famous successor was built uptown on Fifth Ave. The recently renovated cathedral and its Georgian interior are open to the public. In 1999, the cathedral was the site of the memorial mass for John F Kennedy Jr, who lived nearby.

Puck Building (295-309 Lafayette St at Houston St), on the border with SoHo, is a redbrick structure that bears the name of its former resident, the early-20th-century humor magazine. The handsome building, now used for formal affairs, retains a lampooning spirit in the smirks of the two gold-leaf statues of the portly Puck, Shakespeare's famous imp from *A Midsummer Night's Dream*.

Lower East Side   Map pp60-1

This ashen-colored neighborhood still retains much of its historic melancholy from the time when it was New York's premier slum – the bittersweet finale to a trans-Atlantic journey for many homeless immigrants. Early-20th-century residents – Jews, Italians, Irish, Romanians, Hungarians, Poles, Turks and so on – lived in cramped tenement apartment buildings whose hazardous and unsanitary conditions served as an impetus for the implementation of modern housing codes.

Today the Lower East Side attracts a different kind of immigrant: greenhorns from suburbs across America trying to 'make it' in New York as artists, musicians or

---

PICKLE DAYS

There were once over 80 pickle stores in the Lower East Side and even more itinerant pushcart vendors, many of whom were recent immigrants with more energy than capital. Today **Guss' Pickles** (85-87 Orchard St), founded by Russian entrepreneur Izzy Guss, is the last pickle store in the neighborhood and sells sweet-and-sours scooped out of big orange vats that line the sidewalk.

---

fashionable hipsters. More than a dozen late-night bars around Ludlow St are packed on Saturday nights and pulse with an edginess that makes New York the leader of cool.

Stop by the **Lower East Side Visitors Center** (☎ 212-226-9010; 261 Broome St; ☉ 10am-4pm) for a neighborhood walking guide or for information about a free cell-phone **tour** (☎ 800-644-3545; www.talkingstreet.com) narrated by Jerry Stiller. A walking tour (free, Sunday at 11am), guided by a live human, leaves from Katz's Deli, on the corner of Ludlow and Houston Sts.

The subway station at Second Ave (reached via the F train) makes a good starting point for touring the Lower East Side.

ORCHARD ST

The 'Orchard St Bargain District' is the market area above Delancey St defined by Orchard, Ludlow and Essex Sts (it runs east to west). This is where Eastern European merchants once set up pushcarts to sell fruit, vegetables, bread, hot knishes and other odds and ends. Today the 300-odd shops in this modern-day bazaar sell sporting goods, leather belts, hats and a wide array of off-brand 'designer' fashions. Trendy boutiques also have a firm footing in the neighborhood, creating a stark contrast between the new minimalist galleries and the old-style shops with merchandise spilling out into the street.

Although most of the older businesses are not exclusively owned by Orthodox Jews, they still close early on Friday afternoon and remain shuttered on Saturday in observance of the Sabbath. There's an unspoken rule that shop owners should offer their first customer of the day a discount – usually 10% – for good luck, so it helps to arrive at 10am if you're serious about buying something.

Offering to pay in cash may also attract a discount. The visitors center distributes a discount card that is honored by most Lower East Side businesses.

Surviving members of the neighborhood's Jewish era include **Schapiro's Wines** (☎ 212-832-3176; Essex St Market, Essex & Delancey St; ☒ 1pm-5:30pm Mon-Thu, 1-5pm Fri), which sells kosher Passover wines, and well-known **Streit's Matzoh Company** (☎ 212-475-7000; 148-150 Rivington St; ☒ 9am-4:30pm Mon-Thu).

LOWER EAST SIDE TENEMENT MUSEUM

Offering a fresh perspective on the house tour – often the domain of the pampered elite – this **museum** (☎ 212-431-0233; www.tenement .org; 90 Orchard St; adult/child $10/8; ☒ 11am-5:30pm) introduces visitors to struggling immigrant families of the early 20th century. A total of three guided tours recreate the homes of actual residents, with artifacts and stories supplied by their descendents. A walking tour of the Lower East Side is also offered on weekends. In the 'Getting By' tour, you visit a tenement owned by Lucas Glockner, a German-born tailor; this tenement housed an estimated 7000 people over a 72-year period. Pre-dating housing codes, the building lacked indoor plumbing and proper fire escapes. Space was tight, light was scarce and, in terms of space, starter apartments in New York City haven't changed much. The 'Confino Apartment' tour will probably best appeal to children. In this living-history tour, visitors are incorporated into the exhibits with hands-on activities: sitting on the bed, washing clothes, playing the Victrola.

Tickets can be purchased from the museum gift shop, but on weekends advanced reservations are recommended. Tours typically depart every 40 minutes. Visit the website for a schedule of special events, including art exhibits and plays.

LOWER EAST SIDE SYNAGOGUES

Four hundred synagogues once thrived in the neighborhood through the early 20th century. Of those that remain, **First Roumanian-American Congregation** (☎ 212-673-2835; 89 Rivington St at Orchard St) serves a small Orthodox community that was home to many of the previous century's great cantors. The building, somewhat restored to past glory, features a wonderfully ornate wooden sanctuary. Call for tour schedules.

The landmark Moorish-style **Eldridge St Synagogue** (☎ 212-219-0888; www.eldridgestreet.org; 12 Eldridge St; adult/child $5/3; ☒ tours 11am-4pm Sun, 11:30am-2:30pm Tue-Thu), east of the Bowery between Canal and Division Sts, was the first synagogue built for Eastern European Jews and faces one of the oldest surviving blocks of tenements in New York City. Now fully engulfed in Chinatown, the synagogue has dwindled to a small congregation unable to afford the upkeep of the massive building. Since the 1980s, a non-profit group has helped to raise funds for restoration efforts and also conducts tours of the historic building; special musical and cultural events occur throughout the year.

SoHo & Tribeca

Named for a geographic conceit, SoHo (Map pp60-1) is the rectangular area that starts 'SOuth of HOuston St' and extends south to Canal St. Emerging as the city's manufacturing center during post–Civil War boom times, SoHo was quickly filled with hulking cast-iron palaces. The overall effect is haunting: block after block of nearly identical industrial-strength warehouses masquerading as delicate, painted maidens. These multistory buildings housed linen, ribbon and clothing factories – more accurately described as sweatshops – and street-level showcase galleries.

The area fell out of favor as retail businesses relocated uptown and manufacturing concerns moved out of the city. SoHo's huge lofts and cheap rents attracted artists and other members of the 1950s and '60s avant-garde. Political lobbying not only saved the neighborhood from destruction but assured that a 26-block area was declared a legally protected historic district in 1973. To complete the urban cycle, SoHo's original saviors, the artists and the art galleries, were pushed out by mushrooming prices as the area further gentrified into a boutique zone and tourist attraction.

Visit SoHo on a weekday morning, when the neighborhood is populated largely by office workers dressed invariably in sleek black outfits. On Saturday and Sunday, West Broadway (a separate street from Broadway) becomes a sea of suede.

Neighboring Tribeca (Map p63), also named for its geographical location (the 'TRIangle BElow CAnal' St), is an area roughly bordered by Broadway to the east and Chambers St to the south. Mainly a residential neighborhood of old warehouses converted into loft apartments for high-flying Hollywood stars (including Robert De Niro and Harvey Keitel), Tribeca is sometimes despairingly referred to as 'Triburbia' for the pseudo-suburbanites who chose the area for its good public school. Damage from September 11 crippled Tribeca and caused many residents and businesses to move away. With the passing of years, Tribeca has regained some of its previous momentum. One stalwart has been De Niro's Tribeca Productions and Film Center and his offshoot venture, the annual Tribeca Film Festival (www.tribecafilmfestival.org).

SOHO ARCHITECTURAL SITES   Map pp60-1

Just past Prince St is the **Singer Building** (561-563 Broadway), an attractive iron-and-brick structure that was the main warehouse for the famous sewing machine company. Further south, above the shoe stores, you can see what's left of the marble-faced **St Nicholas Hotel** (521-523 Broadway), the 1000-room luxury hotel that was *the* place to stay when it opened in 1854. The hotel, which closed in 1880, was the headquarters of Abraham Lincoln's War Department during the Civil War years.

Referred to as the Parthenon of Cast Iron, the **Haughwout Building** (488 Broadway) was once the headquarters of the EV Haughwout Crockery Company. Built in 1857, it was the first building to use the exotic steam 'elevator' developed by Elisha Otis.

On the southeast corner of the intersection of Prince and Greene Sts, you will see a local landmark: artist Richard Haas' now-fading mural of the front of an apartment building is painted on the bare brick wall of 112 Prince St.

NEW MUSEUM OF CONTEMPORARY ART

This **museum** (Map pp60-1; ☎ 212-219-1222; www.newmuseum.org; 583 Broadway; adult/student/child $6/3/free; ☽ noon-6pm Tue-Sun, noon-8pm Thu), now a memorial to SoHo's reign as queen of the contemporary art world, shows works that are less than 10 years old.

HARRISON ST TOWNHOUSES

The eight townhouses (Map p63) on the block of Harrison St, immediately west of Greenwich St, were all built between 1804

> **HOW TO SAY 'HOUSTON'**
>
> No one really knows for sure why Houston St is pronounced 'how-ston,' though it is assumed that a man named William Houstoun who lived in the area pronounced his surname in that manner. Somewhere along the line the second 'u' in the spelling of the street was dropped.

and 1828 and constitute the largest collection of Federal architecture left in the city. But they were not always neighbors: six of them once stood two blocks away on a stretch of Washington St that no longer exists. In the early 1970s, that area was the site of Washington Market, a wholesale center that was the fruit and vegetable equivalent of the Fulton Fish Market. A new home had to be found for the row houses when the market was relocated uptown to allow the development of the waterfront, including Manhattan Community College and the unattractive concrete apartment complex that now looms over the townhouses. Only the buildings at 31 and 33 Harrison St remain where they were originally constructed.

NEW YORK CITY FIRE MUSEUM

This **museum** (Map pp60-1; ☎ 212-691-1303; www.nycfiremuseum.org; 278 Spring St; adult/child $5/2; ☽ 10am-5pm Tue-Sat, 10am-4pm Sun) occupies a grand old firehouse that dates back to 1904. There's a well-maintained collection of gleaming gold horse-drawn fire-fighting carriages as well as modern-day fire engines. The development of the New York City fire-fighting system, which began with the 'bucket brigades,' is also explained. All the colorful equipment and the museum's particularly friendly staff make this a great place to bring children, even though they are not allowed to hop on any of the engines. A recent addition is a tribute to the 343 firefighters, nearly 25% of the city's force, who were killed on September 11. The exhibit shows footage of ground zero and a memorial wall bearing the names of the fallen.

Greenwich Village   Map pp60-1

A mini-vortex within a magnetic city, Greenwich Village long called artists, poets and radicals to its winding streets of European style. In the 1950s the torch for rebellion was assumed by the Beat generation, the era's most famous group of friends that haunted cafés and bars capturing the raw energy of youth with pen and paper. A young Bob Dylan wandered into the Village's acoustic music scene from the snowdrifts of Minnesota in the 1960s. Gay liberation found a riotous voice here in the 1970s.

Artists and other creative loafers were eventually pushed out by high rents as the Village recaptured its role as a fashionable address, a scenario that persists today.

Generally defined by a northern border on 14th St and a southern demarcation on Houston St, Greenwich Village runs from Lafayette St all the way west to the Hudson River. The area just south of Washington Square Park (including Bleecker St running west to Seventh Ave) is a lively collection of cafés, shops and restaurants. Beyond Seventh Ave is the West Village, a pleasant neighborhood of winding streets and townhouses. Greenwich Village is best reached via subway by trains A, C, E or F to W 4th St, or trains 1 or 9 to Christopher St.

WASHINGTON SQUARE PARK

More urban than sylvan, Washington Square Park has had a troubled career. Like many public spaces in the city, it began as a potter's field, a burial ground for the penniless. It was also the site of public executions, including the hanging of several petty criminals to honor a visit to New York by the French statesman Marquis de Lafayette in 1824. The magnificent old tree near the northwestern corner of the park has a plaque stating it was the 'Hangman's Elm,' though no one is quite sure if it was actually used for executions. Prior to the Giuliani era, this park was also a notorious open-air drug market; among its many clients, David Lee Roth was arrested here in 1993 while trying to buy a $10 bag of marijuana.

The park's heyday came in the early 19th century, when merchants and bankers built fashionable townhouses, known as the **Row**, on both sides of Fifth Ave. Washington Square North, the street that comprises the north border of the park, was the inspiration for *Washington Square*, Henry James' novel of late-19th-century social mores. Edith Wharton, who grew up on W 23rd St, also recorded the expensive pursuits of the Washington Square elite in her novels *The*

Age of Innocence and *The House of Mirth*. A hundred yards up Fifth Ave, to the right, is the Washington Square Mews, a quiet, cobblestoned street of stables that now houses New York University offices. More recent inhabitants of the Row have included painter Edward Hopper and John Dos Passos, author of *Manhattan Transfer*.

Pay particular attention to the **Stanford White Arch**, originally designed in wood to celebrate the centennial of George Washington's inauguration in 1889. The arch proved so popular that it was replaced in stone six years later and adorned with statues of the general in war and in peace (the latter work is by A Stirling Calder, the father of artist Alexander Calder). In 1916, artist Marcel Duchamp climbed to the top of the arch by its internal stairway with a few friends and declared the park the 'Free and Independent Republic of Washington Square.' Today, the anarchy takes place on ground level, as comedians and buskers use the park's permanently dry fountain as a performance space. The site was once used as the terminus and turnaround for the Fifth Ave buses that ran under the arch.

The **Judson Memorial Church** graces the park's south border. This yellow-brick Baptist church honors Adoniram Judson, an

---

NO COVER: MUSIC LANDMARKS

Why is the Rock and Roll Hall of Fame in Cleveland, when everyone knows New York is the 'Big Apple'? This is the top of the heap, king of the hill. If you make it here, never mind making it anywhere else, you've arrived. (Incidentally, jazz musicians are often credited for the term 'Big Apple' but it dates back to the 1920s when it was used by stable hands at a New Orleans race-track to refer to races in New York City.)

Before and during many great musicians' careers, Greenwich Village and the East Village were their sleeping and performing grounds. To impress out-of-towners or annoy loved ones, these are vital pieces of trivia to add to your expansive New York file.

- **Café Wha?** (Map pp60-1; MacDougal St & Minetta Lane) and **Folk City** (Map pp60-1; 11 W 4th St; now Fat Black Pussycat) were both popular performance spots during the protest-music scene of the 1960s.

- Bob Dylan once lived and was inspired to write 'Positively 4th St' at 161 W 4th St.

- One of rock's most romantic album covers, the 1963 *Freewheelin' Bob Dylan*, was shot on Jones St between Bleecker and W 4th St; big shaggy trees now obscure the apartment build-ings' facades.

- Jimi Hendrix lived and recorded at the **Electric Lady Studios** (Map pp60-1; 55 W 8th St at Sixth Ave). The brown-brick building is now a shoe store.

- The cover shot of Led Zeppelin's *Physical Graffiti* album was taken at 96-98 St Marks Place between First Ave and Ave A.

- Charlie Parker lived in the ground-floor apartment at 151 Ave B and Tompkins Square Park from 1950 to 1954, at the height of his career as bebop cofounder.

American missionary who served in Burma in the early 19th century. Designed by Stanford White, this national historic site features stained-glass windows by muralist John La Farge, who was born near the park, and marble frontage designed by Augustus Saint-Gaudens.

One block east of the park, at 245 Greene St, is the building where the Triangle Shirt-waist Fire took place on March 25, 1911. This sweatshop had locked its doors to prevent the young seamstresses from taking unauthorized breaks. The inferno killed 146 young women, many of whom jumped to their deaths from the upper floors because the fire department's ladders did not extend to the top floors of the 10-story building. Every year the New York Fire Department holds a solemn ceremony to commemorate the city's most deadly factory fire.

The southern and eastern portion of the park is dominated by buildings associated with New York University.

East Village
Map pp60-1

Although sharing a surname with Green-wich Village, the East Village has always had an edgier, more subversive reputation.

Hardly a 'village,' the East Village was a tenement landscape, a northern extension of the Lower East Side, where Ukrainian and Polish immigrants established com-munities in the early 20th century. By the 1950s, Columbians, Dominicans and Puerto Ricans settled around the area called 'Loi-saida' (Ave C). The youth-driven forces in the East Village served as a foil to the dreaminess of Greenwich Village. As plain-tive folk songs rose from Greenwich Village, the East Village belched a response – punk rock. Urban realism fueled the music, the political demonstrations in Tompkins Park, the poetry of Allen Ginsberg and the art of Keith Haring. The counterculture wallowed in urban decay as junkies, squatters and hustlers proliferated in the abandoned lots and on street corners. In the last decade, gentrification has moved into the East Village (generally defined by 14th St to E Houston St, and Lafayette St to the East River), even extending its reach into the once notorious slum of Alphabet City, an area marked by Aves A, B, C and D.

Despite the 'Chicken Little' cries of mall-ification, the East Village has some of the city's best thrift stores (p132), experimental theaters, late-night carousing (p125) and restaurants (p119).

The subway stations at Astor Place and Second Ave are good starting points for exploring this neighborhood.

ASTOR PLACE

This square is named after the Astor family, who, in the city's early years, built a fortune on beaver-fur–trading and lived on **Colonnade Row** (428-434 Lafayette St), just south of Astor Place. Four of the original nine marble-faced Greek Revival residences still exist, but they are entombed beneath a layer of black soot. Across the street, in the public library built by John Jacob Astor, stands the **Joseph Papp Public Theater** (425 Lafayette St). It was built in 1848 for the then-phenomenal sum of $500,000. The theater is now one of the city's most important cultural centers and home to the New York Shakespeare Festival.

Astor Place itself is dominated by the large brownstone **Cooper Union**, the public college founded by steel millionaire Peter Cooper in 1859. Just after its completion, Abraham Lincoln condemned slavery in his 'Right Makes Might' speech that he delivered in the Union's Great Hall. The fringed lectern he used still exists, but the auditorium is only open to the public for special events.

Grace Church (E 10th St btwn Fourth Ave & Broadway) is an Episcopal church designed by James Renwick. This Gothic Revival building is made of marble quarried by prisoners at Sing Sing, the state penitentiary in the up-state town of Ossining. At night, its floodlit white marble makes for a strangely elegant sight in this neighborhood of dance clubs,

record stores and pizza parlors. The same architect is thought to have designed **Renwick Triangle** (112-128 E 10th St), a movie-set–perfect group of brownstone Italianate houses one block to the east.

Another significant church is **St Mark's-in-the-Bowery** (☎ 212-674-6377; Second Ave & E 10th St; 🕙 10am-6pm Mon-Fri), also an Episcopal place of worship. It stands on the site of the farm, or *bouwerie*, owned by Dutch Governor Peter Stuyvesant, whose crypt is under the church grounds. The church, damaged by fire in 1978, has been restored with abstract stained-glass windows. This is also a cultural center, hosting poetry readings by the Poetry Project (www.poetryproject.com) and performances by Danspace (www.danspaceproject.org).

OLD MERCHANT'S HOUSE MUSEUM

Not much remains of the neighborhood that existed here before the tenement boom, but this **museum** (☎ 212-777-1089; 29 E 4th St; adult $6, senior & student $4; 🕙 1-5pm Thu-Mon), in the 1831 house of drug importer Seabury Tredwell, is a remarkably well-preserved example of how the business class lived. Occupied by Tredwell's youngest daughter Gertrude until her death in 1933, its original furnishings were still intact when it began life as a museum three years later.

UKRAINIAN MUSEUM

Documenting the cultural legacy of the Ukrainian community, this **museum** (☎ 212-228-0110; 203 Second Ave btwn 12th & 13th St; adult $1.50, senior & student $1; 🕙 1-5pm Wed-Sun) displays folk art, paintings and photographs targeted to

---

COMMUNITY GARDENS

After a stretch of arboreal celibacy in New York City, the community gardens of Alphabet City are breathtaking. A network of gardens were carved out of abandoned lots to give low-income neighborhoods a communal backyard. Trees and flowers were planted, sandboxes were built, found-art sculptures erected, domino games ensued – all within green spaces wedged between buildings or claiming whole blocks. On Saturday and Sunday, most gardens are open to the public to admire the plantings or chat with gardeners; many gardeners are activists within the community and are a good source of information on local politics. The **6 & B Garden** (E 6th St at Ave B; www.6bgarden.org) is a well-organized space that hosts free music events, workshops and yoga sessions; check the website for details. Three dramatic weeping willows, an odd sight in the city, grace the twin plots of **9th St Garden** and **La Plaza Cultural** (E 9th St at Ave C). After a three-year lawsuit, the 9th St gardens were recently spared from the city's plans to raze the gardens in order to build affordable housing; over 150 gardens within Manhattan, however, are still slated for demolition.

a wide audience. Traveling exhibits assembled from its collections have made tours of the US and Ukraine. A new building at 222 E 6th St between Second and Third Aves will open to the public in the fall of 2004.

10TH ST BATHS

Pre-dating spas and even indoor plumbing, the community bathhouse, in the Eastern European tradition, was a cultural ritual more cleansing than a dip under the showerhead. While many of these old baths in Manhattan have closed as the communities dissipated or after the AIDS crisis, the **10th St Baths** (☎ 212-674-9250; 268 E 10th St; 1-day admission $22; 🕐 11am-10pm Mon-Fri, 7:30-10pm Sat & Sun; men only 7:30am-2pm Sun; women only 9am-2pm Wed) have been in existence since 1892. Not as elegant or overbearing as a day spa, this bathhouse of octagonal tile work retains much of its Old World character. Patrons wander in a daze between the different rooms: Russian (dry heat), Turkish (steam heat scented with eucalyptus and lavender oils), redwood sauna, ice cold pool and Swedish shower. The key is to alternate between very hot and very cold temperatures. There's also a small café on the premises. Bathing suits are required for co-ed days.

Chelsea   Map pp64-5

Sophisticated yet friendly, this predominately gay neighborhood offers all the energy of a metropolis without its signature aggressiveness. Roughly bordered by 14th St to the south, 23rd St to the north, the Hudson River to the west and Broadway to the east, this neighborhood was the dry goods and retail area for the Gilded Age, and many of the emporia built to attract well-heeled shoppers are now office buildings. Closer to the Hudson River on Eighth and Ninth Aves, Chelsea is dominated by housing projects and warehouses.

The subway station at 23rd St is a good starting point for those wishing to explore this neighborhood.

HOTEL CHELSEA

Seedy and off-kilter, the **Hotel Chelsea** (222 W 23rd St) has sustained a lengthy reputation as an inspirational bedlam for writers and musicians. More evocative in appearance and spirit of the Big Easy than the Big Apple, Hotel Chelsea (see also p111) is

adorned with ornate cast-iron balconies and no fewer than seven historical plaques announcing its historical relevance. Maybe the hedonistic mood was set in 1953, when Dylan Thomas fell into a coma in his room after a drinking binge at the White Horse Tavern (p125) in the Village; he was rushed to St Vincent's Hospital where he later died. A famous myth persists that Jack Kerouac typed *On the Road* on a single roll of teletype paper during a marathon session at the Chelsea. The climax of Chelsea's self-destructive streak was the 1978 murder of Nancy Spungen by her boyfriend Sid Vicious.

In a saner time, Mark Twain slept here while on tour in 1888, and O Henry wrote many of his famous short stories while living in the hotel. Thomas Wolfe moved into the hotel in 1937 with his manuscript *You Can't Go Home Again.*

CHELSEA ART GALLERIES

New York's gallery scene is a migratory beast, whose habitat of big space and cheap rents is quickly diminishing on the island. Chased out of SoHo, the showcasers for contemporary art have relocated to Chelsea's warehouse district. On the weekends, art groupies don their favorite thrift-store hats and in roving gangs ricochet from one gallery to another. The subject and media come from every imaginable corner and the artists' star power varies from a blip to a meteor. The 'Goings on About Town' section of the *New Yorker* and the *New York* magazine run lists of upcoming shows at Chelsea galleries (on Tenth & Eleventh Ave between W 22nd St and W 26th St). They are generally open from Tuesday to Sunday, 10am to 6pm. Admission is free.

Dia: Chelsea (☎ 212-989-5566; www.diaart.org; 548 W 22nd St; adult/student $6/3; 🕐 noon-6pm Wed-Sun), a sprawling three-floor center of experimental art and installations, was one of the first trailblazers into Chelsea. Exhibiting more of the frontier spirit, Dia has recently opened up an even larger venture in Beacon (p159). Dia: Chelsea will be closed until 2006 for renovations.

Chelsea Art Museum (☎ 212-255-0719; www.chelsea artmuseum.org; 556 W 22nd St; admission $5; 🕐 noon-6pm Wed-Sun), next door to Dia, displays recognized artists dealing with transcultural themes through abstract painting.

Union Square & Around   Map pp64-5

This square (on 14th St and Broadway) was one of New York City's first uptown business districts pre-dating now fashionable Fifth Ave. Throughout the mid-19th century, the square served as a rallying point for the emerging workers' movement and the staging ground for annual May Day parades. Although the name of the square is aptly suited to its affiliation with the labor unions, it was so called because of the convergence at this point of the Bloomingdale Road (now Broadway) and Bowery Road (now Fourth Ave). The square has been abandoned and reclaimed so many times throughout its existence that either state seems entirely temporary. Presently, revitalization is in effect thanks to the **Greenmarket farmers' market** (8am-6pm Mon, Wed & Fri).

FLATIRON DISTRICT

This neighborhood is named after the wedge-shaped **Flatiron Building** (Broadway, Fifth Ave & 23rd St), a technological marvel for its time. Built in 1902, the Flatiron Building used a steel frame to support the exterior walls and floors of each story, a boring architectural tidbit today, but a revolutionary concept then; this design allowed Manhattan to grow heavenward. Standing on a renowned windy corner, the Flatiron attracted young men hoping to glimpse a bit of ankle from the well-covered young ladies. The building's reign as the world's tallest building was cut short in 1909 with the completion of the nearby **Metropolitan Life Tower** (24th St & Madison Ave), which has an impressive clock tower and golden top.

The subway station at 23rd St (by N and R lines) is a good starting point for exploring this neighborhood.

GRAMERCY PARK

The kind of garden area commonly found dotted throughout Paris and other European cities, **Gramercy Park** (Lexington Ave btwn 20th & 21st St) is one of New York's loveliest spaces,. Unfortunately, when the neighborhood was designed on the site of a marsh in 1830, admission to the park was restricted to residents. The tradition still holds, and mere mortals must peer through iron gates at the foliage. Owning a key to the park must surely be an ambition of almost every young New Yorker.

Midtown   Map pp64-5

A dense collection of skyscrapers populates the island's mid-section, where the city's commercial migration north finally came to rest. Times Square, Rockefeller Center, Empire State Building – the area's landmarks (and tourist attractions) are steel-and-glass showcases. These monuments form a man-made mountain range neatly divided into canyons by a grid of streets and governed by a microclimate of wind tunnels. For all of its frigid demeanor, Midtown becomes an urban masterpiece at sunset, when the sun dips low enough in the horizon to illuminate these mine-shaft streets.

TIMES SQUARE

Times Square is an electronic fantasy of flashing lights, dizzying images and 'Big City' energy that has stunned visitors since its electrification in 1901. One lighted billboard for an ocean resort has been credited for starting the advertising orgy of neon lights that exists today. In pre-TV days, the intersection of Broadway and Seventh Ave represented a huge, captive audience. Of its many appellations, the district was finally christened after the city's leading newspaper, the *New York Times*, which is still located here. The area fell into a well-documented decline in the 1960s, as once-proud first-run movie palaces turned into 'triple X' porn theaters. But it has since received an age-defying makeover from theme palaces and media conglomerates that have made it safe and attractive to families and visiting school trips.

The median age of the crowd lined up for a studio visit is usually a good indicator of what TV company (MTV and ABC among others) is encased within Time Square's skyscrapers. Reuters, the US magazine group Condé Nast and German publisher Bertelsmann have also planted headquarters in and around Times Square.

Up to a million people gather here every New Year's Eve to see a brightly lit ball descend from the roof of One Times Square at midnight. Although this event garners international coverage, it lasts just 90 seconds and must have been more dazzling when electric lights were young and magical.

Dreams of 'making it big' on Broadway bring dancers, singers and actors to the theaters of Time Square, further amplifying the area's dramatic energy and optimism (see p127 for more information on ongoing performances and historic theaters).

Times Square Visitor Center (☎ 212-768-1560; www.timessquarebid.org; 1560 Broadway btwn W 46th & W 47th St; ☼ 8am-8pm) sits right in the middle of the famous crossroads of Broadway and Eighth Ave. The center distributes subway maps and MetroCards, has free Internet terminals and a post office. The center can also arrange for you to get your smiling mug posted on a Times Square billboard – claim your birthright, 15 minutes of fame.

EMPIRE STATE BUILDING

New York's original skyline symbol is a limestone classic built in just 410 days during the depths of the Depression at a cost of $41 million. Located on the site of the original Waldorf-Astoria Hotel, the 102-story, 1454ft **Empire State Building** (☎ 212-736-3100; www.esbnyc.com; cnr W 34th St & Fifth Ave; adult/senior/child $11/10/6; ☼ 9:30am-midnight) opened in 1931 and was immediately the most exclusive business address in the city. The famous antenna was originally intended to be a mooring mast for zeppelins, but the Hindenberg disaster put a stop to that plan. One airship accidentally met up with the building: a B25 crashed into the 79th floor on a foggy day in July 1945 and killed 14 people.

Since 1976, the building's top 30 floors have been floodlit in seasonal and holiday colors (eg green for St Patrick's Day in March, red and green for Christmas, pink for Gay Pride weekend in June). This tradition has been copied by many other skyscrapers, lending elegance to the night sky.

Reaching the observatories on the 86th floor means wading through two lines: a security checkpoint and a ticket line. To speed up the process you can order tickets in advance through the building's website. Getting there very early or very late will also reduce the wait time for lines at the top as well. The last tickets are sold at 11:15pm. The Empire State Building is part of the CityPass scheme (see Museum Bargains, p90).

PIERPONT MORGAN LIBRARY

Rare manuscripts, 17th-century watercolors, Italian Renaissance paintings and other pieces from steel magnate JP Morgan's private collection are on display at the **Pierpont Morgan Library** (☎ 212-685-0008; 29 E 36th St & Madison Ave). Morgan spared little expense in his pursuit of ancient works of knowledge or art: there are no fewer than three Gutenberg Bibles in residence here. Currently undergoing an expansion project, the museum will reopen in 2006, but public programs, such as lectures and concerts, are still ongoing; call ☎ 212-590-0333 for a schedule of events.

GRAND CENTRAL TERMINAL

Like a floodgate bisecting Park Ave, **Grand Central Terminal** (cnr E 42nd St & Park Ave) remains one of New York's grandest public spaces despite the decline of rail travel. Entering Grand Central from E 42nd St, or better yet, from an arriving train, leads through low arcades to an expansive concourse with vaulted ceilings (decorated with the constellations of the zodiac) filled with the vibrations of hurried footsteps, hushed conversations and a communal heartbeat. Perch yourself on one of the balconies overlooking the main concourse at around 6pm on a weekday to get a glimpse of the grace this terminal commands under pressure.

Completed in 1913, Grand Central was the terminus for long distance and commuter rail service. Today Grand Central's underground electric tracks only serve commuter trains en route to northern suburbs and Connecticut. But the old dame still merits a special trip for fine dining (see Oyster Bar, p121, or Michael Jordan's Steakhouse, p121).

The **Municipal Art Society** (☎ 212-935-3960) conducts free walking tours through Grand Central every Wednesday at 12:30pm. During the hour-long tour, you will cross a glass catwalk high above the concourse and learn that the ceiling constellation was mistakenly laid out in a 'god's eye view,' with the stars displayed from above rather than below. The tours meet at the visitor information booth in the middle of the terminal.

CHRYSLER BUILDING

Just across from Grand Central Terminal, the 1048ft **Chrysler Building** (cnr Lexington Ave & 42nd St) briefly reigned as the tallest structure in the world until it was superseded by the Empire State Building. Designed by William Van Allen in 1930, the Chrysler Building is a celebration of the car culture, featuring gargoyles that resemble hood ornaments (barely visible from the ground) and a 200ft steel spire that was constructed as one piece and placed at the top of the building as a distinctive crowning touch. The Chrysler will be known primarily as the landmark most often mistaken by tourists for the Empire State Building. The building is not open to the public.

UNITED NATIONS
Overlooking the East River, the **United Nations' headquarters** (UN; ☎ 212-963-8687; First Ave & 46th St; adult/senior/child $10.50/8/6; ☺ tours every 45min 9:30am-4:45pm Mon-Fri, 10am-4:30pm Sat & Sun, no weekend tours Jan & Feb) is technically considered international territory. This means that the 18-acre site has its own fire and security force, postage stamps and conducts business in six official languages (Arabic, French, Chinese, English, Spanish and Russian). An international body that promotes peace and human rights, the UN was created in 1945 by a conference of world leaders who met in San Francisco, California. The complex, appropriately enough, was designed by a large international committee of architects.

Tours of the facility show visitors the General Assembly, where the annual autumn convocation of member nations takes place, the Security Council chamber, where crisis hearings are held year-round, and the Economic & Social Council chamber. A park south of the complex includes Henry Moore's *Reclining Figure* and several other sculptures with a peace theme.

Children younger than five are not admitted. Reservations are not required, but the lines grow long later in the day.

NEW YORK PUBLIC LIBRARY
The main branch of the **New York Public Library** (☎ 212-930-0800; cnr 42nd St & Fifth Ave; admission free; ☺ 11am-7:30pm Tue-Wed, 10am-6pm Thu-Sat) is a monument to learning. Housed in a grand Beaux Arts building designed by Carrére and Hastings, the library ranked as the largest marble structure ever built when it was dedicated in 1911. A vast 3rd-floor reading room decorated with original lamps can hold up to 500 patrons and is a popular rainy-day hideaway. There are over 17 million books in its permanent collection and rotating exhibits display precious manuscripts by just about every author of note in the English language. Free one-hour tours (from Tuesday to Saturday at 11am and 2pm) leave from the information desk in Astor Hall.

Located just behind the library, **Bryant Park** (☎ 212-768-4242; www.bryantpark.org) offers a pleasant tree-filled break for lunching workers or weekend sunbathers. In summer, the park hosts an outdoor movie festival.

ROCKEFELLER CENTER
Built during the height of the Great Depression in the 1930s, the 22-acre **Rockefeller Center** (☎ 212-632-3975; www.rockefellercenter.com; 48th-51st St) gave jobs to 70,000 workers over nine years and was the first project to combine retail, entertainment and office space in what is often referred to as a 'city within a city.' The completion of the center was tainted by a controversy over artwork. A mural painted by Mexican artist Diego Rivera for the lobby of the 70-story RCA (now GE) Building was rejected by the Rockefeller family because it featured the face of Lenin. The fresco was covered during the opening ceremony and was later destroyed. Its replacement (not painted by Rivera) features the more acceptable figure of Abraham Lincoln.

Other architectural details to notice include the tile work above the Sixth Ave entrance to the GE building, the three floodlit cameos along the side of Radio City Music Hall, and the back-lit gilt and stained-glass entrance to the East River Savings Bank building at 41 Rockefeller Plaza, immediately to the north of the skating rink/outdoor-garden café in the heart of the complex.

In the 1930s, construction workers building the center set up a small Christmas tree on the site during the holidays. They inadvertently started a tradition that continues to this day. Every year during the Christmas season a huge pine tree overlooks the Rockefeller Center skating rink. The annual lighting of the Rockefeller Center Christmas tree, the Tuesday after Thanksgiving, attracts thousands of visitors to the area and semi-officially kicks off the city's holiday season.

A 6000-seat Art Deco movie palace, **Radio City Music Hall** (☎ 212-247-4777; www.radiocity.com; 51st St at Sixth Ave; tour adult/senior/child $17/14/10; ☺ tours every 30min 11am-3pm) is a protected landmark. It reopened after extensive renovation to restore the velvet seats and furnishings to the exact state they were in when the building opened in 1932. Even the smoking rooms and toilets are elegant at the 'Showplace of the Nation.' Today Radio City is used for live performances, concerts and the occasional movie premiere. The most celebrated event is the annual Christmas pageant featuring the leggy Rockette dancers. Samuel 'Roxy' Rothafel, the man responsible for the high-kicking chorus line, declared that 'a visit to Radio City is as good as a month in the country.' Any time of the year, you can see the interior by taking a one-hour tour. Tickets are available on a first come, first served basis or in advance through Ticketmaster (www.ticketmaster.com).

The **NBC TV Network** (☎ 212-664-4000; www.nbc .com; tours adult/child $17.75/15.25; ☽ tours every 30min 9:30am-4:30pm Mon-Sat) has its headquarters in the 70-story GE building that looms over Rockefeller Center. The *Today* show broadcasts live (7am to 9am) from the glass-enclosed studios on the street level. Where there's a camera, a crowd usually gathers, and out-of-towners huddle around the studio windows with handwritten messages to folks back home. Tours of the NBC studios leave from the lobby of the GE Building (reservations recommended) and last a little more than one hour; children younger than six are not permitted.

ST PATRICK'S CATHEDRAL
Just across from Rockefeller Center, **St Patrick's Cathedral** (☎ 212-753-2261; Fifth Ave at 50th St; ☽ 6am-9pm) is the main place of worship for the 2.2 million Roman Catholics in the New York diocese. The cathedral, built at a cost of nearly $2 million during the Civil War, originally didn't include the two front spires (added in 1888). The well-lit St Patrick's isn't as gloomy as its Old World counterparts, and the new TV monitors in restricted-view seats are testimony to the church's determination to have its place in the modern world.

Passing by the eight small shrines along the right side of the cathedral brings you past the main altar to the quiet Lady Chapel, dedicated to the Virgin Mary. From here you can see the handsome stained-glass Rose Window above the 7000-pipe church organ. A basement crypt behind the altar contains the coffins of every New York cardinal. The crypt is visible from the altar but closed to the public.

FIFTH AVENUE
Synonymous with the *bon vivant*, Fifth Ave traces its origins to the northern end of Washington Square Park, the premier address for the aristocracy of the Gilded Age. Like a vein of gold, the street extended north to accommodate bigger and better palaces. The industrialists, the Dutch bluebloods, the social climbers – all proved their worth with ostentatious replications of European castles hosting decadent balls and elaborate intrigue. Within several generations, the fortunes were lost or the styles became so tastefully subdued that the heirs sold the addresses for demolition or converted them to the cultural institutions that make up Museum Mile (see p90). The **Villard Houses** (Madison Ave), behind St Patrick's Cathedral, are surviving examples of these grand homes. The six townhouses were built by financier Henry Villard in 1881; they eventually became the property of the Catholic Church and later were sold to become part of the 1000-room Mayfair hotel and the chic and famous restaurant Le Cirque 2000 (p121).

Fifth Ave is still a prestigious address for another fickle sector – upscale fashion stores. Every clothing or accessory empire has a showcase store on Fifth Ave serving as an ambassador to the commoners and the privileged. Exclusive boutiques for Hollywood glitterati tend to gravitate towards Madison Ave and nearby streets (see Shopping in Style, p131, for more information).

Overlooking Grand Army Plaza, **Plaza Hotel** (Fifth Ave at Central Park South) is an enduring institution of the leisure class (p112). During Prohibition, the Plaza was famous for its 'tea' dances attended by the decadent couple F Scott Fitzgerald and his wife Zelda. The couple is said to have night-capped many a drunken evening with a dip in the Pulitzer Fountain that sits in front of the hotel. The Plaza's lobby is still grand even if the clientele is more egalitarian.

MUSEUM OF MODERN ART
One of the country's most important collections, the **Museum of Modern Art** (MoMA; ☎ 212-708-9500; www.moma.org; 11 W 53rd St; ☽ 10:30am-5: 30pm Wed-Mon, 10:30am-8pm Fri) is in the midst of an extensive renovation that will more than double its current exhibition space by the winter of 2004–05. During the renovations, MoMA has relocated portions of its collection to an exhibition space in Queens (p103). MoMA QNS will be holding exhibitions through September 27, 2004.

Among the museum's holdings are first-rate sculptures and paintings including works by Picasso, Van Gogh's *Starry Night*, Matisse's *Dance 1* and Monet's paneled *Water Lilies*. At least once a year, MoMA puts on an important exhibit of one major artist's work; recent retrospectives focused on the abstractionist Piet Mondrian, Picasso's portraiture and American painter Jasper Johns.

The museum places a special emphasis on photography and film, two areas of visual expression that get short shrift at the larger Metropolitan Museum of Art. During the museum's renovation, film showings have moved to **Gramercy Theatre** (☎ 212-708-9480; 127 E 23rd St at Lexington Ave; admission $6).

MUSEUM OF TELEVISION & RADIO

A couch potato's paradise, this **museum** (☎ 212-621-6800; 25 W 52nd St btwn Fifth & Sixth Ave; adult/senior/child $10/8/5; ☺ noon-6pm Tue, Wed, Fri-Sun; noon-8pm Thu) contains a collection of more than 50,000 American TV and radio programs, available with the click of a mouse from the museum's computer catalog. It's a great place to head when it's raining or when you're simply fed up with walking. Nearly everybody checks out their favorite childhood TV programs on the museum's 90 consoles, but the radio-listening room is an unexpected pleasure.

INTREPID SEA-AIR-SPACE MUSEUM

The USS *Intrepid* is an aircraft carrier that served in WWII and in Vietnam. Today it houses the **Intrepid Sea-Air-Space Museum** (☎ 212-245-0072; Pier 86, 12th Ave at W 46th St; ☺ 10am-5pm Mon-Fri & 10am-6pm Sat-Sun Apr-Sep, 10am-5pm Tue-Sun Oct-Mar; adult/child $14/7, military & senior $10). The carrier's flight deck has many fighter planes, and the pier area contains the Growler, a guided-missile submarine, an Apollo space capsule and Vietnam-era tanks, along with the 900ft destroyer *Edson*. Its most recent retiree is the Concorde passenger jet.

The *Intrepid* is the nexus for the Fleet Week celebrations each summer, when thousands of the world's sailors descend upon Manhattan for their own version of *On the Town*.

INTERNATIONAL CENTER OF PHOTOGRAPHY

The city's most important showplace for exhibitions on the careers of major figures in photography (such as fashion photographer and filmmaker William Klein and French photojournalist Henri Cartier-Bresson) is the **International Center of Photography** (ICP; ☎ 212-857-0045; 1133 Sixth Ave & 43rd St; adult/student $10/7; ☺ 10am-5pm Tue-Thu, 10am-8pm Fri, 10am-6pm Sat & Sun).

Central Park   Map pp66-7

This 843-acre rectangular park in the middle of Manhattan was designed to be an oasis from the urban bustle. The downy lawns and meandering wooded paths provide the bit of nature that New Yorkers crave. There are acres of gardens, fathoms of freshwater ponds and miles of trails.

A good stroll through the park begins on the west side at the Columbus Circle entrance, through the Merchants' Gate and up to Sheep Meadow, a wide expanse of green for sunbathers and Frisbee players. Turning right, a pathway (called a transverse) runs along the south side of the meadow to the Carousel, and then the Dairy building, where the park's visitors center is not far from the Wollman ice-skating rink.

Just north of the Dairy, past the statue of Christopher Columbus, is the Mall, enclosed on both sides by a group of 150 American elms. These trees, which have not suffered from the Dutch elm disease that destroyed most of the country's elms, are believed to be the largest surviving stand in the country. At the end of The Mall is **Bethesda Fountain**, a '60s hippie hangout that has been restored. Continue on the path to the right to Bow Bridge. You can cross the bridge to the **Ramble**, a lush wooden expanse that is still a gay pickup area and also a meeting place for dog-owners of all sexual persuasions.

The Ramble gives way to Belvedere Castle and the **Delacorte Theater**, an open-air theater serving as the summer home of the Public Theater/New York Shakespeare Festival (www.publictheater.org). The performances are free, but admission requires lining up for tickets (available from the Public Theater's box office in Astor Place, Map pp60-1, 425 Lafayette St from 1pm to 3pm; the line starts to form at 10am). Immediately beyond is the **Great Lawn**, where the occasional free concert is held, along with annual open-air performances of the New York Philharmonic and Metropolitan

Opera (May through September; visit www.centralpark.org for schedules).

At the W 72nd St park entrance is **Strawberry Fields**, a 3-acre landscape dedicated to the memory of John Lennon; it contains plants from more than 100 nations. This spot was frequently visited by the former Beatles member, who lived in the massive Dakota apartment building across the street. He was shot and killed in front of the building on December 8, 1980.

There are many activities in the park, and more information on what's happening is available at the **Dairy visitors center** (☎ 212-794-6564; www.centralpark.org; ☺ 10am-5pm Tue-Sun), along the 65th St pathway.

The Central Park Conservancy leads one-hour natural history **walking tours** (☎ 212-360-2726) of the park throughout the year.

Without a doubt, the most touristy thing to do in the park is to rent a **horse-drawn carriage** (30 min $40, extra 15min $10) for a spin along the carriage paths. Carriages line up along 59th St (Central Park South), and drivers expect a tip on top of that charge.

Upper East Side   Map pp66-7

The Upper East Side is home to New York's greatest concentration of cultural centers, and Fifth Ave above 57th St is called Museum Mile. The neighborhood is filled with many of the city's most exclusive hotels and residential blocks. From 57th to 86th Sts, the streets between Fifth Ave and Third Ave have some stunning townhouses and brownstones, and walking through this area at nightfall affords a voyeuristic opportunity into the interiors of grand libraries and living rooms in these homes.

The East Side is served by just three subway lines (4, 5 and 6) running up and down Lexington Ave.

FRICK COLLECTION

If you can spare culture-concentration for only one art museum, the choice is simple: the **Frick Collection** (☎ 212-288-0700; www.frick.org; 1 E 70th St at Fifth Ave; adult/senior/student $12/8/5; ☺ 10am-6pm Tue-Thu & Sat, 10am-9pm Fri, 1pm-6pm Sun). Henry Clay Frick, a wealthy steel magnate, had the money and the eye to amass a superb collection of paintings and decorative arts housed in his exquisite 1914 'Millionaire Row' mansion. The paintings are so expertly matched to their surround-

ings that you feel the expansive sky of Jacob van Ruisdael's *Landscape with a Footbridge* or the religious ecstasy of Giovanni Bellini's *St Francis in the Desert*. And for historic irony, Hans Holbein the Younger's portraits of life-long enemies Sir Thomas More and Thomas Cromwell are paired side by side like peeved dinner guests. In the Oval Room, surrounded on almost four sides by larger-than-life portraits of Whistler's women (*Mrs Frederick R Leyland* and *Lady Meux*) posing in dresses he designed makes you wonder why he ever painted his dowdy mother.

Armed with individual cell-phone guides, visitors can survey the museum at their own pace or skip ahead a few rooms to avoid the crowds. It's also worth picking up the guide to the galleries ($1) to fully appreciate the significance of the works on display. For more historical information on Frick and the collection, don't miss the 20-minute movie in the Music Room. The Frick is no secret, so arrive early and prepare to stand in line; the museum regulates how many people are allowed in at a time. Children younger than 10 are not permitted.

TEMPLE EMANU-EL

Five blocks south of the Frick stands **Temple Emanu-El** (☎ 212-744-1400; E 65th St & Fifth Ave; ☺ 10am-5pm Mon-Thu, Sat & Sun; 10am-4pm Fri), the world's largest Reformed Jewish synagogue, which is significant for its Byzantine and Near-Eastern architecture.

WHITNEY MUSEUM OF AMERICAN ART

Housed in an ultra-modern mistake, this **museum** (☎ 212-570-3600/76; www.whitney.org; 945 Madison Ave at 75th St; adult $12, senior $9.50, child under 12 free; ☺ 11am-6pm Wed-Thu, 1-9pm Fri, 11am-6pm Sat & Sun) is a bite-size introduction to 20th-century art. Gertrude Vanderbilt Whitney established its collection in the 1930s; she hosted a salon of prominent artists, including Edward Hopper, in Greenwich Village.

Start a first-time visit on the 5th floor (early-20th-century period) for a chronological evolution of paintings as reality recorders, like George Bellow's famous *Dempsey and Firpo* boxing scene, to nascent abstraction of Joseph Stella's *Brooklyn Bridge: Variation on an Old Theme*. After these appetizers, you're ready for the folly of the mid-century, when painting abandoned reality altogether – Jasper Johns and Pollock are just a few examples in the collection. Warhol, Lichtenstein and Marisol all return to reality but with unprecedented irreverence.

The floors in between show special exhibits of more contemporary works, making the great names of modern art seem like traditionalists.

The **Whitney Museum of American Art at Altira** (Map pp64-5; Philip Morris Bldg, 120 Park Ave; admission free; ☺ 11am-6pm Mon-Fri, 11am-7:30pm Thu), across the street from Grand Central Terminal, is a branch of the collection.

METROPOLITAN MUSEUM OF ART

Like the city of its location, the **Metropolitan Museum of Art** (☎ 212-879-5500; www.metmuseum .org; 1000 Fifth Ave at 82nd St; adult $12, senior $7, child under 12 free; ☺ 9:30am-5:30pm Tue-Thu, 9:30am-9pm Fri & Sat) is powerful, popular and sometimes arrogant in its approach. The Met is virtually a self-contained cultural city-state with two million individual objects in its collection.

Once inside the Great Hall, pick up a floor plan and head to the ticket booths, where you will find a list of exhibits closed for the day along with a lineup of special museum talks. The Met presents more than 30 special exhibitions and installations each year, and clearly marked floor plans show you how to get to them. In the center of the Great Hall is an information desk that offers guidance in several languages (these change depending on the volunteers) and schedules for the day's free walking tours of the museum's highlights. Audio tours of the special exhibits ($6) are rented from a booth to the left of the entrance.

The Met crowds are impossible on rainy Sunday afternoons in summer, though during horrible winter weather you might find the 17-acre museum nearly deserted in the evening. It's best to target exactly what you want to see and head there first, before culture- and crowd-fatigue set in (usually after two hours). Then, put the floor plan away and let yourself get lost as you make your way through the galleries. It's a virtual certainty that you will stumble across something interesting along the way.

A ticket to the Met includes admission to the Cloisters (p95).

GUGGENHEIM MUSEUM

Everything looks great hanging on the walls of the **Guggenheim Museum** (☎ 212-423-3500; www.guggenheim.org; 1071 Fifth Ave; adult $15, senior $10, child under 12 free; ☺ 10am-5:45pm Sat-Wed, 10am-8pm Fri). Designed by Frank Lloyd Wright, the Guggenheim's distinctive spiral space moves visitors conveyor-belt style through the main gallery where a painting can be revisited with only a glance across the room gaining yet another perspective or appreciation. Cézanne, Degas, Vuillard – to name a few – are among the permanent collection, one of the 20th century's greatest private bequests. The Picasso department is quite strong with *Le Moulin de la Galette*, depicting a dancing crowd whose faces are just beginning to morph into geometric shapes. Reality is abandoned altogether in his realistically titled *Head of a Woman*. A 1993 renovation added a 10-story building behind Wright's structure; many complained it made the museum resemble a commode, but it did add space for the 5000-work Guggenheim collection, including the major donation in 1976 of impressionist and modern works by Justin Thannhauser.

NATIONAL ACADEMY OF DESIGN

Founded by painter-inventor Samuel Morse, the **National Academy of Design** (☎ 212-369-4880; www.nationalacademy.org; 1083 Fifth Ave at E 90th St; adult/student $8/4.50; ☺ 11:30am-5:30pm Tue-Sun, 11:30am-8pm Fri) has a permanent collection of paintings and sculptures. Since 1940 the academy's works have been housed in a big mansion designed by Ogden Codman, who also designed the Breakers mansion in Newport, Rhode Island. The academy's house is notable for its marble foyer and spiral staircase

COOPER-HEWITT, NATIONAL DESIGN MUSEUM

An arm of the Smithsonian Institution, the **National Design Museum** (☎ 212-849-8400; www.si.edu/ndm; 2 E 91st St at Fifth Ave; adult $10, senior $7, child under 12 free; ☼ 10am-5pm Tue-Thu, 10am-9pm Fri, 10am-6pm Sat, noon-6pm Sun) sits in the 64-room mansion built by billionaire Andrew Carnegie in 1901 in what those days was so far uptown it was out of town. Carnegie was an avid reader and generous philanthropist, and he dedicated many libraries around the country. The collection, through rotating exhibits, examines design and artistic merit in advertising, shoe design, architecture and engineering.

The museum is free for all from 5pm to 8pm Friday.

JEWISH MUSEUM

Really an art facility, the **Jewish Museum** (☎ 212-423-3200; 1109 Fifth Ave at 92nd St; adult $10, senior & student $7.50; ☼ 11am-5:45pm Sun-Wed, 11am-3pm Fri) examines 4000 years of Jewish ceremony and culture. The building, a 1908 banker's mansion, has more than 30,000 items of Judaica.

MUSEUM OF THE CITY OF NEW YORK

Somewhat duplicating the function of the older New-York Historical Society across town (p93), the **Museum of the City of New York** (☎ 212-534-1672; 1220 Fifth Ave at 103rd St; adult/family $7/12, senior & child $4; ☼ 10am-5pm Wed-Sat) doesn't seem to have a coherent plan to its displays. These two homegrown institutions, though, are more typical of quaint historical museums in small towns across the US – comforting to think that New York is just an overgrown burg.

The museum itself has a notable 2nd-floor gallery that displays entire rooms from demolished homes of New York grandees, an excellent collection of antique dollhouses, teddy bears and toys, along with an exhibition dedicated to Broadway musicals.

ROOSEVELT ISLAND

New York's most planned neighborhood is on a tiny island that's no wider than a football field and sits in the East River between Manhattan and Queens. Once known as

Blackwell's Island after the farming family that lived there, the island was purchased by the city in 1828 and became the location of several public hospitals and an insane asylum. In the 1970s the state of New York built apartments for 10,000 on the island. The planned area along the cobblestoned roadway resembles an Olympic Village, or, as some less kindly put it, a college dorm complex.

Most visitors take the three-minute aerial tramway over, admire the stunning view of the East Side of Manhattan framed by the 59th St Bridge, and head straight back. But it's worth spending an hour or so on the island during good weather, if only to enjoy the quiet and the flat roadway and paths that circle it, making it a perfect spot for both running and picnicking.

The **Roosevelt Island tramway station** (☎ 212-832-4543; cnr 59th St & Second Ave; ticket $2) runs every 15 minutes on the quarter-hour from 6am to 2:30am daily. Roosevelt Island has its own subway station that's accessible from Manhattan via the Q train during the day and the B train on nights and weekends. Just make sure the train you get on lists '21st St–Queensbridge' as its final destination (subway: 63rd St–Lexington).

MUSEO DEL BARRIO

Started as a celebration of Puerto Rican art, this **museum** (☎ 212-831-7272; 1230 Fifth Ave btwn 104th & 105th; adult/child $6/free, senior & student $4; ☼ 11am-5pm Wed-Sun) has expanded to include the folk art of Latin America and Spain. Its galleries now feature pre-Columbian artifacts and a collection of more than 300 *santos*, hand-carved wooden saints in the Spanish Catholic tradition. Temporary exhibits feature the work of local artists who live in Spanish Harlem.

Upper West Side   Map pp66-7

The Upper West Side begins as Broadway emerges from Midtown at Columbus Circle. A number of middle to top-end hotels are along Central Park South, and many celebrities live in the massive apartment buildings that line Central Park West all the way up to 96th St.

LINCOLN CENTER

Replacing a group of tenements that were the real-life inspiration for the musical *West Side Story*, **Lincoln Center** (☎ 212-546-2656, tours

☎ 212-875-5350; Columbus Ave at Broadway; tours adult $12.50, student & senior $9) is a complex of seven large performance spaces built in the 1960s. There's a clean, if architecturally uninspired look to Lincoln Center during the day, but at night the chandeliered interiors look simply beautiful from across Columbus Ave.

For high culture, Lincoln Center is a must-see, because it contains the **Metropolitan Opera House**, adorned by two colorful lobby tapestries by Marc Chagall; the **New York State Theater**, home of the New York City Ballet; and the **New York City Opera**, the low-cost, more daring alternative to the Met. The New York Philharmonic holds its season in **Avery Fisher Hall**.

The Lincoln Center Theater group calls the 1000-seat **Vivian Beaumont Theater** home. The lower levels of the building also contain the smaller and more intimate **Mitzi Newhouse Theater**. To the right of the theaters stands the **New York Public Library for the Performing Arts**, containing the city's largest collection of recorded sound, video and books on film and theater.

The Juilliard School of Music, attached to the complex by a walkway over W 65th St, contains **Alice Tully Hall**, home to the Chamber Music Society of Lincoln Center, and the **Walter Reade Theater**, the city's most comfortable film revival space and the major screening site for the New York Film Festival that is held every September.

Tours of the complex begin at the concourse level each day and explore at least three of the theaters, though just which ones you see depends on production schedules. It's a good idea to call ahead to make a reservation. For more information on the performance companies, call the center.

NEW-YORK HISTORICAL SOCIETY
As the antiquated, hyphenated name implies, the **New-York Historical Society** (☎ 212-873-2400; 2 W 77th St at Central Park West; adult $8, senior & student $5; 🕐 10am-6pm Tue-Sun) is the city's oldest museum. It was founded in 1804 to preserve artifacts of history and culture. It was also New York's only public art museum until the founding of the Metropolitan Museum of Art in the late 19th century, and in this capacity, it obtained John James Audubon's original watercolors for his *Birds of America* survey (they are on display in a 4th-floor gallery).

The museum is somewhat overshadowed by its neighbor, the American Museum of Natural History, and it has suffered severe financial problems in recent years. But it is well worth a visit, because viewing its quirky permanent collection is a bit like traipsing through New York City's attic.

AMERICAN MUSEUM OF NATURAL HISTORY
Founded in 1869, the **American Museum of Natural History** (☎ 212-769-5200; 79th St at Central Park West; adult/child $12/7, senior & student $9; 🕐 10am-5:45pm) today has over 30 million artifacts in its collection. It is no doubt most famous for its three large dinosaur halls, which present the latest knowledge on how these behemoths behaved and theories on why they disappeared. Knowledgeable guides roam the dinosaur halls ready to answer questions, and there are 'please touch' displays that allow you to handle, among other items, the skullcap of a pachycephalasaurus, a plant-eating dinosaur that roamed the earth 65 million years ago.

In February 2000, the giant new **Rose Center for Earth and Space** (space show adult/child $22/13, senior & student $16.50) modernized the collection with the state-of-the-art 3D star show, which is highly recommended. The museum also has an IMAX theater (admission is extra, but combo tickets are available).

The Butterfly Conservancy is a popular recurring exhibition that features 600 butterflies from all over the world (admission is extra, but combo tickets are available).

CHILDREN'S MUSEUM OF MANHATTAN
Featuring discovery centers for toddlers, the **Children's Museum of Manhattan** (☎ 212-721-1223; 212 W 83rd St; adult & child $6, child under 1 free; 🕐 10am-5pm Wed-Sun) also has a postmodern Media Center where technologically savvy kids can work in a TV studio. The museum also runs crafts workshops on weekends. Kids beyond the age of drooling on themselves would be bored here.

COLUMBIA UNIVERSITY
The once all-female Barnard College and **Columbia University** (Map p59; ☎ 212-854-1754, Broadway at W 116th St) are in a spot once far removed from the downtown bustle. Today, the city has enveloped and moved beyond Columbia's gated campus. But the school's main courtyard, with its statue *Alma Mater*

perched on the steps of the Low Library, is still a quiet place to enjoy the sun and read a book. Hamilton Hall, in the southeast corner of the main square, was the famous site of a student takeover in 1968, and since then, it's periodically a place for protests as well as pretty wild student parties. As you would expect, the surrounding neighborhood is filled with inexpensive restaurants, good bookstores and cafés. Take the subway to 116th St–Columbia University.

CATHEDRAL OF ST JOHN THE DIVINE

Just behind the Columbia University campus, the **Cathedral of St John the Divine** (☎ 212-316-7540; Amsterdam Ave at W 111th St; 7am-5pm Mon-Sat) is the largest place of worship in the US, a massive and dark 601ft-long Episcopal cathedral that, upon completion, will be the third-largest church in the world (after St Peter's Basilica in Rome and the newly built Our Lady in Yamoussoukro in the Ivory Coast).

But it's unlikely that St John, which had its cornerstone laid in 1892, will be finished in your lifetime. Work has yet to begin on the stone tower on the left side of the west front or the crossing tower above the pulpit. In 1978, the Episcopal Diocese of New York began training local young people in stone cutting. Other features that are shown on the church's cutaway floor plan near the front entrance, such as a Greek amphitheater, are merely wistful visions of the distant future.

Still, the cathedral is a flourishing place of worship and community activity, the site of holiday concerts, lectures and memorial services for famous New Yorkers. There's even a Poet's Corner just to the left of the front entrance – though, unlike Westminster Abbey, no one is actually buried there. You should also check out the altar designed and built by the late artist Keith Haring.

GENERAL US GRANT NATIONAL MEMORIAL

Popularly known as **Grant's Tomb** (Map p59; ☎ 212-666-1640; Riverside Drive & W 122nd St; admission free; 9am-5pm Wed-Sun), this landmark monument is where Civil War hero and President Ulysses S Grant and his wife Julia are buried. Completed in 1897 – 12 years after Grant's death – the granite structure cost $600,000 and is the largest mausoleum in the country. The building was a graffiti-marred mess for years until the general's relatives threatened to move his body somewhere else and

---

NYC CHARACTER

Often mistaken as rude, New Yorkers are more accurately absorbed, by themselves and by their overpowering city. But it is a kinder, gentler place than years past: the urban maladies have been cured thanks to a strong economy in the 1990s and to the eight-year rule of mayor Rudolph Giuliani. With all the charm of a high school principal, he tamed crime, made the subway run efficiently and demanded almost martial tidiness. An inward evolution has occurred too. Softer emotions of compassion and fraternity, so rarely expressed in this tough city, nourished a populace grieving after the attacks of September 11 and during the rebuilding of the city's wounded southern tip.

---

shamed the National Park Service into cleaning it. Take subway 1 to 125th St.

RIVERSIDE CHURCH

Overlooking the Hudson River, **Riverside Church** (Map p59; ☎ 212-222-5900; 490 Riverside Dr at 122nd St; 9am-4pm) is a gothic marvel built by the Rockefeller family in 1930. The observation deck, 355ft above the ground, is open to the public during good weather ($2), and its 74 carillon bells, the largest grouping in the world, are rung every Sunday at noon and 3pm. Interdenominational services are held on Sunday at 10:45am. Take subway 1 to 116th St–Columbia University.

Harlem
Map p59

Follow the advice in Duke Ellington's famous song and take the 'A' train to Harlem, the storied neighborhood of jazz music, literature and 20th-century emancipation. Frederick Douglass wrote from this vantage point, as did James Baldwin. The Harlem Renaissance bloomed here in the 1920s and '30s after a mass migration of African-Americans out of the South to jobs in New York. Free from the ancestral lands of slavery, writers and poets – like Langston Hughes, Zora Neale Hurston and James Weldon – celebrated their race's identity and struggles within the dominant society. Around the same time, Duke Ellington and Louis Armstrong moved to town with a new musical language – jazz. This peculiar age now had a soundtrack.

Thelonius Monk and Charlie Parker, among others, molded jazz into new expressions. And in Harlem's smoky clubs and grand ballrooms, jazz musicians emceed the forbidden mixing of whites and blacks, a social revolution that would contribute to the dismantling of many slave-era prohibitions.

Harlem has undergone a commercial renaissance in the past five years. Businesses and tourism now thrive where even urban decay was stunted. Young Japanese and European tourists explore the neighborhood by foot, while older Americans tend to sign up for bus tours (much like an urban safari). The best time to visit Harlem is on a Sunday morning when people head to services at the dozens of small churches in the neighborhood. Wednesday is also good, because you can end the day at the Apollo Theater and watch its famous amateur night.

As you explore Harlem, you should note that the major avenues have been renamed in honor of prominent African-Americans, but many locals still call the streets by their original names, making getting around a little confusing. From west to east: Eighth Ave/Central Park West is Frederick Douglass Blvd; Seventh Ave is Adam Clayton Powell Jr Blvd, named for the controversial preacher who served in Congress during the 1960s; Lenox Ave has been renamed for the Muslim activist Malcolm X; and 125th St is also known as Martin Luther King Jr Blvd.

First-time visitors might want to check in at the **Harlem Visitor Information Kiosk** (163 W 125th St at Adam Clayton Powell Jr Blvd; 9am-6pm Mon-Fri) for maps, brochures and friendly advice. People will probably be surprised to discover that Harlem is but one express stop away from the Columbus Circle-59th St station downtown. The trip on the A and D trains takes just five minutes, and the station is only one block from the Apollo Theater and two blocks from Lenox Ave, where there are many soul food restaurants. The 2 and 3 trains from the West Side stop on Lenox Ave at 116th St (site of the Harlem open-air market, p96) and at Lenox and 125th St.

Walking tours of Harlem are sponsored by the Municipal Art Society and Big Onion Walking tours (p107).

APOLLO THEATER

The **Apollo Theater** (212-531-5305; www.apollo theater.com; 253 W 125th St at Frederick Douglas Blvd) has

THE CLOISTERS

Built in the 1930s, the **Cloisters** (Map p59; 212-923-3700; Fort Tryon Park; adult $12, senior & student $7, child under 12 free; 9:30am-5:15pm Tue-Sun Mar-Oct, 9:30am-4:45pm Tue-Sun Nov-Feb) is a strange concept: salvaged fragments of real French and Spanish monasteries have been reassembled to mimic the layout of a monastery for the purposes of curatorship only. It houses the Metropolitan Museum of Art's collection of medieval frescoes, tapestries (including the famous Unicorn tapestries) and paintings. In summer (the best time to visit), concerts are held on the grounds and more than 250 varieties of medieval flowers and herbs grow in the courtyard garden. The museum and the surrounding gardens in Fort Tryon Park are very popular with European visitors and school groups, so get here early during the warm months. The audio guide ($6) does a great job of explaining the collection and the daily lives of medieval monks. To get there, take the A train to Dyckman St.

been Harlem's leading space for political rallies and concerts since 1914. Virtually every major black artist of note in the 1930s and '40s performed here, including Duke Ellington, Ella Fitzgerald and Charlie Parker. After a brief desultory spell as a movie theater and several years of darkness, the Apollo was bought in 1983 and revived as a live venue. It still holds its famous weekly amateur night (Wednesday at 7:30pm; tickets cost $16 to $24) 'where stars are born and legends are made.' Lauren Hill got her start here and other green singers will rise to fame from this stage again. Although the audience leans a little too far toward touristy, amateur night is still great fun. Watching the crowd call for the 'executioner' to yank hapless performers from the stage is often the most entertaining part of the night. Just remember that audience participation is part of the show, so don't be shy about 'putting your hands together.'

On other nights the Apollo hosts performances by established artists and comics. Take subway A, B, C or D to 125th St.

STRIVER'S ROW

While you're in Harlem, check out Striver's Row (W 138th and W 139th between

NEW YORK CITY

GOSPEL SERVICES

Harlem's Sunday services are expressive celebrations with massive gospel choirs and impassioned sermons. The popularity of Sunday service as a tourist attraction has created a clash of cultures with worshippers being put on display for tourist cameras. Some of the churches in Harlem have cut deals with bus operators, and their services are dominated by visitors rather than church members. It's much better to go on your own to a place that welcomes visitors but not tour groups. But be sure to observe the proper etiquette: arrive early, dress in your Sunday best, stay for the entire service, leave your camera at home and join in with an 'Amen' or some hand-clapping. Donating a dollar or two to the collection plate is also appreciated.

Abyssinian Baptist Church (☎ 212-862-7474; 132 W 138th St; 🕙 9am & 11am Sun) was a downtown institution started by an Ethiopian businessman. It moved north to Harlem in 1923, mirroring the migration of the city's black population. Its charismatic pastor Calvin O Butts is an important community activist whose support is sought by politicians of all parties. The church has a superb choir led by Jewel T Thompson, minister of music. Take subway 2 or 3 to 135th St.

Mother African Methodist Episcopal Zion Church (☎ 212-234-1545; 146 W 137th St) graciously takes the overflow from the Abyssinian. Take subway 2 or 3 to 135th St.

Canaan Baptist Church (☎ 212-866-0301; 132 W 116th St at St Nicholas Ave; 🕙 10:45am Sun winter, 10am Sun summer) may be Harlem's friendliest church. It's considerate to show up a bit early and introduce yourself to the parishioners before the service. Take subway 2 or 3 to 116th St.

Frederick Douglass and Adam Clayton Powell Blvds), also known as the St Nicholas Historic District, just east of St Nicholas Park. These row houses and apartments, many designed by Stanford White's firm in the 1890s, were much prized (check out the alleyway signs advising visitors to 'walk their horses'). When whites moved out of the neighborhood, the buildings were occupied by Harlem's black elite, thus giving the area its colloquial name. Striver's Row is one of the most visited blocks in Harlem – so try to be a bit discreet, because the locals (modern-day Harlem elites) are a little sick of all the tourists. Streetside plaques explain more of the area's history.

STUDIO MUSEUM IN HARLEM
Providing working spaces to promising young artists, the **Studio Museum in Harlem** (☎ 212-864-4500; www.studiomuseum.org; 144 W 125th St; adult $7, senior & student $3; 🕙 noon-6pm Wed & Thu, noon-8pm Fri, 10am-6pm Sat & Sun) has given exposure to the crafts and culture of African-Americans for nearly 30 years. Its photography collection includes works by James VanDerZee, the master photographer who chronicled the Harlem Renaissance of the 1920s and '30s.

SCHOMBURG CENTER FOR RESEARCH IN BLACK CULTURE
The nation's largest collection of documents, rare books and photographs recording black history is at the **Schomburg Center for Research in Black Culture** (☎ 212-491-2200; 515 Lenox Ave; admission free; 🕙 10am-6pm Tue-Sat). Arthur Schomburg, born in Puerto Rico to a white father and black mother, started gathering works on black history during the early 20th century while becoming active in the movements for civil rights and Puerto Rican independence.

His collection was purchased by the Carnegie Foundation and eventually expanded and stored in this branch of the New York Public Library. The Schomburg Center has a theater where lectures and concerts are regularly held. To get there, take subway 2 or 3 to 135th St.

HARLEM MARKET
Fashioned to look like an African bazaar, the **Harlem Market** (W 116th St at Lenox Ave; 🕙 10am-5pm) does a brisk business selling tribal masks, oils, traditional clothing and assorted African bric-a-brac. Most of the people at the market used to sell their wares from tables set up along 125th St, but were moved to the open-air site, amid great controversy, in 1995 after retailers complained about their presence. You can also find cheap clothing, leather goods, music cassettes and bootleg videos of films still in first-run theaters. The market is operated by the Malcolm Shabazz Mosque, the former pulpit of Muslim orator Malcolm X, which stands across the street. To get there, take subway 2 or 3 to 116th St.

SPANISH HARLEM

Spanish Harlem is the name given to the area from Fifth Ave above 96th St east to the river. Formerly an Italian neighborhood, it now contains one of the city's biggest Latino communities (Puerto Rican, Dominican and Cuban, mostly). **La Marqueta** (along Park Ave above 110th St) is a colorful, ad-hoc collection of produce stalls that is a signature attraction in 'El Barrio.' Don't miss El Museo del Barrio (p92) for an overview of Latino arts. Every January 5, the museum holds a Three Kings Parade in which hundreds of schoolchildren, along with camels, donkeys and sheep, make their way up Fifth Ave to 116th St, the heart of the neighborhood (subway: 103rd St–Lexington).

The Bronx

☎ 718 / pop 1.3 million

The Bronx – a geographic area that has a curious article before its name, like The Hague – is named after the Bronck family, Dutch farmers who owned a huge tract of property in the area. They gave their name to Bronck's River, which led to the derivation used today.

The borough, once a forest-like respite from the rest of the city, is now home to 1.3 million people and, in spots, remains economically depressed and crime-ridden. Largely ignored by the outside world in the 1970s and '80s, the nightclubs and street corners of the Bronx reinvented the African-American tradition of improvised poetry into the music phenomenon known today as rap. The Morrisania section of the lower Bronx is still riddled with abandoned buildings, while Fieldston, in the northern reaches of the borough, is a privately owned community of Tudor homes occupied by some of the city's richest residents. The Bronx also boasts the quiet and isolated fishing community of City Island as well as the 2764-acre Pelham Bay Park, the city's largest.

An interesting footnote: Jennifer Lopez, Sean 'P Diddy' Combs and Colin Powell all claim a Bronx upbringing.

The **Bronx Tourism Council** (☎ 718-590-3518; www.ilovethebronx.com) offers a visitors' guide to the borough and keeps track of community events. The **Bronx County Historical Society** (☎ 718-881-8900) sponsors weekend walking tours of various sites.

Bronx Tour Trolley (☎ 718-430-1890; www.nyc .gov/parks; free) travels from Fordham Plaza Metro-North station to the Bronx Zoo, New York Botanical Garden, and Arthur Avenue at 187th Street; call for a schedule.

Metro-North (☎ 212-532-4900) leaves from Grand Central Terminal and Harlem-125th St for several destination in the Bronx; buy your ticket from the automatic vending machines in the stations rather than on the train, which will charge you more for the convenience.

YANKEE STADIUM

The legendary **ballpark** (☎ 718-293-6000; www .yankees.com; E 161st St at River Ave; tickets $8-50) is called 'the most famous stadium since the Roman Coliseum.' Throughout summer it hosts 81 home games for the New York Yankees. Gates open 90 minutes before game time, and fans can stroll around Monument Park (behind left field; it closes 45 minutes before game time) where plaques are dedicated to such baseball greats as Babe Ruth, Lou Gehrig, Mickey Mantle and Joe DiMaggio.

Tickets are in high demand, and good seats are hard to come by. Far from the action, bleacher seats are almost always available. The seats don't offer a great view of the game and there's no shade, but the rowdiness of the bleachers crowd might be enough of a spectacle.

You can visit the dugout, the press room and the locker room during a guided **tour** (reservations ☎ 718-579-4531; tickets adult $12, senior & child $6) of the ballpark.

Across the street from the stadium, **Stan's Sports Bar** (57 Murray St btwn W Broadway & Church St) gets particularly raucous, especially when the Yankees play the archrival, Boston Red Sox.

New York Waterway (☎ 800-533-3779; www.ny waterway.com; adult/child $16/12) offers direct service by water taxi to Yankee Stadium departing from Manhattan and points in New Jersey. Or else take subway B, D or 4 to Yankee Stadium.

NEW YORK BOTANICAL GARDEN

The 250-acre **New York Botanical Garden** (☎ 718-817-8700; www.nybg.org; adult/child $13/5, senior & student $11; ☼ 10am-6pm Tue-Sun) features several beautiful gardens and the restored Victorian Enid A Haupt Conservatory, a grand iron and glass edifice that is a New York City landmark. There's also an outdoor Rose Garden, next to the conservatory, and a Rock Garden with a multitiered waterfall. Take subway B or D to Bedford Park Blvd.

BRONX ZOO

Also known by its more politically correct title Bronx Wildlife Conservation Society, the **Bronx Zoo** (☎ 718-367-1010; www.bronxzoo.org; adult $8, senior & child $6; ☼ 10am-5pm Mon-Fri Apr-Oct, 10am-5:30pm Sat & Sun; 10am-4:30pm Nov-Mar) is home to 5000 animals, all in naturalistic settings.

The usual array of lions, tigers and bears can be viewed from the Bengali Express Monorail, which offers a 25-minute narrated journey through the Wild Asia areas. The Jungle World indoor exhibit, which is open year-round, is a 37,000-sq-ft recreation of the Asian tropics with a hundred different species of animals and tropical plants. You'll either be delighted or terrified by the World of Darkness, where bats hover nearly unseen (but not unsmelled).

It's best to visit the zoo in warm weather, because many of the outdoor rides are closed during the winter months and the animals retreat into sheltered areas. To get there, take subway 2 or 5 to East Tremont Ave–West Farm Square

ARTHUR AVE

Just south of Fordham University is the Belmont section of the Bronx, the most authentic Italian neighborhood in the city. This is a living, breathing neighborhood for pure gastronomic exploration (p124).

Belmont is the perfect place to head on a Saturday when many shoppers visit to stock their pantries with real Italian foodstuffs and to visit with the shopkeepers. Most shops are closed Sunday. **Arthur Ave Poultry Market** (☎ 718-733-4006; 2356 Arthur Ave) and **Teitel Brothers Wholesalers** (☎ 718-733-9400; cnr 186th St & Arthur Ave) both sell live chickens, which look yummier than the goose-bumped shapes wrapped up in cellophane at the supermarket.

The **Arthur Ave Retail Market** contains indoor food stalls, including Mike & Sons, a cheese shop with heartbreakingly good aged parmesan and prosciutto. Next to the vegetable stalls, check out the cigar rollers hard at work.

The **Cosenza fresh fish store** (☎ 718-364-8510; 2354 Arthur Ave) sells clams on the half shell to pedestrians from a small table on the street, and clerks at the **Calabria Pork Store** (☎ 718-367-5145; 2338 Arthur Ave) offer free samples of hot and sweet homemade sausages that age on racks suspended from the ceiling.

The **Belmont Italian American Playhouse** (☎ 718-364-4700; 2385 Arthur Ave) is the neighborhood's most lively performance spot. It's the site of a season of new theatrical works that runs from April to December, and it's a place where local authors and musicians perform year-round.

To top off your shopping excursion, don't miss the bakeries on E 187th St.

You can reach Arthur Ave by taking the Metro-North trains from Grand Central to Fordham Rd or the 4 train to the stop of the same name and walking east for 10 to 15 minutes, then turning right at Arthur Ave and continuing south for three blocks.

CITY ISLAND

Surely the oddest and most unexpected neighborhood in the Bronx is City Island, a 1½-mile-long fishing community 15 miles from Midtown Manhattan. City Island has numerous boat slips, is home to three yacht clubs, and it's the place to go if you're interested in diving, sailing or fishing in Long Island Sound. Perhaps the strangest thing about this self-contained little spot cut off from the rest of the Bronx by Pelham Bay Park is that there's hardly a trace of the New York accent found in conversation between the locals – in fact their inflections and accents betray a New England influence.

All of its shops and 20-odd seafood restaurants are along City Island Ave, which runs the length of the island. The short side streets are filled with attractive clapboard houses that overlook the surrounding water, and the main marinas are found on the western side.

You can reach City Island by taking the 6 subway train to its terminus at Pelham Bay Park and getting on the Bx29 bus that runs directly to City Island Ave, or by taking an express bus from Madison Ave in Midtown directly to City Island.

Brooklyn

☎ 718 / pop 2.4 million

Brooklyn is booming. Artists and struggling hipsters have skipped across the river to rejuvenate warehouse districts like Williamsburg and Dumbo. Practical urban couples break up with Manhattan for a Park Slope yard and a bun in the oven. Everything seems a little bigger and calmer in Brooklyn: the sky is a welcome fixture, the sidewalks are ample and neighbors greet one another. More so than ever Brooklyn has a right to flash its trademark claim that 'one out of every seven famous people' in America was born in Brooklyn.

Brooklyn, officially called Kings County, derives its name from the Dutch town of Breukelen. For most of its 350-year history Brooklyn was a collection of farming villages, and its citizens joined greater New York City with great reluctance. Even after the 1898 consolidation, the borough remained independent in spirit: citizens enjoyed Prospect Park, Brooklyn's own version of Central Park, followed the fortunes of the Brooklyn Dodgers baseball team and sun worshipped at the ritzy resort hotels on Coney Island. But much of Brooklyn's separate city pretensions were destroyed in the late 1950s, when the Dodgers moved to the West Coast and many of the borough's residents began moving to the suburbs.

Brooklyn Information & Culture (BRIC; ☎ 718-855-7882; www.brooklynx.org; 2nd fl, 647 Fulton St) issues a free calendar of events and distributes maps and other tourist information. *Brooklyn Bridge*, a monthly magazine available in shops and newsstands, offers a more extensive list of happenings.

BROOKLYN HEIGHTS

This neighborhood of brownstones and mansions near the mouth of the East River developed as a ferry departure point for Lower Manhattan in the early 19th century. Walking along its promenade, you get a stunning view of Manhattan's skyscrapers (framed at the bottom by the far less impressive buildings and warehouses that sit along the waterfront).

The best way to approach Brooklyn is on foot by crossing the Brooklyn Bridge (p75; approximately a 20-minute walk).

Along the main thoroughfare of Atlantic Ave is an area known as Little Arabia, a row of spice and grocery shops. **Sahadi Importing Co** (☎ 718-624-4550; 187-189 Atlantic Ave) is a popular spot for dried fruits, nuts and exotic smells. Across the street, **Oriental Pastry & Grocery** (☎ 718-875-7687; 172 Atlantic Ave) has more than five kinds of date and almond pastries.

BROOKLYN HISTORICAL SOCIETY

This **research library** (☎ 718-222-4111; www.brooklyn history.org; 128 Pierrepont St; ☼ noon-5pm Tue-Sat) also has a museum dedicated to borough history. The museum is housed in a fine terra-cotta auditorium that's a national landmark. Its digitized collection of 31,000 photographs and prints is available for browsing in the 2nd-floor library.

NEW YORK TRANSIT MUSEUM

A block north of Atlantic Ave, the **Transit Museum** (☎ 718-694-1600; www.mta.info; cnr Boerum Place & Schermerhorn St; adult/child $5/3; ☼ 10am-4pm Tue-Fri, noon-5pm Sat & Sun) is in a decommissioned subway station from the 1930s. You pay your admission fee at a subway-style information booth (but here the clerk is friendly). The updated exhibits walk you through the construction of the subway – how construction workers, known as 'sandhogs,' tunneled through the core of the city. Historical photos document what a fiasco it must have been to install an underground railway amid an existing city.

It also has an impressive collection of subway cars from the transit system's first hundred years; most have their original ads still intact. Keep an eye out for the silver car used in the 1995 film *Money Train*, along with the model R-1, the vintage that inspired Duke Ellington's *Take the A Train*.

The transit museum also runs tours of the system in antique subway cars once a year departing from 59th St–Columbus Circle and running to Coney Island. To get to the museum, take the subway to Jay St–Borough Hall.

PROSPECT PARK

Created in 1866, the 526-acre **park** (events line ☎ 718-965-8999; www.prospectpark.org) is considered the greatest achievement of Frederick Law Olmsted and Calvert Vaux, the same landscaping duo that designed Central Park. Though less crowded than its more famous Manhattan sister, Prospect Park offers many of the same activities along its broad meadows, including ice-skating at the **Kate Wollman Rink** (☎ 718-287-6431; adult/child $5/3; ☽ call for hours). There is also the **Lefferts Homestead Children's Historic House Museum** (☎ 718-789-2822; admission free; ☽ 1-4pm Fri-Sun) and a small **zoo** (☎ 718-399-7339; adult/child $5/1; ☽ 10am-5pm Mon-Fri, 10am-5:30pm Sat & Sun). Information on other activities, including park walks, carousel rides and art exhibitions, can be obtained by calling the park office.

Grand Army Plaza stands at the northwest entrance to the park, marked by an 80ft **Soldiers' and Sailors' Monument** constructed in 1898 to commemorate the Union Army's triumph during the Civil War. In summer, you can visit a gallery in the arch that's dedicated to local artists. You can also visit the observation deck that's just below the four-horse bronze chariot. New York City's only structure honoring President John F Kennedy is in a small park with a fountain, just north of the Grand Army arch. The immense Art Deco **Brooklyn Public Library** faces the arch on its south side.

On weekends year-round, a free hourly trolley service makes a loop from Prospect Park to points of interest around the art museum, including the park zoo, ice rink, botanical garden and library. Ask at the museum information desk what time it passes by the entrance. To get to the park, take subway 1 or 2, to Grand Army Plaza, Q or S to Prospect Park, or F to 15th St–Prospect Park.

BROOKLYN MUSEUM OF ART
Were it located anywhere else, the **Brooklyn Museum of Art** (☎ 718-638-5000; www.brooklynmuseum .org; 200 Eastern Pkwy; adult/child $6/free, senior & student $3; ☽ 10am-5pm Wed-Fri, 11am-6pm Sat & Sun) would be considered a premier arts institution. Even though it is overshadowed by the Met, this museum is very much worth a visit. It's never really crowded, even on Sunday, and you can take up an entire day exploring its collection and seeing the nearby botanical gardens (see opposite) and Brooklyn Children's Museum (see opposite).

The museum received a lot of publicity in 1999 when it sponsored the Sensation exhibition of young British artists. One of the featured artists, Chris Ofili, used elephant dung in his portrait of the Virgin Mary, which was attacked by Mayor Giuliani, giving the exhibition (and the mayor) a lot of press coverage. The modern art exhibits at the museum continue in this provocative trend, often dealing with risqué or taboo subjects.

The permanent galleries are dedicated to African, Islamic and Asian art. Particularly good are the modern 3rd-floor galleries containing colorful Egyptian cartonnages (mummy casings) and funerary figurines. The 4th floor, which overlooks a tiled court crowned by a skylight, has period rooms, including a reconstruction of the Jan Schenck House, a 17th-century Dutch settlement in Brooklyn. The 5th floor has colonial portraiture, including a famous Gilbert Stuart painting of George Washington in which the general looks particularly uncomfortable wearing his false teeth, and a collection of 58 Auguste Rodin sculptures. Don't miss the American art wing with pieces ranging from the traditional to the shocking.

On the first Saturday of the month admission is free from 5pm to 11pm. To get to the museum, take subway 1 or 2 to Eastern Pkwy–Brooklyn Museum.

BROOKLYN BOTANIC GARDEN
The 52-acre **botanic garden** (☎ 718-623-7200; 1000 Washington Ave; adult $5, senior & student $3, child under 16 free, admission free 10am-noon Tue & Sat; ☽ 8am-6pm Tue-Fri, 10am-6pm Sat & Sun Apr-Sep; 8am-4:30pm Tue-Fri, 10am-4:30pm Sat & Sun Oct-Mar) has more than 12,000 different plants in its 15 gardens. There's a fanciful Celebrity Path with slate steps honoring famous Brooklynites and a Fragrance Garden that makes for a wonderful walk. The Discovery Garden is a hands-on floral playground for kids and the nearby Children's Garden has been tended by little hands since 1914. To get to the park take subway 1 or 2 to Eastern Pkwy–Brooklyn Museum.

BROOKLYN CHILDREN'S MUSEUM
The world's first museum designed expressly for children, the **Brooklyn Children's Museum** (☎ 718-735-4400; www.bchildmus.org; 145 Brooklyn Ave at St Mark's Ave; admission $4; ☽ 2-5pm Wed-Fri, 10am-5pm Sat & Sun) is full of hands-on exhibits emphasizing art, music and ethnic culture. Each June, the museum holds a festival of custom-made balloons from around the world. Take the C train to Kingston–Throop Ave, or 3 to Kingston.

WILLIAMSBURG
The average age of a Williamsburg resident is just legal, and the pre-requisite look is

straight from a thrift store with an expensive but unkempt haircut. This might be the hippest post-college recovery zone in the nation. Along the main thoroughfare, Bedford St, locals post signs for apartment listings or band mate ads on mini 'democracy walls.' On sunny Sunday mornings, a mix of post-punk, neo-commie, eternally arty crowds gather in the various bars and brunch spots, while the neighborhood's traditional residents (Orthodox Jews, Central Europeans and Latinos) exchange greetings with each other from their stoops or file home after church services.

The area around the Pratt Art School (200 Willoughby Ave) is a popular pub crawl (in part because some places serve underage drinkers); the *Waterfront Weekly* is the free publication covering the neighborhood and is a good source for listings of local music shows, open studio events or street fairs. Williamsburg is best reached by the L train to Bedford Ave.

BROOKLYN BREWERY
Since 1988, the **Brooklyn Brewery** (☎ 718-486-7440; www.brooklynbrewery.com; 79 N 11th St) has made its award-winning Brooklyn Lager under contract at breweries outside the borough. But the beer 'came home' to Brooklyn in 1996 with the opening of a microbrewery in Williamsburg. Housed in a series of buildings that once made up the Hecla Ironworks factory (the firm that made the structural supports for the Waldorf-Astoria Hotel), the brewery has become a Williamsburg institution.

There is a non-smoking tasting room with a display of historical beer bottles and monthly specials. There is often entertainment at night and a happy hour every Friday and Saturday between 6pm and 10pm. On Saturday, there are free tours; call for reservations and hours. To get there, take subway L to Bedford Ave.

DUMBO
New York's penchant for coining geographically inspired handles for neighborhoods has gone too far this time: Down Under the Manhattan Bridge Overpass (Dumbo) – puh-lease. Even if you choke every time you say it, Dumbo is *the* next frontier to be conquered and it is happening fast. Utterly functional, Dumbo's warehouses have

been snatched up by artists and galleries that have been chased out of more expensive real-estate markets elsewhere. If you're in town in late October, be sure to check out the **Dumbo Art Under the Bridge Festival** (☎ 718-694-0831; www.dumboartscenter.org), organized by **Dumbo Arts Center** (DAC; ☎ 718-624-3772; 30 Washington St; ☿ 10am-6pm Thu-Mon). Any other time of the year, hit DAC during one of its five annual shows, which typically contain a Brooklyn theme. Look out for the 'League Treatment Center' awning.

Jacques Torres Chocolate (☎ 718-875-9772; 55 Water St; chocolate $2-5; ☿ 9am-7pm Mon-Sat) is an unlikely neighbor in these parts, but who would bad-mouth a chocolate factory?

St Ann's Warehouse (☎ 718-254-8779; www.artsatstanns.org; 38 Water St) is a cool performance space for cutting-edge theater, musical guests like the late, great Joe Strummer, and tributes to Frank Zappa.

Dumbo is best reached by F to York St or A, or C to High St. Water taxis leave from Fulton Ferry Landing in Manhattan; call New York Water Taxi (☎ 212-742-1969) for more information.

CONEY ISLAND
A trip down memory lane Americana-style, Coney Island was once a bustling amusement park of gaudy fun houses, minor games of chance and bumper car rides. In the amusement park's heyday before WWI, a newspaper report once boasted '300,000 people in Coney Island yesterday. 23 Children Lost.' Coney Island is a bit run-down these days but still offers the simple pleasures of gorging on junk food, riding roller-coaster rides and getting the summer season's first sunburn.

Take subway F, Q or W to Coney Island–Stillwell Ave. As you emerge from the subway station, you'll see a 24-hour coffee shop right in the middle of the station. Hard-bitten patrons sit at a countertop hunched over their meals and dozens of menu items are advertised on the bright yellow walls of the shop. Meanwhile, your nose is assaulted by the smell of sausages, hot dogs, home fries and other greasy delights. Then pass through the doors to Surf Ave, where Russian residents pick up odd tools and electronic equipment at flea market stalls along the street.

Nathan's (Surf Ave; ☿ 8am-4am Mon-Sun), the city's prototypical fast-food stand, has been open at the same spot for more than 75 years and still sells its famous hot dogs ($2.50).

In the Astroland Amusement Park, the 70-year-old wooden **Cyclone** (1000 Surf Ave at Dewey Albert Place; rides $5) is a hair-raising, rickety ride best appreciated from a front-car seat. Along the Boardwalk you will see two relics of Coney Island's past glory: the bright red parachute jump, moved here from the 1939 World Fair in Queens, and the ivy-covered Thunderbolt roller coaster that operated from 1925 to 1983. It's older than the more famous Cyclone.

Coney Island shuts down after Labor Day and opens up sometime around Memorial Day. If you take the Q train, be sure that its final destination is Coney Island as some Q trains terminate in Brighton Beach.

AQUARIUM FOR WILDLIFE CONSERVATION

The **New York Aquarium** (☎ 718-265-3400; adult $11, senior & child $7; ☒ 10am-3pm Mon-Sun), along the Coney Island Boardwalk, has a new name. Its manageable scale makes it a wonderful place for young children. There's a touch pool where kids can handle starfish and other small forms of sea life, and there is a small amphitheater with Sea World–style dolphin shows several times daily. Most children love observing whales and seals from the outside railing that overlooks the tanks or from the observation windows that afford views of the animals in their underwater habitats. You can spend the better part of a day at the aquarium viewing its 10,000 specimens of sea life. Time your visit with feeding time to catch the liveliest part of the day. To get there, take subway F or Q to W 8th St–NY Aquarium.

Queens

☎ 718 / pop 2.2 million

Manhattan has the fame. Brooklyn has the pride. The Bronx has the attitude. Staten Island, the temperament of the put-upon. Where does that leave Queens, a borough of boring, low-slung row houses and a transitional zone between urban Manhattan and suburban Long Island? Only as the most ethnically diverse spot in the United States with 46% of its population claiming foreign birth. The area's cheap rents and proximity to the airports has long made Queens attractive to the newest New Yorkers. According to the New York

---

FLUSHING

Flushing, Queens, was the huge commercial ash heap mentioned in F Scott Fitzgerald's *The Great Gatsby* that travelers passed en route to Long Island.

City government, 1.2 million immigrants entered the city in the 1990s.

With a landmass of 282 sq miles, Queens is the largest borough in New York City. A strange phenomenon has happened over the years – most of the newer immigrant groups have augmented, rather than replaced, those already in Queens. More than 100 minority groups now live in this borough, speaking over 120 different languages or dialects – and its population is over two million.

The No 7 train that cuts through the heart of Queens is dubbed the 'International Express' because many recent immigrants (from Korea, China, Vietnam and Uruguay, to name a few) have established communities along its path. Flushing's center is at the corner of Roosevelt Ave, which runs east–west, and Main St, which runs north–south – right at the subway exit (subway: Main St–Flushing).

The **Queens Council on the Arts** (☎ 718-647-3377; www.queenscouncilarts.org) has a 24-hour hotline on community cultural events; in keeping with the multicultural demographics of the borough, it provides information in English, Spanish, Korean and Chinese.

ISAMU NOGUCHI GARDEN MUSEUM

Tucked away among the East River warehouses in Long Island City, the cinder-block **Isamu Noguchi Garden Museum** (☎ 718-721-2308; www.noguchi.org; 32-37 Vernon Blvd, Long Island City; adult/child $5/3; ☒ 11am-6pm Wed, Sat & Sun Apr-Nov) stands on the site of a studio designed by the Japanese-American sculptor who died in 1988, three years after the museum opened. The 12 galleries and garden contain more than 300 examples of his work.

Just two blocks north, where Broadway meets Vernon Blvd, is the **Socrates Sculpture Park** (☎ 718-956-1819; admission free; ☒ 10am-dusk), a year-round, open-air public space with changing works by local artists on a former illegal waste dump overlooking the East River. The displayed works, including the five wind chimes along the shoreline, have a stark industrial look to them that's in keeping with its location right next to a steel company. Take subway N or W to Broadway.

MOMA QNS
During renovations of its Manhattan exhibition space, MoMA relocated a portion of its holdings (until September 27, 2004) for showing at a converted staple factory, near Queens Blvd. To get to **MoMA QNS** (☎ 212-708-9400; 45-20 33rd St), take subway E, F or V to 23rd St–Ely Ave, G to Long Island City–Court House Sq, or 7 to 45th Rd–Court House Sq.

LOUIS ARMSTRONG HOME & ARCHIVES
Corona, once an Italian neighborhood, was also a place where well-known black jazz musicians bought comfortable houses in the 1920s and '30s. Louis Armstrong lived on 107th St from 1929 until his death in 1971; it's open 10am to 5pm weekdays. Queens College has opened his former home as a **museum** (☎ 718-997-3670; 34-56 107th St; adult/child $8/4; 10am-5pm Tue-Fri, noon-5pm Sat & Sun) for 40-minute guided tours. Take subway 7 to 103rd Street–Corona Plaza.

Staten Island
☎ 718 / pop 443,000
Residents of the 'forgotten borough' of Staten Island have long entertained thoughts of secession from greater New York City. Even still, most New Yorkers know the borough as the place to turn around after a pleasantly breezy ferry ride when the weather turns hellish in summer, or simply as the starting point of the New York City Marathon. Of course, there's more to Staten Island than that, and it's worth a day trip.

The **Staten Island Chamber of Commerce** (☎ 718-727-1900; www.sichamber.com; 130 Bay St; 9am-5pm Mon-Fri) provides information on cultural events and attractions. The daily *Staten Island Advance* covers local news and events.

STATEN ISLAND FERRY
The **ferry** (☎ 718-814-2628; www.siferry.com) is one of New York's best bargains, taking on the free 20-minute, 6-mile journey from Lower Manhattan to Staten Island. The return trip to Manhattan used to be $0.50, but because Staten Island is a Republican-supporting district, Mayor Giuliani abolished the fee. It operates on the half-hour, 24 hours a day,

and only the most brutal weather will keep the ferries in their slips.

This is the low-cost, hassle-free alternative to the crowded boat trips to the Statue of Liberty and Ellis Island. You'll pass within a half-mile of both on the way out to Staten Island, and the views of Manhattan and Brooklyn Heights are breathtaking. It's best to pack a lunch or snack before heading out to the ferry (subway: South Ferry), because the food on the boat itself is dreadful, and the South Ferry terminal, an outdated facility slated for replacement within a few years, doesn't have a decent restaurant.

JACQUES MARCHAIS CENTER OF TIBETAN ART
Home to the largest collection of Tibetan art outside China, the **Jacques Marchais Center** (☎ 718-987-3500; 338 Lighthouse Ave btwn Richmond Rd & Terrace Ct; adult/child $5/2, student & senior $3; 1-5pm Wed-Sun) was built by art dealer Edna Koblentz, who collected the works under an alias that did not betray her gender. It opened to the public in 1947, a year before her death, and includes a number of golden sculptures and religious objects made of human bone. Just about the only authentic thing missing from the home, built in the style of a Tibetan temple, is the smell of yak butter. The museum holds its annual weekend-long Tibetan cultural festival in the early part of October in the outdoor garden amongst the stone Buddhas.

To get to the Marchais Center by public transportation, take the S74 bus from the ferry terminal (it travels along Richmond Rd and is about a 25-minute ride) and ask the driver to let you off at Lighthouse Ave. The museum is at the top of a hill.

There's a bonus in store for those who make the trek out to the museum – just across Lighthouse Ave from the museum, you can get a glimpse of the Wright Residence, the only private home designed by Frank Lloyd Wright ever built in New York City. It's the low-slung, cliffside residence at 48 Manor Court, constructed in 1959 for a private couple.

ACTIVITIES
Running
The **New York Road Runners Club** (NYRRC; Map pp66-7; ☎ 212-860-4455; www.nyrrc.org; 9 E 89th St) organizes weekend runs all over the city as well as the

annual October New York Marathon. Information and assistance for runners can be found at the NYRRC booth at the Engineer's Gate entrance to Central Park at E 90th St.

There are several good spots for solo runs in Manhattan. Central Park's 6-mile roadway loops around the park and is closed to cars each weekday from 10am to 3pm and all weekend. If you don't want to jockey for space with rollerbladers and bikers, try the Jacqueline Kennedy Onassis Reservoir in Central Park, which is encircled by a soft 1.6-mile path.

West St has a runner's pathway along the Hudson River from 23rd St all the way down to Battery Park City, which passes a very pleasant stretch of public park and offers great views of the Jersey shoreline and the Statue of Liberty. The Upper East Side boasts a path that runs along FDR Drive and the East River from 63rd St to about 115th St. If you're alone, it's not advisable to run further north than 105th St, because the path isn't well lit beyond that point.

Bicycling

You're better off peddling through Central Park than muscling through the city streets, although there are bike lanes marked throughout the city and delivery guys loaded down with hot-and-sour soup cycle their way across the island. If you hit the city's pockmarked streets, use a trail bike with wide wheels. Also, wear a helmet and be alert so you don't get 'doored' by a passenger exiting a taxi. **Transportation Alternatives** (Map pp64-5; ☎ 212-629-8080; www.transalt.org; 12th fl, 115 W 30th St) is a bike advocacy group that sponsors free or low-cost weekend trips to the outskirts of the city; its newsletter is available at major bike shops.

Many places rent bicycles for the day, including **Metro Bicycle**. It has seven stores, with one at 6th St and Broadway (Map pp60-1; ☎ 212-663-7531) and another at 545 Sixth Ave (Map pp60-1; ☎ 212-255-5100). Bike rental costs $7 per hour, $35 for over five hours, and $45 overnight.

Fitness Centers

Chelsea Piers (Map pp64-5; ☎ 212-336-6000; 23rd St at Hudson River; day pass $50; 🕑 6am-11pm Mon-Fri, 8am-9pm Sat & Sun) offers a range of activities. This huge complex has a four-level driving range overlooking the river and an indoor ice-skating rink. A huge sports and fitness center offers a running track, swimming pool, workout center, even sand volleyball and rock climbing.

Gyms all over the city offer day passes. Many advertise in the *Village Voice*. One well-located, no-frills gym to keep in mind is the **Prescriptive Fitness Gym** (Map pp64-5; ☎ 212-307-7760; 250 W 54th St; day pass $25).

WALKING TOUR

Greenwich Village is a delight to wander around. The narrow, erratic streets created by capricious streams and animal paths are a welcome antithesis to the city's deliberate grid. In the back alleys and odd corners, generations of New York–lovestruck kids have lived in little shoebox apartments slowly chipping away at their piece of the Big Apple. The tangible excitement of being on the verge of something great is utterly contagious.

The best place to start is the arch at **Washington Square Park** (p81). Head south on Thompson St to the **Village Chess Shop** (**1**; ☎ 212-475-9580; 230 Thompson St; per hour $1; 🕑 noon-midnight), where Village denizens of all levels challenge each other with mental strategy. The game's intense concentration creates one of the quietest places in Manhattan.

Turn right on Bleecker St and head east for two blocks to the corner of MacDougal St – this was the informal center of 1950s literary culture. European-style coffee shops, such as **Le Figaro** (**2**; cnr MacDougal & Bleecker St), served as the meetinghouses for writers, journalists and poets of the era. Surrounded by body-piercing shops and T-shirt stands, this corner has a decidedly touristy feel today.

Turn right onto MacDougal St, where you'll run into **Minetta Tavern** (**3**; ☎ 212-475-3850; 113 MacDougal St at Minetta La), an old Village hangout with a proud wooden bar and crisp white tablecloths. It's a great place to stop for a beer and admire the old caricatures of the 1950s celebrities that used to hang out here. On the opposite corner is **Café Wha? (4)**, a legendary old club where Jimi Hendrix once played; its heyday is long gone.

If you're thirsty for great cappuccino and a sunny sidewalk seat, **Caffe Reggio** (**5**; 119 MacDougal St; coffee $1-4; 🕑 9am-2pm) has a 1902 bronze-and-chrome espresso machine that receives as much exaltation as the Holy Eucharist during a Catholic Mass. Over 80

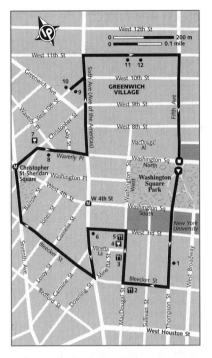

pieces of robust Italian-style paintings encourage imaginings of European chapels.

Head to W 3rd St and hang a left. On the left-hand side of the street, Gerde's **Folk City (6)** once stood where the bar Fat Black Pussycat (11 W 4th St) now resides. One of the most popular venues for folk music, Folk City's tiny stage hosted Joan Baez, Bob Dylan (who supposedly smoked his first joint here), The Clancy Brothers and Peter, Paul & Mary. Folk City moved to 130 W 3rd St in 1969 and closed in 1986.

Turn left at Sixth Ave and work your way to the western extension of Bleecker St. Atmospherically, this is the most interesting part of Bleecker. A brief swath of an Italian community remains anchored around Our Lady of Pompeii church with attendant restaurants and pastry shops. Bookstores, record stores, guitar shops and other browsing are all worthwhile. Check out Carmine and Cornelia Sts for unstructured wandering or to grab a bite to eat.

Turn right into Bleecker St, right again on Seventh Ave and head north three blocks to Christopher St, where a right turn will lead to Stonewall Place, a block-long portion of Christopher St renamed in honor of the historic 1969 gay rebellion at **Stonewall Inn (7**; Stonewall Place). Gay clubs were frequently targeted by police for being centers of 'deviant' behavior, and drag queens and lesbians were arrested for cross-dressing. Police attention was so common that most patrons scattered to avoid trouble or made a game of it. On the night of Judy Garland's funeral, the police raided the Stonewall Inn, a popular after-hours dance club. Instead of compliance, the patrons fought back with fists, high-heeled shoes, pocket change and whatever else could be hurled. Three days of riots followed, and the modern gay pride movement was born. In Stonewall's wake, anti-discrimination legislation on the grounds of sexual orientation was introduced and finally passed in 1986. In the adjoining park between Christopher and Waverly Place, the 1992 statue 'Gay Liberation' marks the turning point in homosexual acceptance by mainstream society.

Heading east (right) on Waverly Place brings you to the three-sided **Northern Dispensary (8**; 165 Waverly Place). It was built in 1831 to combat a cholera epidemic and was New York's oldest public health facility until 1989; it's now awaiting renewal. The Dispensary building creates one of the strangest spots in New York City: the corner of Waverly Place and Waverly Place!

Back on Sixth Ave, turn left and examine the gables and towers of redbrick **Jefferson Market Courthouse (9**; p69), now a public library, and the **Jefferson Market Gardens**, which are sometimes open to the public on weekends. Just behind the courthouse building is **Patchin Place (10**; W 10th St btwn 6th & Greenwich Ave), an enclosed block of flats that was home to both journalist John Reed and poet ee cummings, who once described his apartment at Patchin Place as '…friendly. unscientific. private. human.'

Head to W 11th St and then east. On the right you'll find the tiny **Second Cemetery of the Spanish and Portuguese Synagogue (11)** that was used from 1805 to 1829. Continue along W 11th St and you'll pass a series of traditional row houses, including builder **Andrew Lockwood's House (12)** at No 60. It was built in 1842 on a lot that was originally part of the larger Wouter Van Twiller Farm. Turn right when you reach Fifth Ave and you'll be heading directly back toward the arch in Washington Square Park.

NEW YORK CITY FOR CHILDREN

New York isn't all late-night discos and stuffy museums. Not only do New Yorkers have children, they also take them out, occasionally. (Be warned that New Yorkers feel no shame in stuffing their preteens into industrial-sized strollers for easier city navigation. Seriously, kids old enough to read Michael Crichton novels still qualify for personal chauffeuring.) In addition to the big hits, add these attractions to your family's itinerary.

Central Park   p89

Horse-drawn carriages, rollerblading, a children's zoo, six playgrounds and a famous carousel are just some of the reasons to spend an afternoon in New York's most famous open space. Also check out storytelling at the Hans Christian Andersen statue (11am Saturday) and the Marionette Theater in the Swedish Cottage.

South Street Seaport   p75

Along with the tall ships and children's center here, head to the Seaport for kid-friendly food and fun entertainment like knife jugglers and sandcastle building.

Bronx Zoo   p98

Visiting the oldest wildlife facility in the USA makes a journey to the Bronx worth it.

Staten Island Ferry   p103

Family-oriented activities can be so expensive. To give your wallet and feet a rest, catch a round-trip ride on the Staten Island Ferry complete with Madame Liberty and skyscraper views.

Coney Island   p101

The Boardwalk, the beach, Astroland (and the Cyclone!), Deno's Wonder Wheel Amusement Park, the New York Aquarium, Brooklyn Cyclones baseball team and Nathan's hot dogs. 'Nuff said.

Chelsea Piers   p104

There's something here for kids of all ages: bowling, batting cages, rock-climbing walls and year-round ice- and roller-skating.

QUIRKY NEW YORK CITY
Newspaper Row

No other city in the country has played such a leading role in the political reporting of domestic and world affairs than New York City, and that tradition can trace its roots to Park Row and Nassau St, where the famous dailies had a front-row seat of City Hall. The present ramp to Brooklyn Bridge was the site of Horace Greeley's *New York Tribune* in the mid-1800s. Greeley is often credited for the famous line 'Go West, young man,' an endorsement for the Homestead Act of 1862 that opened up the western frontier. Famous writers, such as Charles Dickens and Henry James, appeared in the pages of the *Tribune*. The damning term of 'yellow journalism' marred the reputations of two Newspaper Row rivals: Joseph Pulitzer's *World* and William Randolph Hearst's *Journal*. In their most grievous sin, both papers reported that the mysterious 1898 sinking of the USS *Maine* in the harbor of Havana, Cuba, was not an accident – an erroneous report that is believed to have initiated the Spanish-American war. Pulitzer's establishment of his namesake award for writing helped repair his damaged image.

Members Only

New York City so masterfully cultivates exclusivity that these Gramercy Park institutions are worth noting only for the fact that ordinary people are denied access. Don't they look luscious from the outside? That's the New York City hook digging into you. **National Arts Club** (Map pp64-5; ☎ 212-475-3424; 15 Gramercy Park South) was designed by Calvert Vaux, one of the men behind the creation of Central Park. It holds exhibitions that are sometimes open to the public. The club has a beautiful vaulted stained-glass ceiling above its wooden bar. **Players Club** (Map pp64-5; 16 Gramercy Park) is an actors' hangout that was created in 1888 by Shakespearean actor Edwin Booth (brother of Abraham Lincoln's assassin John Wilkes Booth) and designed by Stanford White. Its warm wooden interiors, high ceilings and sumptuous leather seating are the epitome of a late-19th-century mansion and give a glimpse of how the rich once lived.

American Museum of the Moving Image

The **American Museum of the Moving Image** (☎ 718-784-0077; www.ammi.org; 35th Ave at 36th St, Astoria; adult/child $10/5, student & senior $7.50; ☉ noon-5pm Wed-Fri, 11am-6pm Sat & Sun) stands in the middle of the Kaufman Astoria Studio complex. This 75-year-old film production center has been the shooting site of everything from the Marx Brothers' *Coconuts* to *Glengarry Glen Ross* and TV's *Cosby Show*. Unfortunately, the studios are not open to public tours, but this museum makes a good effort at showing the mastery behind filmmaking, with galleries showing the makeup and costumes from films such as the *Exorcist* and movie sets from 1987's *Glass Menagerie*, directed by Paul Newman. Film and TV serials are played in a small theater built by conceptual artist Red Grooms, inspired by the 1930s Egyptian-theme movie palaces. The museum also holds interesting film retrospectives year-round, with several movies screened daily. If you decide to make the short 15-minute subway ride out to Queens, go when there's an interesting film on offer, and end your day with a Greek meal on Broadway. Take subway R to Steinway St.

TOURS
Walking Tours

There are many companies and organizations that conduct urban treks with varying themes that offer a more intimate perspective of the city than the rumbling bus tours. **Big Onion Walking Tours** (☎ 212-439-1090; www.big onion.com; adult $12, senior & child $10), established by two Columbia University history doctoral candidates, operates year-round. It specializes in ethnic New York and runs an annual Christmas Day tour of the Jewish Lower East Side. **Adventure on a Shoestring** (☎ 212-265-2663; tour $5) conducts tours of neighborhoods throughout the city as well as thematic tours commemorating special events: Big Apple love affairs on February 14, Irish heritage on March 17, and walks across bridges on their birthdays (complete with birthday cake).

Insider Marketplace (iMar; ☎ 732-636-4650; www.imar.com) acts like an online eBay for tours organized by individual tour guides or city residents. You can find just about anything on this site from tasting tours of Chinatown ($25) to a guided bus tour of hip-hop sites in the Bronx ($65).

The **Municipal Art Society** (☎ 212-439-1049; www.mas.org) is famous for its tours of Grand Central Terminal on Wednesday at 12:30pm (free). It also sponsors architectural and cultural walking tours throughout the city. Visit the website for an upcoming schedule.

Sound Walk (☎ 212-674-7407; www.soundwalk.com) sells CD audio guides to different neighborhoods in New York City. You can buy them online through the website. Sound Walk's website also has a list of stores in NYC that sell its stuff.

Boat & Helicopter Tours

More than one million people a year take the three-hour, 35-mile **Circle Line Full-Island cruise** (Map pp64-5; ☎ 212-563-3200; www.circleline.com; adult/senior/child $26/20/13; ☉ Jun-Sep) that leaves from Pier 83 at 42nd St on the Hudson River. This is *the* tour to take, provided the weather is good and you can enjoy the waterside breezes on an outside deck. The quality of the narration depends on the enthusiasm of the guide; be sure to sit well away from the narrator if you want to avoid the inevitable 'Where are you from?' banter. Visit Circle Line's website for a list of evening music cruises.

World Yacht (Map pp64-5; ☎ 212-439-1049; www.worldyacht.com; tickets $70-80) has well-regarded culinary cruises around Manhattan year-round that leave from Pier 81 at W 41st St. Reservations and proper dress are required.

Liberty Helicopter Tours (☎ 212-967-4550; www.libertyhelicopters.com; per person $56-275) has bird's-eye views of the city that depart from two locations: Midtown at W 30th St and Twelfth Ave (Map pp64-5), and Pier Six on the East River near Whitehall St (Map p63).

FESTIVALS & EVENTS

Hardly a week goes by without a special event taking place in New York. Fifth Ave shuts down several times a year for the major parades, including the granddaddy of all, the St Patrick's Day Parade on March 17. Neighborhood street fairs in summer are celebrated throughout the city. For information on any of the events listed below, call **NYC & Company** (☎ 212-484-1222; www.nycvisit.com). See also the Directory chapter (p288) for more New York City (and State) events.

January
Three Kings Parade (January 5) El Museo del Barrio (p92) sponsors this parade, in which thousands of schoolchildren –

along with camels, donkeys and sheep – make their way up Fifth Ave into the heart of Spanish Harlem.

Chinese New Year The date of the lunar new year varies from late January to early February each year, but the fireworks crackle in Chinatown for days before and after this holiday. Try to catch either the Lion or Dragon Dance Parades.

February

Black History Month The Martin Luther King Jr national holiday (in January) serves as the unofficial kickoff to February's month-long celebration of African-American history. Contact Harlem's Schomburg Center for Research in Black Culture (p96) for events.

March

St Patrick's Day Parade (March 17) For more than 200 years, the city's Irish population has honored their homeland's patron saint with this parade down Fifth Ave. In recent years, a gay Irish group has protested its exclusion from the parade with a demonstration at Fifth Ave and 42nd St.

May

Ninth Avenue International Food Festival In mid-May, Ninth Ave between 42nd and 57th Sts teems with people gorging on ethnic fast food from stalls lining the avenue.

Fleet Week Near the end of the month, thousands of sailors from numerous nations descend on New York for this annual convocation of naval ships and air-rescue teams. Contact the Intrepid Sea-Air-Space Museum (p89) for information.

June

Restaurant Week Every June and November, many top restaurants, from Aquavit (p121) to Vong, participate in this event that gives diners a break: prix fixe meals cost whatever the year ($20.04, $20.05 etc).

Puerto Rican Day Parade Held the second Sunday in June along Fifth Ave from 44th to 86th Sts, this fiesta brings out tens of thousands to dance, eat and frolic.

Buskers Festival A night of 'buskers' (street performers) highlights a series of free concerts and performances at the World Financial Center downtown (☎ 212-945-0505).

Lesbian and Gay Pride Week On the last weekend of June, a huge parade flows down Fifth Ave from Midtown to Greenwich Village. Dance parties take place on the Hudson River piers and clubs are hopping with the rainbow tribe (☎ 212-807-7433; www.nycpride.org).

July

Lincoln Center Events Lincoln Center (p92) hosts an astounding number of events throughout the summer, many of them free, including Lincoln Center Out-of-Doors (☎ 212-875-5108), the Mostly Mozart concert series (☎ 212-875-5399) and the Lincoln Center Festival (☎ 212-875-5928), a biennial event that brings many international actors, singers and acrobats to New York for the first time.

Central Park Summerstage These mostly free musical performances (raucous!) and author readings (poignant!) are held *en plein air* at the Rumsey Playfield behind the park's band shell from mid-June to mid-August (☎ 212-360-2777; www.summerstage.org).

August

Harlem Week Throughout the month, the city's premier black neighborhood celebrates with festivities that culminate in the Harlem Jazz & Music Fest (☎ 212-862-4777).

Fringe Festival This frenzy (more than 1200 performances) stretches over two weeks in mid- to late-August in 20 locations (☎ 212-420-8877; www.fringenyc.org).

September

San Gennaro This 10-day festival honoring Naples' patron saint takes place in the second week of September in Little Italy (www.littleitalynyc.com).

West Indian–American Day Parade On Labor Day, more than one million people take part in a parade along Eastern Parkway in Brooklyn, making this the single largest event of the year (☎ 718-773-4052).

New York Film Festival This major event in the film world takes place at Lincoln Center's Walter Reade Theater (p92), beginning in late September (☎ 212-875-5600).

October

Halloween Parade (October 31; www.halloween-nyc.com) This colorful and wild parade winds its way up Sixth Ave from Broome St, through Greenwich Village, ending in a block party on Christopher St.

December

Rockefeller Center Christmas Tree Lighting At 7pm on the Tuesday after Thanksgiving, the big tree is fired up (☎ 212-632-3975).

Radio City Christmas Spectacular The high-kicking Rockettes are on display all month at the famous theater (☎ 212-247-4777).

New Year's Eve In addition to the annual New Year's Eve festivities in Times Square, the city's celebration features a five-mile midnight run in Central Park (p89; ☎ 212-860-4455), fireworks at the South St Seaport (p75; ☎ 212-732-7678) and First Night, an alcohol-free family event, including ballroom dancing in Grand Central Terminal's main concourse (p86; ☎ 212-883-2476).

SLEEPING

Space doesn't come cheap in New York City, neither do hotel rooms. To sleep in the Big Apple for a $100 a night, especially in the high season (spring and fall), you'll be in a little shoebox with an even tinier private bath, and forget about a view. Most hotels in the bottom of the range feel like

GAY & LESBIAN NEW YORK CITY

For a list of gay clubs and bars catering to every taste, pick up the free sheets *HX/Homo Xtra* (which has listings for her also) and *Next*, available at most restaurants and bars. Chelsea and Greenwich Village spots are predominantly gay male, while lesbians can typically be found in the East Village and Alphabet City. But there is lots of cross-pollination, and many of clubs listed here are mixed (straights and gays).

Barracuda (Map pp64-5; ☎ 212-645-8613; 275 W 22nd St btwn Seventh & Eighth Ave) This cruisy lounge distracts the pick-up game with an engaging drag show. (There's no sign, but look for the glowing red globes.)

xl (Map pp64-5; ☎ 212-995-1400; 357 W 16th St btwn Eighth & Ninth Ave) This high-tech Chelsea favorite scores with the handsome set. Don't miss the bathroom, though you might miss the subtle signage; look for the velvet ropes.

Meow Mix (Map pp60-1; ☎ 212-254-0688; 269 E Houston St btwn Clinton & Suffolk St) A prime lesbian hangout in the East Village that's been going strong for years. It attracts a youthful crowd with live indie girl rock. Happy hours, open jams and DJs all help to get the joint moving and grooving. Men are welcome, but usually have to pay a bit extra to get in.

The following clubs and bars are reviewed elsewhere in the chapter:

Bar d'O (p125) Monday night is lesbian night.

Don Hill's (p129) Trashy transvestite parties with go-go boys, drag shows and anything goes – sounds like a ho-hum weekday?

Henrietta Hudson (p125) A spacious dive bar where girls can be girls.

Marie's Crisis (p125) Share your love of show tunes at this informal piano bar.

Saints (p126) A quiet spot that welcomes a mixed crowd, though it's a predominantly gay bar.

modern high-rise college dorms. Climbing up the price scale, though, brings all sorts of luxuries: chic, designer boutiques that emulate nightclubs, historic hotels that have been muses to musicians and writers, grande dames that overlook Central Park. Some of New York's hotels are such luminaries that even a one-night stand ranks as an attraction.

With the skittish economy, bargain rooms are easier to find than in years past. Several clearinghouses help hotels unload rooms for slow periods by offering discounts (without additional service charges) to the public. Call the following with your travel dates and preferred neighborhood for availability: **Accommodation Plus** (☎ 800-733-7666), **Central Reservation** (☎ 800-950-0232), **Express Hotel Reservation** (☎ 800-356-1123) and **Hotel Discount Network** (☎ 800-869-4986).

The hotels, hostels and B&Bs are listed here by neighborhood, with the less expensive places generally listed first. Unless noted otherwise the prices quoted here are for the high season and do not include city and state taxes (13.625% plus $2 per room per night). Here's a pricing guide for double rooms: budget ($100 or less), mid-range ($100 to $300) and top end ($300 and up).

Lower Manhattan   Map p63

Most of the available hotels below Houston St cater to a business clientele, so most of them offer very good deals on weekends. The downside is that the neighborhood is quite dead once the office workers go home.

Best Western's Seaport Inn (☎ 212-766-6600, 800-468-3569; fax 212-766-6615; 33 Peck Slip btwn Front & Water St; d from $150; ▣) Sitting in the shadow of Brooklyn Bridge, the Seaport Inn is in a faux Federal-style building near cobblestoned streets and the South Street Seaport. If you've only got South Street Seaport on your mind, this is the place to stay; otherwise, you might feel like a castaway.

Millennium Hilton (☎ 212-693-2001, 800-445-8667; 55 Church St; d from $230; ▣) This newcomer rises above the street like a black plinth, peering bleakly into the WTC site across the street. The rooms facing this scene are strangely in demand, while many businesspeople who have to stay here request a room on the other side of the building.

SoHo, Chinatown & Lower East Side
Map pp60-1

Like nightlife? Like wandering around funky urban neighborhoods? Don't care about an 'itinerary'? Then this is the place for you.

ROOM SERVICE IN THE 21ST CENTURY *Mara Vorhees*

In recent years, the Internet has revolutionized many aspects of travel, not the least of which is finding and booking hotel rooms. Savvy surfers now visit bid-for-booking sites and discount hotel sites before they travel, guaranteeing a significantly reduced hotel room rate. These sites can be used for hotels all over the country – if not the world – so anybody who is online has access to hotels' cheapest rates. Here are the best sites and how they work.

www.biddingfortravel.com The goal of this website is to promote informed bidding when using the services of www.priceline.com (below). Visitors are invited to post their successful bidding history on specific hotels so that others learn the lowest acceptable prices. The site is monitored by an administrator, who answers questions and gives advice to subscribers who want to bid.

www.hoteldiscounts.com Enter your destination and dates and the website will provide information and prices for hotels with rooms available. You can book through the website at the discounted rate offered.

www.hotels.com This website uses the same system as www.hoteldiscounts.com and seems to come up with the same results.

www.hotwire.com Choose your dates and your preferred neighborhood (up to four) and www.hotwire.com will provide a general location, list of amenities, price and star-rating for several options. You learn the hotel name and exact location only after you buy your reservation.

www.priceline.com Choose your desired neighborhood, desired star-rating and desired price; enter dates and credit card info. If www.priceline.com finds something that meets your criteria your reservation is automatically booked and you learn the hotel specifics afterwards. There's nothing to stop you from starting very low and gradually increasing your bid so you get the best price possible. Use this site in conjunction with www.biddingfortravel.com for a great hotel deal.

You can shut down the bars on Ludlow St, stagger home and rise the next morning to find a Chinese market in full swing. Not bad for a bed that costs only $100.

Off SoHo Suites (☎ 212-979-9815, 800-633-7646; fax 279-9801; 11 Rivington St btwn Chrystie St & The Bowery; ste $150) Two blocks south of E Houston St, this spot has suites with kitchenettes and offers 10% discounts for stays of a week or more

Sohotel (☎ 212-226-1482, 800-737-0702; fax 212-226-3525; www.pioneerhotel.com; 341 Broome St; d without bath $60-70, d with bath $70-90) Next to the New York Lighting store, a small doorway leads to the 2nd-floor lobby of this budget gem. Rooms are small, but beds are comfortable with nice starched sheets and common areas have a funky paint job.

Greenwich Village & East Village
Map pp60-1

Despite the Village's famous gentrification, visitors can still capture some of the bohemian spirit by staying in inexpensive European-style B&Bs with closet-sized rooms.

St Mark's Hotel (☎ 212-674-2192; fax 212-420-0854; 2 St Marks Place at Third Ave; d $90-120) Smack dab on St Marks Place amidst the toe-ring shops and hot-dog stands, St Mark's has good-sized but sterile rooms. This block is noisy

so you might want to request a room away from the street.

Larchmont Hotel (☎ 212-989-9333; www.larchmont hotel.com; 27 W 11th St; s $70-80, d $90-100) On a pretty tree-lined street, this former residential hotel has shared kitchen and bathroom facilities. The doubles are better value than the singles. Weekend rates increase by $5 to $10.

Washington Square Hotel (☎ 212-777-9515, 800-222-0418; www.washingtonsquarehotel.com; 103 Waverly Place; s $125-145, d $150-160) Within spitting distance of the park, this hotel is a perennial favorite for Greenwich Village pilgrimages. The hotel is decorated in wacky 1980s aesthetic with salmon-colored walls and black faux-lacquered furniture. Book far in advance, as the friendly prices keep this place well-stocked with visitors.

Incentra Village (☎ 212-206-0007; fax 212-604-0625, 32 Eighth Ave btwn W 12th & Jane St; d $120-170, ste $150-200) This is a charming 12-room inn that's gay- and lesbian-friendly and booked solid every weekend. It is well-maintained and quiet with a lovely parlor.

East Village B&B (☎ 212-260-1865; 252 E 7th St; s/d $75/100) The three bedrooms in this Alphabet City apartment are rented out primarily by lesbians, but the all-women guarantee of years past is no longer applied. Because this B&B doesn't have a caretaker in the apartment, it feels more like a sublet. Credit cards are not accepted.

Chelsea & Gramercy Park   Map pp64-5

Many of the city's gay-friendly hotels are quirky inns along Chelsea's attractive side streets. Staying in aristocratic Gramercy Park is perfect for a romantic weekend.

Chelsea Center Hostel (☎ 212-643-0214; www .chelseacenterhostel.com; 313 W 29th St; dm $25-30) Friendly and family-like, this hostel packs two 15-bed dorms into a tiny space, but the foam-mattress beds are in need of a facelift. A small garden and kitchen make up the common areas, and an affiliated property in the East Village handles overflow. The hostel is not signed from the street. Prices include breakfast and taxes.

Chelsea International Hostel (☎ 212-647-0010; www.chelseahostel.com; 251 W 20th St; dm $27, d $40; ☺ to 10pm) Less personal, this modern building is known as a party scene, which congregates in the large outdoor common area reminiscent of a high school quad. Single-sex four-bed dorms come with in-room lockers and are human-sized. If you are dorm-bound in Chelsea, the area's two choices are a bit of a trade-off: do you want comfort or camaraderie? This one probably falls more to the comfort side.

Gershwin Hotel (☎ 212-545-8000; www.gershwin hotel.com; 3 E 27th St; dm $33, d $118-140) Just four blocks north of the Flatiron Building, this arty spot has the aura of a performance space and the room setup of a hostel rather than a hotel. In many ways, it's more bohemian in character than the far more famous (and pricey) Chelsea Hotel. The Gershwin's reputation and popularity make reservations a must, and it's becoming a popular hangout for young travelers who are staying in hostels and hotels elsewhere in the city.

Hotel 17 (☎ 212-475-2845; fax 212-677-8178; 225 E 17th St; s $65-90, d $80-110, tr $90-130; ☐) This is a surprise budget passport into swanky Gramercy Park. All rooms have shared bath and unremarkable decor. In the past, readers have complained that this hotel frequently overbooks; be diligent about confirming your reservation.

Gramercy Park Hotel (☎ 212-475-4320, 800-221-4083; www.thegramercyparkhotel.com; 2 Lexington Ave at E 21st St; d $210-240; ☐) This is a handsome old building standing sentinel over the namesake park (hotel guests get a key to the locked park). The hotel bar with faux-Rococo style furniture and dark velvet wall hangings is a popular watering hole.

Hotel Chelsea (☎ 212-243-3700; fax 212-675-5531; 222 W 23rd St; d from $135) This was once a low-cost hangout and is now cashing in on its fame as a literary landmark. The rooms are uneven in quality and the front desk clerk will snicker if you ask for Sid Vicious' room (since remodeled and re-numbered). Despite the steady increase in rates, the hotel holds steady to an ambience of gritty depravity. Smoking in the rooms is permitted.

Chelsea Inn (☎ 212-645-8989, 800-640-6469; www .chelseainn.com; 46 W 17th St; d without bath $90-100, with bath $130-160, ste $180-240) A set of joined townhouses offer well-sized rooms filled with a motley assortment of worn furniture. The crooked stairs leading to most rooms bypass the front desk, creating the feeling of an apartment building rather than hotel.

Chelsea Savoy Hotel (☎ 212-929-9353; fax 212-741-6309; 204 W 23rd St; s $100-115, d $125-175) Near Hotel Chelsea, this spot doesn't have much

---

ALTERNATIVES TO HOTELS

These networks match visitors with non-traditional accommodations in the city for nightly, weekly and monthly stays.

At Home New York (☎ 800-692-4262; www.athomeny.com) is a service connecting visitors to private properties and B&Bs, with a range of $75 to $150 for B&B singles; private apartments start at $120 per night.

Urban Ventures (☎ 212-879-4229, 800-437-8353; www.gamutrealty.com) has furnished apartments (not sublets) managed by a realty group typically used by business travelers; rates starts at $90 for double occupancy.

Bed & Breakfast Network of New York (☎ 212-645-8134, 800-900-8134) has guest rooms in owner-occupied apartments and apartment sublets throughout Manhattan; rates for singles range from $80 to $100, doubles range from $110 to $150 and apartments start at $150 a night.

in the way of personality but does offer reliable standard-issue rooms.

Inn at Irving Place (☎ 212-533-4600, 800-685-1447; www.innatirving.com; 56 Irving Place at E 17th St; d $325-495) Romantic and stunning, this converted townhouse has high ceilings, arched doors and 12 sumptuously decorated rooms. Just outside the door is an equally impressive row of manicured townhouses and window-box gardens.

Chelsea Pines Inn (☎ 212-929-1023; www.chelsea pinesinn.com; 317 W 14th St; d without bath $90, d with bath $110-139) The rooms in this hotel are named and decorated in honor of such celebrities as Sophia Loren and Paul Newman. The rooms are a healthy size and a complimentary breakfast is served in the garden patio or glassed greenhouse.

Colonial House Inn (☎ 212-633-1612, 800-689-3779; www.colonialhouseinn.com; 318 W 22nd St; r without bath $80-90, d with bath $125) In a converted townhouse, the Colonial House rooms feel like a sparse bachelor's apartment. Artwork by owner Mel Cheren, investor in the 1970s Paradise Garage dance club, decorates the walls. The rooftop deck gives visitors a quintessential New York experience: soaking up the sun or the stars from the 'commoners penthouse.' Discounts are available during the winter months and rates include breakfast. Friday and Saturday rates increase by $25.

Midtown
Map pp64-5

New York's greatest concentration of hotels can be found in its business district, Midtown. The transportation options are many and the big NYC attractions are here too, but Midtown has as much personality as a boardroom meeting. Hotel options range from grandiose for businesspeople on expense accounts, to corporate chains for large touring groups, to some of the city's most historic grande dames. Herald Square and nearby Little Korea begin to assume more 'neighborhood' attributes.

BUDGET & MID-RANGE

Herald Square Hotel (☎ 212-279-4017, 800-727-1888; www.heraldsquarehotel.com; 19 W 31st St; s with/without bath $85/65, d $110-140; 🖳) This no-frills hotel has sunny common spaces, decent-sized rooms and attractive prices. Don't be put off by the Plexiglas-enclosed check-in booth; the clientele is harmless.

Hotel Stanford (☎ 212-563-1500, 800-365-1114; fax 212-629-0043; 43 W 32nd St; s $120-150, d $150-180, ste $200, incl breakfast; 🖳) This is a good choice right in the middle of Little Korea, popular with young business travelers on meager expense accounts. The lobby is shopping-mall shiny with one of the slowest elevators in New York. While you're waiting, you'll have plenty of time to befriend the staff, many of whom have worked here for years.

Wolcott Hotel (☎ 212-268-2900; www.wolcott.com; 4 W 31st St; d $130-150) This 280-room Beaux Art hotel designed by John Duncan, the architect of Grant's Tomb, is a fading star in the grande hotel cosmos. The lobby still retains soaring ceilings and plasterwork dripping with details, but the rooms are ho-hum with outdated hotel decor.

Ameritania Hotel (☎ 212-247-5000; fax 212-247-5000; www.nychotels.com; 1701 Broadway; d from $150; 🖳) Next door to the Ed Sullivan Theater (where the *Late Show with David Letterman* is taped), this modern boutique hotel is decorated in angular shapes and trendy chocolate-brown stripes with a sharp-dressed staff. The rooms sport the greatest tragedy in boutique-mania: futon-style beds that look great in a brochure but sleep like college-days of yore.

Majestic Hotel (☎ 212-247-2000, 800-336-4110; fax 212-581-2248; 210 W 55th St; d $140-300) The Majestic is the new kid on the boutique-hotel block. The cramped lobby approximates a Pier-One version of an Arabian den and a TV screen in the elevator helps detract from the slow journey. Rooms are fashionably decorated with see-through glass bathrooms.

Wellington Hotel (☎ 212-247-3900, 800-652-1212; www.wellingtonhotel.com; 871 Seventh Ave; d $120-200; 🖳) A block south of Carnegie Hall, this well-worn hotel accommodates many touring orchestras and families, who request rooms with kitchenettes. The rooms have received a sunny makeover, but they aren't particularly big.

TOP END

Salisbury Hotel (☎ 212-246-1300; www.nycsalisbury .com; 123 W 57th St; s $279-300, d $300-329, ste from $330; 🖳) A block from Central Park, this hotel has large standard rooms and kitchenettes (with microwaves and refrigerators).

Ritz Carlton (☎ 212-308-9100; www.ritzcarlton.com; 50 Central Park South; d from $650; 🖳) Facing Central Park, this hotel has been remodeled to upmarket proportions. The lobby has a hushed library feel with embroidered couches arranged around delicate Japanese lacquer tables. And for the lottery winners among us, some rooms ($1000) have marvelous views of Central Park where the bordering skyscrapers form a toothy grin around the swath of green.

Royalton (☎ 212-869-4400, 800-635-9013; fax 212-869-8965; 44 W 44th St; d $250-320, ste from $360; 🖥) Publishing executives still love to lunch at the hotel's restaurant – an A-list must – but the hotel itself is easier to book. Ian Schrager has once again created a boutique hotel of form over function so easily a target for criticism. Recreating the claustrophobia of a floating city, the curved hallways lead to efficient quarters with portholes and other nautical details. The bathrooms are probably the best feature of this hotel: Frisbee-sized shower heads, 5ft soak tubs and slate floors make bathing fun again.

Algonquin (☎ 212-840-6800, 888-304-2047; www .algonquinhotel.com; 59 W 44th St; d $190-300; 🖥) Devotees of the *New Yorker* will want to pay homage to this literary temple. In honor of James Thurber, a famous guest, the hotel hallways are papered in recreations of his and other *New Yorker* cartoons. In the 1930s, the downstairs bar became the lunch spot for the Algonquin Round Table, a sharp-tongued group of writers that included Dorothy Parker, Alexander Woollcott and Robert Benchley. If you enter the hotel on a rainy day, remember Robert Benchley's famous quote (uttered under similar weather conditions), 'I'd like to get out of this wet suit and into a dry martini.' The rooms are bright and sunny with cozy beds and furniture that could pass for a real home rather than a sterile hotel room.

Waldorf-Astoria (☎ 212-355-3000, 800-925-3673; fax 212-872-4859; 301 Park Ave; d $250-400, ste from $450; 🖥) This legendary place is where members of the British royal family turn up for fundraising dinners, although the average guest is more likely a suburban mom than a Windsor. The lobby is quietly elegant but, surprisingly, not as grand as you would expect; rooms are tastefully decorated but not excessive in detail.

Plaza Hotel (☎ 212-759-3000, 800-527-4747; fax 212-546-5324; 768 Fifth Ave at Central Park South; d from $350; 🖥) This old gal is just plain famous, especially for the opulent Oak Room. The Beatles, Cary Grant and Grace Kelly are just a few of the big names who have slept here. The hotel even claims a role in the beloved children's books by Wendy Wasserstein featuring Eloise, a precocious six-year-old who lives on the top floor. The grand lobby is quite a treat even for a casual gawker, of which there are many. The rooms run the spectrum from simple to grandiose; the standards are well-appointed with tiled bathrooms but not nearly as luxurious as the lobby would suggest.

Sherry Netherland Hotel (☎ 212-355-2800; www .sherrynetherland.com; 781 Fifth Ave; d $374-525, ste $600-1500; 🖥) The real money stays in this discreet hotel across the street from the garish Plaza. Rooms are decorated with period antiques, rich yellow hues and marble bathrooms, suggestive of guest rooms in inherited townhouses. With 70% of the hotel serving as a residence for old-name families, the hotel is known for its privacy and impeccable manners. On publishing business in New York, Ernest Hemingway preferred to stay here rather than the more popular Plaza.

Times Square   Map pp64-5

Times Square is the default crash pad for hundreds of visitors unfamiliar with other parts of the city. There are plenty of bargains to be had here in hotels that range from simple to corporate, and the district is a hot attraction, especially on New Year's Eve. The drawback is that Times Square doesn't have any full-time residents so it lacks the charm of a neighborhood.

BUDGET & MID-RANGE

Big Apple Hostel (☎ 212-302-2603; www.bigapple hostel.com; 119 W 45th St; dm $30, d $80) A rough approximation of a NYC-college dorm, this spare facility is just off Times Square and is open 24 hours. Four-bed dorms are clean and tight. The drab private rooms aren't much of a bargain in the low season, but if you scored one in high season you'd feel like a highway robber.

Portland Square Hotel (☎ 212-382-0600, 800-388-8988; www.portlandsquarehotel.com; 132 W 47th St; s/d without bath $65/75, d with bath $90-110) This renovated hotel is a good budget option, just steps away from the middle of Times Square. Shared baths are clean and reliable; rooms, especially the singles, are quite small, but rates are an honest indicator of size.

Broadway Inn (☎ 212-997-9200; www.broadway inn.com; 264 W 46th St; s/d $100/139, ste $200, incl breakfast; 🖳) Just across the street from Restaurant Row, this is a former run-down Times Square hotel that has been turned into a reasonably priced small inn with 41 neat rooms. This is a 2nd-floor walk-up; suites have a kitchenette and pull-out bed.

Hotel Edison (☎ 212-840-5000, 800-637-7070; fax 212-596-6850; 228 W 47th St; s/d/tr/q $150/170/185/200) This was once a high-class spot for Broadway stars, but it caters mostly to tourists now. Rooms are solid with a few leftover architectural details from bygone days. The lobby is still a grand Art Deco affair and its colorful coffee shop of powder-blue walls and detailed plasterwork is still a hangout for theater people.

Paramount (☎ 212-764-5500, 800-225-7474; fax 212-354-5237; 235 W 46th St; d from $200; 🖳) Unmarked from the outside, this Ian Schrager hotel used to be the exclusive darling of hip media types; now the economy has everyone minding their purse strings, and the clientele is more diverse. At the time of writing the small rooms were being redecorated to include more business-traveler amenities.

TOP END

Top-end hotels in this area charge roughly $250 to $350 a night for their location – smack dab on Times Square – rather than their distinction. Rates skyrocket around New Year's Eve, especially for rooms with views of One Times Square. Since most of these hotels are chains, attractive discount packages are used to fill rooms in the low season. Options include: **Marriott Marquis** (Map pp64-5; ☎ 212-398-1900; 1535 Broadway); the **Novotel** (Map pp64-5; ☎ 212-315-0100; www.novotel.com; 226 W 52nd St); and the **Doubletree Guest Suites** (Map p64-5; ☎ 212-719-1600; 1568 Broadway at 47th St).

W Hotel Times Square (Map pp64-5; ☎ 212-930-7400; www.whotels.com; 1567 Broadway; d from $340; 🖳) One of five New York properties in the W cult-empire, this pet-friendly Times Square hotel is by far the most womb-like. The street-level entrance leads into a small antechamber surrounded on all sides by a cascading waterfall to an elevator that delivers you into a moody space of paper-thin columns, techno music and an enviously young staff. The rooms are classic W with all the techie gadgets, comfy beds, Aveda bath products and minimalist furniture.

Upper East Side & Upper West Side
Map pp66-7

Most people use the Upper West Side, primarily between W 70th St and W 80th St, as a base for visiting Museum Mile, the Natural History Museum or Lincoln Center. Rooms become hot commodities during the Thanksgiving Day parade. Above W 80th St, there are several inexpensive options that are good for a daytripper who plans to be in bed early. But if you're a night owl, the wad you'll blow on cab rides to return home after a pub crawl is better spent on a hotel closer to the action.

BUDGET & MID-RANGE

Hostelling International – New York (☎ 212-932-2300; fax 212-932-2574; 891 Amsterdam Ave; dm $29-35) This is the only HI facility in the city and it books out its 480 beds quickly during the summer season. As it is open for check-in 24 hours a day, it is a good place to head if you land in town at an odd time of the day. They have four-, six-, eight-, 10- and 12-bed dorms; there is a $3 surcharge per night for nonmembers. The hostel is near a public housing area, so women might prefer to travel in groups late at night.

International Student Center (☎ 212-787-7706; www.nystudentcenter.org; 38 W 88th St at Central Park West; dm $25) In a privileged section of the Upper East Side, this hostel in a converted brownstone welcomes non-NYC residents aged 18 to 30. There are co-ed and single-sex 15-bed dorms (with foam mattresses), an outdoor garden, kitchen facilities and a resident cat with the majestic name of China. The office is open 8am to 11pm, and check-ins must occur within this time.

Hotel Newton (☎ 212-678-6500, 800-643-5553; fax 212-678-6768; 2528 Broadway btwn 94th & 95th St; d $95-130; 🖳) This pet-friendly, 96-room hotel is a good budget option in a predominately Latino neighborhood.

On the Ave (☎ 212-362-1100, 800-497-6028; fax 212-787-9521; 2178 Broadway; d from $160, ste $300; 🖳) Got a hankering for something modern, but the budget can only handle a cookie-cutter chain hotel? This affordable boutique has the prerequisite muted colors and lean-line furniture without a shred of attitude. Europeans, mainly from Italy and Spain, are frequent guests here.

Harlem   Map p59

Two sister hostels in Harlem offer simple accommodations in renovated limestone houses that date back to the 19th century; both are unsigned from the street.

Sugar Hill International House (☎ 212-926-7030; www.sugarhillhostel.com; 722 St Nicholas Ave; dm $25, d $30; 🖵) Six- to eight-person dorms with co-ed and single-sex available; double rooms have shared bath. Weekly rates are available. To get here, take the B or C train to 145th St.

Blue Rabbit (☎ 212-491-3892; 730 St Nicholas Ave; dm $25, d $30) is just down the block from Sugar Hill.

EATING

New York is a crowded culinary cosmos that a mere mortal could never fully conquer. According to urban lore, you could eat out at a different restaurant every night for 46 years without exhausting your options. Some ally themselves with the upscale scene where models and Hollywooders pose and nibble. Others are experts in ethnic cuisine, tracking down hole-in-the-walls for steamed dumplings, *pho*, *samosas* and knishes. And then there is pizza – it's a personal mission for every New Yorker to claim they have discovered the best slice.

To explore the top end of the restaurant world without mortgaging your home, consider making lunch your most formal meal. Menus are typically discounted and tables are easier to garner for the midday meal. For dinner make reservations as far in advance as possible. For places that don't take reservations, expect a line. If New Yorkers see a line they instinctively cue regardless of their previous plans. One more tip: have a fistful of cash on hand as many small restaurants are cash-only.

Lower Manhattan   Map p63

Food is hard to find here after the workers go home and the streets are rolled up, but the lunch offerings are varied.

Pearl Palace (☎ 212-482-0771; 60 Pearl St; dishes $6-9; 🕑 11am-2:30am) This no-frills Indian restaurant fuels workers from nearby Wall St firms. Its weekday buffet lunch ($8) includes a salad bar in addition to tandoori specials. The à la carte menu has many vegetarian options.

Zigolini's (☎ 212-425-7171; 66 Pearl St; dishes $6-8; 🕑 7am-4pm) This family spot specializes in focaccia sandwiches; some of the specials are creatively named after the customers who suggested them. You can even create your own and perhaps achieve New York immortality.

Bridge Café (☎ 212-227-3344; 279 Water St; dishes $20-30; 🕑 11:30am-9pm) Underneath Brooklyn Bridge, this gourmet café is certified as the oldest pub in the city (a hotly contested title). Serving pork tenderloin and delicately seasoned salmon with an extensive wine list, the Bridge Café has come a long way since its days as the Hole in the Wall run by one-armed Charlie (a reference of this 'vicious' dive occurs in the book *Gangs of New York*).

Chinatown   Map p63

Chinatown is great for cheap eats. In shabby cafeteria-style restaurants, families assemble around big round tables deftly sampling the communal dishes with beak-like chopsticks.

Bubble drinks – sweetened soy shakes decorated with colorful balls of tapioca – have sprouted up around town creating the Chinatown version of a soda jerk. To sample these sweet concoctions, stop by **Green Tea Café** (☎ 212-693-2888; 45 Mott St; drinks $3; 🕑 11am-9pm) or **Tea & Tea** (☎ 212-766-9889; 51 Mott St; drinks $3; 🕑 11am-9pm).

BUDGET

Sweet-n-Tart Café (☎ 212-334-8088; 76 Mott St; dishes $5-6; 🕑 11am-10pm) Here's your opportunity to go 'off-roading' through an authentic Chinese menu that isn't altered for English-speaking clientele. Watercress dumplings in soup, Chinese vegetables with oyster sauce and scallion pancakes are some middle-of-the-road standards. Dishes are quite small, so order several to share with your dinner companion.

House of Vegetarian (☎ 212-226-6572; 68 Mott St btwn Canal & Bayard St; dishes $6-8; 🕑 11am-10pm) Vegans should check out this railcar-sized restaurant. The barbecue 'pork' and 'duck' dishes taste so much like the real thing, you'll wonder if the entire menu is a put-on.

Nha Trang (☎ 212-233-5948; 87 Baxter St; dishes $6-10; 🕑 10am-10pm) This Vietnamese spot is often packed at lunch with jurors and lawyers from the nearby city courthouses; they eat at crowded tables with other strangers. A filling meal can be had for less than $10 if you stick with dishes such as barbecued beef on rice vermicelli and shrimp spring rolls. For a legal speedball, chase the meal with the super-rich but delicious Vietnamese-style coffee with condensed milk.

New Pasteur (☎ 212-608-3656; 85 Baxter St; dishes $6-10; ☺ 10am-10pm) A virtually identical menu is available next door if Nha Trang is too crowded to squeeze into.

Great NY Noodle Town (☎ 212-349-0923; 28-1/2 The Bowery; dishes $4-10; ☺ 11am-9pm) The windows of this little storefront are obscured by steam from the big caldrons of soup broth. On a chilly day, their assortment of noodle soups and rice *congee* will chase away any winter blues.

MID-RANGE & TOP END

Hee Win Lai (☎ 212-285-8686; 28-30 Pell St; dishes $15; ☺ 11am-10pm) Cheap and tasty, Hee Win Lai specializes in dim sum at communal tables packed with locals. Just remember, you don't have to know what you are eating to like it.

Peking Duck House (☎ 212-227-1810; 28 Mott St; dishes $20; ☺ 11am-10pm) Former mayor Ed Koch is a proud patron of this Chinatown institution. Everyone says to stick with the specialty: Peking duck. Don't expect to find your meal hanging in the front window, though. This sleek restaurant bucks the typical Chinatown-disdain for decor.

Little Italy   Map pp60-1

Along Mulberry St, restaurants set up outdoor tables overflowing with out-of-town visitors who want a spectacle. Some say the key to a good meal in Little Italy is to avoid restaurants where the manager hangs out in the street trying to drum up business; good luck finding such a thing.

A better rule of thumb is to pick a place that makes you feel comfortable based on your own capricious criteria and order a light meal or dessert rather than blowing a full meal. The complaints on Little Italy restaurants run from mediocre to barely cooked food, so tread lightly.

Please note that Little Italy restaurants are notorious for adding a 25% service charge onto the bills of people they suspect of being tourists (while providing service that does little to justify that percentage tip).

Caffé Roma (☎ 212-226-8413; 385 Broome St; dishes $5; ☺ 9am-9pm) For a midday break, park yourself at an outdoor table with a cannoli and espresso at this famous corner guard.

Lombardi's Pizza (☎ 212-941-7994; 32 Spring St btwn Mott & Mulberry St; dishes $11-14; ☺ 11:30am-11pm Mon-Sat) These ovens are credited with starting the pizza phenomenon. Established in 1905, this brick-oven pizzeria serves only pies and delicious half-moon calzones. The fresh mushroom pie comes with three different kinds of *fungi*. Come early, especially on weekends, as the faithful quickly outnumber seating capacity.

Di Palo Fine Foods (☎ 212-226 2561; 206 Grand St; ☺ 10am-6pm Mon-Sat) One of the neighborhood's last grocery stores, Di Palo's is a good spot for a self-catered Italian picnic. Feast on fresh mozzarella, cold cuts, a loaf of bread and a bottle of wine.

Lower East Side   Map pp60-1

Some of the city's best traditional delis call this immigrant neighborhood home. You'll also find late-night eats for the pub-crawling crowd.

Bereket (☎ 212-475-7700; 187 E Houston St at Orchard St; dishes $5-10) This 24-hour kebab joint is popular with NYC's finest as well as bleary-eyed bar-crawlers.

Katz's Deli (☎ 212-254-2246; 205 E Houston St at Ludlow St; dishes $10; ☺ 7am-2am) You absolutely must make the pastrami pilgrimage to Katz's Deli before you leave New York. There are two things you should know before stumbling inside: first, you must take a ticket as you enter, next you must not reenact the faux climax scene (filmed here) from *When Harry Met Sally*. Throw in a chocolate egg creme for a quieter taste of ecstasy.

teany (Tea NY; ☎ 212-475-9190; 90 Rivington St btwn Ludlow & Orchard St; dishes $7, tea $5; ☺ 11am-10pm) Brainchild of pop maestro Moby, this tea bar and vegan shop imports a soothing mood to New York's frenetic lifestyle. In a pure white basement space filled with power pop tunes (supposedly mixed by Moby himself), guests thumb little notebook–sized menus detailing the 90 varieties of tea harvested from every cool hillside on the planet. Non-meat and non-dairy items, like triangle sandwiches and salads, also grace teany's repertoire.

Yonah Shimmel Bakery (☎ 212-477-2858; 137 E Houston St btwn Eldridge & Forsyth St; dishes $5; ☺ closed Sat) This world-famous bakery is about a century old – not bad for a place that specializes in potato knishes. There are eight varieties of potato knishes, five more of cheese and more bagels and bialys to choose from.

El Castillo de Jagua (☎ 212-982-6412; 113 Rivington St at Essex St; dishes $3-15; ☺ 11am-11pm) This Dominican lunch counter draws in an interesting mix of Lower East Siders, from tattooed musicians waking up at 3pm to Spanish-speaking families catching an early dinner. Huge portions of *bistec salteado* (pepper steak) and *cabrito guisado* (goat stew) give diners a lot to tackle.

SoHo & Tribeca

SoHo and Tribeca are definitely trendy, but there are some exciting food experiments as well as charming bistros to indulge a more sophisticated palate.

BUDGET & MID-RANGE

Souen (Map pp60-1; ☎ 212-807-7421; 210 Sixth Ave at Prince St; dishes $10-12; ☺ 11am-11pm) The city's longtime macrobiotic restaurant, Souen does creative salads, strict macrobiotic mains as well as fish and noodle soups.

Spring Street Natural (Map pp60-1; ☎ 212-966-0290; 62 Spring St at Lafayette; dishes $10-15; ☺ 11am-10pm) A bit of a zoo, this huge restaurant does a brisk business of meatless American classics (grilled tempeh burger) and beautiful salads. Outdoor sidewalk tables catch the rays on a gloriously lazy weekend, and supposedly the organic wines on the menu don't give you a hangover.

Lucky Strike (Map pp60-1; ☎ 212-941-0772; 59 Grand St; dishes $10-15; ☺ 11am-midnight) Sporting a funky garage-band cool, this French bistro scrawls its rotating menu on huge mirrors overlooking the tables. It gets very crowded late on Friday and Saturday when a DJ plays the front room, and is good for a late-night meal when nutrition is more important than grease quota.

Le Jardin Bistro (Map pp60-1; ☎ 212-343-9599; 25 Cleveland Place; dishes $20; ☺ 11am-10pm) When everywhere else is packed for brunch-mania, Le Jardin Bistro is pleasantly off the radar, but squarely on the culinary map. Its sedate backyard patio is shaded by a grape arbor and decorated with ceramic frogs (get it?). Tuna tartare and steamed mussels are luscious options.

Fanelli's Café (Map pp60-1; ☎ 212-226-9412; 94 Prince St; dishes $10-12; ☺ 11am-2am) This dark, smoky bar with a pressed-tin ceiling is a grizzled old-timer predating the artists and the coutures. Burgers and pub grub make up the solid-food portion of the menu.

Balthazar (Map pp60-1; ☎ 212-965-1785; 80 Spring St at Crosby St; dishes $10-20; ☺ noon-1am) A buxom brasserie of Parisian affectation, this celebrity-studded spot is hard to get into; supposedly they have a private reservation line for 'somebodies' rather than 'nobodies.' But the restaurant is so stunning that even the unaffected stare longingly through the floor-to-ceiling windows into the crisp interior. If you manage to score a table, remember to bask in the restaurant's whirlwind of importance.

Walker's (Map p63; ☎ 212-941-0142; 16 N Moore St; dishes $7-13; ☺ 11am-2am) A classic watering hole, Walker's has resisted the downside of gentrification (overpriced food) by staying true to straightforward fare – sliced turkey sandwiches and hamburgers. Jazz combos play Sunday nights and there's no cover charge.

TOP END

Kitchen Club (Map pp60-1; ☎ 212-274-0025; 30 Prince St at Mott St; dishes $20-25; ☺ noon-3:30pm Tue-Fri, 6pm-11:30pm Tue-Sun) Chef-owner Marja Samson works in full view of her dinner guests as if they had been invited to her home rather than wandering anonymously into a restaurant. She's a bit eccentric, if not a performance artist, but her French bulldog, Chibi, might really run the whole affair. The menu dances with Japanese and Western ingredients with the same sort of flamboyance.

Chanterelle (Map p63; ☎ 212-966-6960; 2 Harrison St; prix fixe lunch $38, dinner $84; ☺ noon-3pm, 6-10pm) Extravagant prix fixe meals take the anxiety out of ordering, so you have time to charm your dinner companion at this romantic French restaurant. The seafood sausage is a perennial favorite and the cheese platters are heavenly. Reservations are required weeks in advance.

Nobu (Map p63; ☎ 212-219-0500; 105 Hudson St; prix fixe $120, dishes $15-25; ☺ dinner) Remember the episode of *Iron Chef* when Chef Matsuhisa (Iron Chef Japan) splayed flim-flam chef Bobby Flay? To applaud such a fine cooking battle, save your pennies for a tribute to Chef Matsuhisa at his award-winning restaurant, which helped ignite America's love affair with raw fish. Go for the creative fusions rather than straightforward sushi, which can be found elsewhere at more reasonable prices. If the wait and the prices are too steep, go next door to the less formal **Nobu Next Door** (Map p63; ☎ 212-334-4445; 105 Hudson St; dishes $14-20; ❤️ dinner).

Greenwich Village   Map pp60-1

The Village has an amazing variety of restaurants, from cheap grub shops for NYU students to romantic cafés on Cornelia St.

Pasticceria Bruno and **Rocco's Pastry & Espresso Café** (243 & 245 Bleecker St; dishes $4; ❤️ 10am-6pm) In the Italian enclave of Bleecker St, you can peruse the sweet pastry displays side-by-side a cast of neighborhood personalities.

Jon Vie (☎ 212-242-4440; 492 Sixth Ave btwn 12th & 13th St; dishes $2-4; ❤️ closed Mon) This is a traditional French bakery where you can get a cozy table to enjoy a petit four, black-and-white cookie or a cup of coffee.

Cones (☎ 212-414-1795; 272 Bleecker St; cones $2-3; ❤️ 11am-7pm) Run by self-proclaimed 'ice-cream artisans,' their Italian-style ice creams and sorbets are a great respite from the summer heat.

Shopsin's General Store (☎ 212-924-5160; 54 Carmine St btwn Bedford & Bleecker St; dishes $10-15; ❤️ breakfast & lunch Tue-Sun) Quirky Shopsin's proudly presents diners with a 10-page menu (small type) that reads like a food dictionary covering everything from apple crisp to Senegalese cherry soup. Amazingly it is all good, which begs the question 'how is that possible'? Kenny and Eve Shopsin run the show and have been known to enforce arbitrary rules (absolutely no parties of five even if you sit at separate tables), but most of these horror stories are just restaurant lore. The neighborhood regulars might be the most sensibly dressed in all of New York, so stopping in for lunch is a good pick-me-up if you've been feeling down about your lousy wardrobe.

El Faro (☎ 212-929-8210; 823 Greenwich St; dishes $20; ❤️ dinner) This classic Spanish restaurant is quiet during the week but impossibly crowded on Friday and Saturday nights. The decor hasn't changed in 20 years, nor have the waiters. Main dishes, such as the spicy shrimp Diablo or a million varieties of paella, may seem pricey, but are enough to feed two people.

Rocco (☎ 212-677-0590; 181 Thompson St; dishes $15-20; ❤️ noon-11pm) Just north of Houston St, this old-school trattoria is a favorite for Village eccentrics. The friendly and attentive staff are happy to provide your favorite dish even if it's not on the menu. Don't confuse this

60-year-old establishment with the similarly named restaurant that appeared in the reality TV show.

Marinella (☎ 212-807-7472; 49 Carmine St at Bedford St; dishes $12-16; ❤️ 11am-11pm) This family-friendly restaurant is definitely a locals' spot. Fresh pastas and daily specials are sure-fire bets.

Cornelia St is a charming, tree-lined way with an unbeatable lineup of dining options. **Cornelia St Café** (☎ 212-989-9319; 29 Cornelia St; dishes $7-17, brunch $8.50), with its Parisian-style café tables, is a good spot for an afternoon aperitif to catch the evening breezes across the island. **Pearl Oyster Bar** (☎ 212-691-8211; 18 Cornelia St; dishes $20-25; ❤️ closed Sun) and **Little Havana** (☎ 212-255-2212; 30 Cornelia St; dishes $17-20; ❤️ closed Mon) are other neighborhood favorites.

Tomoe Sushi (☎ 212-777-9346; 172 Thompson St; dishes $15-25; ❤️ Wed-Sat) Reputedly the best sushi in the Village, Tomoe attracts a long line of sushi devotees. If you can catch it on a lean night, you're in for a treat.

Moustache (☎ 212-229-2220; 90 Bedford St btwn Grove & Barrow St; dishes $7-10; ❤️ 11am-10pm) This cramped Middle Eastern restaurant will elevate your appreciation of the lowly chickpea. The restaurant is awash with smells of mint tea and pungent garlic. Surprise, baba-ganoush is really supposed to taste like grilled eggplant, who knew?

Grange Hall (☎ 212-924-5246; 50 Commerce St at Barrow St; dishes $7-15; ❤️ 11am-10pm) This renovated neighborhood tavern has a beautiful wooden bar, serves organic foods and isn't shy about huge portions of American classics. The smoked trout salad appetizer is a meal in itself.

Cowgirl (☎ 212-633-1133; 518 Hudson St at W 10th St; dishes $10-15; ❤️ 11am-midnight) This rowdy frontier-style grub shop shows ninny New Yorkers how the West was won: with huge portions of enchiladas, deep-fried catfish and chicken-fried steak.

Tartine (☎ 212-229-2611; 253 W 11th St; dishes $5-12, brunch $10; ❤️ 10am-10pm) This neighborhood doll claims a sunny corner with outdoor tables and deeply engaged diners. The menu traipses through French bistro fare with a few American surprises. Cash only.

Babbo (☎ 212-777-0303; 110 Waverly Place btwn MacDougal St & 6th Ave; prix fixe $65, dishes $20-30; ❤️ dinner) Part of Mario Batali's Italian empire, exquisite Babbo teaches Americans what real Italian food is. Fluffy gnocchi,

NEW YAWK INVENTIONS

Hot dogs, pretzels, pizza and bagels – while not the sole inventor of these American fast-food classics, New York has religiously upheld their consumption. From streetcarts camped out on a popular corner, whole meals and delicious snacks can be pieced together without ever taking a seat inside a restaurant. Vendors originally hailing from the Middle East whip up brightly spiced meat-and-rice dishes on their portable grills emitting the smells of free advertising. Let the native New Yorkers do the research for you; if there is a line in front of a stall, then you've found the lunchtime score.

Finding the best pizza slice is more aggressively pursued than finding Mr/Mrs Right. An odd little pizza war has been waged in New York among several unrelated pizzerias named Ray's. Legend has it that one of the Ray's was 'the best pizza joint in the city' – the only problem is, no one can decide which one it is! While all claim to be the 'original Ray's,' no one quite seems sure what it was about this Ray's that prompted the good word of mouth. And none can claim the bragging rights of the real truly legendary Lombardi's (p116).

Bagels slathered with an inch-deep of cream cheese can be found at any streetcart or deli, but they achieve regal status at two revered bagel shops: **Ess-a-Bagel** (Map pp64-5; ☎ 212-980-1010; 831 Third Ave btwn E 50th St & E 51st St) and **H&H Bagels** (Map pp66-7; ☎ 212-595-8000; 2239 Broadway at W 80th St). These shops sell the classic hand-rolled, boiled bagels bald and shiny or embedded with sesame and poppy seeds, salt, onion or garlic bits, or everything.

marinated sardines and beef-cheek ravioli are all good explanations for Mario's stately figure. Reservations are difficult, but a few tables a night are open to walk-ins.

Delicia (☎ 212-242-2002; 322 W 11th St; prix fixe $27, dishes $15; 🕑 6-11pm) Fine Brazilian cooking in a cozy basement-level apartment is an unhurried way to unravel an evening. *Feijoada* (a classic Brazilian stew) and *moqueca de camarão* (squash, shrimp and coconut stew), as well as vegetarian options, will further incite your love affair with Brazil.

East Village & Alphabet City   Map pp60-1

Grab a slice of old New York from the Jewish and Ukrainian delis or heavyweight pizza joints. For a second course, foray into the land of ethical eating at one of the vegetarian cult shops.

Stromboli Pizza (☎ 212-673-3691; 83 St Marks Place at First Ave; slice $1.75, pie $10; 🕑 9am-midnight) This prototypical pizza-by-the-slice shop is a major contender for New York's best pizza award. The slices weigh in with a thin crispy crust, a delicate skin of cheese and no oil slicks.

Two Boots (☎ 212-505-2276; 37 Ave A at E 3rd St; pies $10; 🕑 noon-midnight) Marrying the cuisines of the geographic boots (Italy and Louisiana), Two Boots maintains pizza integrity with creative twists. Cornmeal crusts, spicy sauce and kooky toppings offer pizza burnouts a new sensation.

Veselka (☎ 212-228-9682; 144 Second Ave at E 9th St; dishes $5-8; 🕑 24hr) From the street Veselka seems like an ordinary coffee shop, but inside its Ukrainian heritage shines forth. Poppy seed bread, borscht, farina (oldskool porridge that was a favorite of Joey Ramone) are expertly assembled by stern-faced grill chefs. Sometimes their scowls relax into grimaces, and pancake-making takes on a performance art quality.

Second Ave Deli (☎ 212-677-0606; 156 Second Ave at E 10th St; dishes $7-12; 🕑 7am-midnight Sun-Thu, 7-3am Fri-Sat) This quintessential Jewish deli serves huge portions of matzo ball soup (with sprigs of fresh dill), corned beef sandwiches and potato pancakes. Each meal is served with a bowl of coleslaw and a plate of pickles – all to aid in digestion.

Kate's Joint (☎ 212-777-7059; 58 Ave B at E 4th St; dishes $4-10; 🕑 8am-10pm) This no-frills coffeehouse is proof that Alphabet City is still filled with yippies. A varied list of non-meat items, such as Buffalo un-chicken wings, infamous veggie-burgers and fake steak *au poivre*, thumbs its nose at the herd mentality in modern menus and yuppie prices.

Esashi (☎ 212-505-8726; 32 Ave A btwn E 2nd & E 3rd St; sushi $3-5, platters $15-20; 🕑 dinner) Good sushi restaurants are usually so mobbed that eating out feels more like a marathon than fun. Esashi is a refreshing change from the raw-fish race. The space is big enough to seat people comfortably with enough space to hunker down over a lacquered plate of daily specials like wild salmon, fresh octopus and toro. If you need to break out of the California roll rut, try the sanshoku roll (flying fish roe, avocado with tuna and yellow tail).

Quintessence (☎ 212-501-9700; E 10th St btwn First Ave & Ave A; dishes $14; ☽ 11am-10pm) Are you a lost Californian sporting a healthy tan and a toxin-free aura? No, but you just sweated out this morning's hangover at the 10th St Baths? To continue the cleanse, stop into tiny Quintessence, which specializes in 'raw' food (nothing is cooked or overly processed). This doesn't mean just salads, though. Lasagna has an uncooked version, as does the Indian dish *malai kofta*, but Quintessence's juices are by far the best items on the menu.

Chelsea & Gramercy Park   Map pp64-5

Chelsea and Gramercy Park are fraternal gourmet ghettos for fashionable eaters.

BUDGET & MID-RANGE

Empire Diner (☎ 212-243-2736; 210 Tenth Ave btwn W 22nd St &W 23rd St; dishes $5-15; ☽ 24hr) One of the most prominent all-night hangouts in the neighborhood has also become a popular lunch spot for weekend visits to the nearby galleries. Don't expect soggy fries and overcooked burgers; this sophisticated diner knows the difference between feta and Roquefort.

Sucelt Coffee Shop (Map pp60-1; ☎ 212-242-0593; 200 W 14th St; dishes $7; ☽ 8am-6pm) Homesick Cubans keep their lusty figures at this tiny lunch counter serving brightly colored plates of oxtail soup with fried plantains and potatoes. The *café con leche* is chewy and delicious.

Chelsea Market (☎ 212-243-6004; 75 Ninth Ave btwn W 15th & W 16th St; ☽ 9am-7pm) This food emporium is worth a detour not only for its fresh breads and produce stands but for the creative refurbishment of an industrial space. Big slabs of granite, shaped like torture-chamber beds, provide seating for tired toddlers. Indoor waterfalls muffle the echo of severe heels on the concrete floor and other unexpected pieces of art peep out of corners.

'wichcraft (☎ 212-780-0577; 49 E 19th St; dishes $7-10; ☽ 11am-10pm) 'wichcraft delivers savory desserts disguised as gourmet sandwiches. Try the cold cucumber soup, or sandwiches decorated with such combinations as roasted pork loin-pickled pepper relish-fontina or Sicilian tuna-fennel-olives-lemon. The tangy lemon bars are so sweet it will make your fillings itch.

Half King (☎ 212-462-4300; 505 W 23rd St; dishes $15-20; ☽ 11am-3pm) Lots of yarns get spun at this journalist hangout, cooked up by the authors of *The Perfect Storm* (Sebastian Junger) and *Triage* (Scott Anderson). A mighty selection of beers, hearty seafood chowder and crispy fish and chips help fuel the communal efforts to solve the world's problems or to recount assignments in far-flung places. Literary readings are held on Monday nights.

Rocking Horse Café (☎ 212-463-9511; 182 Eighth Ave btwn W 19th & W 20th St; dishes $10-15; ☽ 11am-midnight) The dining room of this Nuevo Latino restaurant looks like an installation of Miró paintings, filled with primary colors and shapes. Frisbee-sized tortilla chips dipped in smoky salsa fill the pre-main wait, a torturous one when you have a date to devour *camarones con papaya* (black tiger prawns, caramelized papaya, poblano chiles with *chipotle* tomato puree).

TOP END

Union Square Café (☎ 212-243-4020; 21 E 16th St btwn Fifth Ave & Union Square W; dishes $20-35; ☽ 11:30am-3:30pm, 6-11pm) Considered one of New York's best restaurants, this New American eatery boasts a delicious yellow-fin burger, tender lamb chops, refreshing desserts and a discounted wine of the night (in addition to a novella wine list). Good luck getting reservations.

Gramercy Tavern (☎ 212-477-0077; 42 E 20th St btwn Broadway & Park Ave; prix fixe $68, dishes $17-20; ☽ 11am-3:30pm, 5-11pm) Another superstar, Gramercy Tavern follows the seasons to match flavors and ingredients into a creative American menu. Savor an appetizer of grilled baby octopus with shaved fennel or a seafood stew spiked with coconut milk and saffron. The main dining room is tough to score a table, but the informal bar takes walk-ins.

Midtown   Map pp64-5

For good eats in Midtown, you've got to go way east or way west; there's a strange dead zone in the middle. Little Korea – the small enclave of Korean restaurants on 31st to 36th Sts between Broadway and Fifth Ave – is a fun evening destination. Little India, roughly Third Ave between E 27th and E 29th St, does a brisk lunchtime business.

BUDGET

Burger Joint (☎ 212-708-7414; 119 W 56th St btwn Sixth & Seventh Ave; dishes $4.50; ☒ closed Sun) Inside the echoing halls of the formal Parker Meridien Hotel, Burger Joint hides, like the Wizard Oz, behind a huge velvet curtain. Follow your nose to the small neon burger sign that marks the doorway into this greasy den serving NYC's best hamburger. Missy Elliott has passed through here, and scrawled her name on the graffiti wall along with other famous burger junkies.

Munson Diner (☎ 212-246-0964; 600 W 49th St at Eleventh Ave; dishes $5-10; ☒ 24hr) Cab drivers and late-night drifters hang out at this greasy spoon where the waitresses will you call you 'Hon.'

Madras Mahal (☎ 212-684-4010; 104 Lexington Ave btwn E 27th & E 28th St; dishes $7-10; ☒ 11am-10pm) In the area known as Little India, Madras Mahal is the only vegetarian restaurant in the city that conforms to kosher rules of preparation. Forget about all the greasy Indian food you've regretted eating; the lunch buffet and the business luncheon specials are delicious to tender eaters.

MID-RANGE

Hangawi (☎ 212-213-0077; 12 E 32nd St btwn Fifth & Madison Ave; dishes $10-20; ☒ 11am-10pm) Vegan and vegetarian versions of Korean classics are reverentially served at this stylish restaurant where diners sit at low tables with recessed floors for foot room. Stone bowl porridges, veggie pancakes and mushroom specials are just a few of the menu's highlights.

Dae Dong Restaurant (☎ 212-967-1900; 17 W 32nd St; dishes $15-20; ☒ 11am-midnight) For some reason going out to cook your own meal is a load of fun. At this Korean barbecue restaurant you get to play chef without having to do the dishes. *Gal-bi gui* (prime beef short rib) and *daeh-ji bul-go-gi gui* (thinly sliced pork loin) come out perfect on the tableside grill. A small army of *ponchon* (Korean appetizers like kim chi, spicy pickles, dried fish) clutter the table for further nibbling.

La Bonne Soupe (☎ 212-586-7650; 48 W 55th St; dishes $10-15; ☒ 11am-11pm) A cute bistro of checkered tablecloths and exposed brick walls, La Bonne Soupe is a much-needed culinary oasis amidst salad bars and power-lunch spots. The space is cramped but the crowd of cooing couples or tweed jackets don't seem to mind; they are more engaged by the good soups (mushroom and barley, French Onion soup or minestrone) as well as French specialties.

Brasserie Les Halles (☎ 212-679-4111; 411 Park Ave S; dishes $12-20; ☒ 11am-11pm) Unpretentious and affordable, this French steakhouse and butcher has landed on some travelers' itineraries thanks to chef Anthony Bourdain's book *Kitchen Confidential*. Follow the subtle hint of a steak knife at each place setting and choose from 'La Grillade' offering no less than five cuts of steak (grown in the good ole USA) plus veal and lamb chops.

TOP END

Michael Jordan's Steakhouse (☎ 212-655-2300; 23 Vanderbilt Ave; ☒ 4-10pm Sun-Thu, 4pm-midnight Fri-Sat) This is smack in the middle of Grand Central Station, on a balcony overlooking the concourse. Despite its celebrity owner (usually a sign of poor food), this place is getting raves for its steak and lobster, though you pay for the setting and the name – about $50 per person.

Oyster Bar & Restaurant (☎ 212-490-6650; Grand Central Terminal; dishes $10-20; ☒ closed Sun) Tucked into the vaulted ceilings of Gustavino tile in Grand Central Terminal, this perennial favorite smells like the ocean and salt marshes that the terminals' trains can deliver you to. Grab a seat at the crowded lunch counter to watch the oysters get shucked or the rounded pots of chowder and bouillabaisse get tended to. On any given day there are at least two dozen types of oysters available from as far away as Washington State.

Aquavit (☎ 212-307-7311; 13 W 54th St btwn Fifth & Sixth Ave; prix fixe $90; ☒ 6-11pm) The main dining room is in a stunning six-story glass-enclosed atrium complete with a silent waterfall. Beginning with an odd twist: Ethiopian-born, Sweden-raised chef Marcus Samuelsson enjoys matching seemingly unmatchables. First he introduced Americans not just to Scandinavian cuisine, but to haute Scandinavian cuisine. Then his James Beard–winning menu pokes holes in food conventions. How about gravlax with beet sorbet or goat-cheese cheesecake? Why not?

Le Cirque 2000 (☎ 212-303-7788; 455 Madison Ave btwn 50th & 51st St; ☒ noon-3:30pm, 6-11pm) Filled with fine crystal and china settings lightened up by a beautiful vaulted mosaic ceiling and stained-glass windows partially obscured by reams of colorful bunting, this

---

PRE-THEATER DINING

Widely touted Restaurant Row is the block of W 46th St between Eighth and Ninth Aves, but locals use the name to refer to almost all the restaurants west of Times Square. Sadly the moniker is more of a marketing tool than a phenomenon. So what's a hungry theatergoer to do? Never fear, honest food is still within striking distance of Times Square. **Joe Allen** (☎ 212-581-6464; 326 W 46th St; dishes $15-20), an official Restaurant Row denizen, is the most reliable of the bunch, serving standard American classics to a conservative crowd. **Basilica** (☎ 212-489-0051; 676 Ninth Ave btwn 46th & 47th St; prix fixe $21) does a well-regarded four-course Italian set menu.

The area that used to be despairingly called Hell's Kitchen is cooking up some great international meals these days. **Zen Palate** (☎ 212-582-1669; 663 Ninth Ave at W 46th St; dishes $10-20) serves an exclusively vegetarian menu of high art and Asian flavors; its attached café is a less formal affair. **Uncle Nick's** (☎ 212-245-7992; 747 Ninth Ave btwn W 50th & 51st St; dishes $12-15) offers a taste of the Aegean with its mouthwatering kebabs; service is hit or miss here. **Grand Sichuan** (p122) delivers authentic and delicious Chinese meals in a banquet-style dining room.

Reservations are recommended for all of these restaurants.

---

elegant spot in the historic Villard Houses features a nightly 'classic' as well as a menu full of innovative, serious cuisine such as tripe à l'Armagnac. The five-course tasting menu ($90) will leave you fat and happy.

Times Square & Hell's Kitchen
Map pp64-5

The options in Times Square proper are straight out of a suburban mall. For a delicious collection of small international eateries head west toward Hell's Kitchen (Ninth Ave between W 42nd St and W 57th St).

Mee Noodle Shop (☎ 212-765-2929; 795 Ninth Ave; dishes $5; ⏰ 11am-11pm) This is part of the city's best chain of cheap Chinese restaurants, serving a hearty bowl of noodle soup. Mee serves the same menu at two other locations: 922 Second Ave at 49th St, and 219 First Ave at 13th St (Map pp60-1).

Island Burgers and Shakes (☎ 212-307-7934; 766 Ninth Ave; dishes $6-8; ⏰ closed Sun) This shoebox-sized place serves churascos, a juicy breast-of-chicken sandwich that comes in more than 50 different varieties. As the menu explains, though, they just don't have the space to make French fries, so consider a baked potato instead.

Grand Sichuan (☎ 212-582-2288; 745 Ninth Ave btwn W 50th & 51st St; dishes $10-15; ⏰ 11am-midnight) Szechuan-style food in America has never before been treated so kindly. Its multipage menu reads like a propaganda newsletter: Grand Sichuan is on a one-restaurant campaign to prove that freshly butchered chickens (the technique of Chinese cooks) are more flavorful and tender than their

American frozen counterparts. Waitstaff are happy to prove the point through a blind taste test. Deeper into the menu are the dishes inspired by Chinese TV dramas, such as the 'green parrot with red mouth' (whole spinach with fresh ginger sauce and red oil). Other winners include the crunchy appetizer of cucumber with garlic and sesame and the ritualistic soup dumplings. Ask for a demo on eating soup dumplings before stumbling into a bite of scalding broth.

Upper East Side
Map pp66-7

Eating options become meager in this posh residential neighborhood. It's a shame, because a steady supply of famished tourists stumble through en route to Museum Mile.

Favia Lite (☎ 212-223-9115; 1140 Second Ave at E 60th St; dishes $15-20; ⏰ 11am-10pm) This is a healthy Italian restaurant near the 59th St Bridge that serves surprisingly tasty pasta main dishes, listing calories and fat content for every menu item. The large grilled-chicken pizza uses skimmed-milk or soy mozzarella upon request.

Lexington Candy Shop (☎ 212-288-0057; 1226 Lexington Ave at E 83rd St; dishes $10-15; ⏰ 11am-8pm) A picture-perfect lunch spot, Lexington Candy Shop comes complete with an old-fashioned soda fountain and some of the most reasonable fare in one of the city's most expensive neighborhoods.

Café Greco (☎ 212-737-4300; 1390 Second Ave btwn 71st & 72nd St; dishes $10-15; ⏰ noon-4pm, 5-11pm) This Greek restaurant serves continental dishes and a good brunch on the weekend.

Upper West Side   Map pp66-7
College grub shops merge with high-powered pre–Lincoln Center dining options. The major avenues that bisect this neighborhood, however, siphon the village ambience of other restaurant zones in the city.

BUDGET & MID-RANGE
Tibet Shambala (☎ 212-721-1270; 488 Amsterdam Ave btwn W 83rd & 84th St; dishes $8-10; ☽ 11am-10pm) The menu is split evenly between meat and vegetarian dishes hailing from the stark land of Tibet.

Café Lalo (☎ 212-496-6031; 201 W 83rd St at Amsterdam Ave; dishes $5; ☽ 9am-9pm) Dessert-lovers rejoice. This attractive café maintains a 14-page menu of pastries, and you can spend an entire rainy afternoon here reading the dozens of newspapers and magazines on offer.

Café con Leche (☎ 212-595-7000; 424 Amsterdam Ave btwn 80th & 81st St; dishes $7-10; ☽ 11am-11pm) A good spot for lunching after the Natural History Museum, this neighborhood café dishes up authentic Latin American fare – rice, beans and plantains accompanying all manner of beef, chicken and seafood dishes – in a casual kid-friendly atmosphere. The feisty paella feeds two.

Hungarian Pastry Shop (☎ 212-866-4230; 1030 Amsterdam Ave; dishes $3-7; ☽ 8am-11pm) Across the street from St John the Divine, this famous Columbia University hangout has been the birthing room for many a sluggish novel and the therapy room for stressed-out students. Try the Hungarian coffee spiked with almond extract and whipped cream – now doesn't life seem better?

Taqueria y Fonda la Mexicana (☎ 212-531-0383; 968 Amsterdam Ave btwn 107th & 108th St; dishes $10; ☽ 11am-1am) Mexican food in New York is sorely underrepresented, making this cramped space all the more attractive, especially if you've worked up an appetite on safari in the northern reaches of Central Park. Tucked into a laid-back neighborhood filled with strolling families and enthusiastic dogs (and their walkers), Taqueria y Fonda serves huge portions of food chaperoned by spicy salsa and warm spongy tortillas. The quesadilla gets a judicious helping of guacamole, cilantro and tomatoes.

TOP END
Tavern on the Green (☎ 212-873-3200; Central Park West at W 67th St; dishes from $30; ☽ 11am-11pm) Once of New York's most famous and scenic restaurants, the consensus is that this is an expensive tourist trap. If you are curious, skip the food and head straight for the back garden and take a cocktail amid the whimsical topiaries.

For planning your own meals, try two neighborhood mainstays: **Zabar's** (☎ 212-787-2000; Broadway at W 80th St) and **Fairway Market** (☎ 212-595-1888; 2127 Broadway at W 74th St).

Harlem   Map p59
Harlem is justifiably famous for its soul food – fried chicken, macaroni and cheese, collards and other Southern home-cooking favorites. Fattening, sweet and salty, soul food makes no apologies for being everything that is unhealthy for you. Don't come to Harlem and order a salad, you'll be disappointed.

Sylvia's (☎ 212-996-0660; 328 Lenox Ave; dishes $8-12; ☽ 11am-10pm) This is by far the most famous restaurant in Harlem. Sylvia is a native South Carolinian who started out in New York working at a neighborhood coffee shop and has expanded to her own full-service restaurant (with Sunday afternoon gospel brunch; call for reservations) and a line of soul-food products. Detractors criticize Sylvia's for being over-rated, but no one knows fried chicken and macaroni and cheese like the crowd that frequents her lunch counter.

Copeland's (☎ 212-234-2357; 549 W 145th St near Broadway; dishes $10-15; ☽ closed Mon) This formal restaurant does a jazz buffet on Friday and Saturday nights ($17 to $20) and gospel buffet on Sunday ($20); if you make reservations, be sure to arrive in your polished best. Next door is a stripped-down cafeteria with leaner prices; a recent sign in the cafeteria apologized to customers for having to raise the price of candied yams by $0.50.

Pan Pan (☎ 212-926-4900; 500 Lenox Ave; dishes $5-8; ☽ 10am-10pm) This is a popular diner with a long takeaway line. Dishes reflect more of a Caribbean flavor with Jamaican meat patties and coffee-and-roll breakfasts.

M&G Soul Food Diner (☎ 212-864-7326; 383 W 125th St; dishes $5-7; ☽ 11am-10pm) Just a short stroll from the Apollo Theater, M&G has a terrific old-school atmosphere with locals bent over their missals and huge plates of food.

The Bronx

The Bronx's most famous culinary neighborhood is in Belmont, an Italian enclave. Some of the restaurants in this eight-block neighborhood have been in business since WWI, including formal **Mario's** (☎ 718-584-1188; 2342 Arthur Ave; dishes $20) and family-style **Ann & Tony's** (☎ 718-933-1469; 2407 Arthur Ave; dishes $10-15). The latter accepts cash only.

On City Island, locals hang out at **Rhodes Restaurant** (☎ 718-885-1538; 288 City Island Ave; dishes $9-12), which serves standard pub specials and burgers.

Brooklyn

Brooklyn has yet to give Manhattan a real culinary rival, but if you're in the neighborhood you won't miss Manhattan's cramped dining rooms and wallet-constricting prices.

Sam's Restaurant (☎ 718-596-3458; 238 Court St, Brooklyn Heights; dishes $10-15; ☼ noon-10pm Wed-Mon) This favorite has a 1940s-style atmosphere, including the menu recommendation 'if your wife can't cook, don't divorce her – eat at Sam's.' Try a classic Italian hero.

Teresa's (☎ 718-797-3996; 80 Montague St, Brooklyn Heights; dishes $5-7; ☼ 7am-10pm) Near Hicks St, Teresa's is a Polish diner with fantastic weekly soups and pierogi. Stop in for a bite after window-shopping along the neighboring streets.

Junior's (☎ 718-852-5257; 386 Flatbush Ave Extension at DeKalb Ave; dishes $10-12; ☼ 11am-9pm) Near the Brooklyn Academy of Music, this spot serves some of the best New York–style cheesecake.

Patsy Grimaldi's Pizza (☎ 718-858-4300; 19 Old Fulton St; ☼ 11am-10pm) At Fulton Landing, this friendly family place serves renowned pizza pies. Descendents of the pioneering Manhattan pizza makers, Patsy Grimaldi uses a coal-fired oven to produce a crispy crust. This is a good spot to reward a crossing of the Brooklyn Bridge.

Coco Roco (☎ 718-965-3376; 392 Fifth Ave btwn 6th & 7th St, Park Slope; dishes $12-17; ☼ 6-11pm) Peruvian food gets a nuevo makeover at this bustling restaurant. Seviche is the hot topic with no less than seven interpretations: red snapper with papaya and ginger, clams with habanero and the finale *seviche de mixto* (mussels, shrimp, squid and red snapper with lime, lettuce, sweet potato and concha). Char-grilled Argentine beef also makes an appearance.

Tom's Restaurant (☎ 718-636-9738; 782 Washington Ave, Park Slope; dishes $5-10; ☼ 7am-midnight) Near the Brooklyn Museum of Art, Tom's Restaurant is a legendary, 70-year-old place that is a must for its egg cream sodas and its filling and hearty breakfasts.

Queens

Queens is a culinary marvel: restaurants serving down-home Mexican, Greek, Asian, Czech, Afghan and others make the borough a great food-hunting adventure.

Uncle George's (☎ 718-626-0593; 33-19 Broadway btwn 33rd & 34th St, Astoria; dishes $5-12; ☼ 24hr) Unabashed diners blow you kisses, baby lambs turn on spits and roasted goat head gives you the hairy eyeball. Rabbit, barbecued pork and red snapper are also available. Don't miss the *tzatziki*, or the roasted lemon potatoes.

Jackson Diner (☎ 718-672-1232; 37-03 74th St, Jackson Heights; dishes $10-20; ☼ 11am-10pm) This dingy converted coffee shop is famous for its *masala dosa* appetizer, a massive crepe with potato, onion and peas, and the *seekh kabob*, a long sausage made of tender lamb. Some consider Jackson Diner to be the best South Indian restaurant in the city.

La Porteña (☎ 718-458-8111; 74-25 37th Ave; dishes $15-18; ☼ 11am-10pm) Just around the corner from Jackson Diner, La Porteña serves Buenos Aires–style barbecue. Meals come to the table with *chimichurri*, a garlic-laden oil and vinegar sauce.

Lemon Ice King of Corona (☎ 718-699-5133; 52-02 108th S, Corona; ☼ 11am-9pm) The signature ice has chunks of lemon and is the perfect refresher for a summer day. The Lemon Ice King is about a mile from the subway. Walk south on 104th St to Corona Ave, turn left and walk two blocks to 52nd Ave; or take the Q23 bus to Forest Hills and get off on 108th St and 52nd Ave on the opposite corner from the shop.

Joe's Shanghai (☎ 718-539-3838; 136-21 37th Ave at Main St; dishes $7-15; ☼ 11am-10pm) Known throughout the city for its noodle dishes and steaming bowls of handmade dumplings, Joe's Shanghai also serves the oddball dish of raw drunken crab (weren't you partying with him last night?).

Shanghai Tang (☎ 718-661-0900; 135-20 40th Rd btwn Roosevelt & 41st Ave; dishes $7-16; ☼ 11am-10pm) The sleekest place in Flushing is the inexpensive Shanghai Tang, where the staff will enthusiastically guide newcomers through the menu choices.

KB Garden (☎ 718-961-9088; 136-28 39th Ave; dishes $3-8; 🕑 11am-10pm) Try a Sunday afternoon feast at KB Garden, where the dim sum will leave nary a dent in your wallet.

DRINKING

Last call in New York is 3:45am, which means most night-crawlers don't hit the streets until midnight. Drinks aren't cheap in Manhattan: beers usually run $7, cocktails $9. Bring along an ID, a chic outfit and plenty of self-assured attitude.

SoHo & Little Italy   Map pp60-1

Ear Inn (☎ 212-226-9060; 326 Spring St) Camped out in the old James Brown House (not the Godfather of Soul), this crusty bar once peered over the banks of the Hudson River and hosted a rough-and-tumble crowd of longshoremen. Today the river has receded, and the bar has moved on to sanitation workers and office-dwellers.

Double Happiness (☎ 212-941-1282; 173 Mott St btwn Broome & Grand St) This basement-level bar tunnels through an old apartment with a narrow skylight room and tables tucked into candlelit corners. Lots of pretty girls scan the crowd for a well-dressed Romeo amongst the wrinkled bards. It isn't signed but look for the steep stone steps.

Chibi's Bar (☎ 212-274-0025; 238 Mott St btwn Prince & Spring St) This romantic sake bar works its magic through smooth sounds of jazz and the refreshing flavors of sake-martinis. One drink packs a powerful punch.

Greenwich Village & West Village
                                        Map pp60-1

Bar d'O (☎ 212-627-1580; 29 Bedford St) This sleek lounge gets all dressed up for its weekly drag acts. Strangely it was voted most romantic bar in the city, proving the theory that nothing says 'I love you' like a she-man.

Chumley's (86 Bedford St btwn Grove & Barrow St) This old speakeasy is said to have inspired the term '86-it' (to get out in a hurry) as code for ducking out one of the alternative entrances before the cops raided the place. Stumbling across it is like discovering a secret society of fellow beer-drinkers. Look for the air-conditioning unit over an unsigned brown door. Cash only.

Corner Bistro (331 W 4th St) This age-old bar is a famous West Village spot for charred hamburgers and other late-night pub fare.

Marie's Crisis (☎ 212-243-9323; 59 Grove St) Devotees of Broadway musicals assemble around the piano and take turns performing for their unintended audience. When the mood is right the whole bar joins in. Cash only.

White Horse Tavern (☎ 212-989-3956; 567 Hudson St) This handsome bar was Dylan Thomas' last drinking hole and has seen almost every New York–based writer while away an evening. Even if you only write letters home to mom, you'll find this low-key pub a nice spot for a spell.

Hudson Bar & Books (☎ 212-229-2642; 636 Hudson St) This cigar bar is an interesting re-creation of a men's club; enjoy a Pimm's cup and recount the polo match; Tuesday night is whiskey night.

Blind Tiger (☎ 212-675-3848; 518 Hudson St at W 10th St) Gregarious, without pretension, this old-timers' joint keeps the good feelings flowing with daily specials on Brooklyn microbrews ($3.50 pints). Belgian beers also join the large selection for the beer aficionados.

Henrietta Hudson (☎ 212-924-3347; 438 Hudson St) This is a spacious lesbian bar and 'girl' where you can play pool or dance to DJ music.

East Village, Alphabet City & Lower East Side   Map pp60-1

Baraza (☎ 212-5309-0811; 133 Ave C btwn E 8th & E 9th St) Cheap *mojitos* help this mixed crowd of sensibly dressed lesbians and insensibly dressed heteros find their Latin-inspired Alpha City groove.

Uncle Ming's (☎ 212-979-8506; 225 Ave B btwn 13th & 14th St) This sexy bar on the 2nd floor over a liquor store has upholstered couches for languidly sipping designer cocktails. The bar is unsigned, adding to its mystery.

Orchard Bar (☎ 212-673-5350; 200 Orchard St) Pencil-thin scene-sters bottleneck around the front door of this long-running bar, but with dedication you can work your way to the back dance floor where DJs coax a groove from the vinyl platters; Wednesday night hosts a break-dance crew.

Luna Lounge (☎ 212-260-2323; 171 Ludlow St) Don't forget your threadbare Cramps T-shirt and blue eyeliner for this 1980s-revival bar. Live bands play nightly (no cover charge).

Arlene's Grocery (95 Stanton St btwn Ludlow & Orchard St) On Monday liquid-courage amateurs mount the stage with a real live band to sing punk and metal tunes.

Welcome to the Johnson's (☎ 212-420-9911; 123 Rivington St at Ludlow St) Credited for making 'white trash' hip, this faux double-wide living room comes with plastic-covered furniture and cheap Pabst Blue Ribbon ($1.50 during happy hour).

Mars Bar (25 E 1st St) A scruffy relic from the heyday of East Village punk, Mars Bar is a graffiti-covered hollow where tattooed kids caress bottles of beer and headbang to their favorite speed-metal riffs. Even with the thrasher tunes, the jukebox is everything you'd want in your home collection.

Swift's Hibernian Lounge (☎ 212-242-9502; 34 E 4th St) You could stage a cattle raid from the wooden tables of this medieval hall–like pub; instead you should just have another pint of Guinness and enjoy the live bands.

KGB (☎ 212-505-3360; 85 E 4th St) Dipped in a blood-red mood, KGB is one of the few bars you can actually have a conversation in; literary meetings and other artistic endeavors are sponsored here as well.

McSorley's Old Ale House (5 E 7th St) With a floor covered in sawdust and a thigh-high bar, McSorley's was the well-known setting for Joseph Mitchell's *New Yorker* short stories. It refused to admit women until the 1970s; today, it often has a long line of tourists waiting to get in.

Union Square   Map pp64-5

Pete's Tavern (☎ 212-473-7676; 124 E 18th St) Short-story writer O Henry is said to have written his Christmas story *The Gift of the Magi* in a front booth in this old-fashioned bar of dark wood and tiled floors; a modern bartender and dime-store historian jokingly theorizes that O Henry used to drink diet sodas.

Old Town Bar and Grill (☎ 212-529-6732; 45 E 18th St) A gruffer sort of place, Old Town fries a mean burger and will fry your cell phone if it rings indoors.

Midtown, Times Square & Hell's Kitchen   Map pp64-5

Siberia (W 40th St at Ninth Ave) Just east of the overpass, this USSR-themed dive bar used to be hidden in a subway stop, which reputedly was a communist propaganda drop point. Now it has moved to a converted garage marked only by an eerie red light over a heavy metal door.

Single Room Occupancy (SRO; W 53rd St at Ninth Ave) This chimney chute of a bar is lit only by flickering candles creating a mini-grotto to tasty beers and wines. It isn't signed, so look for a green moon-shaped light near 360 W 53rd St and ring the bell for entry.

Russian Vodka Room (☎ 212-307-5835; 265 W 52nd St) The outside awning says 'Attitude Adjustment Hour' but only your sobriety will get adjusted at this vodka-piano bar. Infused vodkas (ginger, horseradish, chocolate) go down easier than water and so does the caviar. Like they say in the motherland, 'live for today.'

Rainbow Room (☎ 212-632-5000; 30 Rockefeller Plaza) On the 65th floor of the GE Building, you must wear a jacket to partake in the sky-high outlook of the Empire State Building and beyond.

Upper West Side & Upper East Side

Saints (Map pp66-7; ☎ 212-222-2431; 992 Amsterdam Ave btwn 109th & 110th St) This is a quiet gay bar that welcomes a mixed crowd.

Subway Inn (Map pp66-7; ☎ 212-223-8929; 143 E 60th St) Just above the 59th St–Lexington Ave subway station, commuters and homeless

---

WHAT'S ON WHERE

NYC on Stage (☎ 212-768-1818) Twenty-four-hour information line for music and dance events.

Broadway Line (☎ 212-302-4111) Plays and musicals both on and off the Great White Way.

Clubfone (☎ 212-777-2582) Cabaret events, live music and dance.

All That Chat (www.talkinbroadway.com/forum) Audience members' reviews of new shows.

NYC Theatre (www.nyc.com/theater/) Reviews of on- and off-Broadway plays.

Sheckys (www.sheckys.com) Reviews of bars and clubs.

Broadway World (www.broadwayworld.com) For the latest dish (from trash talking to recommendations) on Broadway performances.

people stop in for the $3.50 Budweisers after a hard day at work. These aren't happy-hour prices, according to the bartender, but the prices tend to make people happy despite the hollow's gloominess.

West End (Map p59; 2911 Broadway btwn 113th & 114th St) A popular Columbia hangout, the West End counts Allen Ginsberg among its famous beer-swilling patrons.

ENTERTAINMENT

New York's entertainment scene is an attraction in its own right: Broadway musicals with legendary actors, high culture that defines the disciplines, emerging bands inventing the next wave in cool and watering holes of beautiful, stylish people. No single source could possibly list everything that happens in the city, but *Time Out* takes a good swing at it. *New York Times* and the *New Yorker* follow stage performances, and dance clubs and smaller music venues take out numerous ads in the *Village Voice*. The free papers such as *Metro* and *New York Press* all round up cultural events and do a good job of covering alternative theater in the East Village.

Theater

The heart of Broadway runs right through Times Square, which has long served as the center of New York's theater world. In general, 'Broadway' productions are those showing in the large theaters around Times Square. For theater locations, see the boxed text (opposite). 'Off Broadway' usually refers to dramas that are performed in smaller (200 seats or fewer) spaces elsewhere in town.

Prominent spots for off-Broadway performances include the following: **PS 122** (Map pp60-1; ☎ 212-477-5288; www.ps122.org; 150 First Ave at 9th St) and **Theater for the New City** (Map pp60-1; ☎ 212-254-1109; www.theaterforthenewcity.net; 155 First Ave btwn E 9th & 10th St). Low-budget, one-person plays and performances pop up at stages and theaters in the East Village.

TICKETS

The **TKTS booth** (☎ 212-768-1818) in the middle of Times Square sells same-day tickets to Broadway and off-Broadway musicals and dramas for half price or 50% off regular box-office rates. Note that TKTS accepts cash or traveler's checks only. Touts offering last-minute discounts to off-Broadway events also canvass the TKTS line with flyers. Box

---

TIMES SQUARE THEATERS

The following theaters appear on the map on pp64-5. For shows, times and reservations call ☎ 212-239-6200 or ☎ 212-307-4100.

Ambassador Theater (219 W 49th St)
Booth Theater (222 W 45th St)
Broadway Theater (1681 Broadway)
Circle In the Square Theater (1633 Broadway)
Eugene O'Neill Theater (230 W 49th St)
Ford Center for the Performing Arts (214 W 42nd St)
Gershwin Theater (222 51st St)
Helen Hayes Theater (240 W 44th St)
Imperial Theater (249 W 45th St)
John Golden Theater (252 W 45th St)
Lunt-Fontanne Theater (205 W 46th St)
Majestic Theater (W 44th St)
Marquis Theater (1535 Broadway at 46th St)
Music Box Theater (239 W 45th St)
Nederlander Theater (208 W 41st Street)
Neil Simon Theater (250 W 52nd St)
New Amsterdam Theater (214 W 42nd St)
Palace Theater (1564 Broadway at 47th St)
Plymouth Theater (236 W 45th St)
Schubert Theater (225 W 44th St)
Walter Kerr Theater (219 W 48th St)
Winter Garden Theater (1634 Broadway at 51st St)

---

offices usually release rush and standing-room tickets on the day of performance. About 6pm ask if there are any unclaimed VIP, press or cast tickets available.

The nearby **Times Square Visitor Center** (☎ 212-869-5453; 1560 Broadway btwn 46th and 47th St) also sells discounted tickets and vouchers to certain shows.

Telecharge (☎ 212-239-6200) is the main contact for Broadway and off-Broadway ticket sales by telephone. **Ticketmaster** (concerts ☎ 212-307-7171, performing arts ☎ 212-307-4100) has a lock on sales for most major concerts and sporting events.

Cinemas

New Yorkers take film very seriously, so going to the cinema can be a trying experience in the evening and on weekends. Independent films and career retrospectives are held at the **Film Forum** (Map pp60-1; ☎ 212-727-8110; 209 W Houston St), and Lincoln Center's **Walter Reade Theater** (Map pp66-7; ☎ 212-875-5600; 165 W 66th St),

---

A LIVE STUDIO AUDIENCE

Getting tickets to the popular network television shows taped in New York City requires star-struck determination. According to the CBS website, the *Late Show with David Letterman*, in the historic Ed Sullivan Theater (Map pp64-5; Broadway and 53rd St), is sold out for the foreseeable future. Cancellations do occur, and tickets are then offered on a first come, first served basis. Call the network's **stand-by ticket office** (☎ 212-247-6497) at 11am for day-of screenings.

Tickets for NBC's *Late Night with Conan O'Brien* can be obtained by calling **NBC Show Tickets** (☎ 212-664-3056) far, far in advance or by visiting the unaffiliated ticket vendor TVtickets.com. *Saturday Night Live* is so popular that tickets are given out on a lottery basis once a year; visit NBC's website (www.nbc.com) for how to join the lottery.

MTV fills its Times Square studio with pop-crazed teenagers for the tapings of *TRL*. To join the low-rise jeans audience, call ☎ 212-398-8549 or email trlcasting@mtvstaff.com. Comedy Central's the *Daily Show with Jon Stewart* enjoys an NYC locale; for tickets call ☎ 212-586-2477.

Most shows require audience members to be 18 years or older; visit the show's website for details.

---

which has wide, screening-room–quality seats. At **Anthology Film Archives** (Map pp60-1; ☎ 212-505-5181; 32 Second Ave), you can see fringe and low-budget European works.

The following specialize in foreign and low-budget independent films: the **Angelika Film Center** (Map pp60-1; ☎ 212-995-2000; cnr Mercer & Houston St); and the **Lincoln Plaza Cinemas** (Map pp66-7; ☎ 212-757-2280; Broadway & 63rd St).

Bryant Park (Map pp64-5; ☎ 212-883-2476; cnr 42nd St & Sixth Ave), right behind the New York Public Library, is the site of open-air film screenings on Monday evenings throughout summer. The park's information booth provides a schedule.

Classical Music & Opera

New York Philharmonic (www.newyorkphilharmonic .org) The renowned Philharmonic performs at **Avery Fisher Hall** (Map pp66-7; ☎ 212-721-6500; Lincoln Center) and still resists deviations from the standard repertoire. It also performs 'rush hour' concerts (lasting just 90 minutes) during the season.

Chamber Music Society of Lincoln Center (☎ 212-875-5788; www.chambermusicsociety.org) This company ranks as the foremost chamber music ensemble in the country. Its main concert season takes place in early autumn at Lincoln Center's **Alice Tully Hall** (Map pp66-7; ☎ 212-721-6500; Lincoln Center).

Metropolitan Opera (☎ 212-362-6000; www.met opera.org) New York's premier opera company offers a spectacular mixture of classics and premieres. It's nearly impossible to get into the first few performances of operas that feature such big stars as Jessye

Norman and Placido Domingo, but once the B-team moves in, tickets become available. It holds its season from September to April in its namesake Lincoln Center theater, **Metropolitan Opera House** (Map pp66-7; ☎ 212-362-6000; Lincoln Center, cnr W 64th St & Amsterdam Ave).

New York City Opera (☎ 212-870-5630) A more daring and affordable opera company takes the stage at the Philip Johnson–designed **New York State Theater** (Map pp66-7; ☎ 212-870-5570; Lincoln Center) for a split season that runs for a few weeks in early autumn and picks up again in the late spring.

Carnegie Hall (Map pp64-5; ☎ 212-247-7800; cnr 57th St & Seventh Ave) Visiting philharmonics and the New York Pops orchestra perform at this storied music hall. A schedule of monthly events is available in the lobby next to the box office.

Brooklyn Academy of Music (☎ 718-636-4100; 30 Lafayette Ave, Brooklyn) This prime outerborough spot for entertainment and is the oldest concert center in the US. It consists of the Majestic Theater and the Brooklyn Opera House, and it hosts concerts, operas and plays all year. You can call to reserve a spot on the bus that leaves from the corner of 51st St and Lexington Ave in Manhattan an hour before a performance. Or take the subway to Atlantic Ave.

Also recommended:

Merkin Concert Hall (Map pp66-7; ☎ 212-501-3330; Lincoln Center, 129 W 67th St) A more intimate venue for classical music.

Symphony Space (Map pp66-7; ☎ 212-864-5400; 2537 Broadway at 95th St)

Town Hall (Map pp64-5; ☎ 212-840-2824; 123 W 43rd St) This is also the site for lectures and readings.

Dance

New York is home to more than half a dozen world-famous dance companies.

New York City Ballet (☎ 212-721-6500; www.nyc ballet.com) Established by Lincoln Kirstein and George Balanchine in 1948, this company performs at the New York State Theater in Lincoln Center (Map pp66-7) during the winter. For generations little girls have fallen in love with ballet due to their performance of the *Nutcracker* during the Christmas holiday.

American Ballet Theater (ABT; ☎ 212-477-3030; www.abt.org) Largely classical pieces are performed by the ABT during the late spring and summer at the Metropolitan Opera House in Lincoln Center (Map pp66-7).

Joyce Theater (Map pp64-5; ☎ 212-242-0800; 175 Eighth Ave at 19th St) The most offbeat dance venue offers noncommercial companies the chance to shine. The Merce Cunningham and Pilabolus dance companies make annual appearances here.

City Center (Map pp64-5; ☎ 212-581-1212; 131 W 55th St btwn Sixth & Seventh Ave) hosts the **Alvin Ailey American Dance Theater** every December and hosts engagements by foreign companies.

Live Music
JAZZ
Jazz at Lincoln Center (Map pp66-7; ☎ 212-258-9800; 33 W 60th St; www.jazzatlincolncenter.org) The premier jazz-arts organization in the country, Jazz at Lincoln Center is headed up by living legend Wynton Marsalis, and hosts tributes to the jazz greats of swing, bebop and Afro-Cuban. The center has found a new home on Columbus Circle in the Frederick P Rose Hall.

Village Vanguard (Map pp60-1; ☎ 212-255-4037; 178 Seventh Ave; tickets $20-30) This basement-level space may be the world's most famous jazz club; it has hosted literally every major star of the past 50 years.

Blue Note (Map pp60-1; ☎ 212-475-8592; 131 W 3rd St; tickets $60) This supper club features some of the most storied names in jazz.

Knitting Factory (Map p63; ☎ 212-219-3055; 74 Leonard St) Spoken word, jazz, folk and experimental music is hosted in four performance spaces.

Fez (Map pp60-1; ☎ 212-533-2680; 380 Lafayette St) The popular Mingus Big Band plays every Thursday; other experimental music is featured the rest of the week.

Iridium (Map pp66-7; ☎ 212-219-3055; 48 W 63rd St) New jazz acts cut their chops here as do legends like McCoy Tyner.

Harlem's Cotton Club era is long gone, but there are still several places to hear jazz in Harlem, both modern and traditional. The old **Lenox Lounge** (Map p59; ☎ 212-722-9566; Lenox Ave & 125th St; tickets $5-15) is worth visiting anytime for its remarkable Art Deco interior.

ROCK, BLUES, FOLK & WORLD
CBGB (Map pp60-1; ☎ 212-982-4052; 315 The Bowery) The prototypical punk club is still going strong after 25-plus years.

Mercury Lounge (Map pp60-1; ☎ 212-260-4700; 217 E Houston St) Big names turn up at this intimate space.

Irving Plaza (Map pp64-5; ☎ 212-777-6800; 17 Irving Place) One of the best clubs of its size hosting indie acts.

Chicago BLUES (Map pp60-1; ☎ 212-924-9755; 73 Eighth Ave btwn 13th & 14th St) Visiting blues masters play at this low-key joint.

Washington Square Church (Map pp60-1; ☎ 212-545-7536; 135 W 4th St) International artists are brought to New York by the World Music Institute for concerts here and at other venues throughout the city.

Back Fence (Map pp60-1; ☎ 212-475-9221; 155 Bleecker St at Thompson) There's never a cover charge for this surviving folk music venue in Greenwich Village, and the bar is manned by 'Good Times' Charlie.

SOB's (Map pp60-1; ☎ 212-243-4940; 204 Varick St) Afro-Cuban sounds emanate from this SoHo club named for Sounds of Brazil.

Clubs

The days of huge underground dance clubs in Manhattan were mightily smitten by the Giuliani administration, which vigorously enforced a previously ignored law forbidding dancing in clubs without expensive cabaret licenses. Dating from the 1930s, this 'No Dancing' law was intended to prevent black-white mixing in Harlem jazz joints. Today's clubbers hope that the present administration will repeal the law, but until then only a few dance clubs remain as memorials to the days of the Tunnel and the Limelight.

Avalon (Map pp64-5; ☎ 212-807-7850; 660 Sixth Ave) Previously part of the Limelight's empire (London, Montreal), this recycled church complete with caged dancing girls has an unmarked door that leads to the bell tower.

Don Hill's (Map pp60-1; ☎ 212-334-1390; 511 Greenwich St at Spring St) This is a favorite with transvestites.

Nell's (Map pp60-1; ☎ 212-675-1567; 246 W 14th St) World beat, hip-hop and reggae fill the spaces of this former lounge.

Spectator Sports

Tickets for important major-league baseball games can be difficult to obtain. The season runs from late March to October and most games begin in the evening (around 7pm) or on weekend afternoons (around 1pm). The two cross-town rivals play a limited number of regular season inter-league games.

The National League **New York Mets** (☎ 718-507-8499; tickets $8-55) play in wind-swept Shea Stadium in Flushing Meadows, Queens; it's a 40-minute journey from Mid-town (subway: Willets Point-Shea Stadium). **NY Waterway** (☎ 800-533-3779; www.nywaterway .com; adult/child $16/12) offers direct service by water taxi to Mets' games departing Man-hattan and points in New Jersey.

The American League **New York Yankees** (☎ 718-293-6000; tickets $8-80) play at their legen-dary namesake stadium in the South Bronx, just 15 minutes from Midtown (subway: 161st St–Yankee Stadium). Like it or not, the New York Yankees are baseball's most famous team. The 26-time world champions claim a historic lineup dating from the 1920s when home-run sensation 'Babe' Ruth was snatched up from the Boston Red Sox. Yan-kee Stadium is still referred to as the 'House that Ruth Built,' because it was partly de-signed to suit his hitting style and was made large enough to fit the many fans who came just to see him. Other Yankee legends who became cultural icons include Lou Gehrig, Joe DiMaggio and Mickey Mantle.

Although New York is a baseball town, its high-profile basketball and hockey teams play in the famous 19,000-seat Madison Square Garden arena (Map pp64-5). The NBA **New York Knicks** (☎ 212-465-6741) and the NHL **New York Rangers** (☎ 212-465-6741) sell a huge number of season tickets, and so, generally, visitors must book seats through **Ticketmaster** (☎ 212-262-3424) or **Madison Square Garden's box office** (☎ 212-456-6741), or deal with the many scalpers who hover around the area on game nights.

Scalpers try to get a premium price for seats that already cost up to $200 for big games. When dealing with scalpers, the best strategy is to wait until after the 7:30pm game time, when prices drop – or merely head to a nearby bar to catch the game on TV.

The US Open Grand Slam tennis tourna-ment (www.usopen.org) is held in Septem-ber at Flushing Meadows Park, also home to Shea Stadium, the ballpark of the New York Mets.

SHOPPING
ANTIQUES

Top-level auctions are held at **Christie's** (Map pp64-5; ☎ 212-492-5485; 20 Rockefeller Plaza), which has sold items from John F Kennedy's es-tate, Marilyn Monroe's dresses and Frank Sinatra's personal items. **Sotheby's** (Map pp66-7; ☎ 212-606-7000; 1334 York Ave) specializes in paint-ings and fine furniture.

There are antique furniture stores on 59th St between Third and Second Aves. More stores are on Broadway, just below Union Square, and along E 12th St.

Vendors selling lighting, rare books, prints and other items of interest can be found at the **Metropolitan Art & Antiques Pavilion** (Map pp64-5; ☎ 212-463-0200; 110 W 19th St), and the **Garage Antiques Building** (Map pp64-5; 110 W 25th St; ☽ Sat & Sun). The nearby **Chelsea flea market** (Map pp64-5; W 25th St & Sixth Ave) is another hot spot for unloved antiques.

CAMERAS

B&H Photo-Video (Map pp64-5; ☎ 800-606-6969, 212-444-6615; 420 Ninth Ave btwn 33rd & 34th St; ☽ 9am-6pm Mon-Thu, 9am-1pm Fri, 10am-5pm Sun) This is a famous New York camera store where bargains can be found, but you need to be a savvy camera-user; the sales team is too aggressive to offer reliable hand-holding.

DESIGNER CLOTHES

Century 21 (Map p63; ☎ 212-227-9092; 25 Church St) This is a legend among savvy New York shoppers. You'll find big bargains on de-signer clothing, perfume, sportswear and kitchen products. It's one of the few dis-count places in New York City where the selection of men's wear is as extensive as the women's department. You never know exactly what's on offer, but you will be guar-anteed to find marked-down Armani shirts and Donna Karan dresses on the racks.

SHOPPING IN STYLE

The funkiest boutiques may be in SoHo, but more formal shopping can be found on Fifth and Madison Aves above 42nd St. Madison Ave is as close as New York comes to a Place Vendome Parisian experience, as designers try to outdo each other in their showplace stores. There are fewer crowds on Sunday, but you won't be able to drop in on any of the avenue's first-rate art galleries, which are closed that day.

Here are a few stores worth noting:

Barney's (Map pp66-7; ☎ 212-826-8900; 660 Madison Ave at E 61st St)

Bergdorf Goodman (Map pp64-5; ☎ 212-753-7300; 754 Fifth Ave at 57th St)

Bloomingdale's (Bloomie's; Map pp66-7; ☎ 212-705-2000; btwn Third Ave & Lexington Ave, E 59th & 60th St)

Brooks Brothers (Map pp64-5) Madison Ave (☎ 212-682-8800; 346 Madison Ave at E 44th St); Fifth Ave (☎ 212-261-9440; 666 Fifth Ave & E 53rd St)

Cartier (Map pp64-5; ☎ 212-753-0111; 653 Fifth Ave at E 52nd St)

Calvin Klein (Map pp66-7; ☎ 212-292-9000; 654 Madison Ave at E 60th St)

Diesel (Map pp66-7; ☎ 212-308-0055; 770 Lexington Ave btwn E 60th & 61st St)

Disney Store (Map pp64-5; ☎ 212-702-0702; 711 Fifth Ave at E 55th St)

Gianni Versace (Map pp64-5; ☎ 212-317-0224; 647 Fifth Ave at 51st St)

Giorgio Armani (Map pp66-7; ☎ 212-988-9191; 760 Madison Ave at E 65th St)

Givenchy (Map pp66-7; ☎ 212-772-1040; 710 Madison Ave at E 63rd St)

Gucci (Map pp64-5; ☎ 212-826-2600; 685 Fifth Ave at E 54th St)

Henri Bendel (Map pp64-5; ☎ 212-247-1100; 712 Fifth Ave at 56th St)

Louis Vuitton (Map pp64-5; ☎ 212-371-6111; 495 E 57th St btwn Fifth at Madison Ave)

Missoni (Map pp66-7; ☎ 212-517-9339; 1009 Madison Ave at E 78th St)

NBA Store (Map pp64-5; ☎ 212-515-6221; 645 Fifth Ave at E 52nd St)

Niketown (Map pp64-5; ☎ 212-891-6453; 6 E 57th St)

Polo/Ralph Lauren (Map pp66-7; ☎ 212-606-2100; 867 Madison Ave at E 72nd St)

Saks Fifth Ave (Map pp64-5; ☎ 212-753-4000; 611 Fifth Ave at E 50th St)

Tiffany & Co (Map pp64-5; ☎ 212-755-8000; 727 Fifth Ave at 57th St)

Yves St Laurent (Map pp66-7; ☎ 212-472-5299; 855 Madison Ave at E 71st St)

Macy's (Map pp64-5; ☎ 212-695-4400; cnr 34th St & Seventh Ave) Most New Yorkers have an affectionate regard for one of the city's last surviving general-interest retailers, in large part because of its sponsorship of a fireworks festival on the Fourth of July and the annual Thanksgiving Day Parade.

MUSIC

J&R Music World (Map p63; ☎ 212-238-9100; 15 Park Row) Just across from City Hall, this sprawling complex is a vast mainstream music store with a very large selection of jazz and hip-hop.

Bleecker St Records (Map pp60-1; ☎ 212-255-7899; 239 Bleecker St) An estimated 70,000 records fill this two-floor store. Happy perusing the 99-cent bin or the 45s.

Other Music (Map pp60-1; ☎ 212-477-8150; 15 E 4th St) Brazenly poised across the street from a Tower Records outlet, this independent music store thrives thanks to its selection of offbeat CDs.

Footlight Records (Map pp60-1; ☎ 212-533-1572; 113 E 12th St; ⊗ closed Mon) Magnificent collection of out-of-print albums and foreign-movie soundtracks find a temporary home here.

etherea (Map pp60-1; ☎ 212-358-1126; 66 Ave A) High-quality DJ records and CDs fill this Alphabet City store.

Wows!Ville Records (Map pp60-1; ☎ 646-654-0935; 125 Second Ave) This is your vinyl connection to New York City punk both dead and gone, and alive and kickin'.

Academy Records & CDs (Map pp64-5; ☎ 212-242-3000; 12 W 18th St) Ever been in a record store where 'early music' meant Gregorian chants? If you list more toward Mozart than Neil Young, you'll love this cramped store of classical and jazz albums.

SHOES, HANDBAGS & BEAUTY PRODUCTS

Low-cost knockoffs of Coach bags and leather backpacks are available in numerous stores along Broadway just above Houston St, on Bleecker St and on W 4th

St immediately off Sixth Ave. More than a dozen stores selling Doc Martens, hiking boots and other sturdy walkers can be found in Greenwich Village on W 8th St between Fifth and Sixth Aves – check ads in the *Village Voice* for specials.

Higher-priced shoe stores can be found in SoHo among the clothing boutiques, including everyone's favorite minimalist **Kate Spade** (Map pp60-1; ☎ 212-274-1991; 454 Broome St).

Kiehl's (Map pp60-1; ☎ 212-475-3400; 109 Third Ave btwn 13th & 14th St) This downtown store has been selling its own line of organic skin-care products since 1851. Stop in to snoop around the tester bottles; if you see something you like, ask for a take-home sample before committing. Their milky moisturizer is heavenly and age-defying.

TOYS

FAO Schwarz (Map pp64-5; ☎ 212-644-9400; 767 Fifth Ave) It may not be the only toy store in the city, but you wouldn't know it from the weekend crowds at FAO Schwarz. There's usually a 25-minute wait to get in during the holiday season. The Barbie salon at the back of the store (entrance on Madison Ave) is wildly popular.

Enchanted Forest (Map pp60-1; ☎ 212-925-6677; 85 Mercer St btwn Spring & Broome St) This is a small and delightful store catering to kids in SoHo. It specializes in teddy bears and hand puppets.

VINTAGE & CHEAP CLOTHING

The East Village and Alphabet City are swimming in vintage stores. But don't expect great bargains, as junk becomes precious retrograde fashions, boutique stores snatch up the good stuff. **Treasure Trends NYC** (Map pp60-1; ☎ 212-777-5514; 204 First Ave) is primarily a used-clothing store for struggling families, secondarily it is a gold-mine of ridiculous fashion (who said hospital scrubs are out?). **Rue St Denis** (Map pp60-1; ☎ 212-260-3388; 174 Ave B at E 11th St) has everything a burgeoning dandy would need: elf shoes, foppish hats and a cravat. **Shake Appeal** (Map pp60-1; ☎ 212-777-8058; 350 E 9th St) definitely has an eye for the past, as evidenced by the owner, who bears an uncanny resemblance to Elvis Costello.

Dozens of shops sell off-brand clothing at wholesale prices in the Garment District, mainly on W 37th St between Eighth and Ninth Aves.

Dave's New York Army & Navy (Map pp64-5; ☎ 212-989-6444, 800-543-8558; 581 Sixth Ave btwn 16th & 17th St) Dave's does an extremely brisk business selling jeans and construction boots to tourists, and as it closes its doors at 6pm on Saturday, there's usually a long line of airplane-bound foreign visitors stocking up on $35 pairs of Levi's.

Paragon Athletic Goods (Map pp64-5; ☎ 212-255-8036; 867 Broadway) Just off Union Square between E 17th and 18th Sts, this store offers a comprehensive selection of sports merchandise, with better prices than the chain stores. Particularly popular are its end-of-season sales on tennis rackets and running shoes.

GETTING THERE & AWAY
Air

New York is served by three major airports.

John F Kennedy Airport (JFK; ☎ 718-244-4444), 15 miles from Midtown Manhattan in southeastern Queens, is where most international flights land. The airport information line will tell you if the airport is closed in bad weather. Until the airport undergoes a much-needed renovation, set to be completed in 2005, it's a place best used only for transit.

La Guardia Airport (LGA; ☎ 718-533-3400), in northern Queens, is 8 miles from Manhattan and services mostly domestic flights, including the air shuttles to Boston and Washington, DC. If you're arriving or departing in the middle of the day, La Guardia is a more convenient choice than JFK. The airport largely serves Northeastern and Canadian destinations.

Newark International Airport (EWR; ☎ 201-961-6000) is in New Jersey, 10 miles directly to the west. It's the hub for Continental Airlines and is also used by international and domestic flights of all major carriers. Newark is the best choice at the moment for foreign visitors, thanks to a new, well-organized international terminal and convenient **Airtrain** (www.panynj.gov/airtrain/) that connects directly with Penn Station in Manhattan. The best feature: a large immigration hall that speeds up passport checks. Moreover, flights to/from Newark International Airport are usually a bit cheaper because of the erroneous perception that the airport is less accessible than JFK.

Bus

All suburban and long-haul buses arrive and depart from the **Port Authority Bus Terminal** (Map

AIRLINE OFFICES

The following international airlines have offices downtown or at the airports:

Aer Lingus (Map pp64-5; ☎ 888-474-7424; 509 Madison Ave)
Aeromexico (Map pp64-5; ☎ 800-237-6639; 37 W 57th St)
Air Canada (Map pp64-5; ☎ 888-247-2262; 15 W 50th St)
Air France (Map pp64-5; ☎ 800-237-2747; 120 W 56th St)
American Airlines (Map pp64-5; ☎ 800-433-7300; 18 W 49th St)
British Airways (Map pp64-5; ☎ 800-247-9297; 530 Fifth Ave)
Continental Airlines (Map pp64-5; ☎ 212-319-9494; 100 E 42nd St)
Delta Airlines (Map pp64-5; ☎ 800-221-1212; 100 E 42nd St)
Finnair (Map pp64-5; ☎ 212-499-9000) 228 E 45th St)
Japan Air Lines (☎ 800-525-3663; JFK Airport)
jetblue (☎ 800-538-2583; JFK Airport)
Philippine Airlines (☎ 800-435-9725; JFK Airport)
Singapore Airlines (Map pp64-5; ☎ 212-644-8801; 55 E 59th St)
Swissair (Map pp64-5; ☎ 800-842-2201; 608 Fifth Ave)
United Airlines (Map pp64-5; ☎ 800-241-6522; 100 E 42nd St)
US Airways (Map pp64-5; ☎ 800-428-4322; 101 Park Ave)
Virgin Atlantic (Map pp64-5; ☎ 800-862-8621; 125 Park Ave)

pp64-5; ☎ 212-564-8484; 41st St and Eighth Ave). **Greyhound** (☎ 212-971-6300, 800-231-2222) links New York with major cities across the country. **Peter Pan Bus Lines** (☎ 800-343-9999) run buses to the nearest major cities, including a daily express to Boston for $30 one-way or $50 for a round-trip.

Port Authority has been modernized and is much improved in recent years. Though it's not as rough as its reputation, you can still be hassled by beggars asking for handouts or offering to carry your bags for tips. You should use city street-smarts if arriving here.

Train

Pennsylvania Station (Penn Station; Map pp64-5; 33rd St btwn Seventh & Eighth Ave) is the departure point for all **Amtrak trains** (☎ 800-872-7245), including the Metroliner service to Princeton, NJ, and Washington, DC. **Long Island Rail Road** (LIRR; ☎ 718-217-5477) serves several hundred thousand commuters each day from a renovated platform area to points in Brooklyn, Queens and the suburbs of Long Island, including the resort areas. **New Jersey Transit** (NJ Transit; ☎ 973-762-5100) also operates trains from Penn Station to the suburbs and the Jersey shore.

One company still departs from Grand Central Terminal (Map pp64-5): **Metro North Rail Road** (New York City ☎ 212-532-4900, outside NYC ☎ 800-638-7646), which serves the northern suburbs and neighboring Connecticut.

GETTING AROUND

The subway is the fastest way to get between uptown and downtown points. The city buses are best used for cross-town trips when traffic has died down.

After 10pm (earlier if traveling alone), take a taxi rather than public transportation.

To/From the Airports

No matter what airport you fly out of, it is advisable to order car service by phone rather than flagging a taxi. You can order a pickup one day in advance and pay by credit card. If you ask for a 'price check' while ordering the ride, the dispatcher can tell you the exact cost of the journey, which should run between $35 to $50 (plus tip), depending on your departure point and the airport destination. **Tel Aviv** (☎ 212-777-7777) is a reliable car service in Manhattan.

When departing for the airports in the middle of the day, allow at least one hour's travel time. The Port Authority of New York and **New Jersey's Air Ride line** (☎ 800-247-7433) offer comprehensive information on transportation to and from all three airports.

New York Airport Service Express bus (☎ 718-875-8200; www.nyairportservice.com) runs buses to and from several stops in Manhattan to JFK and La Guardia and between La Guardia and JFK. The pick-up and drop-off points in Manhattan are Penn Station (Map pp64-5), Port Authority (Map pp64-5) and

Grand Central Terminal (Map pp64-5). See the individual airports below for prices and visit the website for schedules.

Super Shuttle (☎ 800-451-0455; www.supershuttle .com) runs minivans to many hotels in Manhattan from JFK, La Guardia and Newark airports. The fare runs between $17 to $19 depending on the airport.

TO/FROM JOHN F KENNEDY AIRPORT

From JFK, New York Airport Service Express bus costs $13 to $15 one-way for trips to and from Manhattan; buses depart roughly every 15 to 30 minutes from 6am to 11pm.

You can also take the subway to the Howard Beach–JFK station on the A line, which takes at least an hour, and then switch to a free yellow and blue bus at the long-term parking lot to the terminals, which takes another 15 minutes. (You have to haul your luggage up and over several flights of stairs at the Howard Beach terminal.) The AirTrain monorail system connecting JFK airport to Howard Beach–JFK station on the A line should be completed in 2004.

Taxi fare from JFK is a flat rate of $35, plus tolls and tip, to any location in Manhattan.

TO/FROM LA GUARDIA AIRPORT

From La Guardia, New York Airport Service Express bus costs $10 to $12 one-way for trips to and from Manhattan; buses run roughly every 15 to 30 minutes from 7am to 11pm

La Guardia is also accessible via public transportation by taking the subway to the Roosevelt Ave–Jackson Heights and 74th St–Broadway stops in Queens (two linked stations served by five lines). You then take the Q33 bus to the La Guardia main terminals or the Q47 bus to Delta Shuttle's Marine Air Terminal. This journey takes well over an hour and costs $4, not much of a bargain compared to other options. Alternatively, in Upper Manhattan, pick up the M60 bus at one of the signed stops along 125th St; it goes directly to La Guardia for $2.

Taxis to La Guardia from Midtown cost about $20 to $30, plus tolls and tip.

TO/FROM NEWARK INTERNATIONAL AIRPORT

NJ Transit (☎ 973-762-5100) offers a free monorail AirTrain system that connects Newark airport with the nearest train station

(Newark International Airport Station); from here you can take a PATH train to Penn Station in Manhattan ($11.55).

Olympia Trails (☎ 212-964-6233) travels to Newark from Penn Station (Map pp64-5), Port Authority (Map pp64-5) and Grand Central Terminal (Map pp64-5) from 5am to 1:30am daily.

A taxi to Newark will cost about $50.

Bus

City buses operate 24 hours a day, generally along avenues in a south or north direction, and cross-town along the major thoroughfares (including 34th, 42nd and 57th Sts). Buses that begin and end in a certain borough are prefixed accordingly, eg M5 for Manhattan, B39 for Brooklyn, Q32 for Queens, Bx29 for the Bronx. For bus information, call ☎ 718-330-1234.

Bus maps for each borough are available at subway and train stations, and each well-marked bus stop has 'Guide-a-Ride' maps showing the stops for each bus and nearby landmarks. The $2 one-way fares can be paid on the bus, but the onboard machines only accept $1 bills (no change can be made by the driver). An unlimited subway card is also valid on the city's buses. Remember that some 'Limited Stop' buses along major routes pull over only every 10 blocks or so at major cross-streets. 'Express' buses are generally for outer-borough commuters.

Car & Motorcycle

It's a nightmare to have a car in New York. Parking on the street is impossible to find and unsafe for your vehicle, especially if you have a nice sound system or any valuables in the car. For safety and convenience, park in one of the city's many parking garages, which run $25 to $45 a day, depending on the neighborhood. Daily rates do not include in and out privileges and there is also a whopping 18.25% parking tax. Cheaper lots can be found in Manhattan along West St in Chelsea.

Car rental starts at $60 a day for a compact. Car rental companies regularly gouge New Yorkers, and unless you have a special deal offering a cheap car rental (booked before your arrival in conjunction with an air ticket), expect to pay $100 or more a day, with rates of about $300 per weekend.

Ferry

NY Waterway (☎ 800-533-3779; www.nywaterway.com; all-day pass adult/senior & child $15/12; one-stop $4; ☺ 9:15am-4pm Mon-Fri, 11am-7pm Sat & Sun) operates ferry routes around Manhattan as well as routes to Brooklyn and New Jersey. Midday and weekend services travel from the following piers (and attractions): Pier 84 (Map pp64-5; W 44th St, by the Intrepid Sea-Air-Space Museum, p89), to Pier 63 (Map pp64-5; W 23rd St, Chelsea Piers), North Cove (Map p63; World Financial Center, Battery Park City, p72), Pier A (Map p63; Battery Park, p72, Statue of Liberty, p70), Pier 11 (Map p63; Wall St, South Street Seaport, p75) and to Fulton Ferry Landing (Map p63; Brooklyn Bridge, p75, Dumbo, p101).

See the Staten Island Ferry entry (p103) for information on traveling to that borough.

Subway

Mastering this noisy and smelly underground system, operated by **Metropolitan Transportation Authority** (☎ 718-330-1234; www.mta.info), shows the true mettle of a New Yorker and provides countless war stories. The New York subway, 100 years old, is becoming more user-friendly, with automated trains that announce the line and the stop, and recently restored stations. The 656-mile system extends up and down the eastern and western sides of Manhattan into Queens, the Bronx and Brooklyn, and can become indispensable if armed with a subway map (which is given free from station booths) and knowing whether your stop is uptown or downtown from your entrance point (which will help you find the right platform).

Here is an unforeseen impediment: the confounded 'express' train, which operates usually during rush hour making marathon runs up- or downtown with only a handful of stops between. Most express trains are well-marked, but sometimes a regular train will magically turn into an express mid-route. If you're confused, just ask. New Yorkers love to flex their subway knowledge.

Line 6 is the most frequently used tourist train; it runs from Bowling Green at the tip of the island, to Grand Central Terminal, Lexington Ave/59th St (Fifth Ave shopping) and to uptown museums.

One-way rides cost $2 and a magnetic fare card is purchased from vending machines inside the stations. Unlimited day

($7) and week ($21) passes are also available. The vending machines take credit and ATM cards as well as bills.

PATH TRAINS

New Jersey **PATH trains** (☎ 800-234-7284) are part of a separate subway system that runs along Sixth Ave, with stops at 34th, 23rd, 14th, 9th and Christopher Sts to Hoboken, Jersey City and Newark. A second line runs from northern New Jersey to the new World Trade Center station. These reliable trains run every 15 minutes and the one-way fare is $1.50.

Taxi

Taxis are tough to flag during rush hours, rainy weather and busy weekend nights. When a corner is peopled with several couples trying to flag a cab, you should stake out your claim several blocks up the traffic river.

By law cabs are not allowed to refuse your destination (or business); if this happens, record the driver's license number and report them to the city complaint line (☎ 311).

All licensed cabbies drive yellow vehicles that are clearly marked as taxis; gypsy cabs cruise the city in unmarked cars and offer passengers flat, negotiated rates. Unless you know exactly how much your fare should be, don't tangle with the gypsy cabs who are master hustlers.

Taxis cost $2 for the initial charge, with $0.30 for every additional quarter-mile and $0.30 per 90 seconds while stuck in traffic. There's a $0.50 surcharge for rides after 8pm. Tampered meters turn over every 20 seconds or so while the cab is stopped in traffic or at a light, and if you notice it happening, don't hesitate to ask if it is 'running too fast.' If the driver apologizes a bit too energetically, you've probably busted him and can negotiate a lower fare than the meter.

Tips are expected to run 10% to 15%, with a minimum of $0.50.

For hauls that will last 50 blocks or more, it's a good idea to instruct the driver to take a road well away from Midtown traffic. Suggest the West Side Highway or Eleventh Ave if you hail a taxi west of Broadway; on the East Side, the best choice may be Second Ave (heading downtown) or First Ave (uptown), because you can hit a string of green lights in either direction.

See p133 for information on taking a taxi to the airports.

Long Island

Long Island is a reluctant satellite to New York City's powerful gravitational pull. Long ago this island (the largest island in the US at 120 miles from end to end) was a collection of New England–style fishing and farming villages with a small fortress of aristocracy (the Hamptons). In the years following WWII, the western portion became a bedroom suburb for New York City choked by strip malls and superhighways. In the eastern portion, which terminates in two prong-like peninsulas (commonly called the North and South Forks) around Peconic Bay, the farms and open spaces still outnumber settlements and seem immeasurably remote from the concrete of the city. Today, the South Fork is dominated by the Hamptons, a collection of tony villages (Hampton Bays, Southampton, Bridgehampton, East Hampton and Amagansett) where actors, writers and entertainment executives summer in their private estates. The North Fork is working class, although city money is creeping over to this formerly forgotten corner. A burgeoning wine industry has been planted in the North Fork.

For most visitors, a trip to Long Island means a trip to the beach, whether the destination is crowded Jones Beach, quiet Shelter Island or the more showy enclaves of the Hamptons. All of these beaches are within easy reach of New York City via public transportation, which is the best option for summer weekends when traffic jams are particularly hellish. But if you're interested in exploring Long Island's historic mansions or sampling wine in the vineyards of the North Fork, it's best to have a car.

HIGHLIGHTS

■ **Best Place to Spot Celebrities**
East Hampton's Rowdy Hall (p142) is well loved by celebrities and the people who pretend not to notice them.

■ **Best Place to Get a Sunburn**
Take your pick: the south-shore beaches of Fire Island (p138), Jones Beach State Park (p138) or Robert Moses State Park (p138); or on a long bike ride through Shelter Island's Mashomack Nature Preserve (p144).

■ **Best Place to Get an Education**
The Long Island Wine Trail (p144) is an inexpensive and intoxicating education in wine.

■ **Best Bicycle Ride**
Shelter Island (p144) and Orient Point (p143) have miles of thin ribbon roads lapped by sand and sea and refreshingly uncrowded.

■ **Most Unlikely Place to See Taxidermy**
Sagamore Hill (p143), Teddy Roosevelt's home, is packed full of exotic taxidermy animals from his many international safaris.

CLIMATE

Long Island experiences four distinct seasons. Its proximity to the ocean acts as a regulator sparing the island from the extreme temperatures of winter or summer. Winter storms, called nor'easters, often batter the long coastline.

STATE PARKS

Robert Moses State Park (☎ 631-669-0470; Robert Moses Causeway), on the western end of Fire Island (p138), has five miles of ocean beach and a day-use boat area. **Captree State Park** (☎ 631-669-0449; Robert Moses Causeway), at the eastern end of Jones Beach Island, is popular with anglers; the marina has fishing charters and sightseeing boats. **Governor Alfred E Smith/ Sunken Meadow State Park** (☎ 631-269-4333; Rte 25A), on Long Island Sound, has tidal flats and wooded hills that lead to a three-mile beach. **Montauk State Park** (☎ 631-668-3781; Rte 27), on the far eastern tip of the South Fork, offers some of the East Coast's best surf fishing. **Hither Hills State Park** (☎ 631-668-2554; Rte 27) is landscaped with 'walking' or shifting dunes. **Orient Beach State Park** (☎ 631-323-2440; Rte 25), on Long Island's North Fork, fronts Gardiner's Bay and has a rare maritime forest with prickly-pear cactus.

INFORMATION

The **Long Island Convention and Visitors Bureau** (☎ 800-441-4601; www.licvb.com) publishes a free travel guide.

North Fork Promotion Council (☎ 631-477-1383; www.northfork.org), in Southold, can provide a directory of B&Bs, historical sites and wineries for the North Fork area. You can obtain maps, restaurant listings and lodging guides from the local chamber of commerce by calling:

East Hampton (☎ 631-324-0362; www.easthampton .com; 79A Main St)

Greenport-Southold (☎ 631-765-3161; www.green portsoutholdchamber.com)

Montauk (☎ 631-668-2428; www.montaukchamber.com)

Shelter Island (☎ 631-749-0399; www.shelter -island.net)

Southampton (☎ 631-283-8707; www.southampton chamber.com; 76 Main St)

GETTING THERE & AROUND

The Long Island Expressway (I-495, or L-I-E) cuts through the center of the island. The older Rte 25 (the Jericho Turnpike) runs roughly parallel to I-495, then continues to the end of the North Fork at Orient Point. Rte 27 (the Sunrise Highway) runs along the bottom of Long Island from the Brooklyn border and eventually becomes the Montauk Highway (near Southampton), ending up at the South Fork's Montauk Point. A trip from New York City to the end of Long Island takes at least three hours, but on weekends, traffic jams can turn it into a six-hour ordeal.

The **Hampton Jitney bus** (☎ 800-936-0440; www .hamptonjitney.com) leaves several times daily for Long Island's South Fork from four locations in Manhattan (40th St between Lexington and Third Aves; 59th St at Lexington Ave; 69th St at Lexington Ave; 86th St between Lexington and Third Ave). Drivers usually know ways of circumventing summer weekend traffic, making these buses a good alternative to driving a car.

The **Long Island Rail Road** (LIRR; ☎ 631-231-5477, 718-217-5477; www.mta.info/lirr) is a widely used commuter option that reaches New York City's Penn Station. Fares to Greenport and Montauk, the furthest eastern stops, cost $13 to $19 one-way.

THE SOUTH SHORE

The Sunrise Highway leads to Long Island's top beaches, and toniest communities.

JONES BEACH STATE PARK

A mere 33 minutes from Manhattan, **Jones Beach** (☎ 631-785-1600) is the most crowded public beach in the area. Though it's always mobbed, the sand at Jones Beach is clean and it's an enjoyable respite from the city heat. In summer concerts are held at the **Jones Beach Theater** (☎ 516-221-1000). The LIRR offers $15 round-trip fares from Penn Station in New York City to Freeport station on Long Island; the trip takes under 40 minutes and includes a shuttle bus to Jones Beach.

FIRE ISLAND NATIONAL SEASHORE

Sandy beaches, saltwater marshes, evening sunsets and, best of all, no traffic. **Fire Island National Seashore** (☎ 631-289-4810; admission free), a car-free park, runs a narrow 32-mile-long barrier off the southern shore of Long Island. Within the protected zones are 15 hamlets that predated the National

A TOAST TO THE AUTOMOBILE

One of only two points on Fire Island accessible by car, **Robert Moses State Park** is a beautiful stretch of sandy dunes named in honor of New York City's influential civic planner. Through his politically appointed position as a parks commissioner, he retooled the city's landscape in the mid-20th century, eradicating tenements, glorifying the car culture and downplaying public transportation. Unfortunately, Moses had the power of a modern-day Baron Haussmann but none of the master's aesthetic sense; his projects (which included the Triborough Bridge, Lincoln Center and several highways and projects on the Lower East Side) often destroyed entire neighborhoods and routed huge numbers of residents.

Seashore designation. With all this natural beauty, the crowds are a permanent fixture in the summer, and Fire Island is probably the country's leading gay resort area. At the western end of the island, **Robert Moses State Park** (☎ 631-669-0470; Robert Moses Causeway) is better known as a family destination.

Sleeping

Camping spots include **Heckscher Park** (☎ 631-581-4433) in East Islip, and **Watch Hill** (☎ 631-289-9336; www.watchhillfi.com; campsite $28) on Fire Island as part of the National Seashore.

The buildings on Fire Island don't always bear numbered signs. The Ocean Beach zip code (11770) will ensure delivery of mail (during the summer months). **Houser's Hotel** (☎ 631-583-7799; Bay Walk, Ocean Beach; d $150-200) has 12 rooms. Another option is **Four Season Hotel** (☎ 631-588-8295; 468 Denhoff Walk, Ocean Beach; d weekdays/weekend $125/300), open year-round.

Getting There & Away

By car you can get there by taking exit 53 of the Long Island Expressway and traveling south across the Robert Moses Causeway to the public parking facility. Alternatively you can take exit 58 (William Floyd Parkway) to the public parking lot in Smith Point County Park (on Fire Island). There are no cars or bikes allowed within the park.

The three ferry terminals are all close to the Bay Shore, Sayville and Patchogue LIRR stations (train fares from Penn Station are

$8 to $12 one-way). The ferry season runs from early May to November; trips take about 20 minutes and cost an average of $12/6 adult/child for a round-trip, with discounted seasonal passes available. Most ferries depart in order to link directly with a train to/from New York.

Davis Park Ferry Company (☎ 631-475-1665) Travels from Patchogue to Davis Park and Watch Hill.
Fire Island Ferries (☎ 631-665-5045) Runs from Bay Shore to Saltaire, Fair Harbor and Ocean Beach.
Sayville Ferry Service (☎ 631-589-8980) Runs from Sayville to Cherry Grove, Sunken Forest and the Pines.

THE HAMPTONS

The best way to describe the Hamptons is to point out their most prominent feature: the privacy hedgerow. Neatly manicured shrubs form a tall, impenetrable wall along what would otherwise be a scenic drive of majestic houses.

Pedigree used to be the only way to pass beyond the green fence to huge estates and mansions, bearing names as illustrious as their human residents. But as the Hamptons entered the common imagination through writers' stories of wild and extravagant parties, new money invaded the first families' domain. The easy money of the 1980s brought another influx of showier summertime visitors who made their fortunes in the fashion industry and on Wall St.

In recent years the Hamptons have become truly 'hot' as West Coast entertainment moguls purchased large homes here, following in the footsteps of Steven Spielberg. Year-round residents seem annoyed and amused by the show in equal measures. In a subtle wordplay that only Hollywood understands, celebrities come here to be seen but not spotted.

Many of the attractions, restaurants and hotels in the Hamptons close the last week in October and remain shut until late April. About two weeks after Labor Day

SUMMER HOURS

Whenever the opening hours in this chapter mention 'summer,' this means the period from Memorial Day to Labor Day. Call for opening hours after Labor Day as they vary greatly.

LONG ISLAND

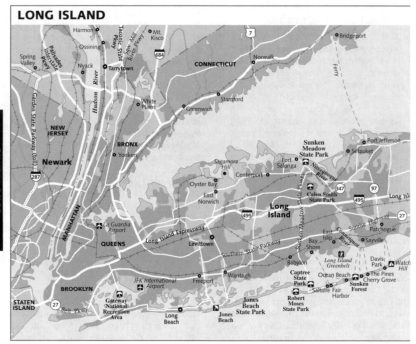

B&B prices drop and traffic jams along the Montauk Highway disappear.

Southampton

☎ 631 / pop 4000

A pleasant village of Cape Cod cottages, Southampton ranks on the second-tier of the Hamptons hierarchy – a community of inherited (but dwindling) fortunes. For the outsider, Southampton has a busy Main St of high-end shopping as well as an art museum and historical sights. You can get maps and brochures about the town at the **chamber of commerce** (☎ 631-283-8707; www.south amptonchamber.com; 76 Main St). Maps and books are available at the well-stocked **Bookhampton** (☎ 631-324-4939; 93 Main St; 8:30am-7pm Mon-Fri, 8:30am-8pm Sat & Sun).

Southampton Historical Museum (☎ 631-283-2494) operates two historic homes in the village: **Rogers Mansion** (17 Meeting House Lane; adult/senior/student $4/3/2; 11am-5pm Tue-Sat, 1-5pm Sun summer), an 1840s Greek-Revival built by a prominent whaling captain, and the austere **Halsey Homestead** (249 S Main St; adult/senior/student $3/2/1; noon-5pm Fri & Sat

summer), a saltbox house built in 1648 just eight years after the first European settlers arrived in the area.

The **Parrish Art Museum** (☎ 631-283-2111; 25 Jobs Lane; adult/child $5/free, student & senior $3; 11am-5pm Wed-Sat, 1-5pm Sun summer) is just a short walk from Main St. It has been open to the public since 1898 and its gallery features the work of major artists like the late Roy Lichtenstein, who had a house nearby.

Sag Harbor

☎ 631 / pop 2300

Known as the 'Un Hamptons,' this salty fishing port on the Peconic Bay is popular with families, surfers and other outsiders of the elite circles. Local perspectives and tips on restaurants, as well as rare books, can be found at **Black Cat Books** (☎ 631-725-8654; Main St Shopping Center; 10am-6pm).

Sag Harbor Whaling & Historical Museum (☎ 631-725-0770; cnr Main & Garden St; adult/child $5/3; 10am-5pm Mon-Sat, 1-5pm Sun May-Oct) celebrates the town's former industry.

Sag Harbor is 7 miles north from Bridge-hampton on Rte 27.

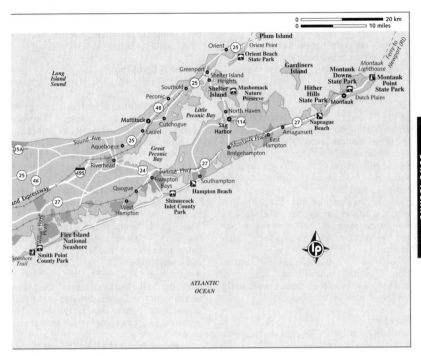

East Hampton & Amagansett

☎ 631

The absolute monarch of the Hamptons, East Hampton (population 1300) provides a refuge for the stinking rich. But the village (more accurately an outdoor shopping resort) is open to anyone who can find a parking space. Maps and books are available at the well-stocked **Bookhampton** (☎ 631-324-4939; 20 Main St; ☼ 8:30am-7pm Mon-Fri, 8:30am-8pm Sat & Sun).

Catch readings and art exhibitions at the **Guild Hall** (☎ 631-324-0806; www.guildhall.org; 158 Main St). Driving or biking down Main Beach along Ocean Ave will afford glimpses of the larger saltbox estates with water views. You can see some other grand (private) houses by turning right at **Lilly Pond Lane** and peeking through the breaks in the high shrubbery. The book *Philistines at the Hedgerow* by Steven Gaines is an entertaining read about the private affairs that these homes have hosted.

Amagansett (population 1000) is basically an extension of East Hampton distinguished by the huge flagpole in the center of the Montauk Highway.

Northeast of town, on Rte 41, is the **Pollock-Krasner House & Study Center** (☎ 631-324-4929; www.pkhouse.org; 830 Springs Fireplace Rd; adult/child $10/free, ☼ Thu-Sat May-Oct), where Jackson Pollock and his wife Lee Krasner lived and worked. Pollock created his famous drip paintings here and the excess paint that extended beyond the canvas is still viewable today. Call for tour schedule.

Montauk

☎ 631 / pop 3800

The landscape becomes windswept and grizzled as you approach Montauk, the furthest tip of the South Fork. This honky-tonk beach town is filled with shifting dunes, cheap beachside motels and T-shirt shops. After the beachgoers head back to school in September, Montauk fills up for sport fishing season (blue fin tuna and bass).

There are six public beaches (some charge parking fees) in Montauk, in addition to the beachfront property of many hotels and motels. Surfing, swimming and kayaking are all popular activities. If you're a cyclist looking for a challenge, peel off to the right

> **MONDAY**
>
> It was once widely held that if you had to make an appearance in the office on Monday, you weren't rich enough to be in the Hamptons.

of Rte 27 and take the **Old Montauk Highway**, an undulating ribbon of asphalt overlooking the ocean. **Montauk Downs State Park** (☎ 631-668-3781; golf fees in/out of state residents $30/65) has a fine public golf course; there are long waits in the summer, so call ahead to reserve a tee time (☎ 631-668-1234).

If all this fun and sun has worn you out, the spa at **Gurney's Inn** (☎ 631-668-2345; www.gurneys-inn.com; 290 Old Montauk Highway; packages from $300) can pamper you into a state of bliss.

Montauk is a feasible car-less destination. The LIRR station is at Edgemere St at Firestone Lane, a 10-minute walk to the center of town and the beaches.

Sleeping

American Hotel (☎ 631-725-3535; www.theamericanhotel.com; Main St, Sag Harbor; d $200-325) In Sag Harbor, this European-style hotel is the only (and most elegant) one in town.

Mill House Inn (☎ 631-324-9766; www.millhouseinn.com; 33 N Main St, East Hampton; d $200-400 incl breakfast) In East Hampton, this B&B is a handsome townhouse with 10 rooms and suites; the rooms on the top floor will afford more privacy. Dogs are allowed.

Sea Breeze Inn (☎ 631-267-3692; 30 Atlantic Ave, Amagansett; s/d without bath $105/175, d with bath $210, incl breakfast) In Amagansett, this guesthouse is just a block away from the LIRR station. Rock, the owner, is a well-seasoned traveler (and big fan of Lonely Planet); the rooms are reminiscent of guest rooms in relatives' homes. Weekly discounts are available.

Hither Hills State Park (☎ 800-456-2267; campsite in/out of state residents $25/50) In Montauk, this state park has camping sheltered behind the dunes.

During summer the motels in more isolated Montauk run a bit cheaper than in other South Fork communities – about $150 a night – but many are booked solid on a monthly basis by groups of students employed at the resorts and restaurants.

You can get a list of accommodations by calling the Montauk tourist office at ☎ 516-668-2428.

Eating & Drinking

Rowdy Hall (☎ 631-324-8555; 10 Main St, East Hampton; mains $10-12; ☒ noon-3:30pm & 5-10pm) This casual restaurant in East Hampton serves the area's biggest hamburger. (Rowdy House was the name of a rollicking boardinghouse and later the rented cottage where Mr and Mrs Bouvier brought their newborn daughter Jacqueline, future Kennedy Onassis.)

Amagansett Farmers Market (☎ 631-267-6600; Main St, Amagansett; ☒ 9am-5pm May-Oct) Fresh flowers for the porch table, corn for the beach clambake and pâté for the afternoon luncheon – the sophisticated farm stand caters to the locals' needs.

Laundry (☎ 631-324-3199; 31 Race Lane, East Hampton; mains $15-36; ☒ 5:30-11pm) One block from the East Hampton train station, this was among the first celebrity-spotting restaurants to open in the Hamptons; it has survived the 'newcomer' buzz to become an old favorite.

Maidstone Arms (☎ 631-324-5006; 207 Main St, East Hampton; mains $15-20; ☒ 8am-11pm summer) Near the junction of Rtes 27 and 114, this historic gem is the most elegant restaurant in town. The menu is subdued American-French with lots of local seafood.

Stephen Talkhouse (☎ 631-267-3117; 161 Main St, East Hampton; ☒ from 7pm) This is a 25-year-old concert venue that has an active bar scene on non-performance nights; Billy Joel and James Taylor have appeared here.

Lobster Roll (☎ 631-267-3740; Rte 27; mains $10-12; ☒ 11:30am-10pm summer) On Rte 27, between the towns of Amagansett and Montauk, a few roadside fish shacks, like this institution, pop up. With its distinctive 'Lunch' sign, the Lobster Roll serves the namesake sandwich as well as fresh steamers and fried clams.

Shagwong Restaurant (☎ 631-668-3050; Main St, Montauk; mains $10-20; ☒ 11:30-2am summer) In Montauk town, this pub-restaurant serves hearty meals and refreshing beer.

Joni's (☎ 631-668-3663; 9 S Edison St, Montauk; mains $4-10; ☒ 11:30am-6pm summer) Off the main drag, Joni's leans toward the vegetarian, health-food aisle with smoothies and wraps.

THE NORTH SHORE

The less-touristed North Shore features gilded Jazz Age mansions, rural roadways and a burgeoning wine industry.

SAGAMORE HILL

Driving through the secluded waterside spot of Oyster Bay brings reminders of robber barons and the Jazz Age. This quiet village – just one hour from New York City – is a refuge for the rich and the location of **Sagamore Hill** (☎ 516-922-4788; 20 Sagamore Hill Rd; adult/child $5/free; 🕙 10am-4pm Mon-Sun Jun-Aug, 10am-4pm Wed-Sun Sep-May). The 23-room mansion was built in 1885 by Theodore Roosevelt. Sagamore Hill eventually served as the summer White House during his tenure in office from 1902 to 1908. It was in this dark Victorian mansion that Roosevelt brokered an end to the Russo-Japanese War, an effort for which he won the Nobel peace prize.

Roosevelt was in many ways the first president of the modern era – he used a telephone (which is still on view in his study) to remain in contact with Washington. Though Roosevelt was also the first chief executive to concern himself with conservation, animal rights activists will no doubt turn pale at the many mounted heads, antlers and leopard skins on display, along with the inkwell made from a rhinoceros foot.

Roosevelt died at Sagamore Hill in 1919 and is buried in a cemetery a mile away. A redbrick Georgian house on the grounds was later occupied by Theodore Roosevelt Jr, and is now a museum charting the 26th president's political career.

In summer, it is best to avoid driving through Oyster Bay village to reach Sagamore Hill; visit www.nps.gov/sahi/travel for a time-saving detour. Tours of the mansion leave on the hour.

VANDERBILT MANSION

Also known as Eagle's Nest, the **Vanderbilt Mansion & Planetarium** (☎ 631-854-5555; 180 Little Neck Rd, Centerport; www.vanderbiltmuseum.org; mansion/planetarium adult $8/7 student & senior $6/5, child $5/4, combo tickets available; 🕙 10am-4pm Tue-Sun) was the estate of Willie Vanderbilt, one of the last major heirs to the Staten Island family railroad fortune. Willie spent most of his life – and money – collecting sea creatures and curiosities from the South Pacific and Egypt; many items of his collection are on display. Please note that the mansion isn't recommended for small children and is not air-conditioned. A planetarium was added to the grounds in 1971, featuring a 60ft 'Sky Theater' and telescope. The site is now owned by Nassau County, which holds community events on the 43-acre site. Finding the Vanderbilt Mansion is tricky: from Rte 25A heading east look for a flashing yellow light in Centerport in front of a fire department and turn left onto Park Circle; this road will bring you to the mansion.

NORTH FORK

Rural and picturesque, the North Fork is dotted with corduroy-striped vineyards, thrifty unadorned villages and small fishing skiffs buoying in sparkling bays. At the jumping-off point for ferries to Shelter Island, Greenport, the main town in the North Fork, is in a tender phase – transitioning from a working waterfront to a nautical-themed tourist attraction. Real estate in the area is being snapped up by weekending city-dwellers, changing the character of the town and augmenting the disparity between the locals and the visitors. Despite its growing pains, Greenport is the perfect base from which to begin an exploration of the area's wineries.

Orient Point

The far tip of the North Fork is where the ferry departs for the casinos in New London, CT. Three miles from the docks is the tiny hamlet of Orient. There's not much of a business district in this tiny 17th-century hamlet, just an old wooden post office and a general store, but Orient is a well-preserved collection of white clapboard houses and former inns. To get to Orient follow the signs for the 'Orient Business District' at the Civil War monument on the side of Rte 25.

Touring around Orient Point makes for a great bike ride. Further out of town, you can bike past the Oyster Ponds just east of Main St and also check out the beach at Orient Beach State Park, which offers some great bird-watching opportunities.

Sleeping & Eating

Silver Sand Motel (☎ 631-477-0011; Silvermere Rd, Greenport; d $150-200) The best place to stay in Greenport is this independent motel (off Rte 25) that claims 36 wooded acres right on Peconic Bay. Still sporting its original Americana turquoise linoleum and Pepto-Bismol pink bathrooms, Silver Sands motel rooms have ridden out the fashion tides to enjoy a retro revival. The horseshoe-shaped motel looks out over a courtyard leading to the sparkling bay and a sandy beach. Cottages and weekly rates are available.

Old Barge (☎ 631-765-4700; 750 Old Main Rd, Southold; mains $15-20) In the Port of Egypt marina, this family-friendly restaurant claims a big waterfront patio and serves sandwiches and burgers.

Pepi's Cucina Di Casa (☎ 631-765-6373; 400 Old Main Rd, Southold; mains $15-25) Next door to the Old Barge is this elegant Italian restaurant. Claiming a water view, Pepi's menu revolves around the sea with local and gulf fish dressed in a variety of sauces.

Aldo's (☎ 631-477-1699; 103-105 Front St, Greenport; mains $20-25) Very New York boutique, this restaurant in downtown Greenport prepares sublime food, especially homemade desserts. Reservations are essential.

Getting There & Away
The **Cross Sound Ferry Company** (☎ 631-323-2525; 860-443-5281) takes passengers and cars from Orient Point, at the tip of the North Fork, to New London, CT, several times a day; reservations are recommended. Cars cost $37, including driver; passengers cost an extra $10 one-way. The company also offers a pedestrian-only hydrofoil shuttle from the terminal to the Foxwoods Casino and Resort in Connecticut for $15 one-way, $25 same-day return. From the ferry dock in New London, shuttle service is available to Foxwoods Casino and Resort and Mohegan Sun casino.

See p145 for information about ferry service from Shelter Island to North Fork.

SHELTER ISLAND
Nearly a third of quiet Shelter Island is dedicated to the **Mashomack Nature Preserve**, and there's an attractive town center in Shelter Island Heights, a cluster of Victorian buildings on the north side of the island. It's a perfect place to explore nature and a true respite from the crowds in the Hamptons.

LONG ISLAND WINERIES

The geography and climate of the North Fork is a near-perfect replication of France's Bordeaux Valley – low humidity, lots of sunshine, well-drained soil and little chance of frost. Merlots, Gewürztraminers and Rieslings produced here have garnered international attention, putting Long Island vintners in league with the European masters.

Judge for yourself by visiting a few of Long Island's 50 wineries, many of which line Rte 25 between Southold (west of Greenport) and Riverhead. The winemakers are more than happy to pour out a few free glasses of their product and 'talk shop' with you; consider this an inexpensive education in wine. You can get more information on touring the wine trail by contacting the **Long Island Wine Council** (☎ 631-369-5887; www.liwines.com).

A few highlights are listed here in west-to-east order; tastings are usually offered from 11am to 5pm during the summer months:

Lenz (☎ 631-734-6010, 800-974-9899; Rte 25, Peconic) One of the oldest wineries on the North Fork, Lenz's Merlot (1997) and Chardonnay (1997) beat out two impressive vineyards. Even other vintages are tasty: from the mellow Chardonnay Gold Label to the dry and fragrant Gewürztraminer.

Bedell Cellars (☎ 631-734-7537; Rte 25, Cutchogue) A favorite of the magazine *Food & Wine*, Bedell's winemaker has been dubbed 'Mr Merlot' for the strong showing of this red.

Pelligrini (☎ 631-734-4111; Rte 25, Cutchogue) Part of the winemaking process is on full display to visitors at this artistically designed winery.

Laurel Lake (☎ 631-298-1420; Rte 25, Laurel) Notable Chardonnays are produced at this Chilean-owned vineyard. Tasting like a hybrid of Riesling and Chardonnay, Windsong white is a vineyard specialty. Live music and family events are often hosted here.

Paumanok (☎ 631-722-8800, Rte 25, Aquebogue) Named after the Indian name for Long Island, Paumanok produces the most consistent wines in this region. Its barrel-fermented Chardonnay, Chenin Blanc, dry Riesling and Sauvignon Blanc prove the vineyard's well-rounded expertise. The knowledgeable and maternal co-owner, Ursula, a native of Germany, frequently pours the tastings herself.

LONG ISLAND OUTDOORS

The eastern portion of Long Island is wild and open, free to tool around on a bike or paddle the marshy inlets.

It's possible to bike along Rte 25 on the North Fork, and along the Hamptons' side roads, especially along the seven-mile Rte 114 (the Sag Harbor Turnpike) from East Hampton to Sag Harbor. The Long Island Greenbelt follows the Connetquot and Nissequoque Rivers for 34 miles from Sunken Meadow State Park (on Long Island Sound) to Heckscher State Park (Great South Bay), passing through wetlands and forest.

There are excellent opportunities for guided walks in the Sunken Forest, located in the middle of the **Fire Island National Seashore** (park office ☎ 516-597-6183). You can also enjoy strolls in the Mashomack Nature Preserve on Shelter Island. Off-season, it's possible to embark on long, uninterrupted walks along the shoreline from East Hampton to Montauk.

Surfers frequently head to the Georgica Jetties, Montauk and Shinnecock Inlet. For more information visit **SurfersInfo.com** (www.surfersinfo.com).

Two-hour kayak explorations of Peconic Bay are offered by **Shelter Island Kayak Tours** (☎ 631-749-1990) for $35 to $55.

Just beyond the Shelter Island Heights Bridge is **Picasso's Bike Shop** (☎ 631-749-0520; Bridge St). Bikes can be rented for $18 a day, and are sturdy enough for a strenuous trek across Shelter Island, or take the ferry to Greenport to explore the North Fork and Orient Point. Call ahead in the summer to reserve bikes.

Sleeping & Eating

For such a small place, Shelter Island is well served by B&Bs, including **Ram's Head Inn** (☎ 631-749-0811; Ram Island Dr; d with/without bath $250/135 incl breakfast). A destination in itself, this waterfront hotel is moored to the mainland by a narrow causeway. The rooms are small but tidy; low-season rates are a bargain. All in all, the Ram's Head is a classic without being fussy, and the rambling grounds are big enough to host lawn games and lazy rendezvous with thick novels

The dining choices on Shelter Island are very seasonal.

Dory (☎ 631-749-8871; mains $15-25; ⏲ 11am-9pm summer) Near the Shelter Island Heights Bridge, Dory is a well-scrubbed restaurant-bar named in honor of an early-17th-century boat invented in Massachusetts.

Shelter Island Pizza (☎ 631-749-0400; Rte 114; pizza $10-12) This simple pizza joint is just another choice in the off-season.

Getting There & Away

The **North Ferry Company** (☎ 631-749-0139) runs boats from the North Fork terminal (near the LIRR station in downtown Greenport) to Shelter Island every 15 to 20 minutes from 6am to 11:45pm; a car and driver are charged $7, additional passengers $1. The trip takes seven minutes.

South Ferry Inc (☎ 631-749-1200) leaves from a dock in North Haven, 3 miles from Sag Harbor. To get to the dock go north on Rte 114 and follow the signs. Ferries leave from 6am to 11:45pm (to 1:45am Friday and Saturday); a car and driver are charged $7, additional passengers $1.

Hudson Valley

HUDSON VALLEY

From a riverbank along the Hudson, it's easy to imagine a New York of another era; when the city itself was (by today's measure) a relatively small port and the skyline was dotted with tall buildings, some even reaching four or five stories. Masted ships sailed this wide river, which reminded German immigrants of their beloved Rhine. Muddy lanes cut through small villages with stone fences, dairy farms and Victorian cottages. On the outskirts of civilization, opulent and extravagant mansions sprouted up – a reminder that fortunes could be made in this young nation.

Today New Yorkers who live in the upstate region closest to the Big Apple still boast of their active but bucolic environment. Small towns dot the river, river traffic is abundant, and dairy farms, roadside produce stands and dirt roads adorn the landscape. This is the same landscape, by the way, captured in the luminous paintings by the famous artists of the Hudson River school (whose work is on view in galleries from New York City to Albany).

'Pick-your-own' fruit and vegetable farms, and hiking and biking trails complement the valley's historic landmarks, which range from Washington Irving's 19th-century Sleepy Hollow haunts near Tarrytown to President Franklin D Roosevelt and Eleanor Roosevelt's home in Hyde Park.

HUDSON VALLEY

HIGHLIGHTS

- **Most Romantic Getaway**
  Strolling along the Hudson at Cold Spring (p158), visiting nearby historic homes or modern-art galleries and dreaming of idyllic futures.

- **Best Proof that a Yard Is an Outdoor Canvas**
  Viewing the Hudson Valley's devotion to landscape art at Storm King Art Center (p152), Clermont State Historic Site (p163) and Innisfree Garden (p164)

- **Best Two Reasons to Read Biographies**
  Visiting the Franklin D Roosevelt National Historic Site (p160) and Eleanor Roosevelt National Historic Site (p160); a truly modern couple, FDR and his wife Eleanor exemplified how compassion and diplomacy can mend a wounded country.

- **Best Use of a Box Factory**
  Checking out Dia: Beacon (p159); this converted factory has smuggled modern art out of the cramped galleries of New York City to give the pieces enough room to overwhelm the viewer.

- **Best Spicy Meal**
  Eating at Santa Fe (p163); this funky restaurant in the artist colony of Tivoli gives credence to 'nouveau' cooking.

CLIMATE

The Hudson Valley has four distinct seasons. The best are fall (32°F to 60°F), when the leaves turn brilliant colors, and spring (40°F to 70°F), when the cottage gardens come to life. Summers are humid and hot (70°F to 90°F) and winters are dreary and cold (-15°F to 32°F) with moderate snowfall. The river helps regulate the overall temperature. And the Hudson Valley's signature green fields are thanks to plentiful rainfall.

STATE PARKS

Hudson Highlands State Park (☎ 845-225-7207; Rte 9D, Beacon; 🕑 dawn-dusk; 🅿 $6), an undeveloped preserve, has 25 miles of hiking trails, including mountaintop trails with spectacular views of the Hudson and the Hudson Highland Range.

Franklin D Roosevelt State Park (☎ 914-245-4434; 2957 Compound Rd/Rte 202, Yorktown Heights; 🕑 dawn-dusk; 🅿 $6) is a popular summertime spot for locals with its spacious picnic areas, lakes and ponds.

Rockefeller State Park Preserve (see p156; ☎ 914-631-1470; Rte 117, Tarrytown; 🕑 dawn-dusk; 🅿 $6) is traversed by carriage paths, alongside rushing rivers, shady woods and vistas of the surrounding countryside.

James Baird State Park (☎ 845-452-1489; 122 Freedom Rd, Pleasant Valley; 🕑 dawn-dusk), about a 10-minute drive southwest from the Millbrook area, is a great day-use park (no camping). It's popular for short hiking, picnicking and biking; a nature center is open on the weekends during July and August.

Fahnestock Memorial Park (☎ 845-225-7207; Rte 301, Carmel; 🕑 dawn-dusk), off Taconic State Parkway, has a large, sandy beach and lake swimming in the highlands of Putnam County. Nature trails include a portion of the Appalachian Trail.

Parts of the Palisades Interstate Park, Bear Mountain State Park (p150) and Harriman State Park (p150) are easy day trips from New York City.

INFORMATION

Dutchess County Tourism (☎ 845-463-4000, 800-445-3131; www.dutchesstourism.com; Suite M-17, 3 Neptune Rd, Poughkeepsie) Covers Poughkeepsie, Red Hook, Rhinebeck, Hyde Park, Millbrook and Beacon.

Hudson Valley Tourism (☎ 800-232-4782) Has its own free guide with information on regional special events.

Rockland County (☎ 800-295-5723; www.rockland.org) Covers Nyack and Harriman and Bear Mountain State Parks.

Westchester County (☎ 800-833-9282; www.westchestertourism.com) Covers Tarrytown and Peekskill.

GETTING THERE & AROUND

If you fly or take the train into this region, be prepared to arrange for a car to get around, especially to the smaller towns.

The main airports in the region are La Guardia in New York City (see p132) and Albany International Airport to the north (see p190). **Stewart International Airport** (☎ 845-564-7200; Rte 17K), 2 miles west of Newburgh, is served by several carriers, including **Delta** (☎ 800-354-9833), **Southeast Airlines** (☎ 800-359-7325), **American Eagle** (☎ 800-433-7300) and **US Airways Express** (☎ 800-428-4322). The fare from Newburgh to Rochester is $272; Newburgh to Buffalo is $389; Newburgh to Boston is $328; and Newburgh to Philadelphia is $308.

Short Line/Coach USA (☎ 800-631-8405; www.shortlinebus.com) offers the best service to the region, including West Point, Bear Mountain State Park and Newburgh. They also offer Hudson Valley day trip packages that include taxi transfer to a particular attraction; check their website for details.

Amtrak's (☎ 800-872-7245; www.amtrak.com) Adirondack line runs the length of the river and connects several of the communities along the eastern shore, from Penn Station in New York City north to Croton-on-Hudson, Poughkeepsie, Rhinecliff-Rhinebeck, Hudson and beyond to Albany and towns in the Adirondacks.

Metro-North (☎ 212-532-4900, 800-638-7646; www.mta.info) Hudson Line runs from Grand Central Station in New York City to eastbank towns such as Tarrytown, Ossining, Peekskill, Beacon and as far north as Poughkeepsie.

To get around, a car is essential, especially to see the countryside and small towns.

Rte 9, the principal scenic north–south road in the Hudson Valley, hugs the east side of the river for the most part; when it strays, Rte 9D near Cold Spring and Rte 9G near Rhinebeck continue the scenic riverside drive. On the west side of the river is Rte 9W.

The area further east of the river is paralleled by the Taconic State Parkway, which connects the towns of Old Chatham, southeast of Albany, and East Fishkill, southeast

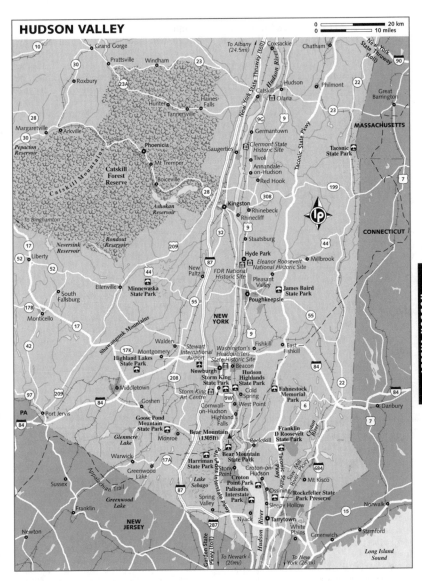

HUDSON VALLEY

of Poughkeepsie in Dutchess County. The Saw Mill River Parkway diagonally traverses the lower eastern valley from southwest to northeast. There it turns into I-684, which runs into I-84 as well as Rte 22, an eastern north–south valley route straddling the state borders of Connecticut, Massachusetts and Vermont.

The lower Hudson Valley further west of the river is traversed by east–west I-287, which runs into north–south I-87 (the New York State Thruway – often called 'Northway'). I-87 continues north into the Catskills region. For Thruway road conditions call ☎ 800-847-8929. Also on the river's west side is the Palisades Interstate Parkway, which begins in Ft Lee, NJ, and runs north through Harriman State Park and ends at Rte 9W in Bear Mountain State Park.

East–west routes include Rtes 17 and 6 in the lower Hudson Valley; I-84 in the mid-Hudson Valley; and Rtes 44, 199 and 308 in the upper Hudson Valley.

There are rental companies in towns such as Poughkeepsie, but the best rates are from the larger towns with airports, in this case Albany – but not Newburgh, which is very expensive.

LOWER HUDSON VALLEY

Heading north from New York City, the lower Hudson Valley stretches north and west from the Tappan Zee Bridge, connecting Nyack and Tarrytown, to Cold Spring just below the Newburgh-Beacon Bridge. It also takes in West Point, Newburgh and Goshen.

NYACK

☎ 845 / pop 6700

Nyack sits on the west bank across the river from Tarrytown. A ferry once connected both towns, but now the towering Tappan Zee Bridge almost overshadows this former manufacturing and boat-building center. Of late, Nyack is a quaint commuter village of New York City. A vibrant arts scene has flourished in and around Nyack, and five times a year the main streets are closed off to host street fairs. The downtown is a pleasant stroll with bookstores and small restaurants.

Information

Ben Franklin Bookshop (☎ 845-358-0440; 17 N Broadway; ☼ 11am-5:30pm Mon-Fri, 11am-6:30pm Sat & Sun) There is a good selection of local history and literature, but the specialty is rare mystery and science fiction.

Farmers Market (Main & Cedar St; ☼ 8:30am-2:30pm Thu May-Nov) In the parking lot.

Nyack Chamber of Commerce (☎ 845-353-2221; www.thenyacks.net; 6 Park St at Main St; ☼ 10am-3pm Mon-Fri) Attractions guide to Nyack.

Pickwick Bookshop (☎ 845-358-9126; 8 S Broadway; ☼ 10am-7pm Mon-Fri, 11am-6pm Sat & Sun) There is a rumpled air to the place and a sprawling corner for children's books. You can easily lose track of time here, as the owner himself does.

Sleeping

Best Western Nyack (☎ 845-358-8100; fax 845-358-3644; 26 Rte 59; d $90-110) Just off the interstate exit, this hotel has reliable rooms in a somewhat sterile setting. From Nyack town, it's at the top of Main St and walking distance to the main drag.

Super 8 Motel (☎ 800-800-8000; www.super8.com; Rte 59 & Waldron Ave; s/d $80/90) Next to McDonald's, this may be the nicest Super 8 on the planet.

Eating

Skylark Café (☎ 845-358-7988; Main St; dishes $6; ☼ 7am-10pm) A combination coffee shop and bar, the Skylark combines the fixtures of every town under one roof. In the mornings the elders sip coffee alongside the winos choking down medicine beers. The food is really of second interest compared to the local characters.

O'Donoghue's (☎ 845-358-0180; 66 Main St; dishes $5-7; ☼ 11am-11pm Tue-Sun) This Irish pub-restaurant serves as an informal community center; if you need a plumber or an apartment, many residents recommend stopping in at OD's. And if you're hungry, the lunch specials get rave reviews.

Getting There & Away

From New York City, take the George Washington Bridge to the Palisades Parkway to I-287/I-87 toward the Tappan Zee Bridge. Get off the interstate at exit 11, the last exit before the Tappan Zee Bridge. Taking a left off the exit ramp will lead you to Rte 59/Main St.

HARRIMAN & BEAR MOUNTAIN STATE PARKS

Just outside of New York City, Harriman State Park and the adjacent Bear Mountain State Park have several well-maintained hiking trails. The Appalachian Trail (see p42) passes through both parks on its way from New Jersey to Connecticut. Admission to the parks is free, but parking is $6 to $8. An Empire Passport (see p286) provides free car entry at all New York State parks.

Harriman State Park is large (72 sq miles) and a good place for a swim; it has three lakes with sandy beaches. Hiking and swimming are the most popular activities in Harriman. For free trail maps, visit the **Park Visitors Center** (☎ 845-786-5003; Palisades

Parkway btwn exit 16 & 17; 8am-6pm summer), in a stone building on the center island.

The three lakes in Harriman are used for both boating and swimming. The good news for swimmers is that no gas motors are permitted; still, lots of rowboats plus a few electric motorboats are available for rent. Lake Tiorati (park office ☎ 845-351-2568) is just below the Appalachian Trail and is another good spot for hiking, swimming, boating, picnicking and, in winter, ice-skating.

Bear Mountain State Park (☎ 845-786-2701; admission free; 8am-sunset; P $6) borders the western bank of the Hudson River. It was once the designated spot for Sing Sing Prison, until President Teddy Roosevelt intervened in 1910. The view from Bear Mountain's peak (1305ft) takes in the Manhattan skyline on a clear day, as well as the river and surrounding mountain greenery. Hiking, fishing, spring-wildflower viewing, fall-foliage viewing and pool swimming are the popular activities; in winter, cross-country skiing, sledding and ice-skating take over.

The **Trailside Museum & Wildlife Center** (☎ 845-786-2701; adult/child $1/0.50; 10am-4:30pm) is across the road from the Bear Mountain Inn and has several exhibits on the geological and natural history of the area. The wildlife center is a refuge of sorts for rescued and wayward animals of the region.

Sleeping & Eating

Beaver Pond Campground (☎ 845-947-2792, 800-456-2267; campsite $13) At Harriman, tent camping is available at Lake Welch, which has basic ground camping and 14-sq-ft wooden platforms with tent stakes.

Lake Sebago Cabins (☎ 845-351-2360, reservations ☎ 800-456-2267; cabins per week $190-370; mid-Apr–mid-Oct) These are a great deal for families or groups of four to six. There are 38 rough cabins here, each with four cots (you can add two more for a fee). You must bring your own bedding and towels. More expensive cabins come with all the amenities of home.

Bear Mountain Inn (☎ 845-786-2731; fax 845-786-0862; d $90-100). Bear Mountain does not have campgrounds but does offer lodge-type accommodations. This mountain-stone and timber inn has been around since the 1920s, and the giant stone fireplaces in the lobby area are worth a visit, even if you stay elsewhere. There are 15 rooms in the main building and four lodges down the road.

Bear Mountain Inn Restaurant (☎ 845-786-2731; dishes $10-15; 11:30am-9pm) The closest sit-down place to eat near the park; the food isn't fantastic, but the views are.

Getting There & Away

Bear Mountain and Harriman State Parks are adjacent to one another. They lie between I-87 to the west and the Palisades Interstate Parkway to the east. I-287 runs to the south of the park system, and Rte 6 marks the northern boundary. To reach Bear Mountain from the south, take Rte 9W to the Bear Mountain exit. You can also take the Palisades Parkway north to exit 19 and follow signs to Bear Mountain State Park. To reach Harriman State Park, take exit 16 from the Palisades Parkway and follow signs to Harriman State Park.

Short Line/Coach USA (☎ 800-631-8405; www.short linebus.com) serves Bear Mountain from New York City's Port Authority ($21 round-trip, 90 minutes). The bus stops at the Bear Mountain Inn.

WEST POINT

☎ 845 / pop 7100

Dedicated to duty, honor and country, the castle-like turrets of the US Military Academy at West Point jut out of the landscape in irregular and imposing tiers, as if carved from the rocky shore. Before an academy was established here, West Point was a key fortification during the Revolutionary War. Sometime between 1778 and 1780, a massive wrought-iron chain (with a log-boom to protect it) was stretched across the river to Constitution Island to prevent British ships from attempting to control river navigation. In 1802, the military academy, the oldest of its kind in the nation, was founded. Notable graduates include famous military heroes, astronauts and presidents.

The campus is impressive. Miles of pathways crisscross a grand preserve of redbrick and gray-stone Gothic- and Federal-style campus buildings, churches and temples, stadiums, a boat landing and panoramic views of the Hudson River. The military presence is tireless even in the landscaping; anything hinting at disorder has been neatly trimmed. Just walking around can make you yearn for a needless haircut. You might even imagine the plight of a young Edgar Allen Poe, a cadet in 1830, who was dismissed for

HUDSON VALLEY

insubordination after only eight months of less-than-military endeavor.

The visitor entrance for the campus is in the village of Highland Falls, which reflects the rather blue-collar aesthetic of a military operation, with just a touch of New England. Here you'll find the **West Point Visitors Center** (☎ 845-938-2638; www.usma.edu; 2107 N South Post Rd; ☺ 9am-4:45pm), about 100 yards south of the military academy's Thayer Gate. Behind the visitors center is the **West Point Museum** (admission free; ☺ 10:30am-4:15pm), which traces the history of warfare, famous generals and historical weapons in addition to West Point history.

Tours

For a glimpse of the cadets' strict military life and a tour of the campus, you must join an organized bus tour. This is a post-9/11 security procedure and is subject to change based on alert-levels issued by the federal government. **West Point Tours** (☎ 845-446-4724; www.westpointtours.com; adult/child $7/4; ☺ 10am-3:30pm Mon-Sat, 11:15am-3:30pm Sun) operates the one-hour tours throughout the day from a kiosk inside the visitors center. Photo identification is required for all visitors. Bus tours take in the following sites on campus: Cadet Chapel, Post Cemetery, Michie Stadium, the Plain (where George Washington drilled the American forces) and other battle monuments. No tours are given on Saturdays during football season.

Sleeping & Eating

Hotel Thayer (☎ 845-446-4731; www.thethayerhotel.com; inside Thayer Gate; d high season $240-260, d low season from $120; ☐) The five-story Gothic-style hotel perched at the entrance gate looks as if it is the command center of the campus. Inside a spit-polished military ambience prevails. Odd-numbered rooms claim a view of the Hudson River, while even-numbered rooms look out over the parade grounds. To enter and leave the campus, guests of the hotel must pass through security checkpoints where machine-gun toting guards inspect the driver and passengers' IDs and car. It is unnerving until they flash an innocent 18-year-old smile.

West Point Motel (☎ 888-349-6788; 156 Main St; d $74-125; ☐) The closest lodging to the campus, this independent motel has standard-issue rooms. Expect rates for all hotels to

increase greatly during graduation and other West Point–related events.

Andy's Restaurant (☎ 845-446-8736; 281 Main St; dishes $5-12; ☺ 5:30am-7pm) Tucked into the squat downtown business district, Andy's gets the morning coffee drinkers, lunchtime work crews and the dinnertime bachelors. To the metallic ringing of the fry cook's spatula, diners feast on Americana specials: stuffed peppers, eggs any style and baked chicken.

Getting There & Away

The main routes into the area are the Palisades Parkway and Rte 9W. Signs for West Point are hard to miss. From Harriman State Park, take Palisades Parkway to the junction with Rte 9W, and then continue north for about 7 miles. **New York Waterway** (☎ 800-533-3779; www.nywaterway.com; cruise $57, cruise & game $80) has boat cruises that depart from New York City for West Point football games.

Short Line/Coach USA (☎ 800-631-8405; www.shortlinebus.com) buses leave New York City's Port Authority for West Point ($38 round-trip, two hours); buses stop at the West Point Visitors Center.

STORM KING ART CENTER

This **art center** (☎ 845-534-3115; www.stormking.org; adult/senior/student $9/7/5; ☺ 11am-5:30pm Wed-Sun Apr-Nov) is a beautiful outdoor walk-through sculpture park featuring some of the finest modern and contemporary sculpture in North America, including works by modern masters Calder, Moore and Noguchi. The setting matches the artwork, angle for angle. There is also a fine indoor museum with a gift- and bookstore. Several picnic areas are available, but the nicest is near Parking Lot B. On weekends only, there is an open-air café that sells sandwiches and soft drinks. Guided walking tours and shuttle bus tours are also available.

Storm King is in Mountainville (not in Storm King State Park), about nine miles southwest of Cornwall-on-Hudson and four miles from West Point. From I-84, I-87 or Rte 9W, exit to Rte 32, where blue-and-white signs will point you to Storm King Art Center on Old Pleasant Hill Rd.

Short Line/Coach USA (☎ 800-631-8405; www.shortlinebus.com) offers day trip packages from New York City's Port Authority to Storm King Art Center ($41 round-trip, includes admission and taxi transfer).

DETOUR – NEWBURGH

Once upon a time, Newburgh was an important whaling village, as were its neighbors Pough-keepsie and Hudson. Newburgh could serve as a textbook of American architecture from the Revolutionary War period to the present. Unfortunately, one chapter of the book would include the demise of such historical towns. The oldest of the town's remaining commercial and residential buildings are in disrepair, and the best views are looking east across the river. History buffs might be able to stomach a visit to this cripple city in order to see **Washington's Headquarters State Historic Site** (☎ 845-562-1195; cnr Washington & Liberty St; adult/child $4/1; ⊙ 10am-5pm Wed-Sat & Mon, 11am-5pm Sun mid-Apr–Oct). It is the home of a small museum where Washington stayed from 1782 to 1783; he was there until the end of the Revolutionary War. The site features several galleries, period furniture and a 50ft map that wraps around an entire room. Plan to spend about an hour here.

By car, Newburgh is north of West Point via Rte 9W. If you're driving north from Newburgh, Rte 9W (between the Newburgh-Beacon Bridge and the Mid-Hudson Bridge at Poughkeepsie) is not as scenic as you might expect. The infrequent river view is hardly worth the string of strip malls, light industry and local traffic. Either jump onto the Northway (I-87), or cross the river and proceed north on Rtes 9D and 9 to the Poughkeepsie area.

TARRYTOWN, SLEEPY HOLLOW & AROUND

☎ 914

Washington Irving, author of the 'The Legend of Sleepy Hollow,' once stated that Tarrytown (population 11,000) got its name from the Dutch farm wives who complained that their husbands tarried a bit too long at the village tavern after selling their farm produce at the nearby markets. The more likely, but less appealing, linguistic explanation finds it a variation of the Dutch *tarwe*, meaning wheat.

Historic Tarrytown has the appearance of a quaint village, but all the energy of a suburb of New York City – a far cry from its rural beginning. Regardless, Tarrytown is the most convenient base for touring a string of historic homes along the river.

In December 1996 the village of North Tarrytown (population 9212) decided that it might do better to attract tourists if it changed its name to Sleepy Hollow – and so it did. Look out for old maps that might bear the old North Tarrytown name.

Information

Historic Hudson Valley (☎ 914-631-8200; www.hudson valley.org) This nonprofit organization maintains five of the most historic sites in the Lower Hudson Valley: Sunnyside, Philipsburg Manor, Kykuit, Van Cortlandt Manor and the Union Church at Pocantico Hills.

Sleepy Hollow/Tarrytown Chamber of Commerce (☎ 914-631-1705; www.sleepyhollowchamber.com; 54 Main St, Tarrytown; ⊙ 10:30am-4pm Mon-Fri)

Sights & Activities

Tarrytown and nearby Sleepy Hollow have one of the largest concentrations of historic house museums. The average person can probably bear oohing-and-aahing at two historic homes a day, so plan your trip accordingly. Thanks to the endearing legacy of the Headless Horseman, Halloween is celebrated here with great enthusiasm.

SUNNYSIDE

Washington Irving once described **Sunnyside** (☎ 914-591-8763; W Sunnyside Lane; adult/senior/child $9/8/5, grounds pass $4; ⊙ 10:30am-4pm Wed-Mon Apr-Oct), his Hudson Valley home, as being 'made up of gable ends and full of angles and corners as an old cocked hat.' Even today, it's easy to imagine Irving staring into the deep forests and ravines and envisioning the Headless Horseman of Sleepy Hollow chasing poor Ichabod Crane. When Washington Irving moved to Sunnyside, it was to combine the watery solitude of this Sleepy Hollow by the river with proximity to the bustling metropolis of New York City. Only 10 years after building Sunnyside on a serene hillside, the railroad came up the river and could not be stopped, even by America's most famous author. Irving cursed the coal-burning steam engine as it passed his home, shaking the ground. He made a compromise of sorts by finally using the train to venture into New York City.

Visitors can see this cottage on a one-hour guided tour. As the costumed tour guide will

HUDSON VALLEY

surely tell you, Irving's old Dutch cottage was cute, cozy, quiet and charming. It's easy to see the age of romanticism at work on the grounds, just as it worked on Irving's imagination. Like all romantics, he found a divine spirit in nature. The formal English hedges are gone, replaced by a carefully designed 'natural' look. The climbing wisteria that Irving planted over a century ago still clings to the house. The house tour reveals how people of leisure spent time at home, took advantage of the daylight hours and often gathered round the piano in the evening.

Sunnyside is 3 miles south of Tarrytown, just off Rte 9. Call for winter opening hours.

LYNDHURST

This **historic home** (☎ 914-631-4481; 635 S Broadway/ Rte 9; adult/senior/student/child $10/9/4/free, grounds pass $4; ☯ 10am-5pm Tue-Sun Apr-Oct) is a classic 19th-century Gothic-revival mansion designed in the 1830s by the leading architect of the genre, Alexander Jackson Davis. The home, which overlooks the Hudson, was built for the mayor of New York City, William Paulding. The landscaping is as spectacular as the building, particularly the rose garden. A small map identifying most of the flora is available for free at the entrance gate when you drive in.

PHILIPSBURG MANOR

Worried your kids think that beef was invented by the supermarket meat department? It is time to introduce them to farming, 17th-century-style, at this educational **manor** (☎ 914-631-3992; N Broadway/Rte 9; adult/senior/child $9/8/5; ☯ 10am-4pm Wed-Mon Apr-Oct). Like many wealthy Europeans, the Dutchman Frederick Philips was awarded a large tract of land here, on which he built a family home, a water-powered gristmill and a Dutch church. Visitors will see farm workers in period dress performing the chores of the day, from tending the vegetable garden to milking the cow. Cocky roosters strut across the grounds and the yard cat Scooter makes friends with everyone. In the pasture you might see a lounging cow beside a muddy stream shaded by a weeping willow – an inadvertent staging of a Hudson River painting. Activities are geared towards kids of all ages and special events, like sheep shearing, are tied to the agricultural calendar.

AMERICAN MANORS

The aristocratic land system that arrived with the Europeans certainly exacted its price from the general population, who had to make do with humble farmhouses and old stone churches. Nevertheless, the monuments of wealth and power are scattered up and down the Hudson River. They often lie deep within a manicured park, where even the gardeners seem to carry the authority of the past.

A word on the word 'manor': in the 17th and 18th centuries, it carried a specific legal meaning similar to its medieval European use, complete with hereditary rights granted by royal charter. With few exceptions, most of these New World mansions are Gothic in mood and proportion – good settings for a scary fireside story.

Two miles north of Tarrytown, Philipsburg is also the starting point for tours to Kykuit (see below).

OLD DUTCH CHURCH & SLEEPY HOLLOW CEMETERY

Across the road from Philipsburg Manor, this 1865 **church** (☎ 914-631-0081) was part of the original manor. Adjacent to the church is the **Sleepy Hollow Cemetery** (admission free; ☯ 8am-4:30pm), formerly the Tarrytown Cemetery until Washington Irving petitioned to rename it to 'keep that beautiful and umbrageous neighborhood sacred from the anti-poetical and all-leveling axe' and 'to secure the patronage of all desirous of sleeping quietly in their graves.'

In fact, Washington Irving is buried here in a section called Beekman Mound; other section names include Poet's Mound and Sunnyside. The whole place has a sort of mysterious air about it. The best time to visit the cemetery is on a foggy morning when the curvy lanes make getting lost seem like a prelude to a horror movie. Stop in at the office for a map of the cemetery.

KYKUIT

Perhaps no family has had a larger influence on 20th-century American history than the Rockefellers, who have left their stamp on business, domestic politics and international relations. The family fortune was founded by

John D Rockefeller (1839–1937), an Ohio-born entrepreneur who bought into an oil refinery in 1859. In the years following the end of the Civil War, his Standard Oil Company evolved into a formidable monopoly with a hammerlock on crude oil processing and sales in the US. By the time the company was broken into 34 different companies by the US Supreme Court in 1911, John D Rockefeller had amassed a fortune worth more than $1 billion. (Standard Oil's constituent parts are now huge businesses in their own right and include Exxon, Mobil, Texaco, Amoco, British Petroleum, Shell, Chevron and Atlantic Richfield.)

A small portion of that fortune went to build this neoclassical mansion, built on a high bluff overlooking the Hudson, known as **Kykuit** (☎ 914-631-9491; 2hr tour adult/senior/student $20/19/17; ☽ 10am-2:45pm Wed-Mon Apr-Nov). It was home to several generations of Rockefellers and parts of the estate are still used by family members. Essentially a fine-arts gallery, it is almost impossible to imagine that people conducted day-to-day rituals inside a building more akin to a bank than a house. Fine porcelain and famous paintings adorn the interior. Outside, the exquisite garden overlooking the Hudson River ('Kykuit' – keye-*cut* – is the Dutch word for 'lookout') is home to modern sculptures by Henry Moore, Alexander Calder, Jacques Lipchitz, Alberto Giacometti, Pablo Picasso and others.

The basement gallery is the most intimate space of Kykuit. This is where Nelson Rockefeller (1908–79), the patriarch's grandson, enjoyed his collection of modern artwork. Nelson Rockefeller served Presidents Roosevelt, Truman and Eisenhower in a variety of positions and helped establish the current site of the Museum of Modern Art (p88) in New York City. He was also elected governor of New York State for four terms. He was a socially liberal Republican who was so self-conscious of his wealth that he used the phrase 'thanks a thousand' to express gratitude. A leading contender for the Republican presidential nomination in the 1960, '64 and '68 elections, he was appointed by President Gerald Ford to serve as vice president following Richard Nixon's resignation in 1974. Even today, the left-wing Republican Party is known derisively as 'Rockefeller Republicans.'

Reservations are essential to visit Kykuit; on weekends chances are slim that you will join a tour if you simply show up in a hopeful mood. If you do decide to trust your luck, go in the morning, get on the day's waiting list, and wait around on the deck in back, or stroll across the bridge to the mill to get away from the mob scene in the gift shop. Children are discouraged from attending tours of Kykuit. All tours leave by shuttle bus from outside the Philipsburg Manor. The basic tour lasts about two hours and includes the house, galleries and garden. More involved tours take in the sculpture garden, the third floor of the house and other add-ons.

UNION CHURCH AT POCANTICO HILLS

This old stone **church** (☎ 914-332-6659; River Rd, Pocantico; admission $4; ☽ 11am-5pm Wed-Fri & Mon, 10am-5pm Sat, 2-5pm Sun, closed Jan-Mar), must be seen from the inside out. It's home to several stained-glass windows by Henri Matisse and Marc Chagall; the modern-art treasures were commissioned by the Rockefeller family and were completed between 1954 and 1965. Most of Chagall's nine windows are dedicated to Old Testament prophets. Matisse's beautiful rose window was his last completed work of art. It is best visited on a sunny day to see the stained glass in its full caliber. Call beforehand if visiting on a Saturday as sometimes the church hosts weddings.

To reach the church, go about 2 miles north from Tarrytown and turn right (east) just before Philipsburg Manor onto Rte 448. The church is about 3 miles away on your right.

VAN CORTLANDT MANOR

This living history **museum** (☎ 914-271-8981, reservations ☎ 914-631-8200; S Riverside Ave, Croton-on-Hudson; adult/senior/child $9/8/5, grounds pass $4; ☽ 10am-5pm Wed-Sun Apr-Oct, 10am-4pm Sat & Sun Nov & Dec) introduces visitors to the Van Cortlandts, an influential Dutch family during the 'new

YULETIDE CHEER

During the month of December, many of the Hudson Valley's historic homes are decorated in period apparel for the holidays. Lights, poinsettias and lots of Victorian lace create the illusion of a romantic past of sleigh rides and parlor games.

nation' period (1790–1815). The home and 200-year-old gardens overlook both the Hudson and the Croton Rivers. The furnishings are a major attraction; perhaps three-quarters of the family's original possessions are on display, from Queen Anne and Chippendale furniture to the colonial kitchen – complete with pots and pans, jugs, mixing bowls and graters. There's not a microwave in sight. There is even a milk room with a stone floor for cold storage. For a telling sign of the politics of the day, notice the gun-slits built into the sides of several outer walls, a reminder of the failure to live peacefully with the native inhabitants of the area.

An annual microbrewery fair is held here in honor of the patriarch Olaf Van Cortlandt who made his fortune as a brewmeister in New Amsterdam (the southern end of Manhattan Island). If you're interested in focusing on a certain historical aspect (decorative arts, herbal medicines or African American history) connected to the site, call the office about the availability of such tours.

ROCKEFELLER STATE PARK PRESERVE

Three miles north of Sleepy Hollow is the entrance to **Rockefeller Preserve** (☎ 914-631-1470; Rte 117; ☷ dawn-dusk; ℗ $6), a peaceful and beautiful getaway from the hustle and bustle that historic touring can stir up. The preserve is a rolling, woodsy expanse of solitude and old fields and pastures marked by low stone walls. A free walking-tour map is available at the small administrative building, and a large notice board tells some of the area's history, from the earliest Munsee-speaking Indian people, to the developers of the New Netherlands (New York) to the Rockefeller benefactors.

A short trail from the entrance will put you on the edge of the small Swan Lake. The preserve's entrance is 1 mile east off Rte 9, about a mile north of Philipsburg Manor

RIVER CRUISES

New York Waterway (☎ 800-533-3779; www.nywaterway.com) offers several tour packages to historic sites. Most cruise boats depart from Pier 78 (W 38th St and Twelfth Ave) in Manhattan:

- **Kykuit Cruise** (adult/senior $64/59) The ticket price includes site admission and the trip lasts a total of 7½ hours; small children are really discouraged from visiting

> ### HUDSON RIVER
>
> The Hudson River begins in the Adirondacks at Lake Tear-of-the-Cloud, atop Mt Marcy. It flows south (over 300 miles) to New York Bay, forming an estuary so large that English navigator Henry Hudson mistook the river for the Northwest Passage, the coveted route to the Far East. Subject to tidal variations, the Hudson acts more like a fjord than a river.

Kykuit – something about noise and vast wealth being incompatible.

- **North Hudson Cruise** (adult/child $15/8) Departs from Tarrytown (at the foot of Main St) for a two-hour trip up the Hudson to Peekskill Mountains.
- **Sleepy Hollow Cruise** (adult/senior/child $46/44/25) Takes in Washington Irving's Sunnyside home and Philipsburg Manor. The ticket price includes boat fare, ground transportation and admission prices. There is a good lunch counter in the gift shop area at Philipsburg Manor.

Sleeping

Accommodations in Tarrytown are corporate facilities geared toward the business traveler. Weekday rates tend to be higher than weekends and if a conference is in town it is difficult to get a room at short notice.

Courtyard by Marriott (☎ 914-631-1122; www.marriott.com; 475 White Plains Blvd/Hwy 119; d $165-200), **Hampton Inn** (☎ 914-592-5680; www.hamptoninn.com; 200 Tarrytown Rd, Elmsford; d $125-150), and **Tarrytown Hilton Inn** (☎ 914-631-5700; www.hilton.com; 455 S Broadway/Hwy 9; d $160-200) are the meager options.

Eating

Bella's Restaurant & Donut Shop (☎ 914-332-0444; 5 S Broadway at Main St; dishes $5-10; ☷ 5am-9pm Mon-Sat, 7am-3pm Sun) One of the best diners in the valley, Bella's donuts will tempt those who swore off donuts years ago. Bella's also serves goulash, pot roast, hearty soups and sandwiches.

Lefteri's Gyro Restaurant (☎ 914-524-9687; 1 N Main St at Broadway; dishes $10-12; ☷ 11am-10pm) For good homemade Greek food, try this small, family-run business. They serve big pita sandwiches (chicken, beef or veggie) and homemade Greek pastries; the 'small' Greek salad is a meal in itself.

Main Street Café (☎ 914-332-9834; 24 Main St; dishes $10-20; ☺ noon-3pm & 5-10pm Tue-Sat, noon-9pm Sun) An upscale American bistro, Main Street Café has standard sandwiches (portobello mushrooms or London broil) and half orders of seafood pasta. In summer, there are outside tables on the Main St sidewalk.

Entertainment

Tarrytown Music Hall (☎ 914-631-3390; 13 Main St) If you start feeling depressed from visiting too many mansions, you can return to 'architectural Earth' with a quick visit to this performing arts center. Housed an 1885 Queen Anne–style building and listed in the National Register of Historic Places, the music hall presents jazz, classical and folk concerts, as well as dance, opera, musicals, drama and children's theater.

Getting There & Away

Tarrytown is just off the Tappan Zee Bridge at the junction of Rte 9 and I-87. If you're coming across the bridge from the west (Nyack), take the first exit (exit 9) after the tollbooth and go to Rte 9, which is the main north–south road in the area.

To reach Tarrytown from Manhattan (about 30 miles), take the West Side Hwy north, which first turns into the Henry Hudson Parkway and then into the Saw Mill River Parkway. Follow the Saw Mill River Parkway to I-287 and go west on it. I-287 merges with I-87, and Tarrytown is at exit 9.

The **Metro-North** (☎ 212-532-4900, 800-638-7646; www.mta.info) Hudson line travels to Tarrytown form New York City's Grand Central Terminal (round-trip $13 to $17, 45 minutes); the station is just south of the New York Waterway dock on Green St between Main and White Sts. There are also train-bus day trip packages; see Metro-North's website for more information.

However, there's a more interesting way to arrive if you don't have a car. **New York Waterway** (☎ 800-533-3779; www.nywaterway.com) operates a Manhattan–Tarrytown trip (Saturday and Sunday, May to November; adult $15, child $8). The tour starts at Pier 78 (W 38th St and Twelfth Ave) in Manhattan at 10:30am and arrives in Tarrytown (foot of Main St) 90 minutes later; the return trip departs at 4:30pm.

FARMERS FOR A DAY

The Hudson Valley has long been a rich agricultural area. Small farms are abundant, and gardening is a common activity. There are hundreds of local farms, produce stands and 'pick-your-own' farms in the region. Mid- to late summer is the best time to visit but check the harvest schedule; depending on the weather, rain and so forth, harvest times vary. Most farms are open daily during summer.

The pick-your-own system works like this: they give you a container (tray or basket), you pick what you want from the seasonal fruits and vegetables, then you weigh your pickings at the register and pay wholesale prices.

Greig Farm (☎ 845-758-1234; ☺ 9am-5pm Apr-Dec) This farm occupies the whole of Pitcher Lane, three miles north of Red Hook, between Rtes 9 and 9G. It's a one-stop produce market with a bakery and education center. Popular produce pickings in the mid- to late summer include asparagus, peas, strawberries, blueberries, blackberries, raspberries and a dozen varieties of apples (Empire, Jonathan, Rome etc) and pumpkins – especially popular before Halloween. There is also a cut-your-own flower garden, as well as a picnic area and a weekend snack bar. Extended opening hours in summer.

Keepsake Farms (☎ 845-897-2266; E Hook Cross Rd; ☺ 9am-6pm May-Sept, until 5 pm in the winter) This is a very good produce market and pick-your-own farm just south of I-84 and a mile west of the Taconic State Parkway (the nearest town is Fishkill). Apples, pumpkin, berries and more are available, but if you are after a certain fruit or vegetable, call ahead to be sure it's harvest time.

Old Chatham Sheepherding Company (☎ 518-795-733; www.blacksheepcheese.com; 155 Shaker Museum Rd, Old Chatham; ☺ 9am-5pm) Makers of locally famous cheese, Old Chatham Sheepherding Company welcomes visitors to its 600-acre farm, the largest sheep dairy in the country. More than 1200 Friesian dairy sheep nibble on young tufts of grass among the rolling hills in this picture-perfect spot. Visitors can watch the milking and production process; bring along a cooler so you can stock up on fresh yogurt, ricotta and Hudson Valley camembert.

HUDSON VALLEY

OSSINING

☎ 914 / pop 24,000

This is a handsome riverside village between Tarrytown and Peekskill on Rte 9. The **Ossining Historical Museum** (☎ 914-941-0001; 196 Croton Ave; admission free) houses Indian artifacts, antique dolls and items from nearby Sing Sing Prison (the opening hours vary, so call ahead). The town used to be called Sing Sing, until the 1820s prison eclipsed the town's good name. Before the death penalty was abolished in New York State in 1965, Sing Sing was the primary facility for electrocution. This and other facts about being sent 'up the river' are available at the small **Ossining Visitors Center & Museum** (☎ 914-941-0009; 95 Broadway; admission free; ☺ 10am-4pm Mon-Sat), inside the community center. An old electric chair and life-size replicas of prison cells are also on display.

PEEKSKILL

☎ 914 / pop 22,400

Peekskill is a homely town with a big adorable heart. The active arts scene, reasonable accommodations and a great bookstore make up for what Peekskill might lack in that trendy faux-antique look.

Manhattan bibliophiles make the trek out here to visit **Bruised Apple** (☎ 914-734-7000; 923 Central Ave; ☺ 10am-6pm Mon-Fri, Sun noon-6pm), a used bookstore featuring floor-to-high-ceiling stacks of used, rare and out-of-print books. There are good sections on local history, travel and exploration and art. A groovy selection of used LPs and CDs competes for collectors' attention as well.

Paramount Center for the Arts (☎ 914-739-2333; 1008 Brown St) shows excellent international and independent films, which generally change every two days. The theater is also the setting for occasional concerts and plays.

Every third Saturday of the month, the **open studios** give the public a chance to view and talk with artists working in Peekskill. Call the Paramount Center for the Arts for details.

Sleeping, Eating & Drinking

Peekskill Inn (☎ 914-739-1500, 800-526-9466; 634 Main St; d $117-130; ☐) Near the junction of Rtes 9 and 6, this pet-friendly motel-inn is perched high on a bluff overlooking the river and a few 'castles on the Rhine' (industrial factories). The staff's enthusiasm for Peekskill

is infectious and you might find yourself more charmed than you had expected. Appalachian Trail hikers frequently stop in for creature comforts (including a swim in the pool) before resuming the journey.

Chola Cuencana Restaurant (☎ 914-737-9041; 1101 Main St; ☺ 9am-8pm; lunch buffet $6) Traveling through the Hudson Valley, it is easy to get bistro-overload. Thankfully, this Ecuadorean restaurant saves people from eating too many mesclun salads. Dust off your Spanish and head here for their enormous down-home lunch buffets (weekdays).

Peekskill Coffee House (☎ 914-739-1287; 101 S Division St; coffee $1.50-3) This cozy coffee shop serves steamy cups of joe as well as Friday night music and poetry readings (no cover, 8pm).

Susan's (☎ 914-737-6624, 12 N Division St; dishes $10-15; ☺ noon-2:30pm & 5:30-9pm Tue-Sat) Right in downtown, Susan's is where most of the town's business is informally decided. The American bistro-style dishes include salmon strudel with spinach and wild rice, Louisiana shrimp and andouille sausage jambalaya.

Getting There & Away

The **Metro-North** (☎ 212-532-4900, 800-638-7646; www.mta.info) Hudson line reaches Peekskill from New York City's Grand Central Terminal (from NYC $20 to $25, one hour); the train station is on Hudson Ave at Railroad Ave, on the riverfront. It's about a half mile to the downtown area. By car, Peekskill is north of Cold Spring on Rte 9.

COLD SPRING

☎ 845 / pop 1900

Cold Spring is a romantic town with prim townhouses lining the narrow streets, and quiet walks along the river in the shadow of Storm King Mountain. Many people take the train here from New York City for a weekend of antiquing. The shops and restaurants are reflective of this affluent and sophisticated clientele. A (free) walking tour sponsored by the **Putnam County Historical Society** (☎ 845-265-4010, 63 Chestnut St; ☺ 10am-4pm Tue-Thu, 2-5pm Sat & Sun) begins at 72 Main St. The tour is offered on Sunday at 2pm from mid-May to mid-November. Call for additional information, or inquire at any of the antique shops on Main St. Midway between Peekskill and Beacon, Cold Spring (on Rte 9D) serves as a more

DETOUR – DIA: BEACON

The Manhattan-based museum Dia (p84) has staked out a satellite in the unlikeliest place: Beacon, a struggling industrial city that the world almost forgot. Now the art world, gasp, leaves New York for the trek to this converted box factory. **Dia: Beacon** (☎ 845-440-0100; 3 Beekman St; adult/student $10/7; ☼ 11am-6pm Thu-Mon Apr-Oct, 11am-4pm Fri-Mon Nov-Mar) comprises 240,000 sq ft of exhibition space that is impressive in its own right. Light streams through the skylights illuminating the enormous raw space of stark white walls and the torturous echoes of squeaking shoes. Before engaging the exhibits, first put yourself in a 'modern-art' state of mind. That's right: modern art doesn't have to be beautiful or realistic or intricate. In order to achieve its goal, modern art has to affect you either by eliciting disgust or wonder. This they will do. Works by John Chamberlain, Andy Warhol, Blinky Palermo and others alter space, distort perception or prove your suspicion that artists are certifiably insane.

Beacon is exit 11 off I-84, from the exit ramp make a right on to Rte 9D south to Season's Restaurant where you'll turn right on to Beekman St. Alternatively Beacon is north of Cold Spring on Rte 9D; follow the street through town and make a left at the city hall, past the I-84 intersection to Beekman St.

scenic base than the roughshod towns of Peekskill and Beacon.

Sleeping & Eating

Pig Hill Inn (☎ 845-265-9247; www.pighillinn.com; 73 Main St; d weekday $120-170, weekend $150-220, incl breakfast) This brick Victorian in the middle of the village has antique-decorated rooms. The more expensive rooms have private baths and the tranquility room comes with a fireplace.

East Side Kitchen (☎ 845-265-7723; 124 Main St; dishes $10-15; ☼ noon-9pm Tue-Sun) A revival-style country general store with mint-green paintwork, this stylish spot has magnificent salads and a loyal clientele of precocious children. How old were you when you were introduced to calamari? These kids have you beat.

The Depot (☎ 845-265-5000; 1 Depot Rd; dishes $10-18) Right by the train tracks, as you'll soon discover, this restaurant is a converted train lounge. In the summer, several umbrella-shaded outdoor tables vibrate slightly as the train goes by. Inside, a lovely horseshoe bar also affords a quick glimpse of the passing trains. Food options range from fish and chicken to burgers and pasta.

Getting There & Away

Cold Spring can be reached by train on the **Metro-North** (☎ 212-532-4900, 800-638-7646; www.mta.info) Hudson Line ($18 to $23, one hour); the train station in Cold Spring is at the foot of Main St. By car Cold Spring is on Rte 9D between Peekskill and Beacon.

MID- & UPPER HUDSON VALLEY

The mid-Hudson Valley extends from the Newburgh–Beacon Bridge (and I-84) north to the area east of the Kingston–Rhinecliff Bridge. It includes Rhinebeck, Red Hook, Poughkeepsie and Hyde Park.

The upper Hudson Valley extends roughly from the area east of the Kingston–Rhinecliff Bridge north to the area between Hudson and New Lebanon. This chapter covers only a portion of the upper Hudson Valley. Communities along the west bank of the Hudson, including the town of Kingston, will be found in the Catskills Region chapter (p168).

HYDE PARK

☎ 845 / pop 20,800

Hyde Park is forever associated with the Roosevelts and their homes, but the surviving town has developed little of its own allure outside of its inherited historic homes.

Sights

History has catapulted FDR to saint-like status for his success in steering the country out of the uncertain events of economic collapse and world war. Intelligent and charming, this golden boy of an accomplished Hudson Valley family married a woman who was as sharp as he but not a society decoration. Fitting for such a modern couple, Hyde Park

---

DETOUR – POUGHKEEPSIE RTE 9

Poughkeepsie (pooh-*kip*-see) is the largest town on the east bank of the Hudson and has suffered the same urban fate as many former factory towns in New York; as industry moved out, decay moved in. There are, however, a few historic sites worth a detour. **Vassar College** (☎ 845-437-7000; www.vassar.edu; 124 College Ave at Raymond Ave), a well-respected liberal arts school, offers tours of its 125-acre campus daily during the summer months. Vassar is also home to the **Francis Lehman Loeb Art Center** (☎ 845-437-5632; http://fllac.vassar.edu; admission free; ☼ 10am-5pm Tue-Sat, 1-5pm Sun), which contains several paintings from the Hudson River school.

Samuel FB Morse Historic Site (☎ 845-454-4500; Locust Grove, 370 South Rd/Rte 9; house adult/senior/student $7/6/3, grounds free; ☼ house 10am-3pm May-Nov, grounds 8am-dusk), a privately owned 1830 mansion about 2 miles south of the Mid-Hudson Bridge, is the former home of telegraph inventor and artist Samuel FB Morse. The house, built in the Tuscan Villa style popular in the mid-19th century, has its picture windows designed to showcase the 150-acre manicured grounds whose carriage roads wind through locust, hemlock and larch trees and gardens galore. It's also home to a beautiful wildlife and bird sanctuary with easy hiking trails and a visitors center, a gallery and a museum shop on the grounds. In addition to the ornate mansion furnishings, some of Morse's old telegraph equipment and paintings are displayed. Check out the mirror in the butler's pantry and kitchen that is carefully positioned for the staff to follow progress at the dining table without disturbing the family or guests.

Although Morse is remembered as one of the great inventors, his passion was painting. He seems to have invented things in order to support his painting. For an eight-year period, he was in and out of court over patent rights, but he continued painting the entire time.

---

boasts a historical monument to both of them. In marked contrast is the ostentatious summer cottage of the Vanderbilts.

FRANKLIN D ROOSEVELT NATIONAL HISTORIC SITE

Even in the staid environment of a historical monument, FDR's compelling and charming persona emerges. This **historic site** (☎ 845-229-9115, reservations ☎ 800-967-2283; 519 Albany Post Rd/Rte 9; adult/child $14/free; ☼ 9am-5pm) includes FDR's home, library-museum, grave site and rose garden.

Guided tours of FDR's home, **Springwood**, take visitors through a surprisingly ordinary home of practical tastes. Winston Churchill spent the night in the bedroom that looks like a 1950s TV show. The home was outfitted with a hand-pulled elevator to transport FDR and his chair to the 2nd floor. Because the tour guides allow visitors to wander around on their own, children have the opportunity to become curious about the site. Tours are popular and reservations are encouraged.

The **Museum of the Franklin D Roosevelt Library** is the nation's first presidential library and the only one that was ever put to use by a sitting president. Several exhibits at the museum highlight Great Depression relief programs, along with exhibits about

Pearl Harbor and America's entry into WWII. The museum features old photos, FDR's voice on tape (from the fireside chats and several speeches), a special wing in memory of Eleanor Roosevelt and FDR's famous 1936 Ford Phaeton car – equipped with special hand controls so he could drive despite the restricted mobility caused by his bout with polio. Roosevelt's White House desk is also here, supposedly just as he left it on his last day at work prior to his death in 1945, less than a year after he was elected to a record fourth term as president.

A new site is **Top Cottage** (☎ 845-229-5320, reservations ☎ 800-967-2283; 4097 Albany Post Rd; adult/child $8/free; ☼ 10am, 1pm & 3pm Thu-Mon May-Oct), FDR's private retreat. The British monarchs and other world figures attended informal diplomacy meetings here; one widely reported event was when King George VI and Queen Elizabeth were served hot dogs at a picnic. Tickets for the site are available from the booth at the FDR National Historic Site.

ELEANOR ROOSEVELT NATIONAL HISTORIC SITE

Better known as **Val-Kill** (Valley Stream; ☎ 845-229-9115, reservations ☎ 800-967-2283; adult/child $8/free; ☼ 9am-5pm May-Oct, 10am-4pm Sat & Sun Nov-Dec & Apr), this site is 2 miles east of Hyde Park. Eleanor herself used to make the drive frequently, but townspeople apparently pulled over to the curb quickly when she came by – not so much out of their respect and admiration for the popular first lady, but rather due to their knowledge of her erratic driving habits.

Eleanor Roosevelt used Val-Kill as a retreat from the main house at Hyde Park, in part to pursue her own interests and maintain her own identity. The cottage, as she called it, was her own place – not FDR's and not his mother's. After the president's death, Eleanor made this her permanent home.

Although she was raised in high society, her house is a simple cottage in the true sense of the word. Unlike many of the famous residences up and down the Hudson, Val-Kill was not meant to impress anyone; comfort was a priority, and you see it immediately in the ordinary and non-matching furniture, the everyday chinaware and the plain water glasses. This was the dinnerware she used to entertain statesmen, kings and queens and the local students she invited for dinner. The grounds are dotted with sugar maple and pine trees, and a road leads to the cottage from the entrance off Rte 9G.

Eleanor was involved in human rights before the term was coined, and she helped establish the International Declaration of Human Rights, earning her the designation 'first lady of the world.' Instead of great works of art, the wood-paneled walls of the cottage are crammed with family photos.

VANDERBILT MANSION NATIONAL HISTORIC SITE

Another valley spectacle of immense wealth, this **mansion** (☎ 845-229-9115, 800-967-2283; Albany Post Rd/Rte 9; adult/child $8/free; ☾ 9am-5pm) housed Frederick, grandson of Cornelius 'Commodore' Vanderbilt, and his wife Louise. Commodore made his money the new-fangled way, he ruthlessly earned it. He started out as a farmer in Staten Island, created a ferry company at the age of 16, and soon bought up all struggling railroads to amass a transportation empire. Despite his power and wealth, Commodore was ostracized from New York society for being a commoner. His descendants, however, rose up the social ladder, partly due to their excessive display of wealth. This beaux arts monument – an eclectic mix of classical Greek, Roman and baroque lines – was merely a country palace used on weekends or seasonal getaways, but was painstakingly decorated to emulate the styles of European aristocracy, including a formal Italian rose garden. Within a generation, the house was so flamboyant that the heirs couldn't find a buyer and ultimately donated it to the public trust. The Vanderbilt Mansion is about 2 miles north of Hyde Park on Rte 9.

STAATSBURGH STATE HISTORIC SITE

About 5 miles north of Hyde Park on Albany Post Rd (Rte 9) in Staatsburg, this **historic site** (formerly Mills Mansion; ☎ 845-889-8851; adult/child $5/1; student & senior $4; ☾ 10am-5pm Sat, noon-5pm Sun Apr-Oct) is an updated Greek-revival-style building with the requisite white columns in front. It was built in 1832 and remodeled in 1896. This is no ordinary addition – it's ostentatious in the extreme. There are guided house tours every half-hour (otherwise, you'd get lost amid the 65 rooms). The palatial grounds are open all year.

HUDSON VALLEY GARDENS

In spring and fall, the best feature of many of the historic homes along the Hudson River are their gardens, many of which were designed with as much care and expense as the homes. Gardens are typically free (unless otherwise noted) and open from dawn to dusk. Lilacs, roses and fall color are major events to plan a visit for. A few highlights include the following:

▪ Montgomery Place & Clermont State Historic Site (p163) – With tree-framed views of the Hudson River and the Catskill Mountains, these nearby estates tie for the honor of most beautiful grounds.

▪ Vanderbilt Mansion Italian Gardens (p161) – This formal rose garden is straight out of a European palace.

▪ Innisfree Garden (p164) – Devoted to landscape art, this garden incorporates wild and sculpted into a seamless balance.

Sleeping & Eating

Mills-Norrie State Park (☎ 800-456-2267; www.reserve america.com; Rte 9, Staatsburg; campsite $14) About 2 miles from Staatsburgh State Historic Park, this 1000-acre park has camping, a marina, boat launch, bicycle paths, sledding, cross-country skiing, nature trails and a museum. You'll also find Norrie Point Environmental Site, which has a small aquarium that replicates conditions of the Hudson River, a museum of New York State wildlife and nature trails. Cabins look out over the river. This is a convenient spot between Hyde Park and tiny Rhinebeck.

Costello's Guest House (☎ 845-229-2559; 21 Main St; d $55-65). Patsy Costello rents out two rooms in her home; the rooms share a bath. She also offers discounts for weekly stays, especially if you're in town to do research on FDR. The house is two blocks from the Vanderbilt mansion, off Rte 9.

Roosevelt Inn (☎ 845-229-2443; fax 845-229-0026; 4360 Albany Post Rd/Rte 9; d from $65, ste $95-135, incl breakfast; 🖭) Hyde Park has some of the most reasonable lodging rates in the entire Hudson Valley thanks to a strip of independent motels. This family-friendly site is halfway between the FDR and Vanderbilt sites. Rooms in the back will be less noisy than those facing the road.

SAMPLING CIA FARE

Bearing the nickname 'CIA,' the **Culinary Institute of America** (reservations ☎ 845-471-6608; www.ciachef.edu; 1946 Campus Drive) is the preeminent culinary school in the US. To sample the creations of America's next generation of chefs, you need reservations at one of the four restaurants on the campus: Ristorante Caterina de' Medici (Italian), Escoffier Restaurant (French), American Bounty Restaurant and St Andrew's Café (the least formal and least expensive). Business-casual attire is recommended and reservations are needed Monday through Friday.

Lunch is served from 11:30am to 1pm, and dinner is served from 6:30pm to 8:30pm. Escoffier and American Bounty are open Tuesday through Saturday, Caterina and St Andrew's Café are open Monday through Friday. The newest addition is the informal Apple Pie Bakery Café, a student-staffed eatery open Monday to Friday.

Eveready Diner (☎ 845-229-8100; Rte 9; dishes $7-10) Between Poughkeepsie and Hyde Park, this busy Art Deco diner has a bit of everything, like Brooklyn egg creams and pastrami sandwiches. Your heart never had it so good.

Getting There & Away

The closest train station is in Poughkeepsie, 10 miles away. By car, take Rte 9 north from Poughkeepsie.

RHINEBECK & AROUND

☎ 845 / pop 3000

With proud Victorian homes and well-pressed residents, Rhinebeck is so pretty and romantic it feels like a movie set, lacking the messiness of ordinary life. Before it became a weekend getaway for well-heeled New Yorkers, the town was a stagecoach stop and still boasts the famous Beekman Arms, America's oldest continuously operating inn. Rates have changed over the years, but a sign in the lobby recalls another era: 'Lodging 3 pence; with breakfast 4 pence; only 5 lodgers to a bed; no boots can be worn in bed.'

Red Hook is a small community that pops up among the winding roads and greens, about 5 miles north of Rhinebeck via Rte 9. With hardware stores and pizza parlors, Red Hook is more functional than its showpiece neighbor. Another interesting village is **Annandale-on-Hudson**, which is just west of Red Hook on Rte 9G.

Sights & Activities

Although there are many historic homes to visit in and around Rhinebeck, the most popular activity is to sleep in late, eat at a fashionable restaurant and stroll the small downtown. If you're a go-getter, stop into one of the historic house museums listed here or even go over to nearby Hyde Park or Millbrook.

OLD RHINEBECK AERODROME

If the Red Baron is a personal hero, you should visit the **Old Rhinebeck Aerodrome** (☎ 845-758-8610; Stone Church Rd; museum adult/senior/child $6/5/2, air show $12/10/5; 🕑 museum 10am-5pm mid-May–Oct, air shows 2pm Sat & Sun mid-Jun–mid-Oct). Between Rhinebeck and Red Hook, this combination museum and air show has vintage planes from WWI and antique cars; you can even take a ride in an open-cockpit plane, but you have to provide your own scarf and goggles.

BARD COLLEGE

Located near Montgomery Place on Rte 9G is Bard College's 600-acre campus. It was founded in 1860 as a school for men, though today it is coed and best known for its devotion to the creative arts. The Frank Gehry–designed building for the performing arts (☎ 845-758-6822) is a recent addition to the campus and hosts opera, music and drama performances, including the acclaimed Bard Music Festival in August.

MONTGOMERY PLACE

In Annandale-on-Hudson, you'll find this 1805 neoclassical riverside villa (☎ 845-758-5461; River Rd/Rte 103; adult/senior/student $7/6/4, grounds pass $3; 10am-5pm Wed-Mon Apr-Oct). The house is impressive, but the grounds are among the prettiest of any of the great estates. Among the 434 acres are gardens, a waterfall, walking trails and views of the Catskill Mountains and the Hudson River. Montgomery Place is north of Rhinebeck, just west of Rte 9G on River Rd, before the entrance to Bard College. Call for winter hours.

CLERMONT STATE HISTORIC SITE

Between Annandale-on-Hudson and Germantown off Rte 9G, this site (☎ 518-537-4240; 1 Clermont Ave; adult/child $5/1, senior & student $4; 11am-5pm Tue-Sun Apr-Oct, 11am-4pm Sat & Sun Nov-Mar), off Woods Rd, is the early-18th-century home of the Robert Livingston family; part of the attraction here is the history of the home and its occupants. The original manor was burned to the ground by the British during the Revolutionary War, but rebuilt soon after. Born in Scotland, the Livingstons made a fortune in the new nation, and a great grandson, Robert R Livingston, was a delegate to the Continental Congress that produced the Declaration of Independence. He also negotiated the Louisiana Purchase of 1803 from Napoleon for Thomas Jefferson. In Paris he also met and became partners with Robert Fulton, who was busy working on a contraption called a steamboat. In 1807, the first steamboat, *North River*, made its appearance on the Hudson River. Later, it was called *Clermont*.

The house is Georgian in style, and original furnishings are on view. The grounds,

which extend down to the river, offer a fine view of the Catskill Mountains across the river. The fragrant lilacs and linden trees are major draws when they bloom. The grounds are open daily all year from 8:30am to sunset. The house is best visited in early evening as the setting sun swathes the world in gold.

Sleeping

Village Inn of Rhinebeck (☎ 845-876-7000; fax 845-876-4756; 6260 Rte 9, Rhinebeck; d weekday $70, weekend $90) This roadside motel has huge rooms with windows that look out over a suburban yard. The owner has an interesting collection of baseball memorabilia displayed in the lobby.

Beekman Arms (☎ 845-876-7077; www.beekmanarms.com; 6387 Mill St/Rte 9, Rhinebeck; d $110-180) At the intersection of Rte 308 in the middle of town, this historic site got its start in 1766 and still retains its cellar-like lobby where dusty travelers rested in front of a crackling fire in the days of stagecoach travel. The rooms in the original inn are exquisite with big cozy beds and roomy bathrooms. The newer, inexpensive motel rooms are often referred to as the 'kennel' because pets tend to be vocal and odiferous guests.

Grand Duchess B&B (☎ 845-758-5818; fax 845-758-3143; 7571 Old Post Rd, Red Hook; d $95-155) This Victorian is a quiet and elegant spot close to the shops in Red Hook and an easy drive to Bard College.

Eating

Rhinebeck Deli (☎ 845-876-3614; 112 E Market St, Rhinebeck; dishes $3-10) In the mornings the so-called town criers assemble around the simple tables for coffee and the leisurely life of retirement. The younger set clamors around the deli counter for take-away sandwiches and meals before scurrying off to work.

Calico Restaurant & Patisserie (☎ 845-876-2749; 6384 Mill St/Rte 9, Rhinebeck; dishes $4-15; 8am-8:30pm Wed-Sat, 8am-4pm Sun) This little tearoom has the best pastries in a town that likes pastries. The menu has recently expanded to include French-inspired bistro fare.

Cripple Creek Restaurant (☎ 845-876-4355; 22 Garden St, Rhinebeck; dishes $18-25; 5-9pm Wed-Mon, later on weekends) In a place where every sandwich-slinger is a CIA graduate (see boxed text on p162), a restaurant has to qualify their credentials. This restaurant, serving eclectic American cuisine, receives the honor as a certain CIA professor's favorite restaurant for special events. In a characterless office park, the restaurant has a long bar, classical music and impressive artwork (check out the Chagall on the wall).

Santa Fe Restaurant (☎ 845-757-4100; 52 Broadway; mains $15-25; ☑ 5-10pm Tue-Sun) In the artist community of Tivoli, west of Red Hook, this hamlet favorite does fresh and interesting nouveau Mexican food. The pulled pork taco has a sultry mix of spicy and sweet, and the restaurant is filled with an eclectic mix of Bard students, young families and professional layabouts.

Getting There & Away
Rhinebeck's train station is in the neighboring hamlet of Rhinecliff, 3 miles away. **Amtrak** (☎ 800-872-7245; www.amtrak.com) trains depart New York City's Penn Station for the trip north along the Hudson River throughout the day ($58 round-trip, 1½ hours). A weekday trolley transports passengers to Rhinebeck; on the weekends, call a **taxi** (☎ 845-876-2010). **Short Line/Coach USA** (☎ 800-631-8405; www.shortlinebus.com) buses make the trip from New York City's Port Authority to the Beekman Arms in downtown Rhinebeck ($50 round-trip, two hours).

By car, take I-87 north to exit 19 and then across the Kingston–Rhinebeck Bridge. Alternatively, Rhinebeck is north of Hyde Park on Rte 9, which becomes very scenic through this stretch.

MILLBROOK & AROUND
☎ 845 / pop 1400
Millbrook lies east of the Hudson in the Taconic Region, midway between the river and the Connecticut border on Rte 44. The area has long been an upscale alternative to the Hamptons in Long Island, and there's a privileged, old-money feel about the area. A maze of backroad retreats, riding trails and genteel country homes seem to appear and disappear among the winding country roads. Nearby Rte 22, which runs north–south near the Connecticut and Massachusetts borders, is also one of the state's most bucolic corridors, dotted with farms and pastures, antique stores and blue-plate family diners.

Millbrook itself is as pretty a little town as you'll find, complete with a village green, shiny fire station and spiffy Main St diner. This is a town with a center, and it's an easy

place to linger. The area counts among its more famous visitors one Timothy Leary (American psychologist and author who advocated the use of LSD and other psychoactive drugs), who spent some of his early LSD-experimenting days around Millbrook at the nearby Hitchcock estate. Some of the townsfolk were scandalized, but it's hard to tell these days if they're bragging or if they're complaining.

Sights & Activities
Every gardener should make the pilgrimage to Millbrook for its stunning landscape creations.

INNISFREE GARDEN
This **garden** (☎ 845-677-8000; 362 Tyrell Rd; weekday/weekend $3/4; ☑ 10am-4pm Wed-Fri May-Oct, 11am-5pm Sat & Sun) is one of the most beautiful in the valley – and there are many. When the great Irish poet William Butler Yeats wrote his poem 'The Lake Isle of Innisfree,' he described a spot in the imagination that is always alive. The 200-acre garden here was designed by Walter Beck, who designed a series of cup gardens, with terraces, streams and stones arranged in meticulous fashion, all of which comes to a delicate rest on the edge of Tyrell Lake – reminiscent of Yeats' 1893 poem, part of which reads: 'And I shall have some peace there, for peace comes dropping slow,/ Dropping from the veils of the morning to where the cricket sings.'

To find Innisfree from Millbrook, head west on Rte 44 at the traffic light, and turn left on Tyrell Rd and follow the signs.

INSTITUTE OF ECOSYSTEM STUDIES
This **center** (☎ 845-677-5359; ☑ ecology shop 11am-5pm Mon-Fri, 9am-5pm Sat, 1-5pm Sun, greenhouse closes 3:30pm) for the study of ecology is between the Taconic State Parkway and the town of Millbrook, just off Rte 44A where a sign will point the way. The institute is a combination arboretum, gardening-education and wetland-ecology center. In addition to being a lovely spot to walk through, you can sign up for courses that last from one day or weekend to a week or six weeks. Courses include natural science illustrating and drawing in the greenhouse. There are also canoe excursion trips to study wetland ecology, as well as other trips. Call for more information or write for a brochure

(Institute of Ecosystem Studies, Box R, Millbrook, NY 12545).

Sleeping

Cottonwood Motel (☎ 845-677-3283; www.cotton woodmotel.com; Rte 44; d weekday $89-110, weekend $115-155) Just outside town, this sparkling white motel is set back from the road so that the din of traffic doesn't echo into your room. The rooms are solid and some have outdoor patios.

Cat in Your Lap B&B (☎ 845-677-3051; Old Rte 82 at the Monument; d $75-125) This pet-friendly farmhouse offers two bedrooms in the main house and barn suites with fireplace and kitchenette. Bill Berensmann, the co-proprietor, is an architect by training and can give you great tips on appreciating the Hudson Valley architecture.

Eating

Millbrook Diner (☎ 845-677-5319; 3266 Franklin Ave/Rte 44; dishes $4-10; ☼ 6am-9pm) Near the village green, this town landmark has basic diner fare of eggs and waffles. The diner's old wooden figurehead is a reputedly the prettiest lady in town (but don't spread this around). The tables inside are adorned with jukebox units, and the food – especially breakfast – is just right.

Allyn's Restaurant & Café (☎ 845-677-5888; 4258 Rte 44; dishes $15-22; ☼ 11:30am-9:30pm Mon, Wed & Thu, 11:30am-10:30pm Fri & Sat, 11:30am-3pm Sun) About 4 miles east of Millbrook, this equestrian-themed restaurant offers excellent daily soups, a nice selection of local wines and a variety of dishes reflecting a Continental-Asian fusion.

Getting There & Away

By car, take the Millbrook exit off of the Taconic Parkway on to Rte 44 east which will lead into town. Rte 44 west connects to Poughkeepsie.

HUDSON & AROUND
☎ 518 / pop 7500

Hudson is another former whaling village, and the architecture is worth a trip through town. Warren St in particular is part of the classic American downtown of small family-owned businesses selling everything from charming junk to the family jewels. Hudson's other claim to fame is its (former) red-light district, said to be the first in the country. Stepping off the well-defined scenic route in Hudson puts you smack dab into urban blight – an odd contrast to the incubator society of New York City that runs along Warren St.

Sights & Activities

An odd assortment of activities await in Hudson. Be sure to cruise the small country lanes for unstructured sightseeing. The roads wind around shady creek beds, vista hills and gnarled apple orchards.

AMERICAN MUSEUM OF FIREFIGHTING

New York State has a proud volunteer firefighting tradition as evidenced by the stoic brick buildings in every town manned during the day by an assortment of local characters sitting out the front in ratty folding chairs. This **museum** (☎ 518-822-1875; 117 Harry Howard Ave; admission free; ☼ 9am-4:30pm) is a one-of-a-kind exhibit displaying 84 fire engines from man-powered carts to engine-powered machines. The oldest fire engine in the collection was built in 1725 and used by Hudson Company No 1. A gooseneck engine from 1811 still bears the battle scars it earned fighting New York City's Great Fire of 1835. The museum docents are happy to explain the history of the equipment, which isn't particularly well signed. The most recent addition is a small touching memorial to the firefighters who lost their lives on 9/11.

OLANA

Using the grounds around his home, **Olana** (☎ 518-828-0135; Rte 9G; adult/senior/child $7/5/2; ☼ 11am-5pm Tue-Sun Apr-Nov, 11am-4pm Sat & Sun Jan-Mar), as a canvas, landscape painter Frederic Edwin Church (1826–1900) set out to create a three-dimensional landscape painting. Church originally planned to build a French chateau on the land he bought in the mid-19th century. But after a trip to the Middle East, he changed his plans and commissioned Calvert Vaux to design a villa with influences of Moorish architecture; the Persianesque project was finished in the late 1870s.

Although some of the views are now spoiled by industrial eyesores along the Hudson's west bank, the house and grounds are still breathtaking and the view from the 'front porch' on a summer afternoon resembles some of the large canvases of the Hudson River school of landscape painters.

HUDSON RIVER SCHOOL OF LANDSCAPE PAINTERS

Big soaring skies and little hamlets along the highway of the day: the Hudson River. The majestic and the ordinary were captured by the Hudson River school of painters. The expansion and prosperity that came in the first decades of the 19th century – especially after the completion of the Erie Canal in 1825 – gave the country a strong national consciousness and, along with it, the freedom to begin exploring distinctly American (that is, non-European) themes. The new artists shunned popular historical themes along with formal portraiture in favor of everyday life – romanticized to be sure, but with a detailed realism that was new to the American art scene around New York. Like Washington Irving, author of 'The Legend of Sleepy Hollow,' the romantic impulse was at work.

Thomas Doughty was the self-taught founder of the school, but its leading spirit was Thomas Cole who was followed by Asher Durand, John Kensett and Frederick Church (who turned his home at Olana into a 'real' landscape painting; see p165). Both Cole and Church injected allegorical elements into their work, but most members of the school worked using a purely representational style, one which some critics found to be uninspired and tedious.

Today, a bright day in the Hudson Valley is sure to bring out a few painters to sit by a quiet riverbank or green hillside with brush in hand and eye on the same landscapes that inspired their famous predecessors.

Olana is open only for guided tours. Call ahead for reservations; tickets sell out quickly. Call for December opening hours.

Olana is about 5 miles south of Hudson on Rte 9G. From downtown Hudson, go south on S 3rd St, which will turn into Rte 23/9G, stay on 9G heading south (away from the Rip Van Winkle Bridge). Look for the sign on the left and go up the hill.

SHAKER MUSEUM & LIBRARY

Even though their numbers have dwindled over the years, the Shakers' legacy is preserved in this fascinating **museum** (☎ 518-794-9100; 88 Shaker Museum Rd, Old Chatham; adult/senior/child $8/6/4; 🕑 10am-5pm Wed-Mon May-Oct). Its location must be put in context: it's close to the border of Massachusetts, home of the Pilgrims and several early religious movements.

The Shakers were an early experimental communal group, one of many to follow the trail of New England religious migration. The original group, known as the United Society of Believers in Christ's Second Appearing, came from England with Mother Ann Lee in 1774. In 1792, the first Shaker community was established in nearby New Lebanon, near the Massachusetts state line.

The Shakers got their nickname from their love of music and dance, all in the name of religious ritual and harvest celebration. The moniker took hold as word

spread of their excited religious services in which members often shook with emotion when seized with the Holy Spirit. The Shakers also had the unique ability to simultaneously entertain the notions of communal living and celibacy.

Recently the museum received a grant to purchase relevant sites in New Lebanon and are planning to build a 50,000-sq-ft museum within the massive ruins of the great stone barn. A timeline of these changes had yet to be announced at the time of writing, so if you're in the area, it is a good idea to call ahead.

The museum is about 20 miles from the town of Hudson via Rte 66.

Sleeping & Eating

St Charles Hotel (☎ 518-822-9900; 16-18 Park Pl; d $100, incl breakfast) Right on the village green, this hotel has several floors of predictable rooms with all the standard amenities.

Hudson City B&B (☎ 518-822-8044; 326 Allen St; d $130-170, incl breakfast) Kenneth Jacobs, proprietor of the historic Joshua T Waterman House, offers six tastefully decorated bedrooms in a historic 1865 townhouse. The house itself is a history and architecture lesson as is the surrounding neighborhood, which was built by the successful shipping magnates of the 1800s.

Columbia Diner (☎ 518-828-1310; 717 Warren St; dishes $6-10) This shiny chrome diner has soothing 1970s colors of fuchsia and beige along with perky waitstaff and Greek lunch classics, like stuffed cabbage and peppers.

Wunderbar & Bistro (☎ 518-828-055; 744 Warren St; dishes $8-14; ☉ 11:30am-2pm & 5-10pm Mon-Fri, 5-10pm Sat) Hudson doesn't have much in the way of indigenous cuisine, instead it borrows liberally from the restaurant culture of New York City. One of many chic bistros that line Warren St, Wunderbar breaks out from the pack with a reasonable lunch special. The menu is straightforward American, like roasted chicken with fries and pork roast with mashed potatoes, and the portions stay true to the American theme of big is beautiful.

Getting There & Away

Hudson's Amtrak train station, on Allen and Front Sts, is within walking distance to the shops and hotels, making a weekend of antiquing an easy car-less affair. You will need a car to visit the surrounding attractions, though. **Amtrak** (☎ 800-872-7245; www.amtrak.com) runs frequent trains from New York City's Penn Station to Hudson ($74 round-trip, two hours).

By car, exit at Ancram-Hudson (Rte 82) off of the Taconic Parkway; follow signs to the Rip Van Winkle Bridge, approximately 9 miles to Rte 9 north, which will take you into Hudson's downtown.

HUDSON VALLEY

Catskills Region

CONTENTS

On a late summer afternoon, when the sun filters through the leafy trees and the shadows turn the surrounding hills a purplish hue, the understated beauty of the Catskills region becomes obvious. A land of lush rounded mountains, brown babbling brooks and small villages laid out along single main streets, the Catskills are a place that seems mostly forgotten. Just half a century ago an over-the-top resort destination, today the Catskills feel a bit left behind in the transition from one millennium to the next. Paint has peeled, junk sits rotting on sagging porches and many restaurants and hotels have limited opening hours (it's best to call ahead).

Yet among the decay gems remain. Don't discount a town on a first drive through just because it looks in disarray: a charming B&B may lurk just around the bend. And despite the hard times, the Catskills are ideal for the outdoor enthusiast – great hiking, skiing and tubing abound. Locals are friendly and eager to show off their lush countryside, situated just a short 2½-hour drive (yet worlds away) from Manhattan. If you're searching for a once heavily beaten, but now forgotten path, the Catskills are worth exploring.

HIGHLIGHTS

■ **Best Ski Town**
Authentic Windham (p179) has cozy après-ski restaurants, one of the best lodgings in the Catskills and a mountain just outside town that provides some of the East's best ski runs.

■ **Best Rock Climbing**
The Mohonk Preserve (p171) and Minnewaska State Park (p171) near the village of New Paltz – even if you don't climb, the setting is fantastic.

■ **Best Place to Get Wet**
Join a tubing trip down Esopus Creek in Phoenicia (p177), the busiest little town in the Catskills.

■ **Best Town for 1960s Nostalgia**
Though the music happened elsewhere, charming Woodstock (p174) connotes those days, and serves up good restaurants, fun festivals and ample off-the-wall shops.

■ **Most Inspiring Waterfall**
The 260ft Kaaterskill Falls (p181) have awed generations of painters, including Thomas Cole who immortalized the scene in his *View of Kaaterskill Falls*.

CATSKILLS REGION

CLIMATE

Summers are hot and muggy and temperatures can soar into the 90°F range. Spring and fall are more pleasant with cooler temperatures and lower humidity. In the fall the fauna puts on a spectacular color show. Winters are cold and snowy, especially in the mountains, although the snow does not fall in as great a quantity as in other parts of the state, such as Buffalo and Syracuse.

STATE PARKS

The Catskills region includes the 1094-sq-mile **Catskill Park**, 40% of which is publicly owned and protected. The park includes the **Catskill Forest Preserve**, established in the late 19th century when the governor of New York signed a law that required these lands 'be forever kept as wild forest lands.' More than 200 miles of hiking trails meander through the preserve, many of them leading to mountain summits.

Near the village of New Paltz are the **Mohonk Preserve** and the **Minnewaska State Park**. Both offer great rock climbing opportunities. Hiking, biking and cross-country skiing can also be undertaken in both parks.

The **Catskill Mountains**, which are part of the Appalachian Range, are older than the Adirondacks and more worn, with few peaks over 3000ft. The tallest are in the north, where downhill and cross-country skiing opportunities attract visitors from throughout the northeastern states. Both the Catskill Mountains and the older **Shawangunk Mountains** to the southeast are havens for hikers, and numerous trails crisscross the area.

GETTING THERE & AROUND

Stewart International Airport (☎ 845-564-2100), to the south in Newburgh, is 20 miles from New Paltz and is the nearest airport to the region. Slightly further and to the north is **Albany International Airport** (☎ 518-242-2300), 60 miles from New Paltz.

Adirondack Trailways (☎ 800-858-8555) offers daily bus service to many towns in the Catskill area, including Kingston, Saugerties, Catskill, Hunter and Woodstock, as well as to Boston, New York City and Albany.

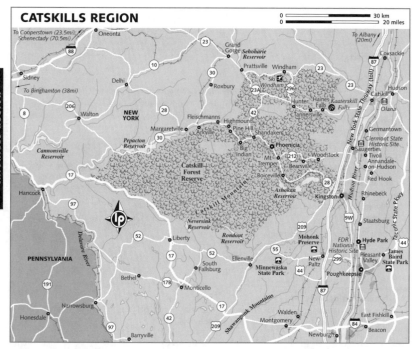

Amtrak (☎ 800-872-7245; www.amtrak.com) runs trains north and south along the east bank of the Hudson River. Two stations are near the Catskills: Rhinecliff, across the river from Kingston, and Hudson, opposite the town of Catskill. Both locations offer bus service around the region via Adirondack Trailways.

Part of the Catskills' charm is the clustering of small villages and towns, most of which are easily accessible by car or motorcycle.

EASTERN CATSKILLS

The west bank of the Hudson River includes the towns of Catskill, Saugerties and Kingston (all along Rte 9W); and the village of New Paltz, in the foothills of the Shawangunk Mountains near the junction of I-87 and Rte 299. Each lies outside the Catskill Forest Preserve. Kingston, New York's first state capital, is the largest town in the region with two distinct historic districts.

NEW PALTZ
☎ 845 / pop 6000
Funky shops and a large selection of restaurants add to this small village's character. Home to a branch of the State University of New York (SUNY–New Paltz), New Paltz has a definite college vibe and is located 9 miles west of the banks of the Hudson River.

Founded by French Huguenot religious refugees in 1677, New Paltz still shows off its original stone architecture on Huguenot St. Those interested in rock climbing and hiking will be drawn to the area, a hot spot for outdoor enthusiasts. Even if you're not into serious hiking or climbing, the surrounding countryside is still beautiful and worth meandering through.

Orientation & Information
New Paltz is easy to reach by car. From I-87 take exit 18 and head west on Rte 299, which turns into the town's main street. Here you will find most of the restaurants and shops within a few blocks.

The **New Paltz Chamber of Commerce** (☎ 845-255-0243; www.newpaltzchamber.org; 259 Main St; ⏲ 10am-4:30pm Mon-Fri) has information about the town and surrounding areas.

Sights & Activities
Outdoor activities are big, but so is wandering around and checking out the historic architecture.

HISTORIC HUGUENOT ST
To get the flavor of the original village, visit the **Huguenot Street Visitors Center** (☎ 845-255-1889; 6 Broadhead Ave; adult/child $8/3; ⏲ 9am-5pm Tue-Sun May-Oct). From here you can join a tour of seven preserved stone houses dating back to the 1680s and a reconstructed French church. Guided tours last 1½ hours.

MOHONK PRESERVE
A full-time conservation, education, research and recreation center, this **preserve** (☎ 845-255-0243; www.mohonkpreserve.org; admission weekend/weekday $8/6; ⏲ dawn-dusk) is located on 6400 acres of woods. There is no camping allowed, but picnicking, great rock climbing, hiking, biking and cross-country skiing (on ungroomed trails) abound. Various guided hikes are offered throughout the year, as well as programs catering especially to children and singles. Take Rte 299 west and go right (west) on Rte 44/55, to the entrance, which is half a mile on the right.

MINNEWASKA STATE PARK
Very popular with rock climbers, this **state park** (☎ 845-255-0752; per car $7; ⏲ dawn-dusk) offers cross-country skiing (groomed trails), hiking, snowshoeing, biking (40 miles of trails), picnicking and swimming in the summer. It's very popular for rock climbing. There is no camping. Take Rte 299 west to Rte 44/55, then go west for 4 miles to the marked entrance.

MOHONK MOUNTAIN HOUSE
Reminiscent of California's lavish Hearst Castle, this **resort** (☎ 845-255-1000; 1000 Mountain Rest Rd; adult/child $10/8), a National Historic Landmark, is worth visiting even if you're not looking to stay the night. The grounds are popular with day hikers in summer and snowshoers in winter. There's a very pricey restaurant (lunch starts at $35), and if you feel like a real splurge you can spend the night – rooms start at about $300. From Rte 299/Main St in New Paltz, turn right immediately after crossing the bridge over the Wallkill River and follow the 'Mohonk' signs. It's about 4 miles out of town.

Sleeping & Eating

New Paltz has sleeping and eating options for all budgets. Parking is readily available and air-conditioning is standard.

New Paltz Hostel (☎ 845-255-6676; www.newpaltz hostel.com; 145 Main St; dm $22, d $57) For clean, cheap accommodation in a communal setting you can't beat the cheery New Paltz Hostel. The walls are filled with artwork, the owners are friendly and there is a kitchen for preparing meals.

Minnewaska Lodge (☎ 845-255-1110; www.minne waskalodge.com; Rte 44/55; d $155-189) Hotel rooms here are slightly lacking in character for the price, but the location, just east of Rte 299, is beautiful and the grounds immaculate. The lodge was built just a few years ago, and there is nothing shabby about it.

Days Inn (☎ 845-883-7373; 601 Main St; d $89) Rooms here are typical of American chain motels, clean and sufficient but with no special touches.

Bacchus Bar & Grille (☎ 914-255-8636; 4 South Chestnut St; lunch $6-10, dinner $13-18) Locals give this place a good review. It specializes in southwestern cuisine and serves more than 300 types of beer. The decor is wood-oriented and you can sit upstairs in the loft.

McGillicuddy's Restaurant & Tap House (☎ 845-256-9289; 84 Main St; mains $6-13) This very popular family-oriented restaurant has a huge menu of American food, serving everything from sandwiches to fajitas to steaks. You're welcome to take the kids here.

Drinking

Being a college town, New Paltz has a decent selection of bars. College hangout **Snugs Tavern** (38 Main St) is dark and dingy and smells like beer but features good happy hour specials and has a few pool tables. For live music try the **Oasis Café** (☎ 845-255-2400; 58 Main St).

Getting There & Around

The **Adirondack Trailways** (☎ 800-858-8555) bus station is on Main St next to the New Paltz Hostel. Routes include Albany ($13, 1½ hours) and Woodstock ($5, one hour).

KINGSTON

☎ 845 / pop 23,450

History runs deep in Kingston, the Catskills' largest town and the state's first capital for a brief period in 1777 when the British drove the provincial congress from New York City.

DETOUR – RTE 9W, EAST OF NEW PALTZ

From New Paltz head east on Rte 299 to Rte 9W, close your eyes and turn either right or left. Either way, you won't be disappointed. The road between the towns of West Park and Marlboro is sprinkled with small wineries well marked by signs. The **Benmarl Winery** (☎ 845-236-4265; 156 Highland Ave, Marlboro; ☺ noon-5pm) is the best known of the bunch. It's perched high on a hill overlooking the Hudson River and produces quite a few award-winning wines. It's open daily for tastings.

The town's layout is relatively simple – the two main tourist areas (the Rondout Historic District and the Stockade District) are separated from each other by a rather seedy stretch of Broadway, the city's main drag.

The best source of information, including free walking tour brochures, is the **Kingston Urban Cultural Park Visitors Center** Rondout Historic District (☎ 845-331-7517, 800-331-1518; 20 Broadway; ☺ 11am-5pm) Stockade District (☎ 845-331-9506; 308 Clinton Ave; ☺ 11am-5pm).

Sights & Activities

The two historic districts make up the bulk of things to see and do in Kingston.

STOCKADE DISTRICT

Filled with sedate stone buildings, many of which have been converted into shops and restaurants, this district dates back to the 17th century. In 1777 the first New York State senate met briefly at the **Senate House State Historic Site** (☎ 845-338-2786; 296 Fair St; adult/child $4/1; ☺ 10am-5pm Mon-Sat year-round, 1-5pm Sun mid-Apr–Oct), dating from circa 1635. The **Old Dutch Church & Cemetery** (☎ 845-334-9355; 272 Wall St) is quiet and shady, and the tombstones date back to the 1700s. New York's first governor, George Clinton, is buried here. The reformed protestant Dutch church, dating from around 1695, has services on Sunday. George Washington visited the church in 1782 and his visit is memorialized in a plaque on the church's exterior wall.

RONDOUT HISTORIC DISTRICT

Once a bustling 19th-century terminal port of the Delaware and Hudson Canal, the

Rondout today is a revived neighborhood and shopping area, boasting quite a few good seafood restaurants and exhibits. It's located at the southeastern end of town.

Within the historic district, the **Trolley Museum of New York** (☎ 845-331-3399; www.tmny.org; 89 E Strand St; adult/child $3/2; noon-5pm Sat & Sun late May–mid-Oct) offers rides on old trolleys and has static displays of trolley, subway and rapid-transit cars from the US and Europe.

River life is celebrated at the **Hudson River Maritime Museum** (☎ 845-338-0071; 50 Rondout Landing; adult/child $10/8; 11am-5pm May-Oct). The museum's gallery has displays of all types of boats. After you've got your fill looking at ships, hop on one for a 15-minute ride on the Rondout Creek to the Hudson River, where you can check out the 1913 Rondout lighthouse.

Sleeping & Eating

Parking is plentiful in Kingston and air-conditioning is standard. There are numerous eating options.

Black Lion Mansion Bed & Breakfast (☎ 845-338-0410; 124 W Chestnut St; d from $100) All rooms in this late-19th-century mansion are decorated differently, and all are stunning. The grand old house has giant windows, sweeping staircases and amazing views of the surrounding mountains.

Adele's Rondout B&B (☎ 845-331-8144; 88 W Chester St; d from $115) This classy Federal-style home is airy and decorated in warm colors with lots of rugs and a large broad porch. The four rooms are well appointed and the owner has a wealth of information about the area.

There are a number of chain hotels just off I-87 at exit 19. The best of the bunch is the **Holiday Inn** (☎ 845-338-0400; www.hikingston.com; 503 Washington Ave; d $139), which boasts a large indoor atrium with a whirlpool.

Twenty Three Broadway (☎ 845-339-2322; 23 Broadway; mains $20; closed Mon & Tue) This new restaurant in the Rondout gets rave reviews from locals and visitors alike. Its interesting menu features starters such as coconut shrimp with Asian pear salad ($9). Mains are heavy on seafood and meat, so the place isn't really suitable for vegetarians.

Ship to Shore Restaurant (☎ 845-334-8887; 15 W Strand St; mains $15-20) This old standby in the Rondout specializes in steaks and progressive American food. It also has sandwiches,

pastas and salads with plenty of options for vegetarians.

Armadillo Bar & Grill (☎ 845-339-1550; 97 Abeel St; mains $12-15; closed Mon) The large menu at this popular Rondout restaurant focuses on a good New York version of Tex-Mex food.

Kingston Cooks (☎ 845-338-2959; 307 Wall St; mains $2-6) This favorite Stockade lunch spot serves cheap, health-conscious food. There is a large selection of sandwiches, fresh salads and smoothies. You can eat in or take the food away.

Jane's Homemade Ice Cream (☎ 845-338-8315; 305 Wall St; mains $2-7) Next door to Kingston Cooks, Jane's is not just about ice cream (although the frozen treat is quite tasty). It also has a large selection of low-fat wraps and Mexican selections. The place even advertises that it has a weight watchers specialist around to help design meals.

Getting There & Around

Adirondack Trailways (☎ 800-858-8555) stops at **Dietz Stadium Diner** (☎ 845-331-0744; 400 Washington Ave). Buses run hourly to New York City ($20, two hours). For those coming by car, Kingston is at exit 19 on I-87, about 90 miles north of New York City. Plan on a two-hour drive from Manhattan.

SAUGERTIES

☎ 845 / pop 5000

Quaint and charming, Saugerties' narrow Main St is lined with historic redbrick buildings filled with antique stores and bookstores and quite a few fine restaurants. Most of the elegant dining establishments are only open for dinner on weekends. The main business district encompasses Partition and Main Sts.

If it's hot out, stop by the **Saugerties beach** (follow the signs from the 9W). You can cool off by swimming in a roped-off area in the river.

There's not really anywhere to stay in Saugerties proper, but the town is only about 15 minutes from Woodstock (p174) where there are plenty of sleeping options, both in the town and on the stretch of highway between Woodstock and Saugerties.

For lunch or an afternoon coffee, stop by **Ann Marie's Café** (☎ 845-246-5532; 74 Partition St; mains $3-7), where you can sit on the sidewalk, sip on an espresso and watch life pass you by. Ann Marie's prepares fresh wraps and has a large breakfast menu. The café is attached to **Ann Marie's Bistro** (mains $20; ☙ dinner Wed-Sat, brunch Sun), which is more upscale than the café. The menu is eclectic, serving everything from ostrich to possum.

Housed in an 1864 funky tavern setting with plenty of outdoor seating, **Café Tamayo** (☎ 845-246-9371; 89 Partition St; mains $15-20; ☙ dinner Thu-Sun) serves new American food. The menu is small with a regional emphasis and gets good reviews.

For live music and a more club-like atmosphere head to **Chowhound Café** (☎ 845-246-5158; 112 Partition St; mains $15-22; ☙ Wed-Sun), where you can eat food from all over the globe – Cajun tacos to Thai fried rice.

Saugerties is 15 miles north of Kingston where Rte 212 meets Rte 9W.

CATSKILL & AROUND
☎ 518 / pop 4400

History and beauty mingle in the tiny town of Catskill, on the banks of the Hudson River at the mouth of Catskill Creek. Home of Thomas Cole, a painter from the 19th-century Hudson River school, Catskill also played an important role supplying booze to those who wanted it during prohibition. Catskill applejack was brewed in the hills surrounding town. The rough terrain made for good hiding, both for moonshine and gangsters, when the law rolled in. As a result Catskill became a favorite haunt of New York City thugs Legs Diamond and Vincent Coll.

The **Thomas Cole House** (☎ 518-731-6490; 218 Spring St; admission $4; ☙ 10am-4pm Fri & Sat, 1-5pm Sun Jun-Aug) has been recently renovated and features exhibits on Cole and his family, including a few paintings by the painter as well as displays on other Hudson River artists. Large and airy, the yellow and white house overlooks the Hudson River.

Started in the 1930s as a conservation project to protect rare and endangered animals from around the world, the **Catskill Game Farm** (☎ 518-678-9595; adult/child $16/13; ☙ 10am-6pm Jun-Aug) has remained popular over the decades. The family-operated complex is a zoo that tends to approximately 2000 animals and runs a successful nursery that breeds wild horses from Mongolia. Children will love the large petting zoo where you can wander amongst tame deer. You can also feed the baby pigs and little lambs by bottle in the farm's nursery. The farm is on Rte 32, just outside of town. Follow the signs.

NORTHERN CATSKILLS

Although much of the central and southern Catskills serve as the nearest weekend getaway from New York City, the northern 'Cats' feels more remote and bucolic. Much of the land here (Greene County and the northernmost parts of Sullivan and Ulster Counties) is part of the Catskill Forest Preserve. The area is known for being rugged, with waterfalls, cliffs, fire towers, old farmsteads, bears, rattlesnakes and rare plant species.

Tourists are not flocking to the Catskills like they used to, and some towns in this area are looking downright shabby. Others, like Woodstock, are thriving and well worth a visit. The northern Catskills towns form a loop of sorts beginning at Woodstock then proceeding west on Rte 28, north on Rte 30, then east on Rte 23 to 23A until you hit I-87. Even if you're not interested in lingering, the loop makes a photographic day drive. The towns are spaced just a few miles apart from each other.

WOODSTOCK
☎ 845 / pop 6200

Best known for the 1960s event that didn't actually happen here, Woodstock is a charming cross between quaint and hip. You will still see a few tie-dyed locals who look like they're in a 1960s time warp, and a handful of shops and businesses retain the names of that magical era: Sunflower, Hibiscus, Pegasus, Once Possessed, Pondicherry and Not Fade Away (from the Buddy Holly song recorded in 1958).

Although '60s nostalgia runs thick in Woodstock, the town's reputation as a legitimate arts colony dates back to the early 1900s. Most of today's residents appear to be artists, musicians or well-heeled folks from downstate who own summer homes here. Chain stores are virtually nonexistent and many quality one-of-a-kind shops line both sides of Tinker St and Mill Hill Rd. With art galleries, fashionable clothing stores, theatrical and musical productions – not to mention a good selection of places to stay and eat – Woodstock should be at the top of your list of towns to visit in the region.

The summer and fall seasons are filled with festivals – there is always something going on. In September the **Woodstock Film**

Festival (☎ 845-679-4265; www.woodstockfilmfestival
.com) takes place over three days and draws
movie aficionados and Hollywood celebrities to town.

Orientation & Information

Woodstock is easily negotiated on foot. A
large parking lot off Tinker St, the village's
main thoroughfare, in the center of town
is a good place to drop off the car. Where
Tinker St meets Rock City and Mill Hill Rds
you will find the village green.

Golden Notebook (☎ 845-679-8000; www.golden
notebook.com; 25 Tinker St; ☯ 10:30am-7pm) is an
excellent small bookstore with helpful
staff knowledgeable about local attractions. Next door is a children's store,
which has a good selection of children's
books on tape.

The active **Woodstock Chamber of Commerce**
(☎ 845-679-6234; www.woodstock-online.com; ☯ 9am-
5pm) has an enthusiastic voice-mail system
that will record your requests for information. You can also stop at Woodstock's
two staffed information booths: on Rock
City Rd, just north of the village green, and
at the junction of Tinker St and Mill Hill
Rd on Rte 212.

Sights & Activities

Seeing Woodstock means strolling about
town, enjoying the friendly feel of the place
and browsing through the galleries and crystal shops. Woodstock's main drags, Tinker
St and Mill Hill Rd, are at the heart of the
action. People-watching is also popular, and
the small village green offers the perfect
vantage point. If you happen to be in town
on Christmas Eve you'll be one of the first to
know how Santa Claus arrives on the green.
This is the best-kept secret around, and it's
never dull; Santa's been known to travel by
camel and hang-glider – on separate occa-
sions, of course.

DOWNTOWN WOODSTOCK

Modern Mythology (☎ 845-679-8811; 12 Tinker St)
stands out among Woodstock's New Age
shops. It sells a plethora of jewelry (some
of which is rather generic-looking), tasteful Woodstock T-shirts, Buddhas and lots
of tarot cards and crystals. Another notable store, if you're into vintage clothing, is
Castaways (☎ 845-679-3459; 36 Mill Hill Rd). It has
lots of resale men's and women's fashions,

including brand names. They also sell new
jewelry and accessories.

About midway through town you'll find
the **Center for Photography** (☎ 845-679-9957; www
.cpw.org; 59 Tinker St; admission free; ☯ noon-5pm
Wed-Sun). This attractive and serious gallery
offers contemporary and historical exhibits,
lectures and photography workshops year-
round. It's well worth checking out.

BYRDCLIFFE ARTS COLONY & THEATER

For generations before the 1969 Woodstock Festival, artists and concertgoers
traveled to **Byrdcliffe** (☎ 845-679-2079) to share
their common vision of peace and justice.
Their hopeful message was set to music by
songwriters and performers, including Pete
Seeger; Peter, Paul & Mary; and Louisiana
bluesman Leadbelly. American artists Bolton Brown and Hervey White, with substantial financial backing from Englishman
Ralph Radcliffe Whitehead, founded the
1500-acre complex in 1902.

Today, the colony hosts artist residen-
cies, craft demonstrations, exhibitions and
performances at the Byrdcliffe Theater. Performances are announced in the *New York
Times* and the local *Woodstock Times*. To
get here, take Rock City Rd north from the
village green to the Glasco Turnpike, head
west to Upper Byrdcliffe Rd, then turn right
and head north to the colony.

KARMA TRIYANA DHARMACHAKRA & OVERLOOK MOUNTAIN

A popular Buddhist center and Tibetan
monastery, **Karma Triyana Dharmachakra** (☎ 845-
679-5906; 352 Meads Mountain Rd) regularly offers
teachings ranging from introductory to advanced. Meditation instruction is available
by appointment free of charge. Meditation
retreats and lectures are also offered year-
round.

Spectacular views of the surrounding
countryside and the Hudson River can be
found at the top of Overlook Mountain.
The 2.4-mile trail starts at the parking lot
across from the monastery. To reach the
monastery from town drive up Rock City
Rd for about 2 miles and look for signs.

OPUS 40

Amazing man-made pathways, pools,
steps and an obelisk are spread over 6.5
acres at **Opus 40** (☎ 845-246-3400; adult/child $6/3;

⊙ noon-5pm Fri-Sun Jun-Sep). Creator Harvey Fite, who meticulously carved and set the bluestone from an abandoned quarry, named it Opus 40 because he expected it to take 40 years to finish. That should have been a tip-off; Fite worked on the quarry his entire life. The **Quarryman's Museum** displays many of Fite's tools. Take Rte 212 east from Woodstock to County Rd 32 east and look for the signs.

Sleeping

Woodstock sleeping establishments have private parking lots.

Twin Gables Guest House (☎ 845-679-9479; 73 Tinker St; d from $64) With tons of character, each room is decorated in a different color scheme with matching walls, floors and bedspreads. A superb location, right in the center of town, makes this a good quirky choice.

Woodstock Inn on the Millstream (☎ 845-679-8211; 38 Tannery Brook Rd; d $107) Tidy white walls and clean rooms are standard at this motel. Quiet and small, it's a three-minute walk from downtown. Each room comes with its own porch, perfect for passing a warm afternoon on.

Bed by the Stream (☎ 845-246-2979; www.bedby thestream.com; Rte 212; d from $79; ⊠) Located in a quiet wooded setting on a stream, this place has a barn-like feel. Rates increase on weekends in summer.

Saugerties-Woodstock KOA (☎ 845-246-4089; campsites $30, cabins $55-79; ⊙ Apr-Nov) Shady wooded sites and small rustic cabins make this campground appealing. It's about halfway between Woodstock and Saugerties on Rte 212.

Eating

Tinker St and Mill Hill Rds have an abundance of good restaurants, bars and bakeries.

Landau Grille (☎ 845-679-8937; 13 Tinker St; mains $8-20) You may have to wait a while to get a table here, but the food is worth it. Sit outside and try one of the fresh, well-presented pasta dishes.

Joshua's (☎ 845-679-5533; 51 Tinker St; breakfast $6-8, mains $12-16) Breakfast is served here until 3pm and there are massive amounts of dishes to choose from. Joshua's also serves Middle Eastern and Israeli dishes. The hummus, *babaganoush* and tabbouleh are good, along with potato latkes, several pasta dishes and a mixed meat grill of lamb, chicken, shrimp, beef and vegetables.

Taco Juan's (☎ 845-679-9673; 31 Tinker St; mains $5-6) For good cheap food in a brightly colored building reminiscent of a bar head to Taco

---

THE WOODSTOCK FESTIVALS

About half a million people – many of them ticketless – descended on Max Yasgur's farm in Bethel, New York (40 miles southeast of the town of Woodstock), from August 15 to 17, 1969, for a music festival billed as 'Three Days of Peace & Music.' The lineup of musicians for the Woodstock Festival – Joan Baez; Joe Cocker & the Grease Band; Country Joe & the Fish; Crosby, Stills & Nash; Arlo Guthrie; Richie Havens; Jimi Hendrix; Santana; John Sebastian; Sha-Na-Na; Sly & the Family Stone; Ten Years After; and The Who – has never been matched.

Festival promoters sold tickets for a remarkable $7 for one day and $18 for three days. The entire event cost only $3 million to stage; unfortunately, less than one-quarter of the half-million concertgoers paid for admission, and the festival had trouble paying its bills.

Despite numerous setbacks ranging from broken toilets to a serious mud problem after a day of rain (earning the festival its 'Hog Farm' nickname), there were no riots and no violence. It was the most successful hippie gathering in the world. The most violent scene probably occurred when activist Abbie Hoffman ran on stage to make a speech, only to be greeted by The Who's Pete Townshend, who promptly bashed him over the head with his electric guitar. Lucky he didn't run into Jimi Hendrix, who often set his guitar on fire.

Promoters trying to cash in on 1960s nostalgia attempted follow-up Woodstock concerts in 1994 and 1999 in Saugerties and Rome, respectively. Both were overhyped and neither was a success.

Alan Gerry, a native to the area and a pioneer in the cable-TV industry, purchased the original Woodstock site in 1996. He landscaped the festival grounds and added a parking lot. Plans are underway for a $40 million performing arts center that will showcase both classical and popular music. The center is slated to open in late 2004 or early 2005.

Johns. Dine on knishes, enchiladas and burritos beneath the rafted ceilings. If you're aching for sweets they also serve ice cream.

Bread Alone (☎ 845-679-2108; 22 Mill Hill Rd; mains $2-5) This is a Catskills chain and a landmark for bread-lovers. Since most folks cannot live by bread alone, the shop also offers fine pastries, morning burritos and eggs, fresh salads and several gourmet deli items.

There are several excellent restaurants just a short drive from Woodstock. Two miles west of the village green on Rte 212 is the small town of Bearsville, where you'll find **Bear Café** (☎ 845-679-5555; mains $20), serving American and French bistro fare in a rather serene brookside setting. The food is excellent and popular with local and New York City celebrities.

The adjacent **Little Bear** (☎ 845-679-8899; mains $6-12), which shares the forest setting with Bear Café, has a well-deserved reputation for serving the best Chinese food north of New York City. The menu offers a few Thai dishes too. In summer sit outside by the creek; in winter try the enclosed porch – there's still a creek view.

Hip country gourmet can be found at the **New World Home Cooking Co** (☎ 845-246-0900; mains $16-20; ☽ 5-11pm) on Rte 212 halfway between Woodstock and Saugerties. The eatery specializes in a Caribbean–Thai–down-home mix; Jamaican jerk chicken is a local favorite, along with *ropa vieja* (Cuban pot roast). Big servings in deep-dish plates are the order of the day.

Entertainment
Gone is the Tinker Street Café, where Bob Dylan often played during the early 1960s, but Woodstock continues to be home to a thriving arts and music scene.

Tinker St Cinema (☎ 845-679-6608; 132 Tinker St) Films at the Woodstock Film Festival are screened here. Other times of the year it features the best in recent and classic international and independent film, with an occasional nod to a good commercial movie. The cinema is on the way out of town, heading towards Bearsville.

Bearsville Theater (☎ 845-679-2100; Rte 212, Bearsville) This venue puts on plays, concerts and stand-up comedy acts. The theater is next to the restaurants Little Bear and Bear Café (see Eating above).

Byrdcliffe Arts Colony & Theater (Sights & Activities above) During summer this venue holds craft demonstrations, art exhibits and theatrical performances.

Maverick Concerts (☎ 845-679-7558; Maverick Rd) Dating back to 1916, this is the oldest chamber music series in the US. Sunday concerts with top performers take place at 3pm from mid-June to early September. Concerts are listed in the *Sunday New York Times*; people often drive up from the city for this. It's off Rte 375.

Getting There & Around
Adirondack Trailways (☎ 800-858-8555) stops at **Houst & Sons hardware store** (☎ 845-679-2115; 4 Mill Hill Rd).

Motorists can reach Woodstock from I-87. Take exit 19 to Rte 28 west, then Rte 375 north, or take exit 20 to Rte 32 west to Rte 212 to town. If you're coming from Mt Tremper in the west, follow Rte 212 east past Bearsville to town.

MT TREMPER
☎ 845 / pop 400
Relaxing in the woods and sampling home-cooked authentic French cuisine are tiny Mt Tremper's main draws. **La Duchesse Anne** (☎ 845-688-5260; 4 Miller Rd; mains $15-20) is set in an old wooden house and serves excellent dishes from France. It's not always open, however, so it's best to call ahead. The restaurant also has a few rooms available, call for rates.

Just around the corner from La Duchesse Anne is **Catskill Rose** (☎ 845-688-7100; Rte 212; mains $15-22; ☽ dinner Thu-Sun), one of the region's better-known restaurants and a favorite among locals. The kitchen features a good selection of both vegetarian and meat dishes; the smoked duck receives rave reviews.

The area also offers hiking and fishing, and is only a short drive to area ski resorts.

Mt Tremper is located less than a mile north of Rte 28 on Rte 212.

PHOENICIA
☎ 845 / pop 381
Cheery and tiny, Phoenicia, north of Mt Tremper, is the center of tubing in the Catskills. Main St consists of just a few blocks but is always bustling. Of all the small towns along Rte 28, Phoenicia offers the summertime visitor the most outdoor excitement.

Visitors can tube on the Esopus Creek, which runs along Rte 28. The more exciting tubing starts 5 miles northwest of town, where water is released from the Schoharie Reservoir, and ends downstream at the bridge in Phoenicia. The floating trip takes about two hours. There is also an easier course that runs southeast from Phoenicia and takes about 1¾ hours. Tubes can come with seats and handles, and outfitters rent paddles and life jackets. The outfitters will drive you to the put-in site.

Town Tinker Tube Rental (☎ 845-688-5553; www .towntinker.com; Bridge St; tubes with/without seats $13/15; ⓥ 9am-6pm mid-May–Sep), half a block south of Main St, is Phoenicia's most popular outfitter. You can rent wet suits and helmets. **FS Tube & Raft Rental** (☎ 845-688-7633; 4 Church St; rental $13; ⓥ 9am-6pm May-Sep) is another option.

Horseback riding also is popular in this region. If you want to hit the trails, head to the **Saddle Up Ranch** (☎ 845-688-7336; 22 Kinsey Rd; per hour $30; ⓥ 10am-5pm Apr-Oct, 10am-5pm weekends & holidays Nov-Mar), which caters to riders of all skill levels. If you're experienced you'll be able to canter. Rides wind through the grassy hills surrounding the ranch. Saddle Up is located off Rte 28 just east of Phoenicia.

The town is geared towards camping and has two good campgrounds. The **Phoenicia Black Bear Campground & RV Park** (☎ 845-688-7407; 17 Bridge Rd; campsites $28) offers shady sites right in town. Prices are based on two people and extra persons pay an additional $10.

Sleepy Hollow Campsite (☎ 845-688-5471; Rte 28; campsites $20), about a mile east of Phoenicia, occupies a beautiful spot right on the Esopus Creek and caters to a lot of RVs, some of which appear not to have moved for years. Campsites are grassy and shady.

Phoenicia Hotel (☎ 845-688-7500; Main St; d $70) is the place to stay in town. The large and popular bar downstairs and the patio area are great for hanging out. Rooms are nothing special, but not shabby.

Attached to the Phoenicia Hotel is the ever-popular **Mizuna Café** (☎ 845-688-7500; Main St; lunch $8, dinner $15-20), one of the few places to eat in town. It's a cheerful eatery with art on the walls, and serves the typical pasta and sandwich options as well as fresh trout from the region.

Plays are performed throughout the year at the **Shandaken Theatrical Society** (☎ 845-688-

2279; 10 Church St; admission $10). Call or stop by the ticket window to see what's showing.

PINE HILL
☎ 845 / pop 300

This small town attracts skiers who come to try out the slopes and trails of the **Belleayre Mountain Ski Center** (☎ 800-942-6904; www .belleayre.com; off Rte 28, Highmount; lift tickets $42). This state-owned resort has a 1404ft vertical drop in a rustic setting. The longest run is more than a mile. Head to the ski area's lake (admission per car is $6) in summer to swim or lie out on the beach. There is also a playground and picnic facilities. The ski area is just east of Pine Hill on Rte 28.

Belleayre Hostel (☎ 845-254-4200; 15 Hostel Dr; dm $20, d from $50) has a variety of room options in a series of wooden structures on a hill just off Main St. The most expensive rooms are the two-bedroom log cabins. These cost between $150 and $200 per night and can sleep up to six people. They resemble small homes, are very clean, and have nice linens. All accommodation is self-catering and there is a big fireplace in the yard for chilly après-ski evenings. There are also pool and table-tennis tables.

Pine Hill Arms Hotel & Restaurant (☎ 845-254-9811; Main St; mains $13-18; ⓥ 5-10pm Wed-Sun) is a big brown barn-like structure with a screened-in porch for dining. The menu includes Cajun and vegetarian specialties. There is live music some weekends.

Pine Hill is on Rte 28, just a few miles east of Fleischmanns.

FLEISCHMANNS
☎ 845 / pop 350

Peeling paint and empty storefronts are an unfortunate reality in Fleischmanns. However, there are gems hidden underneath the decay. The town was originally known as Griffin Corners but was renamed in 1913 to honor Charles Fleischmann, a Hungarian immigrant who developed a bit of land here in the 1880s and assembled a band to greet family members as they arrived at the old train station. The Fleischmann family later gave a park to the town. But Fleischmanns' most famous resident was baseball great Honus Wagner, who played ball here before going on to become one of the all-time great shortstops with the Pittsburgh Pirates.

Fleischmanns is home to **Purple Mountain Press** (☎ 845-254-4062; Main St), an excellent press that specializes in regional history and folklore.

Roberts' Auction (☎ 845-254-4490; Main St) auctions everything from nuts and bolts to antiques every Saturday night at 7pm. You can find items here for as little as a dollar. Come early because the auction draws people from as far away as New York City and seats fill up fast.

Highlands Inn (☎ 845-254-5650; www.thehighlands inn.com; 923 Main St; d from $80) is one of our favorite B&Bs in the Catskills, and a stay here is well worth it. Owners Laura and Doug Smith put tremendous time and effort into decorating this large airy house. Antiques from around the world are placed throughout the inn. Rooms are spotless with a knack for little details – each room is distinct from the others. For entertainment there is a pool table and a big-screen television. Rooms with shared baths are the cheapest.

Fleischmanns is on Rte 28, near the junction with Rte 30.

MARGARETVILLE
☎ 845 / pop 640

Margaretville is the major commercial town in the northern Catskills area and is a good place to stop for supplies.

The **Margaretville Mountain Inn** (☎ 845-586-3933; Walnut St; d from $75) is housed in an 1886 slate-roofed home on top of the mountain overlooking the town. The 2nd-floor rooms have the best views and are more expensive than the 1st-floor rooms. After entering Margaretville from Rte 28 (from the direction of Fleischmanns), make a left at the first light and then make the first right onto Walnut St. Drive up the hill for 1.5 miles to the inn.

Summerfields (☎ 914-586-1111; 127 Main St; lunch $6-8, dinner $15-20) has a good atmosphere and decent food. In summer the outside tiki bar and patio is perfect for drinks. There are lots of wooden bears and some pool tables. The menu is mostly burgers and steaks with a few vegetarian options.

Margaretville is located at the junction of Rtes 28 and 30.

WINDHAM & HUNTER
☎ 518 / pop 2100

This is Catskills ski country. Hunter Mountain is still the Catskills' best-known ski area, but Hunter itself is no longer looking so hot. In the summertime it's a virtual ghost town and even in winter the air of neglect is noticeable. By contrast Windham, just 10 miles away and also home to a ski resort, is much more upbeat with some very good restaurants and, even better, the Albergo Allegria Inn (p180), which provides the best lodging value for money in the region.

Orientation
Hunter is strung out along Rte 23A. It does not retain the village feel that most other towns in the area do. Attractions in Windham can be found on Rte 23 (Main St) and across the covered bridge on Rte 296.

Activities
Both these towns cater to outdoor activities. Besides skiing there is good hiking and mountain biking in the region.

HUNTER MOUNTAIN SKI AREA
Off Rte 23A, **Hunter Mountain** (☎ 518-263-4223; www.huntermtn.com; lift tickets $40) probably makes more snow than any other mountain in the US. The resort draws people from all over the state to its three-mountain complex, which offers 15 lifts, a network of 50 trails and restaurants featuring everything from sushi to burgers.

During summer and fall the mountain stages a series of festivals. The **Hunter Mountain Festivals** (☎ 518-263-4223) feature everything from the International Celtic Festival to the German Alps Festival. Events kick off in the beginning of July and run through October.

SKI WINDHAM
This is the region's second-largest **resort** (☎ 518-734-4300, 800-729-4766; www.skiwindham.com; off South St; lift tickets $40). It's quite a bit smaller than Hunter but still operates a system of 33 trails and five lifts. These trails are open to mountain bikers in the summer. The resort is also the site of craft fairs, antique shows, mountain-bike races and festivals in summer and fall.

Bikes can be rented at **Windham Mountain Outfitters** (☎ 518-734-4700; cnr Rte 296 & South St; bike rental per day $29). The helpful staff here can offer advice on where to ride and provide trail maps.

Sleeping

In winter some places require a two-night minimum stay on weekends; it's best to call ahead.

Albergo Allegria Inn (☎ 518-734-5560; www.albergo usa.com; 43 Rte 296, Windham; d from $73) This immaculately decorated B&B is the best deal in the region. Walking in you'll be shocked that rooms here don't cost double what they do. Even the cheapest rooms come beautifully equipped and a stay in the millennium suite, the inn's most expensive room, is well worth the price ($189 midweek). With deep blue walls, high ceilings, down comforters and a giant whirlpool, this suite was designed with romance in mind. Ask about multiple-day discounts.

Be My Guest (☎ 518-734-5653; www.bemyguest.org; 350 Rte 296, Windham; d summer/winter $75/90) This quaint old house comes complete with a turret. The upper-level porch offers fantastic views of the surrounding countryside, and there is a cozy pink sitting room with a fireplace for cold winter nights. Owner Mary Lawyer also offers astrology readings. Mini-readings cost $25.

Scribner Hollow (☎ 518-263-4211; www.scribner hollow.com; Rte 23A, Hunter; half-board d from $210 per person; ⊠) Possibly the strangest-looking hotel in the Catskills, Scribner is a cavernous place with huge atriums and a bizarre indoor grotto – you can swim through seven waterfalls in the heated pool or rejuvenate in the warm underground spa. Depending on the season and your tastes, you'll either love it or hate it. When it's empty it's a little creepy – think the mansion from *The Shining*. It fills up in winter, however. Each room is individually decorated in styles ranging from 17th-century Spanish adobe to 21st-century futuristic; all of the rooms have cathedral ceilings, some have fireplaces and many have bedroom lofts. 'Future World' features a fireplace and a tiered bathtub with a waterfall; the 'Hunting Lodge' includes log-cabin walls and a bear carpet. Ask to see a few so you can pick one you like.

Forester Motor Lodge (☎ 518-263-4555; Rte 23A, Hunter; d summer/winter $85/110; ⊠) Rooms here are large and clean but very basic. There are good views of Hunter Mountain.

Devil's Tombstone Campground (☎ 845-688-7160; Rte 214, Hunter; campsites $14; ⊠ mid-May–early Sep) In a beautiful location right up against the mountains is this state-run campground.

There is a pleasant pond and lots of trees. Sites are quite basic, with toilets but no showers. To reach Devil's Tombstone head south on Rte 214 from Hunter for 4 miles.

Eating & Drinking

Windham has the better eating options of the two towns. The best nightlife can be found in the town of Tannersville (p182).

Chalet Fondue (☎ 518-734-4650; Rte 296, Windham; mains from $15) The decor at this recommended German restaurant is a cross between ski-lodge hip and southwestern, with wood ceilings and rough white walls. Traditional German dishes such as sauerbraten and Wiener schnitzel go for about $17. They also do Swiss fondue for two with veal and beef for $49. Veggies beware, this place is geared towards carnivores.

Prospect (☎ 518-263-4211; Rte 23A, Hunter, mains from $18) Located inside Scribner Hollow is Prospect, whose small menu features good American and Italian dishes including penne cooked with vodka. Tables overlook the mountain.

Windhaven Pub (☎ 518-734-4280; Rte 296, Windham; mains $5-10) In a dark wood-paneled setting this pub is popular at night for drinks. Its menu focuses mainly on burgers and appetizers.

Hunter Village Inn (☎ 518-263-4788; Rte 23A, Hunter) Hunter's rowdiest nightspot has a large bar and lots of pool tables. It features music and happy hours.

Getting There & Around

To get to Windham from I-87 get off at exit 21 (for the town of Catskill) and take Hwy 23 west for 25 miles.

To reach Hunter from Windham head south on Rte 296 for about 10 miles until you hit Rte 23A.

Adirondack Trailways (☎ 800-858-8555) stops at the **Four Star Food Center** (☎ 518-734-4600; Main St) in Windham and at **Peter's Hunter Auto Repair** (☎ 518-263-4713; Main St) in Hunter.

TANNERSVILLE & AROUND

☎ 518 / pop 450

Tannersville is named for the leather tanning industry that once thrived here. Before the introduction of chemical substitutes, hemlock bark was required in the tanning process. The Catskills, whose hillsides were once covered with hemlocks, provided a convenient source of the raw material. However,

THE LATE, GREAT CATSKILL HOTELS

The area around Tannersville and Haines Falls was home to three of the biggest 19th-century Catskill hotels, the most famous of which was the Catskill Mountain House. Built in the mid-19th century, this resort was the first of its kind: a deluxe hotel built in a remote wilderness on a cliff, with breathtaking views of North/South Lake and the Hudson Valley.

Part of the resort's attraction was its inaccessibility. After a long and difficult journey to the hotel by stage coach, guests were rewarded with spectacular scenery and elegant accommodations. However, the introduction of the automobile allowed vacationers to travel even greater distances from the cities in search of even more magnificent surroundings. By the 1920s, the Catskill Mountain House showed signs of disrepair, and in 1943 it closed permanently. In 1963, the state bought the abandoned hotel and burned it.

Two other deluxe hotels in the area, the 800-room Kaaterskill Hotel and the Laurel House – built at the top of Kaaterskill Falls – met with similar fates. The former burned accidentally in a fire in 1924; the abandoned remains of the latter were burned by the state of New York in 1966.

the mountains were quickly stripped of hemlock in the early days of the industry, and now Tannersville and the surrounding areas are home instead to several exclusive residential developments. For visitors, the town has a rugged mountain feel and offers a few good restaurants and bars for après-ski entertainment.

Tannersville is located east of Hunter on Rte 23A. To reach the best hiking in the area continue heading east on Rte 23A to Haines Falls.

Activities

In summer and fall the area around Tannersville has quite a few good hikes.

KAATERSKILL FALLS HIKES

The inspiration for generations of painters, the 260ft Kaaterskill Falls are the highest in New York (Niagara Falls only measure in at 167ft) and actually make two plunges on Spruce Creek. The Laurel House Hotel, which used to stand at the headwaters of the falls, dammed the creek and released the water over the falls periodically for groups of people who paid $0.25 to watch. Thomas Cole – one of the painters from the Hudson River school – was so impressed with the falls he immortalized them in his work *View of Kaaterskill Falls*.

To get to the base of the falls, drive 1 mile east of Haines Falls on Rte 23A; as the highway begins to dip, you'll see a small parking area on the right. Park here, cross the highway and walk east along the north shoulder for a quarter-mile to the trailhead. The rocky and slightly steep trail travels half

a mile from the highway to the falls. Since this is a popular hike, you should arrive early on weekends.

To get to the top of the falls from Rte 23A, look for a sign in Haines Falls indicating the turnoff for North/South Lake. The trailhead is off Laurel House Rd on the way into North/South Lake.

NORTH/SOUTH LAKE AREA

Two long blue lakes make this one of the most popular outdoor destinations in the Catskills The state-run **lake area** (☎ 518-589-5058; Rte 23A; admission per vehicle $7; ☿ 9am-dusk May-Nov) is particularly brilliant in the fall when the trees turn golden, red and orange. There is a sandy beach and you can rent rowboats to take out on the lake. Good fishing and a plethora of hiking trails round out the area's activities. One favorite trail goes from the North/South Lake campground to the site of the Catskill Mountain House (see The Late, Great Catskill Hotels, above). Camping on one of the more than 200 sites cost $16 per night. Reservations are essential. To get here from Haines Falls, take the marked turnoff for North/South Lake and follow the signs.

Sleeping & Eating

Sleeping options have private parking lots and air-conditioning.

Eggery Inn (☎ 518-589-5363; www.eggeryinn.com; County Rd 16; d from $100) Always popular, this inn in a large house features great views, a big dining room and a woodstove. To reach the inn, turn south on County Rd 16 at the Tannersville traffic light and follow the road for 1.5 miles.

Greene Mountain View Inn (☎ 518-589-9886; www.greenemountainviewinn.com; 132 South Main St; d weekday/weekend $75/100) Reminiscent of another century, rooms here are elegant. The inn has a great lounge made of dark wood with a pool table and a long, solid bar. There is a two-night minimum stay on weekends. To reach the inn, turn south off County Rd 16 at the Tannersville traffic light and follow the signs.

Last Chance Antiques & Cheese Café (☎ 518-589-6424; Main St; mains $8-20) As the name suggests this place specializes in cheese dishes, including fondue, nachos and chili with cheese. Lunch selections such as sandwiches and salads go for about $8. Traditional American-style mains such as meatloaf and mashed potatoes cost about $15. Beer-lovers will enjoy the huge selection of beers from all over the world. The restaurant also sells the antiques and collectibles that cover every inch of its wall space.

Maggie's Krooked Café (☎ 518-589-6101; Main St; mains $8-10) Maggie's has a funky atmosphere, small tables and good food. The breakfasts are great, including a local favorite, the 'SOB Omelet' (South of the Border) made with grilled veggies and salsa. The café is open for breakfast and lunch.

Drinking

Tannersville is the après-ski nightlife spot for those hitting the slopes at Windham and Hunter, with quite a few bars and dance clubs. Locals recommend **Powder** (☎ 518-589-9802; 5969 Main St) and **Slopes** (☎ 518-589-5006; Main St) for dancing and drinking. Both were being renovated at the time of writing, but should be open by the time you read this.

SOUTHERN & WESTERN CATSKILLS

This area includes the infamous 'Borscht Belt' resorts concentrated among the towns of Liberty, Monticello and Ellenville. Once a top-class tourist destination, the area never recovered from the demise of the mega-resorts. Today these towns are some of the Catskills' shabbiest and most depressing. The southern edge of the Catskills, along the Pennsylvania border, is less depressing and offers some good water-oriented activates.

BORSCHT BELT

In the southern foothills of the Catskill Mountains, the famous Catskill resorts are clustered around Monticello and Liberty along Rte 17 and near Minnewaska State Park and Ellenville on Rte 209, north of Rte 17.

These resorts evolved from the boarding-houses that sprang up here in the late 19th and early 20th centuries, when Jewish immigrants sought an escape from the poverty and crowded conditions of New York City. The area became known as the 'Borscht Belt,' and the small boardinghouses grew into enormous (although not especially graceful) resorts, offering guests every imaginable kind of activity, from swimming in Olympic-sized pools to skiing and golfing. As the resorts grew, so did the program of activities, which catered to whole families, from children and teenagers to parents and grandparents. Two major ingredients of the Borscht Belt experience were the food (and lots of it) and the comedians. Woody Allen captures some of this scene in his movies *Annie Hall* and *Broadway Danny Rose*. The 1990 hit film *Dirty Dancing* takes place at one of these resorts during the Borscht Belt's final glory days.

With the advent of jet travel, the resorts went into decline and many closed as guests chose to travel to Florida, the Caribbean and Europe. More recently, Atlantic City has been drawing away a lot of their business. The surviving resorts have redefined themselves with big-name entertainment (from singers and bands like Tom Jones, Neil Sedaka and Frankie Valli & the Four Seasons to such comedians as Jackie Mason, George Carlin and Brett Butler), special-interest promotions

---

DETOUR – MAX YASGUR'S FARM

From Monticello head west on Rte 17B to the town of Bethel where the infamous Wood-stock Music Festival actually took place on Max Yasgur's farm in 1969 (see The Woodstock Festivals, p176). The farm is off Hurd Rd and signs point the way from 17B to the gigantic green field. The site is marked by a stone marker near the road that reads: 'This is the original site of the Woodstock Music and Arts Fair held on Aug. 15, 16, 17, 1969.'

(singles, golfers, tennis players, families celebrating Mother's and Father's Day) and conference facilities.

Kutsher's Country Club (☎ 800-431-1273; www .kutshers.com; Kutsher Rd, Monticello; d per person from $98 incl meals; ⬛), off Rte 42, is one of the last surviving mega-resorts, Kutsher's is a modern family-oriented place with a full activities program for children and adults. There are also indoor and outdoor pools, an 18-hole golf course, a health club and a lake.

ALONG THE DELAWARE RIVER

The Delaware River, dividing New York and Pennsylvania, offers some of the best recreation in the region.

The town of **Narrowsburg**, filled with old, mostly well-preserved buildings, sits on a once-strategic bend in the Delaware River (on Rte 97). The town's 18th-century stockade history is on display at the **Fort Delaware Museum of Colonial History** (☎ 845-252-6660; Rte 97; adult/child $5/3; ☼ 10am-5pm late Jun–Aug, 10am-5pm Sat & Sun Sep-May). The museum is actually a replica of the small Connecticut Yankee settlement that stood on the site between 1755 and 1785, complete with settlers' cabins, blacksmith shop and armory.

Narrowsburg is also one of several points along the river that offers opportunities for water sports. **Lander's Delaware River Trips** (☎ 800-252-3925; www.landersrivertrips.com; ☼ Apr–mid-Oct) is a friendly, family-run operation that does raft and canoe trips ranging from three to six hours, covering 5 to 10 miles of river (depending on river and weather conditions). Rafting and canoe trips cost $30 per day, and tubing trips cost $17. The company also operates a campground ($12 per site) and motel ($80 for a double room). In addition the company has a variety of packages that include accommodation, meals and rafting or canoeing.

The third-oldest inn in the state is another sleeping option in the area. The **Narrowsburg Inn** (☎ 914-252-3998; 176 N Bridge St; d from $54) is looking a little threadbare these days, but is still good value for money. Some rooms share baths.

Another summer river destination is **Barryville**, at the junction of Rtes 97 and 55, along an especially beautiful part of the Delaware River. **Wild & Scenic River Tours** (☎ 800-836-0366; ☼ May-Oct) offers rafting, canoeing and tubing trips. Day trips cost $20, and are family-oriented. The company also offers overnight trips with riverside camping.

Capital District & Mohawk Valley

CONTENTS

A schizophrenic mixture of charming, vibrant towns and decaying industrial cities, this central New York region is crisscrossed by the mighty Hudson, Mohawk, Susquehanna and Chenango Rivers. Rolling green hills, fields full of crops and serene woodlands collide with major interstate highways. The Mohawk Valley is named after the Mohawk Indians, an Iroquois tribe who were New York's first inhabitants.

Rte 20, America's longest highway, runs through Albany and the Mohawk Valley. Settlers hoping to strike it rich in the country's furthest frontiers passed through this road – known as the Great Western Turnpike – en masse between the late 1700s and the early 1800s when it was the main gateway to the West.

The Erie Canal was completed in the region in 1825, and the area became a manufacturing super-center employing thousands of European immigrants. During the factory heyday this was the most densely populated region of the state. Increased poverty and dying industrial towns became a sad reality, however, with the decline of the manufacturing base in the 20th century. Today, the region's main draws are touristic: charismatic Saratoga Springs, with the USA's oldest thoroughbred racetrack, and pristine Cooperstown, home to the National Baseball Hall of Fame. The surprisingly photogenic state capital, Albany, sits astride the Hudson and offers an interesting mixture of architecture, pleasant parks and quiet tree-lined streets.

HIGHLIGHTS

▪ **Best Atmosphere**
One Caroline Street Bistro (p195) in Saratoga Springs. Chic and intimate, the food is as good as the live jazz and blues.

▪ **Best Museums**
The National Baseball Hall of Fame (p197) in Cooperstown and National Museum of Racing & Hall of Fame (p192) in Saratoga Springs.

▪ **Best Underground Experience**
Howe Caverns (p201). Ride an elevator 156ft below ground and tour these expansive caverns just outside Sharon Springs.

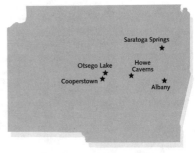

▪ **Best Luxury Splurge**
Otesaga Resort Hotel (p200). This stately landmark is a beautiful Georgian resort right on Otsego Lake in Cooperstown.

▪ **Best Spot to Watch the Horses Run**
The Saratoga Race Course, in Saratoga Springs, is the place to see and be seen (p193).

▪ **Top Diner**
Miss Albany Diner (p189) in Albany, where Americana, nostalgia and good, cheap home-cooking collide.

CAPITAL DISTRICT &
MOHAWK VALLEY

CLIMATE

This region has a varied climate with average January temperatures ranging from 14°F to 22°F. Summer temperatures average around 72°F. Precipitation in the region ranges from 36 to more than 44 inches of rain and snowmelt. The main tourist areas of Albany, Saratoga Springs, Cooperstown and Binghamton operate year-round, although some attractions close in winter.

STATE PARKS

The region has a number of state parks. Many are uncrowded and offer opportunities for swimming, camping, fishing, boating and hiking. The 2000-acre **Saratoga Spa State Park** (p194) in Saratoga Springs contains a complex of buildings, pools and bathhouses designed to rival those found in European health spas. The facilities opened to the public in 1935, and the area officially became a state park in 1962.

Glimmerglass State Park (p199) is at the northern end of the Otsego Lake, about 8 miles north of Cooperstown, and features a swimming beach, campground, hiking and biking trails and a playground in a serene and green location.

For more information on state parks in the region, check out New York State Parks' website www.nysparks.com.

GETTING THERE & AROUND

I-90, the primary east–west highway in the state, follows the Mohawk Valley from Oneida Lake – between Syracuse and Rome – and links the towns of Utica, Herkimer, Canajoharie, Amsterdam and Rotterdam to Albany. From Albany, I-90 dips south to join I-87 (for 8 miles), then crosses the Hudson River and continues to the southeast into Massachusetts. I-88 is the other major east–west highway in the region, connecting Binghamton to Albany, 140 miles to the northeast.

I-87, also known as the Northway, runs north–south and connects Albany to Saratoga Springs, Glens Falls, Lake George and the Adirondacks. The other principle north–south route in the region is Rte 28, which links Oneonta (at the junction of I-88) to Cooperstown and the Adirondacks.

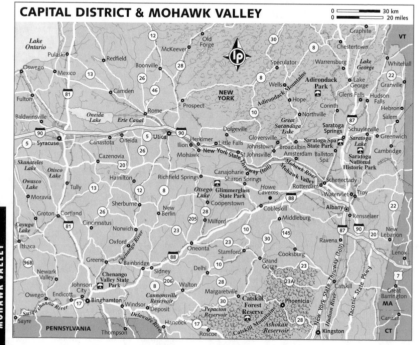

CAPITAL DISTRICT & MOHAWK VALLEY

Adirondack Trailways (☎ 518-436-9651) and **Greyhound** (☎ 800-231-2222) both connect towns and cities in the region. There also is **Amtrak** (☎ 800-872-7245) train service.

THE CAPITAL DISTRICT

This aptly named area's top attractions can be found in its two main cities, Albany and Saratoga Springs.

ALBANY

☎ 518 / pop 95,658

Albany, refreshing and surprising with plenty of wide-open spaces and green parks, is located on the west bank of the Hudson River. The state capital has managed to retain, and retrieve, the historic charm of an old and vibrant northeastern city. The architecture is reminiscent of Europe's grand cities and seems almost out of place in New York – ornate state buildings and brownstone houses grace the downtown area. Neighborhood streets are quiet and tree-lined. The marble and glass buildings of the Empire State Plaza dominate the city center and stand in sharp contrast to the otherwise historic surroundings.

Albany's character is largely defined by its role as the seat of the nation's second-largest state government. Although it continues to be a manufacturing center, the city's service economy allowed Albany to escape the economic devastation dished out to its rust-belt neighbors. In fact, the city enjoys a relatively healthy economy that supports excellent restaurants, revitalized neighborhoods, architectural gems and an array of amenities that make Albany worthy of a visit.

Orientation

Albany is surrounded by interstate highways. The New York State Thruway (I-90) enters Albany from the east and circles the city westward. I-87 comes in from the south, and I-787 completes the circle to the east. The 98-acre Empire State Plaza sits at the center of the city. Washington Ave runs northwest and soon forks into Western and Central Aves. State St divides many street addresses into north and south. Within walking distance of downtown are several historic residential neighborhoods and Washington Park. Filled with restaurants,

bars, retro shops, galleries and even an upscale tattoo parlor in brightly painted brick buildings, Lark St, between Madison and Washington Aves, has earned the saintly nickname of 'Greenwich Village North.'

Information

There are two good stores for used books in town: **Dove & Hudson** (☎ 518-432-4518; 296 Hudson St), at the corner of Dove, and the **Lark Street Bookstore** (☎ 518-465-8126; 115 Lark St). The **Albany Public Library** (☎ 518-427-4300; 161 Washington Ave) is located between Dove and Lark Sts.

The main **post office** (☎ 518-462-1359; 45 Hudson St) is at the corner of Pearl St. There are other post offices in the Empire State Plaza on the concourse level and in the capitol.

The **Albany Heritage Area Visitors Center** (☎ 518-434-0405; www.albany.org; 25 Quackenbush Sq; ☺ 9am-4pm Mon-Fri, 10am-4pm Sat-Sun) at the northeast corner of Broadway and Clinton Aves has the usual vast assortment of brochures, including a self-guided walking tour of the historic downtown area.

Sights & Activities

As befits a large capital city, Albany has a host of things to see and do.

EMPIRE STATE PLAZA

With 98 acres of brilliant white marble and glass buildings and sculpture gardens, the Empire State Plaza, between Madison and State Sts, dwarfs its neighboring structures. Housing legislative offices, courtrooms, various state agencies, a collection of modern art and a performing arts center (referred to by locals as 'the Egg' because of its curvy, modern silhouette), the plaza offers something for everyone. Bring a picnic lunch and eat it by the long reflecting pool in the middle of the plaza, ride the elevator to the free observation deck on the 42nd floor of the Corning Tower Building, or peruse the collection that includes 92 modern art sculptures and paintings – including some by Alexander Calder and David Smith. On weekends locals flock here to roller-skate on the hundreds of feet of marble tiles.

ALBANY INSTITUTE OF HISTORY & ART

Browsing through the **institute's** (☎ 518-463-4478; 125 Washington Ave; adult/child $7/4; ☺ 10am-5pm Wed-Sat, noon-5pm Sun) collection of period furnishings, silver and pewter, decorative arts and fine arts from the Hudson Valley is an excellent way to gain knowledge and insight into the history and culture of the region. Founded in 1791, this museum is one of the oldest in the US and recently went through an extensive renovation. The Hudson River school of landscape painters is represented here with works by Thomas Cole, Asher Durand, James and William Hart and Jasper Cropsey.

NEW YORK STATE CAPITOL BUILDING

A fascinating mixture of Italian and French Renaissance and Romanesque architecture, the **capitol** (☎ 518-474-2418; admission free; ☿ tours 10am, noon, 2pm, 3pm), built between 1867 and 1899, looks as if it would fit in better in Prague than New York. Inside, beyond the pink granite facade, is the Million Dollar Staircase, a series of intersecting stairs and landings. Alongside one of the staircases there are 300 carved portraits of famous New Yorkers and friends of the sculptor. On the senate staircase, carvings depict the evolutionary chain with simpler organisms at the bottom and more complex ones at top. Tours last one hour; it's best to book ahead. The capitol is next to the Plaza between State St and Washington Ave.

WASHINGTON PARK

Perfect for strolling or picnicking, this park is a green oasis in the midst of the city. Designed by Frederick Law Olmstead and Calvert Vaux in the 1870s, it consists of 81 acres of grassy meadows, twisting roads, plenty of trees and long, skinny Washington Lake. On the shores of the lake is the **Washington Park Lake House** (☎ 518-434-4524), complete with pink floors and wrought-iron chandeliers. Plays are performed here nightly for six weeks beginning in early July. There is free seating on the lawn or reserved seating for $6. In summer paddleboat rentals are available, or you can just enjoy a walk in the park and feed the ducks.

NEW YORK STATE MUSEUM

Best described as an experience, this **museum** (☎ 518-474-5877; Madison Ave; suggested donation $2; ☿ 9:30am-5pm) highlights the political, cultural and natural history of New York City and the state through installations built to scale, sound effects and interactive exhibits. Featuring rotating exhibits, the museum is divided

into three major areas: New York Metropolis, Adirondack Wilderness and Upstate New York Native American Peoples. The museum is in the Cultural Education Center at the south end of Empire Plaza, but the entrance is at street level on Madison Ave.

Festivals & Events

Held the second weekend in May, the **Annual Tulip Festival** and **Pinksterfest** (☎ 518-434-1217) are three-day celebrations of the city's Dutch heritage. The festivals include food vendors, crafts and the crowning of a Tulip Queen.

Sleeping

There are a number of independently owned motels along Central Ave within the first 3 miles northwest of the intersection with I-87 (exit 2). The rooms are very basic and inexpensive, but generally clean. Many of Albany's chain motels are by the airport on the western edge of the city. Standards at these motels are generally higher than at the independent motels. All sleeping options either have their own parking lots, or there is off-street parking readily available. Air-conditioning is standard.

BUDGET & MID-RANGE

State Street Mansion (☎ 518-462-6780; 281 State St; d from $79) This renovated guesthouse is a former seminary from around 1881 and is right downtown. Rooms are elegantly furnished. The cheapest rooms have shared baths.

Pine Haven B&B (☎ 518-482-1574; 531 Western Ave; d from $69) Rooms are furnished with antique dressers, iron bed frames, featherbeds and other Victorian amenities. Continental breakfast is served in a dining room with a fireplace that's lit on cold mornings.

Northway Inn (☎ 518-869-0277; 1517 Central Ave; s/d $45/50; ⌨) Rooms here are large and clean, albeit a little shabby, with giant televisions. There is a nice pool and bar.

Western Motel (☎ 518-456-7241; 2019 Western Ave; d $55) North of Washington Park and the downtown area, this place is another inexpensive option that offers very basic rooms. The neighborhood is not the nicest, but it's not too far from the city center.

Comfort Inn (☎ 518-783-1216; 866 Albany-Shaker Rd; d $89; ⌨) This is another option. The motel has 97 rooms.

TOP END

The Desmond (☎ 518-869-8100; www.desmondhotels
.com; 660 Albany-Shaker Rd; d $169; 🖳) This elegant
colonial-style hotel is possibly the nicest
place to stay in Albany. Located near the
airport at exit 4 off I-87, it has lavishly
decorated rooms with plenty of dark-wood
paneling and period furniture. This hotel
includes two heated indoor pools, an exercise room and two restaurants – one casual,
the other formal.

Century House Hotel & Restaurant (☎ 518-
785-0931; 987 New Loudon Rd; d $115; 🖳) This is a
charming hotel in an old Dutch farmhouse
that dates back to 1810. It offers tastefully
decorated rooms, has exquisite grounds
that include a nature trail, and provides a
complimentary breakfast and newspaper
each morning. There is a full-service restaurant and pub, plus tennis courts and a
pool. It's in Latham, just 10 minutes from
Albany, on Rte 9.

New Crowne Plaza (☎ 518-462-6611; cnr State &
Lodge Sts; d $175; 🖳) In the heart of downtown
Albany, this is the poshest place to stay in
the city center. It offers a large indoor pool,
two restaurants and bar with nightly entertainment. Rooms are well appointed and
the service courteous and efficient.

Mansion Hill Inn & Restaurant (☎ 518-465-2038;
www.mansionhill.com; 115 Philip St; d $165, mains $22)
Right downtown, rooms here are comfort-
able with dark-wood furnishings and come
with breakfast. The inn has a restaurant
open for dinner that features wines from
around the world and nouveau-American
cuisine.

Eating

Albany has all kinds of eating options – from
ethnic to classic, cheap to expensive, casual
to formal.

BUDGET

Debbie's Kitchen (☎ 518-463-3829; 456 Madison Ave;
mains $6) Porcelain chickens and still paint-
ings on cheery blue walls give this place a
country kitchen decor, while lava lamps
and wind chimes provide a holistic vibe.
Food is health-oriented, with fresh wraps
and homemade salads.

Mamoun's Mediterranean Restaurant (☎ 518-
434-3901; 206 Washington Ave; mains under $12) Tasty
and authentic Middle Eastern food is
served in a casual environment.

> ### THE CLASSIC AMERICAN DINER
>
> The embodiment of down-home Americana,
> **Miss Albany Diner** (☎ 518-465-9148; 893
> Broadway; mains $8; 🕑 7am-2pm Mon-Fri,
> 9am-2pm Sat & Sun) was designed as an old
> railway car. Nostalgia and good home cook-
> ing are spooned up in equal parts. Known
> for its breakfasts – thick French toast with
> pecan cream cheese filling topped with
> Irish whiskey butterscotch sauce or the MAD
> eggs concoction (eggs on an English muffin
> with curry sauce) – it draws a loyal crowd.
> Weekend mornings you'll find a line at the
> door when the place opens. The diner, which
> dates back to 1941, was originally known as
> Lil's Diner but was renamed after a 1986 ren-
> ovation in preparation for the Albany-based
> filming of William Kennedy's novel *Ironweed*,
> scenes of which were shot here.

Daily Grind Café (☎ 518-427-0464; 204 Lark St;
mains $4-6) This coffee shop is popular with
local college students. It serves decent cappuccino, homemade muffins, croissants
and sandwiches. Try the $6 Belgian waffle
and refillable coffee special.

MID-RANGE & TOP END

Elda's on Lark (☎ 518-449-3532; 205 Lark St; lunch $5-
8, dinner $13-20) This place serves Italian food
in a great atmosphere. There's a martini
lounge with couches for sipping cocktails
and people-watching that has a prohibition-
era speakeasy feel, an elegantly decorated
dining room and 2nd-floor balcony seating.
Jazz is played in the background.

Jack's Oyster House (☎ 518-465-8854; 42 State
St; mains $11-18) Quintessential Albany. The
restaurant's namesake, Jack Rosenstein,
opened his first oyster house in 1913 and
the present one in 1937. The food is as
good as the atmosphere, especially if you
like clams and oysters, which are served on
the half shell or in stews. Jack's also serves
other seafood dishes. Pulitzer-prize–winner
William Kennedy, author of *Ironweed*, immortalized Jack's in a 1985 Esquire article
called 'Jack and the Oyster.'

Nicole's Bistro (☎ 518-465-1111; cnr Clinton St &
Broadway; mains $18) Some say this is Albany's
finest restaurant. It is Albany's oldest Dutch
landmark, dating back to the 1600s. Located in historic Quackenbush Sq, this very

popular French bistro specializes in steak *au poivre*, homemade pastas and rack of lamb. Ambiance is cozy and romantic with lots of old black-and-white photos. Dine in the outdoor garden for lunch or dinner. Try one of the three-course fixed price dinners for $25.

Justin's (☎ 518-436-7008; 301 Lark St; mains from $13) An upscale, creative menu and jazz brunches contribute to the funky vibe here. Justin's is very popular with the college crowd. You have a choice of two menus: the reasonably priced café menu or the more upscale restaurant menu that includes basil pepper salmon, Thai coconut shrimp and jerk chicken, to name but a few dishes. There are daily happy hours.

Quintessence (☎ 518-434-8186; 11 New Scotland Ave; mains $10) In a trendy, stainless-steel diner with a tuxedoed host and a bar where one might expect a counter, this restaurant features international theme menus. Selections include burgers and teriyaki chicken and beef. Sometimes there's live blues and dancing.

Albany Pump Station (☎ 518-447-9000; 19 Quackenbush Sq; mains $8-20) This is an old warehouse converted into a hip brewpub and restaurant with an industrial slant – plenty of exposed pipes. American fare is featured and includes everything from sandwiches and burgers to filet mignon and ribs. The bar stays open late and serves good microbrews.

Drinking & Entertainment

The city's best entertainment sources are the Thursday and Friday editions of the *Times-Union* and *Metroland*, a free alternative weekly. The hippest nightlife is found on Lark St.

Empire State Performing Arts Center (☎ 518-473-1845; The Egg, Empire State Plaza, cnr Madison Ave & Swan St) This is Albany's number one arts venue. It has an 880-seat main theater and a 500-seat recital hall. Concerts and dance and theater performances are held here.

Palace Theatre (☎ 518-465-4663; 19 Clinton Ave) Once a 1930s-era movie theater, this place is now the home of the Albany Symphony Orchestra. It's also a venue for touring music acts and Broadway shows.

Big House Brewing Company (☎ 518-445-2739; 90 N Pearl St) In a renovated warehouse turned into a lively three-story brewpub, Big House boasts several bars, a restaurant, pool, darts and weekend DJ. Dancing takes place on the 3rd floor most nights of the week.

Valentine's (☎ 518 432-6572; 17 New Scotland Ave) Valentine's is Albany's premier club for local bands with big followings and great drink specials can be found here. It has two floors, with bars on each, and at least two bands play most nights of the week. It's located near Dana St.

On Lark St you can check out the **Lionheart Blues Café** (☎ 518-436-9530; 258 Lark St), for good blues, and **Justin's** (☎ 518-436-7008; 301 Lark St), which has jazz on the weekends and is popular with singles.

Getting There & Around

Albany International Airport (☎ 518-869-9611) is in the town of Colonie on Albany-Shaker Rd and is about 10 miles from downtown. Most major carriers serve the airport. Round-trip fares are about $250 to Chicago and $205 to Washington, DC.

Adirondack Trailways (☎ 518-436-9651, 800-858-8555; www.escapemaker.com/adirondacktrailways) and **Greyhound** (☎ 518-434-8095, 800-231-2222; www.greyhound.com) stop at the **Albany Bus Terminal** (☎ 518-427-7060; 34 Hamilton St) at the corner of Broadway. Fares include Atlantic City ($44, 6½ hours), Buffalo ($51, six hours), New York City ($32, three hours) and Montreal ($42, five hours).

The **Amtrak station** (☎ 518-462-5763, 800-872-7245) is across the Hudson River in Rensselaer, about five minutes by car from downtown Albany. Amtrak has daily train service along the Hudson River Valley.

Albany is accessible via I-90 from western New York or Massachusetts and I-87 from southern or northern New York.

Albany city bus Nos 1 and 31 run to/from the airport and various stops in downtown. It costs $0.75 plus zone charges of $0.20 or $0.30. Taxis cost about $20 for the same route.

SARATOGA SPRINGS

☎ 518 / pop 26,000

Already famous for its mineral springs and thoroughbred horseracing, Saratoga Springs became even more popular following the release of the 2003 horseracing movie *Seabiscuit*, filmed in part at the racetrack. A gracious town with Victorian architecture, manicured gardens, luxurious spas, classic pavilions, modern museums and a renowned program of concerts and dance performances, Saratoga Springs is likely

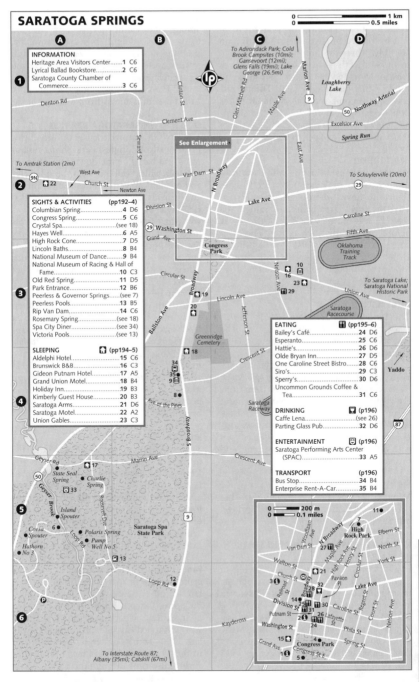

SARATOGA SPRINGS

0 — 1 km
0 — 0.5 miles

INFORMATION
Heritage Area Visitors Center.......1 C6
Lyrical Ballad Bookstore.............2 C6
Saratoga County Chamber of
Commerce................................3 C6

To Adirondack Park; Cold
Brook Campsites (10mi);
Gansevoort (12mi);
Glens Falls (19mi); Lake
George (26.5mi)

To Amtrak Station (2mi)

To Schuylerville (20mi)

SIGHTS & ACTIVITIES (pp192–4)
Columbian Spring......................4 D6
Congress Spring.........................5 C6
Crystal Spa................................(see 18)
Hayes Well.................................6 A5
High Rock Cone...........................7 D5
Lincoln Baths.............................8 B4
National Museum of Dance.........9 B4
National Museum of Racing & Hall of
Fame....................................10 C3
Old Red Spring..........................11 D5
Park Entrance...........................12 B6
Peerless & Governor Springs......(see 7)
Peerless Pools...........................13 B5
Rip Van Dam............................14 C6
Rosemary Spring.......................(see 18)
Spa City Diner...........................(see 34)
Victoria Pools...........................13 B5

SLEEPING (pp194–5)
Aldelphi Hotel..........................15 C6
Brunswick B&B..........................16 C3
Gideon Putnam Hotel................17 A5
Grand Union Motel....................18 B4
Holiday Inn..............................19 B3
Kimberly Guest House...............20 B3
Saratoga Arms.........................21 D6
Saratoga Motel........................22 A2
Union Gables...........................23 C3

EATING (pp195–6)
Bailey's Café............................24 D6
Esperanto................................25 C6
Hattie's...................................26 D6
Olde Bryan Inn.........................27 D5
One Caroline Street Bistro.........28 C6
Siro's.....................................29 C3
Sperry's..................................30 D6
Uncommon Grounds Coffee &
Tea.....................................31 C6

DRINKING (p196)
Caffe Lena................................(see 26)
Parting Glass Pub.....................32 D6

ENTERTAINMENT (p196)
Saratoga Performing Arts Center
(SPAC)................................33 A5

TRANSPORT (p196)
Bus Stop..................................34 B4
Enterprise Rent-A-Car...............35 B4

To Saratoga Lake;
Saratoga National
Historic Park

Saratoga
Racecourse

Yaddo

To Interstate Route 87;
Albany (35mi); Catskill (67mi)

0 — 200 m
0 — 0.1 miles

the most popular destination in the region. Quiet for 47 weeks out of the year, the town is transformed for five weeks beginning in late July, when the thoroughbreds come to town. And with them come the crowds of hardcore horse people, rich society folks and the fans that just like to gawk. Dinner reservations become mandatory, hotel prices double, music and revelers fill the streets and the air is full of a magic and electricity that you just have to see to believe.

Orientation

Saratoga Springs is just 35 miles north of Albany. From I-87, exit 13N (Rte 9) goes right into town, where it becomes Broadway, the town's main drag. Saratoga Spa State Park is on the west side of Broadway before you hit the town center. The racecourse is a few blocks east of Broadway off Union Ave. You can easily walk around the town, although you may want to drive through the state park.

Information

The **Lyrical Ballad Bookstore** (☎ 518-584-8779; 7 Phila St) is an inviting old bookstore. The **post office** is on Broadway at the corner of Church St.

The **Heritage Area Visitors Center** (☎ 518-587-3241; Drink Hall, 297 Broadway; ✆ 9am-4pm Mon-Sat year-round, 9am-4pm Sun Jul & Aug) across from Congress Park can provide maps and brochures of the area. The helpful **Saratoga County Chamber of Commerce** (☎ 518-584-3255; www.saratoga.org; 28 Clinton St; ✆ 9am-5pm Mon-Fri) can set you up with information about lodging, events and promotions.

Sights & Activities

Mineral Springs and horseracing are the two main attractions in Saratoga Springs, but there are other options.

NATIONAL MUSEUM OF RACING & HALL OF FAME

Exhibits on the history of horseracing in England and America and on jockeys, thoroughbreds and breeding are displayed at this state-of-the-art **museum** (☎ 518-584-0400; 191 Union Ave; admission $7; ✆ 10am-4:30pm Mon-Sat, noon-4:30pm Sun, 9am-5pm daily during racing season). Here you'll find the Agua Caliente trophy that Seabiscuit won in Mexico in 1938 (which was lost for about 50 years) and the

leg brace worn by Red Pollard, his jockey, among 20,000 other artifacts. In addition to paintings, sculptures and memorabilia, the museum has interactive exhibits built to scale and a multimedia center where you can watch a famous race of your choice in one of the video booths that line the walls. The museum is across from the racecourse

DOWNTOWN SARATOGA SPRINGS

The city's downtown focuses on Broadway, to the north of Congress Park. Shops, restaurants and bars line the downtown strip. In summer tables spill out onto the sidewalks and at night all genres of music fill the air and crowds pack the streets. The Victorian-style buildings are all immaculate – you won't find any boarded-up storefronts here. Scattered throughout town are almost life-size horse sculptures, each one different. Some sport ice-cream cones for spots; others are extremely glamorous, decked out entirely in glitter.

Although at one time Broadway was lined with one grand hotel after another, today only two of these hotels remain. At 365 Broadway you'll find the beautifully appointed brown and cream Victorian **Adelphi** (p195), built in 1877. At 353 Broadway is the **Rip Van Dam**, built in the Federal style in 1840. Continue north on Broadway through town and the hustle disappears. The road becomes thick with trees and lined with beautiful old homes on spacious lawns.

MINERAL SPRINGS & BATHS

There are public springs throughout the town – a spring even runs through the lobby of the Heritage Area Visitors Center. Except in the coldest weather, spring waters are pumped constantly, spilling from spigots into concrete catch basins or drains. The taste of each and the purported medicinal effects vary greatly. Carry a cup for tasting, although for many the taste may not be appealing.

The small, formally landscaped **Congress Park** is directly across from the visitors center just off Broadway. It is home to Italian sculpture gardens and three springs, including **Congress Spring**, which is inside a Greek Revival-style pavilion. The spring was 'improved' by Gideon Putnam in the late 1700s and its water bottled and sold in the 1820s. **Columbian Spring**, a freshwater spring, also runs through the park.

A DAY AT THE RACES

From late July to August the town is transformed as fans flock to the **Saratoga Race Course** (☎ 518-584-6200; www.nyra.com/saratoga; 267 Union Ave; admission grandstand/clubhouse $3/5; ☉ closed Tue), the oldest active thoroughbred racetrack in the US. Hotel prices soar, the streets are jammed with fancy cars, and the nights are long as gamblers celebrate or commiserate over their wins and losses. You don't have to be a high-stakes player to enjoy the racetrack – entry is still a steal and the minimum bet is just $1. On the way in pick up a copy of the *Post Parade*, which lists each horse's record by race and describes how to place bets.

Once inside, you can walk right up to the fence and stand a few feet from the horses as they charge past. You can also stand near the winner's circle and watch the congratulations bestowed on jockey, owner and horse. Even if you're not into gambling you can still cheer the horses, take in the crowds and enjoy the great musical entertainment. Jazz and folk groups change on a daily basis, and the house Dixieland band guarantees that there is never a lull in the fast-paced, spirited atmosphere.

The track is closed on Tuesday, steeplechase is on Wednesday and Thursday; post time is generally at 1pm. The biggest race of the season is Travers Day in late August. An entire festival, the Travers Festival, is organized in conjunction with this race and runs for a week with a lineup of daily events around town. The last weekend of the season is Final Stretch Weekend, characterized by lots of food and drink and live music downtown.

Parking near the track runs in the neighborhood of $3 to $5. There is free admission from 7am to 9:30am. This is the time to come and watch the horses' morning workouts and get a free tour of the stables. Many people bring their own breakfast and coffee, or splurge at the trackside café for a $12 breakfast buffet.

There are plenty of outdoor-food concessions at the track where you can buy typically over-priced food. As an alternative you can eat at one of the several $15-minimum clubhouse dining rooms, but only if properly attired – 'collared shirts for men, no shorts or abbreviated wear.'

The most popular racetrack hangout, and the place to see and be seen, is **Siro's** (☎ 518-584-4030; 168 Lincoln Ave; ☉ dinner), adjacent to the track at the corner of Lincoln and Nelson Aves. Underneath a striped canvas tent you'll find a long bar where live bands play from 5:30pm to 8:30pm, after which those with dinner reservations move inside to feast on tender cuts of steak or racks of lamb. Dinners aren't cheap – expect to pay about $150 for two people with drinks – but the atmosphere makes it worth it. Dress to impress.

The **Old Red Spring** is at the northern end of High Rock Ave near the intersection with Excelsior Ave, a few blocks from High Rock Park. The spring is high in iron and was called the 'beauty water spring' because it was said to be good for the complexion. It was also used as a cure for eye problems.

The **Rosemary Spring** is behind the Crystal Spa and in front of the Grand Union Motel at 120 S Broadway; although it looks as if it is on private-motel property it is open to the public.

If you want to do more than taste the water, try the **Lincoln Baths** (☎ 518-583-2880; S Broadway; admission from $18; ☉ 9am-4pm Jul-Aug, 9am-4pm Wed-Sun Oct-May, 9am-4pm Wed-Mon Jun-Sep) for a soak. In the Georgian building there are men's and women's sections with semiprivate soaking rooms. Each has a deep tub and a massage table. The customary treatment here is to sit in the bubbly water (which contains 16 minerals) for 20 minutes, and then relax on a table for another 20 minutes. A simple soak starts at $18, but there are also massage packages ($40) and wraps ($70). The baths are on S Broadway between the State Park entrance and the National Museum of Dance.

The **Crystal Spa** (☎ 518-584-2556; 120 S Broadway; admission from $19; ☉ 8:30am-4:30pm Fri-Tue) is the only private-bath facility in town. It pumps water from Rosemary Spring, located behind the building. The facilities and treatments here are more luxurious than those at the Lincoln Baths. The 15 soaking rooms have tile floors. The spa offers an array of soaks, massages, scrubs and facials, which cost anywhere from $19 for a private mineral bath to $80 for a wrap or body scrub. Reservations are required.

SARATOGA SPA STATE PARK

Shortly after the turn of the 20th century the state began buying the springs and the land surrounding them in order to begin a program of conservation and preservation. Construction began on a complex of buildings, pools and bathhouses designed to rival those found in European health spas. The facilities opened to the public in 1935, and in 1962 the area officially became the 2000-acre **Saratoga Spa State Park** (☎ 518-584-2000; off S Broadway; admission $6). Today, although the redbrick buildings are still regal and the grounds well maintained, signs of wear and neglect are visible and the park feels almost dated – as if it never quite made the transition from one century to the next.

At one end of the park is the **Ave of the Pines** and at the other end is **Loop Rd**, leading past half a dozen mineral springs including **Hayes Well**, which is immediately across Loop Rd to the north of the parking lot and is marked by a square cobblestone block about 4ft high and capped with a stone. A spring pours out of one side of the block. On the other side is a one-inch pipe from which you can inhale carbon dioxide – for that 'special' feeling. Do not inhale deeply or your nasal passages will be burned.

In between the Ave of the Pines and Loop Rd are tennis courts, mineral baths, swimming pools, two golf courses, the Saratoga Performing Arts Center and the Gideon Putnam Hotel (p195). The **Victoria Pool** (adult/child $6/3) and the **Peerless Pool** (adult/child $3/1.50) are both inside the park and well marked with signs. They are open for swimming during the summer months.

HIGH ROCK PARK

High Rock Park is a narrow park two blocks east of Broadway. The park itself isn't particularly attractive and is bordered by a few modern townhouses. However, the park's springs are of historical interest. It was here, according to legend, that in 1767 the Mohawk Indians introduced Sir William Johnson to the restorative powers of the highly mineralized water. In doing so the area was opened to commercial development.

High Rock Cone is a cone formed by the mineral deposits of the spring water pumped through it. The cone sits inside a semicircular cement and cobblestone grotto that has a pavilion roof. The water bubbles out very slowly from the top of the cone. **Governor Spring**, about 50ft to the south of the cone, was drilled in 1908 and is named after former New York governor Charles Evans Hughes, who signed a bill protecting the springs. The spring has a strong mineral taste. Behind it is the very mild-tasting **Peerless Spring**.

YADDO

This private **retreat** (☎ 518-584-0746; 312 Union Ave; admission to gardens free; ✆ 8am–dusk), east of the racecourse, has been hosting writers, poets, artists and composers since the 1920s. The massive cut-stone mansion and lush grounds were built and developed by industrialist Spencer Trask and his wife. After their four children were killed in a smallpox epidemic, the Trasks converted the estate into a working community where they hoped artists might 'find the Sacred Fire and light their torches at its flames.' The mansion is still an artists' retreat and is, therefore, off limits to the public. However, the beautifully landscaped gardens – including a mysterious wooded area and formal rose garden – are open to visitors during the day.

NATIONAL MUSEUM OF DANCE

This is the country's only **museum** (☎ 518-584-2225; 99 S Broadway; admission $6.50; ✆ 10am-5pm May-Oct, closed Mon) dedicated to preserving the history and art of American dance; the building has a hall of fame and changing exhibits. Twentieth-century dance is celebrated with enlarged photographs and plaques – you'll find everyone from Fred Astaire to Bill (Bojangles) Robinson. The museum is a must-see for serious dance scholars, but others may not get that much out of it.

Sleeping

Every August hotel prices skyrocket as the town fills up for the five-week racing season. It's advisable to book ahead as many places fill up quickly. Rooms can also be scarce, and prices accordingly high, in May during commencement ceremonies at Skidmore College. Since most people visit Saratoga Springs during the summer season we've quoted rates for this time of year. Off-season rates can be as much as 50% less. During the racing season there is usually a two-night minimum stay on weekends. Most places provide parking lots or off-street parking. Air-conditioning is standard.

BUDGET

Camping is the only truly budget option in Saratoga.

Cold Brook Campsites (☎ 518-584-8038; Gurn Springs Rd; campsites $30; ✆ May–early Oct) This is the nearest campsite to Saratoga, located 10 miles north in Gansevoort. The campground has 272 sites, laundry facilities and hot showers. Take I-87 to exit 16 and go north one mile on Gurn Springs Rd, or follow Rte 50 north out of town.

MID-RANGE

The cheapest places to stay are the independently owned motels outside of town, between I-87 exits 12 and 13N, and along Rte 9 north of town. Slightly more expensive places are between exit 13N and town.

Adelphi Hotel (☎ 518-587-4688; 365 Broadway; d from $185; ✆ May-Oct) This hotel is old Saratoga personified – including its seasonal schedule. The Adelphi was built in 1877 and is elegantly Victorian throughout. Rooms are furnished with lots of pillows and flounced drapes, and there's a garden pool with lots of vegetation. For what you get, it's one of the best deals in town.

Grand Union Motel (☎ 518-584-9000; 120 S Broadway; d from $155) Built like a racing barn, this place has suites named after famous racehorses and simple, no-frills doubles. During race weekends there is a three-night minimum stay. Rates drop to $71 per night during the week in the off-season.

Kimberly Guest House (☎ 518-584-9006; 184 S Broadway; d $150) This place is nothing special. The eight rooms come with kitchens and televisions and some share baths, but it's one of the town's cheaper options and often has last-minute spaces available.

Saratoga Motel (☎ 518-584-0920; 440 Church St; d $110) Rooms here are simple but clean. It's located 1 mile west of town. Rooms go for $55 from November to April.

TOP END

Saratoga Springs has quite a few exquisite places to stay, and is a good city in which to splash out.

Saratoga Arms (☎ 518-584-1775; www.broadwaysaratoga.com; 497 Broadway; d from $300) For some serious luxury, stay at this sprawling Victorian mansion with ornate grand staircases. Fireplaces grace the 16 rooms decked out with carefully chosen antiques. The wraparound porch is perfect for cocktails and celebration after the races.

Gideon Putnam Hotel (☎ 518-584-3000, 800-732-1560; www.gideonputnam.com; 24 Gideon Putnam Rd; d from $235) Its location in the middle of Saratoga Spa State Park makes this the most famous hotel in town. Owned by the state of New York, the Georgian colonial hotel was recently renovated to keep with the vintage elegance of Saratoga. Guests approach the hotel – as one might expect – up a grand driveway. The lobby is expansive, with marble floors, potted palms and period furnishings. Rooms are extremely comfortable, and the hotel has several restaurants and bars.

Union Gables (☎ 518-584-1558, 800-398-1158; 55 Union Ave; d from $265) Just before the racecourse, this is one of the loveliest B&Bs in town. The turn-of-the-20th-century Victorian has 10 spacious, individually decorated rooms. Rates drop from November to April.

Brunswick B&B (☎ 518-585-6715; www.brunswickbb.com; 143 Union Ave; d from $200) In a converted 1886 Victorian house across from the racetrack, this homey place has a comfortable front porch, 10 well-appointed rooms and is wheelchair accessible. It attracts a colorful clientele of racing fans.

Holiday Inn (☎ 518-584-4550; 232 Broadway; d $279; ✆) This is a very upscale Holiday Inn complete with two swimming pools, a restaurant, bar and 150 lavish rooms. Racing season rates are pricey for a Holiday Inn, but there are often rooms here when everywhere else is full. Rates drop to $149 in the off-season.

Eating

Saratoga Springs has the best eating options in the region, including some outstanding fine-dining establishments.

One Caroline Street Bistro (☎ 518-587-8354; 1 Caroline St; mains $17-28) This family-owned place might have the best food in town; it certainly has some of the nicest ambience. Chic and intimate, it has live jazz and blues every night, played at less than ear-shattering levels. The food is homemade and delicious – try the jambalaya ($24), it melts in your mouth. Service is excellent and attentive.

Bailey's Café (☎ 518-583-6060; 37 Phila St; mains $8) Good, inexpensive food is served in an airy, exposed-brick building with stained-glass light fixtures. The kids will love making their own s'mores, and adults can choose from a selection of fresh salads and sandwiches.

CAPITAL DISTRICT &
MOHAWK VALLEY

There is a large outdoor patio with a full bar, and live entertainment Thursday through Saturday. Sunday is open-mike night.

Hattie's (☎ 518-584-4790; 45 Phila St; mains $13-16) Hattie's has been serving Southern fare since 1938. The restaurant is a Saratoga landmark and a very good eatery. Food is served in a casual environment. Lines form early, and waits of more than an hour are common on weekends.

Olde Bryan Inn (☎ 518-587-2990; 123 Maple Ave; mains $8-22) Stone walls, exposed beams and fireplaces give this popular place a rustic look that would seem fake if the inn wasn't in fact a 19th-century building. There are more tables than the space warrants, but the atmosphere is pleasant and no one minds. There are quite a few vegetarian selections.

Sperry's (☎ 518-584-9618; 30½ Caroline St; lunch $8-10, mains $20) Red walls and racing decor are the theme here. The menu is heavy on seafood and meat including Maryland crab cakes with wasabi sauce and jumbo shrimp stuffed with jalapeno horseradish wrapped in bacon. Lunch is salad-oriented. There is a good wine list.

Uncommon Grounds Coffee & Tea (☎ 518-581-0646; 402 Broadway; mains $4-6) A convivial morning or late-night spot for good coffee, pastries, fresh bagels, soups and sandwiches. Inside are bright red walls, outside is a patio heavy on the flowers and wrought iron. It stays open until midnight.

Esperanto (☎ 518-587-4236; 6½ Caroline St; mains $4-6) You can eat your way around the world at this funky little place for less than $10 a plate. There is everything from Thai chicken curry to Louisiana-style jambalaya.

Drinking & Entertainment

Besides the listings here, there are plenty of bars and clubs on Broadway.

Saratoga Performing Arts Center (☎ 518-587-3330; Saratoga Spa State Park; admission $15-56) As if there weren't already enough to draw visitors to town, this center offers world-class entertainment. Located in Saratoga Spa State Park, it's the summer home for both the New York City Ballet and the Philadelphia Orchestra. In addition, the outdoor amphitheater draws in big-name entertainment.

Caffe Lena (☎ 518-583-0022; 47 Phila St) The 'oldest continuously operating coffeehouse in America,' Lena is now run as a nonprofit. The café is a wonderful throwback to the

1960s folk scene, and it is an authentic Saratoga original. It still books top acoustic musicians and is a venue for young performers.

Parting Glass Pub (☎ 518-583-1916; 40-42 Lake Ave) Another Saratoga institution, this is an Irish pub owned and operated by an Italian. Besides the extensive beer selection, the big attraction is the traditional Irish music. The club draws top performers from Ireland and the US.

Getting There & Away

Both Greyhound and Adirondack Trailways stop at the **Spa City Diner** (☎ 518-584-0911; 153 S Broadway). Popular destinations include New York City ($38, four hours) and Albany ($9, 45 minutes).

The **Amtrak station** (☎ 518-587-8354; cnr West Ave & Station Lane) is a couple of miles outside of town. Saratoga Springs is on the Montreal to New York City line ($43, 3½ hours), with one train going north and one south daily.

Saratoga is off I-87 at exit 13N. The exit leads you along Rte 9 past Saratoga Spa State Park and onto Broadway. **Enterprise Rent-A-Car** (☎ 518-587-0687; 180 S Broadway) is a national car-rental agency.

Getting Around

The CDTA Saratoga Springs bus No 98 makes a big loop through town Monday to Saturday. It costs $0.75.

During August racing season, **Upstate Transit** (☎ 518-584-5252) runs a shuttle bus between the track and Broadway (downtown) for $1.

Saratoga Horse Carriage Co (☎ 518-695-3359) runs carriage rides to/from the Gideon Putnam Hotel and points in Saratoga Spa State Park for $25.

MOHAWK VALLEY

COOPERSTOWN

☎ 607 / pop 2300

Down-home America personified, baseball-oriented Cooperstown is a mix of kitsch and culture and is likely the most popular small-town destination in the state. The downtown area is dominated with shops selling everything from baseball cards to T-shirts and bats.

Don't let the commercialism associated with baseball deter you from stopping here. The town has a great deal to recommend

---

DETOUR – SARATOGA NATIONAL HISTORIC PARK

In October 1777, British forces were defeated at the Battle of Saratoga, a major turning point in the campaigns of the Revolutionary War. The battle is commemorated at various sites within the 2800-acre **Saratoga National Historic Park** (☎ 518-664-9821; Rte 32, Stillwater; admission car/person $5/3; ☺ 9am-dusk Apr-Nov), 14 miles east of Saratoga Springs via Rte 29. At the visitors center you can pick up a guide to key battle sites along a 9-mile driving tour that is also accessible to hikers and bikers.

Seven miles north of the visitors center – and still within the park boundaries – is **Schuylerville**, formerly the town of Saratoga. Located on Rte 4 at the southern end of the town is the **Philip Schuyler House** (☎ 518-695-3664; admission free; ☺ 10am-4pm Wed-Sun Jun-Aug). Schuyler was a Revolutionary War general who commanded the northern frontier from his home in Albany. Schuylerville was the site of his summer home, which was burned by British General Burgoyne's retreating forces. The present house was rebuilt in 30 days on the same site and has been carefully restored with period furnishings. Guided tours are available.

Also in Schuylerville is **Saratoga Monument**, a 155ft obelisk commemorating this decisive battle. Dedicated in 1912, the monument sits upon a 300ft hill that affords spectacular views of the surrounding countryside.

---

it, including museums, its location on the forested banks of Otsego Lake, its attractive 19th-century architecture and excellent accommodations and restaurants.

Cooperstown was founded in 1786 by William Cooper, a wealthy land agent and the father of novelist James Fenimore Cooper, author of books such as *The Last of the Mohicans* and *The Deerslayer*. Cooper spent much of his childhood here, as did Stephen Clark, a descendent of Edward Clark who made his money in Singer sewing machines. Stephen Clark was the fortune behind the creation of the three museums that have turned Cooperstown into a popular tourist spot.

An earlier local resident, General Abner Doubleday, was falsely credited with inventing the game of baseball in 1839 (see The Origin of Baseball, p198). Despite the historical inaccuracy, Cooperstown has been home to the National Baseball Hall of Fame and Museum since it opened in 1939. This is the most popular sports museum in the US, attracting more than 400,000 devoted visitors annually. In late July or early August, the town is even more crowded than usual as baseball fans make a pilgrimage here for the annual inductions into the Hall of Fame.

Orientation & Information

Cooperstown is easy to navigate on foot. Chestnut St (Rte 28) is where you'll find many B&Bs and motels. Main St is the heart of town with shops, bars and restaurants.

Otsego Lake and Glimmerglass State Park are to the northeast of town.

The **Cooperstown Chamber of Commerce** (☎ 607-547-9983; www.cooperstownchamber.org; 31 Chestnut St; ☺ 9am-5pm) has information on the town and limited details on accommodations. There is a **visitor information kiosk** on Main St near the flagpole.

Sights & Activities

The draw for most visitors is an equally disparate but interesting mix of museums.

NATIONAL BASEBALL HALL OF FAME & MUSEUM

Baseball's national shrine, the **Hall of Fame** (☎ 607-547-7200; www.baseballhalloffame.org; 25 Main St; adult/child $9.50/4; ☺ 9am-9pm Jun-Aug, 9am-5pm Sep-May), houses all the important baseball artifacts, such as famous players' bats, gloves and uniforms and balls hit by Babe Ruth, Willie Mays and Reggie Jackson just to name a few. Plaques honoring the players – and a handful of managers, umpires and others – who have been voted into the hall are on display. In addition to the thousands of artifacts, the museum has its own movie theater and offers exhibits on every imaginable aspect of baseball. There are many superb interactive statistical exhibits and, for the more serious fans, a library.

DOUBLEDAY FIELD & BATTING RANGE

This is the oldest **baseball diamond** (☎ 607-547-5168; Main St) in the world, and the site of the

THE ORIGIN OF BASEBALL

Although Cooperstown is popularly considered the birthplace of baseball, it almost certainly was not. In 1907, baseball's owners, attempting to establish the American origins of baseball, set up the Mills commission to investigate the issue. The commission took their task seriously and came up with a story establishing baseball as a truly 'American' game, complete with a deceased military hero as its inventor. The inconvenient fact that baseball developed almost directly from the British game of 'rounders' was ignored.

The commission announced that baseball was invented in Cooperstown in 1839 by Abner Doubleday, ignoring the fact that at the time Doubleday was not in his hometown but instead studying at West Point. Doubleday, who died in 1893, was unavailable to comment.

Doubleday or not, the commission's findings were not completely unfounded. Baseball was being played in the 1840s in the urban areas of the northeast, with many organized baseball clubs. In 1876 the National League was formed, giving birth to truly professional ball in the sense that players were now openly paid for their services.

Baseball gained in popularity, and in 1902 the American League was formed, challenging the monopoly of the old National League. The first World Series was played a couple of years later, and modern baseball was in full swing.

Although there were a handful of black players in the National League during the late 19th century, professional baseball was strictly segregated and remained so until after WWII. The major leagues (and their minor league 'farm teams') were reserved for whites only. Black players were relegated to the Negro Leagues, playing under harsh conditions and for little money. In 1947, Jackie Robinson signed with the Brooklyn Dodgers and became the first black player in modern baseball. Other young players from the Negro Leagues followed his lead, and baseball became integrated. However, many of the finest players of that era never had the chance to test their skills against 'all comers.'

Baseball has long been a game of tradition, with statistics and records playing an important part in helping to build its popularity and its place in American mythology. The more recent developments of TV marketing, free agency, player strikes, lockouts, escalating salaries and astronomical profits have often frustrated the game's broad appeal with spectators, but it's still the irrevocable symbol of the National Pastime.

For an extensive overview of the sport, look for Ken Burns' *Baseball*, a PBS documentary series available on video or DVD.

first official game in 1839. It was originally built to accommodate 8000 spectators and then expanded to include 10,000. The field is now available for rent, and on a summer day you'll see local groups playing here. Next to the field is the **Doubleday Batting Range** (10am-9pm May-Oct). Here you can test your batting skills against the same pitching machine used in the major leagues. The Tru-Pitch machines throw 17 different kinds of pitches at various speeds. Children can practice with tennis balls, while hard balls are thrown for older enthusiasts.

FARMERS' MUSEUM & VILLAGE CROSSROADS

The **Farmers' Museum** (☎ 607-547-1450; Lake Rd; adult/child $9/4; 10am-5pm Jun-Sep, 10am-4pm Tue-Sun Apr-May & Oct-Nov) and adjacent Village Crossroads are made up of a dozen 19th-century buildings from the region and moved to Cooperstown on land donated to the New York State Historical Association. The village's buildings – which include a working blacksmith shop, general store, printing office, barn and more – have been very realistically assembled to capture the atmosphere of rural life and to exhibit rural trades and skills. Demonstrations range from farming practices to baking bread and printing.

The nearby **Cardiff Giant** is a 2990-pound carving that, in the 19th century, was once passed off as the petrified skeletal remains of a giant dug up in nearby Cardiff. In reality, cigar-maker George Hull had the giant sculpted out of gypsum. Even after the hoax was discovered people continued to line up – as they do today – to see the 'petrified giant.'

FENIMORE ART MUSEUM

View the country's history through the lives of its literary figures at the **Fenimore Art Museum** (☎ 607-547-1420; Lake Rd; adult/child $9/4; ☻10am-5pm Jun-Sep, 10am-4pm Tue-Sun Apr-May & Oct-Nov). Once the home of Edward Clark, of Singer sewing–machine fame and the town benefactor, the museum was created after heirs to his estate converted an Iroquois bark house on the property. It now displays an outstanding collection of folk art, Native American artifacts and masks, contemporary photography and paintings from the Hudson River school of landscape painters. Included here are Thomas Cole's *Last of the Mohicans* and Gilbert Stuart's *Joseph Brandt*.

The museum also houses memorabilia of the author James Fenimore Cooper. Ironically, Cooper's work is far more popular in other countries than it is in the US, where it came under sharp attack as early as the late 19th century for its romanticized characters, unrealistic and contrived dialogue, and conservative views.

OTSEGO LAKE & GLIMMERGLASS STATE PARK

According to local lore, Judge William Cooper founded the village of Cooperstown in 1786 because of the pristine lakeside setting. His son, author James Fenimore Cooper, called the lake Glimmerglass in his novel *The Deerslayer*, describing it as 'a broad sheet of water, so placid and limpid that it resembled a bed of pure mountain atmosphere compressed into a setting of hills and woods.' The description is fitting. There are three parks for swimming and fishing, plus two small public boat launches, along with two golf courses. Most of the shoreline is protected from development.

Glimmerglass State Park (☎ 607-547-8662; East Lake Rd) is at the northern end of the lake, about 8 miles north of Cooperstown on Rte 80. It's a serene green place and features a swimming beach, many hiking and biking trails, a playground, and a campground (see opposite). It is home to the Glimmerglass Opera (p200).

Sleeping

Cooperstown has a good number of charming B&Bs, as well as cheaper motels and campgrounds. Parking is readily available, and air-conditioning is standard.

BUDGET & MID-RANGE

Landmark Inn (☎ 607-547-7225; www.landmarkinnbnb .com; 64 Chestnut St; d from $150; ▣) This delicate white mansion with magnificent stained-glass windows is set back from the road on a manicured lawn. Inside, classical music, hardwood floors and antiques greet guests. The inn has nine beautifully decorated rooms. A full breakfast is served in the morning.

Cooperstown B&B (☎ 607-547-2893; 88 Chestnut St; d $140) This place has four rooms with beautiful linens and cheery colors. Breakfast is included and served buffet-style – everything from pancakes, French toast, home fries and cinnamon buns. Winter rates drop to $85 per night.

Lake 'n Pines Motel (☎ 607-547-2790, 800-615-5253; 7102 Hwy 80; d $155; ☺) A lakeside sundeck, an indoor and outdoor pool, whirlpool and paddleboats make this place appealing. Located a few miles north of Cooperstown on the west shore of Otsego Lake, it offers nice rooms and cottages to rent daily or weekly.

Mohican Motel (☎ 607-547-5101; 90 Chestnut St; s/d $54/62) Rooms here are cozy, comfortable and good value for money.

Baseballtown Motel (☎ 607-547-2161; 61-63 Main St; d $99) Right downtown, this place has 10 unremarkable but large rooms.

Glimmerglass State Park (☎ 607-547-8662; East Lake Rd; campsites $13) Hot showers and laundry

---

DETOUR – NATIONAL SOCCER HALL OF FAME

Baseball may get all the attention in Cooperstown, but soccer fans can get their fill at this **hall of fame** (☎ 607-432-3351; 18 Stadium Circle, Oneonta; adult/child $8/6.50; ☻ 9am-7pm Jun-Aug), dedicated to the world's most popular sport. Located 22 miles from Cooperstown, the National Soccer Hall of Fame traces the history of soccer in the US from its 1860 origins to the present. Besides the hall of fame there are two floors of exhibits that highlight both men's and women's games. Here you'll see old photos, uniforms and trophies among other memorabilia. There also are interactive displays for children. To reach the museum from Cooperstown take Rte 28 south to I-88, exit 13. The museum is off Brown St.

facilities in beautiful surroundings make this a popular camping option.

Cooperstown Beaver Valley Campground (☎ 800-726-7314; Rte 28; campsites $28) This campground is about 4 miles south of Cooperstown near the town of Index, and has 100 sites and complete facilities, including laundry, hot showers and boat rentals.

TOP END

Otesaga Resort Hotel (☎ 607-547-9931, 800-678-8946; www.otesaga.com; 60 Lake St; d from $355; ☑ May-Nov; ☒) Right on the lake, this is a beautiful Georgian resort with manicured lawns, a golf course, tennis courts, fishing, pool and boat rental. The 136 rooms are large and include four-poster beds, bright colors and oversized tubs in the bathroom. There is swimming in the lake from the resort's private dock. Built in 1909, this stately landmark is well worth visiting for a drink or a meal, even if you don't choose to stay here. Room rates include breakfast and dinner.

Inn at Cooperstown (☎ 607-547-5756; www.innat cooperstown.com; 16 Chestnut St; d $185) Iced tea is served on the veranda every afternoon at this friendly place. Antiques and oil paintings fill the main rooms. If you're looking for televisions or phones in your room stay somewhere else.

Eating

You'll find everything from cheap pizza and sandwiches to top-class dining in Cooperstown.

Blue Mingo Grill (☎ 607-547-7496; 6098 W Lake Rd; mains $20) Eat outside by the lake on a beautiful wooden veranda. The menu is eclectic, international and constantly changing – fresh lobster one week, crispy sea bass or Thai-influenced dishes the next.

Hawkeye Bar & Grill (☎ 607-547-9931; 60 Lake St; lunch $10, dinner $20) Located in the Otesaga Resort Hotel, dining here is a lovely experience and excellent value considering the elegant surroundings. During the warm months you can dine on the lakeside patio. The fare is creative American. Jackets are required for men in the evening.

Hoffman Lane Bistro (☎ 607-547-7055; 2 Hoffman La; mains $15-20) Potted plants and black-and-white photographs lend to a casual environment here. There is a cozy bar and an airy dining room. The menu changes based on the season, and you'll find a

range of dishes including meats, seafood and pastas.

Danny's Main Street Market (☎ 607-547-4053; 92 Main St; mains $4-7) This is a very good old-fashioned deli, with sandwiches made to order, fresh coffee and pastries. You eat on wooden stools.

Doubleday Café (☎ 607-547-5468; 93 Main St; mains under $15) Reliable family dining can be found here, and the café features inexpensive sandwiches as well as some Mexican dishes.

Drinking & Entertainment

In addition to supporting three excellent museums, this tiny town is home to the Glimmerglass Opera.

Alice Busch Opera Theater (☎ 607-547-2255; box office at 18 Chestnut St; tickets $28-104) This is the home of the Glimmerglass Opera about 8 miles north of Cooperstown on Rte 80, opposite the lake. The theater is partially open to the outdoors in summer. The acclaimed Opera Festival is held in July and August. Chamber music concerts, lectures and plays are also staged here during this time.

Taproom at the Tunnicliff Inn (☎ 607-547-9931; 34-36 Pioneer St) Cheap beers make this place a popular late-night hangout.

Bold Dragoon (☎ 607-547-9800; 49 Pioneer St) Loud and rowdy at night, this historic bar always draws a crowd with people spilling out onto the street.

Getting There & Around

Pine Hills Trailways and **Adirondack Trailways** (☎ 800-858-8555 for both) stop in front of the **Chestnut St Deli** (☎ 607-547-5829; 75 Chestnut St). Pine Hills goes to New York City's Port Authority bus terminal ($43, six hours) via Woodstock ($20, three hours) in the Catskills.

By car from I-88, take exit 16 and then Rte 28 north for 18 miles to town. From I-90, take exit 30 to Rte 28 south for 28 miles to town.

A trolley (just $2 for the entire day) runs throughout town daily from June 27 through Labor Day (first Monday in September). From Memorial Day weekend (last Monday in May) to June 27 and after Labor Day through Columbus Day (second Monday in October), the trolley runs on weekends only.

DETOUR – FLY CREEK

Just 2 miles northwest of Cooperstown on Rte 28/80 is the tiny town of Fly Creek, where you can purchase a baseball bat with your name on it and sample old-fashioned apple cider. The **Cooperstown Bat Company** (☎ 518-547-2415) is a factory shop where you can find all kinds of baseball bats, and even watch one being tuned during July and August. You can view collectors bats or purchase a bat of your own with your name inscribed on it.

The town also is home to **Fly Creek Cider Mill & Orchard** (☎ 607-547-9692; ⏰ Jun-Dec), a water-powered cider press that uses original equipment to make great cider.

SHARON SPRINGS
☎ 518 / pop 600

Once known for its sulfur springs and rambling old Victorian hotels, Sharon Springs was until recently in a state of neglect. Today, the town is in a state of revival. New shops have opened along Main St and some of the hotels are operating again. The main reason to visit is for a trip to **Howe Caverns** (☎ 518-296-8990; www.howecaverns.com; adult/child $15/7; ⏰ 9am-6pm), located nearby. The oldest tourist attraction in New York, these heavily commercialized caverns form a labyrinth of caves with high ceilings and glimmering stalactites, stalagmites, a small river and a quarter-mile-long underground lake. Lester Howe discovered the caves in 1842 after he found a dark opening in a ledge. Howe began conducting tours shortly afterwards, and in 1854 his daughter was married in one of the caves. More than 350 weddings have since taken place at the caverns.

Tours include an elevator ride that descends 156ft underground, walks along paved walkways and a boat ride on the lake. Bring a sweater, as the temperature in the caverns stays at 52°F.

On the caverns' property is the **Howe Caverns Motel** (☎ 518-296-8950; Caverns Rd; d $110), a 21-room place with comfortable but unremarkable rooms. A restaurant is attached and serves lunch and dinner (mains $10).

Sharon Springs is located off Rte 20 in Schoharie County 50 miles from Albany. The caverns are off Rte 7.

BINGHAMTON
☎ 607 / pop 53,000

When the Chenango Canal was completed in 1837, Binghamton became a busy link connecting the nearby Pennsylvania coalfields to the Erie Canal and ports beyond. Also known for several gold-domed Russian Orthodox and Ukrainian Catholic churches, Binghamton used to be a major producer of cigars, but a permanent slump in sales made the town shift into the cigarette-producing business. A player during the tech boom in the last decades of the 20th century, the downsizing of this industrial base left Binghamton in a state of decline with high unemployment numbers and rising crime rates. It is home to SUNY-Binghamton and its 12,000 students.

The **Broome County Chamber of Commerce** (☎ 607-772-8860, 800-836-6740; 49 Court St; ⏰ 8:30am-5pm Mon-Fri) has walking- and driving-tour maps of Binghamton and nearby Endicott and Johnson City – collectively known as the Triple Cities.

Ross Park Zoo

Established in 1875, this **zoo** (☎ 607-724-5454; 60 Morgan Rd; adult/child $4.50/3; ⏰ 10am-5pm Apr-Oct) is the fifth-oldest in the country. It features picnic facilities, a gift shop and over 200 exotic animals – everything from snow leopards and Siberian lynxes to white tigers and spectacled bears. The zoo also features Wolf Woods, a 2.5-acre area where timber wolves and endangered red wolves roam outside of cages.

Within the park, **Carousel Museum** is home to a beautifully restored merry-go-round. There are five others in and around town – all wood-carved and all working – but this is a good place to start. The carousels operate from the end of May until early September, weather permitting, and are free.

Sleeping & Eating

A number of budget motels are concentrated on Front St at the city's northern edge. Binghamton is the home of 'spiedies,' a sandwich made of pork, chicken or lamb in a special marinade, grilled and served on a hoagie roll. The obsession never quite gained national notoriety.

Grand Royale Hotel (☎ 607-722-0000; 80 State St; d from $95) Binghamton's only upscale hotel, this place is conveniently located in the downtown business district. Once the city hall, it has been split into 60 rooms that come in various shapes and sizes complete with coffeemaker and refrigerator.

Best Western Binghamton Regency Hotel (☎ 607-722-7575; 225 Water St; d from $80; 🔊) The newest big hotel in Binghamton, this place doubles as a conference center. It is downtown, has 203 rather large rooms and several restaurants at reasonable prices.

Comfort Inn (☎ 607-722-5353; 1156 Front St; d from $70) This 65-room motel is one of the cheaper options.

Lost Dog Café (☎ 607-771-6063; 222 Water St; mains from $10) A popular student hangout, restaurant and late-night coffee house, this funky place serves good food in an eclectic and casual setting. It also features live music.

Ritz Restaurant (☎ 607-773-8876; 27 Chenango St; mains from $10) Dating back to the 1920s, this historic restaurant was renovated in 1999. The menu is largely Greek, but includes everything from gyros to pasta and prime rib to stuffed lobster.

Copper Cricket (☎ 607-729-5620; 266 Main St; mains $13) With a different menu each day, Copper Cricket makes a good lunch or dinner spot and serves American fare. You can dine on the closed-in porch.

Sharkey's (☎ 607-729-9201; 56 Glenwood Ave; mains $5) This hole-in-the wall place serves authentic spiedies.

Getting There & Away

The **bus station** (81 Chenango St) in Binghamton is located in the downtown area. **Adirondack Trailways** (☎ 800-858-8555) has service to Binghamton from New York City ($31, 3½ hours), Albany ($23, three hours) and Syracuse ($11, 1½ hours).

Binghamton is reached most easily by car. Take I-86 from New York City, I-88 from the Albany area or I-81 from Syracuse.

The Adirondacks

The northern hump of New York is a wilderness of rocky peaks ringing mirror-like lakes. Bushy fir and spruce trees claim huge tracts of desirable real estate – some follow a creek bed, others crawl to the summit gaining altitude but losing individual stature. Sprinkled throughout the cloak of green are birch trees – albino matchsticks placed so artistically that a painter must have been involved in this process rather than the cut-throat rules of natural selection.

There aren't many places in the northeast where the vista from a mountain summit is of an undulating landscape of sleeping giants. And there aren't many places where land preservation is a cooperative between publicly and privately owned land. Adirondack Park is just such a place, showing the limits of language and ownership. Established in 1892, Adirondack Park isn't a park in the traditional sense that you pull up to a gate and pay an admission fee. In fact you could drive straight through on the I-87 and not even notice that you had encroached on a wilderness of six million acres covering 20% of the entire state. If you were to take one of the few exits off the interstate, you would find that the small country roads lead to scruffy villages and only about 1300 miles of road, but over 2000 miles of hiking trails, 6000 miles of rivers, and 46 mountains towering over 4000ft. The Hudson River begins on Mt Marcy at Lake Tear-of-the-Clouds.

HIGHLIGHTS

- **Best Campground**
  At Eighth Lake Campground (p224), you can pitch a tent right in front of the lake and watch the moon, stars and sun rise over the placid waters

- **Best Scenic Drive**
  Rte 73 north through Keene Valley into Lake Placid (p220) and Rte 22 north through Westport and Essex (p212)

- **Most Frightening 43 Seconds**
  Bobsled ride at Lake Placid's Verizon Sports Complex (p215)

- **Best Hidden Gem**
  Marcella Sembrich Memorial Studio (p211) in Bolton Landing is an interesting museum dedicated to this famous opera singer

- **Best Day Hike**
  Mt Jo (p216) is a stout peak with easy-to-reach views of wilderness anchored by darling Heart Lake in Lake Placid

CLIMATE

Let's start with the good news: July and August are glorious in the Adirondacks. When the lowlands are sweltering, the Adirondacks are pleasant, almost perfect, though busy. The cold weather sets in quickly, though; July is technically the only killing-frost-free month. By September or October, the days turn crisp and the leaves blush shades of crimson, orange and yellow. Nearly nine months of winter, replete with freezing temperatures (roughly 190 days), snow (up to 10ft a year) and ice, follows like a dreary death march. When the sun finally climbs high enough in the sky to melt the snow, the 'mud season' stands in for spring and black fly season heralds the coming of summer. During the month of June, give or take a week, these tiny, poppy seed–sized biting flies swarm like a plague and the only defense is chemical or the beekeeper-like head nets. An outdoors vacation is quickly ruined by a black fly onset.

STATE PARKS

The New York State **Department of Environmental Conservation** (DEC; ☎ 518-897-1200; Rte 86, Ray Brook) oversees the public areas of the Adirondack Park. Trails are cleared and marked with the assistance from conservation groups such as **Adirondack Mountain Club** (ADK; ☎ 518-523-3441; www.adk.org; Lake Placid). From the road, it's easy to find the trail heads, which are marked by brown wooden signs with yellow lettering. You can set up camp anywhere on state land as long as it isn't above 4000ft, within 150ft of water or within 100ft of a trail. About 60% of

the Adirondacks is privately owned and only a few owners allow public access, so be sure to look for 'No Trespassing' signs.

Of the many preserves and wilderness areas in the Adirondacks, here is a subjective list of destinations.

St Regis Wilderness Canoe Area (p221) encompasses the headwaters of the west and middle branches of the St Regis and Saranac Rivers and a total of 18,000 acres. This wilderness area is off limits to motorized boats and cars, but wide-open for paddlers and anglers.

Like a sparkling string of pearls, a series of narrow lakes called **Fulton Chain of Lakes** (p225) stretches from the pond in Old Forge to Eighth Lake and finally Raquette Lake. From First to Fifth Lake, the waterway is continuous and open to motor craft. Two portages connect the subsequent lakes, which are wild and peaceful. Campsites and lean-tos are available on the mainland and on islands in the middle of these later lakes. Rainbow trout, lake trout and freshwater salmon are common prizes for anglers.

High Peaks (p216) is the most heavily visited region of the park because of its magnificent scenery of 46 tall mountains clustered around Lake Placid–Keene Valley.

Jackrabbit Trail (Adirondack Ski Touring Council; ☎ 518-523-1365; www.lakeplacid.com; Lake Placid) Nearly 35 miles of cross-country ski trails extend from Keene to Saranac Lake, linking the area's major ski trails.

INFORMATION

Adirondack Mountain Club (ADK; ☎ 518-523-3441; www.adk.org; Lake Placid; ☯ 10am-5pm Mon-Fri) This club

---

DON'T GET LOST

There are several excellent books on the Adirondack trail networks. Lonely Planet's *Hiking in the USA* covers a three-day loop in the High Peaks region, a day hike to Mt Marcy and a brief description of the Northville–Lake Placid Trail.

The **Adirondack Mountain Club** (ADK; ☎ 518-523-3441; www.adk.org; Lake Placid) publishes *Adirondack* magazine as well as hiking guides that break up the region into seven parts. Each book includes a large, removable topographical map.

The **Department of Environmental Conservation** (DEC; ☎ 518-897-1200; Rte 86, Ray Brook) in conjunction with the **Adirondack Tourism Council** (☎ 800-487-6867) publishes the following free guides with maps and route descriptions: *Adirondack Great Walks & Day Hikes*, *Adirondack Fishing* and *Adirondack Waterways*.

If you're going to get personal with the Adirondacks, you'll need maps – lots of them. The *Adirondack North Country Regional Map* shows all state-owned land as of 1986. It's available for $2 by mail from the **Adirondack North Country Association** (☎ 518-891-6200; www.adirondack.org; 28 St Bernard St, Saranac Lake, NY 12983).

has been around since 1922 and maintains trails, promotes conservation and outdoor activities and publishes guides and maps to the Adirondacks. It also offers educational programs and operates campgrounds, lean-tos and lodges.

Adirondack Regional Tourism Council (☎ 800-487-6867; Plattsburgh; ☻ 10am-5pm Mon-Fri) General information and publications.

Adirondak Loj & ADK High Peaks Information Center (☎ 518-523-3441; Lake Placid) Operated by ADK, contact this center for lodging and hiking information for the High Peaks.

Department of Environmental Conservation (DEC; ☎ 518-402-9405; www.dec.state.ny.us; 625 Broadway, Albany; ☻ 8:30am-4:45pm Mon-Fri) With regional offices throughout the Adirondacks, contact the DEC for trail and backcountry information and permit, fishing and hunting regulations and licenses.

Newcomb Center Adirondack Park Visitors' Interpretive Center (☎ 518-582-2000; www.northnet.org /adirondackvic; Rte 28; ☻ 9am-7pm Mar-Sep, 9am-5pm Oct-Apr) 14 miles east of the town of Long Lake.

Paul Smith's Adirondack Park Visitors' Interpretive Center (☎ 518-327-3000; www.northnet.org/adirondack vic; Rte 30, north of Paul Smith's College; ☻ 9am-7pm Apr-Sep, 9am-5pm Oct-Mar) One of two Adirondack Park centers, which feature indoor and outdoor exhibits about the park and various educational programs and lectures.

GETTING THERE & AROUND

The region's primary airport is the **Adirondack Regional Airport** (☎ 518-891-4600; Saranac Lake), 17 miles from Lake Placid. **CommutAir** (☎ 800-523-3273) offers commuter service to Albany and Plattsburgh. **Continental Airlines** (☎ 800-523-3273)

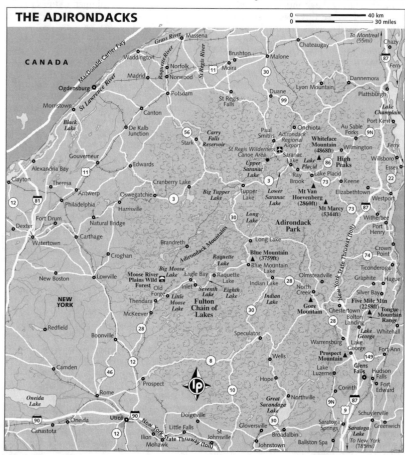

THE ADIRONDACKS

FERRY CROSSINGS

Lake Champlain Ferries (☎ 802-864-9804; www.ferries.com) runs three routes across Lake Champlain between Vermont and the eastern Adirondacks. The northernmost ferry crosses between Grand Isle, VT (outside of Burlington), and Plattsburgh, NY (car and driver one-way $7.75, round-trip $14, additional passengers $2.75; 12-minute crossing; departures 24 hours a day every 15 to 40 minutes). From Plattsburgh you can take Rte 3 south through the northern Adirondacks to Saranac Lake, a distance of about 50 miles.

A scenic ferry travels between Burlington, VT, and Port Kent, NY (car and driver one-way $13.75, round-trip $25, additional passengers $3.25 one way, $6.75 round-trip; one-hour crossing; from 7:30am to 7:30pm mid-May to mid-October). Port Kent is 40 miles from Lake Placid via Rte 373 west to Rte 9N west and then Rte 86 west into Lake Placid.

A southern route connects Charlotte, VT, and Essex, NY (see p212).

The Fort Ti Ferry runs to and from Shoreham (Larabees Point), VT, and Ticonderoga, NY (see p212).

---

serves other destinations but routes flights through Albany or Boston.

Adirondack Trailways (☎ 800-858-8555) is the main bus company in the region. The summer schedule (June to October) is fairly extensive, but winter is more limited. When catching the bus from most Adirondack destinations, tickets must be purchased by paying the driver with the exact fare amount in cash. **Greyhound** (☎ 800-231-2222) has a few routes within the region, and both bus companies offer information about the other's schedules. There is no bus service to the towns of Essex, Blue Mountain Lake, Old Forge or Long Lake.

Amtrak trains arrive at stations in Westport (Rte 9N), 37 miles east of Lake Placid, and Fort Edward/Glens Falls (East St, Fort Edward), 16 miles from Lake George. Both are on the Adirondack line that travels from New York City's Penn Station to Montreal. The journey is quite scenic; the train goes along the Hudson River on and off until Albany, and then through quite a bit of forests.

If you're driving (the best option in this region), I-87 runs north–south from New York City through the eastern portion of the Adirondacks and into Canada. Almost every road through the Adirondack Park could be called a scenic route and most are only two lanes wide. Rte 30 is an especially beautiful road that runs for 160 miles from the Great Sacandaga Lake in the south to Malone outside the northern boundary of the park. Rtes 28 and 3 both enter from the west and intersect with Rte 30 near the middle of the park.

LAKE GEORGE & AROUND

Action in the southeastern area of the park centers on Lake George, the largest lake completely within park boundaries.

LAKE GEORGE
☎ 518 / pop 3500

The 32-mile-long lake – dotted with 365 islands – is often described as the 'Queen of America's Lakes,' in part for its deep-blue, crystal-clear water and wild shorelines. Called Lac du Saint Sacrement by Jesuit missionary Isaac Jacques when he was led here by Native American guides in 1646, the lake was of strategic importance during the French and Indian War (p21).

In 1755, British general William Johnson renamed the lake after King George. More recently, during the mid-20th century, the lake became the haunt of city-weary artists, among them the artist Georgia O'Keeffe and her husband, photographer Alfred Steiglitz, who managed to capture with his camera their quotidian existence along the lake's forested shores.

At the southern end of the lake is Lake George village, crammed with motels and tacky souvenir shops geared toward young families, all of which stand in marked contrast to the otherwise scenic surroundings.

Information
Parking is something neither the Native Americans nor the English of the 18th century had to deal with. Now they do, along with everyone else who comes to Lake

George village. A good place to park is the big lot across the street from the steamboat landing on Beach Rd. It's metered parking, but – good news – you can feed the meter for 10 hours at a time, for $0.50 an hour. Bad news: the meters operate 24 hours daily, seven days a week. There is free parking (if you can get it) on the either side of the street on West Brook Rd; observe the signs. A parking lot in front of Million Dollar Beach charges $6 a day.

Useful organizations in town include the following:

Adirondack Mountain Club Information Center
(ADK; ☎ 518-668-4447; www.adk.org; 814 Goggins Rd; ⏰ 8:30am-5pm Mon-Sat) South of town, ADK's headquarters is the best source of information on the region's outdoor activities. The center is west of the I-87 overpass heading toward Lake Luzerne.

Lake George Chamber of Commerce & Visitors Center (☎ 518-668-5755, 800-705-0059; www.visitlake george.com; Rte 9/Canada St; ⏰ 9am-5pm summer) At the south end of the village opposite Prospect Mountain, on the east side of the street, this center distributes maps of French and Indian War sites.

Post office (☎ 518-668-3386, Canada St) A block north of Beach Rd.

Sights & Activities
MILLION DOLLAR BEACH
This small, sandy **beach** (☎ 518-668-3352; Beach Rd; admission free; ⏰ 9am-6pm late-May–Labor Day), in Lake George Beach State Park, is a short walk south of the town center along the shore of the lake. The beach was originally developed (and so named) for the wealthy clientele of the bygone era of big resorts along the lake. There are picnic facilities here, a bathhouse and on-duty lifeguards. You can find other nice places to swim by heading further north around the lake.

PROSPECT MOUNTAIN
You can drive up the Veterans Memorial Hwy to the top of **Prospect Mountain** (2021ft; admission per car $6; 10am-7:30pm late-May–Oct) for dramatic views of the lake and surrounding mountain ranges, including Vermont's Green Mountains and New Hampshire's White Mountains. The entrance to this two-lane toll road is on Rte 9 south of Lake George Battleground State Historic Site. From here, it's a 5-mile drive to a crest, where you can take a free, air-conditioned bus to the summit (it takes three minutes)

or you can hike for even more spectacular views. There are picnic sites at the summit.

LAKE GEORGE SHIPWRECKS
History buffs, boating enthusiasts and divers will enjoy viewing the remains of seven boats used on the lake during the French and Indian, and Revolutionary Wars in the 18th century. These boats were typical of the flat-bottomed transport vessels called bateaux by English as well as French speakers. Bateaux, which were about 30ft long, were poled or oared across the lake in order to transport troops and supplies. In the summer of 1758, after the British failed to take Fort Ticonderoga (Fort Carillon) from the French, British and American forces sunk over 200 boats to store them for retrieval after the winter. The troops returned in the spring of 1759 to retrieve the bateaux, but they missed many, including those on display.

For more information, contact the **DEC** (☎ 518-897-1200, Rte 86, Ray Brook).

LAKE GEORGE CRUISES
A cruise, even one as short as an hour, is a good way to enjoy the lake and take in the scenery along its shores. Several tour boats leave from Beach Rd on the southern shore of the lake opposite Fort William Henry. Lake cruises vary from one-hour trips around the southern basin to full day tours from south to north and back again. Tours usually depart from early June to Labor Day, but an abbreviated schedule of 'fall color cruises' runs through October.

Lake George Steamboat Co (☎ 518-668-5777, 800-553-2628; www.lakegeorgesteamboat.com) offers lake cruises on their paddleboat *Minne-ha-ha* and on the *Mohican*, and dinner cruises on the *Lac de Saint Sacrement*. Prices and schedules vary; visit the website for detailed information.

LAKE GEORGE HISTORICAL ASSOCIATION MUSEUM
In the old courthouse building, the historical **museum** (☎ 518-668-5044; cnr Canada & Amherst St; admission $3; ⏰ 11am-4pm Sat & Sun May-Jun; 11am-4pm Fri, Sat & Tue, 3-8pm Wed-Thu Jul-Aug) has a well-displayed collection of memorabilia ranging from ice harvesting and logging equipment to quilts and medieval-looking doctors' tools for treating the tuberculosis patients who once frequented the Adirondacks to

'take the cure.' A doctor's bag on display still smells of old medicines from the early 20th century.

Sleeping

Lake George village has dozens of inexpensive roadside motels lining Canada St, the main route through town. Motels on the eastern side of the street have small lakeside beaches or dock access. If you've got children of disparate ages, Lake George village will appeal to a variety of tastes. For more natural surroundings, cabins and cottages line Rte 9 heading north toward Bolton Landing; these offer more lake views and less commercial distractions. Rates are highest from late June through Labor Day weekend.

Park Lane Motel (☎ 518-668-2615; 378 Canada St; d $100-180; 🏊) This tidy representative of the Canada St motels has one large room with a small deck that overlooks the lake, as well as smaller rooms closer to the street. If you're sensitive to traffic noise request a spot closer to the lake. There is a postage stamp–sized beach at the foot of the motel.

Alpine Village (☎ 518-668-2193; Rte 9N; r & cabins $77-155, weekly $500-700; 🏊) North of Lake George village, this shady spot has real log cabins (sleeping up to four people) with roomy porches, four housekeeping units in the main lodge and hotel-style doubles.

The property culminates in a sandy beach on the lake shore. Off-season prices are a steal ($60 to $100).

Melody Manor (☎ 518-644-9750; Rte 9N; d $100-125; 🏊) Claiming one of the best views on the lake, Melody Manor looks out over Huddle Bay, Black and Tongue Mountains. The hotel-style rooms are large and most have balconies or patios. There is a small beach and babbling brook running through the manicured property.

Eating

The food in Lake George village doesn't begin to compare with the scenery, but there are some fair choices. For all restaurants, summer hours are listed here. Fall hours are abbreviated to the weekends; call ahead to confirm.

Prospect Mountain Diner (☎ 518-668-9721; Canada St; dishes $5-7; 🕙 6am-3pm Mon-Thu, 6am-9pm Fri-Sun) At the south end of the village on the west side of Canada St, near the visitors center, this chrome-and-vinyl diner offers fully-fledged desserts masquerading as wholesome breakfasts, like pigs-in-a-blanket (pancakes wrapped around sausage) or apple pancakes with whipped cream. The waitstaff spend more time gossiping and snacking than attending to customers; somehow this neglect adds to the charm.

Mario's (☎ 518-668-2665; 429 Canada St; dishes $12-18; 🕙 4.30pm-late Mon-Sat, 3pm-late Sun) At the Rte 9–Rte 9N split, Mario's assembles honest Italian-American classics like chicken saltimbocca and eggplant parmesan while the neon lights of the village strip scream 'You're on vacation.' The decor is totally canned but after a few of its famous frozen drinks you'll feel like you own the place. In July and August the restaurant does a breakfast buffet.

Old Log Inn (☎ 518-668-3334; Rte 9; dishes $10-15; 🕙 11am-10pm) On Rte 9 north, just past the I-87 overpass, this spiffy restaurant ranks as a favorite with dining locals. Replicating an Adirondack camp, this restaurant-pub runs through an all-American repertoire of surf-and-turf, wraps and pasta dishes.

Entertainment

Lake George Dinner Theatre (☎ 518-668-5781; Holiday Inn Turf, Canada Street/Rte 9; tickets $41-50; 🕙 shows 6:30pm Tue-Sat, 11:30am Wed & Thu mid-Jun–mid-Oct) Opposite the Tiki Lounge, this equity dinner theater does one play each summer, usually

---

LAKE GEORGE CAMPING

The State of New York maintains campgrounds on 92 of the islands in Lake George. For information and reservations in any New York state park, call the **camping reservation system** (☎ 800-456-2267; www.reserveamerica.com). All the island campsites are open from mid-May to mid-September. Canoeing parties sometimes get a tow at the marina to one of the islands, and then paddle around from there. Most state campgrounds charge a $2.75 service fee for the first night.

Long Island (☎ 518-656-9426; campsite $16) On the southern end of the lake, Long Island is reachable by boat from Lake George village, on the eastern side of the lake from Cleverdale, Kattskill Bay and Pilot Knob or on the western side from Diamond Point or Bolton Landing.

Glen Island (☎ 518-644-9696; campsite $16) In the narrows of Lake George (not to be confused with Narrow Island), Glen Island is accessible from Bolton Landing. Glen Island has a camp store.

Narrow Island (☎ 518-499-1288; campsite $16) In the Mother Bunch of Islands in the northern half of the lake, Narrow Island is reachable from Silver Bay on the west side of the lake or Hulett's Landing on the east.

Lake George Islands Public Campgrounds (☎ 518-656-9426, 800-456-2267; campsite $16) On three islands in the middle of Lake George, campgrounds are available with advance reservation; call for details on boat transportation from nearby shore points.

There are a fair number of busy campgrounds around Lake George village.

Lake George Battleground Public Campground (☎ 518-668-3348, Rte 9; campsite $17; ⊙ May–mid-Oct) At the south end of town, this campground has sites in a shady pine grove. It's also a good place to shower at the day-use rates ($6 per car or $1 for walk-ins).

Hearthstone Point Campground (☎ 518-668-5193; Rte 9N; campsite $17; ⊙ mid-May–mid-Sep) Has 250 tent and trailer sites on the lakeshore. It is 2 miles north of Lake George village, between Lake George village and Diamond Point.

---

a Broadway or off-Broadway musical or comedy.

Adirondack Pub & Brewery (☎ 518-668-0002; 33 Canada St) Across the street from Fort Williams Henry, this brew pub–restaurant is a pretty blonde-wood place with amber lighting, respectable enough for families and singles.

The Garrison (☎ 518-668-5281; 220 Beach Rd) East of Million Dollar Beach, the Garrison is a sports pub that will give you a free pitcher of Budweiser if you bring in a college pennant that they don't already have displayed. You'd be surprised at how vast their collection is.

Shopping

Oscar's Adirondack Mountain Smoke House (☎ 800-627-3431; 22 Raymond Lane, Warrensburg; ⊙ 7am-6pm) Oscar's started out as a neighborhood meat market in the 1940s and has expanded into the gift-box business without relocating out of its suburban home-cum-smokehouse. Jerky, sausages and cheese spreads are all made according to the family's 'secret' recipes. Warrensburg is exit 23 off I-87; from the town's main street make a right at the street beside the post office.

Getting There & Away

In Lake George village **Adirondack Trailways** (☎ 800-858-8555) stops at the corner of Amherst and Canada Sts, but tickets can be purchased from **Lake George Hardware Store** (35 Montcalm St). There are typically three buses a day going north and three buses a day going south from here year-round. The fare to New York City is $50 one-way ($100 round-trip).

In Bolton Landing the bus stops at Neuffer's Citgo gas station at the southern end of town. There's one bus that travels north and one that travels south daily during the summer only.

Fort Edward/Glens Falls station (East St, Fort Edward), 16 miles away, is the closest train station to Lake George. Fares on the Amtrak Adirondack line from this station to New York City's Penn Station costs $90 for a round-trip (four hours; two departures per day). **Greater Glens Falls Transit** (☎ 518-792-1085; fares $12.50) runs a shuttle bus between Lake George and the Amtrak station; call 48 hours prior to travel date to arrange transport.

From I-87 (the Northway), exit 21 lets you off at the south end of town on Rte 9, and exit 22 puts you at the north end.

BOLTON LANDING
☎ 518 / pop 2100

Follow the western rim of the lake north-wards to reach the more grown-up town of Bolton Landing.

Sights
MARCELLA SEMBRICH MEMORIAL STUDIO
This serene **hideout** (☎ 518-644-9839; Lake Shore Dr; admission $2; ☺ 10am-12:30pm & 2-5:30pm Jun-Sep) was the home of opera singer Marcella Sembrich, best known for her role as Mimi in *La Bohème*, singing opposite Enrico Caruso. Devoid of scandal, Sembrich passed out of the public's eye with a faithful marriage and a professional reputation. She spent her summers in this cottage working with students on voice and piano. It is said that locals would row past the open windows to hear the practice sessions. The studio contains mementos of the singer's career including opera costumes. The museum is just a few doors north of the Algonquin Restaurant; look for its iron gate on the east side of the street.

Activities
The north of Lake George is less developed and offers hiking, canoeing and kayaking. **ADK** (☎ 518-668-4447, www.adk.org; 814 Goggins Rd, Lake George; ☺ 8:30am-5pm Mon-Sat) can give detailed information on outdoor activities.

HIKING
Off Rte 9N north of Bolton Landing is the trailhead for hikes along the Tongue Mountain range, a peninsula that laps at Lake George. Deer Leap (3.4 miles round-trip, easy), Five Mile Mountain (7 miles round-trip, difficult) and Northwest Bay Trail (10.8 miles round-trip, moderate) offer vistas and shady glens within Tongue Mountain area.

Over 60 miles of trails dissect the eastern side of the lake. Sleeping Beauty (7.8 miles round-trip, moderate) is a switchback trail with open ledges; Buck Mountain (4.6 to 6.6 miles round-trip depending on entrance, difficult) is a vigorous climb rewarded with an open summit with a panorama of Lake George. The trail head for both hikes is off Rte 149 west of Fort Ann.

CANOEING & KAYAKING
There are two island groups in the northern part of Lake George, the Narrows and the

---

NUMBER 2 PENCILS
Some visitors might connect the name Ticonderoga to a long-familiar brand of yellow No 2 pencils, and – in fact – from the mid- to late-18th century, the town was an important graphite mining center.

Mother Bunch, that you can paddle out to for the day or set-up camp (see p210). **Lake George Kayak Co** (☎ 518-644-9366; 4973 Lake Shore Dr, Bolton Landing; kayak half/full day $35/45, canoe full day $50-60) rents kayaks and canoes and does guided tours.

SCENIC DRIVE
The 39-mile drive (via Rte 9N) along the western shore of Lake George from Lake George village north has spectacular views of the lake. After passing Bolton Landing, you will drive through the small towns of Silver Bay and Hague. Grabbing a drink or lunch at **Indian Kettles** (☎ 518-543-6576; Rte 9N) in Hague buys you access to an unusual geographic occurrence. Just beyond the restaurant's back deck are several cauldron-like depressions known as 'kettles,' which were formed when smaller rocks tumbled about in a single spot, eventually eroding the surface to create a hole.

Sleeping & Eating
Carey's Lakeside Cottages (☎ 518-644-3091; Rte 9N; d $84-90, weekly $600-1000; ☺ June–mid-Oct) Just south of the commercial section of Bolton Landing, Carey's Cottages (cash or check only) has handsome wood-paneled motel units with fireplaces as well as housekeeping cottages and efficiencies. All rooms look out over a grassy area and a few of the units even get a lake view.

Sagamore Resort (☎ 518-644-9400, 800-358-3585; 110 Sagamore Rd; d $360-520, condo $750) On a private island, accessible by a bridge, Sagamore Resort is stunning with its sweeping driveway and nearly panoramic view of Lake George. The postcard-perfect hotel was built in the 1920s and the lobby maintains an air of sophistication. The rooms in the historic hotel have been modernized to the point of sterility. The newer condominium units are probably the best value; decorated in an Adirondack country style, they can sleep up to six people and have lots of common space.

Pumpernickel's (☎ 518-644-2106; Lake Shore Dr; dishes $18-20; ☷ 5-9pm May-Oct) Adjacent to the Bolton Pines Motel, Pumpernickel's has German dishes that would stop an invading Prussian army in its tracks. Using everything in the pantry, the roulade is a surprisingly delicious combination of bacon, pickles, onions, mustard and brown gravy all rolled up in a cut of sirloin.

Getting There & Away

See p210 for details about transport to Bolton Landing.

FORT TICONDEROGA

A strategic point during the French and Indian War, **Fort Ticonderoga** (☎ 518-585-2821; Rte 74; adult/senior/child $12/11/6; ☷ 9am-5pm May-Jun & Sep–mid-Oct, 9am-6pm Jul & Aug) is a mile northeast of Ticonderoga town on Rte 74. Originally named Fort Carillon, it was built by the French in 1755 to control the southern reaches of their conquests in America and was strategically located at the southern end of Lake Champlain and the northern end of Lake George. (Its name is a variation on Cheonderoga, a Native American term meaning 'Between Two Waters.') So critical was its location that the fort was attacked a record six times and nicknamed 'Key to the Continent.' In 1758, a French force of only 3500 – under the command of the Marquis de Montcalm – defended the fort against 15,000 British and American colonial troops. However, the following summer British forces under General Jeffrey Amherst captured and re-named the fort.

Sixteen years later, in 1775, Ethan Allen and his Green Mountain Boys captured the fort for the Americans in a surprise attack. Two years after that, General John Burgoyne captured the fort for the British, who abandoned the fortifications and burned the buildings. This historic fort would have been commemorated today with little more than an historical marker if it had not been for the family of William Ferris Pell, who bought the grounds in 1820 and began a complete restoration. Today, it is one of the country's few major historical sites that is privately owned.

Inside the reconstructed buildings are collections of weapons, tools, uniforms and documents from the colonial and revolu-

tionary periods. While the fort is open, there are weekly events, including fife and drum concerts, historical drills and craft demonstrations.

As a side trip on a clear day, you might drive up to **Mt Defiance** (☎ 518-585-2821; Defiance St; admission free; ☷ 9am-5pm mid-May–mid-Oct). It was at the summit that British General John Burgoyne mounted cannons and forced the American forces at Fort Ticonderoga to surrender in 1777. There are fine views from here of Lake Champlain, the valleys and the Green Mountains. From the main road through town (Montcalm St), turn on to Champlain St and veer on to Portage St and finally to Defiance St.

Getting There & Away

The **Fort Ti Ferry** (☎ 802-897-7999; tickets one-way/round-trip $7/12; ☷ 8am-6pm May-Oct) runs to and from Shoreham (Larabees Point), VT, and Ticonderoga, NY. The ferry is the oldest business in Vermont (in continuous operation since 1799), and was originally a military crossing in use during the French and Indian War.

DETOUR – ROUTE 22 TICONDEROGA TO ESSEX

This winding road chases along the shores of smooth, sculpted Lake Champlain. A twist here leads past meadows covered in queen Anne's lace or freshly cut pastures bearing the mower's signature corduroy ribs. In the early morning, the road is as much a commuter route for people as it is for barn swallows and porcupines; in the evening, post-dinner strollers claim the unused lanes and wave politely at the passing cars. Westport and Essex, villages that face the lake and its attendant Green Mountains, seem more like satellites of Vermont, tidy and dignified – unusual exemptions from the brawny industrial towns typically found in the Adirondacks.

In the village of Essex, **Lake Champlain Ferries** (☎ 802-864-9804; www.ferries.com) connects Charlotte, VT, and Essex, NY (car and driver one-way $7.75, $14 round-trip, additional passengers $2.75 one way, $4.50 round-trip; hourly 20-minute crossings). All schedules are subject to change due to ice and weather conditions.

Adirondack Trailways (☎ 800-858-8555) stops at **Hank's General Store** (☎ 518-585-6680; 112 Champlain Ave) in Fort Ti. One-way fares from Ticonderoga are $28 to Lake Placid ($50 round-trip) and $20 to Lake George ($40 round-trip).

LAKE PLACID & AROUND

Gateway to the Adirondack's High Peaks region, Lake Placid gained global fame by twice hosting the Olympic Winter Games.

LAKE PLACID

☎ 518 / pop 2600

A welcome enclave of civilization, Lake Placid village – situated on Mirror Lake – hosted the 1932 and 1980 Winter Olympics. Only two other towns – Innsbruck in Austria and St Moritz in Switzerland – have hosted two Winter Games. Training still occurs in many of the Olympic facilities, and many special events and programs introduce visitors to the winter pursuits of bobsled racing, ice-skating and ski jumping.

Although not as swanky as some mountain resorts, Lake Placid is a year-round destination that runs on the labor of resort gypsies, who use service-industry jobs to fund temporary homes in major outdoor-sports destinations. Perched along the hills of the town are the summer homes of the people whose spending power keeps the resort alive.

Lake Placid became an Olympic center because Dr Melvil Dewey, of Dewey Decimal System fame, opened the Lake Placid Club as a resort here in 1895. The club began winter sports in 1904. The lake that shares a name with the town is north of the town.

Information

The local biweekly newspaper is the *Lake Placid News*. With Pipe & Book (p220) sells good maps of the region. Other useful places in town:

Lake Placid (Essex County) Visitors Bureau
(☎ 518-523-2445, 800-447-5224; www.lakeplacid.com; 216 Main St; ⏰ 8am-5pm Mon-Fri, 9am-4pm Sat-Sun)
In the large brownstone building connected to the new Olympic Center at the south end of town. You can pick up the helpful booklet that lists all places to stay in Lake Placid and surrounding towns.

Post office In the fork between Main St and Parkside Drive downtown.

FOREVER WILD

The publicly owned lands in the Adirondack region make up the Adirondack Forest Preserve, which is 40% of Adirondack Park; the preserve is protected from development by the designation 'forever wild' in the state Constitution. Privately held land in the park designation is subject to state regulation and zoning to limit development. Only in a few population centers, like Lake Placid, will you find shopping centers and chain stores. When the park was first established, a blue line was used on an official map to designate the borders. Residents who live within the park's boundaries speak with understandable pride of living within the 'Blue Line.'

Sights

Lake Placid has so many things to do that whole vacations are anchored to this one destination.

OLYMPIC SITES

Of the five Olympic venues, three of the facilities are located in Lake Placid proper; these include the Olympic Center, MacKenzie-Intervale Ski Jumping Complex and Verizon Sports Complex. The visitors bureau distributes weekly schedules for Olympic venue events, and you can buy tickets there too. You can visit the following Olympic sites separately or all together on the all-inclusive **Summer Passport** (www.orda.org; adult $19, child 0-6 free), available from mid-June to mid-October; it can be bought at the Olympic venues. Most sites are open daily from mid-December to mid-March and mid-May to mid-October from 9am from to 4pm; call the individual venues for off-season hours. In addition to the sites covered here, the Winter Passport ($39) includes admission for ice skating, a gondola ride at Whiteface Mountain and a cross-country trail pass.

The **Olympic Center** (☎ 518-523-1655, 800-462-6236; 218 Main St) is the large white building next to the visitors bureau. It was used for the 1980 Olympics and houses four ice-skating rinks. You can watch athletes training here for free or take in an ice show or hockey game. Bring a jacket or sweater; even in the summer the ice is cold. Inside the center, the **Lake Placid Winter Olympic Museum** (adult/senior/

THE ADIRONDACKS

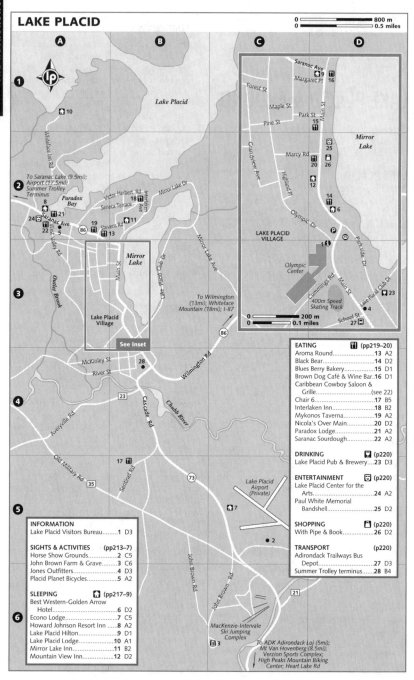

LAKE PLACID

0 _____ 800 m
0 _____ 0.5 miles

Lake Placid

Mirror Lake

Saranac Ave
Margaret Pl
Forest St
Maple St
Park St
Pine St
Marcy Rd
Cranberry Ave
Highland Pl
Olympic Dr

LAKE PLACID VILLAGE

Olympic Center

400m Speed Skating Track

0 _____ 200 m
0 _____ 0.1 miles

Park-side Dr
Main St
Cummings Rd
School St
Lake Placid Club Dr

Whiteface Inn Rd

To Saranac Lake (9.5mi);
Airport (17.5mi);
Summer Trolley
Terminus

Paradox Bay

Victor Herbert Rd
Immelen
Seneca Terrace
Saranac Ave
Stevens Rd

Mirror Lake

Mirror Lake Dr
Mirror Lake Ave

Lake Placid Village

See Inset

To Wilmington
(13mi); Whiteface
Mountain (18mi); I-87

West Valley Rd
Onida Brook
Main St
Lake Placid Dr

McKinley St
River St
Wilmington Rd
Cascade Rd
Chubb River

Averyville Rd
Old Military Rd
Sentinel Rd

Lake Placid
Airport
(Private)

John Brown Rd

MacKenzie-Intervale
Ski Jumping
Complex

To ADK Adirondack Loj (5mi);
Mt Van Hovenberg (8.5mi);
Verzion Sports Complex;
High Peaks Mountain Biking
Center, Heart Lake Rd

INFORMATION
Lake Placid Visitors Bureau.........1 D3

SIGHTS & ACTIVITIES (pp213–7)
Horse Show Grounds.................2 C5
John Brown Farm & Grave.........3 C6
Jones Outfitters........................4 D3
Placid Planet Bicycles...............5 A2

SLEEPING (pp217–9)
Best Western-Golden Arrow
 Hotel.....................................6 D2
Econo Lodge.............................7 C5
Howard Johnson Resort Inn 8 A2
Lake Placid Hilton.....................9 D1
Lake Placid Lodge....................10 A1
Mirror Lake Inn........................11 B2
Mountain View Inn...................12 D2

EATING (pp219–20)
Aroma Round.........................13 A2
Black Bear..............................14 D2
Blues Berry Bakery..................15 D1
Brown Dog Café & Wine Bar..16 D1
Caribbean Cowboy Saloon &
 Grille..............................(see 22)
Chair 6..................................17 B5
Interlaken Inn.........................18 B2
Mykonos Taverna....................19 A2
Nicola's Over Main..................20 D2
Paradox Lodge........................21 A2
Saranac Sourdough.................22 A2

DRINKING (p220)
Lake Placid Pub & Brewery....23 D3

ENTERTAINMENT (p220)
Lake Placid Center for the
 Arts...................................24 A2
Paul White Memorial
 Bandshell............................25 D2

SHOPPING (p220)
With Pipe & Book....................26 D2

TRANSPORT (p220)
Adirondack Trailways Bus
 Depot.................................27 D3
Summer Trolley terminus......28 B4

DETOUR – WHITEFACE MOUNTAIN

Whiteface Mountain (4868ft) is a popular ski destination for its 65 miles of trail and the greatest vertical drop (3430ft) in the eastern part of the US. Whiteface hosted alpine events for the 1980 Olympic Games.

Rentals and passes for downhill skiing and snowboarding in winter and mountain biking and hiking in summer can be arranged from the **Whiteface base lodge** (518-946-2255; www.whiteface.com; Rte 86, Wilmington). You can also take a gondola ride (adult $12) up to the summit of Little Whiteface Mountain for views of Lake Placid and the surrounding High Peaks and a panoramic view during fall foliage season.

Although hiking trails go to the top of Whiteface, you can also drive to the **Whiteface Mountain Memorial Highway** (car & driver $9, additional passenger $6; 8:30am-5pm Jun-Oct). To get there, drive 17 miles north on Rte 86 to Wilmington and then take Rte 431 for roughly 8 miles up the 4900ft mountain (the only Adirondack High Peak accessible by car). On clear days, you can view the surrounding peaks and mountain ranges as far off as Montreal and Vermont.

For more information on skiing Whiteface, see the New York State Outdoors chapter (p46).

The town of Wilmington serves the ski resort with accommodations and restaurants. **Wilmington Notch Campground** (518-946-7172, 800-456-2267; Rte 86; campsite $13; mid-Apr–mid-Oct) This is a simple public camp between Lake Placid and Wilmington on Rte 86. Many travelers use it as a base for hiking and fishing trips. The campground leads to the Ausable River.

Wilkommen Hof (518-946-7669, 800-541-9119; Rte 86; d without bath $64-75, d with bath $100-130), south of the four-way stop in town, is a converted farmhouse with a German theme. It has a comfortable common area with fireplace and television, a sauna and hot tub. Rooms are simply decorated and there are family suites. Rates include a full breakfast. In winter the Yosts family serves a German dinner for $30 by reservation. They also are a good source of information about mountain biking in the area.

child $4/3/2; 10am-5pm) displays memorabilia from the 1932 and 1980 Olympics. It was on the adjacent speed skating oval that speed skater Eric Heiden made history by winning five individual gold medals.

MacKenzie-Intervale Ski Jumping Complex (518-523-1655, 518-523-2202; Rte 73; adult $8, senior & child $5), located southeast of town, is the training facility for the US Olympic ski jump teams. There are 90m (the bunny jump) and 120m towers. Thanks to artificial surfaces, ski jumpers train here all year. When there is no snow, ski jumping takes place on a porcelain in-run and plastic-covered landing hill. You can take a chair lift followed by an elevator ride to the top of the 26-story viewing room of the 120m ski jump tower. A recorded loop tape introduces you to the ins-and-outs of this death-defying sport. You can also venture out to view the starting ramp. Next door is the **Kodak Sports Park**, a freestyle aerial ski jump training center. TV does not do this sport justice. Skiers launch off a jump, then perform aerial flips and tricks to land neatly into a 17ft-deep, 750,000-gallon pool of water. The exhilaration and fear that a

spectator feels is akin to a rollercoaster ride.

Verizon Sports Complex (518-523-4436; Rte 73, Mt Van Hoevenberg), seven miles south of Lake Placid, is the site of the Olympic bobsled run, as well as newly constructed luge and skeleton tracks, and cross-country skiing trails. Trolley tours of the bobsled and luge areas are available (tickets adult $5, child $4). Winter and summer bobsled rides are available to the public (tickets $30 per person). During the winter (mid-December to mid-March), bobsled rides on the half-mile 1980 Olympic track reach speeds of over 50mph (as compared to speeds of over 80mph during professional competitions on a newer track); when there's no snow 'wheeled' bobsleds run on a concrete track, reaching speeds of over 45mph. All bobsled rides are piloted by professional drivers and brakemen. Good luck anyway.

Whiteface Mountain, in nearby Wilmington, also hosted several Olympic events in 1980 (see above).

Ever flirted with the idea of being a winter Olympiad? **Gold Medal Adventure** (www.goldmedaladventure.org) will introduce you to luge, bobsled and ski jumping through daylong clinics.

JOHN BROWN FARM & GRAVE

The famous American abolitionist who was hanged for leading a raid on the US Arsenal at Harpers Ferry, WV, is buried outside Lake Placid in North Elba. The **historic site** (☎ 518-523-3900; John Brown Rd; admission $1; ☷ 10am-5pm Wed-Sat & 1-5pm Sun May-Oct), off Rte 73, includes Brown's farm and his gravestone, as well as those of two of his sons and nine other men killed in Harpers Ferry.

Brown was born in Connecticut in 1800 and lived in Ohio for a number of years; he moved to North Elba in 1849 to participate in a radical social experiment led by Gerrit Smith. The plan was to give land to any free black man who wished to farm it. Brown moved to North Elba to teach farming practices. It was here that he and his followers organized the raid, hoping to use the captured arms to launch a general rebellion. On October 16, 1859, Brown and a group of followers attacked the federal arsenal. They were captured on October 18 and hanged on December 2.

There is a self-guided tour of the farm building, the 244-acre farm and the graves. You can walk around the grounds and look at the graves any time of year. Take Rte 86 from town to Rte 73 south. Drive 1.7 miles to the fork with a sign noting the 'John Brown Historic Site.' Drive half a mile down this road (John Brown Rd) to the farm.

HIGH PEAKS

A spectacular range of tall peaks, 46 of which measure over 4000ft, dominate the Lake Placid–Keene Valley area. Mt Marcy (5344ft) is the most popular peak to tackle, followed closely behind by Algonquin (5114ft), Haystack, Nippletop and Santanoni. Peak baggers who have scaled all 46 peaks debate endlessly about which mountain affords the best view. In winter most of these hiking trails, especially Avalanche Pass, are used by downhill skiers. Rock-climbers scale up Wallface Mountain.

Phelps Trail (9.5 miles) is the eastern approach to Mt Marcy and starts at the main crossroads in Keene Valley. Another well-known trail is the 130-mile Northville–Lake Placid Trail, which starts near Great Sacandaga Lake in the southern Adirondacks and winds through high meadows and dense pine forests into the High Peaks area. The shortest approach to Mt Marcy starts at the ADK Adirondak Loj/High Peaks Information Center in Lake Placid. From the center's parking lot, Mt Marcy is 7.4 miles and Algonquin is 4 miles. To get to the ADK property, take Rte 73 south of Lake Placid for about 2 miles to Adirondak Loj Rd (also known as Heart Lake Rd). Drive on Adirondak Loj Rd for 5 miles. Parking for hikers is $9 a day and $30 a week for ADK nonmembers ($3 and $10 respectively for ADK members).

Although the views feel like looking down from Mount Olympus, the trails are not an escape from humanity. These are popular routes, especially in summer, and a veritable restaurant row for hungry bears who prefer ramen noodles over foraging for berries. Apprize yourself on how to handle and store food in bear country before rumbling with these not-so-gentle beasts.

ADK High Peaks Information Center (☎ 518-523-3441; www.adk.org; Adirondak Loj Rd, Lake Placid) should be the first stop for planning a hiking or skiing trip through the High Peaks. They have maps, trail guides and other useful information for staying on the trails and avoiding bears. The center has an information number (☎ 518-523-3518) for daily weather and trail conditions in the North Country.

Activities
HIKING & SKIING

Most trails (used for hiking in summer and skiing in winter) start at or near the ADK Loj–High Peaks Information Center on Adirondak Loj Rd off of Rte 73 south of Lake Placid. One of the best short hiking options in the area is Mt Jo (2.3 miles round-trip, moderate), named in 1877 after Josephine Schofield, who was engaged to Henry Van Hoevenberg, but she died before they were to be married. The trail to the summit rises dramatically over Heart Lake. Take the short steep trail up the mountain and the long gentler trail down, or the long trail both ways with small children. Red pine, silver birch and maple adorn the way, and both routes take roughly the same time. From the boulder ledge at the summit, you can see Indian Pass and half a dozen of the High Peaks, including Mts Marcy and Algonquin.

Mt Van Hoevenberg (4.4 miles round-trip, moderate) is a healthy stroll through

WARNING TO HIKERS

Be careful hiking in the Adirondacks. Although the mountains are deceptively gentle in appearance, the terrain is, in fact, difficult. Add to this the sheer size of the wilderness, and the result is the nearly annual tragedy, often involving an experienced, lone hiker who wanders from the established trails. In the summer of 1990, 38-year-old David Boomhower got lost while on a solo 10-day hike along the popular 130-mile Northville–Lake Placid Trail. He left on June 5 and died in early August after trying to survive on insects, snails and plants. One of the final entries in his journal, found after his death, reads 'Just what happened? I didn't bring enough food, ran out, and also encountered a string of bad weather. Took [unreadable] trail... Somehow got lost off that... I'm surprised they haven't found me....'

the woods garnering views of the High Peaks. To get to the trailhead, go 4 miles on Adirondak Loj Rd heading toward the ADK Loj and keep an eye out for a sign that reads 'South Meadows, Marcy Dam, Johns Brook.' Turn left at the sign and follow the dirt road. to another sign for Mt Van Hoevenberg. Other hikes of moderate difficulty in the Lake Placid area include Avalanche Lake (10 miles round-trip) and Rocky Falls (4.5 miles round-trip).

In addition to the state trails, **Verizon Sports Complex** (Mt Van Hoevenberg, Rte 73; day trail pass adult/child $12/10) has 50 kilometers of cross-country trails as well as clinics and equipment rental.

BICYCLING

The Lake Placid area is great bicycling country, even hosting annual Iron Man competitions. Country-road and off-road trails are abundant and road shoulders tend to be wide enough for cars to safely pass. Any of the several bike shops in town can provide you with maps and rentals. Half a day of cycling, for example, could take you around the River Rd loop, a trip of about 12 miles.

Placid Planet Bicycles (☎ 518-523-4128; 51 Saranac Ave; mountain/road bike per day $30/35) does sales, repairs and rentals, and they'll help you with maps and suggestions for either off-road or country-road cycling.

In summer, the cross-country ski trails at Mt Van Hoevenberg (p216) and Whiteface Mountain (p215) are open to mountain bikers, both experienced and novice. Trail fees are $6 and bikes and helmets are available to rent at the **High Peaks Mountain Biking Center** (☎ 518-523-4436; Verizon Sports Complex, Rte 73).

FISHING & CANOEING

The west branch of the Ausable River (*oh*-sable) is one of the most fabled trout streams in the northeast. **Jones Outfitters** (☎ 518-523-3468; 37 Main St; fly-fishing half/full day $145/195) teaches and leads fly fishing trips all year. Jones also takes trips to the lake, just out the front door, and the Chubb, Saranac and Bog Rivers. You'll understand how serious these folks are about fish with a quick glance at the chalk board outside the shop. In summer, it lists the names of hatch flies that the fish are biting; poetic entries include Yellow Sallys, Red Quills, Olive Caddis and Stonefly Nymphs. Canoes and kayaks can also be rented here for $15 per hour or $38 per day.

Middle Earth Expeditions (☎ 518-523-9572; Rte 73) is a year-round outfitter specializing in wilderness canoe and fishing trips and whitewater rafting in spring, summer and fall; call for directions from Lake Placid.

Sleeping

A note on seasons and prices: Lake Placid is a premier resort area, and the press of the Olympic stamp is everywhere. There are bargains to be had, but prices are the highest in the Adirondacks. The high season is generally the summer months from mid-June to early September, followed by the winter ski season from about a week before Christmas until mid-March; weekend rates can be higher year-round. Rates are lower, often considerably so, after mid-October and mid-March – unless a 'special event' is scheduled. It's often worth asking about possible discounts during off-season.

Wilmington, 12 miles east of Lake Placid, offers additional (and sometimes cheaper) accommodations, as does Saranac Lake, west of Lake Placid.

Most of the cheaper motels extend along Saranac Ave on the way into town from Rte 86 to the west. Saranac Ave is a busy thoroughfare and many of the hotels are flimsily constructed with rooms facing the noisy road. Main St is where you want to be; that's

BUNK DOWN AMID HIGH PEAKS

ADK Adirondak Loj (518-523-3441; www.adk.org; Heart Lake Rd/Adirondak Loj Rd; campsite $23-32, dm $34-45, d $110) Sitting on Heart Lake at the feet of the High Peaks, this large lodge serves as a base for exploring the nearby hiking and skiing trails. Inside, there is a common room with rocking chairs in front of a large fireplace, over which is hung a moose head; there's also a good library of books and magazines on the Adirondacks. Accommodations include private rooms, four- to six-person dorms and 18-person dorms all with wooden bunks, thick and firm mattresses and, if you're lucky enough to get a bunk facing the lake, great views. Private rooms have double beds. A favorite detail of the Loj: there are 46 beds to match the 46 high peaks of the Adirondacks.

There is also an adjacent campground with tent, lean-tos and canvas cabin sites in a pretty woods. This is your best choice in the bottom-end accommodations bracket – if not in any bracket – and it's open to members and nonmembers alike.

All Loj room rates include breakfast; if you want dinner ($14), arrange it in advance. The food is served family-style at long tables. Breakfast is $5 for those in cabins, lean-tos and tents. Trail lunches can be ordered in advance for $5.50.

John Brooks Lodge (JBL; dm $38-41; lean-to $17) About 3.5 miles by foot from the Adirondak Loj is another affiliated facility. It has bunk rooms for 10 to four people. During nonsummer months, the rates for dorm beds drop to $15 to $17.

ADK also maintains two backcountry cabins, **Grace Camp** (per night $120), sleeping six, and **Camp Peggy O'Brien** (per night $240), which sleeps 12. These camps are a 3.3 mile walk from the town of Keene Valley on Rte 73, about 15 miles southeast of Lake Placid. They're open all year and have bunks, tables, firewood, cooking stoves (you bring the fuel) and cooking equipment. There are also lean-tos around Grace Camp and Camp Peggy O'Brien.

ADK members get a 10% discount on everything.

where you'll find the shops, restaurants and Olympic sites, although the hotels' proximity to these attractions fetches a higher price.

MID-RANGE
Howard Johnson Resort Inn (518-523-9555; fax 518-523-4765; 90 Saranac Ave; d $85-150, ste $250;) Perched on a small hill overlooking Paradox Bay, pet-friendly Howard Johnson offers the best noise-free options on Saranac Ave. There is also a small waterfront lounge area. The affiliated restaurant wins praise from locals for having Lake Placid's best breakfast.

Econo Lodge (518-523-2817; Cascade Rd/Rte 73; d weekday $80-100, weekend $125) About a mile south of the Olympic Center, this well-managed chain has simple motel-style rooms in an area of town that is a quieter option than Saranac Ave.

Mountain View Inn (518-523-2439, 800-499-2668; 140 Main St; d $87-145;) Across the street from the Best Western, this is the cheapest hotel on Main St; it is also the last independent hotel on the block. The name is a bit misleading, rooms have views of nothing in the back or a crowded street scene in the front; some might squeak a view of the lake.

Best Western-Golden Arrow Hotel (518-523-3353, 800-582-5540; 150 Main St; d $90-200, ste per week $400-1500;) Possibly the best choice in town, Best Western is right on the lake and has a beach, heated pool, saunas, Jacuzzi and racquetball court. Rooms are furnished in upmarket motel style and are pet-friendly.

TOP END
Lake Placid Hilton (518-523-4411, 800-755-5598; cnr Main St & Saranac Ave; d $80-270;) This corporate hotel is really a complex of several buildings. The best rooms – all of which have a view of Mirror Lake or the mountains – are in the tallest of these buildings. Rooms (pet-friendly) are big, nicely furnished and each has a balcony. Ask for information about ski packages that include lift tickets to Whiteface Mountain and about late-January and spring specials.

Mirror Lake Inn (518-523-2544; fax 518-523-2871; 5 Mirror Lake Dr; d from $400;) This is an Adirondack classic, and one of the most elegant retreats in upstate New York. It offers afternoon tea, a restaurant, private beach, canoeing, tennis, spa, lakeside dining and the list goes on. The rooms in the main lodge are exquisite split-level suites with well-polished blonde wood and huge views of the lake. The newer wings of the hotel have personality-less rooms that still boast a finishing-school price tag.

Lake Placid Lodge (☎ 518-523-2700, 877-523-2700; fax 518-523-1124; Whiteface Inn Rd; d from $375; ☒ ☒) This grand 1880s hunting lodge has been converted into a romantic getaway and gallery of Adirondack furnishings. Rustic and remote, the lodge overlooks the west end of Lake Placid and offers everything from stone fireplaces and sunset cruises to swimming and snowshoeing. Pets are welcome; however, children under 12 are not. If you can't afford a room at least come for a drink in the sylvan-styled bar.

Eating

Lake Placid has fine gourmet dining as well as simple grub shops. The options on Main St are plentiful but more interested in being tourist-troughs. If the food is disappointing at these Main St restaurants, the lakeside scenery is more than a mouthful.

BUDGET & MID-RANGE

Aroma Round (☎ 518-523-3818; 18 Saranac Ave; dishes $2-4) Within walking distance to Main St, this rounded lookout cabin is a nice spot to begin the day or just to lounge around in the upholstered couches. It has a fireplace, books, puzzles to play and a good coffee bar.

Blues Berry Bakery (☎ 518-523-4539; 26 Main St; dishes $2-5) Describing himself as the 'only liberal baker in Lake Placid' Rainer Schnaars makes tasty apple strudel, blueberry scones and other baked goods.

Saranac Sourdough (☎ 518-523-4897; 89 Saranac Ave; dishes $4-7) Across the street from Howard Johnson's, this precious café is decorated like a country hollow kitchen. At morning coffee time, it's a great place to eavesdrop on local gossip. You can also stop in for deli sandwiches and pick up supplies for a picnic basket.

Black Bear (☎ 518-523-9886; 157 Main St; dishes $6-10) This family friendly restaurant does affordable and dependable cafeteria-style food, including a soup and salad bar. Breakfast is the biggest draw. The tables at the rear of the restaurant look out over the lake.

Chair 6 (☎ 518-523-3630; 46 Sentinel Rd; dishes $4-5; ☺ 6am-3pm Wed-Sun) Lots of bleary-eyed, bed-headed locals wander in to this simple kitchen set-up in the ground floor of a suburban house. Fluffy and tart buttermilk pancakes, breakfast burritos and eggs any style comprise the breakfast menu. Sandwiches and soups make up the lunch fare. This is the closest restaurant to the ADK hiking trails and campground.

Brown Dog Café & Wine Bar (☎ 518-523-3036; 3 Main St; dishes $5-15; ☺ 11am-9pm) Across the street from the Lake Placid Hilton, this storefront café has indulgent salads, veggie deli sandwiches and dinner bistro fare. Every Saturday evening, it hosts a multi-course meal paired with wines.

Caribbean Cowboy Saloon & Grille (☎ 518-523-3836; 89 Saranac Ave; dishes $10-15; ☺ 5-10pm) Behind Saranac Sourdough, this rollicking restaurant offers an eclectic menu of spicy chicken and fish dishes as well as Asian-influenced vegetarian options. This is where the young and tipsy hang out, ushered into oblivion with candy-sweet drink specialties. An odd lot shuts the place down, including one summer visitor who played Star Wars on the bagpipes.

Nicola's Over Main (☎ 518-523-4430; 90 Main St; dishes $18-20; ☺ 5-11pm) Recreating the festive mood of Carnival, this Mediterranean restaurant has an open kitchen boisterously preparing steaks, seafood and pasta dishes.

Mykonos Taverna (☎ 518-523-1164; 38 Saranac Ave; dishes $15-20; ☺ 11:30am-2pm & 5-9:30pm) This pleasant family-owned Greek eatery has tasty soups and salads, moussaka, pilaf and kabobs.

TOP END

Interlaken Inn (☎ 518-523-3180; 15 Interlaken Ave; dishes $25-30; ☺ 5:30-9:30pm) The inn is in an old Victorian house with appropriately stunning interior. The continental treatment of seafood and land-dwellers is creative and draws from the Adirondack's thick forests. A mushroom forager delivers freshly harvest fungi. The bitter greens salad is surprisingly delicious as is the duck breast with sweet potato sauce and braised leeks. Reservations are recommended and dress is business casual.

Paradox Lodge (☎ 518-523-9078; 76 Saranac Ave; dishes $25-30; ☺ 6-8:30pm) Eating in the dining room of this Victorian B&B is like visiting a friend's house for a dinner party. Chef Moses bangs away in the kitchen while his unflappable wife, Nan, ushers diners, food and wine to their tables. Veal with morels and cognac fill the air with tantalizing aromas.

Lobster bisque and other fish dishes also maintain a loyal clientele. Reservations are recommended.

Entertainment

Lake Placid Center for the Arts (☎ 518-523-2512; www.lakeplacidarts.org; 91 Saranac Ave) This is a year-round, multi-purpose center that presents professional theatrical, music and dance performances, shows films and conducts workshops.

Lake Placid Sinfonetta (☎ 518-523-2051) A summer orchestra of 19 professional musicians presents a six-week season of concerts in July and August. They use a variety of locations, including Sunday night performances at the Lake Placid Center for the Arts. Free outdoor 'cushion concerts,' which some boaters attend by floating over to listen, are performed Wednesday nights at the Paul White Memorial Bandshell downtown along Mirror Lake.

Lake Placid Pub and Brewery (☎ 518-523-3813) Salvaged church-stained glass adds a touch of reverence to this local microbrewery. Try the Ubu Ale, a chocolate ale named after a chocolate Labrador who used to frequent the place. Downstairs is PJ O'Neil's, a rowdy bar that often has two-for-one specials.

Shopping

With Pipe & Book (☎ 518-523-9096; 91 Main St) This great browsing store has a number of rooms upstairs and downstairs, and sells fine pipes and natural blended tobaccos. They also have a great selection of new, rare and used books, as well as scenic prints and good hiking and driving maps of the Adirondack region. Opening hours are erratic.

Getting There & Around

Adirondack Trailways (☎ 800-858-8555) stops at 326 Main St. A one-way ticket from Lake Placid to New York City will cost $63 (round-trip $126).

Coming from New York City by car, take the Palisades Parkway to I-87 north to exit 24 (Albany). Continue on I-87 to Rte 73, then 30 miles west to Lake Placid. From Montreal, Take Autoroute 15 south to the Champlain crossing, where it connects with I-87 south. Take exit 34 west to Rte 9N and west to Rte 86.

Lake Placid is within reach of the Adirondack Regional Airport (see p206).

Placid Express (☎ 518-523-2445) runs a free trolley service from the southern end of Main St to the Tops Shopping Center on Saranac Ave. From June to September 1, the trolley runs daily from 7:30am to 10pm with stops every 15 to 20 minutes. From May to June and September to October, the schedule is abbreviated to weekends (9am to 10pm on Saturday, 9am to 6pm Sunday) with stops every 30 minutes.

SARANAC LAKE

☎ 518 / pop 5000

Situated in the middle of a chain of lakes, including the Upper, Middle and Lower Saranac, the village of Saranac Lake was a major tuberculosis treatment center in the late-19th century. (As late as 1930, tuberculosis – or consumption, as it was more commonly referred to then – killed more Americans than heart disease.)

The first sanitarium for the treatment of tuberculosis was established here in 1884 by Dr Edward Livingston Trudeau, a young New York physician who was diagnosed with tuberculosis at the beginning of his career. Instead of heading to the tuberculosis sanatoria of Europe, he decided to return to a place he had once visited for pleasure, the Adirondacks. After a great deal of hardship, he opened the Adirondack Cottage Sanitarium, just northeast of the remote village of Saranac Lake, which in the 1880s was a 32-mile stagecoach ride from the nearest railroad station.

The town isn't as prissy as nearby Lake Placid; evidence of bitter winters and meager wages shows on the buildings' chipped-paint facades and asthma-inducing cars. Without the pretensions of wealth, Saranac is free to be kind to everyone who passes through.

Information

Several banks and ATMs are on Broadway, Church and Main Sts.

Adirondack Medical Center (☎ 518-891-4141; Lake Colby Dr) Northwest of downtown; the major hospital in the region.

American Village (☎ 518-891-2150; 28 Bloomingdale Ave) For laundry.

Blue Line Sport Shop (☎ 518-891-4680; 82 Main St; ⏰ 8:30am-5:30pm Mon-Sat, 9am-3pm Sun) It has hiking and camping supplies, rents cross-country skis ($15 a day) and has everything and anything to do with fishing.

Fact & Fiction Bookshop (☎ 518-891-8067; 17 Broadway; ☒ 9:30am-6pm) Carries a plentiful supply of books on local history and fiction.

Post office (60 Broadway)

Saranac Lake Chamber of Commerce (☎ 518-891-1990, 800-347-1992; www.saranaclake.com; 30 Main St; ☒ 8:30am-5:30pm Mon-Fri, 10am-3pm Sat-Sun summer) In the municipal building; publishes booklets describing wilderness areas and places to stay.

Sights & Activities

This town of Saranac offers interesting strolling opportunities and the surrounding wilderness, while not as dramatic as the High Peaks region, is remote and secluded.

ROBERT LOUIS STEVENSON COTTAGE

The **house** (☎ 518-891-1462; 11 Stevenson La; adult/child $5/free; ☒ 9:30am-noon & 1-4:30pm Tue-Sun Jul–mid-Sep) was Stevenson's home for the winter of 1887–88, when he came to Saranac to 'take the cure' for tuberculosis. His days were spent on the front porch breathing in the cold winter air so as to 'freeze' the lungs and cure the disease. To keep the body warm, he was wrapped with heavy woolen blankets and warmed bricks. This amateur museum contains the largest collection of Stevenson memorabilia in the US, including old photos, clothing, ice skates and a lock of the author's hair. Stevenson wrote the essays 'The Master of Ballantrae,' 'The Wrong Box' and 'A Christmas Sermon' here. Take Main St north to Bloomingdale Ave, turn south on Pine St to Stevenson Lane.

COTTAGE ROW

A little-known area on the outskirts of the town should be of interest to history buffs. There are a number of historic 'cure cottages' dating from the days when Saranac Lake was a mecca for people (Stevenson and baseball great Christie Mathison) seeking a cure for tuberculosis. The best-restored houses are on Park Ave between Catherine and Grove Sts.

SIX NATIONS INDIAN MUSEUM

About 14 miles north of Saranac Lake and a mile from Onchiota on County Rd 30, this **museum** (☎ 518-891-2299; adult/child $2/1; ☒ 10am-6pm Jul-Sep) helps to preserve the culture of the Iroquois Confederation, originally comprised of the Mohawk, Seneca, Onondaga, Oneida and Cayuga tribes, and later the Tuscaroras. On display in the museum are artifacts, historic documents and models of typical Iroquois villages, as well as contemporary Iroquois crafts. The museum stands as a reminder to visitors that the Native American culture and history long predates their contact with Europeans.

CANOEING

Around Upper Saranac Lake, the St Regis Wilderness Canoe Area is prized by canoeists. This area is composed of 58 lakes and ponds where you can canoe for weeks, or put in for a leisurely afternoon. There are no motorized boats, cars or roads in the area.

In the St Regis area, Fish Creek Ponds Loop is a good trip to make with small children. This trip can take from one to three days, and begins and ends at Fish Creek public campground. The 10-mile loop connects the ponds of Fish Creek, Little Square, Floodwood, Rollins, Whey and Copperas. There are only three portages, each less than a quarter mile.

Another modest 10-mile trip through the area is between Saranac Inn and Paul Smith's College. Also known as the Seven Carries route, the trip begins with a 1.5-mile portage to Little Green Pond, and crosses the ponds of Little Clear, St Regis, Green, Little Long, Bear and Bog, and the lakes of Upper St Regis and Spitfire. The average portage here is no more than a quarter mile.

Another popular trip includes the St Regis area to Tupper Lake, a trip of three to four days.

There are many outdoor outfitters in the area that can help you organize a canoe trip. **Adirondack Lakes & Trails Outfitters** (☎ 518-891-7450, 800-491-0414; 541 Lake Flower Ave/Rte 86; ☒ 9am-5pm), on the south end of town across from Pizza Hut, gives guided tours and has equipment rentals for canoeing, kayaking, skiing, hiking and camping. It has extended summer hours.

Mac's Canoe Livery (☎ 518-891-1176; 5859 Rte 30, Lake Clear) is one of the best sources in the area for canoes in summer (and cross-country skiing and snowshoeing in winter). Mac's concentrates on the adjacent St Regis area and is about a mile west of Lake Clear on Rte 30, near the New York State Fish Hatchery. Guided trips are $250 for one to three people.

Sleeping

BUDGET

Saranac Lakes Islands Campground (☎ 518-891-3170, 800-456-2267; campsite $14) This is a collection of 87 state-maintained campsites in and around Lower and Middle Saranac Lakes. Sites are considered primitive, but have tables, pit fireplaces and toilets. Small power boats are permitted on Lower Saranac Lake, so canoeists and hikers tend to prefer Middle Saranac Lake. It's also where you'll find a fine little sandy beach reachable by an easy half-mile trail. To get there, head west on Rte 3 from the village of Saranac Lake at the junction of Rte 86. Go 8.5 miles, and look for a small parking lot and trail on the right (north).

Adirondack Motel (☎ 518-891-2116, 800-416-0117; 23 Lake Flower Ave/Rte 86; d $90) This family-run motel right in town with lakefront view is clean and quiet. Rooms are large and some have kitchenettes. Rates in the off-season can dip as low as $50 and pets are welcome.

Gauthier's Saranac Motor Inn (☎ 518-891-1950; 143 Lake Flower Ave/Rte 86; d $90-130; ☒) Also on the lake, Gauthier's has canoes and kayaks for guests' use. Some rooms overlook the lake and have kitchenettes. The owner is involved with canoe racing in the area.

Lake Flower Inn (☎ 518-891-2310; 15 Lake Flower Ave; d $88-108; ☒) This is a cozy and clean spot with 14 rooms facing the lake. Low season rates drop to $48 to $78 and pets are welcome.

Hillman's Cottages (☎ 518-891-2263; Lake Colby Dr/Rte 86; d $70-100) On the road leading to Mt Pisgah, Hillman's (cash only) has cute wooden cottages decorated in a simple country-style. Warm summer evenings are passed in the small grassy yard.

MID-RANGE & TOP END

Sunday Pond B&B (☎ 518-891-1531; Rte 30; d $75) In the village of Saranac Inn, Sunday Pond was named for the pond in the back of the wooded property. Sunday Pond is a rustic outpost with old quilts, antiques and two screened-in porches. There are five rooms, one with private bath. Dinner is available with 24-hour notice. Visitors can go mountain biking, fishing, canoeing and hiking from here. (They'll make you a trail lunch.) To get there from Saranac Lake take Rte 86 to Rte 186 for 7 miles to Rte 30. It is a 10- to 15-minute drive from Saranac Lake and just opposite the St Regis Wilderness

Canoe Area (which has excellent cross-country ski trails).

Hotel Saranac (☎ 518-891-2200, 800-937-0211; 101 Main St; d $100-195) The town's famous old hotel has recently gotten a makeover. It is a large red-brick Italianate hotel run by hospitality management students of Paul Smith's College. When the hotel was built in 1927 it was noticed for its big-city, non-woodsy look. There are 88 modestly furnished and comfortable rooms. The ones on higher floors have good lake views.

Porcupine B&B (☎ 518-891-5160; 350 Park Ave; d $112-240) Just off of Catherine St, this 1903 cure 'cottage' is on the elegant side, with handsomely decorated rooms, all with bath and two with fireplaces. Two rooms also have small porches where you can take a modern cure on a sunny morning. There are two large living rooms, each with fireplace. Children are not allowed.

Eating

BUDGET & MID-RANGE

Lakeview Deli (☎ 518-891-2101; 102 River St; dishes $4-6; ⏲ 7am-7pm Mon-Fri, 9am-6pm Sat & Sun) Facing the lake, this little deli serves excellent sandwiches made to order, along with its own fresh breads and soups. Most items are under $5. There are a few tables, but most people order to go.

Nori's Whole Foods (☎ 518-891-6079; 65 Main St; ⏲ 9am-8pm Mon-Fri, 10am-4pm Sat & Sun) Behind Sears, this health food store sells some vegan and vegetarian items that you can eat at the one table up front.

Belvedere Restaurant (☎ 518-891-9873; 57 Bloomingdale Ave/Rte 3; dishes $10-15; ⏲ 11:30am-2pm Tue-Sat, 5-9:30pm) When people in Saranac celebrate, they usually pick the 'Bel,' an Italian family restaurant (cash only). If the dining room is too crowded, you can eat at the bar where all the action takes place.

Casa del Sol (☎ 518-891-0977; 154 Lake Flower Ave/Rte 86; dishes $7-10; ⏲ 11am-10pm) Just outside town as you arrive from Lake Placid, this faux-adobe spot will transport you to the Southwest, and their neon-colored drinks will transport you to oblivion. But before you dive into the margaritas, the Casa has the best Mexican food for many miles around. All the selections – burritos, tostadas, flautas, chimichangas – use fresh ingredients and the portions are large. But forego the salsa, which is really a bland tomato topping.

TOP END

AP Smith's (☎ 518-891-2200; 101 Main St; mains $14-18; ☺ 7am-1:30pm, 5-9pm) Inside the Hotel Saranac, this restaurant is run by chefs and hospitality students from Paul Smith's College. AP Smith's has a Sunday buffet brunch with waffles, omelets, eggs and desserts. It also serves American lunches, such as Reubens, tuna melts and other sandwiches. Dinners can include grilled lamb, Thai-style duck and Adirondack trout. Some have described the food as Russian roulette, sometimes it is amazing, sometimes it is a disaster. The students also make the house wine during summer stints in the south of France.

Wawbeek's Restaurant (☎ 518-359-2656; 553 Panther Mountain Rd; dishes $22-30; ☺ 5-9pm Wed-Sun) This old-fashioned lodge of hand-hewn logs and expert craftsmanship is an Adirondack classic in the great camp tradition. The menu brings the harvest of the forest to the table with maple-roasted duck, rainbow trout, strawberry salads and medallions of venison. Reservations are recommended. It is 1 mile north of Rte 3 near Upper Saranac Lake, a 20-minute drive out of town.

Entertainment

Waterhole No 3 (☎ 518-891-9502; 43 Main St; cover for bands $3-10) Across the street from the town hall, the Waterhole is a beer and whiskey kind of place that features good local music from rock to folk.

Pendragon Theatre (☎ 518-891-1854; 148 River St; adult/student $20/16) Saranac's year-round professional theatre and arts center hosts performances of classic plays and musicals.

Getting There & Away

Adirondack Airport is 5 miles from Saranac Lake.

Adirondack Trailways (☎ 800-858-8555) stops at Hotel Saranac (101 Main St). One-way fares are $3 to Lake Placid and $65 to New York City. Round trips are double the price.

For more details on reaching Saranac Lake, see Lake Placid (p220).

CENTRAL ADIRONDACKS

Outdoor recreation options expand the deeper travelers venture into the Adirondacks, with paddling in the Fulton Chain of Lakes a high point.

BLUE MOUNTAIN LAKE & AROUND
☎ 518 / pop 126

In the geographic center of the Adirondacks, Blue Mountain Lake is enclosed in demure mountains and dotted with heavenly blue ponds and lakes. Paddling through the quiet waterways to outcast islands or pitching a tent in front of such a vista invokes sheer awe.

The **Indian Lake Chamber of Commerce** (☎ 518-648-5112; Rte 28; ☺ 8am-4pm Mon-Fri, 6am-6pm Sat, 10am-6pm Sun) has a small office about 11 miles east of Blue Mountain Lake that provides tourist information for the area. The post office at Blue Mountain Lake is in the middle of the village.

For more information about public lands around Blue Mountain lake, contact New York **Department of Conservation** (☎ 518-863-4545; 701 S Main St, Northville).

Sights & Activities

Blue Mountain houses the Adirondack Museum, a cultural chronicler of this remote area. In addition, it is the gateway to the Fulton Chain of Lakes (p225) and to a network of excellent hiking trails.

ADIRONDACK MUSEUM

One of the finest regional museums in the US, the **Adirondack Museum** (☎ 518-352-7311; Rte 30; adult/senior/child $14/13/7; ☺ 10am-5pm late May–mid-Oct), just north of the intersection with Rte 28, is housed in a complex of 22 detached buildings overlooking Blue Mountain Lake. Each building focuses on different aspects of Adirondack life. You can wander through indoor and outdoor exhibits of rustic Adirondack furniture displayed in a restored Victorian cottage, a typical 19th-century luxury resort hotel room, a hermits' camp or the reassembled Bill Gates Diner (a former private railroad car – doubtfully related to the Microsoft billionaire), originally located in Bolton Landing. In addition, there are exhibits depicting the history and lore of the logging and mining industries of the region. Boating enthusiasts in particular will want to explore the popular exhibit on boat building, which includes fine examples of watercraft, ranging from dugout and birch-bark canoes to speedboats.

Allow at least three hours and plan to break your visit with some lunch so you don't get overloaded.

SAGAMORE GREAT CAMP

This **wilderness retreat** (☎ 315-354-5311; www.saga more.org; Sagamore Rd, Raquette Lake; adult/child $9/3; ☻ tours 10am & 1:30pm Jun-Sep, 10am & 1:30pm Sat & Sun Oct) was one of many 'great camps' built between the end of the Civil War and the beginning of WWI, when the rich and stylish built expensive and exclusive getaways. Sagamore, which was built in 1897, is typical in its architectural layout: there are servant and worker complexes and guest complexes. The buildings designed for the workers are in the board-and-batten style. Comfortable enough, but no match for the guest quarters, which defined the rustic wood-and-stone style of architecture still popular throughout the region. The interior of the buildings is covered in bark sheathing and log railings.

The camp is now a National Historic Landmark that provided the model for subsequent National Park Service sites. The camp offers residential programs ranging from mountain music to camps for grandparents and their grandchildren. Also, visitors can go on two-hour guided tours of the 27 rustic buildings on the grounds. For residential program information, call ☎ 315-354-5311 ext 21.

Also on the grounds is the **Adirondack Boat Building School** (☎ 315-354-5311; classes $700-1500), which hosts canoe-construction courses throughout the summer and fall. In the nine-day course, students build their own boats that instructors promise will be waterworthy.

From Blue Mountain Lake, take Rte 28 west 12 miles to Raquette Lake, and take Sagamore Rd 4 miles south to the camp.

HIKING & PADDLING

Blue Mountain (elevation 3759ft, nearly 2000ft above Blue Mountain Lake; 4 miles round-trip, difficult) is a popular family hike that starts out leisurely and morphs into a steady climb. The trail head is 1.6 miles north from the junction of Rtes 28 and 30 and about an eighth of a mile past the Adirondack Museum. Castle Rock (1 mile round-trip, easy), just behind the Adirondack Museum, is a rocky ledge that looks out over Blue Mountain Lake. For other hikes, pick up a copy of *Hiking in the Indian Lake-Blue Mountain Lake Region* from the Indian Lake Chamber of Commerce office (p223).

If interested in exploring the water routes here, talk to **Blue Mt Outfitters** (☎ 518-352-7306;

144 Main St; canoe/kayak rental per day $25/30), just north of the junction of Rtes 28 and 30. It functions as a complete outfitters, general store and information clearing house, and owners Ernie and Kim LaPrairie know the area well. They rent equipment and provide guided canoe and kayak trips and canoe instruction. They also rent guideboats, a unique Adirondack invention that outdoor guides used to transport hunting parties.

Sleeping

Blue Mountain is a summer and fall destination so accommodations are open from mid-May to mid-October and closed for winter and spring.

Golden Beach Campground (☎ 315-354-4230; Rte 28; campsite $14; ☻ May-Sep) Between Eighth and Seventh Lake, this has a sandy beach and is popular with families.

Eighth Lake Campground (☎ 315-354-4120, 800-456-2267; www.reserveamerica.com; Rte 28, Eighth Lake; campsite $14; ☻ mid-Apr–mid-Nov) Midway between Inlet and Raquette Lake, this state campground has pretty sites facing Eighth Lake. There are 125 tent and trailer sites, a beach and picnic area, showers and toilets.

Hemlock Hall B&B (☎ 518-352-7706, winter ☎ 518-359-9065; d $100-175, incl breakfast & dinner) Hemlock Hall commands a spectacular view of Blue Mountain Lake and is set off far enough from the road to feel isolated. There is a large lodge with eight rooms in the main building, 10 cabins and four motel units in a shaded pine forest overlooking the lake. The main lodge has an enormous stone fireplace and an inviting porch. Hemlock Hall has its own beach and canoes. Most of the cottages are on the hill right above the lake. The dining room is open to the public for breakfast and dinner, but you must call ahead for reservations. Kids eat half price. To get there take Rte 30 north from the intersection with Rte 28; after a quarter mile you should see the sign for the lodge and Maple Lodge Rd. If you get to the Adirondack Museum, you've gone too far.

Point Breeze Motel (☎ 518-648-5555; Rte 30, Indian Lake; d $50-65) Set way back from the road on Indian Lake, this family-run place is a quirky find. The motel rooms are made of knotty pine and display paintings and quilts made by the owners, Don and Jean Langley. The decor aesthetic has stalled around 1973, but so have the prices. Cabins and weekly rates are also available. Point Breeze is two miles from Indian Lake town and 12 miles southeast of Blue Mountain Lake. They accept cash and check only.

Big Moose Inn (☎ 315-357-2042; www.bigmoose inn.com; Big Moose Lake, Eagle Bay; d without bath $65-80, d with bath $125-160) An ideal spot for couples, Big Moose Inn has comfortable rooms of varying sizes and amenities. The Inn is perched over Big Moose Lake, a motorized lake with a few summer cottages sprinkled along the shore. To get here from Blue Mountain Lake, take Rte 28 north heading toward Old Forge to the village of Eagle Bay, turn left on Big Moose Rd and the inn is 5 miles on the right.

Eating
There is a scarcity of restaurants and cafés in Blue Mountain Lake village. For alternatives, go west to Old Forge, east to Indian Lake or north to Long Lake for more options.

Adirondack Museum Café (☎ 518-352-7311; Rte 30, Blue Mountain Lake; dishes $5-7) This is a good spot for lunch with a lovely view of the lake.

Burkes Diner (Rte 28; dishes $3-7) Look for a faded sign, 'Good Food Here,' as you head west on Rte 28 about 4 miles west of the Rte 30 junction, on the south side of the road across from the Mobil gas station. This is a local spot for coffee and eggs and eavesdropping on conversations. If you get to Raquette Lake, you missed it.

Entertainment
Adirondack Lakes Center for the Arts (☎ 518-352-7715; ☺ gallery 10am-4pm Mon-Fri) This is a visual and performing arts center near the junction of Rtes 28 and 30. Evening performances include folk music, classical music and storytelling. During the day, the center runs a series of workshops – for children and adults – that include canoe construction, wildlife photography and basket making. There is a gallery and gift shop.

Getting There & Around
Blue Mountain Lake is at the junction of Rte 28 and Rte 30, and is not serviced by public bus options.

OLD FORGE & AROUND
☎ 315 / pop 1587
The western entry point to the Adirondacks, Old Forge (and the neighboring village of Thendara) is as *au naturel* as a woodlands

screen saver. Chock-full of street-side motels, amusement parks and pancake houses, Old Forge appeals to the moonlighting outdoors-enthusiast, one who likes to play outside but sleep inside. The area is the snowmobiling capital of the region during winter, and summer attracts canoe and hiking buffs.

Contact the Old Forge **tourist information center** (☎ 315-369-6983; Main St; ☺ 8am-5pm Mon-Sat & 9am-5pm Sun), across the road from McDonald's, for seasonal events information and for a map of mountain biking and hiking trails.

Most shops and businesses are along Rte 28 (Main St), including the post office and a coin laundry.

Sights & Activities
Although the town of Old Forge is straight-up Americana funland, the wilderness around the town is some of the most remote in the park.

ADIRONDACK SCENIC RAILROAD
This **scenic railroad** (www.adirondackrr.com; adult/senior/child $12/11/5) is a project of the Adirondacks Railway Preservation Society in nearby Thendara (just west of Old Forge) and operates vintage open-window coaches through some very pretty country between the old Thendara and Minnehaha stations, complete with fake, weekly train robberies. Trips take about an hour and run Wednesday to Sunday from late June to August and for fall color from mid-September to mid-October. Weekend trips are made in May and September.

FULTON CHAIN OF LAKES
Made up of eight lakes – from the pond at Old Forge to Eighth Lake – this cluster of waterways covers over 2000 acres and stretches for about 20 miles from Old Forge to Raquette Lake. Carved out over 10,000 years ago by massive glaciers, the Fulton lakes were once the primary route into the interior of the Adirondacks. Native Americans used these lakes, which run southwest to northeast, to crisscross the region, carrying their canoes from lake to lake.

In the early 19th century, the railroad opened the region to development as a resort area, and the early trappers and hunters of the region often became the guides of rich sportsmen from the industrial capitals of the East Coast. Today, the area draws all sorts of water-sports enthusiasts. Old Forge to Third Lake is popular with boaters. Canoeists are often advised to begin around Sixth Lake to avoid the heavy motorized traffic.

The **Adirondack Classic** (☎ 518-891-2744), also known as the 90-miler, is a 90-mile race (and party) from Old Forge to Saranac Lake. It takes place in early September, on the weekend following the Labor Day holiday and lasts three days. The route goes through a number of northern lake towns including Tupper Lake, Saranac Lake and Paul Smith's. Some portage is required.

For a more leisurely day trip, you can canoe down the North Branch of the Moose River, at the put-in behind Tickner's Adirondack Canoe Outfitters (see next). The trip, which takes about four hours, is easy and scenic as the river twists its way along the gently curved banks of hardwood forests and grassy wetlands. Take along a picnic to enjoy on one of the many small sandy beaches. There is one portage of about 300 yards along the route. For an even easier canoeing trip, you might try Nick's Lake, 2 miles from Old Forge.

Third Lake to Seventh Lake, and Seventh Lake to Raquette Lake are popular with canoeists. Most portages are under a mile.

If you arrive in the area without a boat, you can rent one at the marinas on most lakes, or try **Tickner's Adirondack Canoe Outfitters** (☎ 315-369-6286; 1 Riverside Dr, Old Forge; canoe per day $22), behind Keye's Pancake House. Tickner's also offers shuttle service and river-rail trips that include canoeing down the Moose River and riding back to town on the Adirondack Scenic Railroad (from $42).

HIKING & FISHING

For fishing trips and car camping, the Moose River Plains Wild Forest has an extensive road system connecting small lakes and ponds. Lost Ponds (2 miles round-trip, easy) leads to a popular fishing hole for brook trout. Spring wildflowers and bird-watching are other draws to this area. The Ha-de-ron-dah Wilderness is one of the least used areas of the park recommendable for extended backpacking trips. Middle Settlement Lake (6.4 miles round-trip, moderate) is one spur leading into this area;

the trail connects to a small lake and lean-tos. For maps and advice, see the Old Forge tourist information centre (p225).

Sleeping & Eating

There is no shortage of basic motels along Rte 28 between the towns of Blue Mountain Lake and Old Forge.

Limekiln Lake Campground (☎ 315-357-4401; Rte 28; campsite $14; ☽ May-Sep) Between Old Forge and Blue Mountain Lake, Limekiln is about 3 miles southeast of the town of Inlet and Rte 28. This is a big public campground, with room for RVs. Boat rentals are available.

Alger Island Campground (☎ 315-369-3224; campsite $12; ☽ May-Sep) A more interesting campsite is available for boaters only. Alger Island is about 8 miles east of Old Forge near the foot of Fourth Lake. Minimal facilities include toilets but no showers. There are 15 lean-tos and two tent sites, in addition to a picnic area and hiking trail that circles the 40-acre island.

Nick's Lake Campground (☎ 315-369-3314; 800-456-2267; Rte 28; campsite $16; ☽ May-Sep) From Rte 28 through Old Forge, turn onto the road beside the school and follow the signs.

Moose River House B&B (☎ 315-369-3104; 12 Birch St; d with/without bath $125/90) In the village of Thendara, this Victorian themed B&B has four rooms, two with private bath.

Van Auken's Inne & Restaurant (☎ 315-369-3033; fax 315-369-3808; www.vanaukensinne.com; Forge St, Thendara; d $70-90) This town landmark is across the street from the Adirondack Scenic Railroad station. It's a beautiful old white Victorian building with a long front porch. Their seasonal hours are complicated, so call beforehand.

Seventh Lake House Restaurant (☎ 315-357-6028; 479 Rte 28; dishes $10-20; ☽ daily Jun-Sep, Sat & Sun Oct-May) Above the village of Inlet, at the west edge of Seventh Lake, this is one of the best dinner spots west of Blue Mountain Lake. The fare is contemporary American, but the owners call it 'civilized dining in the wilderness.'

Farm Restaurant (☎ 315-369-6199; Rte 28, Thendara; dishes $7-15; ☽ 7am-2pm summer) Across the street from the post office in Thendara, this place has character written all over it, from the food to the antiques to Frank, the owner.

Thousand Islands & St Lawrence Seaway

CONTENTS

The watery world of the Thousand Islands and the St Lawrence Seaway is nothing short of fantastic. The stunning blue waters of Lake Ontario and the St Lawrence River provide a vivid backdrop to the small towns and villages, many with a weathered hard-times feel, sprinkled throughout the region. The air is crisp and clean and the breathtaking views in abundance, with never-ending pink and purple sunsets and a distinct off-the-beaten-path allure. If you arrive from crowded New York City or industrial Syracuse you'll feel as if you've stepped into another world. Life moves slower in this part of the state, way up north by the Canadian border.

The lower part of the St Lawrence River, at the outflow of Lake Ontario, is dotted with 1864 small islands known as the Thousand Islands. Some of these islands are so small they appear only as specks on a map. Appearances, in this case, are not deceiving: most of the islands are home to a few solitary trees, a jumble of rocks, or a single – albeit magnificent – vacation house. A few islands are large enough to support small towns, summer camps, state parks and dense growths of pines, birches and oaks. The region's big activity, especially in Clayton, is fishing for muskie, northern pike and largemouth bass.

Running through the center of the river is the St Lawrence Seaway, a major transit line for huge oil, grain and ore transports traveling from the Atlantic through the Great Lakes.

HIGHLIGHTS

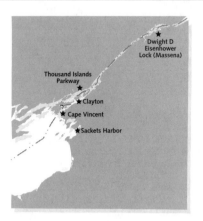

■ **Best Drive**
Canada's Thousand Islands Parkway offers the region's most scenic coastline, with breathtaking views piling up one after the other (p232).

■ **Best Package Option**
The sleeping, eating and activities packages at the Thousand Islands Inn in Clayton: everything from fishing trips to wreck-diving adventures (p235).

■ **Best Town**
Sackets Harbor tops the quaintness charts, with splendid lake views, rich history and good restaurants (p237).

■ **Best Place to Stay**
HI-AYH Tibbetts Point Lighthouse Hostel in Cape Vincent. If you don't mind dorms, you'll get crashing waves, rugged coastlines and out-of-this world sunset views at this unique place (p236).

■ **Best Place to See Big Ships**
Dwight D Eisenhower Lock in Massena. It's stunning to see a 700ft oceangoing ship passing through the narrow canal (p238).

CLIMATE

Winters in the Thousand Islands and St Lawrence Seaway are long, harsh and snowy. Many tourist attractions, hotels and restaurants close in September or October and do not open again until April, May or even June. The peak tourist season is July and August when temperatures average in the 70s and 80s Fahrenheit. Temperatures (and crowds) drop in September and it's a good time to visit, especially when the foliage begins to change. Leaves usually peak in October.

NATIONAL & STATE PARKS

The **St Lawrence Islands National Park** in Canada is the region's best. With about 9 sq km of land area it is the smallest national park in the Canadian system. Primarily water-based, its 21 granite islands and numerous tiny islets are a unique river landscape strewn along 80km (50 miles) of the upper St Lawrence River between Kingston, in the west, and Brockville, in the east. It has plenty of opportunities for camping (p234), although most of the sites are only accessible by boat.

There are numerous US state parks in the region, many on the islands themselves, which also offer good camping and hiking opportunities. Among them is **Wellesley Island State Park** (p232), near Alexandria Bay, which spreads over 2600 acres and has hiking trails, a beach, a campground, miniature and nine-hole golf courses and a marina. The park also has an excellent nature center.

Robert Moses State Park (p238) is another option. Located near Massena, it's one of the prettiest parks in the northeast, situated on both the mainland and Barnhart Island. The park is spacious and serene, with lots of animals. There are white-tailed deer, beaver, bobcat and coyote along with several songbirds, waterfowl and birds of prey. The park (and beach) is open year-round, and there is a visitors center and a nature interpretive center.

GETTING THERE & AROUND

The region has limited commercial-airline service. **US Airways** (☎ 800-428-4322) has daily routes from its hub in Pittsburgh, PA, and Watertown, NY. United, American and Delta serve Syracuse, which is 45 miles south of Watertown via I-81.

Both **Greyhound** (☎ 800-231-2222; www.greyhound.com) and **Adirondack Trailways** (☎ 800-858-8555) serve parts of the Thousand Islands region; call their offices or check their websites for schedules and bus-depot locations. During summer **Thousand Islands Bus Line** (☎ 315-788-8146) runs from Watertown to several Thousand Islands towns, including Alexandria Bay and Clayton.

Syracuse, 45 miles south of Watertown, has the nearest Amtrak terminal to the region. VIA rail in Canada makes a stop at nearby Cornwall (a Canadian city across from Massena) and continues to Montreal.

A car is almost essential to explore much of the Thousand Islands region. I-81 is the main north–south road in the region and connects Syracuse to Watertown and the St Lawrence Seaway at the international border between Canada and the US via the Thousand Islands International Bridge. From I-81, the primary road heading northeast is Rte 12/37, which connects Alexandria Bay, Ogdensburg and Massena. Rte 11 is another southwest–northeast road connecting Watertown to Malone in the northern Adirondacks.

From New York City, take I-80 west to Rte 380 north to I-81 north; or take I-87 north to I-90 west to I-81 north. From Philadelphia, take Rte 476 north to I-81 north. From Boston, take I-90 west to I-81.

The only auto ferry across the St Lawrence River leaves from Cape Vincent at the source of the river, and goes to Wolfe Island, where another ferry travels to the Canadian mainland.

THOUSAND ISLANDS

The towns of the Thousand Islands – Alexandria Bay, Clayton, Cape Vincent and Sackets Harbor – are all within easy driving distance of each other, so it's possible to stay in one and eat in another. Drives between the villages offer stunning views and all can be reached via the scenic Seaway Trail (see boxed text on p237), which at times hugs the St Lawrence River and Lake Ontario.

ALEXANDRIA BAY & AROUND

☎ 315 / pop 1300

With a slightly tacky, yet old-fashioned feel, Alexandria Bay (Alex Bay) is a popular tourist destination and one of the largest towns in the area. Fading neon signs and boarded-up buildings share the tree-lined streets with

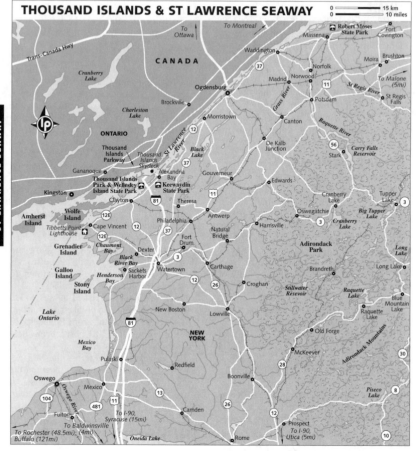

1950s-era mom-and-pop stores, homegrown motels and kitschy souvenir shops. The village boasts some good attractions and gorgeous watery vistas – especially at sunset.

At the turn of the 20th century, Alex Bay was a bustling resort town boasting several large hotels. Today these grand hotels are gone, but many of the estates – built during the same time on privately owned islands – remain. The largest of these estates is George Boldt's castle on Heart Island, located outside of town.

Alex Bay does get crowded with tourists from mid-June through August. But its location – near the Thousand Islands International Bridge, 4 miles north of I-81 on the St Lawrence River – makes it a good base from which to explore the region. If you have a limited amount of time, you can take a boat tour from here to explore the nearby islands. If time is not a factor, rent a boat and meander the waterways.

Orientation & Information

The village's commercial strip is made up of James, Market and Church Sts. Here you will find shops, tour-boat companies, bars and restaurants. The area is easily walkable, taking up just a few blocks.

The **Alexandria Bay Chamber of Commerce** (☎ 315-482-9531, 800-541-2110; 11 Market St; ☀ 9am-5pm mid-May–early Oct, 9am-5pm Mon-Fri early Oct–mid-May), off James St, has information on the region. The **1000 Islands International Council**

STORIES OF THE THOUSAND ISLANDS

Some of the islands are tiny. Some contain lavish homes or gorgeous campgrounds; others are home to just a scraggly tree and a few rocks. Many have stories to tell. We've searched for some of the strangest.

The **Price is Right Island** was given away on the *Price is Right* game show in 1964.

Longue View Island is the only artificial island; it was created by a doting husband wishing to build a summer home for his wife. The story goes that the man searched long and hard for an island to suit his wife's tastes, but when he couldn't find one he decided to build his own by filling in the area between two shoals. He then constructed a luxurious mansion. His efforts were fruitless – his wife ended up running away with another man.

The Skull and Bones Society, a famous secret society at Yale University, owns **Deer Island**. President George W Bush was a member of this society when he attended Yale.

Grindstone Island was the home of the last existing one-room schoolhouse in New York State, which didn't close its doors until 1989. The schoolhouse accommodated children between kindergarten and the 6th grade in its one room.

The Thousand Islands Bridge Authority gave **Florence Island** to Arthur Godfrey in exchange for free advertising. Godfrey sung the song 'Florence on the St Lawrence.'

Abbie Hoffman lived incognito on **Wellesley Island**, under the name Barry Freed, after jumping bail in 1974 on cocaine charges. At one point in time the Thousand Islands Golf Club on Wellesley Island was the most exclusive club in the world – it cost $100,000 to join and another $10,000 a year to stay a member.

Church services are held in the water on the large crescent-shaped inlet that's **Half Moon Bay** in the St Lawrence River near Gananoque, Ontario. During July and August parishioners enjoy open skies as they sit in boats of every sort – skiffs to rowboats to luxury cruisers – on the river and listen to the interdenominational worship services. Visiting ministers or local clergymen conduct the services on a natural stone pulpit. Ushers paddling about in their canoes pass out prayer books and hymnals to the floating congregation.

(☎ 315-482-2520, 800-847-5263; Collins Landing; ☺ 8am-5pm Apr-Oct) is under the Thousand Islands Bridge and promotes tourism along the St Lawrence River in both New York and Ontario. It is a good source of information on fishing, camping and attractions for the entire region.

For information on boat and houseboat rentals in the area, contact **Remar Shipyard** (☎ 315-686-4170; 510 Theresa St, Clayton), 10 miles southwest of Alex Bay.

Sights & Activities

There is nothing much to see in Alex Bay itself. Sightseeing focuses on island-hopping.

BOLDT CASTLE

Billed as the site of the 'saddest true love story ever told,' it's hard to skip this 127-room, Rhineland-inspired stone **castle** (☎ 315-482-2501; adult/child $4.75/3; ☺ 10am-6pm mid-May–mid-Oct) on Heart Island, across from Alex Bay, even if it is a tourist trap. The story begins in 1900, when George Boldt, who had worked his way up from the kitchen to ownership

of New York City's Waldorf-Astoria Hotel, decided to have a castle built for his wife, Louise. He bought Heart Island and had it reshaped into a heart. As the castle was nearing completion in 1904, with $2.5 million invested, Louise died. Boldt stopped all work on the estate, and the building and grounds were left to decay until 1977, when the Thousand Islands Bridge Authority took over the castle and began the slow process of renovation.

The castle, with its numerous towers, is quite dramatic from the outside. It's the view from the inside, however, that sends chills down your spine. Romantic yet haunting, the tramping of hundreds of visitors' feet can't take away the cold, eerie feel the place gives off. During its long period of abandonment much of the interior was stripped of its marble and exotic wood detailing, leaving only bare walls, but this bareness seems to befit the castle's tragic tale.

The only way to reach the castle is by boat (see Tours, p232).

WELLESLEY ISLAND STATE PARK

Spread over 2600 acres on Wellesley Island, this **state park** (admission $6) has hiking trails, a beach, a campground, miniature and nine-hole golf courses and a marina. At the southeast end of the park is **Minna Anthony Common Nature Center** (☎ 315-482-2479; admission free; ☼ 8am-6pm daily), which includes a museum and wildlife sanctuary and encompasses a 600-acre peninsula. There are fascinating collections of live fish and amphibians, and an observation hive of busy honeybees.

One of the best activities offered by the center is the Ecology Canoe Paddle, a daily ride in a 36ft canoe along river shorelines with a guide who is knowledgeable about the natural history of the St Lawrence River. The trip lasts about two hours, and the cost is $2 for adults and $1 for children.

Loons, geese, eagles, robins and blue jays will keep bird-watchers busy. If you have time, rent a canoe and explore the park's watery fringes.

To reach Wellesley Island State Park you must cross the Thousand Islands Bridge. Built in 1938, this skinny steel suspension bridge extends over five spans and stretches for 7 miles. The park lies at the end of the first span (Exit 51) coming from the I-81 and the US mainland. There is a $2 toll to cross the bridge going northbound, but it's free southbound.

THOUSAND ISLANDS PARK

Also on Wellesley Island is the town of Thousand Islands Park. Originally a Methodist camp meeting ground, today it's home to summer residents who carefully maintain elaborate 19th-century Victorian homes painted in an array of pastels and decorated with ornate carvings, shingled roofs and more gables than you can count.

Thousand Islands Park was once a private golf club, and membership came with a hefty price tag – $100,000 got you initiated, then you had to fork over another $10,000 a year to stay in. Today, the place is on the National Registry of Historic Places and features its own movie theater, playground, library and post office. Unlike the old days, visitors are free to wander around, although some residents will seem less than thrilled that you're there.

DETOUR – ATTRACTIONS IN CANADA

Once you've finished touring Wellesley Island continue across the Thousand Islands Bridge into Canada and visit the **Thousand Islands Skydeck** (☎ 613-659-2335; Hill Island, Canada; ☼ 8.30am-7pm May, 8.30am-9pm Jun-Aug, 9am-6pm Sep-Oct). You can ride an elevator to the top of this 395ft observation tower, which offers excellent views of the islands and the river. To enter Canada, US citizens may be asked to show valid ID or passport at the border; international visitors need a passport. When you're finished continue across the bridge to the Canadian mainland and look for signs for the **Thousand Islands Parkway**. The parkway runs parallel to Hwy 401 for 25 miles between Gananoque and Brockville, and offers some of the most scenic coastline in the region. Breathtaking views pile up one after the other. If you want to get out, there's a paved path that runs along the parkway's length. Be sure to bring a camera.

The town is south of the state park at the very tip of Wellesley Island. It is well signposted.

Tours

The only way to reach Boldt Castle (and all the other islands in the St Lawrence River) is by boat. Many companies offer tours. **Uncle Sam Boat Tours** (☎ 315-482-2611, 800-253-9229; 45 James St; adult/child $7/4; ☼ May-Oct) runs an hourly shuttle on triple-deck paddle wheelers to Heart Island. Once there you can stay as long as you like. The company also offers a variety of dinner and sightseeing tours.

Motor and platoon boats as well as canoes to explore the islands independently can be rented through **O'Briens U-Drive** (☎ 315-482-9548; 51 Walton St). Boats are rented by the hour, day or week and you're provided with maps of the river and advice on where to go. Call for prices.

Sleeping

There sleeping options for all budgets in Alex Bay. Many places shut down from October to April when the snow starts piling up. Most places have private parking lots, or else there is off-street parking. Air-conditioning is standard.

BUDGET & MID-RANGE

Bach's Alexandria Bay Inn (☎ 315-482-9697; 2 Church St; d from $60) Painted in pale lavender with purple trim, this lovely Italianate Victorian sits just off the downtown area, across from the St Lawrence River. Rooms are handsomely furnished and antiques abound – there's even a Persian rug supposedly purchased during the prohibition for $20 and a bottle of old whiskey.

Maple Crest Motel (☎ 315-482-9518; 11 Crossmon St; d $85) This charming little place feels much more like a B&B than a motel. Located in a white house that's been expanded to create motel rooms, it has a nice front porch with chairs and plenty of flowers. Breakfast is included. Rooms are simple, but have personal touches like teddy bears on the bed. The owners are very friendly. If you are traveling alone you may get a discount.

SS Suellen B&B (☎ 315-482-2137; 26 Otter St; d $95; 🔉) This place has three rooms in a renovated and compact suburban-style house. The B&B has its own boat access. It closes from October to mid-April.

Edgewood Resort (☎ 315-482-9922, 888-334-3966; 22467 Edgewood Park Rd; d from $85; 🔉) With beautifully landscaped grounds, Edgewood is right on the river just west of downtown. The resort's 160 rooms are in motel buildings with contemporary, if unexceptional, decor. There is a restaurant and bar, a beach and a dock.

TOP END

Alex Bay has a number of large resorts as well a few top-end inns and B&Bs.

Hart House (☎ 315-482-5683; www.harthouseinn.com; 21979 Club House Rd; d from $125) In a rambling old house on Wellesley Island, this elegant B&B has seven beautifully decorated rooms and open all year. There are special packages in the winter. Extra touches include candlelit breakfasts and a cozy great room. In winter there is cross-country skiing from the back door.

Riveredge (☎ 315-482-9917, 800-365-6987; www .riveredge.com; 17 Holland St; d $170; 🔉) Rebuilt in the late 1980s after a devastating fire, this is the nicest of the large resorts in town. The 129 rooms all have views of the river. The channel-view rooms are the nicest as they open up to the most spectacular scenery. Rooms are furnished with armoires and double beds and are decorated with paintings by local artists. The most luxurious rooms have Jacuzzis. There are indoor and outdoor pools, an exercise room and a boat dock. Rates vary greatly depending on the room and the season. In the winter the cheapest rooms go for $100. During the fall and spring these rooms cost $126 and there are numerous packages throughout the year. The resort also has a fine-dining restaurant, a casual restaurant and a lounge.

Bonnie Castle (☎ 315-482-4511, 800-955-4511; www.bonniecastle.com; Outer Holland St; d from $114; 🔉) One of the most popular resorts with the locals is this expansive place. Rooms come with wet bars, but are distinctly motel-like. That said, amenities abound: there are tennis courts, an entertainment complex, private beach, nightclub, miniature golf courses, swimming pools and restaurants. Winter rates are a steal – come during the week and you'll only pay $48 for a double.

Eating & Drinking

Alex Bay's best upscale dining options are at the restaurants in the Riveredge, Edgewood or Bonnie Castle resorts, and many visitors choose to dine here. There are several informal dining spots in the downtown area and a string of fast-food joints. Again, many local places shut during the winter.

Port Shamrock (☎ 315-482-6217; 2 James St; mains $6) Right on the water, there are excellent sunset views from the large outdoor patio here. Food is burger- and sandwich-oriented, but the burgers are very large.

WHAT'S IN A NAME?

There are competing ideas as to how the Thousand Islands were created. An Iroquois legend has it that the Great Spirit, or Master of Life, created a bountiful and beautiful land for the Indian nations that had agreed not to fight each other. When the nations broke their promise, the Great Spirit sent messengers to retrieve the paradise in a huge blanket. As the land was being lifted into the sky, it fell out of the blanket and broke into thousands of pieces, creating the Thousand Islands. Modern geologic legend suggests that the islands are part of a granite mass that was crushed, twisted and pushed above the surface over time.

CAMPING

Camping is understandably very popular in the Thousand Islands, and there are campgrounds in both the US and Canadian state parks on the various islands of the St Lawrence River. For general information about camping in the Thousand Islands area, call ☎ 315-482-2593 (for US parks) and ☎ 613-923-5261 (for Canadian parks).

Wellesley Island State Park (☎ 315-482-2722; on I-81; campsite $13) This is the largest US campground in the area. The park has 430 sites (including 10 cabins) and hot showers and extends from the St Lawrence River to Eel Bay. Campsites accommodate up to six people. Follow the signs after crossing the Thousand Islands Bridge onto Wellesley Island. The campground is 2 miles west of exit 51 on I-81.

Keewaydin State Park (☎ 315-482-3331; Rte 12; campsite $13; ☺ May-Sep) This is one of the prettiest parks in the region, with several old gazebos. There are 41 campsites. The park is on Rte 12 half a mile west of Alex Bay.

St Lawrence Islands National Park (☎ 613-923-5261; Box 468, RR 3, Mallorytown Landing, Ontario, Canada; campsite C$10) With about 9 sq km of land area this is the smallest national park in the Canadian system. Primarily water-based, its 21 granite islands and numerous tiny islets are a unique river landscape strewn along 80km of the upper St Lawrence River between Kingston, in the west, and Brockville, in the east. The park has 21 campsites – 15 are open for camping and the rest are for day use. All of the sites are easily accessible by boat from either side of the river, but only one accessible by car. They all have outhouses, and almost all have water pumps and shelter, usually cabins with camp stoves. The Canadian government even provides firewood.

The one car-accessible site is at **Mallorytown Landing**, at the park headquarters. This site has flush toilets, running water and a boat launch for getting to Grenadier Island. It is 15 miles north of the Thousand Islands Bridge, on the Canadian mainland. Take Canada Rte 401 north and look carefully for the sign for Mallorytown Landing, which is easy to miss. You'll see a parking area and boat launch on your right along the river. The park's headquarters is hidden behind the greenery on the side of the road opposite the parking area.

As for the other island camping sites in St Lawrence Islands National Park, you'll find **Stovin**, off the coast of the Canadian city of Brockville; **East**, **West**, **North** and **Centre Grenadier** and **Adelaide**, on or near Grenadier Island; **Georgina**, between Hill Island and the Canadian mainland near the town of Ivy Lea; **Mulcaster**, between Wellesley Island and Canada; **Camelot**, **Endymion**, **Gordon**, **Thwartway**, **Mermaid**, **Aubrey**, **Beaurivage** and **McDonald**, between Grindstone Island, offshore from Clayton, NY, and the Canadian city of Gananoque; and **Milton** and **Cedar**, off the shore of the Canadian town of Kingston.

There is no reservation system for the St Lawrence Islands National Park campsites. On summer weekends, many sites fill up by Friday, so you may want to think about arriving on Thursday night. In addition to camping fees, you will pay a mooring fee (C$6 to C$18) for your boat. All payments are done on a self-registration system. You calculate camping and mooring fees and put them in an envelope and deposit it in a slot at the site.

Cavallario's Steak & Seafood House (☎ 315-482-9867; 26 Church St; mains $18-22; ☺ dinner) The facade here has been made to look like a castle, and the interior is decorated in a red velvet 'knight' motif, including armor and weapons. The dinner selections are standard medieval fare, such as steak and seafood. The restaurant is half a block south of James St.

Brass Tacks (☎ 315-482-9805; 24 James St; mains $5-7) This low-key tavern serves salads, burgers and sandwiches, as well as a few Mexican dishes such as deep-fried jalapenos and fajitas.

Dockside Pub (☎ 315-482-9849; 17 Market St; mains $5-10) This pub has a sports theme. Located near the water, it's popular with locals. Food focuses on pizza, salads and sandwiches.

Bootleggers Café Nightclub (☎ 315-482-3303; cnr James & Church St) This is a popular nightspot with a long bar, pool tables, dartboards and nightly drink specials. It closes in winter (mid-October to mid-April).

Getting There & Around

From the south, take I-81 to just before its northern terminus at the Thousand Islands

Bridge and exit at Rte 12. Alex Bay is 4 miles to the east. From the northeast, take Rte 37 along the St Lawrence Seaway to Alex Bay.

CLAYTON
☎ 315 / pop 2100

Weathered-looking buildings and a few galleries and antique stores make up the small downtown of sleepy Clayton, which has a distinct lived-in and less touristy vibe than other places in the region. Once a shipbuilding and lumbering port, Clayton, 11 miles southwest of Alex Bay, today provides services for summer island residents and fishermen, fishing being the place's big draw.

Downtown is just a few blocks of James St and Riverside Dr. The **Clayton Chamber of Commerce** (☎ 315-686-3771; 510 Riverside Dr; ⏱ 9am-5pm Jul-Sep, 9am-4pm Mon-Fri Oct-Jun) can give you lists of licensed fishing guides.

Sights & Activities
Clayton has a few museums around town.

ANTIQUE BOAT MUSEUM
One hundred and fifty freshwater boats ranging from a Native American dugout to birch-bark canoes reside at this **museum** (☎ 315-686-4104; 750 Mary St; adult/child $6/2; ⏱ 9am-5pm May-Oct). In addition there are examples of the St Lawrence Skiff and the thickly varnished Kris-Kraft pleasure boats that once belonged to the region's millionaire summer residents. It also contains extensive historical exhibits – the most unique of these focuses on Clayton's prohibition-era rum-running days when liquor was smuggled across the border from Canada on everything from sleds to skates.

THOUSAND ISLANDS MUSEUM
This **museum** (☎ 315-686-5794; 312 James St; adult/child $6/2; ⏱ 10am-4pm May-Oct) is the home of the 'Muskie Hall of Fame,' the region's most prized fish; there is a replica of the world-record muskellunge – it weighted 69lb, 15oz. In addition there is a giant collection of hand-carved decoys, a popular regional folk art, and assorted fishing paraphernalia on display.

HOUSEBOAT RENTALS
Exploring the region on a houseboat is a popular activity. Unfortunately, high insurance costs have forced most of the rental companies that once operated in the towns along the St Lawrence to close. Although many still operate in Canada, in the US **Remar Houseboat Rental** (☎ 315-686-3579; 510 Theresa St) is the lone survivor. Call for prices and advance reservations. The company will provide you with operating instructions.

Sleeping & Eating
Clayton has a couple of good options for sleeping and eating.

Thousand Islands Inn (☎ 315-686-3030; www.1000-islands.com; 335 Riverside Dr; d from $60) This place claims to have invented Thousand Islands salad dressing in its restaurant. Whether or not that's true, the inn is the best place to stay in town. It's a charming old brick hotel with large rooms, and it offers a dizzying array of packages, the most interesting of which are the wreck-diving packages. The exceptionally clear water of the St Lawrence, along with an abundance of well-preserved wrecks, make the area a popular dive spot. The inn offers specials that include two nights accommodation, meals and two days of diving for $450 per person. The place also does charter fishing trips and adventure packages that include tours of the area. Check the website for more information.

The inn has a restaurant (mains $13 to $20) with early-bird dinner specials and a great fisherman's bar made of rough wooden planks.

Bertrands Motel (☎ 315-686-3641; 229 James St; s/d $60/70) This white, two-story motel in the middle of town caters to anglers. Rooms are basic, but large and clean.

The Clipper Inn (☎ 315-686-3842; Rte 12; mains $15-20; ⏱ dinner) This is one of the finest dining spots in the Thousand Islands region. Daily specials generally feature fresh seafood, prime rib and pasta. It's very popular with locals.

Koffee Kove (☎ 315-686-2472; 220 James St; mains $3-8) This sandwich shop/diner is a family-oriented restaurant with wooden tables and chairs and a big mural of the Thousand Islands on the wall. It does good chili and breakfasts and has a different dinner special each night.

CAPE VINCENT
☎ 315 / pop 760

Situated on the cape where the St Lawrence River meets Lake Ontario, Cape Vincent boasts stupendous scenery. A drive around the roads hugging the water, especially heading towards the Tibbetts Point Lighthouse, reveals crashing waves, rugged coastline and outstanding sunsets.

The town was named for Vincent LeRay de Chaumount, who came here seeking asylum for the failing Napoleonic government, and Napoleon's brother and sister lived here briefly before returning to France. The village celebrates its French heritage every mid-July with a festival called French Heritage Day.

There are few attractions in Cape Vincent; the emphasis is on black-bass fishing. The main street, Broadway, is lined with towering trees, big old houses and just a few places to eat. Wander down any of the numerous side streets, however, and the road will literally stop at the water's edge, where there will be a conveniently placed bench on which to sit and contemplate.

Cape Vincent Chamber of Commerce (☎ 315-654-2481; 175 James St; ☒ 9am-5pm Mon-Fri), near the ferry dock, can give information about fishing licenses and guides. Next to the chamber is the **Cape Vincent Historical Museum** (☎ 315-654-4400; 175 N James St; ☒ 10am-4pm Mon-Sat year-round, noon-4pm Sun Jul-Aug). This little museum documents the town's history, and has a collection of tiny figures created out of scrap metal by a local farmer.

Sleeping & Eating

Cape Vincent has two excellent lodging choices, perhaps the best (and most unique) in the region. Eating is more of a problem – options are quite limited and you may want to drive to either Alex Bay or Sackets Harbor for dinner.

HI-AYH Tibbetts Point Lighthouse Hostel (☎ 315-654-3450; 33439 County Rte 6; dm $15) For sure one of the most unique and picturesque hostels in the country, this place is on the grounds of a lakeside lighthouse built in 1854. The 69ft white conical stucco lighthouse is still used by the coast guard. Dorms are in two white houses that used to be the lighthouse-keepers' quarters and the entire place is on the National Historic Register. Even if you don't usually stay in hostels we'd suggest at least checking this one out. The drive alone is worth the trip, as the road hugs the edge of the lake. The hostel is right on the point and you can sit

in the garden and listen to the waves crash about as the sun goes down. The hostel is open from mid-May to late October, following the Wolfe Island ferry schedule that runs from town (see below). There is a 9.30am to 5pm lockout.

The hostel is 3 miles west of town. To get there, take Rte 12E west from Clayton into Cape Vincent, which becomes Broadway as you enter town. Continue west on Broadway, which becomes Lighthouse Rd and leads you to the lighthouse/hostel.

Buccaneer Motel and B&B (☎ 315-654-2975; 230 N Point St; d $75-185) Right on the river in a beautiful location, the B&B part of this place features a gorgeously decorated lounge with floral cushioned wicker couches facing floor-to-ceiling glass windows from which you can watch the boats pass by. If it's warm sit outside on the lawn in big cushioned chairs or lounge in the hammock. The B&B has four well-appointed rooms that come with a big breakfast, but it is only open in summer. The motel is next door and has 10 rooms that extend along a single corridor. The rooms are nicely decorated with dark-wood furniture. The motel is open year-round.

Roxy Motel (☎ 315-654-2456; 111 E Broadway; d $50; mains $10-12) This place is a little rough around the edges, but that's part of its charm. The motel's restaurant is a hole-in-the-wall joint with aging photos of anglers and mounted fish on the walls. It's known for its Friday-night fish fry. There are pool tables and a bar. Upstairs are 10 simple guestrooms.

Captain Jack's (☎ 315-654-3333; 361 Club St; mains $6-18) Perched on the marina in a weathered old building, this restaurant and bar has a good outdoor patio and pool tables inside. Food is only served on Friday and Saturday nights, however, although the bar is open daily. The menu focuses on fish with cheaper sandwich options also available.

Getting There & Around

Cape Vincent is on Rte 12E, 28 miles southwest of Alex Bay.

Wolfe Island Ferries (☎ 315-783-0638; ☒ 8am-7pm May-Oct) makes 11 trips daily (weather permitting) each way between Cape Vincent and Wolfe Island, Canada. The crossing takes 10 minutes and costs $6 for a car,

---

DETOUR – SEAWAY TRAIL

Leisurely making its way through small towns and villages, the New York State Seaway Trail is a 450-mile scenic driving and bicycling route on a series of highways following the seaway through New York (and northern Pennsylvania) along the St Lawrence River, Lake Ontario and Lake Erie. The well-marked trail includes Rtes 104, 3, 12E, 12 and 37 (from Oswego to Massena) and provides an interesting alternative to superhighways. Green and white 'Seaway Trail' signs help guide you along the historic route. There are also 42 brown and white interpretive signs along the trail, marking events that took place here during the War of 1812. Much of the trail makes for magnificent driving – you'll hug the deep, deep blue waters of Lake Ontario sprinkled with colorful fishing boats or meander through fields, across streams and past dilapidated red barns.

$1 for passengers. The ferry then continues from Wolfe Island to Kingston, Canada, which takes another 35 minutes and is free. The schedule may change slightly each year. The ferry dock in Cape Vincent is at the north terminus of James St.

SACKETS HARBOR

☎ 315 / pop 1400

Sackets Harbor is one of those places you stumble upon, perhaps not expecting much, and are taken away by its charm. Perched on a bluff overlooking the shores of Lake Ontario, it's a picturesque village with a strong sense of history. When the sun is out, making the lake sparkle, and the trees are starting to change colors, it's a stunning place to photograph.

The Americans won a key naval battle here at the expense of the British during the War of 1812. After the war, the harbor's strategic importance made it a major shipping point. That lasted until the 1850s, when the railroad arrived. Today much of the town depends on seasonal tourism. Guides working out of nearby Lake Ontario ports feature trophy fishing for salmon and lake trout. An annual Oktoberfest celebrates the town's history during the second week of October.

The **Sackets Harbor Chamber of Commerce** (☎ 315-646-1700; 301 W Main St; 🕙 10am-4pm Jun-Aug) can provide information on fishing guides and licenses. The **Sackets Harbor Visitors Center** (☎ 315-646-2321) shares the same building and hours as the chamber.

The **Sackets Harbor Battlefield State Historic Site** (☎ 315-646-3634; cnr Main & Washington St; admission $1; 🕙 10am-5pm Wed-Sat year-round, 1-5pm Sun May-Aug) is a former naval base (which was maintained until the 1870s in case of a military attack by Canada) where two battles were fought during the War of 1812. The site has a small house-museum tour through the commandant's 1850s four-story residence, as well as a hands-on exhibit of the naval battles, where children can pretend to shoot at the British boats. The grounds stay open year-round and are quite pleasant with numerous benches perched on the edge of the lake. Every mid-July the Battle of Sackets Harbor is re-enacted at the site.

In the heart of town is **Ontario Place** (☎ 315-646-8000; www.ontarioplacehotel.com; 103 General Smith Dr; d from $80), a classy old waterfront hotel with 28 large rooms and 10 whirlpool suites.

The **Barracks Inn Restaurant** (☎ 315-646-2376; 42 Madison Barracks; mains from $14) is part of the old Madison Barracks, which used to house thousands of soldiers during the War of 1812. Today the barracks, a mile east of the village center, have been converted into apartments and restaurants. History is palatable here, and the food is fresh. Seafood and steak mains with an Italian flavor dominate. There is a nice outside dining area overlooking the lake and harbor. As with many establishments in the area, the restaurant is only open from June until Labor Day weekend.

Tin Pan Galley (☎ 315-646-3812; 110 Main St; mains from $10) is the perfect place for an afternoon cocktail. Sit on wrought-iron chairs in the garden – there's even a fountain. It's an informal place serving breakfast, lunch and dinner.

The **Sackets Harbor Brewing Company** (☎ 315-646-2739; 212 W Main St; mains $10-16) is perched right on the harbor overlooking the marina. It has a large seafood menu, but also does pastas and salads. There is seating inside or out. Inside the decor is dark wood, but quite inviting.

ST LAWRENCE SEAWAY

In 1959, the long-sought joint effort of the Canadian and US governments to create a deepwater channel between the Atlantic Ocean and the Great Lakes paid off and the St Lawrence Seaway opened. The Canadians led the effort, and the US joined in when it became apparent that the canal might be built without its involvement – or benefit.

Now operated jointly by both countries, the seaway is a system of 15 locks that allows cargo vessels to travel 2350 miles (8½ sailing days) from the Atlantic Ocean to Duluth, Minnesota, on Lake Superior. Along the way, the water level rises 602ft. The channel is extremely narrow in some places, notably off Alexandria Bay, where a 1976 oil spill wreaked havoc on the ecosystem. The area has never fully recovered. Of the 15 locks, two belong to the US, including the Dwight D Eisenhower Lock near Massena. From here, you can watch ships passing through the lock and learn how the system works.

MASSENA
☎ 315 / pop 11,200
Before the engineering marvel of the St Lawrence Seaway and Eisenhower Lock, Massena was a small industrial town dominated by an aluminum plant. In 1900, Henry Warren led an ambitious canal-digging enterprise between the Grass River and the St Lawrence River. The water in the new canal dropped 45ft in about 3 miles, creating a power source that spurred the town's growth. Today the main reason to stop by this small industrial city is to view the St Lawrence Seaway, which can accommodate ships up to 730ft long and 76ft wide. When the ships pass by it can be an awesome sight.

Sights & Activities
Sights in Massena focus on the seaway, but when you're tired of looking at ships stop by the Robert Moses State Park – it's delightful.

DWIGHT D EISENHOWER LOCK
To see a 700ft oceangoing ship (or 'laker') passing through the narrow canal at Massena is stunning. The best place to see it happen is at the **Eisenhower Lock Visitors Center** (☎ 315-769-2049; Barnhart Island Rd; ☻ 8am-9pm Jun-Aug), just off Rte 37. There are two viewing decks, one above the other. The process takes about 10 minutes, displaces 22 million gallons of water, and involves raising or lowering the ships 42ft into the seaway.

To make sure you get to see a ship passing through, call **Seaway Eisenhower** (☎ 315-769-2422) to hear a 24-hour recorded message giving the estimated arrival times (and ship names) of both ocean-bound and lake-bound ships.

ROBERT MOSES STATE PARK
One of the prettiest **parks** (☎ 315-769-8663; admission $5) in the northeast, Robert Moses is spacious and serene. Situated on both the mainland and Barnhart Island, many animals call the habitat home, including white-tailed deer, beaver, shy (they say) bobcat and coyote, along with several song-

---

DETOUR – OGDENSBURG

Following the banks of the St Lawrence, Ogdensburg is roughly midway between Alexandria Bay and Massena. The town is the oldest settlement in New York and traces its roots back to 1748 when the French established Fort La Presentation. The reason to visit Ogdensburg is for the **Frederic Remington Museum** (☎ 315-393-2425; 303 Washington St; admission $6; ☻ 10am-5pm Mon-Sat, 1-5pm Sun May-Oct, 11am-5pm Tues-Sat Nov-Apr). The town is the artist's boyhood home. The museum houses the largest collection of Remington's bronze sculptures, oil paintings and pen-and-ink sketches, as well as many of the artist's personal effects. Born in 1861, Remington is best known as a chronicler of the American Western experience. He left Yale at 19 and moved to the West, where he spent five years capturing what he saw (frontiersmen and cowboys riding on horseback, soldiers fighting and Native Americans hunting) in photographs, illustrations for newspapers and sketches that would later serve as the basis for his work in bronze and on canvas.

Remington died in 1909 at his home in Connecticut. After his death, his widow returned to Ogdensburg and rented a home, which opened as a museum shortly after her death in 1923.

birds, waterfowl and birds of prey. There is a visitors center and a nature interpretive center with wildlife, natural history and environmental displays, as well as a campground (see opposite). Robert Moses State Park is one of several 'carry in – carry out' parks in New York. Trash barrels have been removed from day-use areas, placing faith in visitors to hang on to their own garbage. The park is reached via a tunnel that passes under the Eisenhower Lock.

Sleeping & Eating

Sleeping options in Massena are slim. You can camp or stay at a chain motel.

Massena EconoLodge & Baurenstraube Restaurant (☎ 315-764-0246; Rte 37W; d $75; mains from $10) This is a relatively upscale EconoLodge off the main motel strip about 2.5 miles west of town. There is also a good German restaurant on the premises that features all-you-can-eat buffets on Friday and Saturday night.

Super 8 Motel (☎ 315-764-1065; Rte 37 & Grove St; d $64) About three blocks from downtown Massena, this motel is decent enough with friendly service and clean, typical rooms.

Robert Moses State Park (☎ 315-769-8663; campsite $13; 🕑 mid-May–mid-Oct) The park has 168 sites.

Viola's Restaurant (☎ 315-764-0329; 209 Center St; mains from $10) Good northern Italian food is served here in casual surroundings.

Getting There & Around

Adirondack Trailways (☎ 800-858-8555) operates bus service between Massena and Lake George ($34, four hours). **Greyhound** (☎ 800-231-2222) operates between Massena and Syracuse ($23, four hours)

Massena is on Rte 37, and most people reach the town by car via I-81 and Rte 12 from the west, via I-87 and Rte 374 from Plattsburgh and via Rtes 20 and 401 from Montreal.

Finger Lakes Region

Rolling green hills planted with rows of corn, long skinny lakes and some of New York's most picturesque villages all comprise the quintessential Finger Lakes experience. It's a good region to get lost in, to take things as slowly as they come. Many roads hug the lakes and turning just a few miles off the main drag will lead you past grapes ripening on the vines, along fields of wildflowers and toward small wineries perfect for an afternoon of ice wine tasting.

The Finger Lakes region derives its name from the 11 lakes running north to south in the western part of the state. Iroquois legend says the lakes are actually the fingerprints of the Great Spirit, created when he reached out his hand to bless the land. Geologists have a different take: they say constant grinding from Ice Age glaciers created the lake valleys, among the deepest on the continent. This geography has yielded a surprisingly productive wine region.

Physical beauty is only one chapter of the Finger Lakes story, however. Civil rights history and women's suffrage runs deep here – Seneca Falls is the birthplace of the American women's rights movement. The area also played an important literary role – Mark Twain wrote some of his most infamous works in the region.

The region is often divided into the Northern Tier – including Canandaigua, Geneva and Seneca Falls – and the Southern Tier – including Ithaca, Corning and Watkins Glen.

FINGER LAKES REGION

HIGHLIGHTS

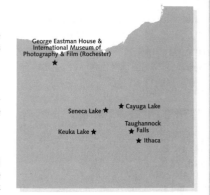

■ **Best Time to Have a Designated Driver**
Driving the lakeside wine trails (p259) on the shores of Seneca, Keuka and Cayuga Lakes and stopping off for late afternoon tastings

■ **Best Reason to Linger**
Visiting a myriad of charming lakeside villages, including lush Ithaca (p242); home to Cornell University

■ **Best History Lesson**
Exploring the region's rich legacy of civil rights and women's suffrage (p256); the area is home to Harriet Tubman, Frederick Douglass and Elizabeth Cady Stanton

■ **Wettest Weekend Spot**
Taughannock Falls (p247), the highest straight waterfall east of the Rocky Mountains

■ **Best Photographer's Pilgrimage**
Rochester's excellent George Eastman House & International Museum of Photography & Film (p260)

CLIMATE

The Finger Lakes experiences four distinct seasons. Winters are cold with temperatures dropping below 0°F. Syracuse and Rochester are famous for a phenomenon known as 'lake effect snow.' The cold white flakes accumulate quickly and bury the cities for months at a time. Summers in the region are hot and muggy with temperatures soaring above 90°F. Fall and spring are good times to visit. Humidity drops and temperatures are moderate. Autumn is particularly splendid when the myriad of trees put on a magnificent color show.

STATE PARKS

The region's spectacular natural sites include the many gorges and waterfalls in **Watkins Glen State Park** (p248) and in the state parks around Ithaca (p244). **Taughannock Falls** (p247), at 215ft, is the highest waterfall around, even higher than its better-known counterpart in Niagara. All of this water creates a multitude of boating, fishing and swimming opportunities. Cycling, hiking and cross-country skiing round out the area's recreational offerings. The region also is home to the **Finger Lakes National Forest** (p250), the smallest national forest in the country and the only one in New York. The Genesee River in **Letchworth State Park** runs for 17 miles beneath a 600ft gorge.

INFORMATION

Finger Lakes Tourism (☎ 315-536-7488; www.finger lakes.org; 309 Lake St, Penn Yan; ☯ 8am-4.30pm) A regional information center.

GETTING THERE & AROUND

For motorists, the area is easily accessible by car. The trip from New York to Ithaca City is a 5½-hour drive; from Philadelphia to Ithaca is a 6½-hour drive.

In the Northern Tier, Rte 20 runs east to west and skirts the northern fringe of most of the lakes. I-90 (the New York State Thruway) links Rochester and Syracuse. On the region's southern edge, Rte 17 connects the towns of Bath, Corning, Elmira and Oswego. In the west, I-390 drops south from Rochester, and in the east I-81 links Syracuse with Cortland. The primary north–south routes within the region are Rtes 21, 14 and 89, which parallel the western shores of Canandaigua, Seneca and Cayuga Lakes.

Public transportation outside Rochester, Syracuse and Ithaca is limited. You must have a car to explore many of the lakeside communities.

If traveling to this region by air or train, see p255 and p262.

SOUTHERN TIER

The towns of the Southern Tier – including Ithaca, Corning and Watkins Glen – derive their appeal from their proximity to the lakes, their village greens and their rural pace. Rte 17 runs through many of them, linking Bath, Corning, Elmira and Oswego. Rte 13 connects Ithaca with these southernmost towns.

ITHACA

☎ 607 / pop 29,287

Surrounded by steep hills and rocky gorges at the edge of Cayuga Lake, Ithaca is a handsome college town dominated by the distinguished Ivy-league ambience of Cornell University. With a permanent population of just about 30,000, Ithaca nearly doubles in size when students return to session at Cornell and nearby Ithaca College, a music conservatory and fine-arts school.

A fusion of old and new buildings, Ithaca is a relaxed, culturally rich place where residential and business districts share the space with creeks and waterfalls. Arrive on an early fall evening, when there's a hint of chill in the air, and the small downtown will be packed. Diners fill outdoor tables at numerous hip restaurants, mimes compete for your attention and small change, various genres of music spill out of the many bars, and window shoppers check out the secondhand bookstores, eclectic shops and art galleries before heading off to catch a show at one of the local theaters.

Orientation

Ithaca's compact downtown is dominated by Ithaca Commons, a pedestrian mall spread along State St. At the east end of the Commons runs Aurora St, which is choke full of restaurants and bars. One block north of the Commons, at the corner of Seneca and Cayuga Sts, stands the DeWitt Mall, a former schoolhouse now home to about 20 shops, galleries and restaurants. Perched high on a

FINGER LAKES REGION

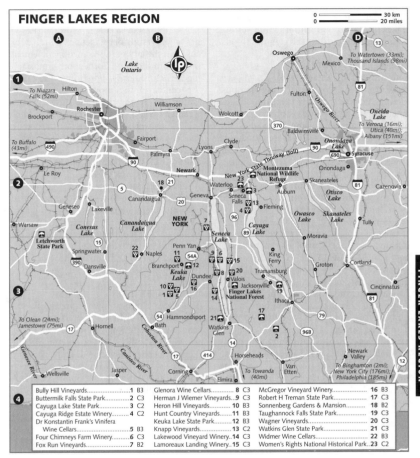

Bully Hill Vineyards	1	B3	Glenora Wine Cellars	8	C3	McGregor Vineyard Winery	16 B3
Buttermilk Falls State Park	2	C3	Herman J Wiemer Vineyards	9	C3	Robert H Treman State Park	17 C3
Cayuga Lake State Park	3	C2	Heron Hill Vineyards	10	B3	Sonnenberg Gardens & Mansion	18 B2
Cayuga Ridge Estate Winery	4	C2	Hunt Country Vineyards	11	B3	Taughannock Falls State Park	19 C3
Dr Konstantin Frank's Vinifera			Keuka Lake State Park	12	B3	Wagner Vineyards	20 C3
Wine Cellars	5	B3	Knapp Vineyards	13	C2	Watkins Glen State Park	21 C3
Four Chimneys Farm Winery	6	C3	Lakewood Vineyard Winery	14	C3	Widmer Wine Cellars	22 B3
Fox Run Vineyards	7	B2	Lamoreaux Landing Winery	15	C3	Women's Rights National Historical Park	23 C2

steep hill to the east of town is Cornell University. The surrounding streets, steep and narrow, comprise Collegetown. On another hill to the south of town is Ithaca College. The campus is flanked by two gorges, Cascadilla Gorge to the south and Fall Creek Gorge to the north, both of which wind their way to Cayuga Lake.

Information

Bookery I and **Bookery II** (☎ 607-273-5055; DeWitt Mall, 215 N Cayuga St) Used, rare and out-of-print books and a rambling collection of contemporary prose, poetry, travel and children's books.

Borealis Bookstore (☎ 607-272-7752; 111 N Aurora St) Specializes in literature, mystery, philosophy and New Age titles.

Cayuga Medical Center (☎ 607-274-4011; 101 Dates Dr) Near Cayuga Lake in the northwest corner of town.

Historic Ithaca and Tompkins County (☎ 607-273-6633; Clinton House, 116 N Cayuga St; 10am-6pm Mon-Sat) Offers free walking-tour brochures of historic downtown sites.

Ithaca/Tompkins County Convention & Visitors Bureau (☎ 607-272-1313, 800-284-8422; www.visitithaca.com; 904 E Shore Drive; 9am-5pm Mon-Fri year-round, 10am-5pm Sat & Sun Jun-Oct) Off Rte 13. Has a good selection of information on the area.

Post office (☎ 607-272-5455; cnr Buffalo & Tioga St; 9am-5pm Mon-Fri, 9am-1pm Sat) Downtown.

Sights & Activities

Most sights and activities in the area are geared for walking, so bring comfortable

FINGER LAKES REGION

shoes. The magnificent landscape around Ithaca provides opportunities for serious hiking or simple strolls through the woods.

CORNELL UNIVERSITY

Founded in 1865, **Cornell** (☎ 607-254-4636; www .cornell.edu) has a lovely, inviting campus, mixing old and new architecture, shaded arcadian walkways and panoramic views of Cayuga Lake. For prime vistas, go to the fifth floor of the **Herbert F. Johnson Museum of Art** (☎ 607-255-6464; University Ave at Central Ave; admission free; ☯ 10am-5pm Tue-Sat), which houses a major Asian collection, as well as pre-Columbian, American and European exhibits. This striking modern structure, designed by acclaimed architect IM Pei, is known on campus as the 'sewing-machine building.'

Cornell's classic Ivy League landscaping includes the **Cornell University Plantations** (☎ 607-255-3020; Plantations Rd; admission free; ☯ 9am-4pm Mon-Fri Sep-Apr, 9am-4pm daily May-Aug) near the eastern end of campus, which is an elaborate and diverse complex with an arboretum, a botanical garden housing an array of poisonous plants and the ever popular 'weed garden.' The plantations contain many miles of nature trails, including paths through Cascadilla and Fall Creek Gorges.

For something different check out the **Wilder Brian Collection** (Uris Hall, cnr East Ave & Tower Rd). Once containing 1600 specimens, today only eight brains remain. Burt Wilder, Cornell's first zoologist, began collecting the brains in the late 1800s. He was trying to prove the size and shape of the brain was directly proportional to a person's race, intelligence and sex. Wilder's research eventually led him to an opposite conclusion. In 1911 he shocked the scientific community by announcing there was no difference between the brains of white and black men.

DOWNTOWN ITHACA

Jam-packed with restaurants, bars and upscale shops in late 19th-century buildings, the pedestrian-only **Ithaca Commons** runs along State St between Aurora and Cayuga Sts and along Tioga St between Seneca and State Sts, and stays hopping day and night.

One block north of the Commons is the **DeWitt Mall**. Once a school building, it now houses about 20 shops, restaurants and galleries, the most famous of which is the **Moosewood Restaurant** (see the boxed text on p246).

The **Tompkins County Museum** (☎ 607-273-8284; 401 E State St; admission free; ☯ 11am-5pm Tue-Sat) has an interesting permanent exhibit that focuses on the city's little-known involvement in the film industry. For a short time starting in 1914, Ithaca – not Hollywood – was the center of the movie-making empire. Unfortunately, the city's often-frigid winter weather made it less than perfect for filmmaking and in 1920, after a few films were shot in the city, the industry headed west.

SAPSUCKER WOODS SANCTUARY

This **sanctuary** (☎ 607-254-2473; 159 Sapsucker Woods Rd; admission free; visitors center ☯ 8am-5pm Mon-Thu, 8am-4pm Fri, 10am-4pm Sat) might turn you into a bird-watcher. The Cornell Lab of Ornithology operates an observatory overlooking a bird-feeding garden and a 10-acre pond full of waterfowl and other wildlife. You can also track birds on the 4 miles of trails, open year-round from dawn to dusk.

ITHACA AREA HIKING

The water tumbles down more than 500ft and forms 10 different waterfalls at **Buttermilk Falls State Park** (☎ 607-273-5761; car $4), two miles south of Ithaca on Rte 13. The park also features ragged cliffs, roaring rapids, a natural swimming hole, deep gorge trails and a campground (p245). A popular trail in the park runs alongside the falls then climbs up to Pinnacle Rock and Treman Lake.

A 3-mile gorge trail that passes 12 cascades, including Devil's Kitchen and Lucifer Falls is the reason to visit **Robert H Treman State Park** (☎ 607-273-3440; car $4), on Rte 13 south of the city. This trail is part of the **Finger Lakes Trail** (www.fingerlakestrail.org), which connects the Appalachian Trail with Canada's Bruce Trail. The entire 776-mile footpath, bordered by waterfalls, glens and glacial lakes, is off-limits to motor vehicles.

Circle Greenway (☎ 607-274-6570) refers to a 10-mile walking circuit that links a series of 30-minute to three-hour walks in and around Ithaca, including Fall Creek, the Waterfront, the Commons and Six Mile Creek Gorge, a mostly level walk that winds through a wildflower preserve. A map is available from either city hall, at the corner of Green and Cayuga Sts, or from the convention & visitors bureau (p243).

ARTSY ITHACA

If you're in the market for some art, you could do a lot worse than Ithaca. About 50 local artists have banded together to form the Greater Ithaca Art Trail. Visitors call ahead to set up self-guided tours to the artists' studios. The artists work in various mediums; you'll find everything from sculpture to handcrafted jewelry to pottery to photography. Though the quality varies, much of it is quite good. Inside the studios you'll often get a chance to see the artists at work and they're happy to sell you finished products. Brochures and maps to the trail are available at visitors centers throughout the area. During October the artists have open studio weekends where you do not have to call ahead to visit. To read profiles of the various artists and download maps to the region, visit www.arttrail.com.

Festivals & Events

Billed as an artistic celebration, the four-day Ithaca Festival, held in the city in late May, showcases performances of more than 1000 local artists and attracts about 35,000 people. For more information go to www.ithacafestival.org.

Sleeping

Ithaca has accommodations options to meet every budget. B&Bs are usually non-smoking and air-conditioning is a standard feature in most places. Parking is plentiful. Note that during major events weekends at Cornell and Ithaca prices may jump and rooms fill up quickly.

BUDGET & MID-RANGE

Buttermilk Falls B&B (☎ 607-272-6767; fax 607-273-3947; 110 E Buttermilk Falls Rd; d from $95) Near the foot of the falls at the edge of town, this charming B&B features large rooms filled with antiques – if you want to splurge go for the room with the double Jacuzzi. The brick building dates back to the early 1800s, and the hosts are well versed on the area. To get there take Rte 13 south towards the falls.

Hillside Inn (☎ 607-272-1000; 518 Stewart Ave; d from $60) This no-frills motel is the best budget option in town. Adjacent to the Cornell campus, rooms are rather tiny and vaguely resemble college dorms; but it's clean and within walking distance to the Commons.

Best Western University Inn (☎ 607-272-6100; www.bestwestern.com/universityinnchapelhill; 1020 Ellis Hollow Rd; d from $119 incl breakfast; 🐾) An attractive motel within walking distance of Cornell, this Best Western provides standard US chain motel rooms with very friendly service.

Buttermilk Falls State Park (☎ 800-456-2267; www.nysparks.state.ny.us; Rte 13; campsite $13) Two miles south of town, the park has 60 campsites in a beautiful setting.

Robert H Treman State Park (☎ 607-273-3440; www.nysparks.state.ny.us; Rte 13; campsite $13, cabin $40; 🕑 mid-May–Nov) Five miles south of Ithaca, nestled within the spectacular state park, are more than 70 campsites and 14 cabins.

TOP END

Statler Hotel (☎ 607-257-2500, 800-541-2501; www.statlerhotel.cornell.edu; 11 East Ave; d from $155) Cornell University's hotel management training school, the 132-room Statler, is the hotel of choice for visiting parents and professors. It matches the campus in quality. Amenities include three restaurants, big banquet rooms, a 93-seat amphitheater and rooms with VCRs and computer modem hookup. There is also free transportation from the airport.

La Tourelle Country Inn (☎ 607-273-2734, 800-765-1492; www.latourelleinn.com; 1550 Danby Rd; d from $149; 🐾) Comfortable, unpretentious, inviting and convenient, La Tourelle sits on a hill with great views of Cayuga Lake, and is close to walking trails. Serve it up year-round on the tennis court affectionately known as the 'bubble.' The inn is 2 miles south of town on Rte 96B.

Holiday Inn (☎ 607-272-1000; www.holidayinnithaca.com; 222 S Cayuga St; d from $150; 🐾) Conveniently located just off the Commons, the Holiday Inn offers the usual full-service upscale chain hotel amenities: comfortable rooms, spotless bathrooms and all the cable channels. It fills up quickly during special events weekends so book ahead.

Eating

Ithaca might have the best variety of eateries in all of upstate New York. Many of the area's restaurants use fresh and seasonal ingredients to prepare international, gourmet and vegetarian fare fit for every budget.

FINGER LAKES REGION

Simeon's on the Commons (☎ 607-272-2212; 224 W State St; mains $10-20) A beautifully laid-out restaurant featuring an ornate Victorian long bar with gilded mirrors and chandelier fans. The outdoor tables get packed on summer nights. Try the Gorgonzola and pear salad ($8).

Lost Dog Café (☎ 607-277-9143; 106-112 S Cayuga St; mains $14) This ultrahip eatery has a mosaic bar and East meets West decor in the dining room. A red wall shares space with exposed brick and Buddha statues; Thai elephants mingle with modern art murals. The food is excellent. The upstairs features a very chilled lounge with lots of candles and couches. Live music on weekends.

John Thomas Steakhouse (☎ 607-273-3464; 1552 Danby Rd; mains from $20) Set in a 150-year-old restored country farmhouse adjacent to La Tourelle Country Inn, this top steakhouse features dry-aged beef, as well as lamb, seafood and chicken mains. This is one of Ithaca's best dining spots, with everything prepared fresh on the premises.

Just a Taste Wine & Tapas Bar (☎ 607-277-9463; 116 N Aurora St; tapas $3-6) A wine rack takes up half of one wall and a large assortment of Spanish tapas is served in a small intimate setting.

Café DeWitt (☎ 607-273-3473; 215 N Cayuga St; mains from $5; ⏰ 8:30am-2:30pm Mon-Sat) Ithaca's favorite breakfast spot, Café DeWitt spreads across the old schoolhouse walkway in the DeWitt Mall, adjacent to the eclectic shops. Fish tanks along one wall provide eye stimulation as you wait for your food to arrive. Try one of the 'create your own omelets' ($4.50 plus $0.60 per filling); everything from brie to mushrooms is available.

Asia Cuisine (☎ 607-256-8818; 126 N Aurora St; mains $6-10) This popular eatery serves big portions of inexpensive Korean and Chinese food in an unpretentious atmosphere. The menu spans the continent.

Drinking

Ithaca has a number of bars, pubs and clubs. The Commons area and the streets around Cornell University are good bets for nightlife.

ABC Café (☎ 607-277-4770; 308 Stewart Ave) This bright Collegetown café has lots of artwork on the walls and features folk music, Sunday jazz and weekly open mike nights. It also doubles as a popular vegetarian restaurant.

THE FRESH FOOD REVOLUTION

If you ever wondered where the recipes came from in the popular vegetarian cookbook series, the *Moosewood Restaurant*, look no further. The answer lies in an Ithaca restaurant of the same name. **Moosewood Restaurant** (☎ 607-273-9610; 215 N Cayuga St; mains from $10) rightly takes some credit for elevating vegetarian cooking to a loftier plane. Despite its vegetarian roots, Moosewood offers a fresh fish dish Thursday through Sunday. Be forewarned: there is usually a line to get in, made less tiresome by reading the flyers on the long bulletin board by the inside entrance. Once inside it's a casual place with lots of rustic tables and chairs and comfy couches.

Chapter House Brewpub (☎ 607-277-9782; 400 Stewart Ave) Dark wood paneling and a vast selection of beers evoke a British pub. Cornell students pack this Collegetown place most nights of the week.

Kopes Garage (☎ 607-273-9108; 110 N Aurora St) One of the newer spots in Ithaca, Kopes serves inexpensive, freshly prepared pub food for under $10. The bar is the real draw; it takes up half the restaurant and is usually packed.

Entertainment

Ithaca supports a thriving theater and performing arts scene. Call the Ticket Center at **Clinton House** (☎ 607-273-4497, 800-284-8422; 116 N Cayuga St) for more information.

Hangar Theatre (☎ 607-273-8588; www.hangar theatre.org; Rte 89) This is a popular professional summer theater series that includes the Kiddstuff summer children's theater. Look for the bright red building in Cass Park, just off Rte 89 west of the inlet to Cayuga Lake.

Kitchen Theatre Company (KTC; ☎ 607-272-0403; www.kitchentheatre.com; 116 S Cayuga St) This well-respected company presents contemporary productions in the historic Clinton House.

State Theatre (☎ 607-277-7477; www.statetheatre ofithaca.com; 107 W State St) This newly renovated landmark building reopened its doors in December 2001 after extensive renovations. It showcases everything from West African drummers to ballet to comedy.

Cinemapolis (☎ 607-277-6115; 171 E State St) This movie theater focuses almost exclusively on feature foreign and independent films.

Nines (☎ 607-272-1888; 311 College Ave) A popular rock, reggae and blues club featuring the best of local and touring bands.

Shopping

Ithaca Farmers' Market (☎ 607-273-7109; www.ithaca market.com; 535 3rd St; ⏰ 9am-2pm Sat, 10am-2pm Sun Apr-Dec) Stock up on organic supplies at this wonderful outdoor market where samples are served in abundance: summer berries, autumn apples, Finger Lakes wines, bread and cookies just out of the oven, as well as hot meals that range from Mexican to macrobiotic dishes.

The market doubles as a local arts-and-crafts showcase and features painters, jewelers and musicians. Everything sold here has been made within a 30-mile radius of town. Most weekends feature free performances by everyone from bluegrass musicians to belly dancers, table tennis players to turkey callers. The main market takes place at Steamboat Landing just off Rte 13; a smaller version is held in DeWitt Park on Tuesday from 9am to 2pm.

Getting There & Around

Tompkins County Airport (☎ 607-257-0456) is five miles northeast of Ithaca via Rte 13. Served by Continental Airlines and US Airways, this modest airport offers daily services to Newark, New York City, White Plains, Syracuse, Pittsburgh, Philadelphia and Boston. To travel from the Tompkins County Airport to town by taxi, contact **Ithaca Dispatch** (☎ 607-277-2227) or **Cayuga Taxi** (☎ 607-277-8294). The fare from downtown Ithaca to the airport is about $15.

To travel from Ithaca to Hancock International Airport in Syracuse, contact **Ithaca Airline Limousine Shuttle Service** (☎ 607-273-3030) or **Cayuga Taxi** (☎ 607-277-8294). The fare is $95.

The **bus terminal** (☎ 607-277-8800; 710 W State St at Fulton St) serves as a depot for **Adirondack Trailways** (☎ 800-858-8555) and **Greyhound** (☎ 800-231-2222). Destinations include New York City ($39, five hours), Syracuse ($10, 1½ hours) and Philadelphia, via Scranton, ($54, nine hours).

Car travelers will find Ithaca at the crossroads of Rtes 13 and 96, about 50 miles

northwest of Binghamton and 55 miles southeast of Syracuse. If you're coming from the southeast (ie New York City), take I-88 west to Rte 17; at exit 64, head north on Rte 96 to 96B and follow that into Ithaca. From I-81 to the east, take exit 11 or exit 12 to Rte 13 west. From the west, take Rte 224 east to Rte 13 north, which brings you to the south of town. From Watkins Glen, take Rte 414 north to Rte 79 east, which takes you right into Ithaca.

Taxi service is available 24 hours a day from **Cayuga Taxi** (☎ 607-277-8294).

TRUMANSBURG

☎ 607 / pop 1600

Tiny Trumansburg, a one-street town about 15 miles north of Ithaca on Rte 96, is the gateway to stupendous **Taughannock Falls State Park** (☎ 607-387-6739; campsite $13; ⏰ camping late March–mid-October). The 215ft-high Taughannock Falls – 30ft higher than their more famous neighbor Niagara – drop down a steep gorge in a misty cloud of thunder and are the highest straight falls this side of the Rocky Mountains. There are five miles of hiking trails throughout the park. You can see the falls from two lookout points on one trail, or hike on a trail that follows the streambed to the falls.

The park has a campground with 76 sites, 16 cabins, boat facilities, a small swimming beach and picnic areas with fire pits. Children can clamber about on an excellent playground with large wooden towers.

During the snow season head over to the **Podunk Ski Touring Center and Ski Shop** (☎ 607-387-6716; 6383 Podunk Rd; admission from $12) for cross-country skiing. There are quite a few trails and the cost includes rentals and trail fee. Guests can use the sauna and then roll in the snow. To reach the ski center from Ithaca, take Rte 96 north past Jacksonville and then make a left on Cold Springs Rd and another left on Podunk Rd. The center is about a quarter mile up the road.

Well situated for wine tasting and gorge hiking is the **Taughannock Farms Inn** (☎ 607-387-7711; www.t-farms.com; 2030 Gorge Rd; d from $105; mains from $20), a Victorian estate 8 miles north of Ithaca on Rte 89 directly across from Taughannock Falls State Park. The Inn, which overlooks Cayuga Lake, has 13 bright guest rooms equipped with heavy wooden furniture. The restaurant serves American cuisine and features fine wines from the Finger Lakes region.

If you're hungry try the **Rongovian Embassy to the USA** (☎ 607-387-3334; 1 W Main St; mains $8-10). The place does good pizzas and doubles as one of the best clubs in the area for live music. There's something for everyone here. Depending on the night of the week you'll hear jazz, country, rock, reggae or blues.

Three doors down is **Ron Don's** (☎ 607-387-5622; 19 W Main St; mains $3-5), a cheap choice good for breakfasts and burgers.

WATKINS GLEN
☎ 607 / pop 2149

Watkins Glen, at the southern tip of Seneca Lake, is famous for an unlikely duo of attractions: its world class car-racing track and a spectacular natural gorge with waterfalls. In town the main drag of Franklin St grows steadily more interesting as you approach the lake, and the harbor area is quite charming. Ten blocks further up kitschy souvenir shops predominate, many with a Nascar theme. In 1973 Watkins Glen hosted the largest single day rock-and-roll concert ever presented – more than 600,000 people gathered to take in groups such as the Allman Brothers and the Grateful Dead.

The **Schuyler County Chamber of Commerce** (☎ 607-535-4300; www.schuylerny.com; 100 Franklin St; ☼ 9am-5pm Mon-Fri) provides area and race information.

Sights & Activities
The main draws in Watkins Glen's are car racing and hiking.

WATKINS GLEN INTERNATIONAL
This **track** (☎ 607-535-2481; www.theglen.com; off County Rd 16; admission $10-50; ☼ Jun-Oct) is well known for car racing. Cars used to race on a 6.6-mile course through town streets, but saner minds built a 2.3-mile course in its present location in 1956. The track has since gone through some ups and downs, but today hosts major Nascar and grand prix races, including the Winston Cup Race in August.

Race season runs from June to October, and ticket prices depend on the race and how close you want to be to cars trying to break the sound barrier. You can also bring your RV and park next to the track during some races for $35 to $110. To reach the track, take Rte 414 north through town to County Rd 16 and then follow the signs three miles to the track.

WATKINS GLEN STATE PARK
This **park** (☎ 607-535-4511; ☼ May-Oct/Nov) was operated as a private tourist attraction until the state bought it in 1906. It has 19 waterfalls, grottoes and many summer tourists who walk along a dazzling self-guided 1.5-mile gorge trail with 832 stone steps. The entrance to the park is on Franklin St between 10th and 11th Sts. You can camp here, too (p250). In the summertime there is a large pool for swimming. Day visitors can bring hot dogs and burgers and use one of the many grills.

PLEASANT VALLEY WINE COMPANY TASTING ROOM
Located in a big barn-like structure, this **tasting room** (☎ 607-535-4867; 2 N Franklin St; admission free) makes a good substitute if you don't have time to discover the region's wine trails. The oldest commercial winery in the country, Pleasant Valley opened on the shores of Keuka Lake in 1860. A few years later the company hired French champagne makers and a Boston taster gushed that the Pleasant Valley's bubbly was 'the great Champagne of the Western World.' The owners then adopted the name Great Western for the company. Great Western is now part of Taylor Vineyards, the largest producer in the state and second largest in the US. Today the wines are mediocre, although for cheap whites we enjoyed the peach chardonnay ($4 per bottle). You can taste as much as you like for free here. Call ahead for opening hours.

CAPTAIN BILL'S SENECA LAKE CRUISES
You can take one-hour boat cruises (hourly) with **Captain Bill's** (☎ 607-535-4541; foot of Franklin St; adult/child $8.50/4; ☼ mid-May–mid-Oct) on Seneca Lake. The cruises take you past waterfalls and cliffs featuring paintings by Native Americans and provide narration of the region's history. Captain Bill's also offers dinner cruises ($33, three hours), moonlight cocktail cruises ($10, two hours) and even a cruise designed just for teens ($12, three hours).

Sleeping
On summer race weekends the town books up and prices jump. During these times

FOUR FAVORITE FINGER LAKES WINERIES

Bully Hill Vineyards

Perched high on a hill with a bird's-eye view of Keuka Lake, this **vineyard** (☎ 607-868-3610; www.bullyhill.com; Rte 76, Hammondsport; admission free; ☉ 10am-6pm Mon-Sat, 11am-6pm Sun), off Rte 54A, is the most eccentric in the region – where else can you purchase women's thong panties with a glow-in-the-dark goat on them?

Bully Hill used to be the original Taylor wine company, founded by Walter S Taylor. But Walter, who died in April 2001, was never allowed to tell you this. A 1977 lawsuit by Coca-Cola, which bought the newer and larger Taylor Wine Company in nearby Pleasant Valley, prevented him from using his name or the paintings of any ancestors on his wine labels. So he responded by putting paintings of his goat on many labels and proclaiming: 'They have my name and heritage, but they didn't get my goat.'

The wines aren't the best in the region, but they certainly have the most interesting labels. Taylor designed most himself, and a few take subtle jabs at the lawsuit. The winery does 45-minute tours followed by a tasting that is both informative and hysterical – you'll be giggling before you even touch the booze.

The winery also is home to the **Wine Museum of Greyton H Taylor**, which tells the story of the Taylor family history and the history of winemaking in the region. It features original artwork by Walter S Taylor.

Bully Hill has a charming restaurant, open for lunch daily until 4pm. It features an interesting menu in the $6-8 range.

Glenora Wine Cellars

This **winery** (☎ 607-243-5511; www.glenora.com; 5435 Rte 14, Dundee; admission free; ☉ 10am-6pm) has one of the most picturesque settings in the region with a commanding view of Seneca Lake. Besides the tasting room there is the Verasions Restaurant and the Inn at Glenora. The place is tasteful and blends into the surrounding environment perfectly. Tastings are informal – you sample what you want as many times as you want. The only drawback is that there is little explanation of the various wines you are sampling.

Rooms at the Inn start at $99 (November to April) and $130 (May to October); but there are often extremely good weekday specials that include room, dinner and breakfast for two for $215.

Dr Konstantin Frank's Vinifera Wine Cellars

Between Hammondsport and the Rte 54 junction, this **winery** (☎ 607-868-4884; www.drfrankwines.com; 9749 Middle Rd, Rte 76; admission free; ☉ 9am-5pm Mon-Sat, noon-5pm Sun) is home to some of the best wines in the region, and to the vinifera revolution in Finger Lakes winemaking.

The winery, run by Dr Konstantin Frank's son and grandchildren, is known for its Johannisberg Riesling, pinot noir and champagne. There are no tours, but free tastings are conducted in a modest building with inviting white walls, a solid brown wooden bar, and excellent lake views. The organized tastings are very informative and allow you to sample a range of wines.

Hunt Country Vineyards

On the northwestern side of Keuka Lake, this **winery** (☎ 315-595-2812; www.huntcountryvineyards.com; 4021 Italy Hill Rd; admission free; ☉ 10am-5pm Mon-Sat, noon-5pm Sun) is nestled among the grape vines in a white barn with green doors. The winery is best known for its superb ice wine, which melts in your mouth and has delicious honey and apricot undertones. It is said to resemble the best European dessert wines. Ice wines are made from grapes that freeze on the vine, usually in December. The winery allows you to taste four wines and offers 15 to 20 minute walking tours of the property.

many places require a two-night minimum stay. B&Bs are usually non-smoking and air-conditioning is standard in almost all places.

Idlewilde Inn (☎ 607-535-3081; 1 Lakeview Ave; d $85 incl breakfast) In a distinctive pink-roofed Victorian with a wraparound porch overlooking Seneca Lake, this charming place has 18 rooms. The cheapest rooms have shared baths. The price includes a full breakfast. The inn doesn't allow children under 12.

Seneca Lodge (☎ 607-535-2014; south entrance Watkins Glen State Park; cabin from $38, d from $63) There is a variety of sleeping options. Choose from the small, inexpensive wooden cabins, chalet-style A-frames or more luxurious motel rooms. The lodge has a dining room in a giant log cabin with a large outdoor patio. The restaurant serves American dishes – everything from lobster tail to rib-eye. Dinners ($11 to $15) comes with salad bar, bread, vegetables and potatoes.

Villager Motel (☎ 607-535-7159; 106 4th St; d from $60; 🏊) When the air turns chilly you can still swim at the Villager Motel's indoor heated pool. Despite its rather uninspiring brick building, it's right downtown and has a good selection of rooms. The motel-style rooms are the cheapest, but for a little more you can get nicer furnishings in the B&B-style rooms.

Watkins Glen KOA (☎ 607-535-7404; www.watkins glenkoa.com; Rte 414; campsite $25-30, cabin from $45; ⌛ late Apr–late Oct) More than 100 sites, plus a few rustic cabins, are spread about this densely wooded 90-acre campground. There's a swimming pool, a small mini-golf course and a small pond for fishing. To reach the KOA, take Rte 414 about 4.5 miles south of the junction with Rte 14.

Watkins Glen State Park (☎ 607-535-4511; Franklin St btwn 10th & 11th St; campsite $15-20; ⌛ mid-May–late Oct) There are more than 300 sites among the trees here. There also are picnic tables, a cooking area and a large pavilion.

Finger Lakes National Forest (☎ 607-546-4470; off Rte 414; campsite $5) The smallest national forest in the country (and the only one in New York State), this 16,000-acre site has more than 70 miles of hiking trails, fishing, ponds and a basic campground (Blueberry Patch Camp). Located between Cayuga and Seneca Lakes 8 miles north of Watkins Glen via Rte 414.

Eating

Watkins Glen has eating options for all budgets.

Seneca Harbor Station (☎ 607-535-6101; foot of Franklin St; mains $16-20) Watkins Glen's classiest restaurant is right on the docks. Floor-to-ceiling windows provide fabulous views of the lake; and there is a large deck on which to sit back, sip Finger Lakes wine and watch the sunset. The menu is seafood-oriented to match the seafaring theme inside.

Wildflower Café (☎ 607-535-9797; 301 N Franklin St; mains $15-18) The Cajun-influenced Wildflower Café serves jambalaya and jerk chicken, but also features American stand-bys like pizza, pasta, ribs and seafood. There are a number of vegetarian options on the large menu. Food is served in an old-fashioned atmosphere.

Jerlando's Ristorante (☎ 607-535-4254; 400 N Franklin St; mains under $10) This small, cheerful eatery with green checked tablecloths smells delicious upon entry. Large servings of simple Italian classics as well as pizzas and a selection of 'healthy dishes' are served in an unpretentious country kitchen atmosphere.

Getting There & Away

Watkins Glen is at the southern tip of Seneca Lake, on Rte 14.

CORNING

☎ 607 / pop 10,842

The focus and draw of Corning is glass. From the sculptors and shows at the Corning Museum of Glass to the downtown glass shops and artists' glassblowing studios, all this glass has helped make Corning the state's third-largest tourist destination. The town itself is quite pleasant, especially the historic Market St area which was restored to its 19th-century origins after the Chemung River flooded downtown Corning in 1972.

Orientation & Information

Corning's historic downtown centers around the Market St area. Here you will find numerous glass shops, restaurants, bars and the Rockwell Museum.

The **Greater Corning Chamber of Commerce** (☎ 607-936-4686; 42 E Market St; ⌛ 9am-5pm Mon-Fri) has information on the area. The **Finger Lakes Wine Country Visitors Center** (☎ 607-974-8271; 151 Centerway; ⌛ 9am-5pm Sep-Jun, 9am-8pm Jul & Aug) is located inside the Corning Museum of

Glass. This helpful desk provides brochures and lots of information about visiting the region's numerous wine trails.

Sights & Activities

Corning has two excellent museums – perhaps two of the most interesting in the region – that should not be missed.

CORNING MUSEUM OF GLASS

Housed in a building made of giant sheets of glass, this astounding **museum** (☎ 607-974-8271; www.cmog.org; 151 Centerway; adult/child $12/6; ✆ 9am-5pm Sep-Jun, 9am-8pm Jul & Aug) received a $62 million face-lift recently and is now sleeker than ever. In the entrance hall a 1400-pound neon-yellow glass sculpture with 500 individually blown glass elements attached is just a teaser for what you'll find inside. You'll experience the Glass Innovation Center, which informs you about the latest scientific advances in glassmaking, the largest Glass Sculpture Gallery in the world, and a glass exhibit showcasing more than 10,000 objects, some dating back to 1400 BC. The museum also includes the Hot Glass Show, where you can observe glassblowing up close and the Steuben Factory where craftspeople ply the glass trade. When you are done checking out the museum stop by the gift shop. If you can make it with glass they have it here. Dedicate at least three hours at the museum.

ROCKWELL MUSEUM

Old American Western art, early examples of Steuben glass and antique toys are on display at this **museum** (☎ 607-937-5386; www.rockwellmuseum.org; 111 Cedar St; adult/child $7/5; ✆ 9am-5pm Mon-Sat, 11am-5pm Sun), located in the historic Market St area. The displays by Frederic Remington, Charles M Russell and 1830s landscapes by the 'explorer artists' are especially noteworthy. Displays are divided into three themes: the Indian, the Landscape and the Cowboy. The museum is said to house the largest collection of American Western art in the east.

Sleeping & Eating

Most of Corning's eating options are in the historic downtown area.

Rosewood Inn B&B (☎ 607-962-3253; www.rosewoodinn.com; 134 E First St; d from $95) Corning's best sleeping option, the inn dates back to 1855 and is housed in an elaborately decorated Victorian house with seven rooms. Afternoon tea is served in an elegant parlor with antique rocking chairs, period wallpaper and oriental rugs. Check out the winter packages.

Radisson Hotel Corning (☎ 607-962-5000; 125 Denison Parkway E; d $99) This plush upscale chain hotel is centrally located close to historic Market St. Its 177 rooms are spacious and well appointed. The service is friendly and professional.

Gate House Motel (☎ 607-936-4131; 145 E Corning Rd; d $45) On the outskirts of town, this no-frills motel offers clean rooms in a squat red building.

Market Street Brewing Co (☎ 607-936-2337; 63-65 W Market St; mains $6-18) If the weather cooperates dine outside in the beer garden or on the rooftop patio. The menu is exhaustive – you can order a $6 burger or an $18 steak. Wash it down with a fresh local brew.

Old World Café & Ice Cream Parlor (☎ 607-936-1953; cnr Market & Centerway St; mains $5-6) The kids will love this old-fashioned ice cream parlor featuring all sorts of ice cream, sundaes and shakes (from $3) as well as pink floral-patterned walls. There also is a giant selection of salads and sandwiches.

Pelham's Upstate Tuna Co (☎ 607-936-8862; 73 E Market St; mains $11-17; ✆ dinner) Here customers cook for themselves. You buy your favorite chicken teriyaki or fish kabobs and start grilling with your fellow diners. The restaurant is an ultrahip establishment with an ornate columned faux marble bar.

Getting There & Away

About 20 miles southwest of Watkins Glen, Corning is at the intersection of Rtes 414 and 17, a short hop west of the intersection of Rtes 17 and 15.

HAMMONDSPORT

☎ 607 / pop 700

Perfectly situated for wine tasting, tiny Hammondsport is a quaint Victorian town with a pleasant green square lined with shops, and a few restaurants and lodgings. A short walk down the main drag, Sheather St, takes you to Keuka Lake where you'll find a quiet park and two public beaches.

For sleeping and eating check out the **Village Tavern & Inn** (☎ 607-569-2528; 39 Mechanic St; d from $79; mains from $15) on the town square. The restaurant is classy, yet cozy, with candles,

---

DETOUR – MARK TWAIN STUDY, EXHIBIT & GRAVE SITE

Samuel Clemens (1835–1910), whose better-known pen name Mark Twain is synonymous with the very best American storytelling, is Elmira's most famous resident. Today the town contains his study, an exhibit on his life and his final resting spot. Twain was a humorist, newspaperman, lecturer and the author of *The Adventures of Tom Sawyer*, among other titles. Famous for reporting the world as he found it, he once wrote: 'Tell the truth – that way you don't have to remember anything.'

Twain spent more than 20 summers in Elmira. His wife Olivia Langdon grew up in the area and Twain wrote quite a few of his most famous books while summering at her family's Quarry Farm. A gallery of photos, along with Twain's original study, was moved to **Elmira College** (☎ 607-735-1914; 1 Park Pl; admission free; 9am-5pm Mon-Sat Jun-Sep) in 1952. The study contains his 1880s Remington Rand typewriter; Twain claimed to be the first author in the world to submit typewritten manuscripts to a publisher. There also is a video about Twain's life, and Elmira college students conduct the informative tours.

Twain is buried in **Woodlawn Cemetery** in the Langdon family plot. The wooded cemetery is perched on a hill overlooking the town. Twain's gravestone is simple, proclaiming only his name and dates of birth and death. To reach the cemetery follow the well-marked signs throughout the town.

Elmira is just off Rte 17, at exit 56, between Corning and Ithaca.

---

tiny white lights and lots to look at on the walls. It serves a huge selection of Finger Lakes wines and more than 99 beers. The large menu concentrates on meats, pastas and seafood. Don't miss the slightly sweet freshly baked bread. There is live piano music on the weekends. The inn has eight studio-apartment–style rooms complete with kitchens.

The **Park Inn** (☎ 607-569-9387; 37 Sheather St; d from $79; mains from $10), also on the square, has five simple rooms above a small tavern/restaurant that serves lunch and dinner. It has a very lively and popular bar.

The **Hammondsport Motel** (☎ 607-569-2600; cnr William & Water St; d from $64; Apr-Nov) might not be the best-looking place in town, but its location right on the lake has top views at reasonable prices.

Half a block north of the square and half a block from the lake, **JS Hubbs B&B** (☎ 607-569-2440; 17 Sheather St; d $89) is in a big, green house built in 1840. It has four large rooms all with private bath, though some of the toilets are a little cramped. The B&B includes two very large common rooms with a TV and piano, a small greenhouse and a parking area.

Try the **Crooked Lake Ice Cream Co** (☎ 607-569-2751; 35 Sheather St; mains from $3) for breakfast and informal lunch or great ice cream (from $2) in an old-fashioned setting on the town square. The food is a little greasy, but not bad.

Hammondsport lies on Rte 54A just off Rte 54.

NORTHERN TIER

An indelible part of this area's history begins with the construction of the legendary Erie Canal. When it first opened in 1825, it was the engineering marvel of the day. A great wave of westward migration followed, along with the construction of several lateral canals. Today parts of the canal remain, other parts have been filled in (Erie Blvd in Syracuse, for instance, is actually the old canal). Rte 20, which connects many of the towns at the northern ends of the lakes, is a direct descendent of the canal's development, and considered among the loveliest drives in New York.

Towns with the most notable historical architecture in this region, particularly Greek Revival mansions, tend to be in the Northern Tier, a more citified and urban environment than the southern half of the region. The Northern Tier encompasses the industrial centers of Syracuse and Rochester, in addition to smaller towns such as Canandaigua, Geneva and Seneca Falls.

SYRACUSE
☎ 315 / pop 146,306

Syracuse, at the southern end of Onondaga Lake, stands in sharp contrast to the more pastoral portions of the Finger Lakes region. The salt industry that prospered here in the 19th century made Syracuse a working-class town at heart. With the completion of the Erie Canal the city's image as an industrial center took hold. By the 1960s and '70s, however, it suffered the same fate as many of its rust-belt neighbors; employers and workers discovered the suburbs and the downtown decayed. Today, the Armory Sq neighborhood, a collection of trendy shops and cafés, represents the downtown's attempt at revival.

Syracuse is enlivened by the presence of Syracuse University's large student body, but commerce and industry still dominate the city's image. Railroads and highways crisscross each other. The downtown skyline is really more of a 'brickline,' with striking examples of Victorian Gothic, Art Deco and limestone Romanesque. There's no mistaking Syracuse for suburbia.

Orientation & Information

Clinton Sq, where Erie Blvd and Genesee St meet, marks the heart of downtown Syracuse. The city's main business district, dominated by Salina and Montgomery Sts, is just south of the square. Syracuse University is on a hill to the southeast. To the northeast is Onondaga Lake. I-81 and I-690 pass right through town, to the dismay of many. Downtown sights are within easy walking distance of each other.

Syracuse Convention & Visitors Bureau (☎ 315-470-1910; www.syracusecvb.org; 572 S Salina St; ☒ 8.30am-5pm Mon-Fri) Provides walking tour maps of downtown.

Erie Canal Museum (☎ 315-471-0593; 318 Erie Blvd E; ☒ 10am-5pm) Also houses a visitors center.

Main post office (☎ 315-452-3401; 5640 E Taft Rd; ☒ 9am-5pm Mon-Fri, 9am-1pm Sat)

Sights & Activities

As befits a large city, Syracuse has a host of sights and activities.

ERIE CANAL MUSEUM

Perhaps the most impressive artifact in this **museum** (☎ 315-471-0593; 318 Erie Blvd E at Montgomery St; admission free; ☒ 10am-5pm) is the 65ft-long reconstructed canal boat that contains original personal effects of some of its first passengers. Of note is a heartbreaking letter by an Irishwoman who had just buried her husband at sea. The museum is housed in the 1850 Weighlock Building. Boats were once towed along the canal (now Erie Blvd) into the building, and locks at the

front and rear were closed and the water drained out. Each boat then lay on a huge wooden cradle and scale, which weighed it and determined the tax. The museum also features a visitors center, historical exhibits and a sculpture garden.

AMORY SQUARE DISTRICT

Syracuse's trendiest area, and the city's best attempt at downtown revival, is filled with funky boutiques, used record stores, chic restaurants and hip bars in restored red-brick buildings. If too much coolness causes distress don't fear. There are casual sports bars, Irish pubs and blue-collar restaurants mixed in for good measure. If you visit before the first snows, you'll find outdoor tables packed with patrons trying their best to ignore the cold blustery winds. The district centers around the junction of Franklin and Walton Sts and makes a fine pit stop.

CANAL CRUISES

Mid-Lakes Navigation Co (☎ 315-685-8500, 800-545-4318; Dutchman's Landing; ☒ mid-Apr–early Nov), off Rte 370, offers a variety of Erie Canal cruises. The shortest excursions are the lunch tours ($19) and champagne dinner cruises ($35); a Sunday brunch cruise costs $30. The four-hour cruise for $29 ($20 for children), with a buffet lunch that includes salads and sandwiches, might be better value.

For the more adventurous, two- and three-day overnight cruises are available. These range from about $250 to $375 per person, including all meals and transportation to and from area hotels. Two-day cruises, in particular, sell out early; reservations are necessary during the busy summer season.

Cruises depart from Dutchman's Landing, about 7 miles northwest of Syracuse via Rte 370. From Syracuse, take I-81 to I-90 west to exit 38 (Rte 57). Turn left to reach Rte 370, then right at River Rd and right again at Hillsdale Rd.

ONONDAGA HISTORICAL ASSOCIATION MUSEUM

This county **museum** (☎ 315-428-1864; 321 Montgomery St; admission free; ☒ noon-4pm Wed-Fri, 11am-4pm Sat) might be one of the best small museums in the state. It covers the entire scope of New York history from the Onondaga Nation to the Erie Canal and the salt industry. Nineteenth-century fashion, old photos, Iroquois culture and antique typewriters are among the featured displays.

MILTON J RUBENSTEIN MUSEUM OF SCIENCE & TECHNOLOGY

Housed in the old armory, the **Museum of Science & Technology** (MOST; ☎ 315-425-9068; cnr Franklin & W Jefferson St; adult/child $5/4; 🕑 11am-5pm Tue-Sun) has several exhibits designed for children, including the Silverman Planetarium, which features daily star shows and hands-on exhibits in the old 1863 stables. MOST's newest edition is the Bristol Omnitheater, where a combination IMAX-museum ticket costs $9.75 for adults and $7.75 for children.

TIPPERARY HILL

Head to Syracuse's oldest Irish neighborhood to see the country's only upside-down traffic light found at the intersection of Tompkins and Lowell Sts. The neighborhood begins west of downtown where West Fayette and West Genesee Sts meet. Legend has it that when the traffic light was first installed (right-side up) residents were so outraged that British red was placed above Irish green they immediately destroyed the light's lenses. Realizing this was a battle they could not win, city officials reversed the lenses to placate the neighborhood.

Festivals & Events

The **New York State Fair** (☎ 315-487-7711; 581 State Fair Blvd) comes to town for 12 days every year, ending on Labor Day weekend in September. The fair features food, music, amusement rides, agricultural and livestock competitions, and business and industrial exhibits. It attracts about 85,000 people. Take exit 7 off I-670.

Sleeping

Syracuse features accommodations options for all budgets. Most places have private parking lots and air-conditioning.

Dickenson House on James (☎ 315-423-4777; www.dickensonhouse.com; 1504 James St; d from $110) Each room is named for a different person, mostly famous writers, and each is uniquely decorated. We particularly liked the Byron Room with its deep blue walls and mahogany Queen Anne period furnishings.

Bed & Breakfast Wellington (☎ 315-474-3641, 800-724-5006; www.bbwellington.com; 707 Danforth St; d $105)

Located on a quiet residential street, this B&B, housed in a 1914 Tudor home, was designed by Ward Wellington Ward. The sturdy wood-and-stucco house contains a fireplace and four porches, as well as a fridge stocked with sodas and juices.

Hotel Syracuse Radisson Plaza (☎ 315-422-5121, 800-333-3333; www.radisson.com; 500 S Warren St; d from $100; 🖳) The buildings surrounding the Hotel Syracuse make it look deserted, but inside it has been recently remodeled and expanded. Built in the 1920s, the hotel is registered with Historic Hotels of America, and the lobby is a grand place with high ceilings, chandeliers and gilding. Rooms are somewhat small but well appointed.

HI-AYH Downing International Hostel (☎ 315-472-5788; www.hiayh.org/hostels/newyork/syracuse.cfm; 535 Oak St; dm $14) Budget travelers can head to this hostel in a big house with 31 beds in separate-sex dorm rooms. There is a large basement kitchen and small library. There is a 9am to 5pm lockout and 11pm curfew. The hostel is a mile northeast of downtown in a residential neighborhood.

There are a few moderately priced motels at Carrier Circle. (To reach the area, take I-690 east about 2.5 miles to Thompson Rd north).

John Milton Inn (☎ 315-463-8555; Carrier Circle; d $35) This place has inexpensive but clean rooms.

Wyndham Syracuse (☎ 315-432-0200; www.wyndhamnewyorkhotels.com/properties/syracuse/index.html; Carrier Circle; d $155; 🖳) The luxury hotel at Carrier Circle, the Wyndham has a heated indoor-outdoor pool, sauna, whirlpool, tanning salon and more.

Eating

Check the Armory Sq district for a host of eating options.

Pastabilities (☎ 315-474-1153; 311 S Franklin St; mains $11; 🕑 closed Sun) Always packed at lunch, this eatery makes a wide variety of pastas in unusual flavors such as paprika lasagna. The dining area is a crisply designed narrow room lined with booths and a bar; music in a garden courtyard adds to the summertime atmosphere.

Lemon Grass (☎ 315-475-1111; 238 W Jefferson St; mains $15) Excellent Pacific rim cuisine is served at this very classy restaurant near the Armory. The decor includes white linen tablecloths and black-and-white Thai artwork.

Pascale Wine Bar & Restaurant (☎ 315-471-3040; 204 W Fayette; pizza $8, mains $20) In a historic building, Pascale Wine Bar has an interesting French-American menu with a good selection of Finger Lakes wines. It also does unusual pizzas.

PJ Dorsey's (☎ 315-478-3023; 116 Walton St; pub fare $6-10, mains $17-20) A great place for people-watching, PJ Dorsey's is located in the heart of the Armory Sq district with outdoor tables in summer. Inside are lots of booths and walls plastered with carefully painted beer labels. Dinners focus on steaks and seafood.

Mulrooney's (☎ 315-479-6163; 239 W Fayette St; mains from $9) This is a sports bar with pub food. Come hungry – the servings are plentiful and cheap.

Nancy's Coffee Café (☎ 315-476-6550; 290 W Jefferson St) Worth a visit for good coffee and espresso drinks, homemade gourmet deserts and a good view of pedestrian traffic and Armory Sq.

Entertainment

The performing arts scene is particularly strong in Syracuse. Many restaurants turn into popular bars at night.

Syracuse Symphony Orchestra (☎ 315-424-8200; John H Mulroy Civic Center, 411 Montgomery St) Classical and popular music concerts are performed from October to May. Call for concert schedule and prices.

Landmark Theatre (☎ 315-475-7979; 362 S Salina St) This is a flourishing 1928 architectural leftover from Hollywood's make-believe tropical-vaudeville movie-palace days. The Landmark showcases everything from touring stage shows to rock-and-roll concerts.

Salt City Center for the Performing Arts (☎ 315-474-1122; 601 S Crouse Ave) Musicals, dramas and comedies are presented year-round.

Syracuse Stage (☎ 315-424-8210; 820 E Genesee St) This is the area's only professional theater. From September to May it presents a mix of contemporary and classical drama.

Dinosaur Bar Barbecue (☎ 315-476-4937; 246 W Willow St) This blues bar and restaurant attracts an unlikely mix of bikers, tattooed waitresses, students, business professionals and anyone else who likes to eat ribs while gazing at the walls crowded with old signs, car parts and bumper stickers ('No Feeding the Cooks'). Most dishes are under $8, including racks of ribs (pork or beef), chili, red beans and sausage, chicken sandwiches and homemade desserts. At night, the Dinosaur draws crowds with live blues and recorded music.

Foundation (☎ 315-472-2665; 314 S Franklin St) This is a live-music and dance club inside an industrial-looking black-and-chrome warehouse across from the Pastabilities restaurant in Armory Sq. The music ranges from blues to hardcore metal and acid jazz. During the summer a courtyard barbecue pit adds to the festive atmosphere.

Happy Endings Coffeehouse (☎ 315-475-1853; 317 S Clinton St) This place has live music featuring local singer-songwriters as well as poetry readings.

Getting There & Around

Hancock International Airport (☎ 315-454-4330) offers daily services by a number of major airlines. Regular fares from Philadelphia and Chicago are about $230 round-trip, but there are usually specials. The airport is north of the city; take I-81 and exit at 27.

A **Regional Transportation Center** (☎ 315-478-1936) houses both the bus and train station served by **Greyhound/Trailways** (☎ 800-231-2222) and **Amtrak** (☎ 800-872-7245). Located on the north side of town, the transportation center is only a five-minute drive from downtown.

Those traveling by car will have no trouble reaching Syracuse. Two major highways cross it: I-81 and I-90 (the NY State Thruway).

If you need a taxi anywhere in the Syracuse area, call **Dependable Taxi** (☎ 315-475-0030). It costs about $20 to get from the airport to downtown.

SKANEATELES

☎ 315 / pop 2600

Picturesque, small and quiet, Skaneateles ('skinny-atlas') just might be the nicest small town in the Finger Lakes region. It sits at the top of one of the prettiest, deepest and smallest of the Finger Lakes, Skaneateles Lake, and has an almost romantic air to it. There's not much to do here, which makes it attractive to many people. The town centre covers just a few blocks around Genesee and Jordan Sts, which are packed with quite a few interesting shops, chic restaurants and bars. Genesee St runs parallel to the lake, and there is a good swimming beach halfway through town.

The best place to stay in town is the **Sherwood Inn** (☎ 315-685-3405; www.thesherwoodinn.com; 26 W Genesee St; d from $100; mains $18-25), a classic New York colonial inn that dates back to 1807, when it was a stagecoach stop. Each of the 20 rooms is a bit different, though all feature antique furnishings. Prices differ depending on the room and all are cheaper between January and April. The classy restaurant overlooks the lake and serves continental cuisine.

At the other end of the Skaneateles spectrum, **Doug's Fish Fry** (☎ 315-685-3288; 8 Jordan St; mains under $7) is good, greasy, loud and cheap. The fish is trucked in from Boston daily, and the menu includes seafood gumbo, steamed clams, baked beans and fries. For a splurge try the whole lobster with two sides for $17. Doug's also has ice cream and sundaes.

SENECA FALLS
☎ 315 / pop 6800

Rich in women's suffrage history, Seneca Falls was the home of Elizabeth Cady Stanton and the 1848 women's rights convention she organized. The convention, along with a Declaration of Sentiments written by Stanton that was approved at the convention, is credited with initiating the struggle towards women's rights and suffrage in the United States. Stanton and her abolitionist husband Henry Stanton moved to Seneca Falls from Boston in 1847. At the time the town was a transportation hub and the entire Finger Lakes region was at the center of the abolitionist movement.

Today, Seneca Falls streets are lined with stately homes on large grassy lawns and lots of leafy trees. The village's downtown is not as picturesque as other Finger Lakes towns, but most people come to learn about the past. The downtown area centers around Fall St. For area information, stop by the **Heritage Area Visitors Center** (☎ 315-568-2703; 115 Fall St; ⌚ 10am-4pm Mon-Sat, noon-4pm Sun), which also houses exhibits on the town's history and women's suffrage.

Sights & Activities

The women's rights movement dominates Seneca Falls' sights.

WOMEN'S RIGHTS NATIONAL HISTORICAL PARK

This is actually a federal complex composed of a **visitors center** (☎ 315-568-2991; 136 Fall St; admission $3; ⌚ 9am-5pm) packed with exhibits on the convention, its leaders and what life was like in the times in which they lived; what's left of the Wesleyan Chapel, site of the 1848 Women's Rights Convention; and the

Elizabeth Cady Stanton House. The Stanton House has been restored in the spirit of historical accuracy: the original wallpaper has been copied and replaced, and the few pieces of original furniture that could be located, including her writing desk and piano, have been placed in the house. There also is a bronze cast of Stanton's hand clasping Susan B Anthony's. The two women met shortly after the 1848 convention and worked together for the rest of their lives. Allocate at least two hours to view the historic park.

NATIONAL WOMEN'S HALL OF FAME

This small private **museum** (☎ 315-568-8060; 76 Fall St; admission $3; ⌚ 9:30am-5pm Mon-Sat, noon-4pm Sun May-Oct; 10am-4pm Wed-Sat, noon-4pm Sun Nov-Apr) has large wall plaques describing the achievements of an expanding number of women in the arts, athletics and humanitarian fields: everyone from Elizabeth Bailey and 'Mother' Seton to Jane Adams, Marian Anderson, Sojourner Truth and Emily Dickinson. It's a good place to come if you like a quiet, reflective museum experience, although the place is a little barren and could use a few more exhibits.

MONTEZUMA NATIONAL WILDLIFE REFUGE

This **refuge** (☎ 315-568-5987; 3395 Rte 5 & 20 E; admission free; ⌚ dawn-dusk Apr-Nov), located about 5 miles east of Seneca Falls at the north end of Cayuga Lake, is a major stopover point for waterfowl on their way south from Canada and a must-see for bird lovers. From the middle of September until the ponds freeze, Canada geese and ducks stop by, many of them arriving in November. From mid-August to mid-October (with a mid-September peak), shorebirds like herons, egrets and sandpipers come through. From late February to April Canada and snow geese and some ducks come back. Mid-May is peak warbler season. About 315 species of birds have been spotted in the refuge since its establishment in 1937.

The refuge is spread over 6300 acres and has a visitors center, nature trail for hiking, a driving trail and two observation towers.

The refuge is on Rtes 5 and 20. To get there from Rte 89, turn east onto Rtes 5 and 20. From I-90, take exit 41 to Rte 414 south to Rte 318 east to Rtes 5 and 20 east.

DETOUR – HARRIET TUBMAN HOUSE

From Seneca Falls drive east on Rte 20 and Rte 5 for 20 miles until you hit the city of Auburn, home of Harriet Tubman. Her house sits on a 26-acre plot of land, next door to the AME Zion Church. The home, a simple white two-story structure with a long front porch, is one of four buildings on the property.

Tubman was born into slavery in Maryland in 1820 or 1821. In 1849, she escaped and fled first to Philadelphia and then to Canada. During the next dozen or so years she made 19 trips at night, mostly solitary, to the south to rescue more than 300 slaves. She settled in Auburn after the Civil War. Her good friend, William Seward, lived nearby. Seward, a fellow abolitionist and US Senator, sold her the property for a modest sum.

The AME Zion Church administers the **Tubman House** (☎ 315-252-2081; 180 South St; adult/child $3/2; ◔ 10am-3pm Tue-Sat Jun-Sep). Rev Paul G Carter, or a member of his family, will lead you on a tour of the homestead. First you'll be taken into a small museum that includes a well-made and very informative video of Tubman's life. Afterwards you'll be taken into Tubman's house. Few of her belongings remain, but it's still a moving experience.

Following a visit to the Tubman House, you can head to the **Fort Hill Cemetery** (☎ 315-253-8132; 19 Fort St; ◔ 9am-4pm Mon-Fri) where Tubman and William Seward are buried. The site was originally a Native American burial ground dating back to 1100 AD.

Sleeping & Eating

Seneca Falls has a limited selection of sleeping and eating options.

Hubbell House B&B (☎ 315-568-9690; www.hubbell housebb.com; 42 Cayuga St; d from $85) This three-story Gothic Revival home was built in 1855 and vaguely resembles a gingerbread house. It's an elegant place with four guest rooms and a wonderful wraparound screened porch overlooking Van Cleef Lake. The B&B has a private dock from which you can go swimming, or take out a rowboat.

Van Cleef Homestead B&B (☎ 315-568-2275; 86 Cayuga St; d from $90; ☒) This Federal-style home was built by Seneca Falls' first permanent resident, Lawrence Van Cleef. It has three nicely decorated rooms.

Cayuga Lake State Park (☎ 315-568-5163; Rte 89; campsite $17; ◔ May-Nov) This state park contains almost 300 sites. To get there, take Lake Rd east from town for 3 miles, then go 4 miles south on Rte 89.

Pump House (☎ 315-578-9109; 16 Rumsey St; mains $6-14) This restaurant offers a large selection of healthy dishes as well as steaks, pasta and seafood.

Downtown Deli (☎ 315-568-9943; 53 Fall St; mains $4) A cheaper alternative, the Downtown Deli serves up big sandwiches and subs in a casual environment. Standard deli-diner items include hot pastrami, chili, pizza and (on the children's menu) macaroni and cheese.

Getting There & Away

Seneca Falls is on Rte 20, 3 miles west of Cayuga Lake.

GENEVA

☎ 315 / pop 13,600

There is little to see or do in Geneva, located at the northern tip of Seneca Lake, but the town itself is easy on the eyes. Stately homes and the buildings of Hobart and William Smith College share Main St with plenty of trees. Geneva lies at the intersection of Rtes 20 and 14. For tourist information, contact the **Geneva Area Chamber of Commerce** (☎ 315-789-1776; 1 Lakeside Drive; ◔ 9am-5pm Mon-Fri).

If there is one reason to go to Geneva, it's to visit the amazing **Belhurst Castle** (☎ 315-781-0201; www.belhurstcastle.com; Rte 14; d from $125; lunch $9, dinner $22), south of town. Belhurst is a large, red 1889 Medina stone originally built on the lake for Carrie Harron Collins, a descendent of Henry Clay, a great 19th-century American statesman known for resolving bitter political conflicts. The 13 rooms have polished woodwork, stone and plaster walls, solid oak doors and gas fireplaces. The grounds are beautifully kept up. The dining room has lake views and a choice menu. There also is a cozy bar with old paintings and green walls. Even if you can't stay, stop by for the all-you-can-eat buffet lunch – it's a very good deal. During the off-season (November to April) room rates drop by as much as 50 percent.

FINGER LAKES REGION

Seven miles north of town on Rte 14 is the pleasant **Cheerful Valley Campground** (☎ 315-781-1222; Rte 14; campsite $18), which has 160 sites near the river. Services include a coin laundry and pool.

For casual dining on the lake check out **Crow's Nest on Seneca Lake** (☎ 315-781-0600; 415 Boody's Hill Rd; mains $6-16), which serves sandwiches, salads, seafood and steaks. The restaurant is just off Rte 96A.

PENN YAN

☎ 315 / pop 5200

The area around Penn Yan, at the northern tip of Keuka Lake on Rte 54, is Finger Lakes farm country. Driving towards the village you'll pass fields of corn, grain silos and red barns. The tiny village consists of just a few shops and restaurants, but is ideally situated as a base for wine tasting. The name Penn Yan is an amalgamation of 'Pennsylvania' and 'Yankee' because most of the early settlers came from Pennsylvania and New England.

The village's biggest claim to fame is its spot as the world's largest producer of buckwheat. Penn Yan is home to the **Buckwheat Harvest Festival** (☎ 315-536-7434), held the fourth weekend in September. If you're around the region at this time it's worth stopping by to sample everything buckwheat: ice cream, pizza, shortcake and numerous other buckwheat delights. The festivities also include games, arts and crafts and a parade.

Otherwise the town's limited attractions include the **Windmill Farmers' Market** (☎ 315-536-3032; 🕐 8.30am-4.30pm Sat May-Dec) on Rte 54 about 6 miles south of the Elm St intersection downtown. Mennonites, who still travel by horse and buggy, come from the surrounding area to sell good produce, jams, molasses and baked goods at this indoor-outdoor farmers' market.

The best place to stay in town is the **Fox Inn** (☎ 315-536-3101; 158 Main St; d from $105), which has four rooms plus a two-bedroom suite, and, best of all, the ghosts of two former inhabitants, according to the 19th-century diary of a Penn Yan dentist. You can't miss its yellow facade and two-story white columns. There's a huge garden out back.

Otherwise you can try the **Colonial Motel** (☎ 315-536-3056; 175 W Lake Rd; d from $75), which has 17 unremarkable rooms with kitchenettes, but a nice location just across from the lake. Take Rte 14A south to W Lake Drive, then go 1.4 miles to get there.

The **Keuka Lake State Park** (☎ 315-536-3666; 3370 Pepper Rd Bluff Point; campsite $15; 🕐 May–mid-Oct) includes 150 campsites on 620 acres and it has a good view of the lake. In winter the state park offers hiking and cross-country skiing opportunities. In summer a gravel-covered beach is open for swimming and there are a few boat launches. The park is reached via Hwy 54A.

The local dining choices are slim. Your best bet is **Lloyd's Ltd** (☎ 315-536-9029; 3 Main St; mains from $4), which sells inexpensive pub food like hamburgers, sandwiches and pizza and has a vast selection of imported bottled beer.

CANANDAIGUA

☎ 716 / pop 11,200

The late-Victorian flavored town of Canandaigua is a sprawling place anchored around bustling Main St where you will find stately homes and Greek Revival buildings set well back from the road. The town sits on the northern tip of Canandaigua Lake and gets nicer the further north you go on Main St away from the lake. The name Canandaigua comes from the Seneca 'Kanandarque,' which means 'Chosen Spot,' and the site was the main village in the Seneca Nation. This was where Susan B Anthony was tried for voting in the 19th century, found guilty and fined $100. She refused to pay and the authorities didn't have the nerve to imprison her. When the Susan B Anthony dollar coin was issued in 1979, the Canandaigua National Bank paid her fine with 100 of the new coins. (Despite her legacy, though, this dollar coin has never caught on with the American public.)

Canandaigua lies at the intersection of Rtes 5 and 20. For tourist information about the town, contact the **Canandaigua Chamber of Commerce** (☎ 716-394-4400; 113 Main St; 🕐 9am-5pm Mon-Fri).

The main attraction in town is the **Sonnenberg Gardens and Mansion** (☎ 716-394-4922; 151 Charlotte St; adult/child $8/3; 🕐 9:30am-5:30pm Jun-Oct). This handsome 50-acre estate includes nine formal gardens, an arboretum and an 1887 stone mansion with a tasting room for the Canandaigua Wine Co. The grounds are regarded as some of the finest Victorian gardens in the US.

FINGER LAKES REGION

DETOUR – WINE TRAILS

Finger Lakes vineyards come in all varieties: some have magnificent lake views. Others sit back off seemingly lost byways. Some are large, some small. A few are commercial enterprises with large tasting rooms and gift shops. Still others are family-run affairs in the back of a faded barn. Since the Finger Lakes became known for winemaking about 25 years ago, more and more vineyards have been cropping up in the region.

Much of the region's wine revolution can be credited to Dr Konstantin Frank. For years New York winemakers used native labrusca grapes, which make great jam but mediocre wine, because they believed that European vinifera grapes could not survive in the state. Enter Dr Frank. Born of German parents in the Ukraine in 1899, Frank held a doctorate in plant sciences and had been director of a large state-owned vineyard in the Ukraine. In 1953 he came to the US and eventually was hired by Charles Fournier, who was working at the Urbana Wine Co (which later became Gold Seal).

Fournier and Frank experimented with grafting native American rootstock to European vinifera buds to prove the latter could grow in New York. Frank's experiments led to the growth of the state's huge wine industry. He later opened his own winery – Dr Konstantin Frank's Vinifera Wine Cellars (see p249) – although it wasn't successful until his son Willy Frank took over in the 1980s and the business expanded beyond experimentation to the production of fine wines.

Today the Finger Lakes region is home to more than half of the state's wineries. And New York is now the second-largest wine-producing state in the US, after California, with annual sales of over $300 million. The long-held opinion that New York wines were too 'grapey' is changing as premium vineyards appear and occasionally win awards once conceded to California wines.

To explore the region all you need is a car and sharp eyes. To find the wineries look for the 'Wine Trails' signs, but beware it will take months (and you will be very, very drunk) to visit every vineyard in the region.

The trails often hug lakeside roads with wineries on one side an water on the other, and even if you're not much of a wine drinker, it's worth exploring the trails for the magnificent drives alone. Many places stay open year-round. Most offer free tastings, some offer cellar tours, and still others have restaurants and lodges attached.

The **New York Wine & Grape Foundation** (☎ 315-536-7442; 350 Elm St, Penn Yan) can provide information about all Finger Lakes wineries and brochures for various wine trails. Roads on which the 'trails' run are:

- On the west side of Keuka Lake, take Rte 54A north between Hammondsport and Branch-port and then Rte 54 to Penn Yan at the top of Keuka Lake.
- On the west side of Seneca Lake, take Rte 14 north from Watkins Glen to Geneva.
- On the east side of Seneca Lake, follow Rte 414 north from Watkins Glen to Rte 96A.
- On the west side of Cayuga Lake, take Rte 89 north from Ithaca.

Canandaigua's sleeping and eating options tend to be housed in the same buildings. Options include the **Canandaigua Inn on the Lake** (☎ 585-394-7800; www.visitinnonthelake.com; 770 S Main St; d from $130, mains $18; ⚊), an upscale hotel on the waterfront with 147 well-appointed rooms and a wonderful indoor swimming pool. The inn's restaurant serves contemporary American cuisine in a dining room with lake views.

Kellogg's Pan-Tree Inn (☎ 585-394-3909; 130 Lakeshore Dr; d from $65, mains $8) is also located on the lakefront and provides good access to the beach. It caters to families and has 15 rooms and a relaxed restaurant known for its pancakes (you can order them all day), homemade baked goods and creamed codfish.

Thendara Inn (☎ 585-394-4868; 4356 E Lake Rd; d from $115, mains $20) is perched high on a hill overlooking the lake, has five antique furnished guest rooms and an excellent restaurant (dinner only) which serves American cuisine in three dining rooms with sweeping lake views.

Try **Koozina's** (☎ 585-396-0360; 699 S Main St; mains $9) if you're in the mood for inexpensive wood oven pizza or pastas.

ROCHESTER

☎ 585 / pop 219,773

Rochester spreads across and around the Genesee River in western New York, a few miles south of Lake Ontario. The city, New York's third largest, has a small, modern downtown that's encircled by an expressway (but somewhat deserted at night), and a number of neighborhoods with old homes and mansions from its industrial glory days.

During the 19th century, Rochester attracted several important figures. The abolitionist Frederick Douglass published his *North Star* newspaper here beginning in 1847, and Susan B Anthony was arrested for voting here in 1872 (but she was tried in Canandaigua). In 1853 John Bausch and Henry Lomb opened a small optical shop that grew to global dimensions. In the 1880s a inquisitive bank clerk named George Eastman experimented with photographic techniques in his mother's kitchen; the Eastman Kodak Company followed. Even the Xerox Corporation got its start in Rochester, as the Haloid Company in 1906.

The prosperity of Kodak and others benefited Rochester throughout most of the later 19th and 20th centuries. Beginning in the 1960s, however, Rochester experienced the hard economic times of many industrial cities, earning its place along the rust belt. During the late '90s, the economy rebounded, and the city has a lively, if slightly bland, feel.

Orientation & Information

The central downtown area of Rochester is encircled by the 'Inner Loop,' part of I-490. The Genesee River runs north–south through the western portion of downtown. The High Falls are two blocks north of the Inner Loop. Park Ave, a popular restaurant and shopping district, is just east of downtown. East Ave is Rochester's 'museum and mansion row.'

Brownbag Bookshop (☎ 716-271-2494; 678 Monroe Ave; ☉ 9am-6pm) Sells used books.

Greater Rochester Visitors' Association (☎ 585-546-3070; www.visitrochester.com; 45 East Ave; ☉ 8.30am-5pm Mon-Fri, 9am-5pm Sat, 10am-3pm Sun) Good information about the area.

Main post office (☎ 716-272-5952; 1335 Jefferson Rd; ☉ 9am-5pm Mon-Fri, 9am-1pm Sat)

Sights & Activities

Rochester contains several exceptional museums that shouldn't be missed.

GEORGE EASTMAN HOUSE & INTERNATIONAL MUSEUM OF PHOTOGRAPHY & FILM

The **house** (☎ 585-271-3361; 900 East Ave; adult/child $8/3; ☉ 10am-5pm Tue-Sat, 1-5pm Sun) that Kodak built is a 1905 colonial-Revival mansion. Daily docent tours begin at 10:30am and 2pm (2pm only on Sundays), but you can easily explore the exhibits on your own with a self-guided map.

The museum, connected to the house by a long corridor filled with photos and history, boasts the world's largest collection of historic films, photographs, cameras and books about photography and film with rotating exhibits of original photographs and equipment.

Serious students of photography can also make an appointment to view some of the 400,000 photographs dating from 1839 to the present (via videodisk or actual images); the motion-picture collection of 25,000 films and 3 million publicity stills and posters; the 15,000 cameras and pieces of equipment in the 'technology vault' and the 51,000 titles in the Menschel Library. Visitors can also step outside to take in the restored gardens on this 12-acre estate.

STRONG MUSEUM

A hands-on history center for children and home of the National Toy Hall of Fame, the **Strong Museum** (☎ 585-263-2700; cnr Chestnut St & Woodbury Blvd; adult/child $7/5; ☉ 10am-5pm Mon-Thu & Sat, 10am-8pm Fri, noon-5pm Sun) features an enormous collection of middle-class Americana. A working 1918 carousel and an operating 1950s diner at the museum's glass atrium entrance set the tone for a whimsical and interactive learning environment: you can step into Sesame Street, pilot a giant helicopter or produce your own television show. Want to travel through time? No problem, the TimeLab exhibit allows you to do just that while learning about American food, fashion and politics.

Although it's not officially described as a children's museum, the Strong is very popular with kids, probably because it offers a great deal for them to do – including trying on clothes from other eras. But it does manage to bridge the generation gap with such ongoing exhibits as 'When Barbie Dated GI Joe – Toying with the Cold War.' Plastic Godzillas, trigger-happy cowboys, dainty dolls and tiny cooking sets from the 1950s and '60s show period stereotypes of boys and girls.

Allocate at least a few hours for this amazing museum, one of the region's best.

SUSAN B ANTHONY HOUSE & MT HOPE CEMETERY

The **Susan B Anthony House** (☎ 585-235-6124; 17 Madison St; adult/child $7/5; ☿ 11am-5pm Tue-Sun Jun-Aug) was the famous feminist's home from 1866 to 1906. She helped write the *History of Woman Suffrage* in her attic, and she was arrested here in 1872 after she tried to vote.

At the corner of Mt Hope and Elmwood Aves south of downtown, the Mt Hope Cemetery features a rolling expanse of 196 acres that attracts walkers, cyclists and sun lovers. Dating from 1838, the chapel, crematorium and other buildings represent neo-Gothic, Moorish Revival and Italianate styles. Mt Hope is the final resting place of Frederick Douglass, Susan B Anthony, Buffalo Bill's children and George Washington's drummer boy, among other luminaries.

Sleeping

As befits a big city, Rochester has a variety of sleeping options. B&Bs are generally non-smoking and most everywhere comes with air-conditioning. Parking is not a problem.

Hyatt Regency Rochester (☎ 585-546-1234; www .rochester.hyatt.com; 125 E Main St; d from $130; ☒) This is the best large hotel in town and is connected to the convention center by an enclosed skyway. Amenities include excellent service, a pool, health club and the Palladio restaurant.

Dartmouth House B&B (☎ 585-271-7872; www.dart mouthhouse.com; 215 Dartmouth St; d from $95) This B&B is ideally located between Monroe and East Aves and within walking distance of several restaurants and museums. The 1905 English Tudor home has four luxurious guest rooms. The hosts are very well versed on the area.

428 Mt Vernon (☎ 585-271-0792; www.428mt vernon.com; 428 Mt Vernon Ave; d $125) The seven spacious rooms in this Victorian house are filled with antique furniture.

Strathallan Hotel (☎ 585-461-5010; www.strathallan .com; 550 East Ave; d from $120; ☒) This 150-room

---

THE HOUSE OF JELL-O

Paul B Wait, a carpenter, invented Jell-O – the trademark for a gelatin desert and metaphor for the weak of knee – in 1897 in the town of LeRoy, southwest of Rochester. Orator Woodward bought the rights for Jell-O for $450 in 1899, and in 1925 the Woodward family sold them for $60 million.

The Jell-O Gallery at the **LeRoy House Historic Museum** (☎ 716-768-7433; 23 E Main St, LeRoy; admission $3; ☿ 10am-4pm Mon-Sat, 1-4pm Sun, closed weekends Nov-Apr) tells the story of this original bit of Americana. LeRoy is about a 30-minute drive southwest of Rochester (about 3 miles south of exit 47 off I-90).

---

hotel is set among several mansions and boasts of service to match the neighborhood. Most rooms have balconies, and all have fridges and small kitchenettes. Newly renovated, it has a rooftop bar.

Days Inn Historic (☎ 585-325-5010; www.daysinn .com; 384 East Ave; d from $69; ☒) Located in town, this place is within walking distance of several restaurants, museums and galleries.

Decent, and usually cheaper, motels are outside town near the highways. Near the airport, take I-390 to exit 18 west (Brooks Ave/Airport exit). Go one block to Buell Rd and turn right. Several discount motel chains line the first block of Buell, including **Motel 6** (☎ 585-436-2170; www.motel6.com; 155 Buell Rd; d from $50; ☒).

Eating

You'll find several good, inexpensive eateries along Monroe Ave, a popular restaurant-row destination southeast of the Inner Loop between Union and Alexander Sts. It's a popular street to stroll, with its variety of restaurants, herb shops, and used clothing and antique stores.

Richardson's Canal House (☎ 585-248-5000; 1474 Marsh Rd; mains $25) Richardson's is a Rochester institution. Housed in a restored 1818 Erie Canal tavern it is both elegant and highly acclaimed. French and American cuisine is served by candlelight. Richardson's is near the Victor Rd exit of I-490.

Raj Mahal (☎ 585-546-2315; 324 Monroe Ave; mains $15) Serving excellent mostly North Indian food (tandoori etc) and several vegetarian dishes, this restaurant is located at the corner of Alexander St. You can watch your food being prepared through a glass window.

Olive Tree (☎ 585-454-3510; 165 Monroe Ave; mains $16) This restaurant is housed in a restored 1864 brick storefront with a summer garden. The menu features nouvelle Greek cuisine that emphasizes fresh ingredients. It also features Greek wines and beers.

Highland Park Diner (☎ 585-461-5040; 960 S Clinton Ave; sandwiches from $5) This is a restored 'Orleans' style diner boasting 'real food at real prices.'

Entertainment

CLUBS

Rochester's downtown club scene is spread among three areas, starting with the hip East End district around the Eastman School of Music.

Center at High Falls (☎ 585-423-0000; 60 Browns Race) The Center is in the High Falls district and you can get a bit of everything here including three nightclubs with jazz and dance music, plus a sports bar and outdoor patio.

Jillian's (☎ 585-454-6530; 61 Commercial St) Around the corner from High Falls, Jillian's is an unlikely combination of restaurant, bowling alley, billiard room and dance spot.

Milestones Tavern & Music Room (☎ 585-325-6490; 170 East Ave) Nightly live music is on the menu here. The place brings in regional and, occasionally, national acts.

THEATER & MUSIC

The Geva Theatre Center (☎ 585-232-4382; www.geva theatre.org; 75 Woodbury Blvd) At the corner of Clinton Ave S, this is Rochester's premiere professional theater. The performance season runs from September through June.

Little Theatres (☎ 585-232-4699; 240 East Ave; admission $3) Revivals and new independent movies on are shown on five screens in a classic Art Deco building in the East End district.

Eastman School of Music (☎ 585-274-1100; 26 Gibbs St) One of the world's premiere music schools has regularly scheduled jazz and classical concerts by students and visitors. More than 700 performances are staged annually. The Rochester Philharmonic Orchestra also performs here.

Getting There & Around

Greater Rochester International Airport (☎ 716-464-6000; Brooks Ave), at I-390 exit 18, is served by most major American carriers. The typical round-trip fare from Chicago is around $253, from New York City $155, and from Philadelphia $230. Usually there are specials.

The **bus terminal** (☎ 800-295-5555; 187 Midtown Plaza) is on the corner of Broad and Chestnut Sts. Buses go to Buffalo, Syracuse, Niagara Falls and points further east like Albany and New York City. Trains from the **Amtrak train station** (☎ 585-454-2894, 800-872-7245; 320 Central Ave) run east through Syracuse to New York City, west to Buffalo and other points.

If you're coming by car, Rochester is about 10 miles north of I-90 via I-390 (Genesee Expressway) or I-490, which circles the center of town.

The Skyway system is an enclosed network of walkways connecting downtown buildings. The Skyway begins at Main St near the Genesee River, runs three blocks east to Elm St and then three blocks south to a parking garage on Woodbury Blvd.

Western New York

With 40 million gallons of water per minute hurtling downward and extending outward into a cloud of mist, Niagara Falls is western New York's most revered tourist attraction, and the state's most famous after New York City. Honeymooners, daredevils, artists and families all traipse through the Niagara Reservation State Park to spend a minute, an hour or a day staring at the power and magnificence of the falls. The water, before it plunges over the edge, is a multitude of colors that change with the shifting light – from a cold glacial blue to almost turquoise or pale sea-green.

The falls are not the only reason to visit this part of the state. Just a short drive away is the vibrant city of Buffalo. In a state of revival, it is home to numerous art galleries, fascinating architecture – some of which was designed by Frank Lloyd Wright – and a thriving theater scene. It's also the home of Buffalo wings and Buffalo Bills football. South of Buffalo, the Chautauqua Institution hosts a well-known summer retreat, which includes lectures and courses on music, dance, theater and art. The courses attract about 180,000 visitors to this tranquil lakeside community. In addition the area is home to wonderful Allegany State Park, with miles of hiking trails, stream-fishing and year-round camping; to the town of Lockport, where you can relive life on the Erie Canal; and to Jamestown, home of Lucille Ball of *I Love Lucy* fame.

HIGHLIGHTS

■ **Wettest Natural Wonder**
Niagara Falls. Need we say more? Forty million gallons of water hurtling downward creates a tremendous cloud of mist (p271).

■ **Best Bar**
Buffalo's Anchor Bar. Home of the Buffalo wing, and a low-key place where you can chow delicious wings and drink beer (p270).

■ **Best Summer Retreat**
Chautauqua Institution. Quiet charm, famous porches and a summer educational series (p278).

■ **Best Year-Round Park**
Allegany State Park. Camp and hike year-round, or in winter go ice-fishing, cross-country skiing and snowmobiling (p282).

■ **Best-Kept Secret**
Buffalo. The city famous for snow has much more: vibrant arts, good theater, excellent restaurants, bars and Frank Lloyd Wright–designed buildings (p265).

CLIMATE

Buffalo is famous for a phenomenon known as 'lake-effect snow.' Storms gain strength as they blow from the northwest to the southeast over the Great Lakes and tend to dump all concentrated precipitation on the eastern shores. During the winter snow falls often and in great quantities, although locals will tell you it's a lot lighter here than over in Syracuse. Winter temperatures in the region are low, with highs only about 21°F in January. Temperatures climb in April where they reach around 50°F and by July temperatures can soar into the 90°F range. Although an ice-covered Niagara Falls can be a spectacular site to view, most of region is most comfortably visited during the warmer months.

STATE PARKS

There are a number of state parks in western New York. The most famous is the **Niagara Reservation State Park** (p274), from which you have stunning views of the state's number two tourist attraction and one of the natural wonders of the world. The state park is the oldest in the country and receives about 12 million visitors per year.

North of Niagara Falls is the 150-acre **Artpark** (p278), a National Historic Landmark Site, and the only state park in the country entirely dedicated to the visual and performing arts.

Also north of Niagara Falls is the **Fort Niagara State Park** (p277), which includes the Old Fort Niagara, a fully restored fort built in the 1700s.

At the state's western edge lies the 65,000-acre **Allegany State Park** (p282), which includes over 80 miles of hiking trails. The park is open year-round but is best known for its winter facilities, which include ice-fishing, snowmobiling and cross-country skiing.

GETTING THERE & AROUND

I-90 stretches from New York's southwest corner to Buffalo, then runs east toward Rochester. The other major east–west road is Rte 17/I-86 near the Pennsylvania border; Rte 417, which branches off Rte 17/I-86 just east of Allegany State Park, is certainly one of the prettiest drives in all New York. Other east–west roads are Rte 20, which heads east from Buffalo to the Finger Lakes; and Rte 104, which heads east from Niagara Falls to Rochester.

Buses between Niagara Falls and Buffalo run up to five times daily. Amtrak has service between New York City and Buffalo.

GREATER BUFFALO

Famous for its winter snowfalls, Buffalo has been heating up as an outpost for art, theater and architecture.

BUFFALO

☎ 716 / pop 310,500

A mixture of edgy and hip, Buffalo is like a gawky teenager unsure just how she wants to reinvent herself. Spunky yet awkward, she can't quite decide whether to shake off her old rust-belt image of decaying factories, disappearing industry, snow and poverty and take on a new persona of cultural hub extraordinaire, serious art destination and maybe even New York City of the north.

Walk the tree-lined streets of New York State's second-largest city and everywhere you look you'll see revival. A crowded coffee house full of modern art and bright red walls, a sleek new bar done up in black-and-white where the cool come to play, and the largest collection of theaters in the state outside of New York City. Peruse the local newspapers and you'll see advertisements for gallery openings, for concerts, for film, art and food festivals.

Yet walk these same streets, lined with historic buildings from early skyscrapers to 19th-century residences, buildings designed by America's foremost architects – Frank Lloyd Wright, Louis Sullivan and Henry Hobson Richardson – in the early morning or late afternoon, when no one's about, and you'll feel something almost akin to danger in the air. Although it's more a feeling than a threat, there are still boarded-up buildings here, and problems with rising crime rates and dodgy streets you just don't want to walk down.

Buffalo's a city in transition. But despite its problems, we're betting this transition is going to be a good one.

Orientation

Buffalo's major streets radiate outward from its downtown business district. Because Lake Erie forms the city's western

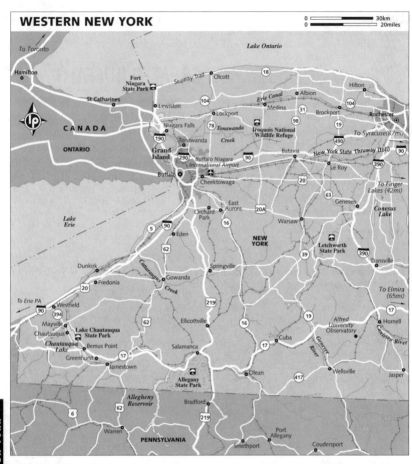

WESTERN NEW YORK

and southern borders, most of the city's major streets begin in the downtown area and run to the north and the east. Niagara Sq serves as a point of orientation in the downtown. The visitors bureau and city hall are nearby.

From Niagara Sq in the downtown area, Niagara St branches out to the northwest and Delaware Ave to the north. Main St is three blocks east of Delaware Ave and runs north to south. Main St is closed to traffic downtown from the Buffalo & Erie County Naval & Military Park (Naval Park) to near Goodell St. A Metro rail public transportation line runs up the center of Main St and this car-free pedestrian area is designated 'Buffalo Place.'

North of downtown is the historic district of Allentown. Good walking-tour maps are available from the visitors bureau. Between Allen and North Sts in Allentown is the Elmwood strip, a trendy and lively area of shops, eateries and bookstores.

Buffalo is a city where it helps to have a car to see things; the most interesting sights are far apart.

Information

Rust Belt Books (☎ 716-885-9535; 202 Allen St) is an eclectic bookshop in the Allentown neighborhood that has all genres of reading material and helpful staff.

The **Greater Buffalo Convention & Visitors Bureau** (☎ 716-852-2356, 800-283-3256; www.buffalocvb.org;

617 Main St; 8am-5pm Mon-Fri) houses a visitors center in the Market Arcade. The center provides a wide selection of travel brochures and maps.

The local newspaper is the *Buffalo News*; *ArtVoice* is the giveaway arts paper in town and a good source of information for gallery openings, concerts and theater productions.

Sights & Activities

There is something for everyone in Buffalo, from museums to fascinating architecture to galleries.

ALBRIGHT-KNOX ART GALLERY

Housed in a wonderful Greek Revival building this **museum** (716-882-8700; 1285 Elmwood Ave; adult/child $5/4; 11am-5pm Tue-Sat, noon-5pm Sun) is the heart of Buffalo's art scene. World-renowned for an excellent collection of contemporary art, the Albright-Knox Art Gallery was the first museum in the US to purchase works by Picasso and Matisse. It's best known for its collection of 20th-century works from all the major currents, from abstract expressionism to pop art. The collection also contains paintings and sculpture from other historic periods. The museum is north of the downtown near Scajaquada Parkway.

THEATER DISTRICT

The restored Theater District begins one block north of the Hyatt hotel. The 20-block area extends west as far as Delaware Ave and north to Tupper St. Here you'll find about a half-dozen theaters, along with restaurants, galleries and shops. Chippewa St, in the heart of the district, is known for its nightlife. Quiet during the day, at night the street comes alive. Whether it's a pre-theater cocktail or a night of barhopping, Chippewa St does not disappoint.

The crown jewel of the Theater District is **Shea's Performing Arts Center** (716-847-1410; www.sheas.org; 646 Main St). The interior dates back to 1926 and was designed by Louis Comfort Tiffany. Formerly a movie palace, opulence reins supreme here – from the 15ft Tiffany chandeliers to the marble floors. The center was almost demolished in 1975 but is now fully restored. It showcases first-run musicals, opera, dance and concerts.

Buffalo's theater season runs from September to May. Pick up the free weekly *ArtVoice* (www.artvoice.com) for performance schedules.

Other theaters in the district include: Ujima Theater Co in the **Alleyway Theatre** (716-852-2600; 1 Curtain Up Alley), a small, intimate theater company that showcases new plays; **Theater Loft** (716-883-0380; 545 Elmwood Ave), a professional company dedicated to performing works by African-American and other playwrights; The Theater of Youth at the newly renovated **Allendale Theatre** (716-884-4400; 203 Allen St), in historic Allentown, which has staged plays for children and young adults for 20 years; and **Irish Classical Theatre** (716-853-4282; 625 Main St) in a new, state-of-the-art center that mounts productions by renowned Irish and international playwrights.

ORIGINAL AMERICAN KAZOO FACTORY

The only **metal kazoo factory** (716-992-3960; 8703 S Main St; admission free; 10am-5pm Tue-Sat, noon-5pm Sun) in the world, this is a one-of-a-kind place. It's a combination of factory, museum and gift shop. Established in 1916, the factory paid $5000 for its first kazoo patent and still makes the instruments in the same manner it always has – using sheet metal and die presses. The factory showcases strange kazoo facts – the record for the most kazoos played at once was set in Rochester on January 2, 1986 and totaled 54,500. It also has a large kazoo display. There are even kazoos shaped like liquor bottles produced to celebrate the end of the Prohibition. The factory is about 30 minutes south of town in Eden on Rte 62.

PEDALING HISTORY BICYCLE MUSEUM

This **museum** (716-662-3853; 3943 N Buffalo Rd; adult/child $6/4; 11am-5pm Mon-Sat, 1:30-5pm Sun Apr–mid-Jan, closed Tue-Thu mid-Jan–Mar) is the only one in the country dedicated exclusively to bicycles. There are 300 bikes and other related paraphernalia on display, as well as exhibits tracing the history of bicycling. The museum is in Orchard Park, about 12 miles southwest of downtown on Rte 20A.

Tours

Theodore Roosevelt Inaugural National Historic Site (716-884-0095; Wilcox Mansion, 641 Delaware Ave) offers self-guided audio walking tours of Buffalo's architectural sites. The cost is $5 for the tape, plus a $25 deposit (you return

WESTERN NEW YORK

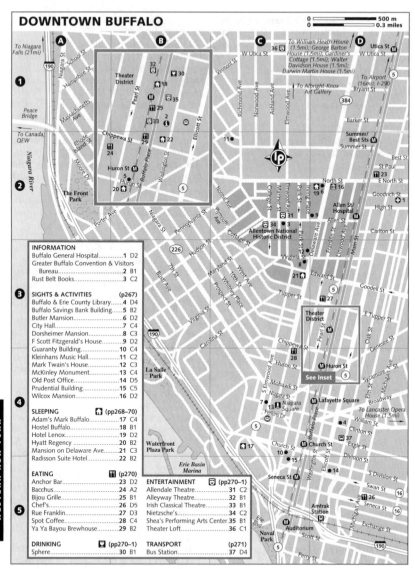

DOWNTOWN BUFFALO

0 — 500 m
0 — 0.3 miles

it at the end) and cassette players can also be rented for a nominal fee.

Sleeping

Sleeping options in Buffalo are mostly limited to chain hotels and motels, although many of these places are quite posh. For quality, rates are generally lower in Buffalo than other cities of comparable size in the state. Parking is available in private lots on accommodation grounds. Air-conditioning is standard.

BUDGET

Hostel Buffalo (☎ 716-852-5222; www.hostelbuffalo .com; 667 Main St; dm $22, d $51) In the heart of

BUFFALO ARCHITECTURE

You can explore Buffalo's architectural treasures in greater depth if you take advantage of one of the excellent self-guided or guided architectural tours (p267) sponsored by the Theodore Roosevelt Inaugural National Historic Site. If you are already versed in American architecture and would prefer going it alone, you might pick up a copy of Reyner Banham's book *Buffalo Architecture: A Guide*, which is available in many local bookstores.

The largest concentration of Frank Lloyd Wright homes is north of the downtown area near Delaware Park, which was designed by landscape architect Frederick Law Olmsted. Most of these residences are privately owned except **Darwin Martin House** (☎ 716-831-3485; 125 Jewett Pkwy; adult/child $7/3.50; ☒ tours Tue & Thu), which is owned by SUNY-Buffalo. Call for exact hours of tours. Others include the **William Heath House** (76 Soldiers Place), at the corner of Bird Ave; **George Barton House** (118 Summit), which is definitely worth a look; **Gardiner's Cottage** (285 Woodward Ave); and **Walter Davidson House** (57 Tillinghast Place). The homes can be distinguished from others in the neighborhood by their sleek and strong horizontal lines.

Frank Lloyd Wright's mentor, architect Louis Sullivan, and his partner Dankmar Adler, designed the **Prudential Building** on Church St. Sullivan is generally regarded as the father of the skyscraper. One of the finest examples of early skyscraper design is Sullivan's **Guaranty Building** (28 Church St), near Pearl St. Built in 1895, the building was beautifully restored in 1983.

There are a number of other interesting buildings downtown, such as the art-deco **City hall** (Niagara Sq), the **old post office** (cnr Ellicott & Swan St) and the former **Buffalo Savings Bank building** (cnr Main & Huron St). Henry Hobson Richardson designed nine of the buildings at the **Buffalo State Psychiatric Hospital** (400 Forest Ave). These red sandstone buildings are excellent examples of the Romanesque Revival Richardson championed in the latter half of the 19th century. The **McKinley Monument**, designed by Carrère and Hastings and sculpted by A Philmister Proctor, is in the middle of Niagara Sq.

The beautiful residential neighborhood of Allentown is just southwest of the intersection of Delaware and North Sts. The streets of this National Historic District are lined with restored 19th-century homes, galleries and restaurants. Walk by the 1869 **Dorsheimer Mansion** (434 Delaware St), which was designed by Henry Hobson Richardson, and the 1899 **Butler Mansion** (672 Delaware St), designed by Stanford White.

The Finnish architects Eliel and Eero Saarinen designed the modernist **Kleinhans Music Hall** (☎ 716-883-3560) on Symphony Circle. The building is famous for its modern, curving lines and acoustic excellence.

F Scott Fitzgerald's childhood home is at 29 Irving Place. **Mark Twain** lived at 472 Delaware Ave while working for the *Buffalo Morning Express*. The one historic home open to visitors is the **Wilcox Mansion** (☎ 716-884-0095; 641 Delaware Ave; adult/child $3/1; ☒ 9am-5pm Mon-Fri, noon-5pm Sat & Sun). Now a National Historic Site and museum, this was the site of Teddy Roosevelt's inauguration following President William McKinley's assassination.

the Theater District, this big, airy hostel is in a historic building and has 52 beds in immaculate dorms. There is no lockout during summer and the staff is knowledgeable about what's happening in Buffalo.

Hotel Lenox (☎ 716-884-1700, 800-825-3669; 140 North St; s/d $59/69) This is an old classic in the city's historic Allentown district. The good-sized rooms are furnished with mismatched but sturdy furniture and include kitchenettes.

Sleep Inn (☎ 716-626-4000; 100 Holtz Rd; d $69) By the airport, this chain motel offers clean, comfortable rooms.

MID-RANGE

Adam's Mark Buffalo (☎ 716-845-5100; 120 Church St; d from $99; ☒) Located at the corner of Lower Terrace, this is the largest hotel in western New York, and a luxurious complex overlooking Lake Erie and the entire downtown. The lobby features marble floors and a waterfall, and the hotel has its own health club. Ask about discounts and weekend specials.

Radisson Suite Hotel (☎ 716-854-5500; 601 Main St; d from $112; ☒) Downtown and adjacent to the historic Market Arcade annex, this is another solid choice. Amenities match the price.

TOP END

Mansion on Delaware Avenue (☎ 716-886-3300; www.themansionondelaware.com; 414 Delaware Ave; d from $135) This is Buffalo's hippest establishment. Ultra-swanky, the 134-year-old mansion was turned into a 28-room hotel just a few years ago. The most unique feature is the hotel 'butlers,' who drop off and pick up guests at nearby restaurants free of charge.

Hyatt Regency (☎ 716-856-1234; 2 Fountain Plaza; d from $140; ⊠) This is truly a luxurious place. It's in the Theater District on the Buffalo Place pedestrian mall along Main St. The brick and stone building was originally an office tower that was converted into a hotel in 1984. Even if you don't stay here, it's a fun place to explore. The lobby is a plant-filled atrium. There are three restaurants, a bar, indoor pool and sun garden.

Eating

In culinary terms, Buffalo is best known for its Buffalo-style chicken wings and beef on weck. Buffalo wings are covered in a spicy red chili sauce (unlike the honey-mustard sauce of lesser-known Rochester wings) and are served with creamy blue-cheese dressing and celery sticks. Beef on weck is sliced roast beef on kummelweck, a hard roll impregnated with salt and sometimes caraway seeds. Both items are featured on menus throughout the city.

Ya Ya Bayou Brewhouse (☎ 716-854-9292; 617 Main St; mains $7-16; ⊗ dinner) This hip place serves Cajun mains in a red-walled, purple-carpeted and mirrored environment. The food is outstanding.

Spot Coffee (☎ 716-854-7768; cnr Delaware Ave & Chippewa St) For delicious coffee and assorted sandwiches and pastries baked from scratch on-site, try this western New York chain. There are bright walls filled with artwork and plenty of couches to chill out on. Sometimes there is live music at night.

Rue Franklin (☎ 716-852-4416; 341 Franklin St; mains $21-26; ⊗ dinner) For excellent French cuisine try Rue Franklin, located in a brick townhouse just north of town. The menu is small and changes seasonally.

Chef's (☎ 716-856-9170; 291 Seneca St; mains from $10) Another Buffalo institution, the main building of this Italian restaurant is an unpretentious three-story brownstone connected to two one-story additions. The decor is simple and the food is good. Dishes

ANCHOR BAR

Your vocabulary need only consist of four words at Buffalo's most famous restaurant – mild, medium, hot or suicidal. Okay, maybe five – beer appears to also be essential. The **Anchor Bar** (☎ 716-886-8920; 1047 Main St; mains $6-15) claims to have invented Buffalo chicken wings in 1964. Located in a marginal neighborhood, the bar still packs in crowds most days of the week. Inside the redbrick building is a tin-ceiling bar backed with a hundred baseball caps, license plates and other memorabilia. You can also dine in one of the two modern – but less imaginative – dining rooms. Wings come in single and double orders ($8/12). Often when a place becomes notorious, the quality decreases. Not here. The wings remain mouthwatering. And it's not just the sauce – the chicken is also perfect (not too fatty). You'll find yourself still eating long after you're full. Besides wings, the Anchor Bar has a full menu of seafood, pasta, pizza, chicken and sandwiches, but most people just eat the wings.

(most with tomato sauce) are offered in small and large portions. Typical dishes are spaghetti with meatballs or sausages, or ravioli stuffed with meatballs, mushrooms or sausages. Chef's is in an industrial neighborhood a few blocks east of Main St.

Bacchus (☎ 716-854-9563; 56 Chippewa St; tapas $8) Perfect for before or after the theater, this is a very swanky tapas and wine bar with a black-and-white theme. The menu is innovative and the wine list extensive.

Bijou Grille (☎ 716-847-1512; 643 Main St; mains $6-22) An array of American cuisine is served in an art-deco environment in the heart of the Theater District. The grille also has a long bar, and there's outdoor dining in the summertime.

Drinking & Entertainment

Buffalo has a thriving entertainment scene, and visitors can find worthwhile offerings every night. The best sources for information on nightlife and theater productions are the Friday edition of the *Buffalo News* and *ArtVoice*. The Chippewa District downtown has numerous bars and clubs, as does Elmwood Ave in the Allentown historic district. Tickets to sporting events and theater productions can be purchased through **Ticketmaster** (☎ 716-852-5000).

Sphere (☎ 716-852-3900; 681 Main St) Buffalo's most popular nightclub, Sphere is a massive establishment with numerous rooms, a great design, and an overwhelming feeling of coolness. Lines form to get in the door on weekends, and the place also showcases live music.

Nietzsche's (☎ 716-886-8539; 248 Allen St) This old standby brings in everything from popular rock and blues bands to country, reggae and folk groups. It's a casual club with a good little dance floor.

The Buffalo Philharmonic Orchestra (☎ 716-885-5000; 370 Pennsylvania Ave) This orchestra performs at the Saarinen-designed Kleinhans Music Hall, one of five acoustically perfect concert halls in the country.

Lancaster Opera House (☎ 716-683-1776; 21 Central Ave) A restored 350-seat, early-20th-century theater, the opera house puts on plays, musicals and concerts.

Buffalo Bills football team (☎ 716-649-0015) This NFL team plays at Ralph Wilson Stadium in Orchard Park from September to December, barring yet another trip to the Superbowl. This team is well known for playing great games until the national championship comes along.

Getting There & Around

Buffalo Niagara International Airport (☎ 716-630-6000; Genesee St) is in Cheektowaga about 16 miles from downtown and is served by numerous carriers. Some average round-trip fares are Boston ($260), New York City ($160) and Chicago ($260). A taxi from the airport costs about $30.

New York Trailways (☎ 716-855-7531, 800-295-5555), **Greyhound** (☎ 800-231-2222) and **NFTA** (☎ 716-285-7211) operate out of the **Metro Transportation Center** (cnr Ellicott & Eagle Sts). NFTA operates bus No 40 between Niagara Falls and Buffalo every day. Express bus No 60 runs between Niagara Falls and Buffalo five times a day from Monday to Friday. Two express buses leave Niagara Falls for Buffalo before 7am and three buses leave Buffalo for Niagara Falls roughly between 4:30pm and 5pm. The fare for both buses is $2.

Amtrak stops in Buffalo at the downtown **Buffalo Exchange Station** (☎ 716-683-8440; cnr Exchange & Oak Sts) and has trains to New York City ($75, eight hours).

Buffalo is reached by I-90 from the east and south and by I-190 from Niagara Falls to the north. The QEW in Canada to the west leads to the Peace Bridge over the Niagara River and into Buffalo at Moore Dr.

Taxi companies around town include:
Airport Taxi Service/ITA Shuttle (☎ 716-633-8318, 800-551-9369)
City Service Taxi (☎ 716-852-4000, 800-439-7006)
Liberty Cab (☎ 716-877-7111, 800-455-8294)

NIAGARA FALLS & AROUND

Straddling Canada and the US, Niagara Falls has long attracted travelers, daredevils and honeymooners to its misty shores.

NIAGARA FALLS
☎ 716 / pop 56,000

Writing about the falls, the French missionary, Father Hennepin, observed that 'the waters which fall from this horrible precipice do foam and boil after the most hideous manner imaginable.' In a more irreverent vein, Oscar Wilde remarked that he would have been more impressed if the falls had flowed upward. It's unlikely the two gentlemen had much in common.

When describing the falls, it is important to note that there are actually two cataracts, or high waterfalls. The Canadian, or **Horseshoe Falls**, are the larger and more impressive. They are 2500ft across and plunge 170ft down. The smaller **American Falls** are 1100ft across and fall 180ft. Sometimes referred to as a separate cataract, **Bridal Veil Falls** actually form the western portion of the American Falls. The parkland called **Goat Island** sits in the middle of the Niagara River. The middle of the river makes up part of the international border between Canada and the US, the longest unprotected border in the world.

Originally about 200,000 cu ft per second (or 5.5 billion gallons per hour) of water flowed over the falls, but today between a half and three-quarters of the water is diverted to run power turbines in the US and Canada. About 10% of the water flows over the American Falls and 90% over the Canadian Horseshoe Falls.

The falls were formed about 12,000 years ago as glaciers melted, releasing water from

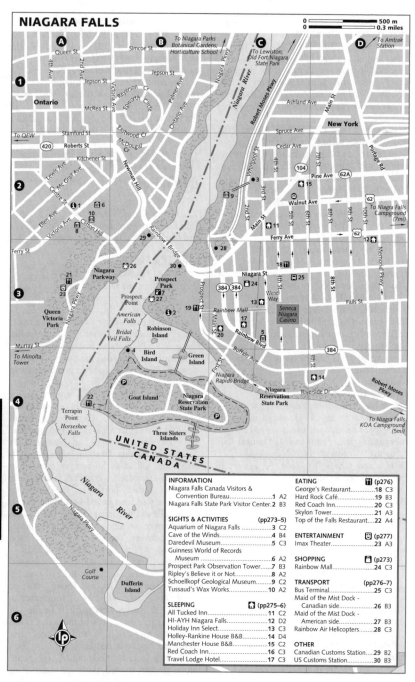

NIAGARA FALLS

0 _____ 500 m
0 _____ 0.3 miles

WESTERN NEW YORK

INFORMATION	
Niagara Falls Canada Visitors &	
Convention Bureau	1 A2
Niagara Falls State Park Visitor Center	2 B3

SIGHTS & ACTIVITIES	(pp273–5)
Aquarium of Niagara Falls	3 C2
Cave of the Winds	4 B4
Daredevil Museum	5 C3
Guinness World of Records	
Museum	6 A2
Prospect Park Observation Tower	7 B3
Ripley's Believe it or Not	8 A2
Schoellkopf Geological Museum	9 C2
Tussaud's Wax Works	10 A2

SLEEPING	(pp275–6)
All Tucked Inn	11 C2
HI-AYH Niagara Falls	12 D2
Holiday Inn Select	13 C3
Holley-Rankine House B&B	14 D4
Manchester House B&B	15 C2
Red Coach Inn	16 C3
Travel Lodge Hotel	17 C3

EATING	(p276)
George's Restaurant	18 C3
Hard Rock Café	19 B3
Red Coach Inn	20 C3
Skylon Tower	21 A3
Top of the Falls Restaurant	22 A4

ENTERTAINMENT	(p277)
Imax Theater	23 A3

SHOPPING	(p273)
Rainbow Mall	24 C3

TRANSPORT	(pp276–7)
Bus Terminal	25 C3
Maid of the Mist Dock -	
Canadian side	26 B3
Maid of the Mist Dock -	
American side	27 B3
Rainbow Air Helicopters	28 C3

OTHER	
Canadian Customs Station	29 B2
US Customs Station	30 B3

the Great Lakes along what became the Niagara River. The 37-mile-long Niagara River connects Lake Erie and Lake Ontario. As it flows through the city of Niagara Falls, the river is actually flowing northward. The water cut through rock over time creating a waterfall. When they were formed, the falls were 7 miles downstream from their present location. The edge of the falls continues to erode upstream at the rate of about one inch every year. Note the piles of boulders at the base of the falls.

In 1969 the American Falls were actually shut off for a period of time. A dam was built across the river and the flow diverted to the Horseshoe Falls because the Army Corps of Engineers wanted to study how to prevent further erosion. Gleeful tourists walked along the dry riverbed, and among the things found were 12 buckets of coins and two bodies.

The falls are illuminated at night throughout the year on a changing monthly schedule, but roughly according to the sunset times. The Festival of Lights refers to the lighting of all the trees in the parks adjacent to the falls, and runs from late November to the first week in January.

The sheer power and beauty of the falls – a spectacular 40 million gallons of water per minute hurtling downward and extending outward into a cloud of mist – have made them a popular destination. After New York City, this is the most popular travelers' spot in New York. As early as 1803, Napoleon's nephew Jerome Bonaparte is said to have made a visit here with his bride. And the challenge of surviving a trip over the falls has attracted a number of curious and daring individuals (see boxed text, p274). Even for the less adventurous, simply viewing and experiencing the falls up close can be an exciting and memorable experience.

Unfortunately, while the falls themselves are amazing, the towns of Niagara Falls fit every cliché in the book – cheesy, tacky, and 1950s kitsch. Cheap souvenir shops share space with faded arcades and wax museums, and to find much charm in either town would be difficult to say the least. That said, the falls are the main attraction, and while it's hard to find a good place to eat, there are a handful of good places to stay.

Orientation

There are actually two towns of Niagara Falls: Niagara Falls, NY, and Niagara Falls, Ontario (Canada), situated across from one another on the opposite banks of the Niagara River. The town of Niagara Falls, NY, is relatively easy to navigate. Its downtown is laid out on a grid pattern with numbered streets running north to south and named ones running east to west, with the exception of a few streets that run diagonally. Prospect Park extends along the Niagara River, creating a vast green strip. Niagara St runs east–west to the Rainbow Bridge gateway to Canada. Most of the major attractions are south of Niagara St, along the river. The Niagara Reservation State Park, on the American side, includes Goat Island, Prospect Point and the Schoellkopf Geological Museum.

See Niagara Falls – the Canadian Side (p277) for coverage across the river.

Information

Throughout the town, you'll come across privately owned information centers that offer accommodations and tour packages. Services vary in quality, but the staff can be helpful in answering questions and providing more general assistance.

The **Niagara Falls State Park Visitors Center** (☎ 716-278-1796; Prospect Park; ✆ 8am-10:15pm) is adjacent to the falls in a swanky building. It is run by the state and has tons of information about the falls and surrounding areas.

You can park for free in the lot of the Rainbow Mall right downtown and walk to everything you'll need to see.

Sight & Activities

Obviously, the falls are the main draw here. And the most pertinent questions is: which side offers the better view? The answer is to check out both sides. For the best panoramic view, cross over to the Canadian side. Views from the American side are considered less satisfactory because you're generally standing too close for comfort, or at an angle that makes viewing difficult. On the other hand, the American side allows you (you have no choice) to feel the immense power of the falls. You can easily walk or drive across **Rainbow Bridge** to Canada. It costs $2.50 per round-trip to drive. Either way you have to go through customs for both countries and non-American or Canadian residents should

NIAGARA FALLS DAREDEVILS

Since early in the 19th century, stuntsters have been attracted to the falls, challenging the raging waters on tightropes and in barrels, kayaks and rubber inner tubes. Some not-so-daring visitors have even gone over the falls unintentionally.

In 1829, Sam Patch started the craziness by leaping twice from a platform about 100ft above the gorge at the foot of the falls. The next person to challenge the falls was Englishman Bobby Leach, who went over in a steel barrel on July 25, 1911. He was so battered and bruised that he needed six months in hospital to recuperate. Fifteen years later, while in New Zealand, Leach slipped on an orange peel, broke his leg and died from ensuing complications.

Jean Lussier of Quebec designed an innovative vehicle with a steel frame and 32 inner tubes and went over on July 4, 1928. He emerged an hour later in perfect health. For years afterwards Lussier sold small pieces of his inner tubes for $0.50 apiece.

The first recorded woman plunger was Anna Edson Taylor, who, at 63, decided the way to fame was to go over the falls in an oak barrel. On October 24, 1901, Taylor and her barrel went over. Less than 20 minutes later, the barrel was pulled to shore and Taylor told a reporter, 'I would sooner walk up to the mouth of a canon knowing it was going to blow me to pieces.'

Only one is recorded to have gone over the falls unintentionally – and lived. On July 9, 1960, Jim Honeycutt took 17-year-old Deanne Woodward and her seven-year-old brother Roger out for a boat ride on the upper Niagara River above the falls. To give the children a thrill, Honeycutt maneuvered the boat close to the falls, but then the engine failed, the boat flipped, and all three were rushing towards the edge of the falls. Deanne was pulled out at Terrapin Point on Goat Island very close to the brink. Honeycutt and Roger Woodward went over. Amazingly, Roger survived and was picked up by the *Maid of the Mist* tour boat, but Honeycutt died.

The most daring – and perhaps the stupidest (though the competition is stiff) – attempt of all was that of Tennessee's Jessie W Sharp, who shot the falls in a 12.5ft polyethylene kayak on June 5, 1990. Sharp had planned to ride the rapids beyond the falls to Lewiston, NY, where he had made dinner reservations. He skipped wearing a helmet so his face would be recognizable on film. It was, but his body was never found.

Tightrope walkers have also challenged the falls. The most famous, Jean François Gravelet – known as 'Blondin' – walked across many times beginning in the summer of 1859, varying his routine each time to continue to attract attention – somersaulting on the rope, cooking an omelette or pulling up a bottle of champagne from the *Maid of the Mist* to refresh himself. He even once carried his trusting manager across on his back.

On October 20, 2003, an unidentified man, apparently attempting suicide, plunged headfirst over the falls and survived. He was led away in handcuffs. The current maximum fine for performing a stunt without a license (and they don't grant licenses anyway) is $10,000. This fine is payable if you live to tell about it.

The greatest daredevil escapes are documented in the **Daredevil Museum** (☎ 716-282-4046; 303 Rainbow Blvd; admission free; ☺ 9am-10pm), a small informal exhibit area in the back of one of the town's souvenir shops.

have their passports ready. Americans and Canadians technically just need identification cards, but in an age of increased security it would be a good idea to bring a passport just in case.

NIAGARA RESERVATION STATE PARK

The oldest state park in the country includes **Goat Island**, a half-mile-long island connected to the US mainland by free pedestrian and car bridges. From the island you can walk to **Three Sisters Islands**, a series of rapids approaching Horseshoe Falls. You can also walk down to **Terrapin Point**, the closest viewing point to Horseshoe Falls. From this spit of land you can imagine 17-year-old Deanne Woodward being rescued from shooting over the brink after her boat capsized (see boxed text, p274).

To experience the falls up close, take an elevator down from Goat Island to the **Cave of the Winds** (☎ 716-278-1730; adult/child $6/5; ☺ Jun-Oct), where you'll walk along wooden walkways within 25ft of the cataracts. You'll be provided with a yellow raincoat to protect you from the heavy mist. It's a rather dramatic experience.

There is free parking at the eastern end of Goat Island close to Three Sisters Islands, or a $5 parking lot near Terrapin Point on the western side of the island.

SCHOELLKOPF GEOLOGICAL MUSEUM
Housing exhibits and explaining the geology of the region, this **museum** (☎ 716-278-1780; Niagara Reservation State Park; admission $1; ☉ 9am-5pm) overlooks the Niagara Gorge. A 15-minute three-screen slide show sketches the geology of the gorge. Information on nature trails surrounding the museum is also available. There are free guided tours along the rim or you can descend to the base of the falls. Walks vary in length and difficulty, but all are designed to be both informative and fun.

AQUARIUM OF NIAGARA FALLS
More than 1500 varieties of fish, sharks and other aquatic animals are on display at this first-rate **aquarium** (☎ 716-285-3575; 701 Whirlpool St; adult/child $6.50/4.50; ☉ 9am-5pm). Check out Peruvian penguins, moray eels, sea lions and Atlantic bottlenose dolphins, among others. There are various feedings each day and an observation deck provides good gorge views. The museum is linked to the geological museum by a footbridge. There is free parking.

SENECA NIAGARA CASINO
Gamblers will want to check out this brand new **casino** (☎ 716-299-1100; www.seneca niagaracasino.com; 310 4th St) with more than 2900 slot machines and tables for blackjack, craps and poker among other games. In addition there is a 426-seat theater featuring everything from comedy to rock-and-roll, a nightclub with DJs and live bands, and a number of restaurants.

Tours
Although you can view the falls by walking or by a combination of driving and walking, many visitors prefer to take in the sights on a narrated bus tour. Typically, tours include stops on both sides of the border. On the US side, the major sights generally include a boat ride on the *Maid of the Mist* and visits to Prospect Park and Goat Island. On the Canadian side, you will visit the tunnels behind the falls and the Minolta Observation Tower.

Check to see what the current tour stops are and compare the package rate with the costs for admission to the individual sights.

MAID OF THE MIST TOURS
Since 1846, Niagara Falls' biggest tourist attraction has been a boat ride on the **Maid of the Mist** (☎ 716-284-8897, Canada ☎ 905-358-5781; adult/child $10.50/6.25; ☉ 9am-6pm May–Oct), which leaves from the base of the Prospect Park Observation Tower. If you only have time for one attraction, this should be it. You'll be supplied with a large yellow raincoat before heading for the base of the American Falls and Horseshoe Falls, where you can best experience the power and the fury of the water hurtling over the cliffs above. Even with a raincoat, expect to get wet. The trip lasts half an hour. *Maid of the Mist* also leaves from the dock at Clifton Hill St and River Rd in Canada.

OTHER TOURS
For informal and very inexpensive sightseeing, hop on the **Viewmobile** (☎ 716-278-1730; adult/child $4.50/3.50; ☉ Oct–Apr), an open trolley operated by the park. The tour goes around Goat Island and over to Prospect Park in a loop, stopping at five various sights. Riders can get on and off at any stop and pick up the next passing trolley.

You can arrange to fly over the falls by contacting **Rainbow Air Helicopters** (☎ 716-284-2800; 454 Main St). Flights last about 10 minutes. Call for prices.

Sleeping
Niagara Falls has sleeping options in all price ranges.

BUDGET
HI-AYH Niagara Falls (☎ 716-282-3700; 1101 Ferry Ave; dm $18) This hostel has seven dormitory rooms with four, six or eight bunks to a room, a large living room, and laundry and kitchen facilities. During summer, guests receive discount coupons for the *Maid of the Mist* boat tours and other attractions. You can also rent a bike for $10 a day. There's a 9:30am to 4pm lockout and an 11:30pm curfew.

Niagara Falls KOA Campground (☎ 716-773-7583; 2570 Grand Island Blvd; campsite $25; ☉ Apr–mid-Nov; 🐾) On Grand Island, about 5 miles south of Niagara Falls, this campground has a pool, laundry facilities, camp store, miniature golf course and more. Take exit N-19 from I-190 on Grand Island.

Niagara Falls Campground (☎ 716-731-3434, 800-525-8505; 2405 Niagara Falls Blvd/Rte 62; campsite $21) About 7 miles east of Niagara Falls, this is another option.

MID-RANGE

Rte 62 (Niagara Falls Blvd), as it nears Niagara Falls, is overloaded with inexpensive motels.

Travel Lodge Hotel/Falls View (☎ 716-285-9321; 201 Rainbow Blvd; d from $59) Scruffy on the outside but considerably more lavish inside, this place is in the old Niagara Hotel, built in 1924. The 193 redecorated guest rooms can't restore the hotel to its former charm, but it's still a decent value. The grand lobby, done up with faux gold trim and many columns, is a dim reminder of better days. There is a cocktail lounge and restaurant. Prices vary according to weekday/weekend and views of the falls (best from the 6th floor and up).

Manchester House B&B (☎ 716-285-5717; 800-489-3009; 653 Main St; d $90) In a private home built in 1903, this is a pleasant place with four rooms. The owners know the area well. Take advantage of the sitting room with its gas fireplace, television and music. From October to May rates drop to $60.

All Tucked Inn (☎ 716-282-0919; 574 3rd St; d from $49) This place has 10 clean rooms with basic furnishings. Two rooms have private baths and the others have sinks and share three clean bathrooms. There are no phones or televisions, and there is generally a 1am curfew.

TOP END

Holley-Rankine House B&B (☎ 716-285-4790, 800-845-6649; 525 Riverside Drive; d $100) In a large Gothic stone house across from Niagara River, the long, comfortable living room with fireplace looks out over the river. There's also a nice stone terrace. The B&B has five rooms and includes a full breakfast.

Red Coach Inn (☎ 716-282-1459; 2 Buffalo Ave; d from $109) The inn offers one- and two-bedroom suites furnished with European antique reproductions. The inn is above the Red Coach restaurant in a 1920s Tudor-style building. The suites at the front of the inn have views of the street and river; rooms in the back of the building have a view of the parking lot.

Holiday Inn Select (☎ 716-285-3361; www.hiselect.com/niagarafalls; 300 3rd St; d $129; ⚏) The newest and the nicest of the area's full-service hotels, this place has 397 luxurious guest rooms featuring high-speed internet access and coffee makers, as well as a restaurant, lounge, indoor pool, whirlpool and sauna.

Eating

Food isn't the main attraction in Niagara Falls. Choices are few and far between, and tend to be spread out.

Red Coach Inn (☎ 716-282-1459; 2 Buffalo Ave; mains $12-25) The restaurant at this inn is one of the best options in town. The dining room is decorated with faux wood beams and chandeliers, and diners are seated in comfortable captain's chairs at oak tables. Dinners feature steak, prime rib and lobster tail. Lunches are cheaper and focus on soups and sandwiches.

Top of the Falls Restaurant (☎ 716-278-0337; Goat Island; lunch $6-9, mains $13-25) Excellent views of the falls are on display through large plate-glass windows and are particularly brilliant at sunset. The restaurant is at Terrapin Point at the tip of Goat Island. Dinners focus on pastas and upscale American cuisine like sesame-seared tuna and honey-barbecue salmon. On Friday night there is a fish fry ($13). Lunch features salads, wraps and pizza. There is also a bar.

Hard Rock Café (☎ 716-282-0007; 333 Prospect St; mains from $10) Serving classic American fare, this Hard Rock Café is like every other one around the world. You'll find plenty of rock-and-roll memorabilia on the walls, a large souvenir shop, and so-so food. But hey, people come for the experience more than anything. It's a good place to take the kids.

George's Restaurant (☎ 716-284-5766; 420 Niagara St; mains $4-6) A simple neighborhood restaurant in an orange building, George's has $4 breakfast specials, sandwiches for under $5 and dinner selections such as meatloaf with mashed potatoes.

Getting There & Around

AIR

Buffalo's airport, which is 30 miles away, is the nearest. To reach the airport from Niagara Falls, go to the bus stop in front of the Niagara Falls Official Information Center at 4th and Niagara Sts, and get the No 40 bus to downtown Buffalo (ask for a transfer). From

Buffalo, take the No 24 bus to the airport. The entire trip takes nearly two hours, and the cost is $2.

Alternately, the **ITA Buffalo Airport Shuttle** (☎ 800-551-9369) runs three times a day between Niagara Falls and the Buffalo airport ($25, 30 minutes). The shuttle service also operates taxis that fit up to five people for $50.

CAR & MOTORCYCLE
You can get to Niagara Falls by I-190 from the south, a toll road from Buffalo, or by Rte 62, a commercial strip that extends all the way from Buffalo to the falls. From Canada, the QEW (Rte 420) highway leads to the Rainbow Bridge, which dumps cars right downtown next to the American Falls.

TRAIN
Amtrak (☎ 716-285-4224) stops at Lockport Rd and 27th St, one block east of Hyde Park Blvd. There is daily service to Buffalo ($14, 50 minutes).

NIAGARA FALLS – THE CANADIAN SIDE
The beautifully landscaped Queen Victoria Park affords the best view of the falls from either side of the river, and it's a short drive, or short walk, across the bridge. Weather permitting, pedestrians often arrive sooner than drivers due to the long line of cars at the international border.

The **Niagara Falls Canada Visitors & Convention Bureau** (☎ 905-356-6061, 800-563-2557; 5433 Victoria Ave; ☼ 9am-5pm) has restaurant and lodging information, and suggestions for enjoying the falls and other parts of the region.

Most Americans and Canadians will encounter little trouble as they cross from one side to the other. Nevertheless, you should have proof of citizenship with you, and it's best to also bring a passport. Citizens of other countries should possess proper documents. If you're renting a car in the US and considering crossing the border, ask the rental agency if you'll need any additional documents.

The Canadian side of the falls is even more touristy than the American side. The downtown area is not as spread out as on the American side, and the business district concentrates around Clifton Hill. Here you will find one kitsch museum after another, from **Tussaud's Wax Works** to **Ripley's Believe It or Not** and the **Guinness World of Records Museum**.

While the US side can boast of offering the most thrilling proximity to the falls, the Canadians can rightly claim the best panorama. The long perspective across the river from **Queen Victoria Park** is magnificent and perhaps easier to take in, like a long leisurely breath – as opposed to the powerful gasp of the roaring water at the US vantage point.

The Canadian government has developed the **Niagara Parkway**, a beautiful scenic drive along the Niagara River north to Lake Ontario, and it is a worthwhile drive.

The **IMAX Theater** (☎ 905-374-4629; 6170 Buchanan Ave; admission $7; ☼ 9am-6pm) is home to the spectacular giant screen (six stories tall), which – among other things – dramatizes (and occasionally eulogizes) the daredevils, tightrope walkers and others of questionable decision-making powers who have pitted their wits and bodies against the power and splendor of the falls (see boxed text, p274).

For food, check out the buffet-style dining and outstanding views from the restaurant atop the 520ft-high **Skylon Tower** (☎ 905-356-2651; Minolta Tower, 5200 Robinson Rd; mains adult/child $30/12). Views that stretch more than a mile on a clear day can be taken in from the tower **observation deck** (adult/child $8/5).

Summertime Friday evenings feature a fireworks display, and the Winter Festival of Lights (lighting the trees in the parks adjacent to the falls) takes place every winter from late November until the first week of January.

FORT NIAGARA STATE PARK
Strategically located at the mouth of the Niagara River with splendid views of Lake Ontario, this state park is about 15 miles north of the town of Niagara Falls, and contains **Old Fort Niagara** (☎ 716-745-7611; adult/child $7/4; ☼ 9am-4:30pm). The fort was built by the French in 1726, but was captured by the British during the French and Indian War in 1759 (p21). The US took over in 1796 after the British retreated across the river to Fort George in Canada. The fully restored fort is a commanding place and includes a French castle dating back to 1726 and a well that's supposedly haunted by a headless ghost in constant search of its head. The state park, which surrounds the fort, offers numerous easy hiking trails and a swimming pool.

To reach the park from Niagara Falls, travel north on Robert Moses Parkway for

WESTERN NEW YORK

DETOUR – LEWISTON

This historic 19th-century village (population 2781) is home to many buildings on the National Historic Landmarks list, including a McDonald's restaurant in an 1824 Frontier House (460 Center St). But the main reason to visit Lewiston is for the 150-acre performing and visual arts park, **Artpark** (☎ 716-754-4375; 450 S 4th St; ◷ 8am-dusk; **P** $5), at the southern edge of town.

A National Historic Landmark Site, Artpark is the only state park in the country devoted to this medium. Located on land rich in both Native American and pioneer history, the park runs along the historic Niagara River Gorge. During the summer events including acrobatics, theater and dance workshops and storytelling take place. Several archaeological sites, including a Hopewell Mound from one of the earliest Native American cultures, along with good hiking trails and fishing spots, can be found in the park.

Dicamaillo's (☎ 716-754-2218; 535 Center St) is a good place to stop for an afternoon treat. Operating since 1920, it's one of the oldest (and tastiest) bakeries in the region.

To reach Lewiston from Niagara Falls, travel north on the Robert Moses Parkway for about 10 miles.

12 miles and take the Fort Niagara State Park exit.

LOCKPORT
☎ 716 / pop 8552

The story goes that this town's contribution to America was the fire hydrant and the game of volleyball. In an ironic twist, according to the legend, the man who invented the fire hydrant also had a factory. This factory was later reduced to rubble in a fire. As for volleyball, residents first used a basketball, but after a slew of broken fingers invented something lighter.

The highlight of a trip to Lockport is to take a two-hour cruise on the Erie Canal, offered by **Lockport Locks & Erie Canal Tours** (☎ 716-693-3260; 210 Market St; adult/child $12.50/8; ◷ May-Oct). The narrated boat trips take passengers through Locks 34 and 35, a process that involves raising and lowering the barge in the same manner it was done during the canal's golden age in the 1800s.

Travel through five locks, industrial ruins and a tunnel more than 2000ft long with another canal trip option, the **Lockport Cave and Underground Boat Ride** (☎ 716-438-0174; 21 Main St; adult/child $8/6; ◷ 10am-8pm May-Sep). The tunnel was blasted out of solid rock in the 1850s.

If you choose to spend the night in Lockport you'll have a choice of chain motels or campgrounds – all located on Niagara Falls Blvd before you reach town. One option is the **Quality Inn** (☎ 716-283-0621; 7708 Niagara Falls Blvd; d from $80), which has 70 motel-quality rooms.

Lockport is 20 miles east of Niagara Falls on Rte 31/270.

CHAUTAUQUA & AROUND

Southwestern New York offers winter sports, a world-renowned lecture center and hometown tributes to America's most beloved redheaded comedienne, Lucille Ball.

CHAUTAUQUA
☎ 716

In western New York's bucolic wine and farm country is the township of Chautauqua (pronounced sha-*taw*-kwah), 65 miles southwest of Buffalo on Chautauqua Lake (named by the Seneca tribe and meaning 'bag tied in the middle,' referring to the shape of the lake). While 400 to 1100 people live here year-round, the majority of activity takes place during the nine-week summer tourist season.

Chautauqua includes several villages, the lake and the Chautauqua Institution, which hosts lectures, concerts, workshops, and dance and theater productions for approximately 180,000 visitors each summer. A throwback to a bygone era, the institution has been designated a National Historic District. Comprising 215 acres inside its gates, the institution is a 'town' full of small winding streets and beautifully maintained Victorian buildings and gardens with a tranquil atmosphere. Between attending lectures, taking music classes or swimming, visitors loll about on front porches and garden benches or stroll the locust-tree–covered grounds. Cars are banned (except for loading and emergencies), and given its 'Sunday School' roots, alcohol is permitted but it is not sold, and no drinking is allowed in public. Life here is as unstructured as you wish to make it. The psychologist William James, brother to Henry James, referred to Chautauqua – in a less than complimentary tone – as a 'middle-class paradise, without a sin, without a victim, without a blot, without a tear.'

The institution does appeal to a broad audience through its diverse course offerings, ranging from writing to puppetry, from personal interaction and adjustment to archery. Lectures and entertainment are also designed to attract people of different ages and backgrounds.

You can visit the town in one day, but most visitors arrange for stays of a weekend, a week or longer. In fact, many visitors return year after year for generations, bringing with them children and grandchildren. To receive information about the upcoming summer session, a schedule of entertainment and the various packages offered by the institution, write or call them at the **Chautauqua Institution** (☎ 716-357-6200, 800-836-2737; www.chautauqua-inst.org; PO Box 28, 1 Ames Ave, Chautauqua, NY 14722) or check out the website.

Orientation

The village is between Rte 394 and Chautauqua Lake. There are five gates to the Chautauqua Institution, but visitors must enter through the main gate (off Rte 394). At the center of the community is Bestor Plaza. Around the plaza are the Colonnade (a building housing the institution's offices), the post office, library and a few restaurants. Brick Walk extends along the north side of the plaza. One block east of Bestor Plaza is the amphitheater.

Information

The institution's **business offices** (☎ 716-357-6200, 800-836-2787; www.chautauqua-inst.org; ☼ 9am-5pm Jun-Aug) are in the Colonnade building. There is an information desk in the **Colonnade lobby** (☎ 716-357-6257) and at the **main gate** (☎ 716-357-6263).

Located in the Welcome Center at the Chautauqua Institution main gate, the **Chautauqua Country Visitors Bureau** (☎ 716-357-4569, 800-242-4569; Main Gate; ☼ 9am-5pm Jun-Aug) is another source of information.

The institution is open from late June to August. The use of cars on the grounds is restricted. Parking lots near the entrance gates charge $4 a day and long-term parking ($111 per season) is available at the **main gate parking office** (☎ 716-357-6225).

Sights & Activities

Everyone over 13 who enters the institution, including residents, must buy a gate ticket at the main gate. Day passes cost $11 and evening passes are $25. Entrance is free on Sunday. Large events in the amphitheater have festival seating, and popular performances and lectures fill up quickly. The amphitheater is a 5000-seat, roofed outdoor structure that houses an enormous Massey pipe organ.

LECTURES

The lecture series at Chautauqua enjoys national renown. President Franklin D Roosevelt gave his 'I Hate War' speech at the Chautauqua amphitheater in 1936. Nine other US presidents, from Ulysses S Grant to Bill Clinton, have lectured here, as have Leo Tolstoy and William Jennings Bryan. Today, every weekday morning during the nine-week season a different lecture is given in the amphitheater. Lectures are organized around broad seasonal or weekly themes, such as racism and ethnicity, emerging democracies, science and technology, and ethics and public life. The lectures are followed by question-and-answer sessions. In addition, the Chautauqua Literary & Scientific Circle invites authors to speak on their work, as does the School of Art.

CHAUTAUQUA LITERARY & SCIENTIFIC CIRCLE

Founded in 1878 (making it the oldest book club in America), the circle is a four-year home-study program. In its early years, the circle served as correspondence courses do today. In particular, they reached out to men and women from small rural towns that had little access to formal advanced study. The circle also played an important role in the creation of adult education programs in the US. Today, each graduating class comes to the Hall of Philosophy, an open-air plaza, for a graduation ceremony.

WESTERN NEW YORK

On the floor of the hall are tile plaques representing many circle classes of the past.

RELIGION
There are morning Christian services most days of the week. On Sunday, sermons are given by visiting theologians. Throughout the season, lectures and discussions on religion and spirituality are far more ecumenical. Past speakers have included Norman Vincent Peale, Jesse Jackson, Elie Wiesel and Mrs Coretta Scott King.

SUMMER SCHOOLS
The institution houses four schools of fine and performing arts for art, dance, music and drama. Auditions are required and competition is rigorous. There are also over 200 **Special Studies courses** (☎ 716-357-6234/6255) that do not require participants to audition. These one-week courses include studies in literature, languages, art, dance and music. They cost from $40 to over $100, depending on fees for materials.

Parents who bring their children to Chautauqua can enroll them in a variety of programs geared to children of different ages and interests. There is day care, children's school, boys' and girls' clubs and youth activities. Contact the **Chautauqua Institution business office** (☎ 716-357-6200) for current listings.

RECREATION
On Chautauqua Lake fishing is probably the most popular summertime activity, along with water-skiing and boating. Fish that abound in Chautauqua Lake include muskellunge, walleye, northern pike, crappie, carp, perch, sunfish, bass and trout.

The **sports club** (☎ 716-357-6281) on the lake rents sailboats and canoes, and there is dock space for those who bring their own boats. The club also fields a number of softball, volleyball and basketball teams in the Chautauqua leagues.

The **Chautauqua Yacht Club** (☎ 716-357-4001) has weekly races during the summer and teaches sailing through the **Special Studies program** (☎ 716-357-6255).

There are four **public swimming beaches** (☎ 716-357-6255/6309) on the lake within the grounds of the institution and eight tennis courts near the main gate.

Bike Rent (☎ 716-357-9032; Massey Ave; ⏰ 9am-6pm Mon-Sun) does just that.

PALESTINE PARK
The park, which is reflective of the institution's religious beginnings, is a to-scale replica of the Holy Land complete with the Sea of Galilee, Dead Sea and other topographical features. The park is near Miller Bell Tower on Lake St, the road that runs along the lake.

Entertainment
MUSIC
The Chautauqua Symphony Orchestra is comprised of American and international musicians and is conducted by Uriel Siegel, as well as guest conductors. The institution also presents a nine-concert chamber music series, guest recitals and student recitals.

Larger concerts and performances take place in the amphitheater. Past performers include Glenn Miller, Peter, Paul & Mary, 10,000 Maniacs (originally from the local Jamestown area), the Beach Boys, Bill Cosby and Natalie Cole.

The Chautauqua Opera stages four operas each season. Tickets are $16 to $39, or you can attend all four for $60 to $140.

DANCE & THEATER
Jean-Pierre Bonnedoux, a former dancer with the New York City Ballet and the Paris Opera, is the artistic director of the Chautauqua Dance Company. Each season they put on performances of modern dance and ballet. The Chautauqua Conservatory Theater Company presents four plays each season in Normal Hall.

Sleeping
The **Chautauqua CVB Accommodations Referral Service** (☎ 716-357-6373, 800-242-4569) can assist you in finding housing for your stay at the institution. Or you can drop by the information office in the Colonnade and pick up a copy of the Accommodations Directory that is updated before each season. A list of accommodations and prices are also listed on the institution's website. The Athenaeum Hotel is the only accommodation owned and operated by the institution. All other places are privately owned and operated. The best budget options are generally rooms in houses or guesthouses. At the upper end are the hotels and condos, some of which offer vacation packages ranging from a weekend to one week. The packages

include accommodations, a gate ticket and tickets for selected events.

BUDGET

Rose Cottage (☎ 716-357-5375; 2 Roberts; s/d $60/65) Rooms are in an 1877 cottage just one house away from the amphitheater in the middle of town. Weekly rates run between $420 and $455. There are 12 rooms.

27 Scott (☎ 716-357-3011, off-season ☎ 716-484-1438; 27 Scott St; s/d $45/60) In a central location, this guesthouse has three single and two double rooms, allows pets, and rents by the week ($275 to $385).

The Cooper (☎ 716-357-3885; 15 Roberts Ave; s/d $55/65) Near the amphitheater and the lake, this place does not allow alcohol. It rents rooms by the week ($250 to $300) and the season ($2250 to $2700).

MID-RANGE

Gleason (☎ 716-357-2595; 12 N Lake Drive; s/d weekly $525-950) This is a large lakefront house with a grand front porch complete with wicker rocking chairs. There is a shared guest kitchen for cooking. The 24 rooms are rented on a weekly basis.

Wind Rush Cottage (☎ 716-357-9853; 18 Simpson St; d from $65) This Victorian cottage is just one block from the lake and the amphitheater and features private and shared porches. It has four rooms, is open year-round, and also has weekly rentals ($850 to $1250).

Sheldon Hall (☎ 716-664-4691; Sheldon Hall Rd; d from $80) In the hamlet of Greenhurst, 5 miles west of Rte 17/I-86 at the Jamestown exit, is this restored turn-of-the-20th-century summer home once favored by boat captains who dropped in from Lake Erie. Sheldon Hall has a 50ft boathouse and an upstairs ballroom. There are 10 guest rooms, most with private bath; all include a full breakfast. It is open summer only from Memorial Day to Labor Day.

TOP END

Athenaeum Hotel (☎ 716-357-4444, 800-821-1881; s/d from $178/314) For many, this hotel defines the Chautauqua experience. The large white-and-green Victorian building overlooks the lake. Originally built in 1881, the hotel was renovated in 1983. The rooms all have high ceilings and are comfortably furnished with Victorian period reproductions. Room rates include three meals a day. The more expensive rooms have lake views. The hotel offers discounts for longer stays. Nonguests can also eat in the Athenaeum restaurant, which has fixed-price meals. Breakfast ($15) and lunch ($20) are casual, but dinner ($33.50) is quite formal (at dinner the hotel suggests that 'ladies are to be dressed in their loveliest and gentlemen, neckties and jackets, please'). Dinners are a five-course affair.

Eating

During the summer session, you can pick up fresh produce and baked goods at the farmers' market Monday through Saturday from 7am to 11am. The market is at the main gate building.

Sadie J's (☎ 716-357-5245; cnr Pratt & Ramble St; mains from $6) Next to the Colonnade, this place is open year-round. You can buy reasonably priced soup and deli sandwiches here.

Tally-Ho (☎ 357-3325; 16 Morris Ave; mains $7-17) This casual restaurant serves everything from salads and burgers to pasta and steaks.

Getting There & Around

The Chautauqua Institution is in the middle of the town of Chautauqua about 65 miles south of Buffalo. Take I-90 to the Westfield exit and then Rte 394 to the entrance. From the south it's 16 miles northwest of Jamestown on Rte 394.

There is a free shuttle bus and tram service running around the grounds from 8:20am to 8:20pm, as well as after amphitheater and Norton Hall events.

JAMESTOWN

☎ 716 / pop 31,730

Comedienne Lucille Ball was born in this city at the southeastern end of Chautauqua Lake. A working class city, Jamestown is a mixture of boarded up storefronts, elegant Victorian homes and red brick buildings.

Jamestown's love affair with its favorite daughter is evident throughout the city. Tribute is paid to Lucille Ball at the **Lucy-Desi Museum** (☎ 716-484-7070; 212 Pine St; adult/child $5/3.50; ⏰ 10am-5:30pm Mon-Sat, 1-5pm Sun). Lucy was born in Jamestown in 1911 to a telephone lineman and a concert pianist, and her parents encouraged her to act. At 15 she took a bus to New York City and landed a job in the chorus of the Broadway musical *Stepping Stones*. She was fired shortly after and struggled for seven more years before she

WESTERN NEW YORK

DETOUR – ALLEGANY STATE PARK

Popular year-round, this **park** (☎ 716-354-9121) is particularly fantastic in the winter when you can indulge in ice-fishing, snowmobiling and cross-country skiing. About 25 miles east of Chautauqua along scenic Rte 17/I-86, the 65,000-acre state park offers more than 80 miles of hiking trails. Swimming off two sandy beaches, horseback riding, biking and fishing are popular summer activities. There is year-round camping ($15 per site). Both tent sites and winterized cabins are available. The cost for visiting the park is $6 a day per car.

Nearby is the **Seneca-Iroquois National Museum** (☎ 716-945-1738; Broad St; adult/child $4/3; ☺ 10am-5pm Tue-Sat Apr-Oct), in the Allegheny Indian Reservation. The word 'National' in the museum's name refers to the Iroquois confederacy, which included the Seneca nation.

met Desi Arnaz during the filming of *Too Many Girls* in 1940. The rest is history.

Audio- and video-taped interviews and clips from movies and TV tell the personal story of Lucille Ball and Desi Arnaz. There are tapes of every single *I Love Lucy* episode available for viewing as well as a two-hour video of the TV show that runs continuously throughout the day. In all, close to 2000 items from Lucy's estate are showcased, including photographs, awards, letters and ball gowns.

There are other Lucy landmarks sprinkled throughout town, including the **Lucille Ball Little Theater of Jamestown** (☎ 716-483-1095; 18 E 2nd St), the largest community theater in New York State and the place where Lucy made her stage debut; and the **Reg Lenna Civic Center** (☎ 716-664-2465; 116 E 3rd St) that Lucy frequented as a child. On display is more Lucy memorabilia, including her dancing boots and favorite hair products. The center is open only during performances or by appointment. **Jones Bakery** (☎ 716-484-1988; 209 Pine St) is famous for making a Swedish rye that Lucy continued to purchase even after becoming famous – after she moved to Hollywood she had the bread shipped out to her. Today, the bread is made the same way and sold in the store.

The town pays further homage to Lucy twice a year. The Lucy-Desi Days festival is in late May and in August it's Lucy mania all over again when Jamestown celebrates her birthday.

Even restaurants have cashed in on the Lucy craze. At **Kaldi's Coffee House** (☎ 716-484-8909; 106 Third St; mains $4-6) you can order sandwiches named after various *I Love Lucy* events. For sleeping try the **Holiday Inn** (☎ 716-664-3400; 150 W 4th St; d from $90) in the heart of downtown. It has 149 comfortable rooms.

Jamestown is 18 miles south of Chautauqua. From I-86 take exit 12 south to the center of town.

Directory

CONTENTS

ACCOMMODATIONS

The region offers a comfortable array of accommodations from campsites to lavish inns. In the high season or on busy weekends, you will want to make reservations for accommodations as far in advance as possible. If you're just passing through the region, motels are fairly plentiful off the major interstates. But for the road-tripper on the back roads, it is surprising how few towns, especially in the Adirondacks, Hudson Valley and on Long Island, don't have a simple in-town motel. So it is worth setting up a skeleton itinerary and making reservations to avoid the late-night hotel scramble.

The rates given in this book are typically high-season rates; low-season rates can drop as much as 50%, but rarely will you find a room for less than $70. In seasonal destinations like the Adirondacks, hotels typically

PRACTICALITIES

- Electric current is 110 to 120 volts, 60-cycle. Appliances built to take 220 to 240 volt, 50-cycle current (as in Europe and Asia) will need a converter (transformer) and a US-style plug adapter with two flat pins, or three (two flat, one round) pins.

- Photography supplies are readily available throughout the state. Observe photography restrictions in museums and cultural institutions to help preserve sensitive collections.

- Sales tax is 8.25%. Hotel rooms in New York City are subject to 13.625% tax plus $2 per night occupancy tax.

- The US uses a modified version of the British Imperial measuring system. Although the metric system has made some inroads, most Americans continue to resist its imposition. There's a conversion chart on the inside front cover.

- The USA uses the National Television System Committee (NTSC) color TV and video standard. It isn't compatible with PAL and SECAM standards used in Africa, Europe, Asia and Australia, unless converted.

- There are hundreds of dailies covering regional and municipal news in New York State. The most famous is the *New York Times*, which is an international and national leader in reporting and writing. The *Wall St Journal* follows business news. There isn't a state-wide paper, but Albany's *Times Union* covers the legislative action in the state house. Major population centers serve as watchdogs in their respective regions.

- All major TV networks are carried by various local affiliates.

- Talk radio is popular in New York State. The AM dial is filled with local and national conservative bloodhounds as well as the much maligned shock jock, Howard Stern.

close after Labor Day or Columbus Day and reopen around Memorial Day.

Most hotels and motels have smoking and nonsmoking rooms, and sensitive noses can tell the difference. Some hotels allow pets, so ask in advance if you fall on either side of the canine-feline divide. If you arrive in town without hotel arrangements, feel free to ask to see a room before committing.

B&Bs & Guesthouses
North American B&Bs aren't the casual, inexpensive accommodations found in Britain or Ireland. Operated out of the family home, many B&Bs strive to create a romantic atmosphere with an elaborate breakfast and handsome furnishings in a historic home, and rates typically reflect these efforts ($150 to $200). The plus to B&Bs is that you have access to a knowledgeable local who can give restaurant recommendations and talk village politics, but B&Bs are personality-driven establishments with little room for privacy or anonymity. Because rooms are limited, reservations are required at B&Bs and many don't accept children under 12.

Accommodations at a guesthouse are the poorer cousin to the refined B&Bs. Often just a spare room in someone's home with a shared bath, guesthouses are some of the cheapest and cleanest lodgings you'll find. Sadly these aren't as prolific as B&Bs.

Camping
New York State's public campgrounds are some of the best around. Sites are shady, facilities are clean and the campground is usually removed from the road near hiking trails and canoeing ponds. All **reservations** (☎ 800-456-2267; www.reserveamerica.com) are made through a central system.

Backcountry camping in the Catskills or Adirondacks is relatively simple; unless otherwise marked, you cannot camp within 150ft of roads, trails, lakes, ponds, streams or other bodies of water. Groups of 10 or more persons or stays of more than three days in one place require a permit from the New York State forest ranger. Lean-tos are available on a first come, first serve basis.

Kampgrounds of America (KOA; ☎ 406-248-7444; www.koa.com) is a national network and publishes a free annual directory of its sites. Of the private campgrounds, KOAs are the

most reliable with extras like playgrounds and swimming pools. The KOA cabins are also good in a pinch for basic electrified lodging. Other private campgrounds are a real gamble; many are too close to the highway, the bathrooms aren't clean or you have to pay for a hot-water shower.

Woodall's North American Campground Directory (www.woodalls.com) is a huge tome listing campgrounds throughout the USA and Canada.

Hostels
The hostelling network is less widespread in the US than in other countries. New York City has a reasonable selection. Lake Placid and New Paltz have independent hostels with all the hostel amenities. The Internet guide to hostelling (www.hostels.com) lists hostels in New York State.

Hostelling International USA (HI-USA; ☎ 301-495-1240; www.hiayh.org; membership adult/senior $28/18) has hostels in Buffalo, Niagara Falls, Syracuse, Cape Vincent and New York City. You must be a US resident to join HI-USA, foreigners should buy an HI membership in their home countries. If you didn't join HI or HI-USA you can still stay in US hostels by buying 'Welcome Stamps' for each night you stay in a hostel. Six stamps on your stamp card qualifies you for a valid one-year HI-USA membership.

Most hostels provide sheets, but call ahead to verify. Dorms are typically segregated by sex. Some hostels have a curfew (around 10pm). Most prohibit alcohol and some require you to do a small housekeeping chore. Most also have kitchen and laundry facilities, information and advertising boards, TV room and lounge area.

Motels & Hotels
While the accommodations in this book focus on the independently owned establishments, the chain motels and hotels are often worth looking into, especially in low season, for any promotional discounts. While the reputation of the roadside motel is a bit frayed, New York State's motels can be real gems. Some are situated on attractive lots by the water and run by friendly proprietors who know the area. A sort of family-reunion atmosphere reigns at the long-time establishments that have built up a loyal clientele. Swimming pools and

common areas are pluses for families traveling with children. Many motels and hotels also have refrigerators and some units have efficiencies or housekeeping units (small kitchen areas).

BUSINESS HOURS

Generally, public and private office hours are 9am to 5pm Monday through Friday. Customary banking hours are 9am to 5pm weekdays, but many banks have extended customer hours on Saturday (10am to 2pm). Post offices are open 9am to 4pm or 5:30pm weekdays, and some are open from 10am to midday on Saturday.

In large cities, a few supermarkets, convenience stores, restaurants and the main post office are open 24 hours. Many shops are open until 9pm, especially on Saturday, and have abbreviated hours on Sunday (typically from noon to 5pm).

Most attractions, government offices and some stores are closed on public holidays.

CHILDREN

From the Olympic venues at Lake Placid to Niagara Falls, children will dig New York State. Even the adult-oriented romantic spots in the Hudson Valley can be counterbalanced with a trip to a pick-your-own farm. If the kids get too antsy in the hotel room, take them to the municipal playground to get their yah-yahs out.

Most hotels and motels have family-sized rooms with hideaway beds or cots. Also ask about efficiencies or housekeeping units, which come with kitchen facilities. B&Bs typically do not allow children under the age of 12, and most kids wouldn't find the faux-romantic atmosphere of a B&B very comfortable either.

Some restaurants offer a limited selection of inexpensive, smaller-portioned child-friendly foods; ask for the children's menu. Diners are an interesting alternative to the generic fast-food restaurants that typically entrap families.

Museums and sightseeing activities offer reduced prices for children. They often have games and puzzles that engage the children in art appreciation; ask at the front desk.

For general information on traveling with kids, read Lonely Planet's *Travel with Children* by Cathy Lanigan.

CLIMATE CHARTS

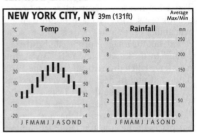

NEW YORK CITY, NY 39m (131ft) — Average Max/Min — Temp — Rainfall

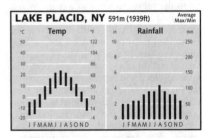

LAKE PLACID, NY 591m (1939ft) — Average Max/Min — Temp — Rainfall

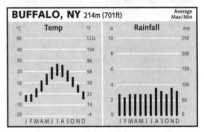

BUFFALO, NY 214m (701ft) — Average Max/Min — Temp — Rainfall

COURSES

While most courses in the region are geared toward people who live in the state, a few respected organizations offer weeklong sessions primarily in the summertime. The Sagamore Great Camp, also known as Sagamore Institute, in Raquette Lake (p244) has an extensive calendar of family and adult courses ranging from canoe building to fly-fishing. The Chautauqua Institution (p278) in western New York also hosts family-oriented seminars, lectures and performances. The Culinary Institute of America (see boxed text on p162) in Hyde Park has a variety of cooking courses.

The area is full of outfitters who will organize and lead canoeing, kayaking, bicycling and fishing trips.

DIRECTORY

DANGERS & ANNOYANCES

The USA has a widespread reputation as a dangerous, violent place because of the availability of firearms. This is true to some extent, but the image is propagated and exaggerated by the media. New York City's crime rates have fallen dramatically since the 1970s (and continue to decline). Nevertheless, all cities suffer to some degree from crimes of pickpockets and physical violence.

Highways can be some of the most dangerous places in the country. Don't let children go to the restroom alone at a highway rest stop and exercise caution when stopping in a rest stop at night. While driving, if your car is bumped from behind, don't stop – keep going to a well-lit area with lots of people, a service station or even a police station. The same applies if you experience car trouble on the highway; try to get into a town or a gas station where help is more reliable.

Street people and panhandlers may approach visitors in the larger cities and towns asking for money. It's an individual judgment call as to whether you believe their stories and offer them money or anything else, though it's immensely preferable to give to a recognized charity. If you do give, don't wave a full wallet around – carry some change in a separate pocket.

Tourist areas tend to be more prone to theft than assault. Avoid unnecessary displays of money or jewelry. Carry valuables in a money belt or pouch underneath your clothing for maximum safety. Lock valuables in your suitcase in your hotel room or put them in the hotel safe when you're not there. Don't leave anything visible in your car when you park it in a city, particularly at night. Always lock your car when you leave it.

If you don't know your way around a city, stick to the well-lit streets and aim to use ATMs in well-trafficked areas.

Dial ☎ 911 if you need emergency assistance of any kind. This is free from any phone.

DISABLED TRAVELERS

The USA is a world leader in providing facilities for the disabled. The Americans with Disabilities Act (ADA) is a federal law that requires public buildings (including hotels, restaurants, theaters and museums) and public transportation to be wheelchair-accessible. Telephone companies are required to provide relay operators for the hearing impaired and many banks provide ATM instructions in braille. You'll find audible crossing signals, and at busier roadway intersections there are curbs with wheelchair ramps.

Larger private and chain hotels have suites for disabled guests. Major car-rental agencies offer hand-controlled models at no extra charge. Major airlines, intercity buses and Amtrak trains allow guide dogs to accompany passengers and frequently sell two-for-one packages when seriously disabled passengers require attendants. Airlines also provide assistance for connecting, boarding and disembarking the flight – mention that you will need assistance when making your reservation. (Note: airlines must accept wheelchairs as checked baggage and have an onboard chair available, though some advance notice may be required on smaller aircraft.) The more populous the area, the greater the likelihood of facilities for the disabled. Wherever you're headed, it is always a wise idea to call ahead to arrange your accommodations and transportation.

For New York residents with permanent disabilities, the Access Pass provides free admission to New York parks and recreation areas. To obtain an application for a pass, call ☎ 518-474-0456, or write to Access Pass, State Parks, Albany, NY 12238.

The following organizations and tour providers specialize in the needs of disabled travelers:

Access-Able Travel Source (☎ 303-232-2979; www .access-able.com; PO Box 1796, Wheat Ridge, CO 80034) Provides travel information for accessibility and also operates Travelin' Talk network (www.travelintalk.net).

Mobility International USA (MIUSA; ☎ 541-343-1284; www.miusa.org; PO Box 10767, Eugene, OR 97440)

Society for the Advancement of Travel for the Handicapped (SATH; ☎ 212-447-7284; www.sath.org; ste 610, 347 Fifth Ave, New York, NY 10016) Publishes *Open World* magazine.

DISCOUNT CARDS

If you plan on doing a lot of driving in the USA, it might be beneficial to join your national automobile association. Members of the American Automobile Association (AAA) or an affiliated automobile club may be entitled to lodging, car rental and sightseeing admission discounts. More importantly, membership gives you access to AAA road service in an emergency.

If you're a student, bring your school or college identification or get the International Student Identity Card (ISIC) so that you can take advantage of student discounts. The GO 25 card, issued to those aged 12 to 25, can help you get a reduced rate on airfares, car rental and other travel expenses. Both the ISIC and GO 25 card are issued at many budget travel agencies, colleges and universities.

An Empire Passport can be bought from any New York State park office. It costs $60 and is good for day-use vehicle entry to state parks and forest preserves for one year.

FESTIVALS & EVENTS

Every community has a harvest festival or celebration of its noteworthy agriculture product (from wine to milk), as well as memorials to present-day or colonial-era settlers. Contact the **state visitors center** (☎ 800-225-5697) for exact dates. Listed below are just a few of New York's noteworthy festivals:

January

Chinese New Year Begins at the end of January or beginning of February and lasts two weeks; the first day is celebrated with parades, firecrackers, fireworks and food. New York City's Chinatown (p76) is the place to see and hear the spectacle.

March

St Patrick's Day (March 17) The region's premier parade is held in New York City (p108).

May

Lucy-Desi Days Honors the stars of *I Love Lucy* in Lucille Ball's hometown of Jamestown, late May (p281).

Ithaca Festival Musicians converge on this pretty college town for a four-day creative celebration in late May. There's a kick-off parade, including a Volvo ballet, a circus of stilt walkers, and lots of food (p245).

July

Saratoga Springs Horseracing season runs from late July to August (p193).

Chautauqua Institution Its well-respected lecture series is held in western New York throughout the summer (p278).

August

New York State Fair Held the last weeks in August in Syracuse with a carnival, animal and food competitions and lots of junk food (p254).

September

US Open Tennis Tournament Showcases the world's top tennis players in this two-week championship held in Flushing Meadows, Queens (p130).

Woodstock Film Festival Screens up-and-coming directors as well as indie heavy-hitters in early fall-late summer (p174).

Adirondack Canoe Classic A 90-mile canoe race that paddles and portages its way from Old Forge to Saranac Lake in early September (p225).

October

Halloween (October 31) Best celebrated in Tarrytown and Sleepy Hollow (p153), the towns that inspired Washington Irving's *The Legend of Sleepy Hollow*.

November

New York Marathon The New York Road Runners Club (p103) sponsors this annual 26.2-mile road race, in which some 25,000 runners travel through all five boroughs on the first weekend in November.

Thanksgiving Day On this national holiday, Macy's sponsors its famous parade in New York City, with huge floats that travel down Broadway from W 72nd St to Herald Sq.

December

New Year's Eve is December 31 and huge crowds pack into New York City's Times Square to watch the ball drop (p85).

GAY & LESBIAN TRAVELERS

New York City was the birthplace of the gay rights movement and is still a center for gays. The Hudson Valley and Long Island, which fall within New York City's influence, are refuges to gay and straight couples escaping the hectic city. Rural areas of New York operate with more skepticism toward different lifestyles, although New Paltz has recently started facilitating gay marriages.

The **Lesbian, Gay, Bisexual & Transgender Center** (☎ 212-620-7310; www.gaycenter.org; 208 W 13th St, New York, NY) list events in New York City. A useful website is www.gay.com, with information on travel to gay-friendly cities, accommodations and entertainment. The **Out & About Newsletter** (☎ 800-929-2268; www.outandabout.com) also provides information about gay-friendly hotels, restaurants, clubs, gyms and shops in New York City.

Damron (☎ 415-255-0404, 800-462-6654; www.damron.com) publishes well-regarded male and female gay-friendly guides; their website has a searchable database for hotel recommendations throughout New York State.

If you experience discrimination or harassment, contact the **Lambda Legal Defense Fund** (☎ 212-995-8585) in New York City.

HOLIDAYS
Public Holidays
On national public holidays banks, schools and government offices (including post offices) are closed, and transportation, museums and other services are on a Sunday schedule. Many stores, however, will maintain regular business hours. Holidays falling on weekends are usually observed the following Monday. See p287 for religious and regional celebrations that may not enjoy a government closing.

New Year's Day January 1.
Martin Luther King Jr Day Third Monday of January; it celebrates the civil rights leader's birthday (January 15, 1929).
Presidents' Day Third Monday of February; it celebrates the birthdays of Abraham Lincoln (February 12, 1809) and George Washington (February 22, 1732).
Memorial Day Last Monday in May; it honors the war dead (and is also the unofficial first day of the summer tourist season).
Independence Day July 4; more commonly called 4th of July, this day celebrates the adoption of the Declaration of Independence in 1776; notable fireworks demonstrations are held at New York Harbor.
Labor Day First Monday of September; it honors working people (and is the unofficial end of the summer tourist season).
Columbus Day Second Monday of October; it commemorates the landing of Christopher Columbus in the Bahamas on October 12, 1492.
Veterans' Day November 11; it honors the nation's war veterans.
Thanksgiving Fourth Thursday of November; it's a day of giving thanks and is traditionally celebrated with a turkey dinner; there is a parade in New York City.
Christmas December 25; Christmas Eve is as much of an event as the day itself, with church services, caroling in the streets and last-minute shopping.

School Holidays
Schools in the region observe major holidays with the longest break for Christmas and New Year. Spring break (in February or March) is rarely scheduled during 'spring-like' weather, but lasts a glorious week. The summer vacation usually starts in early June and runs until early September.

INSURANCE
A travel insurance policy to cover theft, loss and medical problems is a good idea. This should cover you not only for medical expenses and luggage theft or loss, but also for cancellations or delays in your travel arrangements, and everyone should be covered for the worst possible case, such as an accident requiring hospital treatment and a flight home. Coverage depends on your insurance and type of ticket, so ask both your insurer and ticket-issuing agency to explain the finer points.

Many travel agencies sell medical and emergency repatriation policies but these can be expensive for what you get. It's advisable to discuss travel insurance with your health care provider or regular insurance agent for comparison of coverage and costs. Make sure you have a separate record of all your ticket details or, better still, a photocopy of the ticket. Also, make a copy of your travel insurance policy in case you lose the original.

Purchase travel insurance as early as possible. If you buy it the week before you fly, you may find, for example, that you're not covered for delays to your flight caused by strikes or industrial action. Insurance may seem expensive, but it's nowhere near the cost of a medical emergency in the USA.

The following companies offer various sorts of travel and health insurance:
Access America, Inc (☎ 866-807-3982; www.access america.com; PO Box 90315, Richmond, VA 23286-4991)
Europ Assistance (☎ 0870 737 5720; www.europ-assistance.co.uk; Sussex House, Perrymount Rd, Haywards Heath, West Sussex, RH16 1DN, UK)
TripInsurance.com (☎ 800-423-3632; PO Box 9159, Van Nuys, CA 91409-9159)

INTERNATIONAL VISITORS
Regulations for visiting foreign nationals to the US are subject to change; check out the US Department of State's website for current information (www.travel.state.gov /visa_services).

Passports & Visas
After 9/11, obtaining visas for entering the US has become more complicated and difficult. Apply early to avoid delays and disappointment. Also be prepared to appear at the nearest US embassy for a personal interview, if necessary.

To enter the USA, Canadians must have proof of Canadian citizenship, such as a citizenship card with photo ID or a passport. Visitors from other countries must have a valid passport, and most visitors also require a US visa. There's a reciprocal visa-waiver program that allows citizens of certain countries to enter the USA, but there are certain passport requirements and visiting restrictions that apply. See the 'Visa Waiver Program' page (www.travel.state.gov/vwp) of the State Department's website for up-to-date details.

The 'Nonimmigrant Visas' page (www.travel.state.gov/nonimmigrantvisas) of the State Department's website has all the details on how and where to apply for a visa and what to do if denied. If you are denied a visa, a friend or relative in the US can write a letter for reconsideration on your behalf. Some US residents have also found it necessary to write to their congressperson to ask for help in getting a visa for a friend or relative.

It's easy to make trips across the border to Canada, but upon return to the USA, non-Americans may be subject to full immigration examination. Always take your passport and documents of funds, roundtrip air tickets, etc, when crossing the border. You'll want to time your jaunt into Canada within a comfortable margin of your legal stay to avoid zealous immigration officials. Citizens of most western countries don't need a visa for Canada, so it's no problem to cross to the Canadian side of Niagara Falls or to Quebec. All foreign travelers entering the USA by bus from Canada may be closely scrutinized – a roundtrip ticket that takes you back to Canada will make the border officials less suspicious.

Customs

US customs allows each person over the age of 21 to bring 1L of liquor and 200 cigarettes duty free into the USA. US citizens are allowed to import, duty-free, $400 worth of gifts from abroad, and non-US citizens are allowed to bring in $100 worth. If you're carrying more than $10,000 in US and foreign cash, traveler's checks, money orders and the like, you need to declare the excess amount. There is no legal restriction on the amount that may be imported, but undeclared sums may be subject to confiscation.

US Embassies & Consulates

This is a quick list of US diplomatic offices; for additional embassies or consulates, see the US State Department 'Embassies' website (www.travel.state.gov/links):

Australia (☎ 02-6214-5600; http://canberra.usembassy.gov; 21 Moonah Place, Yarralumla, ACT 2600)
Canada (☎ 613-238-5335; www.usembassycanada.gov; 490 Sussex Dr, Ottawa, ON K1N 1G8)
France (visa questions ☎ 0 810 26 46 26, embassy switchboard ☎ 1 43 12 22 22; www.amb-usa.fr; 2 rue Saint-Florentin, 75382 Paris, Cedex 08)
Germany (☎ 0190-85 00 55; www.usembassy.de; Clayallee 170, 14195 Berlin)
Israel (☎ 972-3-519-7575; www.usembassy-israel.org.il; 71 Hayarkon St, Tel Aviv 63903)
Italy (☎ 06-4674-1; www.usis.it; Via Vittorio Veneto 119/A, 00187 Rome)
Japan (☎ 3-224-5000; http://japan.usembassy.gov; 1-10-5 Akasaka Chome, Minato-ku, Tokyo)
Mexico (☎ 5-080-2000; www.usembassy-mexico.gov; Paseo de la Reforma 305, Colonia Cuauhtémoc, 06500 México, DF)
UK (☎ 020-7499-9000; www.usembassy.org.uk; 24 Grosvenor Sq, London W1A 1AE)

CONSULATES IN NEW YORK

The presence of the United Nations in New York City means that nearly every country in the world maintains diplomatic offices in Manhattan.

Australia (Map p64-5; ☎ 212-245-4000; www.australianyc.org; International Bldg, 636 Fifth Ave, New York, NY 10011)
Canada (Map p64-5; ☎ 212-596-1628; www.canadianembassy.org; 1251 Ave of the Americas/Sixth Ave, New York, NY 10020-1175)
France (Map p66-7; ☎ 212-606-3699; www.consulfrance-newyork.org; 934 Fifth Ave, New York, NY 10021)
Germany (Map p64-5; ☎ 212-610-9700; www.germany-info.org; 871 United Nations Plaza, New York, NY 10017)
Italy (Map p64-5; ☎ 212-439-8600; www.italconsulnyc.org; 690 Park Ave, New York, NY 10021)
UK (British Information Services; Map p64-5; ☎ 212-745-0200; www.britainusa.com/ny/; 845 Third Ave, New York, NY 10017)

YOUR OWN EMBASSY

As a foreign visitor, it's important to realize what the embassy of the country of which you're a citizen can and can't do. Generally speaking, it won't help much in an emergency situation if the trouble you're in is your own fault. Remember that while in the US, you're bound by US state and federal laws. Your embassy won't be sympathetic if you're jailed for committing a crime locally, even if such an action is legal in your own country. In genuine emergencies you might get some assistance, but only if other channels are exhausted. If your tickets, money and documents are stolen, your embassy might help get you a new passport, but it won't give you a free ticket home or a loan for onward travel – you're expected to have insurance. Your embassy will help someone in your home country get in touch with you.

INTERNET ACCESS

Most public libraries have a public computer with Internet access. Copy centers (such as Kinko's) or corporate hotels have Internet access for a charge of about $10 to $15 an hour. Some hostels also offer Internet access to their guests. Many hotels also have dedicated dataports in guest rooms for dial-up service, a few have high-speed. Don't plug your computer modem line directly into a hotel room telephone outlet – many a computer has met an untimely death this way. New York City has free wireless Internet zones in many of the city's parks.

LEGAL MATTERS

If you're stopped by the police for any reason, bear in mind that there's no system of paying on-the-spot fines. For traffic offenses, the police officer will explain your options to you. Attempting to pay the fine to the officer is frowned upon at best and may lead to a charge of bribery to compound your troubles. Should the officer decide that you should pay up front, he or she can take you directly to the magistrate instead of allowing you the usual 30-day period to pay.

If you're arrested for more serious offenses, you're allowed to remain silent, entitled to have an attorney present during interrogation and are presumed innocent until proven guilty. There's no legal reason to speak to a police officer if you don't wish to. Any arrested person is legally allowed (and given) the right to make one phone call. If you don't have a lawyer or family member to help you, call your embassy or consulate. The police will give you the number on request.

Driver's License & International Driving Permits

Foreign visitors with a legal driver's license from the home country can legally drive in New York State. An International Driving Permit (IDP) is a useful adjunct and may have more credibility with US traffic police, especially if your home license has no photo or is in a foreign language. Your home automobile association can issue an IDP, valid for one year, for a small fee. You must carry your home license together with the IDP. The minimum driving age in New York State is 18.

Drinking

The minimum age for drinking alcohol in New York State is 21. You'll need a government-issued photo ID (such as a passport or US driver's license) to prove your age.

Drinking & Driving

Stiff fines, jail time and other penalties may be incurred if you're caught driving under the influence (DUI). The blood alcohol limit is 0.08%. During holidays and special events, road blocks with Breathalyzer tests are sometimes set up to deter drunk drivers. Refusing a Breathalyzer, urine or blood test is treated as if you'd taken the test and failed.

MAPS

Lonely Planet publishes a useful laminated foldout map of New York City with bus and subway information. City and town maps are available, for free or at low cost, from local tourist offices and chambers of commerce. These vary from useless to very detailed.

If you're doing a lot of driving around the state, it is handy to have DeLorme's *New York Atlas & Gazetteer*; it contains detailed topographic and highway maps at a scale of 1:150,000 and labels hiking, fishing and camping sites directly on the map. The atlas is sold in grocery stores and bookstores throughout the state.

If you want to explore the little country roads then you'll need a county map, which gives more detail than the DeLorme atlas. Sold in most gas stations, **Jimapco** (☎ 518-899-5091; www.jimapco.com) makes the best county maps.

Hikers shouldn't set out on backcountry trips without the appropriate **US Geological Survey** (USGS; ☎ 888-275-8747; www.usgs.gov) topographical maps at a scale of 1:24,000. They're superb close-up maps for hiking, backpacking or intensive exploration by car. Jimapco publishes the best commercial topographic maps for all hiking regions in New York State.

MONEY

It is useful to have a healthy supply of cash on hand as some small hotels and restaurants do not accept credit cards. Banks and ATMs are widely distributed throughout the state and can provide access to your personal bank account, including overseas accounts, for a service charge. Most New York ATMs charge $1.50 to $2 for non-bank members and your home bank will piggybank a charge as well. To avoid service charges, visit a teller window and do a cash advance on your debit card (not your credit card). Exchange rates on foreign currency conversion at ATMs are typically fair. Check with your bank about compatibility with foreign ATMs and currency conversion charges.

Banks in major cities exchange cash or traveler's checks in major foreign currencies. Traveler's checks in US dollars can be used at most restaurants, hotels, gas stations and big stores as if they were cash. Get them in $50 and $100 denominations. Traveler's checks in a foreign currency can only be changed at a bank or at one of the few exchange counters. This can be inconvenient and might require an exchange fee, and you may not get a good exchange rate.

Nearly all banks buy and sell Canadian currency. If you're changing US to Canadian dollars, you're more likely to get a better rate at a Canadian bank. Almost any business on either side of the US–Canadian border will honor a fair exchange rate, so you should be aware of what it is.

You'll need a credit (not a debit) card to rent a car in the US. A credit card also comes in handy if you are making reservations over the phone.

If fraud occurs, you can more easily contest charges on a credit card than on a debit card, which pulls directly from your account. Regardless of which type of card you use, monitor your account daily for any unexplained activity. Carry copies of your credit card numbers and telephone numbers to report stolen cards separately from the cards themselves. If you lose your credit cards or they are stolen, contact the company immediately.

Be careful about where you carry your money and cards. Don't leave valuables in your car overnight or in plain view when the car is parked. Keep money and credit cards in an inside, protected pocket, rather than in a handbag or in an outside pocket.

For exchange rates, see inside front cover.

POST

The **US Postal Service** (USPS; ☎ 800-275-8777; www.usps.com) is reliable and inexpensive, though Americans often complain about it. Private shippers such as **United Parcel Service** (UPS; ☎ 800-742-5877; www.ups.com) and **Federal Express** (FedEx; ☎ 800-463-3339; www.fedex.com) ship much of the nation's parcels and important time-sensitive documents to both domestic and foreign destinations.

Postal Rates

Rates for 1st-class mail within the USA are $0.37 for letters up to 1oz, $0.23 for each additional ounce and $0.23 for postcards. The cost for parcels airmailed anywhere within the USA is $3.20 for 2lbs or less, increasing by $1 per pound up to $6 for 5lbs. For heavier items, rates differ according to the distance mailed. Books, periodicals and computer disks can be sent by a cheaper 4th-class rate.

International airmail rates are typically $0.70 for a postcard and $0.80 for a letter.

Receiving Mail

Poste restante is called 'general delivery' in the USA. If you're sending (or expecting) mail to be held at the post office in a city or town, it should be addressed:

Your name
c/o General Delivery, Station Name
Town, State, ZIP Code
USA

Mail is usually held for 10 days before it's returned to the sender: You might request your correspondents to write 'hold for arrival' on their letters. When you pick up mail, bring some photo identification. Your passport is best.

SENIOR TRAVELERS

Though the age when the benefits begin varies, travelers from 50 years and up can receive cut rates and benefits unknown to their younger fellows. Be sure to inquire about such rates at hotels, museums and restaurants.

The National Park Service issues Golden Age Passports to people 62 years or older for national historic sites and national refuges. New York also offers a similar passport to New York State residents 62 or older for free access to state parks, state historic sites and arboretums.

In the Adirondacks, the Sagamore Institute operates an Elderhostel program for grandparents and grandchildren. Reservations a year in advance are recommended. For information, contact **Sagamore Great Camp** (☎ 315-354-5311; www.sagamore.org; PO Box 146, Raquette Lake, NY 13436).

National advocacy groups that can help in planning your travels include the following:
American Association of Retired Persons (for membership ☎ 800-424-3410; www.aarp.org; PO Box 199, Long Beach, CA 90801) The AARP is an advocacy group for Americans 50-plus and is a good resource for travel bargains. Annual membership costs $12.50.
Elderhostel (☎ 877-426-8056; www.elderhostel.org; 11 Avenue de Lafayette, Boston, MA 02110) Elderhostel is a nonprofit organization offering seniors academic college courses throughout the USA and Canada. Programs last one to three weeks, include meals and accommodations and are open to people 55-plus and their companions.

SOLO TRAVELERS

People tend to be curious and impressed by solo travelers, especially women. If you sit at the bar in a restaurant, the bartender or other solos will be more likely to strike up a conversation with you than if you are shoved in an isolating table. Even going into bars alone won't present a problem as long as you keep your guard up. During the summer and fall when people are still on vacation, they are excited to talk to people from other places or to share their own experiences about their favorite destinations. Campgrounds tend to be more friendly places than sterile hotels, but many of the family-run motels run a close second behind campgrounds in terms of a fraternity.

Solo hikers should take extra precautions; sign in at the hiker's log, stay on the path and carry an ID with you.

New York City for solos is a mixed bag. You might wander into a place and find engaging conversation or you might get the 'too-cool-for-you' treatment. The city somehow manages to seduce and repulse visitors when it is least expected.

TELEPHONE

Payphones from public streets are quickly disappearing because of the proliferation of cell phones. Check in hotel lobbies, gas stations and diners for the few remaining dinosaurs. Verizon manages payphones in most of New York State.

If you're calling from abroad, the international country code for the USA is ☎ 1. Phone numbers within the USA consist of a three-digit area code followed by a seven-digit local number. If you're calling locally, just dial the seven-digit number. If you're calling a town in another area code, dial ☎ 1 + the three-digit area code + the seven-digit number.

To make an international call direct, dial ☎ 011 + country code + area code + the phone number. Country codes are typically listed in the front matter of the phone book.

If making a local call ($0.35 to $0.50) use the exact change. If you are making a long-distance call, purchase a pre-paid calling card from CVS or other drug stores. Calling cards can also be used on some hotel phones without incurring an additional service charge from the hotel, but call the front desk to verify their policy.

Aimed specifically at travelers, Lonely Planet's ekno Communication Card offers cheap international calls, a range of messaging services and free email. For local calls, you're usually better off with a local card. You can join online at www.ekno.lonelyplanet.com, or by phone from the continental USA by dialing ☎ 800-707-0031. Once you've joined the service, to use ekno from the continental USA, dial ☎ 800-706-1333.

TIME

New York is five hours behind GMT/UTC, two hours ahead of US Mountain Time and three hours ahead of US Pacific Time.

TOURIST INFORMATION

In many towns free visitor information is given by the chamber of commerce (also called Convention and Visitors' Bureau or CVB), a membership organization for local businesses (hotels, restaurants etc).

New York State Division of Tourism (☎ 800-225-5697; www.iloveny.state.ny.us; PO Box 2603, Albany, NY 12220-0603) publishes a handy guide to the entire state, offers accommodations listings, travel ideas and a calendar of special events.

TOURS

For car-less New Yorkers escaping the city, **Short Line/Coach USA Bus Co** (☎ 800-631-8405; www.shortlinebus.com) has a variety of day tours to places in the Hudson Valley that would otherwise be impossible to reach without a car. **New York Waterway** (☎ 800-533-3779; www.nywaterway.com) offers similar excursions to destinations along the Hudson River. Different aspects of New York City's history can be learned through one of the many walking tours on offer (p107).

WOMEN TRAVELERS

Common sense is usually the only vigilance women will need to navigate through New York. Exercise caution in unfamiliar neighborhoods or cities, especially at night. Don't ride the New York City subway alone after 9pm; take a cab instead. Don't accept rides from strangers or invitations where you'll be alone with a stranger. Avoid telling people what hotel you are staying at. Heed your gut instinct – if a situation gives you an itchy feeling, remove yourself from it.

If you're nervous about visiting New York City, stay in Chelsea (see p111), a predominantly male gay neighborhood, at one of the smaller, personable inns. You won't have to worry about unwanted advances in this neighborhood.

For woman-oriented news and travel tips, visit www.journeywoman.com.

Transportation

TRANSPORTATION

THINGS CHANGE...

The information is this chapter is particularly vulnerable to change: prices for international travel are volatile, routes are introduced and/or canceled, schedules change, special deals come and go, and rules and visa requirements are amended. Flying in America has been in a state of flux since the September 11 terrorist attacks, and it's likely that requirements for international visitors will change greatly in the future. Airlines and governments seem to take a perverse pleasure in making price structures and regulations as complicated as possible. The travel industry is highly competitive and there are many hidden costs and benefits.

Get opinions, quotes and advice from as many airlines and travel agents as possible and make sure you understand how a fare (and any ticket you may buy) works before you part with your hard-earned money. The details given in this chapter should be regarded as pointers and are not a substitute for your own careful, up-to-date research.

New York sits at the crossroads between the northeastern states of New England and the rest of continental US. New York City is one of the country's major entry and exit points for international traffic.

Whether you're coming from a domestic location or from abroad, the quickest way to travel is by airplane. Within the USA you can also travel by bus, train or car, but that eats into your vacation time. In New York itself you can fly between major cities or drive. A car provides the easiest access to the region. You'll be able to travel to areas where bus and train travel is limited, and it will give you the flexibility to travel at your own pace.

GETTING THERE & AWAY

This section focuses on getting to the major transportation hubs in the region from the major US ports of entry and other parts of world. Whichever way you're traveling, make sure you take out travel insurance (p289).

ENTERING THE COUNTRY

Most international travelers enter New York via airplane, although there are border crossings with Canada at Niagara Falls, Alexandria Bay and near Plattsburgh. Following the September 11, 2001 terrorist attacks on New York City and Washington, DC, air travel in the US has changed. You can expect extensive baggage screening procedures and personal searches. Non-US citizens, especially residents of Middle Eastern, Asian and African countries, should be prepared for an exhaustive questioning process at immigration. You can expect questions on what you're going to do in the US, how long you plan to stay, and exactly why you chose to visit. Although this process is time-consuming, once finished most visitors will be allowed into the country. Crossing the border into the USA from Canada used to be a relaxed process – US citizens often passed with just a driver's license. Following the terrorist attacks this process has become more time-consuming. Expect more substantial questioning and possible vehicle searches for both residents of the US and travelers from other countries.

AIR

Most air travelers to the region arrive at John F Kennedy (JFK), La Guardia (LGA) or Newark Airport (EWR), which is actually across the river in New Jersey. Almost all international airlines allowed to fly into the US have flights into JFK, as it is one of the country's major international hubs. Fares to and from this airport, especially from points in Europe and Africa, are often the cheapest in the country. Other major airports in New York are located in Buffalo (BUF), Syracuse (SYR), Albany (ALB), Saranac Lake (SLK) and Newburgh (SWF). All the large US carriers have multiple daily flights between these cities.

Airlines flying to and from New York include:

Aer Lingus (☎ 800-474-7424; www.aerlingus.com)
Aeromexico (☎ 800-237-6639; www.aeromexico.com)
Air Canada (☎ 800-776-3000; www.aircanada.com)
Air France (☎ 800-321-4538; www.airfrance.com)
American Airlines (☎ 800-433-7300; www.american airlines.com)
British Airways (☎ 800-247-9297; www.britishairways .com)
Continental Airlines (☎ 800-523-3273; www .continental.com)
Delta Airlines (☎ 800-221-1212; www.delta.com)
Japan Airlines (☎ 800-525-3663; www.japanair.com)
Korean Air (☎ 800-438-5000; www.koreanair.com)
Northwest Airlines (☎ 800-225-2525; www.nwa.com)
Olympic Airways (☎ 800-838-3825; www.olympic -airways.com)
Philippine Airlines (☎ 800-435-9725; www.philippine air.com)
Qantas (☎ 800-227-4500; www.qantasusa.com)
Singapore Airlines (☎ 800-742-3333; www.singapore air.com)
Swiss International Air Lines (☎ 877- 359-7947; www.swiss.com)
United Airlines (☎ 800-241-6522; www.united.com)
US Airways (☎ 800-428-4322; www.usairways.com)
Virgin Atlantic (☎ 203-750-2000; www.virgin-atlantic .com)

LAND

Although major rail lines and interstates connect New York with the rest of the US, public transportation to remote areas is limited.

Border Crossings

New York shares an international border with Canada. There are major border crossings at Alexandria Bay and Niagara Falls. From Alexandria Bay you can cross the Thousand Islands Bridge into Canada. At Niagara Falls the crossing is via the Rainbow Bridge. Both borders are open 24

BOOK YOUR OWN TRAVEL

Online travel agencies have become very popular and often offer great deals on flights, as well as packages that include flight, hotel and car rental. The top US sites, which allow bookings originating outside or inside the US, are **Travelocity** (www.travelocity.com), **Expedia** (www.expedia.com) and **Orbitz** (www .orbitz.com). If you are looking for flights that originate inside the US (but you can travel to either international or domestic destinations) and are not choosy about specifics, try **Priceline** (www.priceline.com) or **Hotwire** (www.hotwire.com). Both offer heavily discounted fares, however you cannot choose your airline or flight time, only the date. With Priceline you name the price you want to pay and the website will search to see if any airline is willing to accept it. If one is, your credit card will be charged immediately and you will not be able to change or cancel the flights. Hotwire works in a similar manner.

---

hours. Non-US citizens will need a passport to cross between the countries. Prepare to be questioned and to possibly have your car searched. US citizens may be able to cross the border with a valid picture identification card, but should bring a passport along just in case. Politeness and cooperation go a long way toward a smooth entrance into either the US or Canada.

Bus

Big, comfortable, air-conditioned buses connect most cities and some towns in the USA. However, as the private auto is king, and air service is faster in this large country, bus service is limited. Bus lines don't serve places off main routes. If you are traveling long distances it's often the same price, if not cheaper, to fly, and you'll get there a lot faster. For instance it costs about $169 to travel from New York City to Los Angeles by bus and the trip takes about three days. Airfares between the two cities usually hover between $200 and $300, with some even cheaper flights available.

Greyhound (☎ 800-231-2222; www.greyhound.com) is the country's major long-distance carrier, and its routes also connect most major Canadian cities with the main continental US cities.

TRANSPORTATION

Car & Motorcycle

If driving to New York from another state, I-95 is the major north–south route along the East Coast and stretches from the Canadian (Maine–New Brunswick) border to Miami, Florida. I-95 becomes a toll road between New York City and the Delaware Memorial Bridge (this portion is the NJ Turnpike). It's well traveled by trucks, smelly in places, and often completely congested. The other main north–south route, I-81, runs from the New York–Ontario border through Pennsylvania to Maryland, Virginia and Tennessee.

I-90 extends east–west from Boston, Massachusetts, across New York and continues all the way to Seattle, Washington, on the Pacific Northwest coast some 3000 miles away. I-80 runs from New York City all the way to San Francisco on the West Coast.

If coming from Canada, automobile drivers and motorcyclists need their vehicle's registration papers and liability insurance.

There are plenty of gas stations on even minor roads in the US, and roadside assistance is readily available if your vehicle breaks down.

Train

Amtrak (☎ 800-872-7245; www.amtrak.com) operates most passenger rail services, and this region (part of the northeast rail system) features some of the most heavily traveled routes. Long-distance travelers from the west and southwest must make connections in Chicago. The most popular routes run between New York City and Boston ($85, three hours) and Washington, DC ($89, 2½ hours). It's often faster and less of a hassle to take a train rather than a plane between these cities, because trains go into the city centers, while the airports are in the suburbs.

GETTING AROUND

New York State is best negotiated in a private vehicle. Public transportation doesn't reach many of the interesting, more isolated places, so having your own car can be a major advantage and it's worth considering car rental for at least a part of your trip. You can use public transportation to towns and cities, then rent a car locally to get to places not served by public transportation. This option is usually more expensive than just renting a car and driving yourself everywhere, but it can cut down on long-distance driving. If you need to stick to public transportation, buses provide a more extensive network than trains, though train travel can be quicker.

AIR

The region is served by most domestic airlines. Cheap airfares can often be found between cities in New York if you book at least seven days in advance and you are not choosy about what time or day you fly. If you're arriving from abroad or another major US airport, it's often cheaper to buy a through ticket to small airports as part of your fare rather than buying them separately.

BOAT

You can rent boats to travel New York State's 524-mile canal system, which is made up of four waterways: the Erie, Cayuga-Seneca, Oswego and Champlain Canals. These link with lakes and rivers across the state and connect Hudson River with the Great Lakes and the waterways of the northeast. The Champlain Canal heads north from Albany to Lake Champlain and west along the Erie Canal to Buffalo and the Great Lakes. The Erie Canal meets the Oswego Canal at Three Rivers, west of Syracuse. For more information, contact **New York State Canals** (☎ 800-422-6254; www.canals.state.ny.us).

BUS

Buses go to more places than airplanes or trains, but the routes still leave a lot out, bypassing some prime destinations. Local carriers generally serve towns that aren't on major routes. Greyhound and other bus lines often share the same terminal. Buses normally provide the cheapest form of public transportation, and fares are even cheaper if you travel Monday to Thursday; Friday to Sunday, any fare goes up several dollars. For specific fares, check the information given under specific towns and cities.

Carriers

Greyhound (☎ 800-231-2222; www.greyhound.com) is the main long-distance carrier for the region with the most extensive routes. Sometimes its terminals are in undesirable parts of town, however the buses are reasonably comfortable and they usually run on time. The company has a good safety record.

Greyhound connects large towns along major highways one or two times a day, stopping at smaller towns on the way. In many small towns, Greyhound doesn't maintain terminals but merely stops at a given location, such as a service station, grocery store or fast-food restaurant (which may be the only choice for a meal – bring your own food if burgers and fries are unappealing). At these 'terminals,' passengers may be able to buy a ticket, but usually you pay the driver (with exact change) upon boarding. Note that all buses are nonsmoking.

Greyhound works in conjunction with **Bonanza Bus Lines** (☎ 800-556-3815; www.bonanza bus.com) and **Peter Pan Bus Lines** (☎ 800-343-9999; www.peterpanbus.com). Bonanza connects New York City with upstate New York and New England. Peter Pan operates between Washington, DC, and Boston via Philadelphia and New York City, and it also runs to Atlantic City, New Jersey.

Capitol Trailways (☎ 800-333-8444; www.capitol trailways.com) runs between Washington, DC, and Baltimore, Maryland and also has stops in New York State, at New York City, Syracuse, Binghamton and Buffalo. The family-owned **Adirondack Trailways** (☎ 800-858-8555; www .escapemaker.com/adirondacktrailways) runs to many major towns in the state.

Buying Tickets

Tickets can be purchased over the phone with a credit card or more conveniently on the bus companies' websites. The tickets can be mailed to you if you buy them at least 10 days in advance, or they can be picked up at the terminal (make sure to bring proper identification). Greyhound terminals also accept American Express, traveler's checks, post-office money orders and cash. Reservations are made with ticket purchases only.

You can often get discounted tickets if you buy them seven or 21 days in advance, and Greyhound often runs special promotional fares.

CAR & MOTORCYCLE

Driving or motorcycling is by far the most convenient way of getting around the countryside, seeing small towns and visiting out-of-the-way places. With your own mode of transportation, you have independence and flexibility. Driving can work out reasonably cheap if two or more people share the cost.

Many US cities and towns owe their sprawl to the popularity of the automobile. Satellite communities – with their shopping malls, fast-food restaurants and motels – exist along highways and at the intersections of important routes. The attractions you've come to see may be downtown, but the only affordable accommodations may well be a number of miles away in one of these commercial strips, and the only means of access will be a car or motorcycle.

On the down side, the independence you enjoy using your own vehicle tends to isolate you from the local people. The larger cities, with their one-way traffic systems and complex network of highways into, through and around town, can be confusing and wearing on the nerves. Finding a convenient place to park in unfamiliar city centers can be difficult and expensive.

For young travelers (under 25 and especially under 21), car travel is scarcely an option. Car rentals are expensive or unavailable, and if you buy a car, insurance can be prohibitive.

Driving License

Most foreign visitors can drive in the USA for up to a year with a license from their home country. An International Driving Permit (IDP) is a useful adjunct and may have more credibility with US traffic police, especially if your home license has no picture or is in a foreign language. Your automobile association can issue an IDP, valid for one year, for a small fee. You must carry your home license together with the IDP.

Hire

To rent a car, you must have a valid driver's license (your out-of-state or home license will do) and present a major credit card or else a large cash deposit. You normally need to be at least 25 years of age, but some companies rent to drivers aged 21 to 24 for an additional daily fee.

The major rental agencies are as follows:
Alamo (☎ 800-327-9633; www.alamo.com)
Avis (☎ 800-831-2847; www.avis.com)
Budget (☎ 800-527-0700; www.budget.com)
Dollar (☎ 800-800-4000; www.dollar.com)
Enterprise (☎ 800-325-8007; www.enterprise.com)
Hertz (☎ 800-654-3131; www.hertz.com)
National (☎ 800-227-7368; www.nationalcar.com)
Thrifty (☎ 800-367-2277; www. thrifty.com)

TRANSPORTATION

Rent-a-Wreck (☎ 800-535-1391; www.rentawreck.com) offers older vehicles at lower prices, but you will have a mileage limit – usually between 100 and 200 miles per day. Smaller local companies sometimes offer better prices than the major companies; consult the yellow pages under 'Automobiles.'

Rental prices vary greatly in relation to region, season, day of the week and the type or size of the car. Some rental agencies have bargain rates for weekend or week-long rentals, especially outside peak season or in conjunction with airline tickets. If you're arranging a rental before you get to the USA, check the options with your travel agent or check out websites such as www.travelocity.com, www.expedia.com or www.priceline.com, which will allow you to choose from different models of cars, prices and companies. These rates are often cheaper than going through the rental companies directly.

It's also possible to rent an RV (recreational vehicle; also known as a motor home), which is basically a vanlike vehicle that usually has beds, a stove or microwave oven, a toilet and a shower. These can range in size from a camper slightly bigger than a pickup truck to a 30ft behemoth. The benefits of renting an RV is that it can make for a fun trip with friends and family, and you can conceivably save money on accommodations and food, especially if you're in a large group. Many campgrounds throughout the US have special sites designated for RVs, with electrical, water and sewage hookups. The downside is that RVs can be very expensive to rent, especially when you consider the hefty amount of gas they require (and don't forget the cost of the campsites). They are cumbersome, difficult to drive and even more difficult to park. If you're spending much time in cities, parking and driving an RV will probably turn out to be more trouble than it's worth. If you are thinking about renting an RV, be sure to consider the total cost, and if you or no one in your group has ever driven a very large vehicle, you might want to reconsider your choice.

One of the more common RV rental companies is **Cruise America** (☎ 800-327-7799; www.cruiseamerica.com). The pricing scheme is very complicated and depends on the size of the vehicle and where, when and how long you'd like to rent. A standard RV that sleeps up to five people could be $380 to $670 for three nights with a mileage allowance of 500 miles, whereas a large RV that sleeps up to seven people could be $460 to $830 for the same rental period and mileage allowance. Check with the rental company for details and special deals.

You're normally expected to return any rental, car or otherwise, to where you picked it up; you can arrange to drop the vehicle off elsewhere, but you'll have to pay a surcharge to do so.

Insurance

There are several types of insurance to consider. Liability insurance, which covers damage you may cause to another vehicle, is required by law but isn't always included in rental contracts because many Americans are covered for rental cars under their regular car liability insurance policy. You do need liability coverage, but don't pay extra if the coverage already included with the rental is sufficient. Liability insurance is also called 'third-party coverage.'

A Collision Damage Waiver (CDW), also called a Loss Damage Waiver (LDW), is usually optional; you don't need to buy this waiver to rent, but it does cover the full value of the vehicle in case of an accident, except when the accident is caused by acts of nature or fire. For a mid-sized car, the cost for this extra coverage is around $15 per day. Agencies also add a daily fee for each additional driver.

Some credit cards cover your CDW if you charge the full cost of rental to your card. If you opt to do that, you'll need to sign the waiver, declining the coverage. If you already have collision insurance on your personal policy, the credit card covers the large deductible. To find out extents and details, contact your credit card company.

Road Rules

You must be at least 16 years old to drive; in New York City, you must be at least 18, regardless of whether you are licensed to drive in other states. Speed limits are 65mph on interstate highways and freeways unless otherwise posted (but you're likely to find traffic moving at around 70mph); some interstate highways have limits of 55mph. On undivided highways, speed limits vary from 30mph to 50mph. In cities and towns, they're usually 25mph to 35mph, lower near schools and medical facilities.

Wearing a seat belt is compulsory, and children under four must use approved safety seats. No child should sit in the front-passenger seat of a car equipped with a front-passenger seat air bag. Air bags, which inflate at 200mph, are designed to protect a full-size, full-weight adult and can seriously injure or kill a small or light person.

Motorcyclists and their passengers must wear helmets. Drinking and driving is a serious offense in the US and police take their jobs seriously. Even just two drinks, drunk in relatively quick succession, can make you too legally intoxicated to drive. A Driving Under the Influence (DUI) charge comes with hefty fines, loss of your license, time in court and usually some jail time. During weekends, especially around holidays, police often set up DUI checkpoints where your car may be stopped and you may be given a field sobriety test. If you refuse to take a Breathalyzer test you will automatically lose your license for one year.

New York is the only state in the country that has banned drivers from using cell phones. If you are caught you can be fined.

HITCHHIKING

Travelers who hitch should understand they're taking a serious risk. It's potentially dangerous and definitely not recommended. Most Americans don't do it and drivers are reluctant to pick up hitchhikers anyway. This may be less so in rural parts, but traffic can be sparse, and you might get stranded.

If you do hitch, be extremely careful when accepting a lift. If in doubt, don't do it. Ask the driver where they're going rather than telling them where you want to go. Hitching in pairs may be a fraction safer, and you should let someone else know where you're planning to go.

Hitching on freeways is prohibited – there's usually a sign at the on-ramp stating 'no pedestrians beyond this point,' and anyone caught hitching past there can be arrested. Police routinely check hitchhikers' identification, and you may be asked to show some money to prove you aren't destitute.

Even hitching to and from a hiking trailhead should be avoided – try to arrange something at a ranger station or with other hikers. If you're broke, there are alternatives to hitching – look for rideshares at hostels or ask at campgrounds.

LOCAL TRANSPORTATION

Comprehensive local bus networks exist in big cities and most of the larger towns, though some popular destinations have no public transportation. Other towns have bus systems with limited hours and routes, which make them unreliable as a primary means of local transportation.

New York City (which has an extensive subway and bus system, plus the Metro-North Railroad and the Long Island Rail Road) has an extensive urban and suburban transportation system.

Most towns of any size have a taxi service. Taxis can be expensive but aren't so outrageous if shared with two or three people. You can hail them on the street when their center roof-light is lit. Check the yellow pages under 'Taxi' for phone numbers and services. Drivers almost always expect a tip of about 12% to 18% of the fare.

The Staten Island Ferry services New York City, but most ways of getting around a town by boat or ferry are as part of a guided tour.

TRAIN

Amtrak (☎ 800-872-7245; www.amtrak.com) connects the major cities in the region with stops at smaller towns along the routes. The main Amtrak routes radiate from New York City north to the cities of Albany, Schenectady, Rouses Point (near the Quebec border) and Montreal, Quebec, and northwest to the New York cities of Utica, Syracuse, Buffalo and Niagara Falls.

Long Island Rail Road (LIRR; ☎ 516-822-5477, 718-217-5477) joins New York City with Long Island. **Metro-North Railroad** (☎ 212-532-4900) serves New York City's northern suburbs (Westchester) and Connecticut. **Port Authority Trans-Hudson** (PATH; ☎ 800-234-7284) connects the city to New Jersey's northern cities (including Newark, Hoboken and Jersey City).

In some areas, privately owned tourist trains offer scenic day trips through the countryside or other attractions. Some of the trains travel on narrow-gauge railroads built by former mining companies; they are usually steam-powered.

Health

CONTENTS

The North American continent encompasses an extraordinary range of climates and terrains, from the freezing heights of the Rockies to tropical areas in southern Florida. Because of the high level of hygiene here, infectious diseases will not be a significant concern for most travelers, who will experience nothing worse than a little diarrhea or a mild respiratory infection.

BEFORE YOU GO

INSURANCE

The USA offers possibly the finest health care in the world. The problem is that, unless you have good insurance, it can be prohibitively expensive. It's essential to purchase travel health insurance if your regular policy doesn't cover you when you're abroad.

Bring any medications you may need in their original containers, clearly labeled. A signed, dated letter from your physician that describes all medical conditions and medications, including generic names, is also a good idea.

If your health insurance does not cover you for medical expenses abroad, consider getting supplemental insurance. Check the Subwwway section of the Lonely Planet website (www.lonelyplanet.com /subwwway) for more information. Find out in advance if your insurance plan will make payments directly to providers or reimburse you later for overseas health expenditures.

RECOMMENDED VACCINATIONS

No special vaccines are required or recommended for travel to the USA.

ONLINE RESOURCES

There is a wealth of travel health advice on the Internet. The World Health Organization publishes a superb book, called *International Travel and Health*, which is revised annually and is available online at no cost at www.who.int/ith/. Another website of general interest is MD Travel Health at www.mdtravelhealth.com, which provides complete travel health recommendations for every country, updated daily, also at no cost.

It's usually a good idea to consult your government's travel health website before departure, if one is available:
Australia (www.dfat.gov.au/travel/)
Canada (www.hc-sc.gc.ca/pphb-dgspsp/tmp-pmv /pub_e.html)
UK (www.doh.gov.uk/traveladvice/index.htm)
US (www.cdc.gov/travel/)

IN THE USA

AVAILABILITY & COST OF HEALTH CARE

In general, if you have a medical emergency, the best bet is to find the nearest hospital and go to its emergency room. If the problem isn't urgent, you can call a nearby hospital and ask for a referral to a local physician, which is usually cheaper than a trip to the emergency room. You should avoid stand-alone, for-profit urgent care centers, which tend to perform large numbers of expensive tests, even for minor illnesses.

Pharmacies are abundantly supplied, but you may find that some medications which are available over the counter in your home country require a prescription in the USA, and, as always, if you don't have insurance to cover the cost of prescriptions, they can be shockingly expensive.

INFECTIOUS DISEASES

In addition to more common ailments, there are several infectious diseases that are unknown or uncommon outside North

America. Most are acquired by mosquito or tick bites.

West Nile Virus

These infections were unknown in the USA until a few years ago, but have now been reported in almost all 50 states. The virus is transmitted by culex mosquitoes, which are active in late summer and early fall and generally bite after dusk. Most infections are mild or asymptomatic, but the virus may infect the central nervous system, leading to fever, headache, confusion, lethargy, coma and sometimes death. There is no treatment for West Nile virus. For the latest update on the areas affected by West Nile, go to the **US Geological Survey website** (http://westnilemaps.usgs.gov/).

Lyme Disease

This disease has been reported from many states, but most documented cases occur in the northeastern part of the country, especially New York, New Jersey, Connecticut and Massachusetts. Lyme disease is transmitted by deer ticks, which are only 1mm to 2mm long. Most cases occur in late spring and summer. The Center for Disease Control (CDC) has an informative, if slightly scary, web page on Lyme disease (www.cdc.gov/ncidod/dvbid/lyme/).

The first symptom is usually an expanding red rash that is often pale in the center, known as a bull's eye rash. However, in many cases, no rash is observed. Flu-like symptoms are common, including fever, headache, joint pains, body aches and malaise. When the infection is treated promptly with an appropriate antibiotic, usually doxycycline or amoxicillin, the cure rate is high. Luckily, since the tick must be attached for 36 hours or more to transmit Lyme disease, most cases can be prevented by performing a thorough tick check after you've been outdoors.

Rabies

Rabies is a viral infection of the brain and spinal cord that is almost always fatal. The rabies virus is carried in the saliva of infected animals and is typically transmitted through an animal bite, though contamination of any break in the skin with infected saliva may result in rabies. In the US, most cases of human rabies are related to exposure to bats. Rabies may also be contracted from raccoons, skunks, foxes and unvaccinated cats and dogs.

If there is any possibility, however small, that you have been exposed to rabies, you should seek preventative treatment, which consists of rabies immune globulin and rabies vaccine and is quite safe. In particular, any contact with a bat should be discussed with health authorities, because bats have small teeth and may not leave obvious bite marks. If you wake up to find a bat in your room, or discover a bat in a room with small children, rabies prophylaxis may be necessary.

Giardiasis

This parasitic infection of the small intestine occurs throughout North America and the world. Symptoms may include nausea, bloating, cramps and diarrhea, and may last for weeks. To protect yourself from giardiasis, you should avoid drinking directly from lakes, ponds, streams and rivers, which may be contaminated by animal or human feces. The infection can also be transmitted from person to person if proper hand-washing is not performed. Giardiasis is easily diagnosed by a stool test and readily treated with antibiotics.

HIV/AIDS

As with most parts of the world, HIV infection occurs throughout the US. You should never assume, on the basis of someone's background or appearance, that they're free of this or any other sexually transmitted disease. Be sure to use a condom for all sexual encounters.

ENVIRONMENTAL HAZARDS
Bites & Stings

Common sense approaches to these concerns are the most effective: wear boots when hiking to protect from snakes, wear long sleeves and pants to protect from ticks and mosquitoes. If you're bitten, don't overreact. Stay calm and follow the recommended treatment.

MOSQUITO BITES

When traveling in areas where West Nile or other mosquito-borne illnesses have been reported, keep yourself covered (wear long sleeves, long pants, hats and shoes rather than sandals) and apply a good insect repellent, preferably one containing DEET, to exposed skin and clothing. In general, adults and children over 12 should use preparations containing 25% to 35% DEET, which usually lasts about six hours. Children between two and 12 years of age should use preparations containing no more than 10% DEET, applied sparingly, which will usually last about three hours. Neurologic toxicity has been reported from DEET, especially in children, but appears to be extremely uncommon and generally related to overuse. DEET-containing compounds should not be used on children under age two.

Insect repellents containing certain botanical products, including oil of eucalyptus and soybean oil, are effective but last only 1½ to two hours. Products based on citronella are not effective.

Visit the CDC's website (www.cdc.gov /ncidod/dvbid/westnile/prevention_info .htm) for prevention information.

TICK BITES

Ticks are parasitic arachnids that may be present in brush, forest and grasslands, where hikers often get them on their legs or in their boots. Adult ticks suck blood from hosts by burrowing into the skin and can carry infections such as Lyme disease (p301).

Always check your body for ticks after walking through high grass or thickly forested area. If ticks are found unattached, they can simply be brushed off. If a tick is found attached, press down around the tick's head with tweezers, grab the head and gently pull upwards – do not twist it. (If no tweezers are available, use your fingers, but protect them from contamination with a piece of tissue or

paper.) Do not rub oil, alcohol or petroleum jelly on it. If you get sick in the next couple of weeks, consult a doctor.

ANIMAL BITES

Do not attempt to pet, handle or feed any animal, with the exception of domestic animals known to be free of any infectious disease. Most animal injuries are directly related to a person's attempt to touch or feed the animal.

Any bite or scratch by a mammal, including bats, should be promptly and thoroughly cleansed with large amounts of soap and water, followed by application of an antiseptic such as iodine or alcohol. The local health authorities should be contacted immediately for possible postexposure rabies treatment, whether or not you've been immunized against rabies. It may also be advisable to start an antibiotic, since wounds caused by animal bites and scratches frequently become infected.

SNAKE BITES

There are several varieties of venomous snakes in the USA, but unlike those in some other countries they do not cause instantaneous death, and antivenins are available. First aid is to place a light constricting bandage over the bite, keep the wounded part below the level of the heart and move it as little as possible. Stay calm and get to a medical facility as soon as possible. Bring the dead snake for identification if you can, but don't risk being bitten again. Do not use the mythic 'cut an X and suck out the venom' trick; this causes more damage to snakebite victims than the bites themselves.

Behind the Scenes

THIS BOOK

The 1st edition of *New York, New Jersey & Pennsylvania* was researched and written by Tom Smallman, David Ellis, Michael Clark and Eric Wakin. The first three returned to update the 2nd edition. This edition of *New York State* was written by China Williams and Becca Blond. The boxed text 'Room Service in the 21st Century' was written by Mara Vorhees.

THANKS from the authors

China Williams Many thanks to Sam and Elsa Huxley who kindly let me camp out in their spare bedroom and talk during the playoffs; y'all went the distance. More thanks to my other NYC peeps: Heather and Jason, Giles, Kate, Felicity, Ian and Schimmey. And a nod to Brooklyn for Victoria, Sarah and Candy. Thanks to Jean Murphy in Saranac Lake, the state's bookstore owners and canoe outfitters, the guard at the Lake George Campground who gave me her map, and the couple from Rochester who shared their campfire. Top of my list goes to my hubby, Matt, for picking me up and taking me home after a long, tiring trip. The last breath goes to Jay Cooke, Becca Blond and the LP staffers.

Becca Blond I'd like to dedicate my portion of this book to Lou Gonzales, who passed away in March 2003 and always acted like a second mother to me in Colorado. Next, thanks to Janette and Steve Miret and Vera Fortino for their outstanding hospitality

and for their geyser searching efforts in Saratoga Springs. I'm also indebted to Kevin Burket for all his pretrip advice. A big thanks goes to my parents, David and Patricia Blond, sister Jessica and grandma Jennie for their continued support. Thanks to my roommates Lani Houseman and Jason 'Sponge Bob' Rickey for putting up with the maps in the kitchen and my constant out-loud mumblings. At Lonely Planet thanks to my commissioning editor Jay Cooke, who responded enthusiastically and gave invaluable advice, and to my coauthor China Williams. Finally, thanks for your constant support: Natalie Swetye, Jamie Torres, Ian Hay, Jesi Hannold, Patricia Caron, Dave Courage, Andrew Stone, Joanna Harma, Gina and Bill Hethcock, Carol and Bill Holland, Coree Thompson, Pascale Nyby and Brittany, Spanky, Gavin, Cassie and Moe.

CREDITS

Series Publishing Manager Susan Rimerman oversaw the redevelopment of the regional guides series with the help of Virginia Maxwell and Maria Donohoe, who also steered the development of this title as Regional Publishing Manager. The series was designed by James Hardy, with mapping development by Paul Piaia. The series development team included Shahara Ahmed, Jenny Blake, Anna Bolger, Erin Corrigan, Nadine Fogale, Dave McClymont, Leonie Mugavin, Rachel Peart, Lynne Preston, Howard Ralley, Valerie Sinzdak and Bart Wright.

BEHIND THE SCENES

This title was commissioned and developed in Lonely Planet's Oakland office by Jay Cooke. Cartography for this guide was developed by Anthony Phelan. Eoin Dunlevy and Andrew Weatherill were the project managers. Coordinating editor Barbara Delissen was assisted by Carolyn Bain, Thalia Kalkipsakis and Charlotte Keown, and coordinating cartographer Joelene Kowalski was assisted by Simon Tillema and Celia Wood. The book was laid out by Jacqui Saunders and Laura Jane. Ruth Askevold designed the cover and Maria Vallianos prepared the artwork.

Thanks also to Martin Heng, Melanie Dankel, Kate McDonald, Sally Darmody, Jennifer Garrett and of course to China Williams and Becca Blond.

THANKS from Lonely Planet
Many thanks to the travelers who used the last edition and wrote to us with helpful hints, useful advice and interesting anecdotes:

A Robin J Andrus, Matt Azeles **B** Gene Bauston, Kirsten Bayly, Amy Bean, Matt Bellingham, Cecilia Bergold, Margaret Boulos, Murray Bruce, Martin Bucheli, Harry Burgess **C** Angela Carper, Hua Chee Ooi, G Chettino, Chungwah Chow, Ruth Corcoran, Linda Corriveau, Agustin Cot **D** Ake Dahllof, Anke Dekkers-de Wit, Dhawa Dhondup, Jonathan R Drew, Christian Dupont **E** Allan Engelhardt, RA Escoffey, Caroline Evans, Mike Evans **F** Bert Flower, Christopher Frankland, Iain Franklin, Loek Frederiks, Linda Fuchs Mescher **G** Peter T Gachot, Lantin Gaelle, Ben Godfrey, Robert J Goetschkes, Isidoro & Letizia Gorianz, Tara Govind, Jane Grantham, Simone Groothuis **H** Kay Hand, Esther Hardiman, Rob Hart, Emma Holmbro, Thng Hui Hong, B Hudgins, Irene Hughes **I** Dave Ingold **J** Jani Jaderholm, Amanda James **K** Felicia Kahn, Roswitha Kleineidam, GWM Kremer **L** Maxime Lachance, Gero Lange, Jeffrey Laurenti, Franz J Leinweber, Mikelson Leong, Henretta Leslie, Beverly Leu, Andy Levitt, Harrison Lipscomb, Paul Littlefair **M** Sarah Manocha, Michael Matthes, Robert McCarroll, Lisa Meyer, Keith Miller, Stephanie Monaghan, Genevieve Moreland, Wendy Mulligan **N** Robert Normandin **O** Robin O'Donoghue, Richard Owen **P** Simon Parker, David Patch, Stuart Pattullo, Mark W Pickens **R** Kale Rahul, Glen Rajaram, Steve Rogowski, Aaron Romero, Mariette Rommers, Rob Ruschak **S** Kenji Saito, Barry Samuels, Catherine Saunderson, Martina Schoefberger, Elisha Schoonmaker, Dennis Shore, Karen Smith, Maurice & Anne Smith, Anne Sofie Bay, Raymond Soon, Petra Sprenger, Christopher Staake, Jane Stirling, David Strasburg, Julia Suzuki **T** Lim Tai Wei, Scott Toulson, John & Maria Trimboli **V** Bodil van Dijk, Ruud van Leeuwen **W** T Watanabe, David Webster, Christophe Weyers, Martin White, Scott Williams, Trevor Wilson **Y** Terence Yorks

ACKNOWLEDGMENTS
Many thanks to the following for the use of their content:

Globe on back cover © Mountain High Maps 1993 Digital Wisdom, Inc.

Index

INDEX

MAP LEGEND

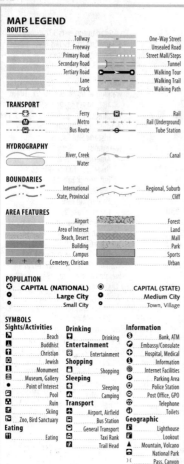

ROUTES
- Tollway
- Freeway
- Primary Road
- Secondary Road
- Tertiary Road
- Lane
- Track
- One-Way Street
- Unsealed Road
- Street Mall/Steps
- Tunnel
- Walking Tour
- Walking Trail
- Walking Path

TRANSPORT
- Ferry
- Metro
- Bus Route
- Rail
- Rail (Underground)
- Tube Station

HYDROGRAPHY
- River, Creek
- Water
- Canal

BOUNDARIES
- International
- State, Provincial
- Regional, Suburb
- Cliff

AREA FEATURES
- Airport
- Area of Interest
- Beach, Desert
- Building
- Campus
- Cemetery, Christian
- Forest
- Land
- Mall
- Park
- Sports
- Urban

POPULATION
- CAPITAL (NATIONAL)
- CAPITAL (STATE)
- Large City
- Medium City
- Small City
- Town, Village

SYMBOLS

Sights/Activities
- Beach
- Buddhist
- Christian
- Jewish
- Monument
- Museum, Gallery
- Point of Interest
- Pool
- Ruin
- Skiing
- Zoo, Bird Sanctuary

Eating
- Eating

Drinking
- Drinking

Entertainment
- Entertainment

Shopping
- Shopping

Sleeping
- Sleeping
- Camping

Transport
- Airport, Airfield
- Bus Station
- General Transport
- Taxi Rank
- Trail Head

Information
- Bank, ATM
- Embassy/Consulate
- Hospital, Medical
- Information
- Internet Facilities
- Parking Area
- Police Station
- Post Office, GPO
- Telephone
- Toilets

Geographic
- Lighthouse
- Lookout
- Mountain, Volcano
- National Park
- Pass, Canyon
- River Flow
- Waterfall

LONELY PLANET OFFICES

Australia
Head Office
Locked Bag 1, Footscray, Victoria 3011
☎ 03 8379 8000, fax 03 8379 8111
talk2us@lonelyplanet.com.au

USA
150 Linden St, Oakland, CA 94607
☎ 510 893 8555, toll free 800 275 8555
fax 510 893 8572, info@lonelyplanet.com

UK
72–82 Rosebery Ave,
Clerkenwell, London EC1R 4RW
☎ 020 7841 9000, fax 020 7841 9001
go@lonelyplanet.co.uk

France
1 rue du Dahomey, 75011 Paris
☎ 01 55 25 33 00, fax 01 55 25 33 01
bip@lonelyplanet.fr, www.lonelyplanet.fr

Published by Lonely Planet Publications Pty Ltd
ABN 36 005 607 983

© Lonely Planet 2004

© photographers as indicated 2004

Cover photographs: Emery Park, NY, James Schwabel/Panoramic Images/NGSImages.com (front); Brooklyn Bridge, Jeff Greenberg/LPI (back). Many of the images in this guide are available for licensing from Lonely Planet Images: www.lonelyplanetimages.com.

Printed through Colorcraft Ltd, Hong Kong.
Printed in China